Managing Capital Flows

The Search for a Framework

Edited by

Masahiro Kawai

Dean and CEO of the Asian Development Bank Institute, Japan

Mario B. Lamberte

Director of Research of the Asian Development Bank Institute, Japan

A JOINT PUBLICATION OF THE ASIAN DEVELOPMENT BANK INSTITUTE AND EDWARD ELGAR PUBLISHING

Edward Elgar
Cheltenham, UK • Northampton, MA, USA

© Asian Development Bank Institute 2010

All rights reserved. No part of this publication may be reproduced, stored in a retrieval system or transmitted in any form or by any means, electronic, mechanical or photocopying, recording, or otherwise without the prior permission of the publisher.

Published by
Edward Elgar Publishing Limited
The Lypiatts
15 Lansdown Road
Cheltenham
Glos GL50 2JA
UK

Edward Elgar Publishing, Inc.
William Pratt House
9 Dewey Court
Northampton
Massachusetts 01060
USA

A catalogue record for this book
is available from the British Library

Library of Congress Control Number: 2009941241

ISBN 978 1 84844 787 5

Typeset by Servis Filmsetting Ltd, Stockport, Cheshire
Printed and bound by MPG Books Group, UK

Contents

List of contributors	vii
Preface by Masahiro Kawai	ix
List of abbreviations	xi

Introduction Masahiro Kawai and Mario B. Lamberte	1

PART I   MANAGING CAPITAL FLOWS IN EMERGING ASIA AND REVIEW OF THE LITERATURE

1	Managing capital flows: emerging Asia's experiences, policy issues and challenges *Masahiro Kawai and Mario B. Lamberte*	9
2	A survey of the literature on managing capital inflows *Masahiro Kawai and Shinji Takagi*	46

PART II   PERSPECTIVE PAPERS

3	Central banks and capital flows *Stephen Grenville*	75
4	Managing large capital inflows: taking stock of international experiences *Susan Schadler*	105
5	Managing recent hot money inflows in Asia *Robert N. McCauley*	129
6	Crises, capital controls and financial integration *Eduardo Levy-Yeyati, Sergio L. Schmukler and Neeltje van Horen*	160
7	Managing capital flows: experiences from Central and Eastern Europe *Jürgen von Hagen and Iulia Siedschlag*	192

PART III COUNTRY STUDIES

8 Managing capital flows: the case of the People's Republic of China — 217
    Yongding Yu

9 Managing capital flows: the case of India — 239
    Ajay Shah and Ila Patnaik

10 Managing capital flows: the case of Indonesia — 260
    Ira S. Titiheruw and Raymond Atje

11 Managing capital flows: the case of the Republic of Korea — 280
    Soyoung Kim and Doo Yong Yang

12 Managing capital flows: the case of Malaysia — 305
    Kee Kuan Foong

13 Managing capital flows: the case of the Philippines — 330
    Josef T. Yap

14 Managing capital flows: the case of Singapore — 361
    Hwee Kwan Chow

15 Managing capital flows: the case of Thailand — 386
    Kanit Sangsubhan

16 Managing capital flows: the case of Viet Nam — 411
    Tri Thanh Vo and Chi Quang Pham

Index — 439

Contributors

Raymond Atje, Head, Economics Department, Centre for Strategic and International Studies, Jakarta, Indonesia.

Hwee Kwan Chow, Associate Dean and Practice Associate Professor, School of Economics, Singapore Management University, Singapore.

Kee Kuan Foong, Senior Research Fellow, Malaysian Institute of Economic Research, Kuala Lumpur, Malaysia.

Stephen Grenville, Visiting Fellow at the Lowy Institute for International Policy, Sydney and Adjunct Professor at the Crawford School, Australian National University, Canberra, Australia.

Masahiro Kawai, Dean and CEO, Asian Development Bank Institute, Tokyo, Japan.

Soyoung Kim, Professor, Department of Economics, Seoul National University, Seoul, Republic of Korea.

Mario B. Lamberte, Director of Research, Asian Development Bank Institute, Tokyo, Japan.

Eduardo Levy-Yeyati, Head of Latin American Research, Barclays Capital and Faculty, Barcelona Graduate School of Economics, Barcelona, Spain.

Robert N. McCauley, Senior Adviser, Monetary and Economic Department, Bank for International Settlements, Basel, Switzerland.

Ila Patnaik, Senior Fellow, National Institute for Public Finance and Policy, New Delhi, India.

Chi Quang Pham, Research Fellow, Edinburgh Business School, Heriot-Watt University, Edinburgh, UK.

Kanit Sangsubhan, Director, Fiscal Policy Research Institute, Ministry of Finance, Bangkok, Thailand.

Susan Schadler, Senior Fellow, The Atlantic Council, Washington, DC, USA.

Sergio L. Schmukler, Lead Economist, Development Research Group, World Bank, Washington, DC, USA.

Ajay Shah, Senior Fellow, National Institute for Public Finance and Policy, New Delhi, India.

Iulia Siedschlag, Associate Research Professor and Head of the Centre for International Economics and Competitiveness, Economic and Social Research Institute, Dublin, Ireland.

Shinji Takagi, Professor, Osaka University, Osaka, Japan.

Ira S. Titiheruw, Senior Research Fellow, Centre for Strategic and International Studies, Jakarta, Indonesia.

Neeltje van Horen, Senior Economist, Research Department, Dutch Central Bank and Researcher at Economics Department of the University of Amsterdam, Amsterdam, Netherlands.

Tri Thanh Vo, Vice-President, Central Institute for Economic Management, Hanoi, Viet Nam.

Jürgen von Hagen, Professor of Economics, Department of Economics, University of Bonn, Bonn, Germany; Indiana University Kelley School of Business, Indiana, USA; Research Fellow, CEPR, London, UK.

Doo Yong Yang, Associate Professor, College of International Studies, Kyung Hee University, Gyeonggi, Republic of Korea.

Josef T. Yap, President, Philippine Institute for Development Studies, Makati, Philippines.

Yongding Yu, Professor and Director-General, Institute of World Economics and Politics, Chinese Academy of Social Sciences, Beijing, People's Republic of China.

Preface

Sustained economic growth can contribute significantly to poverty reduction, as evidenced by marked declines in poverty incidence for economies that have enjoyed long periods of economic growth. But a financial crisis could disrupt growth and frustrate such development. While crisis-hit economies will recover from the crisis, they may not return to the pre-crisis growth path. Because a crisis can have long-term development implications, the Asian Development Bank Institute (ADBI) is keen to make a contribution to the understanding of the causes of a crisis and to the formulation of policy measures that ADB's developing member countries could adopt to avoid a crisis.

Many fast growing economies in Asia suffered from a financial crisis in 1997–98, which could be attributed largely to their inability to deal with large capital flow volatility. Although few deny the benefits of capital inflows for recipient economies, they often create problems especially if they are substantial and volatile. Massive capital inflows can create too much bank lending, excessive investment, and speculative activities, which can lead to goods price inflation, asset market bubbles, and potential vulnerabilities in bank, household, and corporate balance sheets. Moreover, sudden stops or reversals in capital inflows could lead to a currency crisis, the bursting of asset price bubbles, investment collapse, banking sector stress, and economic difficulties.

Since the recovery from the Asian financial crisis, many economies in the region have experienced massive private capital inflows against the backdrop of current account surpluses over many consecutive years. Cognizant of the implications of potentially volatile capital flows for the sustainability of Asian economies' growth, Thailand's former Finance Minister Chalongphob Sussangkarn made a request at ADB's Annual Meeting in Kyoto in May 2007 to conduct a study on capital flows in Asia, the results of which could be inputs for the region's policymakers in managing capital flows from national and regional perspectives. In response, ADB tasked ADBI to conduct the study. ADBI's research proposal, which laid the groundwork for this book project involving experts from leading think tanks in the region, was presented at the informal meeting of the ASEAN Finance Ministers held in Washington in October 2007. Most of this study was conducted in the first half of 2008 before the visible eruption of the global financial crisis.

Following the failure of Lehman Brothers in September 2008, the world economy experienced the worst global financial and economic crisis since the Great Depression. The economies of several European peripheral countries were severely damaged by a sudden stop in inward flow, and/or withdrawal, of capital. Even though Asian economies were not affected much by capital flow volatility with a few exceptions, they were hit hard by the downturn in export demand. But Asian economies have quickly recovered and are now leading global growth. There are signs that capital of a largely short-term nature is returning to Asia in a significant way, raising serious concern among policymakers in the region who are trying to prevent rapid appreciation of their currencies against the US dollar and to contain inflation and increases in asset prices to stabilize their economies and sustain the recovery. Indeed, following Brazil's move, Taipei,China; Indonesia; and the Republic of Korea have recently imposed capital controls to limit speculative capital inflows.

These recent developments suggest that managing capital inflows remains an important policy issue for many emerging market economies that needs to be studied rigorously and debated openly. This study clearly benefited from lessons learned from the impact of the global financial crisis on international capital flows. With the publication of this book, ADBI hopes to contribute to the debate by providing analyses that can help policymakers develop a framework for managing capital flows that is consistent with prudent macroeconomic and financial sector stability.

Masahiro Kawai
Dean and CEO, Asian Development Bank Institute

Abbreviations

ABMI	Asian Bond Markets Initiative
ABS	Australian Bureau of Statistics
ADB	Asian Development Bank
ADBI	Asian Development Bank Institute
ADM	Asian Dollar Market
AREAER	Annual Report on Exchange Arrangements and Exchange Restrictions
ASEAN	Association of Southeast Asian Nations
BBC	Basket-Band-Crawl
BI	Bank Indonesia
BIBF	Bangkok International Banking Facility
BIS	Bank for International Settlements
BNM	Bank Negara Malaysia
BOK	Bank of Korea
BOP	Balance of Payments
BOT	Bank of Thailand
BSP	Bangko Sentral ng Pilipinas
CBB	Central Bank Bills
CEE	Central and Eastern European (countries)
CEIC	China Economic Information Center
CIP	Covered Interest Parity
CMI	Chiang Mai Initiative
CPF	Central Provident Fund
CPI	Consumer Price Index
DR	Depositary Receipts
EAE	Emerging Asian Economy
EC	European Commission
ECB	European Central Bank
ECB	External Commercial Borrowing (India)
ECLAC	Economic Commission for Latin America and the Caribbean (United Nations)
EEC	European Economic Community
EMDB	Emerging Market Database
EMEAP	Executives' Meeting of East Asia-Pacific Central Banks
EMP	Exchange Market Pressure

EMU	Economic and Monetary Union
ERM	Exchange Rate Mechanism
EU	European Union
FASBI	Fasilitas Bank Indonesia
FDI	Foreign Direct Investment
FIF	Foreign Investment Fund
FII	Foreign Institutional Investors
FPRI	Fiscal Policy Research Institute
FTC	Fine Tuning Contraction
GDP	Gross Domestic Product
GND	Grama Niladhari Division
GoI	Government of Indonesia
GOI	Government of India
IADB	Inter-American Development Bank
ICAPM	Intertemporal Capital Asset Pricing Model
ICT	Information and communication technology
IFA	International Financial Architecture
IMF	International Monetary Fund
IOSCO	International Organization of Securities Commission
IPO	Initial Public Offering
IRF	Impulse Response Functions
IS/LM	Investment Saving/Liquidity Preference Money Supply
IT	Inflation Targeting
JSCB	Joint Stock Commercial Bank
JSX	Jakarta Stock Exchange
KLCI	Kuala Lumpur Composite Index
LIBOR	London Inter-Bank Offered Rates
LOOP	Law of One Price
MAS	Monetary Authority of Singapore
MHPI	Malaysia House Price Index
MOF	Ministry of Finance
MSB	Monetary Stabilization Bonds
MSS	Market Stabilization Scheme
NASDAQ	National Association of Securities Dealers Automated Quotation System
NDA	Net Domestic Asset
NEER	Nominal Effective Exchange Rate
NFA	Net Foreign Asset
NGO	Non-government organization
NOP	Net Open Position
NPL	Non-Performing Loans
NYSE	New York Stock Exchange

OECD	Organisation for Economic Co-operation and Development
PBI	Bank Indonesia Regulation
PBOC	People's Bank of China
PER	Price Equity Ratio
PPP	Public-Private Partnership
PRC	People's Republic of China
QDII	Qualified Domestic Institutional Investors
QFII	Qualified Foreign Institutional Investors
RBA	Reserve Bank of Australia
RBI	Reserve Bank of India
REER	Real Effective Exchange Rate
RP	Repurchase Rate
SAFE	State Administration of Foreign Exchange
SBI	*Sertifikat Bank Indonesia* (Government Bonds)
SBV	State Bank of Vietnam
SCIC	State Capital Investment Corporation
SDA	Special Deposit Account
SET	Stock Exchange of Thailand
SGS	Singapore Government Securities
SME	Small and medium-sized enterprise
SOCB	State-Owned Commercial Bank
SOE	State-Owned Enterprise
SSC	State Securities Commission
SUN	Indonesian Government's State Debt Security
TWI	Trade-Weighted Index
UIP	Uncovered Interest Parity
UN	United Nations
UNCTAD	United Nations Conference on Trade and Development
UNDP	United Nations Development Programme
UNEP	United Nations Environment Programme
URR	Unremunerated Reserve Requirements
VAR	Vector Autoregression
VECM	Vector Error Correction Model
WB	World Bank
WTO	World Trade Organization

Note: Throughout this book the term 'billion' refers to 1000 million; the term 'trillion' refers to 1000 billion.

Introduction
Masahiro Kawai and Mario B. Lamberte

In 1997–98, emerging Asian economies were subjected to a crisis, with Thailand, Republic of Korea (hereafter Korea), Indonesia, and Malaysia being the most affected economies. The crisis was preceded by surges in private capital inflows of a largely short-term nature, creating double mismatches of currencies and maturities, and inflating asset prices, followed by a sudden stop and massive reversals of capital flows. With central banks of crisis-affected countries not being able to hold the line, currencies depreciated sharply, exposing the weaknesses of the banking system.

Although the crisis devastated several emerging Asian economies, the recovery of crisis-hit countries proved to be remarkable, facilitated by comprehensive government reforms and a favorable external environment. Since the recovery from the Asian financial crisis, most emerging Asian economies have enjoyed current account surpluses, attracting more foreign capital, and accumulating international reserves that have reached new heights. Yet, these very same developments pose major policy challenges to policymakers in the region.

Massive capital inflows put pressure on the currency to appreciate; this has prompted monetary authorities in the region to intervene in the foreign exchange markets. However, the tendencies of emerging Asia's currencies to appreciate against the US dollar continue, threatening their competitiveness. Policymakers in the region are faced with questions on best policy responses and regional cooperation initiatives to utilize capital inflows while maintaining macroeconomic stability.

Against this background, the Asian Development Bank Institute (ADBI) organized a series of conferences to provide a forum for policymakers, academics, and private sector participants to identify, study, and debate issues on capital flows and alternative measures for managing such flows. As these papers have been largely prepared as a basis for policy dialogue among national and regional policymakers, we hope that they would help shape the development of a framework for managing capital flows in the region.

The sixteen chapters in this volume are the fruit of the collaborative efforts of the participants in this project. The chapters are grouped into three parts: (i) Managing Capital Flows in Emerging Asia and Review of the Literature (Chapters 1 and 2); (ii) Perspective Papers (Chapters 3 to 7); and (iii) Country Studies (Chapters 8 to16).

The first chapter, by Masahiro Kawai and Mario B. Lamberte, which partly draws from the analyses made by various chapters of this book, provides a comprehensive discussion of the experiences of Asia's emerging economies with surges in capital inflows and in managing such inflows. They argue that following the restoration of the US and European financial stability and the easing of the ongoing global credit crunch precipitated by the US subprime crisis, capital inflows to emerging Asian economies (EAEs) will likely resume in a big way and pose serious policy challenges to EAEs for macroeconomic management, exchange rate policy, and financial sector supervision. In the final section of the chapter, the authors suggest possible policy measures to manage capital flows that are consistent with macroeconomic and financial sector stability. They include, among others, improving prudential regulations, using capital controls at the time of inflow surges rather than as a permanent measure in a country where the regulatory authorities have the administrative capacity to enforce them, making the fiscal stance countercyclical to surges in capital inflows, rebalancing growth, and exploring regional collective action such as exchange rate coordination and strengthening of regional financial market surveillance and integration.

Chapter 2 by Masahiro Kawai and Shinji Takagi presents a succinct literature survey focusing on developing and emerging market economies. More specifically, they review empirical work on the benefits of free capital mobility and discuss the evolution of thinking on capital account liberalization, the use of capital controls as an instrument of managing capital inflows, and the effectiveness and limitations of conventional macroeconomic and structural instruments. The authors point out that the literature provides little practical guidance on capital account liberalization, except to advocate the need for pursuing sound macroeconomic policies and establishing an effective framework of prudential regulation. They stress the need for additional work to develop tools to identify and quantify the various risks of capital inflows.

Chapter 3 by Stephen Grenville discusses key operational questions confronting policymakers, particularly those directed to central bankers. Grenville addresses the question of why capital flows cause problems to economies, particularly emerging market economies, and discusses policy responses that might be grouped into two categories: those preventative measures put in place *before* the crisis, and those used to try to ameliorate the unfolding crisis. He suggests a practical research agenda that would encompass the design parameters of a managed float, reserve holdings, and intervention policies, including the possibility of using state-contingent assets and government foreign/domestic debt management, as well as conventional reserves.

Chapter 4 by Susan Schadler reviews episodes of large capital inflows of economies in several regions since the early 1990s and investigates the macroeconomic characteristics of successful episodes. Schadler finds that only a modest portion of the capital inflow episodes have ended in crisis, and overheating pressures have not in general been severe. While all regions experienced some crises, proportionately more emerging Asia episodes had hard landings. She points out that much attention has been given to the issue of whether sterilized intervention or capital controls are effective in managing capital flows, but insufficient attention has been accorded to fiscal policy which she argues is most likely to have a strong and constructive effect.

Chapter 5 by Robert N. McCauley surveys the nature of hot money inflows into Asia since the peak of the US dollar in the first quarter of 2002 and the policy responses to them. McCauley points out that the most important qualitative change since 2002 involved foreign bank flows, which have returned to net inflows after five years of pay-down after the 1997–98 financial crisis. Carry trades, although difficult to measure, appear to have become important. He observes that capital inflows have become more volatile in recent episodes and that the authorities in the region have adopted measures both to encourage outflows and to discourage inflows to deal with such volatility. McCauley concludes that progress in Asia toward fuller capital account convertibility has the character of two steps forward, one step back, rather than a monotonic process.

Chapter 6 by Eduardo Levy-Yeyati, Sergio L. Schmukler, and Neeltje van Horen analyzes the effects of capital controls and crises on the integration of emerging economies with the international financial system. The authors characterize the behavior of the cross-market premium around crises and changes in different types of capital controls by computing summary statistics and by using an event-study methodology. They find that controls on cross-country capital movement appear to work as intended and segment markets effectively. They also find that when crises erupt, the cross-market premium becomes volatile, reflecting the shocks that markets receive and the difficulties in performing instantaneous arbitrage. The authors conclude that cross-market premium could be used as a tool to measure capital market integration, particularly during periods of capital controls and crises.

Chapter 7 by Jürgen von Hagen and Iulia Siedschlag discusses the experience of Central and Eastern European countries which recently joined the European Union with capital account liberalization and discusses some lessons and implications for EAEs. The authors find that since 2000, the group of fast liberalizers has experienced larger net capital flows than the gradual liberalizers. They argue that fiscal policy is the more appropriate policy instrument for dealing with large capital inflows and add that more effective spending controls and improved budgeting procedures rather than higher taxes will best promote macroeconomic stability.

The next nine chapters detail the experiences of emerging Asian economies in managing capital flows. They analyze the types and magnitude of capital flows, their impacts on the domestic economy, and effectiveness of national authorities' responses, and discuss policy implications.

In Chapter 8, Yongding Yu provides a comprehensive account of the evolution of the People's Republic of China's (PRC) management of capital flows. The PRC's successful management has been crucial in achieving high growth rates and macroeconomic stability, and should be treated as part of a long-term economic reform and liberalization program, not merely a way to reduce the pressure on the Chinese yuan to appreciate. With the lowering of the interest rate in the US, Yu argues that the objective of tightening monetary conditions has become increasingly difficult to achieve. Thus, he recommends that the PRC maintain capital controls whenever possible so that the People's Bank of China can implement an independent monetary policy to sustain the economy's growth in the next decade.

In Chapter 9, Ajay Shah and Ila Patnaik point out that there is a substantial mismatch between the needs of India, a fast-growing and fast-globalizing trillion dollar economy, and the present policy framework of capital controls and monetary policy. The authors argue that at this point in India's progression towards integration into the world economy, the rapid dismantling of capital controls appears to be the best strategy. However, this opening up needs to be accompanied by a monetary policy reform, a shift towards greater exchange rate flexibility, and the creation of currency derivatives markets. They point out that the lack of defined goals of the central bank is the most important weakness of the Indian policy environment.

In Chapter 10, Ira S. Titiheruw and Raymond Atje examine capital flows in Indonesia's post-Asian financial crisis period and the country's economic performance. They observe that the government shifted its development financing away from reliance on foreign currency to local currency bonds, which have attracted foreign capital inflows. Foreign capital inflows have remained volatile, as was apparent during the mini crisis in 2005. Currently, the government and the monetary authority direct their attention towards achieving sounder economic fundamentals such as maintaining fiscal restraint and controlling inflation. The monetary authority has undertaken some measures to monitor capital flows in both directions which can help improve its capability to respond in a timely manner against any eventuality.

In Chapter 11, Soyoung Kim and Doo Yong Yang document the recent trend in capital inflows and asset prices in Korea, and review how a surge in capital inflows can increase asset prices. They find that capital inflows shocks increased the stock prices but not land prices. The effects of capital inflows on the nominal and real exchange rates are limited, and this is related to the accumulation of foreign exchange reserves. Aside from encouraging capital outflows and exploring the use of fiscal policy to counter the effects of massive capital inflows, the authors suggest that Korea expand its risk management policies on credit expansion into the equity and real estate market.

In Chapter 12, Kee Kuan Foong discusses issues pertaining to capital flows in Malaysia under two regimes: fixed exchange rate and managed float exchange rate. In recent years, massive net inflow of portfolio funds generated a rise in liquidity in the financial system. To overcome inflationary pressure and to stabilize interest rates, the monetary authority conducted sterilization operations combined with prudential lending procedures, which effectively lowered credit growth. The author also explores other policy measures to overcome the negative effects of capital flows. He points to fiscal policy which Malaysia is trying to use in conjunction with sterilization to handle surges in foreign capital.

In Chapter 13, Josef T. Yap examines the impacts of foreign currency inflows on the Philippines' domestic economy and evaluates policy responses of the country's monetary authority. He finds that capital inflows could lead to an increase in reserves, a real appreciation of the peso against the basket of major trading partners' currencies, domestic liquidity, and inflation; but they appear to have no significant impact on domestic interest rate, consumption, investment, and government expenditures. Results of his analysis lead him to conclude that the reserve accumulation and subsequent sterilization has not undermined the policy of inflation targeting. To revive domestic private investment, Yap recommends efficient utilization of overseas remittances, which are quite substantial in the Philippines.

In Chapter 14, Hwee Kwan Chow finds that Singapore's experience with capital flows after the Asian crisis appears to have been somewhat benign. She argues that it is the overall package of policies – including strong economic fundamentals and a robust financial system, prudent policy management on both the fiscal and monetary side, and credible exchange rate policy aligned with underlying fundamentals – and having the latitude to react promptly and on a sufficiently large scale to economic and financial developments that serve to increase Singapore's resilience towards disruptive swings in capital flows.

In Chapter 15, Kanit Sangsubhan points out that since the beginning of 2005, capital inflows in Thailand have increased substantially, leading to a gradual appreciation of the baht. It is estimated that a 12 per cent appreciation of the baht reduces the profits of the real sector by 6.4 per cent. Foreign exchange rate intervention made by the Bank of Thailand caused a build-up of foreign exchange reserves within a short time. In view of the negative impact of capital controls imposed on equity, bond, and currency transactions, Sangsubhan suggests that it is better to explore other strategies to reduce pressure on the baht, such as exploring several channels of capital outflows as tools for capital outflow management. He argues that monetary policy should be conducted to stabilize long-term inflation through intermediate instruments such as exchange rate.

In Chapter 16, Tri Thanh Vo and Chi Quang Pham note that the recent surges in capital inflows have led to a financial boom in Viet Nam with commensurate increase in risks, especially in the context of macroeconomic policy inconsistencies and weaknesses in financial sector supervision. In their assessment, they find that the macroeconomic policy responses so far (up to February 2008) seem to be less effective in stabilizing the economy and in reducing policy inconsistencies as well as financial risks. The authors recommend a broad reform package including tackling the bottlenecks in the economy (the weaknesses of economic institutions, infrastructure, and human resources), modernizing the State Bank of Vietnam, and strengthening risk management in the banking sector and financial supervision system. They argue for a firm commitment to combating high inflation and combining tight monetary policy with a more flexible exchange rate and tight fiscal policy.

Finally, we would like to take this opportunity to thank our paper writers, who painstakingly prepared the papers and ably addressed the reviewers' comments and suggestions, participants of the conferences for their insightful comments and guidance on the draft papers presented during the conferences, and all those who have been involved in preparing this book, particularly Elsbeth E. Gregorio for editorial assistance, Hiroyuki Kiyota and Elvira Kurmanalieva for research assistance, and Kayo Tsuchiya for administrative assistance.

PART I

Managing Capital Flows in Emerging Asia and Review of the Literature

1. Managing capital flows: emerging Asia's experiences, policy issues and challenges

Masahiro Kawai and Mario B. Lamberte

1.1 INTRODUCTION

Capital inflows provide emerging market economies with invaluable benefits in pursuing economic development and growth by enabling them to finance needed investment, smooth consumption, diversify risks, and expand economic opportunities. However, large capital flows, if not managed properly, can expose capital-recipient countries to at least three types of risks (Kawai and Takagi, Chapter 2, this book). The first is macroeconomic risk. Capital inflows could accelerate the growth of domestic credit, create economic overheating including inflation, and cause the real exchange rate to appreciate, thus affecting macroeconomic performance in a way not consistent or compatible with domestic policy objectives such as sustainable economic growth with price stability. The second is risk of financial instability. Capital inflows could create maturity and currency mismatches in the balance sheets of private sector debtors (particularly banks and corporations), push up equity and other asset prices, and potentially reduce the quality of assets, thereby contributing to greater financial fragility. The third is risk of capital flow reversal. Capital inflows could stop suddenly or even reverse themselves within a short period, resulting in depleted reserves or sharp currency depreciation. About 15 per cent of the large capital inflow episodes over the past 20 years ended in crisis, with emerging Asia experiencing proportionately more episodes of hard landings (Schadler, Chapter 4, this book), the most devastating of which occurred in 1997–98. Thus emerging Asian economies (EAEs)[1] need to manage these risks well to fully enjoy the benefits of capital inflows.

EAEs posted remarkable growth rates during the period 2000–07, with the People's Republic of China (PRC) showing the fastest growth rate. This is also the period when the region experienced current account surpluses, in contrast to the years before the Asian financial crisis (Table 1.1). In 2008, the world witnessed the eruption of systemic financial crises in the United States and Europe, simultaneous contractions of output, a dramatic shrinkage of international trade and investment, and rises in unemployment in these and many other affected economies including Asian economies. Although growth rates in almost all EAEs slowed in 2008, these still compare well with those of developing economies in other regions such as central and eastern Europe (3 per cent on average) and Western Hemisphere (4.2 per cent on average).[2] Also, most EAEs have continued to post current account surpluses in 2008. One unhealthy development is the dramatic fall in investment ratios of crisis-economies after the Asian financial crisis. In contrast, the investment ratios of the PRC, India, and Viet Nam have risen markedly and exceeded those of crisis-affected economies in recent years.

Despite sizeable current account surpluses, most EAEs had received significant private capital inflows. The International Monetary Fund (IMF) (2007) identified India, Pakistan, Thailand, and Viet Nam as Asian economies that were experiencing capital inflow episodes in the late summer of 2007. However, situations had changed considerably beginning in the last quarter of 2007 as the US subprime crisis deepened, which in the following year evolved into a global financial and economic crisis. In 2008, capital inflows in EAEs had slowed substantially and in some economies had stopped or reversed, causing currencies across the region to depreciate vis-à-vis the US dollar. However, once the global financial system has stabilized, major international financial institutions have successfully repaired their balance sheets, and cash-rich institutional investors begin to change their assessment of risks in emerging economies, capital inflows in EAEs are expected to resurge, which would most likely present the same major challenges that confronted policymakers in the region before the onset of the global financial and economic crisis. This makes it more compelling to put in place policy measures to deal with surges in capital inflows that are consistent with the objectives of macroeconomic and financial sector stability.

This chapter draws on the analyses presented in succeeding chapters of this book and other sources of information. The remainder of this chapter is organized as follows. Section 1.2 discusses the degree of capital account openness of EAEs and patterns of capital flows from 1990 to 2008, but with special focus on recent capital inflow episodes. Section 1.3 analyzes impacts of capital flows on EAEs while Section 1.4 examines the policy responses of nine EAEs to surges in capital inflows. Section 1.5 discusses policy challenges facing EAEs, especially following the restoration of US and European financial stability and the easing of the ongoing global

Table 1.1 GDP growth rates, current account balance, and investment ratio: emerging Asian economies

Economies	GDP growth (%)			Current account (% of GDP)			Investment ratio (% of GDP)		
	1990–96	2000–07	2008	1990–96	2000–07	2008	1990–96	2000–07	2008
Cambodia (CAM)	5.8	9.5	6.7	−5.0	−4.1	−10.2	10.8	18.5	n/a
China, People's Republic (PRC)	10.7	10.1	9.0	1.1	4.8	9.8	31.2	38.9	42.0
Hong Kong, China (HKG)	4.6	5.3	2.4	n/a	9.3	14.2	28.2	22.5	19.7
India (IND)	5.8	7.3	6.7	−1.3	−0.1	−3.0	22.6	27.6	34.8
Indonesia (INO)	7.5	5.0	6.1	−2.5	2.8	0.1	27.9	21.5	27.6
Korea, Republic of (KOR)	7.9	5.2	2.2	−1.6	1.8	−0.7	37.3	29.0	29.3
Lao PDR (LAO)	6.5	6.7	7.8	−14.3	−2.3	0.0	n/a	28.5	0.0
Malaysia (MAL)	9.5	5.6	4.6	−5.5	11.8	17.6	38.7	22.5	19.6
Myanmar (MYA)	5.5	8.0	n/a	−0.6	0.0	0.0	13.2	n/a	n/a
Philippines (PHI)	2.8	5.0	3.8	−4.0	0.9	2.3	22.4	16.6	14.8
Singapore (SIN)	8.8	6.0	1.1	12.4	17.6	14.9	34.5	25.1	28.5
Taipei,China (TAP)	6.9	4.1	0.1	n/a	7.1	6.4	n/a	20.3	21.2
Thailand (THA)	8.6	5.0	2.9	−7.0	2.9	0.0	40.4	25.3	27.3
Viet Nam (VIE)	7.9	7.6	6.2	−8.4	−1.8	−11.8	20.2	32.4	36.0

Sources: International Financial Statistics (IMF); World Development Indicators (World Bank); national statistics.

credit crunch. The last section discusses possible policy measures EAEs could individually and collectively adopt to effectively manage surges in capital inflows consistent with the objectives of macroeconomic and financial sector stability.

1.2 CAPITAL FLOWS IN EMERGING ASIAN ECONOMIES

Capital inflows in EAEs have been facilitated by liberalization of the capital account as well as certain 'push' and 'pull' factors. The push factors included low interest rates globally, slow growth and the lack of investment opportunities, and deregulation that allowed greater global risk diversification in industrial economies. The pull factors included the robust economic performance and the improved investment climate in EAEs, which are the results of a series of trade, financial-sector, and legal reforms and other economic liberalization measures.

1.2.1 Degree of Capital Account Openness

The degree of capital account liberalization varies across EAEs. This can be gathered from results using both *de jure* and *de facto* measurements of capital account liberalization. As regards *de jure* measurement, Chinn and Ito (2008) have constructed an index that measures the extent of financial openness of a country based on information reported by the IMF in its Annual Report on Exchange Arrangements and Exchange Restrictions (AREAER). A higher index value indicates greater degree of financial openness. As shown in Figure 1.1, Hong Kong, China and Singapore rank very high in terms of financial openness. At the other extreme is Myanmar, followed by the PRC, Viet Nam, India, and Lao PDR.

The *de jure* approach in measuring the degree of a country's capital account openness may not reflect real situations; that is, *de facto*, a country may have a more open capital account and therefore be more integrated with the international financial system. Lane and Milesi-Ferretti (2006) have developed a volume-based measure of international financial integration, defined as the ratio of the sum of stock of assets and liabilities to gross domestic product (GDP), and compiled data for 145 countries over the period 1970–2004.[3] Table 1.2 shows the evolution of this ratio for EAEs from 1990 to 2004. The ratio has been generally rising for all countries. Although India's ratio of total foreign assets and liabilities to GDP has remained low, nevertheless it has been rising through the years.

In summary, although most EAEs have maintained various types of controls on cross-border capital flows as reported in the IMF's AREAER, their capital accounts are much more open than they appear to be, as suggested by the high and generally rising ratios of total stocks of foreign assets and liabilities to GDP in recent years.

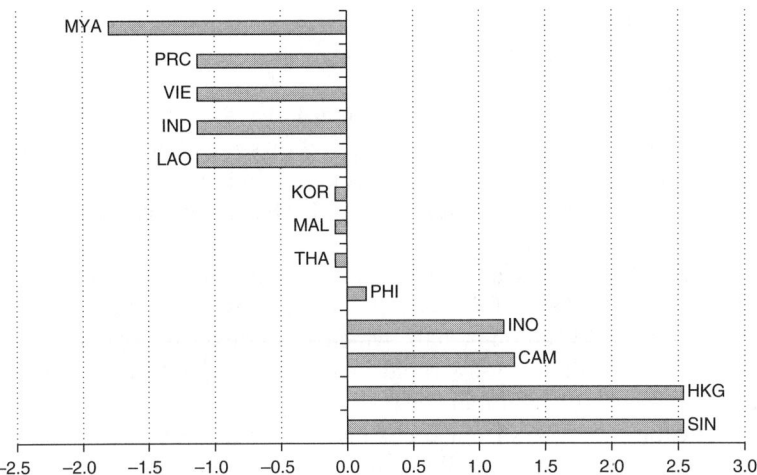

Source: Chinn and Ito (2008).

Figure 1.1 Degree of openness of the capital account: de jure, 2006

Table 1.2 Ratio of total stock of assets and liabilities to GDP, emerging Asia, 1990–2004 (%)

Economies	1990	1995	2000	2004
Cambodia (CAM)		96.3	176.8	177.3
China, People's Republic of (PRC)	38.9	58.7	84.7	102.8
Hong Kong, China (HKG)	1462.9	1338.6	1246.5	1414.6
India (IND)	30.2	39.7	42.3	57.8
Indonesia (INO)	80.6	86.2	136.8	100.7
Korea, Republic of (KOR)	35.4	50.9	82.7	109.2
Lao PDR (LAO)	215.3	147.5	198.7	170.4
Malaysia (MAL)	121.6	160.8	185.5	224.1
Philippines (PHI)	95.0	97.3	143.3	137.3
Singapore (SIN)	361.3	419.5	809.5	1023.2
Taipei,China (TAP)	103.4	97.7	132.3	272.1
Thailand (THA)	68.8	114.4	142.7	119.1
Viet Nam (VN)		96.2	110.7	110.8

Sources: Lane and Milesi-Ferretti (2006), except for TAP whose data were obtained from China Economic Information Center (CEIC) database.

1.2.2 Patterns of Capital Flows

Magnitude of capital flows

EAEs experienced a resurgence in capital flows after the 1997–98 Asian financial crisis. Total capital flows (i.e., inflows plus outflows) reached a record high of $1542 billion in 2007 from $53 billion in 1990 (Table 1.3). In relation to GDP, total capital flows in EAEs also increased to 21.6 per cent in 2007 from 3.4 per cent in 1990.

Capital inflows in EAEs generally trended upward after 1990, reaching $885 billion in 2007. The PRC's capital inflows rose dramatically in recent years, posting $241 billion in 2007, which accounted for 27 per cent of the total in EAEs. India also saw rapid increases in capital inflows in recent years, reaching $101 billion in 2007.

Total capital outflows from EAEs have also been generally rising since 1990, accelerating more rapidly in recent years to reach US$657 billion in 2007. Capital flows in the region have therefore become increasingly two-way in recent years. The PRC and Hong Kong, China had the largest amount of capital outflows in 2007, amounting to $171 and $153 billion, respectively. Together, they accounted for almost half of the total outflows in EAEs that year, followed by Singapore and the Republic of Korea (hereafter Korea). Countries with large capital outflows appear to be seeking risk diversification in their wealth holding.

Even though more than half of the net capital inflows to emerging market economies went to transition economies of eastern and central Europe, EAEs' share has increased while flows to Latin America have remained weak. EAEs' net capital inflows recorded $227.5 billion in 2007, which was equivalent to 3 per cent of their combined GDP.

Situations changed considerably in 2008 as EAEs felt the effects of the global financial and economic crisis. More specifically, capital inflows in EAEs slowed substantially and in some economies stopped or reversed as foreign investors liquidated their investments, particularly portfolio investments. In fact, this trend started in the second half of 2007 when foreign investors liquidated over $12 billion in August and November in six Asian markets with daily transaction reporting (McCauley, Chapter 5, this book). As a whole, EAEs experienced a negative net capital inflow of $15 billion in 2008.

Composition of capital flows

Figure 1.2 presents the composition of capital inflows and outflows as a percentage of GDP. Foreign direct investment (FDI) began to take the dominant role in total capital inflows in the middle of the 1990s. By the late 1990s, FDI accounted for more than half of all private capital inflows

Table 1.3 Magnitude of capital flows in emerging Asia, 1990–2008 (US$ billion)

Items	1990	1991	1992	1993	1994	1995	1996	1997	1998	1999
Gross capital flows	53.1	55.3	84.9	150.7	171.3	228.4	278.4	298.3	-183.2	176.4
% of GDP	3.4	3.3	4.7	7.6	7.3	8.2	9.0	10.0	-6.2	5.3
Gross capital inflows	43.2	51.1	59.2	104.5	118.9	161.5	196.2	151.3	-118.2	91.7
% of GDP	2.8	3.1	3.3	5.3	5.1	5.8	6.4	5.1	-4.0	2.7
Gross capital outflows	9.9	4.2	25.7	46.2	52.5	67.0	82.1	147.0	-65.0	84.7
% of GDP	0.6	0.3	1.4	2.3	2.2	2.4	2.7	4.9	-2.2	2.5
Net inflows	33.3	46.9	33.5	58.3	66.4	94.5	114.1	4.3	-53.3	6.9
% of GDP	2.1	2.8	1.9	2.9	2.8	3.4	3.7	0.1	-1.8	0.2

Items	2000	2001	2002	2003	2004	2005	2006	2007	2008
Gross capital flows	377.6	87.3	121.3	342.0	548.2	664.9	1059.8	1541.9	237.2
% of GDP	10.3	2.3	2.7	6.4	8.8	9.0	11.8	21.0	2.8
Gross capital inflows	186.0	52.3	74.5	195.3	338.3	361.6	531.5	884.7	111.2
% of GDP	5.1	1.3	1.7	3.7	5.4	4.9	5.9	12.0	1.3
Gross capital outflows	191.7	35.0	46.8	146.7	210.0	303.3	528.3	657.2	126.0
% of GDP	5.2	0.9	1.0	2.8	3.4	4.1	5.9	8.9	1.5
Net inflows	-5.7	17.3	27.7	48.5	128.3	58.3	3.2	227.5	-14.8
% of GDP	-0.2	0.4	0.6	0.9	2.1	0.8	0.0	3.1	-0.2

Sources: International Financial Statistics (IMF); World Development Indicators (World Bank); CEIC.

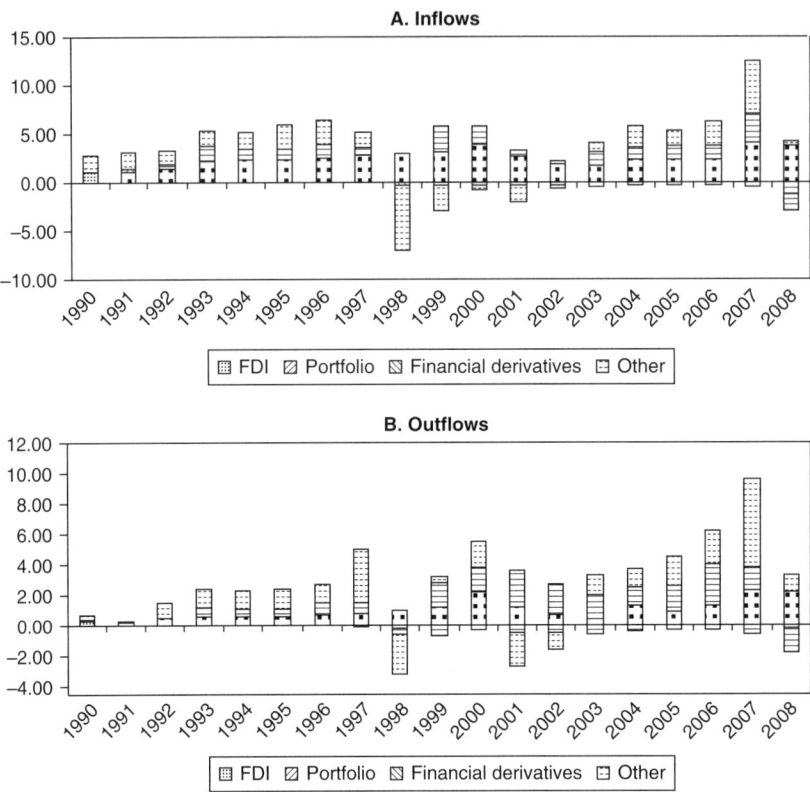

Sources: International Financial Statistics (IMF); World Development Indicators (World Bank); CEIC.

Figure 1.2 Composition of capital inflows and outflows (% GDP)

to EAEs. Total FDI inflows in EAEs amounted to $320 billion in 2008, of which 46 per cent went to the PRC. It is noteworthy that the share of portfolio investment inflows was generally higher after the Asian financial crisis, except in 2008 when portfolio flows reversed themselves.

Portfolio equity inflows in EAEs increased after the Asian financial crisis. Most Asian economies reduced barriers to investment on equity markets to recapitalize ailing banks and non-financial corporations. As a result, equity inflows rapidly increased in 1999, but momentum was reversed in 2000 due to the bursting of the information technology (IT) bubble and the subsequent recession in the US. Portfolio equity inflows resurged in recent years from $10 billion in 2002 to $109 billion in 2007. The recent increases in equity inflows in EAEs were dominated by the

PRC and India. In 2008, however, equity inflows in EAEs turned negative (−$63 billion) and showed volatile movements as the global financial and economic crisis deepened.

Unlike portfolio equity inflows, debt securities inflows were a relatively small component of capital inflows in EAEs. Underdevelopment of the local currency bond market was pointed out as one of the main reasons behind the Asian financial crisis. Several policy initiatives have been undertaken to promote local-currency denominated bond markets, and the size of regional bond markets has been expanding. In recent years, debt securities inflows have been increasing, especially for Korea.

Bank financing in EAEs was relatively small in the 1990s except in the three years prior to 1997–98 crisis. After the Asian financial crisis, bank financing accounted for a negligible proportion of capital inflows in Asia up until 2006 and 2007 when it rose sharply to almost $70 billion each year, with Korea accounting for almost two-thirds of the total. In 2008, bank financing turned negative (−$12 billion), with Korea accounting for almost all of it.

As the amount of total capital outflows increased after the Asian financial crisis, the composition of capital outflows also changed. More specifically, the ratio of portfolio investment outflows to GDP became significantly higher after the Asian financial crisis. Equity outflows rose consistently from 2004, reaching $205 billion in 2007, but dropped to $44 billion in 2008. Hong Kong, China; Korea; and Taipei,China were dominant equity investors abroad.

Portfolio debt securities outflows also rose consistently from 2004. The PRC's debt securities outflows reached US$109 billion in 2006, which was 60 per cent of EAEs' total portfolio debt securities for the year. In 2007 and 2008, however, the PRC's debt securities outflows turned negative, indicating that some investments in securities abroad were repatriated.

There was a significant rise in FDI outflows in 2007 and 2008. A large part of it was contributed by the PRC; Hong Kong, China; Korea; Singapore; and Taipei,China.

Volatility of net short-term capital flows varies greatly among EAEs during the period 2000–07 (Table 1.4). When measured as a standard deviation of the ratio of net short-term capital flows to GDP, volatility of net short-term capital flows in emerging Asia appears comparable with that of Latin America and central and eastern European economies. However, when measured as a standard deviation of the ratio of net short-term capital flows to broad money, volatility of net short-term capital flows in EAEs is generally lower than that of Latin America and central and eastern European economies.

Table 1.4 Volatility of net capital flows in emerging Asia, 2000–08 (standard deviation of net capital flows excluding FDI)

	% of GDP	% of Broad Money
A. Emerging Asian Economies		
Cambodia	3.0	16.9
China, People's Republic of	1.7	1.1
Hong Kong, China	20.9	6.2
India	2.1	8.7
Indonesia	1.3	2.8
Korea, Republic of	2.1	1.7
Lao PDR	0.2	11.8
Malaysia	8.1	3.4
Myanmar	0.0	0.0
Philippines	1.6	3.9
Singapore	7.1	5.7
Taipei,China	4.6	2.2
Thailand	4.3	3.0
Viet Nam	5.8	7.5
B. Latin America		
Argentina	7.7	61.2
Brazil	2.4	8.7
Chile	4.1	7.5
Costa Rica	1.8	7.6
Venezuela, Rep. Bol.	2.7	15.6
C. Central and Eastern Europe		
Bulgaria	8.0	13.9
Czech Republic	2.8	4.8
Estonia	6.1	12.3
Hungary	4.2	8.5
Latvia	7.1	11.9
Lithuania	3.7	7.1
Poland	2.5	5.4

Sources: Balance of Payments Statistics (IMF); and World Development Indicators (World Bank).

1.3 IMPACT OF CAPITAL FLOWS

The combination of persistent current account surpluses, rising capital inflows, and accumulation of foreign exchange reserves in Asia with persistent US deficits exerted upward pressure on the exchange rates in EAEs.

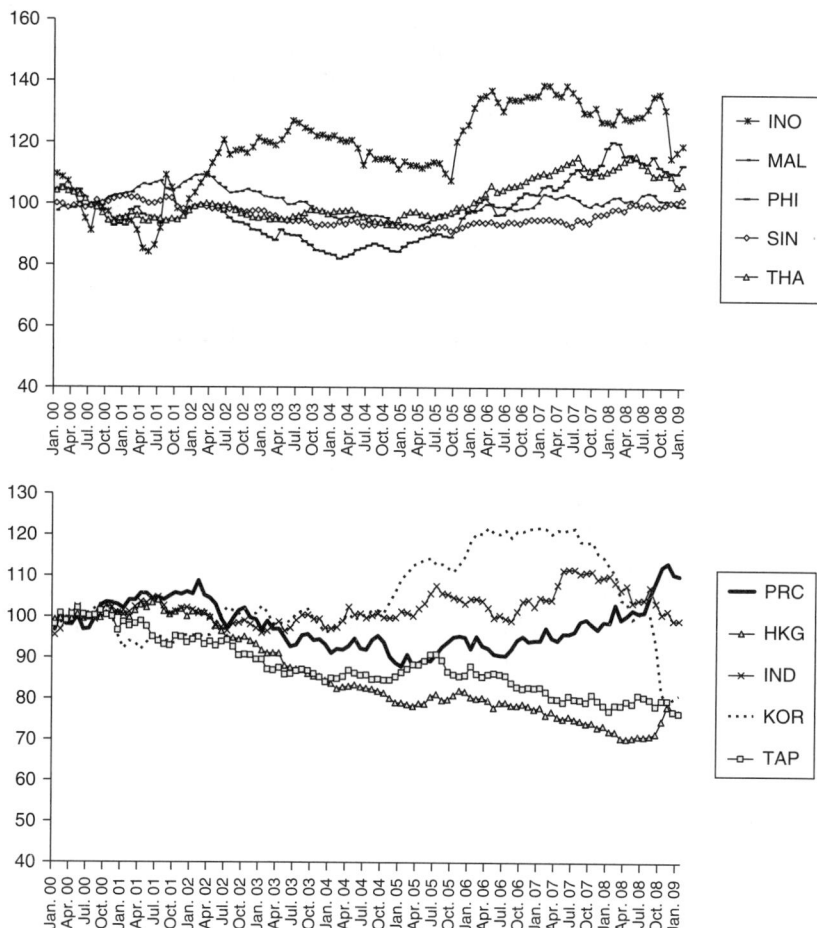

Source: Bank for International Settlements.

Figure 1.3 Real effective exchange rates, emerging Asian economies 2000–09 (2000 = 100)

More specifically, real effective exchange rates in EAEs, except Hong Kong, China and Taipei,China, generally tended to appreciate after 2004 (Figure 1.3). This trend, however, was reversed in most economies in the region starting in late 2007 due to substantial nominal depreciation in their currencies brought about by a large increase in capital outflows.

Accumulation of massive foreign exchange reserves is one of the most significant changes in the region's landscape since the Asian financial crisis. Total reserves held by EAEs rose from $214 billion or 5 per cent of GDP in 1990 to $3.4 trillion or 25 per cent of GDP in 2007, with the PRC contributing almost three-fifths of the total (Table 1.5). The reserve accumulation was the result of intervention in the currency market to stabilize exchange rates vis-à-vis the US dollar with varying degrees. In 2008, some economies in the region such as India, Korea, and Malaysia experienced a substantial decline in foreign exchange reserves compared to 2007 levels as a result of their intervention in the foreign exchange market to slow the depreciation of their respective currencies resulting from reversal in capital flows. The declines in foreign exchange reserves in these economies were, however, more than offset by increases in foreign exchange reserves in the PRC; Hong Kong, China; Singapore; Taipei,China; and Thailand.

Most EAEs exhibited relatively stable growth in money supply after 1998 (Table 1.6). In 2006 and 2007, however, many EAEs experienced higher increases in the growth rate in money supply. This suggests that central banks in the region only partially sterilized their intervention in the foreign exchange market to moderate the impact of surges in capital inflows on money supply.

After the Asian financial crisis, goods and services price inflation stayed generally at lower levels, albeit inflation rates in Indonesia, Lao PDR, and Myanmar were generally higher than those of other EAEs (Table 1.7). However, inflation rates for many EAEs rose markedly in 2008 as a result not only of the monetary impact of rising foreign exchange reserves, but more importantly of increases in the prices of oil, food, and other commodities in the global markets. This situation appears to be temporary as commodity and food prices declined sharply in the last few months of 2008 and continued to decline well into the first quarter of 2009, thereby easing inflationary pressure.

Unlike goods and services price inflation, equity prices in most EAEs increased markedly between 2003 and 2007 (Figure 1.4). Indonesia, India, and the PRC showed strong price hikes in equity markets during this period. Capital inflows to the stock markets of EAEs increased the demand for stocks. Since stocks in these economies are few, such an increase in demand raised equity prices to levels not supported by fundamentals. However, significant reversals in equity price booms started in October 2008 due to the worsening of the US subprime mortgage crisis that caused a global liquidity crunch and increased risks in global equity markets. Economies that saw significant increases in equity prices before the US subprime mortgage crisis experienced sharp falls in equity prices as foreign investors withdrew substantial amounts of investments from equity markets in these economies. Although equity prices started to recover in April 2009, at the end of June 2009, they had not yet reached

Table 1.5 Foreign exchange reserves, emerging Asian economies (US$ billion)

Economies	1990	1995	2000	2001	2002	2003	2004	2005	2006	2007	2008
Cambodia	0.0	0.2	0.5	0.6	0.8	0.8	0.9	1.0	1.2	1.8	2.3
% of GDP	0.0	5.6	13.7	14.7	18.1	17.5	17.8	15.2	15.9	20.9	22.2
China, People's Republic of	29.6	75.4	168.3	215.6	291.1	408.2	614.5	821.5	1068.5	1530.3	1949.3
% of GDP	8.3	10.4	14.0	16.3	20.0	24.9	31.8	36.7	40.2	45.2	45.0
Hong Kong, China	24.6	55.4	107.5	111.2	111.9	118.4	123.5	124.2	133.2	152.6	182.5
% of GDP	32.0	38.4	63.7	66.7	68.4	74.7	74.5	69.9	70.2	73.7	84.7
India	1.5	17.9	37.9	45.9	67.7	98.9	126.6	131.9	170.7	267.0	247.4
% of GDP	0.5	5.0	8.2	9.6	13.3	16.4	18.2	16.2	18.7	23.4	20.2
Indonesia	7.5	13.7	28.5	27.2	31.0	35.0	35.0	33.1	41.1	55.0	49.6
% of GDP	6.5	6.8	17.3	16.6	15.5	14.7	13.7	11.5	11.3	12.7	9.7
Korea, Republic of	14.8	32.7	96.1	102.8	121.3	155.3	199.0	210.3	238.9	262.2	201.1
% of GDP	5.6	6.3	18.0	20.4	21.1	24.1	27.6	24.9	25.1	25.0	21.6
Lao PDR	0.0	0.1	0.1	0.1	0.2	0.2	0.2	0.2	0.3	0.5	0.6
% of GDP	0.2	5.2	8.0	7.4	10.5	9.8	8.9	8.1	9.9	12.6	11.9
Malaysia	9.8	23.8	28.3	29.5	33.4	43.8	65.9	69.9	82.1	101.0	91.1
% of GDP	22.2	26.8	31.4	33.5	35.1	42.1	55.6	53.6	52.6	54.1	41.2
Myanmar	0.3	0.6	0.2	0.4	0.5	0.6	0.7	0.8	1.2	0.0	0.0
% of GDP	1.3	0.5	0.1	0.1	0.1	0.0	0.0	0.0	0.0	0.0	0.0
Philippines	0.9	6.4	13.1	13.5	13.3	13.7	13.1	15.9	20.0	30.2	33.2
% of GDP	2.1	8.6	17.4	17.7	17.5	16.9	14.5	16.1	17.0	21.0	19.9
Singapore	27.8	68.8	80.2	75.7	82.2	96.2	112.6	116.2	136.3	163.0	174.2
% of GDP	75.4	81.6	86.5	88.4	93.1	103.3	102.7	96.0	97.9	97.6	95.7

Table 1.5 (continued)

Economies	1990	1995	2000	2001	2002	2003	2004	2005	2006	2007	2008
Taipei,China	72.4	90.3	106.7	122.2	161.7	206.6	241.7	253.3	266.1	270.3	291.7
% of GDP	44.0	33.0	33.2	41.9	54.3	67.6	73.0	71.2	72.6	70.3	74.6
Thailand	13.3	36.0	32.0	32.4	38.0	41.1	48.7	50.7	65.3	85.2	108.7
% of GDP	15.6	21.4	26.1	28.0	30.0	28.7	30.1	28.7	31.7	34.7	39.8
Viet Nam	0.0	1.3	3.4	3.7	4.1	6.2	7.0	9.1	13.4	23.6	23.9
% of GDP	0.0	6.4	11.0	11.3	11.7	15.7	15.5	17.0	21.9	33.4	26.4
Total	213.7	422.5	703.0	780.7	957.2	1224.9	1589.4	1838.1	2238.3	2942.7	3355.6
% of GDP	4.7	5.3	8.4	9.8	11.4	12.8	14.7	15.4	16.7	24.9	24.9

Sources: International Financial Statistics (IMF); World Development Indicators (World Bank); CEIC.

Table 1.6   Growth rates of money supply, 1991–2008 (%)

Economies	1990–94 (Ave.)	1995–99 (Ave.)	2000	2001	2002	2003	2004	2005	2006	2007	2008
Cambodia	35.6	26.7	26.9	20.5	31.1	15.4	28.3	15.8	40.5	61.8	5.4
China, People's Republic of	33.9	21.0	12.3	15.0	18.3	19.6	14.4	17.9	16.0	16.6	17.8
Hong Kong, China	11.6	10.3	9.3	−0.3	−0.9	8.4	9.3	5.1	15.4	20.8	2.7
India	17.5	16.5	15.2	14.3	16.8	13.0	16.7	15.6	21.6	22.3	20.5
Indonesia	19.4	31.0	16.6	11.9	4.8	7.9	8.9	16.4	14.9	19.3	14.9
Korea, Republic of	21.1	17.9	5.2	8.4	13.8	2.9	6.3	6.9	12.2	11.4	11.8
Lao PDR	33.8	60.1	46.0	13.7	37.6	20.1	21.6	7.9	26.7	38.7	18.3
Malaysia	16.7	16.3	5.2	2.2	5.8	11.1	25.4	15.4	16.6	11.0	13.3
Myanmar	33.9	33.6	42.5	43.9	34.7	1.4	32.4	27.3	27.2	30.0	14.8
Philippines	21.6	19.2	8.1	3.6	10.4	3.6	9.9	6.4	19.6	5.4	15.6
Singapore	12.8	13.5	−2.0	5.9	−0.3	8.1	6.2	6.2	19.4	13.4	12.0
Taipei,China	16.0	8.7	6.5	4.4	2.6	5.8	7.4	6.6	5.3	0.9	7.0
Thailand	18.7	11.5	3.7	4.2	2.6	4.9	5.4	8.2	6.0	1.3	9.2
Viet Nam	13.2	40.1	35.4	27.3	13.3	33.1	31.1	30.9	29.7	49.1	20.7

Sources: International Financial Statistics (IMF); CEIC; various central banks.

the levels achieved before the onset of the global financial and economic crisis.

1.4 POLICY RESPONSES TO CAPITAL FLOWS

Policy responses of EAEs' monetary authorities during recent surges in capital inflows can be classified into three categories: intervention in the foreign exchange market; reduction in interest rates; and capital controls. A summary of such responses largely based on the nine country studies conducted by various authors for this book is discussed below.

1.4.1   Intervention in the Foreign Exchange Markets

During recent episodes of surges in capital inflows, all nine economies intervened in the foreign exchange market to reduce pressure on their domestic currencies to appreciate so as to maintain price competitiveness of their exports, but sterilized such intervention to a large extent through various ways.[4]

Table 1.7 Annual inflation rates, 1990–2008 (%)

Economies	1990–94 (Ave.)	1995–99 (Ave.)	2000	2001	2002	2003	2004	2005	2006	2007	2008
Cambodia	96.8	6.0	−0.8	0.7	3.7	−20.0	5.3	8.4	4.2	14.0	12.5
China, People's Republic of	12.4	3.1	0.9	−0.1	−0.6	2.7	3.2	1.4	2.0	6.6	2.8
Hong Kong, China	9.9	2.6	−2.1	−3.6	−1.5	−1.9	0.3	1.4	2.3	3.8	2.0
India	10.3	8.6	3.2	5.2	4.0	2.9	4.6	5.3	6.7	5.5	9.7
Indonesia	8.9	20.8	9.3	12.5	9.9	5.2	6.4	17.1	6.6	5.4	11.1
Korea, Republic of	6.9	4.3	2.8	3.2	3.7	3.4	3.0	2.6	2.1	3.6	4.1
Lao PDR	12.3	55.8	10.6	7.5	15.2	12.6	8.6	8.8	4.7	5.6	3.2
Malaysia	2.9	3.4	1.2	1.2	1.6	1.2	2.2	3.3	3.1	2.2	4.3
Myanmar	n/a	27.6	3.8	53.8	54.0	8.0	7.7	12.6	38.7	28.8	9.2
Philippines	10.6	7.8	6.5	4.5	2.5	3.9	8.6	6.7	4.3	3.9	8.0
Singapore	2.8	0.8	2.1	−0.6	0.4	0.7	1.3	1.3	0.8	3.9	5.4
Taipei,China	3.8	1.9	1.6	−1.7	0.8	−0.1	1.6	2.2	0.7	3.3	3.8
Thailand	4.2	5.0	1.4	0.7	1.7	1.7	3.0	5.8	3.5	3.2	0.4
Viet Nam	34.3	4.4	−0.6	0.9	4.1	3.1	9.8	8.8	6.7	12.6	19.9

Source: World Economic Outlook Database (IMF) October 2009, http://www.imf.org/external/pubs/ft/weo/2009/02/weodata/ (accessed 14 December 2009).

The People's Bank of China (PBOC) initially used treasury bonds in June 2002 to deal with surges in foreign exchange inflows (Laurens and Maino, 2007). When it ran out of treasury bonds, the PBOC started selling its own low-yielding central bank bills (CBBs) to commercial banks. To complement the open market sale of CBBs, the PBOC reversed its policy of reducing the reserve requirement and raised the reserve requirement ratio 15 times during the period September 2003 to end-2007. According to Yu (Chapter 8, this book) the PBOC was able to sterilize 8 trillion yuan of the 11 trillion yuan high-powered money it created as of October 2007 when it intervened in the foreign exchange market.

The Reserve Bank of India (RBI) conducted open market sales of government securities from its portfolio to neutralize the effect of its purchases of foreign exchange on the monetary base. However, it ran out of government securities in late 2003 (Shah and Patnaik, Chapter 9, this book). In January 2004, the Government of India (GOI) and RBI agreed to put in place the Market Stabilization Scheme (MSS), which authorizes the latter to sell bonds on behalf of the government for the purpose of sterilization. As pointed out by Shah and Patnaik, a key strength of MSS lies in the

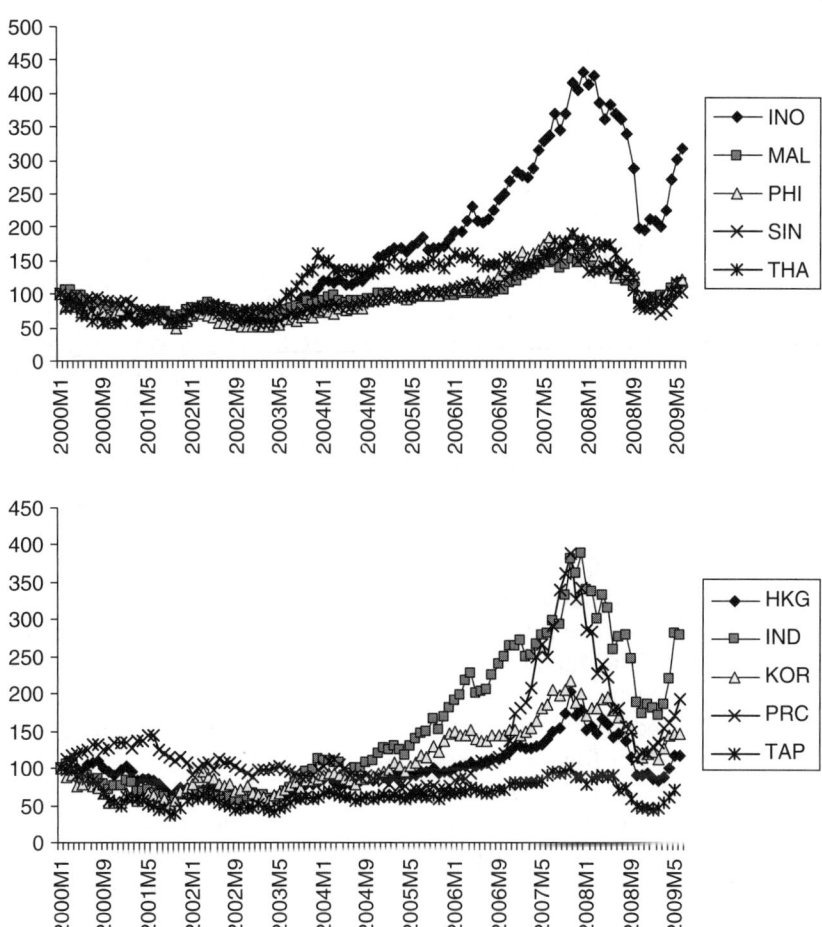

Sources: Reports of various stock exchanges.

Figure 1.4 Stock price indices, emerging Asian economies, 2000–09 (Jan. 2000 = 100)

fact that it makes the cost of sterilized intervention more transparent; that is, interest payments for MSS face scrutiny in the budget process. To complement its sterilized purchases of foreign exchange, RBI raised reserve requirement ratios, thus reversing its policy of phasing out reserve requirements.

Bank Indonesia (BI) intervened in the foreign exchange market but partially sterilized such intervention mainly using one-month and three-month

Bank Indonesia Certificates (SBI). SBIs' interest rates were more than 8 per cent, which attracted more portfolio inflows especially since non-residents are allowed to hold such certificates.[5] Since the BI was committed to its inflation-targeting monetary framework and had been confronted by depreciation threats rather than appreciation, it allowed the exchange rate to partially absorb the impact of capital inflows (Titiheruw and Atje, Chapter 10, this book).

The Bank of Korea (BOK) used its own monetary stabilization bonds (MSBs) to sterilize the effect of its intervention in the foreign exchange market on money supply. Since the stock of MSBs had risen so much after several years of intervention in the foreign exchange market, making it more costly for the BOK to use the MSBs for sterilization purposes, the Korean government came in to assist the BOK in its sterilization measure by selling government securities and depositing the proceeds with the BOK. As in India, such an approach makes the cost of sterilized intervention more transparent. In addition to such measures, the BOK also increased the average reserve requirement ratio in 2006 (Kim and Yang, Chapter 11, this book).

Bank Negara Malaysia conducted sterilized operations to overcome inflationary pressure and to stabilize interest rates in the face of massive inflows of portfolio funds. As pointed out by Foong (Chapter 12, this book), net domestic assets declined in 2004 possibly due to a sterilization measure effected by the monetary authority aimed at neutralizing the impact of large portfolio inflow speculating on the currency.

The Bangko Sentral ng Pilipinas (BSP), the central bank of the Philippines, had been intervening more heavily in the foreign exchange market after the Asian financial crisis and tried to sterilize its intervention (Yap, Chapter 13, this book). Aside from its open market operation to mop up excess liquidity, the BSP also raised the regular and liquidity reserve ratios in July 2005. As the BSP found the need to intervene more heavily in the market to reduce liquidity, it opened in 2007 a special deposit account (SDA) facility to banks. The BSP later relaxed the rules on the SDA allowing non-bank government corporations, and banks' pension funds and trust operations to deposit excess liquidity in this facility.

Singapore is in a completely different situation from the rest of the EAEs included in this study. It was running budget surpluses averaging around 5 per cent of GDP after the Asian financial crisis and was experiencing net positive contributions to its Central Provident Fund (CPF). Both had the effect of withdrawing funds from the domestic financial system, causing the money supply to shrink and putting pressure on the Singapore dollar to appreciate. To avoid such appreciation, the Monetary Authority of Singapore (MAS) re-injected funds into the domestic financial system through its foreign exchange operations, using the Singapore dollar to purchase the US dollar (Chow, Chapter 14, this book).

The Bank of Thailand (BOT) had been intervening in the foreign exchange market to prevent rapid appreciation of the baht in the face of massive influx of foreign capital using treasury bonds. The intervention was intensified in July 2007 when the baht hit its strongest value against the US dollar. With a considerable increase in reserves during August and September 2007, the BOT sold foreign currency in the forward market for hedging purposes. Accompanied by other measures such as lowering the repurchase rate, this intervention helped in stabilizing the onshore exchange rate of the baht. However, the baht continued to appreciate in the offshore market (Sangsubhan, Chapter 15, this book).

The State Bank of Vietnam (SBV) engaged in sterilized intervention in the foreign exchange market using treasury bills and its own central bank bills. In June 2007, it raised the reserve requirement ratio for deposits under 12 months from 5 per cent to 10 per cent. Such measures were apparently ineffective as the money supply expanded sharply in 2007, exerting more pressure on inflation (Vo and Pham, Chapter 16, this book). By the end of December 2007, the SBV widened the trading band of VND/US$ to ± 0.75 per cent and raised the reserve requirement ratios by one percentage point. The SBV issued 365-day bills in March 2008 with a coupon rate of 7.8 per cent, which was slightly higher than the SBV refinancing rate but lower than the rediscount rate, and required commercial banks to purchase such bills. This measure forced banks to run to the inter-bank market, causing the inter-bank rates to go up to 25–30 per cent. The SBV tried to loosen up the liquidity in the inter-bank market by pumping more money into the system. Since the deposit rate started to rise as banks competed intensively to mobilize deposits to comply with the compulsory purchase of the 365-day bills, the SBV stepped in to control the situation by issuing a directive requiring all commercial banks not to raise the annual deposit rates to more than 12 per cent and by promising to meet liquidity of the banking system through the inter-bank market at reasonable rates.

1.4.2 Interest Rate Policy

Interest rate differentials can exist and persist because foreign and domestic assets are not perfect substitutes. However, in an environment wherein there are fewer restrictions on inflows and outflows of capital and domestic currency is expected to appreciate further, a sufficiently large interest rate differential can attract more interest-sensitive foreign capital. Thus, monetary authorities need to narrow that gap by lowering domestic interest rates without necessarily changing their monetary stance.

In the PRC, the PBOC was very careful in its move to tighten monetary policy by raising the interest rate because it was concerned with the impact of carry trade (Yu, Chapter 8, this book). Thus, it managed the domestic interest rate to maintain a 3-per cent spread in favor of the US$ London Inter-Bank Offered Rates (LIBOR) with the intention of letting the yuan appreciate at the rate of 3 per cent per annum.

In India, the RBI raised the reverse repurchase rate by 50 basis points and the repurchase rate by 125 basis to 6.0 per cent and 7.75 per cent, respectively, between January 2006 and April 2007, but reduced the interest rates on non-resident deposits (RBI, 2007). Bank Indonesia gradually brought down the BI rate from 12.75 per cent in January 2006 to 8 per cent in December 2007, and maintained that level up until April 2008 (Bank Indonesia, various monthly reports). In the Philippines, the BSP reduced its policy rate five times during the period March 2007–March 2008 from 7.5 per cent to 5 per cent (BSP, various reports). In Thailand, the BOT also reduced its key policy rate five times during the period January–July 2007 from 4.75 per cent to 3.25 per cent (Sangsubhan, Chapter 15, this book).

The situation in Viet Nam was quite different from other EAEs. Interest rates were left unchanged throughout 2006 and 2007, but to contain the recent surge in the money supply, the SBV raised all official interest rates on 1 February 2007 from 6.5 per cent to 7.5 per cent for the refinancing rate, from 4.5 per cent to 6 per cent for the discount rate, and from 8.25 per cent to 8.75 per cent for the basic rate (Vo and Pham, Chapter 16, this book).

1.4.3 Capital Controls

Although there have been recent impositions of capital controls to slow down inflows of foreign capital – moves such as Thailand's imposition of the 30 per cent unremunerated reserve requirement on all capital inflows, which later on was lifted; Korea's re-imposition of limits on lending in foreign currency to Korean firms; and Indonesia's move to limit rupiah transaction and foreign exchange credit to restrict speculative movements – the general trend in the region is towards liberalization of the capital account. Table 1.8 presents some measures to manage capital flows adopted by the nine economies included in the study since 2000.[6] Briefly discussed below are the cases of the PRC, India, and Viet Nam, which appear to have lower degrees of capital account openness *de jure*.

The PRC's process of liberalizing its capital account started in the mid-1980s, but was put on hold when a financial crisis struck the region in 1997–98. The process was re-launched after the PRC acceded to the World Trade Organization (WTO) and accelerated in 2003 to reduce appreciation of the yuan and improve resource allocation (Yu, Chapter 8,

Table 1.8 *Some measures to manage capital flows adopted by emerging Asian economies since 2000*

Emerging Asian economies	Capital controls	
	Inflows	Outflows
China, People's Republic of	After the PRC's World Trade Organization (WTO) accession, FDI flows were liberalized entirely. Non-residents are allowed to open yuan accounts in the PRC and to buy A shares via the Qualified Foreign Institutional Investors (QFII). The authorities relaxed restriction on domestic institutions' issuance of bonds abroad.	The authorities relaxed rules on Chinese enterprises' overseas investment. Residents are allowed to convert yuan to foreign exchanges up to $50 000 per annum. The range of qualified students who are allowed to bring out large quantities of foreign exchanges for studying abroad has been widened. Residents are allowed to buy foreign equities via the Qualified Domestic Institutional Investor (QDII) scheme.
India	Portfolio inflows are allowed through Foreign Institutional Investors (FIIs). In 2007, the government introduced fresh capital controls against 'participatory notes,' which are over-the-counter (OTC) derivatives sold by a financial firm which is a registered FII to an investor who is not registered.	Individuals are now permitted to take $200 000 per person per year out of the country. Since 2004, Indian companies have been allowed to invest in entities abroad up to 200% of their net worth in a year.
Indonesia	The government exerted effort to attract foreign investments. The Investment Law of March 2007 provides equal treatment between domestic and foreign investors, binding international arbitration, elimination of forced divestiture (considered as a guarantee against nationalization), land use rights up to 95 years (from	

Table 1.8 (continued)

Emerging Asian economies	Capital controls	
	Inflows	Outflows
	35 years previously), and extended residency permits for foreign investors. Bank Indonesia has moved to limit rupiah transaction and foreign exchange credit to restrict speculative movements.	
Korea, Republic of	Re-imposed limits on lending in foreign currency to Korean firms.	All direct restrictions on original transactions of current and capital transactions have been removed with the exception of the ceiling of $3 million on overseas real estate investments. In 2005, the government granted tax incentives to portfolio investments abroad.
Malaysia		The authorities imposed no restriction on repatriation of capital, profits, dividends, interest, fees or rental by foreign direct investors or portfolio investors. Licensed onshore bank and approved merchant banks may invest abroad as long as they comply with certain laws. Residents, companies and individuals with no domestic borrowing are free to invest abroad. Investment banks are allowed to undertake foreign currency business subject to a comprehensive supervisory review on the capacity of the investment banks.

Table 1.8 (continued)

Emerging Asian economies	Capital controls	
	Inflows	Outflows
Philippines		The Bangko Sentral ng Pilipinas (BSP) encouraged private sector capital outflows through further liberalization of foreign exchange transactions such as: a symmetrical limit of 20% of unimpaired capital (oversold/overbought positions); increased limit of outward investment by Philippine residents to $12 million/year; and increased limit on allowable foreign exchange purchases by residents from banks to cover payments to foreign beneficiaries for non-trade purposes without supporting from $5000 to $10 000.
Singapore		Restrictions on the non-internationalization of the Singapore dollar were progressively liberalized. The last measure which came into effect in May 2004 stipulates that non-resident non-financial issuers of Singapore dollar bonds and equities are no longer required to swap their Singapore dollar proceeds into foreign currencies before remitting them abroad.
Thailand	The Bank of Thailand (BOT) imposed 30% unremunerated reserve requirement on all capital inflows less than 1 year on 18 Dec. 2006, but reversed the following day in the case of inflows to the equity market. This was removed in March 2008.	The authorities relaxed the regulation on foreign portfolio investment by institutional investors. Allowed companies registered in the Stock Exchange of Thailand to purchase foreign currencies to purchase assets abroad up to $100 million per year.

Table 1.8 (continued)

Emerging Asian economies	Capital controls	
	Inflows	Outflows
Viet Nam	The government moved towards unifying domestic and foreign investment regulations to establish a level playing field for both domestic and foreign investors. Beginning in 2004, foreign invested enterprises (FIEs) have been allowed to transform themselves into shareholding companies. The government also provided guidelines for purchasing and selling securities by foreigners at the securities trading centers.	

Sources: Yu (Chapter 8, this book); Shah and Patnaik (Chapter 9, this book); Titiheruw and Atje (Chapter 10, this book); Kim and Yang (Chapter 11, this book); Foong (Chapter 12, this book); Yap (Chapter 13, this book); Chow (Chapter 14, this book); Sangsubhan (Chapter 15, this book); Vo and Pham (Chapter 16, this book); and publications of central banks of the nine emerging Asian economies.

this book). The liberalization of the capital account produced some visible results. For instance, under its Qualified Domestic Institutional Investors (QDII) scheme which was introduced in June 2006, a total of $26.8 billion was remitted outward for purposes of investing in foreign equities. Under its Qualified Foreign Institutional Investors (QFII) scheme, 47 QFIIs were granted an aggregate investment quota of about $10 billion as of 30 October 2007.

The PRC's QFII scheme was, however, more restrictive compared to the scheme used by India. More specifically, India's Foreign Institutional Investors (FII) scheme had no quantitative restrictions or limitations on which global financial firms can participate in the Indian market (Shah and Patnaik, Chapter 9, this book). India's newly introduced capital control against participatory notes, which aimed at reducing capital inflows that were causing difficulties for the implementation of the pegged exchange rate, appeared to have limited impact. However, India's relaxation of controls on outward capital flows produced the intended results, with outbound flows rising to 2.1 per cent of fixed capital formation in 2006.

In Viet Nam, the authorities planned to relax regulations on capital outflow. It issued in December 2005 the Ordinance of Foreign Exchange Management that would permit individuals to obtain foreign loans and domestic economic entities to lend overseas if they met certain conditions. However, implementation of this ordinance has been delayed due to problems related to the effective monitoring of external debts (Vo and Pham, Chapter 16, this book).

1.5 CHALLENGES TO EMERGING ASIA

Since the outbreak of the US subprime crisis, private capital inflows have dwindled, and in some countries these inflows have stopped or even reversed: the global financial crisis has already induced capital outflows from many EAEs, thereby causing currency depreciation and sharp falls in stock market prices on a global scale.[7] One of the reasons for capital flow reversals is that many US financial institutions have been trying to secure needed cash and capital by deleveraging their overextended balance sheets – that is, by selling both domestic and foreign assets and reducing the need to refinance their asset-side activities. As a result, many Asian economies are now facing steeply higher risk premiums, and their access to the international capital markets is severely curtailed. Particularly vulnerable to this new development are countries that had enjoyed large capital inflows with large current account deficits, large external debt, and high inflation rates.

The recession in the industrialized countries in 2008 has adversely affected Asia's real economic activity through trade channels. The weak demand for EAEs's products – due to the negative growth of the US, European, and Japanese economies – slowed their exports and FDI inflows, further reducing their economic growth. Nonetheless, EAEs as a whole have performed better in terms of output growth and banking system stability than other emerging economies that are similarly affected by the global financial and economic crisis, and are expected to recover and post healthy growth rates sooner than other emerging economies.

Following the restoration of US and European financial stability and the easing of the ongoing global credit crunch, capital inflows to EAEs will likely resume in a big way given the robustness of the region's economy relative to those of the US and Europe. In addition, emerging economies in eastern and central Europe, which received more than half of net capital inflows to emerging economies before the onset of the global financial and economic crisis, are less likely to attract significant amounts of foreign capital in the next few years considering the huge tasks they currently face in stabilizing their economies and repairing their financial systems. This will pose serious policy challenges to EAEs for macroeconomic management, exchange rate policy, and financial sector supervision. Allowing one's currency to appreciate in response to significant capital inflows is desirable for better macroeconomic and financial-sector outcomes – from the perspective of containing domestic inflationary pressure and incipient asset price bubbles and reducing financial sector vulnerability – as it can prevent the accumulation of foreign exchange reserves, ensure more prudent monetary policymaking, and set the ground for facilitating possible external adjustment. However, it could damage international price competitiveness of the country concerned.

1.6 POLICY ISSUES

To manage persistently large capital inflows, policymakers in EAEs must address the following questions:

- Of the measures tried before, which work better and why?
- What other domestic policy options should be mobilized?
- Is there scope for collective action, particularly at the regional level?

This section discusses possible policy measures to manage surges in capital inflows, which are summarized in Table 1.9.

1.6.1 Doing More of What Has Been Tried Before

Sterilized intervention   Sterilization has been the favorite tool applied by many EAEs to prevent nominal and real exchange rate appreciation and economic overheating. Between 2000 and 2007, intervention in the foreign exchange market was unidirectional, making sterilization an increasingly costly method of preventing overheating of the economy. The need to allow greater exchange rate flexibility in times of surges in capital inflows is thus becoming more compelling. Making this an attractive policy option for the region's authorities is an important challenge that is explored below.

As of end-2008, EAEs' total foreign exchange reserves accounted for more than half of the world's total reserves. Although reserve accumulation can be regarded as a means of self-insurance against exposure to sudden stops or reversals of capital inflows, however, there is a growing consensus – based on standard measures of reserve adequacy, e.g., in

Table 1.9 Summary of policy measures

Policy tools	Intended outcome	Possible limitations	Evidence on effectiveness	Recommended policy responses
Macroeconomic measures				
Sterilized intervention	Prevent nominal and real appreciation while neutralizing the growth of base money	Rising quasi-fiscal cost; higher interest rates that attract additional inflows; unable to prevent real appreciation over the medium term due to eventual inflation	Some evidence of effectiveness in the short term, but not in the medium to long term	Limit the use of sterilized intervention as a short-run measure; reduce international reserves through a reserve-sharing arrangement (like a multilateralized Chiang Mai Initiative)
Greater exchange rate flexibility	Direct monetary policy for macroeconomic management; discourage speculative capital inflows by creating two-way risks	Loss of international price competitiveness	Limited evidence on the response of speculative flows	Allow greater flexibility through regional cooperation (see the discussion of regional collective action)
Fiscal policy tightening	Contain inflationary pressure; discourage capital inflows by reducing interest rate pressure; prevent real appreciation	Lack of flexibility and timeliness; a natural limit to the degree of tightening; reduction of the provision of some basic services and infrastructure investment; possibility of a positive signaling effect to attract additional inflows	Some evidence of effectiveness in preventing real appreciation and keeping better growth performance following capital flow reversals	Exploit the automatic stabilizer function of the budget; that is, the government may implement planned infrastructure investment and basic services delivery without increasing spending out of higher tax revenues or reducing tax rates

Table 1.9 (continued)

Policy tools	Intended outcome	Possible limitations	Evidence on effectiveness	Recommended policy responses
Structural measures				
Financial sector reform	Minimize the negative impact of capital flow reversals by promoting risk management	Not achievable in the short run	n.a.	Strengthen financial-sector supervision and regulation; develop and deepen capital markets
Controls on capital inflows	Limit capital inflows	High administrative capacity required, which is lacking in many emerging market economies	Some evidence of effectiveness in lengthening the maturity of inflows without much impact on the volume; effectiveness tends to weaken over time	For financially open economies, carefully design selective, temporary, market-based controls and avoid a system of extensive administrative controls. For financially closed economies, pursue capital account liberalization in a well-sequenced way together with institutional development
Easing restrictions on capital outflows	Reduce net inflows by encouraging outflows; allow residents to diversify risks	Insufficient pent-up demand for foreign assets; possibility of a positive signaling effect to attract additional inflows	Some evidence of promoting additional capital inflows	Ease outflow controls together with complementary measures such as strengthening financial sector supervision

Rebalancing growth	Reduce current account surpluses by refocusing sources of growth from external to domestic demand; contain upward pressure on the real exchange rate	Policymakers' reluctance to abandon existing policies	For former crisis economies, stimulate infrastructure investment. For PRC, reduce corporate and household savings and redirect investment toward social sector protection
Further trade liberalization	Reduce current account surpluses by encouraging imports; contain upward pressure on the real exchange rate	Failure of net imports to rise when the tradables sector becomes more competitive as a result; possibility of a positive signaling effect to attract additional inflows	Sustain ongoing efforts to liberalize trade
Collective action			
Global solutions			
Greater transparency	Minimize the volatility of capital flows by strengthening the role of fundamentals	Lack of sufficient attention to fundamentals by market participants	Support ongoing international transparency initiatives
Countercyclicality in financial regulation	Minimize herd behavior resulting from imperfect and asymmetric information	Unlikely to receive wide support	Consider this measure as part of the agenda for future research

Also: "Occurrence of crises despite the rise in transparency" appears under the risk column for Greater transparency, and n.a. entries appear in the recommendation column for Collective action / Global solutions rows.

Table 1.9 (continued)

Policy tools	Intended outcome	Possible limitations	Evidence on effectiveness	Recommended policy responses
Regional solutions				
Regional exchange rate coordination	Maintain macroeconomic and financial-sector stability without much affecting international price competitiveness	Not viable without a mechanism for conducting intensive policy dialogue and cooperation	n.a.	Utilize existing policy dialogue processes such as ASEAN+3 ERPD and EMEAP to achieve collective currency appreciation
Regional financial market surveillance/integration	Monitor regional financial markets and capital flows; mitigate the impact of investor herd behavior and financial contagion	Not viable without an effective institution	n.a.	Establish a new, high-level 'Asian Financial Stability Dialogue' on regional financial-sector issues
Regional cooperation on capacity building	Enhance capacity of financial regulators and supervisors to manage increasing financial risks in the markets	Not viable without an effective institution	n.a.	Include this measure among important functions of the 'Asian Financial Stability Dialogue'

terms of months of imports of goods and services, and ratios of foreign exchange reserves relative to external debt, GDP, or domestic money supply – that these foreign exchange reserves are excessive. Even though it is difficult to come up with a reliable estimate of the optimal level of reserves, the current total foreign reserves in Asia exceed the level that is needed for mitigating abrupt capital reversals or external financing in a crisis. The countries' apparent desire for large reserves may be reduced if there is a credible reserve-sharing arrangement at least at the regional level. Such an arrangement, like an expanded, multilateralized Chiang Mai Initiative (CMI), would collectively insure member countries against short-term capital reversals without each member holding unnecessarily large reserves, which is costly. Indeed, the recent agreement by ASEAN+3 finance ministers to multilateralize the CMI with $120 billion is a positive step for regional currency and financial stability.

Strengthening national financial markets One important lesson learned from the Asian financial crisis and from the recent global financial crisis is that the banks and other financial institutions must be well governed and their risk management capacity must be high. Thus, there is now great appreciation of the importance of financial-sector supervision and regulation in each country, in inducing banks and non-bank financial institutions to manage large capital inflows in a prudent way. Efforts must be intensified to: (i) improve prudential regulations such as limiting the practice of concentrating lending to a few individuals or business entities and maintaining adequate capital; (ii) ensure stronger governance and risk management of financial institutions through greater transparency and better disclosure; and (iii) enhance the capacities of regulatory bodies and strengthen their coordination.

At the same time, reforms to accelerate the development and deepening of domestic capital markets and to put in place efficient market infrastructure must be pursued to enhance the absorptive capacity of domestic financial markets to match large capital inflows. The Asian Bond Markets Initiative (ABMI) is in support of such national efforts. The growth of domestic capital markets would provide alternative channels for intermediating ample domestic savings and foreign funds for domestic investment and would help alleviate the burden put solely on the banking sector.

Controls on capital inflows Capital controls are a common tool for limiting capital inflows in emerging market economies. While capital controls can take a variety of forms, for countries that have substantially liberalized the capital account, more market-based controls – such as the Chilean unremunerated reserve requirement imposed on capital inflows – have been the predominant option in recent years. Thailand adopted this measure in December 2006, but encountered a severe side effect of rapidly falling stock prices (McCauley, Chapter 5, this book), suggesting that designing and implementing capital inflow control is not an easy task. To these economies, returning to the days of draconian capital controls or recreating a system of extensive administrative controls is no longer a viable option.

Evidence on the effectiveness of capital inflow controls is mixed (Kawai and Takagi, Chapter 2, this book). Country experiences suggest that the best market-based controls can be expected to lengthen the maturity of inflows; such controls can have little impact on the volume. The effectiveness of capital control measures tends to weaken over time as market agents find ways to circumvent them. At the same time, capital controls can produce adverse effects: they tend to increase domestic financing costs, reduce market discipline, lead to inefficient allocations of financial capital, distort decision-making at the firm level, and can be difficult and costly to enforce.[8] To the extent that capital controls are effective only for relatively short periods of time, such measures might be used at the time of inflow surges rather than as a permanent measure (Grenville, Chapter 3, this book). But again, effective implementation is not an easy task. Administering capital controls requires highly competent country regulatory authorities as they must constantly look out for unwanted flows – often disguised – entering through other channels.

The story may be different for countries such as the PRC and India, which have not substantially opened their capital accounts and have maintained restrictions on some types of capital transactions. In a way, they have been successful in managing the process of gradual capital account liberalization by moving to adopt investor-based controls and prudential-like measures. Capital account liberalization needs to be well-sequenced, proceed within an integrated framework to improve macroeconomic and financial-sector management, and be accompanied by the development of institutions that can ensure markets' continued stability.[9]

Easing restrictions on capital outflows Countries with significant capital controls have tried easing restrictions on capital outflows in a limited manner to reduce net capital inflows. Easing restrictions on capital outflows is expected to generate some capital outflows, reduce the size of net capital inflows, and hence mitigate the upward pressure on exchange rates. This is the policy that many East Asian economies, like Japan, Korea, and Taipei,China used to pursue during periods of large balance of payments surpluses. It has been adopted by the PRC and India in recent years.

As these measures are expanded, it must be kept in mind that a more liberal capital outflow policy could invite more capital inflows. Thus, to be effective, these measures need to be combined with other measures mentioned above, such as strengthening financial sector supervision.

1.6.2 Exploring Other Options

The countries in the region can explore other policy options that they have not rigorously pursued in the past in order to contain, mitigate, or cope with the adverse impact of surges in capital inflows.

Fiscal policy tightening In EAEs, fiscal policy has not yet been explored thoroughly as an instrument for managing large capital inflows. Although there is no definitive theoretical presumption on the impact of fiscal policy on capital flows, evidence from country experiences suggests that countries that use fiscal tightening tend to perform better than others in managing the adverse consequences of large capital inflows (Schadler, Chapter 4, this book). Tightening fiscal policy, or more generally making the fiscal policy stance countercyclical to surges in capital inflows has often been found to help reduce the risk of an overheating economy and the appreciation pressure on the domestic currency. This lessens the need for the monetary authorities to engage in costly and often ineffective sterilized intervention in the foreign exchange market. Exploring ways to make fiscal policy flexible in the face of surges in capital inflows, therefore, should receive high priority.

The appropriateness of this policy for EAEs must be assessed carefully because in recent years, most economies in the region have been running very slim fiscal deficits, if not fiscal surpluses. Tightening fiscal policy further can be achieved only if governments are willing to forego the provision of some basic services or curtail much needed investment in infrastructure. A realistic option in the face of surges in capital inflows and the associated economic boom would be to exploit the automatic stabilizer function of the budget. That is, the government may implement planned infrastructure investment and basic services delivery without increasing spending, out of higher tax revenues or reducing tax rates. This automatic fiscal tightening can offset the impact of the economic boom associated with surges in capital inflows and lead to a better macroeconomic outcome.

Rebalancing growth In the context of the economies affected by the 1997–98 financial crisis – Indonesia, Korea, Malaysia, the Philippines, and Thailand – there is a need to increase private investment, thus refocusing the engine of growth from external demand to domestic demand. Public investment especially in soft and physical infrastructure is a key measure to stimulate domestic demand in the short run.

In the context of the PRC, there is a need to reduce savings. The PRC's investment-GDP ratio is very high and the savings-GDP ratio is even higher. The challenge for the PRC is to reduce savings, particularly corporate savings, and redirect investment towards soft investment with high social rates of return. One effective way would be for the authorities to absorb a large portion of corporate savings (or undistributed profits) through lower interest subsidies to, and/or collection of larger dividends from, state-owned enterprises and through generally higher taxes on private corporations. The revenues could be spent on social sector protection (such as health, education, pension reform), environmental improvement, energy efficiency, and rural sector development.

Although these measures are not intended to contain or mitigate the adverse impacts of large capital inflows, they are desirable not only in and of themselves, but also in order to reduce the current account surpluses and hence to minimize upward pressure on the exchange rate.

1.6.3 Scope for Collective Action

The broad consensus in the academic literature, as well as our review of recent country experience in Asia, seems to suggest that none of the available tools to deal with large capital inflows at the individual country level is a panacea, as each involves significant costs or brings about other policy challenges. If policies taken by individual countries are of limited effectiveness, is there any room for collective policy action by a group of countries to deal with large capital inflows? Not surprisingly, relatively little has been said about the potential for collective action, given the presence of general skepticism among economists and policymakers on such approaches and the resulting reluctance of countries to pursue them. However, in the absence of effective national measures to manage excessive capital flows, and given the frequent and compelling need to do something about them, it is time to start thinking outside the box.

Global solutions On the global level, we have observed over the past several decades that there is cyclicality in global capital flows and that the pattern of capital inflows to specific emerging market economies closely matches that of global capital flows into all emerging and developing countries. One global solution, therefore, is to reduce the cyclicality of global capital flows.

The global initiatives of recent years have focused mainly on transparency as a way to minimize the volatility of capital flows. Behind the transparency initiatives is the idea that better quality information leads to a global allocation of resources that is based more on economic fundamentals, hence leading to a more efficient and stable global flow of capital. While there is no doubt that transparency can minimize surprises in the revelation of unfavorable information and hence sudden reversals, it is difficult to believe that transparency alone can eliminate the broader boom-and-bust cycles of capital flows (Metcalfe and Persaud, 2003).

The volatility of global capital flows may well be intrinsic to the way financial markets operate. Proponents of such a view point to evidence suggesting that the incidence of crises has not declined despite the increase in transparency, as evidenced by the US subprime crisis. From this perspective, the role of imperfect and asymmetric information is the key in creating herd behavior or 'information cascades' that lead to market myopia. 'Supply-side' reforms in advanced economies' financial markets can be a solution to the problem. Ocampo and Chiappe (2003), for example, proposed that a countercyclical element be included in the regulation of financial intermediation and capital flows (see also Griffith-Jones and Ocampo, 2003). However, such drastic reforms of the regulation of capital flows in source countries are not forthcoming and are unlikely to receive wide support in the near future.

Regional exchange rate coordination If no effective global responses are forthcoming, a search for a cooperative solution could begin in the Asian region. At the regional level, collective action can expand the menu of options available to individual countries. There are three relevant dimensions to regional cooperation in Asia: exchange rate cooperation, financial market supervision and integration, and capacity building on financial supervision and regulation.

If loss of competitiveness is the reason for not allowing its currency to appreciate, a country can cooperate with its competitor neighbors in similar circumstances to take the action simultaneously. Collective currency appreciation is a solution to this dilemma because it allows the economies experiencing large capital inflows to maintain macroeconomic and financial stability without much affecting the international price competitiveness and, hence, the growth prospects of individual countries within Asia (Kawai, 2008). Such collective appreciation would spread the adjustment costs across Asia, thus minimizing and balancing the costs from the perspective of individual economies.

In order for collective currency appreciation to become a viable policy option, there must be an effective mechanism of intensive policy dialogue and cooperation. The existing policy dialogue processes among the region's finance ministers (such as ASEAN+3)[10] and central bank governors (such as the Executives' Meeting of East Asia-Pacific Central Banks (EMEAP)) can play a critical role in fostering the establishment of such a mechanism.

Regional financial market surveillance and integration One of the main factors behind the severity and simultaneity of the Asian financial crisis was the large impact of swings in international investor sentiments and the spread of the contagious effects throughout the region. To mitigate the impact of investor herd behavior and financial contagion, it is critical for the region's policymakers to intensify their monitoring of financial markets and exchange information on a continuous basis. From this perspective, the surveillance and monitoring of regional financial markets is an important area for regional cooperation. The recent agreement by ASEAN+3 to set up a surveillance unit is indeed a welcome development.

It is high time for the region to introduce institutions that conduct meaningful financial market surveillance and address common issues for financial market deepening and integration. This could be best accomplished by establishing a new, high-level 'Asian Financial Stability Dialogue' on regional financial-sector issues (ADB, 2008). This forum would bring together all responsible authorities – including finance ministries, central banks, and financial supervisors and regulators – to address financial market vulnerabilities, regional capital flows, common issues for financial-sector supervision and regulation, and efforts at regional financial integration through greater harmonization of standards and market practices.

Capacity building The lessons of the Asian crisis reiterated the need for a sound regulatory and supervisory framework. The role of regulation and supervision in such a situation is to promote financial market stability and minimize systemic risk. Regulators and supervisors must therefore be well trained so that they are better prepared to handle increasing financial risks in the markets, including financial contagion. In line with this, regional cooperation on capacity building for financial regulators and supervisors can be enhanced. This would be another important function for the proposed 'Asian Financial Stability Dialogue'.

NOTES

1. In this book, EAEs include: Cambodia (CAM); People's Republic of China (PRC); Hong Kong, China (HKG); India (IND); Indonesia (INO); Republic of Korea (KOR); Lao PDR (LAO); Malaysia (MAL); Myanmar (MYA); the Philippines (PHI); Singapore (SIN); Taipei,China (TAP); Thailand (THA); and Viet Nam (VN).
2. See IMF (2009).
3. The database takes into account valuation effects and corrects for cross-country differences in definitions of items.
4. Kawai and Takagi (Chapter 2, this book) pointed out that sterilization can be any measure such as exchange of domestic bonds for foreign assets, often through open market operations, raising reserve requirement ratios, central bank borrowing from

commercial banks, and shifting of government deposits from commercial banks to the central bank, that attempts to offset the growth of monetary aggregates coming from reserve inflows.
5. See also McCauley (Chapter 5, this book) for a related discussion on this issue.
6. Only a few key measures are mentioned in the table to illustrate the direction of capital controls.
7. McCauley (Chapter 5, this book) pointed out that, in August and November 2007 alone when the US subprime crisis deepened, foreign investors liquidated over $12 billion in six Asian markets, namely, India; Indonesia; Korea; the Philippines; Taipei,China and Thailand.
8. See also Levy-Yeyati, Schmukler and van Horen (Chapter 6, this book). More specifically, they found that capital controls and crises do affect the integration of capital markets using data from firms from emerging economies that simultaneously trade their stocks in domestic and international stock markets.
9. See Kawai and Takagi (Chapter 2, this book) for a discussion of pace and sequencing of capital account liberalization, and von Hagen and Siedschlag (Chapter 7, this book) for the cases of Central and Eastern European economies.
10. ASEAN+3 consists of the 10 members of the Association of Southeast Asian Nations (ASEAN) plus the PRC, Japan, and Korea.

REFERENCES

Asian Development Bank (ADB) (2008), *Emerging Asian Regionalism: A Partnership for Shared Prosperity*, Manila: Asian Development Bank.
Chinn, M.D. and H. Ito (2008), 'A new measure of financial openness', *Journal of Comparative Policy Analysis*, **10**(3), September, 309–22.
Griffith-Jones, S. and J.A. Ocampo (2003), *What Progress on International Financial Reform? Why So Limited?*, Stockholm: Almqvist & Wiksell International.
IMF (2009), *World Economic Outlook Update*, April, Washington, DC: International Monetary Fund.
Kawai, M. (2008), 'Toward a regional exchange rate regime in East Asia', *Pacific Economic Review* **13**(1), February 83–103.
Lane, P.R. and G.M. Milesi-Ferretti (2006), 'The external wealth of nations Mark II: revised and extended estimates of foreign assets and liabilities, 1970–2004', IMF Working Paper No. 06/69.
Laurens, B. and R. Maino (2007), 'China: strengthening monetary policy implementation', IMF Working Paper No. 07/14.
Metcalfe, M. and A. Persaud (2003), 'Do we need to go beyond disclosure?', in B. Schneider (ed.), *The Road to International Financial Stability: Are Key Financial Standards the Answer?*, Basingstoke, Hampshire, UK and New York: Palgrave Macmillan.
Ocampo, J.A., and M.L. Chiappe (2003), *Counter-Cyclical Prudential and Capital Account Regulations in Developing Countries*, Stockholm: Almqvist & Wiksell International.
Reserve Bank of India (RBI) (2007), 'Annual report 2006–07', available at: http://rbidocs.rbiorg.in/rdocs/Annual Report/PDFs/79542.pdf.

2. A survey of the literature on managing capital inflows
Masahiro Kawai and Shinji Takagi

2.1 INTRODUCTION

This chapter presents a brief survey of the literature on managing capital inflows, with a focus on developing and emerging market economies. The rest of the chapter is organized as follows. Section 2.2 discusses the economic characteristics of capital inflows, including a review of empirical work on the benefits of free capital mobility. Section 2.3 provides an overview of the evolution of thinking on the pace and sequencing of capital account liberalization. Section 2.4 discusses the use of capital controls as an instrument of managing capital inflows, while Section 2.5 reviews the effectiveness and limitations of conventional macroeconomic and structural (microeconomic) instruments. Finally, Section 2.6 presents concluding remarks.

2.2 CHARACTERISTICS OF CAPITAL INFLOWS

2.2.1 Measuring the Benefits of Capital Mobility

In a perfect world, capital moves from a country with a lower rate of return to a country with a higher rate of return. Compared with what would be the case under autarky, the higher-return country both invests and consumes more in the current period, and consumes more in the future while paying back the interest on international borrowing from greater income. On the other hand, the lower-return country produces more but invests less in the current period, and augments its consumption in the future from the interest income from international lending. It is easy to show that welfare is improved in both countries as interest rates are equalized internationally. In a perfect world, free capital mobility is welfare-enhancing (Fischer, 1998).

There is disagreement over the benefits of unfettered international capital flows because we do not live in a perfect world. There are at least three reasons why free capital flows may not be optimal (Eichengreen et al., 1998; Cooper, 1999; Stiglitz, 2000). First, information is imperfect and asymmetric, especially in financial transactions. It is not possible to know the rate of return from investment with certainty, and borrowers typically know more about the probability of repayment than the lender. Neither is there a guarantee that borrowed funds are invested as promised. Second, there can be distortions in the real economy. If certain industries are protected for political reasons, capital inflows could reduce welfare by increasing production in industries with little comparative advantage. Third, the marginal rate of tax on capital differs from country to country. Thus, capital may in reality flow from a high tax country to a low tax country, irrespective of the productivity of capital.

Much of the empirical work on the benefits of capital flows has focused on the contribution of capital account openness to economic growth. Although capital inflows should at least in theory contribute to faster growth (especially in developing countries) through more efficient resource allocation, enhancing domestic savings, and transferring technological or managerial know-how, evidence is inconclusive at best (see Edison et al., 2002 for a survey).[1] For example, while Quinn (1997) finds a positive association between capital account liberalization and economic growth, Grilli and Milesi-Ferretti (1995) and Rodrik (1998) fail to find any such relationship. The more recent study of Prasad et al. (2003), by using the ratio of the gross stock of foreign financial assets and liabilities to GDP as the measure of capital account openness, concludes that financial integration is neither a necessary nor a sufficient condition for achieving a high rate of growth.

The inconclusiveness of these studies may be due to a fundamental misspecification of the way they test the benefits of capital account openness. It may be that the growth-enhancing effect of openness is a one-time event (such as a permanent increase in the level of GDP) that follows an opening of the capital account in a given country, rather than permanent differences in growth rates across countries. A series of studies that directly tested the one-time benefit of a discrete change in capital account policy – which Henry (2007) calls the policy-experiment approach – have drawn a much less ambiguous conclusion about the positive impact of stock market liberalization on growth and investment.[2] For example, Henry (2000) used event study techniques to show that stock market liberalization was followed by a temporary increase in the growth rate of private investment in major emerging market economies, while Bekaert et al. (2005) gave evidence that the impact of stock market liberalization on real per capital GDP growth was 1 per cent on average for a large number of countries.

The positive impact of capital account openness on growth is also less ambiguous for foreign direct investment (FDI). Reisen and Soto (2001), for example, examined a panel data of 44 countries over 1986–97 and found that FDI (as well as equity) inflows, but not any other type of capital inflows, are positively correlated with subsequent economic growth. Moreover, there is some evidence of a 'threshold effect', whereby a country's absorptive capacity must exceed a certain amount in order to exploit the benefits of capital inflows (Prasad et al., 2003; also Arteta et al., 2001; and Eichengreen and Leblang, 2002). This may reflect the role of human capital in translating capital inflows into productive activities (Borensztein et al., 1998) or the possibility that FDI inflows, the type of inflows known to contribute to growth, are attracted only to countries with a sufficient degree of governance or rule of law.

Empirical evidence on the other theoretical benefits of capital account openness is limited, but available evidence seems to suggest that, contrary to a theoretical prediction, developing countries with larger financial flows typically experience greater volatility in consumption. Kose et al. (2003), for example, show that the volatility of consumption relative to income rose from the 1980s to the 1990s for 'more financially integrated developing countries' while the volatility fell for both industrial countries and less financially integrated developing countries. This implies that the risk diversification role of international capital flows has been of limited usefulness for developing countries.[3] As noted in Prasad et al. (2003), the limited risk diversification role of capital account openness may be related to the procyclicality of developing country access to international capital markets, such that they tend to receive more inflows when times are good than when they are bad (Kaminsky et al., 2004). As an extreme case of greater volatility, some emerging market economies experienced a 'sudden stop' (Dornbusch et al., 1995; Calvo and Reinhart, 2000) in international capital inflows in the 1990s and early 2000s, with a severe adverse impact on macroeconomic performance.[4]

2.2.2 Recent Features of Capital Flows

The post-World War II international monetary system was based on the notion that unfettered international capital flows were not welfare-enhancing. The idea that free capital mobility is incompatible with a free trading system was well accepted in academia and the mainstream policymaking community when the International Monetary Fund (IMF) was established (Bloomfield, 1946). Consequently, the IMF Articles of Agreement granted member countries the right to maintain controls over capital transactions, though not on current transactions (see also James,

1996). It was only in the context of extensive trade liberalization that the majority of industrial countries began to liberalize capital flows; given a degree of substitutability between current and capital transactions, capital controls became less effective and more distortionary.[5] More recently, an increasing number of emerging market and developing countries have followed suit.

Cyclicality has been an important feature of capital flows into emerging and developing countries (see Schadler, Chapter 4, this book, for more discussion). Capital flows almost dried up in the early 1980s in the aftermath of a developing country debt crisis, but they increased sharply in the early 1990s. In the background was the liberalization of the capital account in an increasing number of emerging market economies in Asia, Latin America and Eastern Europe, but there were also various 'pull' and 'push' factors. The pull factors included higher rate of return on capital and improved investment climate in these countries, which had resulted from a series of trade, financial, and other economic liberalization measures, and the development of a legal framework to protect investor rights. On the other hand, the push factors included low interest rates, slow growth, lack of investment opportunities, and deregulation that allowed greater global risk diversification in industrial countries. Chuhan et al. (1998) showed that, during 1988–92, the pull factors were more important in Asia, while they were as important as the push factors in Latin America (see also Fernandez-Arias and Montiel, 1995; Calvo et al., 1996).

The magnitude of capital inflows experienced by some of these countries, especially in Asia, was massive indeed. For example, the total volume of capital inflows amounted to 52 per cent of GDP in Thailand and 46 per cent in Malaysia between 1988 and 1995. As country after country experienced an accumulation of international reserves and an expansion of the money supply (under a dollar peg policy), a current account deficit (as a counterpart of capital inflows), a rapid rise in equity and real estate prices, and expanding domestic consumption, the challenge of addressing the economic consequence of large capital inflows began to be referred to as the 'capital inflow problem'.

The sharp decline that followed the 1997–98 Asian financial crisis was reversed with a sudden recovery in 2003, which may well have been the beginning of another upward cycle. During the recent wave, however, the nature of the inflows appears to have changed. Whereas in the 1990s, inflows into emerging markets occurred against the background of a large current account deficit, more recently the emerging market economies have collectively registered a current account surplus. This is particularly pronounced among the Asian countries, where they have been net capital exporters though their gross inflows have been large. Not only has this presented the countries with greater currency appreciation pressure than during the previous episode of inflows, but it has also raised the interesting question as to whether it is only net inflows that matter for policymakers or whether gross inflows also matter (Schadler, Chapter 4, this book).

It must be acknowledged that emerging markets are inevitable recipients of capital inflows in the process of building their capital labor ratio up to the levels prevailing in mature economies (Grenville, Chapter 3, this book; Schadler, Chapter 4, this book). At the same time, it is difficult to believe that capital flows can be so volatile if they are driven by such fundamental economic factors alone. Recent experience suggests that there is also a geographical component to the pattern and size of net capital inflows (which Schadler calls the 'neighborhood' effect). For these reasons, some believe that speculation, herd behavior, and other non-economic factors play a significant role in the determination of capital flows (Cooper, 1999). Indeed, there is some empirical evidence to suggest that foreign investors tend to display greater herding behavior than domestic investors in emerging stock markets (see Bikhchandani and Sharma, 2001).

2.2.3 Controlling the Risks of Capital Inflows

In considering the risks of capital inflows and the possible policy responses to them, we must make a clear distinction between two types of inflows. One is inflows that are driven by fundamental factors (such as a disparity in capital labor ratios across countries) and thus expected to be sustained over time. Emerging markets that open the capital account provide the world with profitable investment opportunities through higher interest rates; moreover, the existing stock of financial assets in those economies may also become attractive to foreign investors. Under these circumstances, countries must accept the inevitability of a pickup in international capital inflows and an appreciating real exchange rate (Grenville, Chapter 3, this book). The other type of capital inflows is not driven by economic fundamentals and may thus be reversed in the future. In some sense, such capital inflows can legitimately be considered 'excessive', relative to some sustainable or desirable level.

Regardless of the type, the rationale for managing capital inflows rests on the presence of an imperfection, whether it is in the absorptive capacity of a recipient or the nature of the inflows themselves. Recent experience shows that, with a weak regulatory framework, large capital inflows can exceed the absorptive capacity of a country's banking system, leading to inappropriate lending decisions and a subsequent buildup of financial system fragility. If capital flows are largely driven by economic fundamentals but the absorptive capacity is weak, the challenge to policymakers is not to stop the capital inflows or to prevent the real exchange rate appreciation altogether, but to align the magnitude to the capacity in the short run while building the necessary infrastructure, including the risk management skills of financial institutions. If capital flows are driven by speculation or herd behavior, the challenge is more daunting. Policymakers must somehow limit the emergence of an asset price bubble and the country's vulnerability to capital flow reversal, including from contagion from elsewhere. Although how to measure the risks of capital inflows is a complex issue, we can at least conceptually consider the following three types of risks:

- *Macroeconomic risks* Capital inflows could accelerate the growth of credit (or even create loss of monetary control), cause the real exchange rate to appreciate, cause inflation, and affect other macroeconomic variables in a way inconsistent or incompatible with immediate domestic policy objectives, such as price stability, exchange rate stability, and export promotion (see Fernandez-Arias and Montiel, 1995). Grenville (Chapter 3, this book), however, argues that the macroeconomic consequences of recent capital inflows, including on monetary control and inflation, have not been so large, although the impact on real exchange rates may have been (Schadler, Chapter 4, this book).

- *Financial stability risk* Capital inflows could push up equity and other asset prices, reduce the quality of assets, and adversely affect the maturity and currency composition of the balance sheets of the private sector (particularly banks and corporations), thereby contributing to greater financial fragility. Recent experience suggests that the impact of capital inflows on asset prices has been particularly significant (Grenville, Chapter 3, this book; Schadler, Chapter 4, this book).

- *Risk of capital flow reversal* Capital inflows could reverse themselves suddenly, with a potential for the depletion of reserves or sharp currency depreciation. Schadler (Chapter 4, this book) notes that about 15 per cent of the capital inflow episodes over the past 20 years ended in crisis.[6] It is mainly against this crisis risk that many countries in Asia have accumulated large foreign exchange reserves as a form of self-insurance.

Conventional wisdom in the economics literature has typically focused on the third type of risk and holds that long-term flows are less risky than short-term flows because they are presumably less speculative (Claessens et al., 1995; Carlson and Hernandez, 2002); the ratio of short-term debt-to-reserves, for example, has been shown to increase the probability of currency crisis (Rodrik and Velasco, 1999). Among the long-term flows, FDI flows are considered particularly desirable because they are related to underlying real considerations and are also empirically less reversible (Chuhan et al., 1996; Lipsey, 1999; Schadler, Chapter 4, this book). Athukorala (2003) shows in the context of the East Asian crisis that no major discontinuity in FDI inflows (except for a brief and modest decline) was detected in the region, with only a limited outflow at the height of the crisis.

The post-Asian crisis policy debate focused on vulnerabilities inherent in the balance sheet of an economy, especially maturity and currency mismatches (Allen et al., 2002). A maturity mismatch refers to a gap between the maturity structure of assets and liabilities, while a currency mismatch arises when assets and liabilities are denominated in different currencies. Vulnerabilities develop when assets are long term and liabilities short term, or when assets are denominated (or revenues are due) in domestic currency and liabilities are denominated in foreign currency.[7] These balance sheet risks are minimized when countries borrow more long term and less in foreign currencies. Some have highlighted the imperfections in the global financial market that limit the ability of emerging market economies to borrow abroad in their own currencies ('original sin') as a factor responsible for the currency mismatch that typically builds up in emerging market balance sheets (see Eichengreen et al., 2003 for a discussion of the relationship between currency mismatch and original sin), and have suggested the need to develop local currency bond markets (Burger and Warnock, 2006).[8]

The conventional wisdom notwithstanding, determining the precise risk characteristic of a particular capital transaction in practice is not a simple matter, especially in a financially liberalized, open economy. What ultimately determines the associated crisis risk is the liquidity of the instrument, not necessarily the maturity or the currency of denomination.[9] With sufficient liquidity, domestic currency-denominated bonds (or equities and FDI positions, for that matter) can be easily sold by foreign investors in the secondary market, and the proceeds can be exchanged for foreign currency in the foreign exchange market. Detragiache and Spilimbergo (2001) found that for 1971–98, the probability of debt default was not influenced by the amount of short-term debt once adjustment was made for the endogeneity of maturity structure (see also Frankel and Rose, 1996 for a similar result).[10] Jomo (2003), noting that the 1997 exodus of foreign investors forced market capitalization to fall to a fourth of its peak value, draws a lesson from the Malaysian crisis that equity flows are 'more easily reversible'. Bussiere and Mulder (1999) give evidence that a higher ratio of FDI to GDP was not significantly associated with less crisis vulnerability during 1997–98, especially with a large current account deficit and an overvalued exchange rate.

In short, the risk of capital inflows is specific to each transaction. In the words of Andrew Sheng (2008, p. 19), measuring the risk requires a 'forensic investigation' because each capital transaction has its own unique characteristics and works through the financial system differently. Even for FDI, not all flows are equal. Jinjarak (2007), for example, provides empirical evidence that vertical FDI activity (in which the output of subsidiaries is exported back to the parent abroad) is much more sensitive to host country risks than vertical FDI (see Aizenman and Marion, 2004 for the underlying theory). Based on the experience of Malaysia, Doraisami (2007) highlights a macroeconomic risk of FDI by noting that substantial FDI inflows had created a large export sector and made the country vulnerable to a sudden decline in export growth. A policymaker must conduct a sort of simulation exercise to know the macroeconomic, financial, and reversal risks of a capital inflow by tracing how it moves through the system and, in the event of a sudden withdrawal, what the likely impact of it would be.

2.3 PACE AND SEQUENCING OF CAPITAL ACCOUNT LIBERALIZATION

For countries that are still in the process of opening the capital account, how best and how fast to proceed remains an unresolved issue. There is no presumption that the resource requirements of implementing a quick transition are either smaller or larger than those of managing a long transition process or administering capital controls (see Nsouli et al., 2002 for a discussion of several conceptual issues). Developing effective regulatory frameworks takes time, but a lengthy process may create wrong incentives and distortions. There are also political considerations. A big-bang approach may be appropriate if a prolonged transition is likely to create resistance from vested interests or if different elements of the existing system are so dependent upon each other that a piecemeal reform is not possible without creating significant distortions. A gradualist approach, on the other hand, may be more appropriate if it takes time to build consensus or if a slower process is more conducive to minimizing the adjustment costs.

The early contributions to the scholarly literature were based on the

'Southern Cone' experience of Argentina, Chile and Uruguay in the late 1970s, and emphasized the importance of achieving macroeconomic stabilization, financial liberalization, and trade liberalization before opening the capital account (McKinnon, 1982; Edwards, 1984). The literature then shifted toward advocating the big-bang approach in the early 1990s, particularly in the context of transition economies, arguing that the lack of credibility in the reform made it more appropriate to act quickly (Funke, 1993). In extending the big-bang approach to non-transition contexts, some argued that the best route to an efficient financial sector was to liberalize the capital account quickly, as it would allow market discipline to operate on the banking system (Guitian, 1996). Others used the presumed ineffectiveness of capital controls to argue for faster liberalization, given their distortionary effects (Mathieson and Rojas-Suarez, 1993).

The emerging market crises of the 1990s were a watershed event in the evolution of thinking on the pace of capital account liberalization. Although they were all complex phenomena with multiple causes, some saw in them a role played by capital account liberalization. These observers recognized that liberalized systems could create dangers by allowing market participants to 'undertake greater and sometimes imprudent risks', so that 'sound prudential policies to ensure proper private incentives for risk management' would be necessary to safeguard the benefits from capital account liberalization (Eichengreen et al., 1998, p. 1). It was in this context that 'sequencing' emerged as an operational concept in the policy-oriented literature, largely developed at the IMF.

The new sequencing literature stresses the importance of an 'integrated' approach, which considers capital account liberalization as part of a more comprehensive program of economic reform and coordinates it with appropriate macroeconomic and exchange rate policies, as well as policies to strengthen the financial system (Johnston et al., 1999). In this approach, emphasis is placed on the sequence by which the necessary preconditions – including not only current account liberalization, macroeconomic stability, and financial sector liberalization but also establishing an effective system of prudential supervision – are to be met and the various components of the capital account are to be liberalized. IMF staff have developed an operational framework, based on several sets of country experience, to sequence capital account liberalization in coordination with other closely related policies (Ishii et al., 2002).

The integrated approach acknowledges that no simple rule exists for sequencing, and that the detailed plan for coordinating capital account liberalization with other policies must be based on an assessment of specific circumstances and therefore requires judgment (Ingves, 2003). Subject to this disclaimer, the broad principles are to pursue macroeconomic policies and structural reforms that promote financial sector stability, while gradually liberalizing the capital account as preconditions are met. Elements of sound macroeconomic policies might include fiscal discipline, prudent external debt management, a flexible exchange rate, and transparency in the conduct of monetary and exchange rate policies. Financial policies must be designed to promote prudent risk management, supported by, among others, a strong capital base and strict disclosure requirements. As these conditions are met, FDI is liberalized first, followed by portfolio flows. Consistent with the conventional wisdom, long-term flows are to be liberalized before short-term flows.

While few would disagree with the concepts embodied in this approach, it has proved difficult to apply in practice. The Asian Policy Forum (2002, p. 4) described this as including 'virtually every conceivable aspect of microeconomic, institutional, and macroeconomic policy possible', 'unnecessarily complex', and 'unoperational'. The exhortation that one must gradually open the capital account by pursuing good policies, establishing good institutions, and paying attention to attendant risks, is hardly an operational guide to policy, especially when it does not explain how to measure risks and provide clear criteria for prioritizing them. As already noted, it is a complex task to measure the risks of capital inflows. But as long as risks are not properly identified, any approach to capital account liberalization can only be based on intuition and guesswork.

There is also an issue of feasibility. The conventional argument that certain types of inflows should be liberalized before others may not work in practice. For example, much has been said about the 'wrong' sequencing followed by the Republic of Korea in liberalizing short-term bank flows before long-term portfolio flows (Cho, 2001). However, different types of short-term capital transactions are highly substitutable not only for each other, but also for long-term capital transactions. The Thai experience shows that, when the authorities tightened control over short-term Bangkok International Banking Facility (BIBF) inflows in 1995,[11] inflows through loans, portfolio investment, and nonresident bank deposits rose markedly so that the overall volume was little affected (Siamwalla et al., 2003).

Although the new orthodoxy on capital account liberalization may have served as a deterrent to rapid capital account liberalization, countries with a partially open capital account usually do not have the luxury of time with which to establish all the right preconditions. With economic liberalization, it becomes increasingly difficult to maintain comprehensive capital controls, making any remaining controls necessarily selective. They are inherently distortionary. In addition, as greater trade flows create loopholes in the control regime, any remaining controls are bound to lose effectiveness over time. For example, multinational corporations can sell goods and services to overseas parent firms at very low bookkeeping prices, thereby transferring real value out of the country, while foreign investors wanting to circumvent the controls can swap their funds for the overseas assets of a domestic resident. In the words of Eichengreen et al. (1998, p. 27), there is therefore 'no generally applicable cookbook recipe for the sequence of steps to undertake' in capital account liberalization.

2.4 USE OF CAPITAL CONTROLS

Some countries with an otherwise open capital account have experimented with the use of direct controls on inflows (see Ariyoshi et al., 2000 for a selective review; also Independent Evaluation Office (IEO), 2005). More recently, Russia and Croatia introduced controls in 2004 and, in December 2006, Thailand followed in an attempt to stem the tide of capital inflows and the resulting appreciation pressure on the currency.[12] These recent controls have typically taken the form of unremunerated reserve requirements (URRs) that mandate a certain percentage of inflows to be deposited with the central bank for a given period of time.[13] These controls also tend to be temporary, as the countries have been the beneficiaries of substantial capital inflows in the past and no longer have the option of isolating themselves permanently from the rest of the world. The controls are lifted when the triggering situation ceases to exist.

URRs are different from the conventional controls in at least three respects. First, URRs are designed for a country with an otherwise open capital account, to manage – not prevent – capital inflows. Second, they work on capital inflows not through administrative means but through the price incentives of international investors. Third, the amount of 'tax' on capital inflows is negatively related to the length of the investment. Hence, URRs are more effective on short-term (and presumably more speculative) flows than on long-term flows that are believed to be driven more by fundamental economic factors. For these reasons, URRs are considered to be less distortionary and abrasive, and have received sympathy even from some advocates of free capital mobility (Fischer, 1998).

There is a large empirical literature on the effectiveness of URRs based on the experience of Chile in the 1990s. The results remain inconclusive not only because they are sensitive to the choice of methodology as in any empirical work but more importantly because URRs were endogenous to the volume of capital flows.[14] Broad consensus, however, seems to be that: (i) URRs reduced the volume of capital inflows in the short run, but lost effectiveness over time; (ii) they lengthened the maturity of inflows; (iii) they were effective in raising relative domestic interests but not in preventing real exchange rate appreciation; and (iv) they had greater (adverse) impact on small and medium-sized firms (that rely on bank borrowing) than on large firms with access to a wider range of financing instruments (Nadal-De Simone and Sorsa, 1999; Gallego et al., 2002; Le Fort and Lehmann, 2003; Ffrench-Davis and Tapia, 2004). In terms of financial vulnerability, Edwards (1999) provides preliminary evidence that URRs might have protected Chile's financial markets from small shocks originating abroad though not from contagion from very large shocks, such as during the East Asian crisis.

Based on a broader group of countries, Dooley (1996) argued that the empirical literature is generally skeptical of the ability of capital controls to affect such variables as the volume or composition of private capital flows, international reserves, or the level of exchange rates, especially in the longer run. The more recent review of empirical literature by Magud and Reinhart (2007) concludes that capital controls can alter relative interest rates and lengthen the maturity of inflows, but cannot reduce the volume of net flows (their effect on real exchange rates is uncertain).[15] While the macroeconomic effect may be limited, the microeconomic effect is less ambiguous. Desai et al. (2006) provide evidence that capital controls raise local borrowing costs for affiliates of multinational corporations and, coupled with the cost of circumventing the controls, discourage FDI inflows. Wei and Zhang (2007), based on a large sample of countries, provide some evidence that exchange controls, including capital controls, reduce trade presumably because firms face a higher cost of meeting the associated inspection and reporting requirements.[16]

Experience suggests that capital controls lose more of their effectiveness as they become more permanent because time will allow economic agents to find ways of evasion. Controls that are introduced in an otherwise liberalized regime are also necessarily selective, and are therefore less effective than the comprehensive controls of a tightly controlled regime that cover all transactions. In a highly open economy with a commitment to transparency and accountability, there is a limit to the coverage of capital controls and the rigor with which they can be enforced (Schadler, Chapter 4, this book). Some transactions thus become inevitably exempted from the application of controls, making any remaining controls less effective, as well as more distortionary, as exempted transactions create loopholes. In surveying the empirical literature on the microeconomic effects of capital controls, Forbes (2007) concludes that evidence indicating distortions in the allocation of resources is compelling.

A more promising alternative to the use of transaction-based capital controls may be 'prudential' regulations, to the extent that, being targeted at financial institutions and large corporations, they are easier for the authorities to monitor and enforce.[17] Such measures might include reporting or approval requirements, making prescribed institutions eligible for capital transactions, limits on short-term external borrowing, and limitations on foreign currency exposure. Although coverage is necessarily limited, they can still be expected to control a significant portion of capital inflows. Grenville (Chapter 3, this book) argues that limiting the role of financial institutions in intermediating inflows and subjecting the exposure of their customers to prudential scrutiny would help contain the adverse impact of a currency crisis.

Investor-based controls are another promising alternative to transactions-based controls, at least as a tool of managing the process of liberalization. For example, the use of such devices as the qualified foreign investor scheme in the People's Republic of China (PRC) and the foreign institutional investor (and more recently non-resident Indians or NRI) classification in India seem to have a measure of effectiveness in managing the process of capital account opening, presumably because it is always easier to track down who is investing than how inflows are coming. Kimball and Xiao (2005) show that, for the period 1996–2004, the PRC's financial openness and capital flow volatility were considerably lower than those of other emerging market economies, indicating the effectiveness of capital controls. Shah and Patnaik (2005) likewise note that India has experienced a rapid expansion of capital inflows in recent years without experiencing a corresponding increase in volatility (despite the relatively small share of FDI).

Administrative capacity is a prerequisite for the effectiveness of any capital control measure, prudential or otherwise. Johnston and Ryan (1994) show, from a sample of 55 countries during 1985–92, that capital controls were more effective in industrial countries than in developing countries, reflecting the difference in the competence of bureaucratic systems. Among the emerging market economies, bureaucratic competence is credited for the reasonable effectiveness with which capital control measures were enforced in Chile and Malaysia during the 1990s (Kawai and Takagi, 2004).

2.5 MACROECONOMIC AND STRUCTURAL MEASURES TO MANAGE CAPITAL INFLOWS

If capital inflows are driven largely by economic fundamentals, authorities must sooner or later accept the inevitability of allowing the real exchange rate to appreciate. In fact, real exchange rate appreciation is the only sustainable response to a permanent increase in capital inflows and a fundamental revaluation of domestic relative to foreign assets. Exchange rate appreciation is also the most effective response to large capital inflows, regardless of the cause of the inflows, because it avoids the myriad limitations and side-effects attendant to other policy responses (see below). This is how most industrial countries respond to large capital inflows.

Policymakers, however, are generally reluctant to allow the exchange rate to appreciate. Many emerging market economies are more limited than industrial countries in the depth of financial markets, industrial diversification, and risk tolerance to allow the exchange rate to fluctuate widely in response to a sudden (and especially temporary) surge in capital inflows. Grenville (Chapter 3, this book) notes that emerging market currencies are particularly subject to sudden 'gyrations' during the transition to mature market status, because there is no anchor that guides the path of the exchange rate as the currencies appreciate in real terms over time.

Moreover, loss of international price competitiveness is an overriding concern of the authorities when they resist allowing the exchange rate to appreciate. Preventing the real exchange rate from appreciating may not be a sustainable policy over the long run, but it takes time for capital inflows to work through the system to have impact on inflation (hence to cause real appreciation), whereas nominal appreciation will lead to an immediate adjustment in the real exchange rate.

2.5.1 Macroeconomic Measures

In general, three broad categories of macroeconomic measures are available to countries facing surges in capital inflows, if they are not willing to allow the nominal exchange rate to appreciate: (i) sterilized intervention (sterilization), (ii) greater exchange rate flexibility, and (iii) fiscal tightening (preferably through an expenditure cut). During earlier episodes of large inflows, each of these measures was used by various countries, with differing degrees of intensity and effectiveness (Schadler et al., 1993; Fernandez-Arias and Montiel, 1995; IEO, 2005; IMF, 2007; Grenville, Chapter 3, this book; and Schadler, Chapter 4, this book).

(i) Sterilization has been the most commonly used instrument; Reinhart and Reinhart (1998) call it 'the policy of first recourse'. Narrowly defined, sterilization involves the exchange of domestic bonds for foreign assets, often through open market operations, designed to neutralize the increase in base money arising from purchases of foreign currency. In a number of emerging market economies where the market for government debt is not well developed, the central banks have often created their

own debt instruments for this purpose. Through sterilized intervention, countries experiencing surges in capital inflows can maintain the nominal exchange rate while also preventing the capital inflow from increasing the balance of base money.

Sterilized intervention works only if two conditions are met.[18] First, domestic and foreign assets must be imperfect substitutes, such that the exchange of one type of asset for another alters the relative rates of return. Second, the interest cost of the operation must be manageable, as sterilization typically carries quasi-fiscal costs that arise from the exchange of high-yielding domestic debt for low-yielding foreign assets (Calvo, 1991). There is a broad consensus that the first condition does not hold between industrial country assets and therefore the effectiveness of sterilized intervention is limited at best for industrial countries. Between industrial country assets and emerging market assets, however, substitutability may be sufficiently low to allow sterilized intervention to have some effectiveness, though available evidence is mixed at best (Ishii et al., 2006).[19] On the other hand, the interest rate differential rises as substitutability declines, so that greater effectiveness can also mean more limited sustainability.[20]

More broadly, sterilization can be any measure (such as raising reserve requirements; central bank borrowing from commercial banks; and shifting of government deposits from commercial banks to the central bank) that attempts to offset the growth of monetary aggregates coming from reserve inflows. Tightening monetary conditions when there is a genuine demand for credit, however, will create a further incentive to borrow from abroad. If reserve requirements are raised to tighten monetary policy, it may end up raising the cost of financial intermediation and create a distortion in the allocation of resources. In either case, sterilization can be self-defeating, by raising the level of interest rates and encouraging further capital inflows, as was observed in several emerging market economies, including Indonesia and Malaysia in the 1990s (Reinhart and Reinhart, 1998). It is also of limited usefulness in preventing real appreciation over the medium term as inflation eventually picks up (IMF, 2007; Schadler, Chapter 4, this book).

(ii) Greater exchange rate flexibility is another possible response. Here, greater exchange rate flexibility does not mean nominal exchange rate appreciation, which is the very outcome the authorities are trying to avoid in the first place. Rather, it is meant to introduce two-way risks and thereby discourage speculative capital inflows. This usually involves, in the context of a *de facto* peg or a tightly managed float, introducing a wider band of fluctuation. The effectiveness of this instrument depends on how much the authorities are willing to allow the exchange rate to

move. If the fluctuation band is set narrow, the disincentive for speculative inflows would also be limited. If the band is set large, the potential for large nominal appreciation would also become great. Empirical evidence is inconclusive as to the deterrence effect of greater exchange rate variability on speculative flows (Reinhart and Reinhart, 1998).

(iii) Fiscal tightening is arguably the most assured response to a surge in capital inflows because it involves a reduction in the absorption of real resources by the public sector to offset the domestic impact of resource transfers from abroad. To the extent that it is a real response, it should work to contain inflationary pressure and to prevent a real appreciation of the currency. In addition, fiscal tightening could reduce pressure on interest rates, thus directly reducing incentives for interest rate-induced capital inflows (Schadler, Chapter 4, this book), as well as restrain appreciating pressure by limiting the increase in the relative price of non-tradable goods. Provided that government consumption is more intensive in the use of non-tradable goods, fiscal tightening would cause domestic demand to shift from tradable to non-tradable goods, and domestic production to shift from non-tradable to tradable goods. Indeed, the empirical result reported in IMF (2007) suggests that fiscal tightening has helped limit real exchange rate appreciation in a group of emerging market and advanced economies.

Fiscal tightening, however, has at least three limitations as a response to capital inflows. First, fiscal policy lacks flexibility because it often requires parliamentary action. Second, there is a limit to how much fiscal policy can be tightened, especially in a democratic society and if there is little fiscal space to begin with. Third, fiscal tightening may have the perverse effect of attracting additional capital inflows by providing a signal that the authorities are pursuing a sound, disciplined macroeconomic policy. It should be countered, however, that such a positive signaling effect is likely transitory; over time, sustainable fiscal policy should help attract only the most stable and committed types of capital (Schadler, Chapter 4, this book).

2.5.2 Structural Measures

Structural or microeconomic measures to deal with surges in capital inflows are many, but three types of measures are the most common: (i) financial sector reform; (ii) easing restrictions on capital outflows; and (iii) further trade liberalization (Schadler et al., 1993; IEO, 2005).

(i) Financial sector reform including improving the system of prudential supervision and developing capital markets, is not meant to reduce

the volume of inflows, but to minimize any negative impact should a crisis occur. If banks are well capitalized and diversified, they are more likely to be resilient to potential capital flow reversals and associated macroeconomic shocks. Having an alternative to bank finance promotes greater risk diversification in the economy (as well as allowing the corporate sector to maintain access to corporate financing even when the banking sector is adversely affected). Thus, financial sector reform may help minimize the financial stability risk of capital inflows. This is a long process, however, as a well-supervised financial sector or efficient capital markets cannot be produced overnight.

(ii) Easing restrictions on capital outflows may have two motives. The first is to subject domestic financial markets to greater international competition and to allow residents to diversify their risks; the second is to reduce net capital inflows by encouraging outflows (Schadler et al., 1993). The impact of this measure depends on whether there is a sufficient pent up demand for foreign assets. If not, the easing of outflow controls can send a positive signal to markets and, by making it easier to repatriate funds, even lead to additional net capital inflows (Bartolini and Drazen, 1997). This may be what actually happened in Malaysia and Thailand in the previous surge of capital inflows (Reinhart and Reinhart, 1998).

(iii) Further trade liberalization (through tariff reductions and the like) could help contain increases in foreign exchange reserves by encouraging more imports, at least temporarily. Trade liberalization has also been used to increase productivity in the non-tradable sector, so that pressures on the real exchange rate could be eased (Reinhart and Reinhart, 1998). Over time, however, trade reforms may improve export competitiveness by reducing the price of imported inputs and may not contribute much to reducing net imports. Moreover, they may encourage further capital inflows by showing a signal of authorities' commitment to a liberal and open international economic policy regime.

2.5.3 Exploring Policy Options

The existing literature, as well as past experience, suggests that conventional policy options offer no panacea for countries facing large inflows of capital (see Table 2.1 for an overview of the discussion). The proper policy response therefore must appropriately weigh various country-specific factors, including the policy objectives, the causes and sustainability of the inflows, and the political and other constraints on the use of instruments. If the cause of the excessive inflow is a domestic distortion (such as a tax

Table 2.1 Conventional policy responses and implications

	Policy tool	Intended outcome	Possible limitations	Empirical evidence on effectiveness
Macroeconomic measures	Sterilized intervention	To prevent nominal appreciation while neutralizing the growth of base money	Quasi-fiscal cost limits sustainability; higher interest rates attract additional inflows	Limited effectiveness in preventing real appreciation over the medium term, as inflation eventually picks up
	Greater exchange rate flexibility	To discourage speculative capital inflows by introducing two-way risks	Risk of exchange rate appreciation	Limited evidence on the response of speculative flows
	Fiscal tightening	To contain inflationary pressure and prevent real appreciation by curtailing aggregate demand (especially on non-tradables); to discourage capital inflows by reducing interest rate pressure	Lack of flexibility; there is a natural limit to the size of tightening; possibility of a positive signaling effect to attract additional inflows (at least in the short run)	Some evidence of effectiveness in preventing real appreciation; some evidence of better growth performance following a capital flow reversal
Structural measures	Financial sector reform	To minimize the negative impact of a capital flow reversal by promoting better risk management	Process takes time	n.a.

63

Table 2.1 (continued)

Policy tool	Intended outcome	Possible limitations	Empirical evidence on effectiveness
Easing restrictions on capital outflows	To allow residents to diversify risks; to reduce net inflows by encouraging outflows	There may not be enough pent-up demand for foreign assets; possibility of a positive signaling effect to attract additional inflows	Some evidence of promoting additional capital inflows
Further trade liberalization	To contain increases in foreign exchange reserves by encouraging more imports; to contain pressure on the real exchange rate by raising productivity in the non-tradable sector	Net imports may not increase if the tradable goods sector becomes more competitive as a result; possibility of a positive signaling effect to attract additional inflows	n.a.

benefit for foreign investment), for example, the proper response is to remove that distortion. To enhance the effectiveness of fiscal policy as an instrument of managing capital inflows, governments may find it useful to establish fiscal rules, whereby they aim, for example, to achieve a cyclically adjusted fiscal surplus. This will alleviate the procyclicality of fiscal policy that is typical of developing and emerging market economies (Kaminsky et al., 2004) and protect the authorities from the political pressure of increasing spending when times are good. Such a rule has been successfully adopted in Chile (IMF, 2007; Schadler, Chapter 4, this book).

Over the medium term, effectiveness and feasibility may not be the only consideration because large capital inflows may sooner or later come to a stop. The IMF (2007), based on the experience of a large number of emerging market economies over the past two decades, concludes that the adverse impact on GDP growth of a sudden stop in capital inflows tended to be more moderate when the authorities had used fiscal restraint during the period of large inflows. By contrast, the authorities who resisted nominal appreciation through intervention during the capital inflow period tended subsequently to face more serious adverse macroeconomic consequences when the surge stopped. The difference in outcomes appears to be related to how successfully the authorities could limit the extent of real appreciation. Schadler (Chapter 4, this book), noting that fiscal policy has rarely been tightened during surges in capital inflows, calls for greater attention to fiscal policy as an effective tool of inflow management.

2.6 CONCLUSION

How to manage capital inflows remains an important policy issue for many emerging market economies. The issue has assumed even greater importance in recent years as the volume of capital flows picked up against the background of increasing global financial integration. In this environment, even countries without a fully open capital account can no longer consider themselves immune from the risks of capital inflows as they liberalize their trade regime and domestic financial system. Current account convertibility substantially reduces the ability of a control regime to manage capital flows, while financial liberalization increases substitutability among different types of capital account transactions. Once a certain threshold of economic openness and financial market development is reached, a partially open capital account may not effectively protect an economy from the volatility of international capital flows.

The literature provides little practical guidance on capital account liberalization, except to advocate the need for pursuing sound macroeconomic policies and establishing an effective framework of prudential regulation. The difficulty of identifying the precise sequencing of steps comes from the fact that the risks of capital inflows are specific to each transaction and are difficult to measure. Countries with a fully open capital account may resort to the use of temporary capital controls or prudential regulations, but it requires a high degree of administrative capacity to implement them effectively. With respect to the use of conventional macroeconomic measures, the existing literature may provide guidance on good practice, suggesting for example the greater effectiveness of fiscal tightening relative to other measures. Even so, each of the measures, including fiscal tightening, comes with limitations in terms of effectiveness, flexibility, or sustainability.

NOTES

1. Empirical work involves a joint test of the effect of liberalization on growth and the particular method of quantifying the degree of liberalization or effectiveness of capital controls. Empirical results are therefore sensitive to the quantitative measure of capital account openness as well as the choice of sample and methodology. Another complication is the endogeneity of capital controls, which makes it difficult to disentangle the effect of capital controls per se from that of the macroeconomic and international environments within which they are introduced.
2. These studies have focused on stock market liberalization because, compared with other types of capital account liberalization, it is a more easily identifiable policy shift and its theoretical prediction is clearer. Martell and Stulz (2003) compare the equity market liberalization of a country to the initial public offering (IPO) of a firm.
3. Tesar (1995), noting that international consumption correlations were generally low, argued that the utility gains from international risk sharing were small even among industrial countries. Recent data seem to suggest that consumption correlations have increased considerably among industrial countries.
4. Calvo and Reinhart (2000) show that a sudden stop of capital inflows has been a recurring feature of currency crises in emerging market economies, but not in advanced industrial economies.
5. Abdelal (2007) discusses the place of capital transactions in the international monetary system. See Thiel (2003) for the role played by the Organisation for Economic Co-operation and Development (OECD) in the liberalization of capital flows among industrial countries.
6. The definition of a crisis is based on three metrics: (i) a depreciation greater than 20 per cent; (ii) a drop in real government primary expenditure exceeding 20 per cent of GDP; and (iii) a drop in output.
7. Another source of balance sheet vulnerability is domestic liability dollarization, which has been shown to increase the probability of sudden stops in emerging market economies (Calvo et al., 2004).
8. Reducing the currency mismatch only shifts the exposure to foreigners. Grenville (Chapter 3, this book) notes that, unless foreign investors are more stable holders of currency exposure, the vulnerabilities remain.
9. At the time of a crisis, however, otherwise liquid assets may become highly illiquid, limiting the ability of investors to sell them without incurring a substantial capital loss.
10. Countries that are more at risk of default may become unable to borrow at long maturities. If long-term borrowing does not reduce the risk of crisis, it is not clear if an

economy benefits by borrowing long term, given a higher premium on long-term debt (Alfaro and Kanczuk, 2007).
11. The BIBF was established in 1993, with the stated objective of making Bangkok an international financial center by providing tax benefits to international banks. Responding to a subsequent surge in short-term capital inflows, in 1995 the authorities introduced various measures, including a 7 per cent reserve requirement on non-resident baht accounts with a maturity of less than one year and on short-term borrowing of finance companies; limits for open short and long foreign currency positions (with lower limits for short positions); and reporting requirements for banks on foreign exchange risk control measures (Johnston et al., 1999). To target the BIBF in particular, they also raised the minimum level of 'out-in' flows from $500 000 to $2 million (Siamwalla et al., 2003).
12. Following the introduction of a 30 per cent reserve requirement, stock prices declined sharply, prompting the authorities to announce that the control measure would not apply to foreign inflows to the Thai stock exchange.
13. URRs have precedents in the earlier capital control regimes of some industrial countries, such as Japan and Australia in the 1970s. The Japanese authorities, for example, managed the volume of capital inflows by altering the rate of marginal reserve requirement on so-called free-yen accounts for non-residents.
14. In Chile, URRs were frequently revised in response to the strength of capital inflows, in terms of both coverage and reserve requirements.
15. The empirical works reviewed by Magud and Reinhart (2007) covered the controls introduced by Brazil, Chile, Colombia, the Czech Republic, Malaysia, and Thailand mostly in the 1990s. The overall conclusion, however, is heavily weighted by the experience of Chile, for which much more work has been done.
16. It should be noted that the authors do not make a distinction between capital controls per se and other types of exchange controls that affect foreign exchange transactions.
17. Though on the outflow side, evidence suggests that Japan's prudential controls on the foreign investment behavior of institutional investors (such as insurance companies) were effective. See Fukao (1990) and Koo (1993).
18. In the short run, there is an additional announcement or signaling effect. This cannot be sustained in the longer run, however, unless there is a change in the stance of monetary policy as has been anticipated by the markets.
19. Ishii et al. (2006), based on an analysis of daily data, show that intervention had a small but statistically significant impact on the exchange rate level in Mexico, but not in Turkey.
20. Grenville (Chapter 3, this book), however, estimates that the cost of funding the foreign exchange reserves was relatively modest, at around or less than 1 per cent of GDP, for major Asian emerging market economies.

REFERENCES

Abdelal, R. (2007), *Capital Rules: The Construction of Global Finance*, Cambridge, MA: Harvard University Press.
Aizenman, J. and N. Marion (2004), 'The merits of horizontal versus vertical FDI in the presence of uncertainty', *Journal of International Economics*, **62**, 125–48.
Alfaro, L. and F. Kanczuk (2007), 'Debt maturity: is long-term debt optimal?', NBER Working Paper No. 13119.
Allen, M., C. Rosenberg, C. Keller, B. Setser and N. Roubini (2002), 'A balance sheet approach to financial crisis', Working Paper 02/210, International Monetary Fund.
Ariyoshi, A., K. Habermeier, B. Laurens, I. Okter-Robe, J.I. Canales-Kriljenko

and A. Kirilenko (2000), 'Capital controls: country experiences with their use and liberalization', Occasional Paper 190, International Monetary Fund.

Arteta, C., B. Eichengreen and C. Wyplosz (2001), 'When does capital account liberalization help more than it hurts?', NBER Working Paper No. 8414.

Asian Policy Forum (2002), 'Policy proposal for sequencing the PRC's domestic and external financial liberalization', Asian Development Bank Institute, Tokyo.

Athukorala, P. (2003), 'Foreign direct investment in crisis and recovery: lessons from the 1997–1998 Asian Crisis', *Australian Economic History Review*, **43**, 197–213.

Bartolini, L. and A. Drazen (1997), 'Capital-account liberalization as a signal', *American Economic Review*, **87**, March, 138–54.

Bekaert, G., C.R. Harvey, and C. Lundblad (2005), 'Does financial liberalization spur growth?', *Journal of Financial Economics*, **77**, 3–55.

Bikhchandani, S. and S. Sharma (2001), 'Herd behavior in financial markets', *International Monetary Fund Staff Papers*, **47**, 279–310.

Bloomfield, A.I. (1946), 'Postwar control of international capital movements', *American Economic Review*, **36**, 687–709.

Borensztein, E., J. De Gregorio and J.W. Lee (1998), 'How does foreign direct investment affect economic growth?', *Journal of International Economics*, **45**, 115–35.

Burger, J. and F. Warnock (2006), 'Local currency bond markets', *International Monetary Fund Staff Papers*, **53**, 133–46.

Bussiere, M. and C. Mulder (1999), 'External vulnerability in emerging market economies: how high liquidity can offset weak fundamentals and the effects of contagion', Working Paper 99/88, International Monetary Fund.

Calvo, G. (1991), 'The perils of sterilization', *International Monetary Fund Staff Papers*, **38**, 921–6.

Calvo, G. and C. Reinhart (2000), 'When capital flows come to a sudden stop: consequences and policy', in P.B. Kenen and A.K. Swoboda (eds), *Reforming the International Monetary and Financial System*, Washington, DC: International Monetary Fund, pp. 175–201.

Calvo, G., L. Leiderman and C. Reinhart (1996), 'Inflows of capital to developing countries in the 1990s', *Journal of Economic Perspectives*, **10**, 123–39.

Calvo, G., A. Izquierdo and L.F. Mejia (2004), 'On the empirics of sudden stops: the relevance of balance-sheet effect', NBER Working Paper No. 10520.

Carlson, M. and L. Hernandez (2002), 'Determinants and repercussions of the composition of capital inflows', IMF Working Paper 02/86.

Cho, Y.J. (2001), 'The role of poorly phased liberalization in Korea's financial crisis', in G. Caprio, P. Honohan, and J.E. Stiglitz (eds), *Financial Liberalization: How Far, How Fast?*, Cambridge and New York: Cambridge University Press, pp. 159–87.

Chuhan, P., G. Perez-Quiros and H. Popper (1996), 'International capital flows: do short-term investment and direct investment differ?', Policy Research Working Paper No. 1669, World Bank.

Chuhan, P., S. Claessens and N. Mamingi (1998), 'Equity and bond flows to Latin America and Asia: the role of global and country factors', *Journal of Development Economics*, **55**, 439–63.

Claessens, S., M. Dooley and A. Warner (1995), 'Portfolio capital flows: hot or cold', *The World Bank Economic Review*, **9**, 153–74.

Cooper, R. (1999), 'Should capital controls be banished?', *Brookings Papers on Economic Activity*, **1**, 89–125.
Desai, M., G. Fritz Foley and J. Hines, Jr (2006), 'Capital controls, liberalizations, and foreign direct investment', *Review of Financial Studies*, **19**, 1433–64.
Detragiache, E. and A. Spilimbergo (2001), 'Crises and liquidity: evidence and interpretation', IMF Working Paper 01/2.
Dooley, M. (1996), 'A survey of literature on controls over international capital transactions', *International Monetary Fund Staff Papers*, **43**, 639–87.
Doraisami, A.G. (2007), 'Financial crisis in Malaysia: did FDI flows contribute to vulnerability?', *Journal of International Development*, **19**, 949–62.
Dornbusch, R., I. Goldfajn and R. Valdes (1995), 'Currency crises and collapses', *Brookings Papers on Economic Activity*, **2**, 219–93.
Edison, H., M. Klein, L. Ricci and T. Slok (2002), 'Capital account liberalization and economic performance: survey and synthesis', IMF Working Paper 02/120.
Edwards, S. (1984), 'The Order of Liberalization of the External Sector in Developing Countries', Princeton Essays in International Finance 156, Princeton, NJ: International Economics Section, Princeton University.
Edwards, S. (1999), 'How effective are capital controls?', *Journal of Economic Perspectives*, **13**, 65–84.
Eichengreen, B. and D. Leblang (2002), 'Capital account liberalization and growth: was Mr. Mahathir right?', NBER Working Paper No. 9427.
Eichengreen, B., M. Mussa, G. Dell'Ariccia, E. Detragiache, G. M. Milesi-Ferretti and A. Tweedie (1998), 'Capital account liberalization: theoretical and practical aspects', Occasional Paper 172, International Monetary Fund.
Eichengreen, B., R. Hausmann and U. Panizza (2003), 'Currency mismatches, debt intolerance, and original sin: why they are not the same and why it matters', NBER Working Paper No. 10036.
Fernandez-Arias, E. and P. Montiel (1995), 'The surge in capital inflows to developing countries: prospects and policy response', Policy Research Working Paper No. 1473, World Bank.
Ffrench-Davis, R. and H. Tapia (2004), 'The Chilean-style of capital controls: an empirical assessment', United Nations Economic Commission for Latin America and the Caribbean.
Fischer, S. (1998), 'Capital account liberalization and the role of the IMF', in S. Fischer, R.N. Cooper, R. Dornbusch, P.M. Garber, C. Massad, J.J. Polak, D. Rodrik and S.S. Tarapore, *Should the IMF Pursue Capital-Account Convertibility?*, Princeton Essays in International Finance No. 207, May, Princeton, NJ: International Economics Section, Princeton University, pp. 1–10.
Forbes, K. (2007), 'The microeconomic evidence on capital controls: no free lunch', in S. Edwards (ed.), *Capital Controls and Capital Flows in Emerging Economies: Policies, Practices, and Consequences*, Chicago: University of Chicago Press, pp. 171–99.
Frankel, J. and A. Rose (1996), 'Currency crashes in emerging markets: an empirical treatment', *Journal of International Economics*, **41**, 351–66.
Fukao, M. (1990), 'Liberalization of Japan's foreign exchange controls and structural changes in the balance of payments', *Bank of Japan Monetary and Economic Studies*, **8**, 101–65.
Funke, N. (1993), 'Timing and sequencing of reforms: competing views and role of credibility', *Kyklos*, **46**, 337–62.

Gallego, F., L. Hernandez and K. Schmidt-Hebbel (2002), 'Capital controls in Chile: were they effective?', in L. Hernandez and K. Schmidt-Hebbel (eds), *Banking, Financial Integration, and International Crises*, Santiago: Central Bank of Chile.
Grilli, V. and G.M. Milesi-Ferretti (1995), 'Economic effects and structural determinants of capital controls', *International Monetary Fund Staff Papers*, **42**, 54–88.
Guitian, M. (1996), 'The issue of capital account convertibility: a gap between norms and reality', in S.M. Nsouli and M. Guitian (eds), *Currency Convertibility in the Middle East and North Africa*, Washington: International Monetary Fund, pp. 169–88.
Henry, P.B. (2000), 'Do stock market liberalizations cause investment booms?', *Journal of Financial Economics*, **58**, 301–34.
Henry, P.B. (2007), 'Capital account liberalization: theory, evidence, and speculation', *Journal of Economic Literature*, **45**, December, 887–935.
IEO (Independent Evaluation Office) (2005), 'The IMF's approach to capital account liberalization', International Monetary Fund.
IMF (International Monetary Fund) (2007), 'Managing large capital inflows', *World Economic Outlook*, Washington: International Monetary Fund, Chapter 3.
Ingves, S. (2003), 'Sequencing capital account liberalization and financial sector stability', in A.F.P. Bakker and B. Chapple (eds), *Capital Liberalization in Transition Countries: Lessons from the Past and for the Future*, Cheltenham, UK and Northampton, MA, USA: Edward Elgar, pp. 43–57.
Ishii, S., K. Habermeier, J.I. Canales-Kriljenko, B. Laurens, J. Leimone and J. Vadasz (2002), 'Capital account liberalization and financial sector stability', Occasional Paper 211, International Monetary Fund.
Ishii, S., J.I. Canales-Kriljenko, R. Guimaraes and C. Karacadag (2006), 'Official foreign exchange intervention', Occasional Paper 249, International Monetary Fund.
James, H. (1996), *International Monetary Cooperation Since Bretton Woods*, Washington: International Monetary Fund and Oxford: Oxford University Press.
Jinjarak, Y. (2007), 'Foreign direct investment and macroeconomic risk', *Journal of Comparative Economics*, **35**, 509–19.
Johnston, R.B. and C. Ryan (1994), 'The impact of controls on capital movements on the private capital accounts of countries' balance of payments: empirical estimates and policy implications', Working Paper No. 94/78, International Monetary Fund.
Johnston, R.B., S.M. Darbar and C. Echeverria (1999), 'Sequencing capital account liberalization: lessons from Chile, Indonesia, Korea, and Thailand', in R.B. Johnston and V. Sundarajan (eds), *Sequencing Financial Sector Reforms: Country Experiences and Issues*, Washington: International Monetary Fund, pp. 245–383.
Jomo, K. S. (2003), 'Capital flows into and from Malaysia', in S. Griffith-Jones, R. Gottschalk and J. Cailloux (eds), *International Capital Flows in Calm and Turbulent Times: The Need for New International Architecture*, Ann Arbor: University of Michigan Press, pp. 107–61.
Kaminsky, G.L., C. Reinhart and C. Vegh (2004), 'When it rains, it pours: procyclical capital flows and macroeconomic policies', NBER Working Paper No. 10780.

Kawai, M and S. Takagi (2004), 'Rethinking capital controls: the Malaysian experience', in S. Chirathivat, E.M. Claassen and J. Schroeder (eds), *East Asia's Monetary Future: Integration in the Global Economy*, Cheltenham, UK and Northampton, MA, USA: Edward Elgar, pp. 182–214.

Kimball, D. and F. Xiao (2005), 'Effectiveness and effects of China's capital controls', *China & World Economy*, **13**, July/August, 58–69.

Koo, R.C. (1993), 'International capital flows and an open economy: the Japanese experience', in S. Takagi (ed.), *Japanese Capital Markets: New Developments in Regulations and Institutions*, Oxford: Basil Blackwell, pp. 78–129.

Kose, M.A., E. Prasad and M. Terrones (2003), 'Financial integration and macroeconomic volatility', *International Monetary Fund Staff Papers*, **50**, 119–42.

Le Fort, G. and S. Lehmann (2003), 'The unremunerated reserve requirement and net capital flows: Chile in the 1990s', *CEPAL Review*, No. 81, United Nations Economic Commission for Latin America and the Caribbean.

Lipsey, R. (1999), 'The role of foreign direct investment in international capital flows', NBER Working Paper No. 7094.

Magud, N. and C. Reinhart (2007), 'Capital controls: an evaluation', in S. Edwards (eds), *Capital Controls and Capital Flows in Emerging Economies: Policies, Practices, and Consequences*, Chicago: University of Chicago Press, pp. 645–74.

Martell, R. and R. Stulz (2003), 'Equity-market liberalizations as country IPO's', *American Economic Review*, **93**, 97–101.

Mathieson, D. and L. Rojas-Suarez (1993), 'Liberalization of the capital account: experiences and issues', Occasional Paper 103, International Monetary Fund.

McKinnon, R. (1982), 'The order of economic liberalization: lessons from Chile and Argentina', *Carnegie-Rochester Conference Series on Public Policy*, **17**, 159–86.

Nadal-De Simone, F. and P. Sorsa (1999), 'A review of capital account restrictions in Chile in the 1990s', Working Paper 99/52, International Monetary Fund.

Nsouli, S., M. Rached and N. Funke (2002), 'The speed of adjustment and the sequencing of economic reforms: issues and guidelines for policymakers', Working Paper 02/132, International Monetary Fund.

Prasad, E., K. Rogoff, S. Wei and M. Ayhan Kose (2003), 'Effects of financial globalization on developing countries: some empirical evidence', Occasional Paper 220, International Monetary Fund.

Quinn, D. (1997), 'The correlates of change in international financial regulation', *American Political Science Review*, **91**, 531–51.

Reinhart, C.M. and V.R. Reinhart (1998), 'Some lessons for policy makers who deal with the mixed blessing of capital inflows', in M. Kahler (ed.), *Capital Flows and Financial Crises*, New York: Council on Foreign Relations, pp. 93–127.

Reisen, H. and M. Soto (2001), 'Which types of capital inflows foster developing-country growth?', *International Finance*, **4**, 1–14.

Rodrik, D. (1998), 'Who needs capital-account convertibility?', in S. Fischer, R.N. Cooper, R. Dornbusch, P.M. Garber, C. Massad, J.J. Polak, D. Rodrik and S.S. Tarapore, *Should the IMF Pursue Capital-Account Convertibility?*, Princeton Essays in International Finance, No. 207, May, Princeton, NJ: International Economics Section, Princeton University, pp. 55–65.

Rodrik, D. and A. Velasco (1999), 'Short-term capital flows', NBER Working Paper No. 7364.

Schadler, S., M. Carkovic, A. Bennett and R. Kahn (1993), 'Recent experiences with surges in capital inflows', Occasional Paper 108, International Monetary Fund.

Shah, A. and I. Patnaik (2005), 'India's experience with capital controls: the elusive quest for a sustainable current account deficit', NBER Working Paper No. 11387.

Sheng, A. (2008), 'The fetish of liquidity: liquidity, leverage and moral hazard – lessons from Asian and subprime crises', paper presented at the G20 Seminar on Competition in the Financial Sector, Bali, 16–17 February.

Siamwalla, A., Y. Vajraqupta and P. Vichyanond (2003), 'Foreign capital flows to Thailand: determinants and impact', in S. Griffith-Jones, R. Gottschalk and J. Cailloux (eds), *International Capital Flows in Calm and Turbulent Times: The Need for New International Architecture*, Ann Arbor: University of Michigan Press, pp. 75–106.

Stiglitz, J. (2000), 'Capital market liberalization, economic growth and instability', *World Development*, **28**, 1075–86.

Tesar, L.L. (1995), 'Evaluating the gains from international risk sharing', *Carnegie-Rochester Conference Series on Public Policy*, **42**, 95–143.

Thiel, E. (2003), 'Recent codes-based liberalization in the OECD', in A.F.P. Bakker and B. Chapple (eds), *Capital Liberalization in Transition Countries: Lessons from the Past and the Future*, Cheltenham, UK and Northampton, MA, USA: Edward Elgar, pp. 85–104.

Wei, S. and Z. Zhang (2007), 'Collateral damage: exchange controls and international trade', Working Paper 07/08, International Monetary Fund.

PART II

Perspective Papers

3. Central banks and capital flows
Stephen Grenville

3.1 HOW HAVE INTERNATIONAL CAPITAL FLOWS CHANGED THE POLICY ENVIRONMENT?

We start with the presumption that international capital flows, like international trade flows, are a Good Thing. They give the opportunity for a capital-constrained emerging country to tap into the world supply of savings, not only increasing the quantity of funds available to it, but also reducing the cost (just as globalized trade opens up opportunities to buy more cheaply). The Feldstein/Horioka (1980) paradox suggests that there is room for much more international trade in capital to allow investment to take place in those countries with high marginal productivity of capital, whether or not they are also high savers.

Over time, the paradox seems to be lessening. This would lead us to expect that on average over time, international capital will flow from the mature countries to the emerging countries, and that these flows will become larger over time as the path of transmission becomes smoother, information become more available and institutional channels develop more depth. How long can these inflows be expected to persist? The simple answer is 'as long as there is a difference in the marginal return to capital'.

We can remind ourselves of how these flows affect the macro-economy. If there is an autonomous increase in inflow, this can only be absorbed in terms of real goods and services if the exchange rate appreciates and the current account moves in the direction of deficit by the same amount as the capital flow.[1] This is the transfer problem that Keynes (1929) discussed. Two things are worth noting: that the exchange rate has to appreciate; and that the capital flow, accompanied by a current account deficit, adds as much to supply as it does to demand.

3.1.1 Macro-economics: Structural Interest Differentials

Emerging countries are likely to be high growth, high productivity, high profit economies, as they move towards the best-practice production frontier.[2] While this is a jerky 'punctuated evolution', with diversions and setbacks caused by poor domestic policies, inefficiencies and shocks, there is enough inherent dynamism and profitability in this transition to the frontier to ensure that the equilibrium interest rate in these emerging economies will, on average, be higher than in mature countries, because the return on physical capital is higher. One way of expressing this idea is to say that the Wicksellian 'natural' interest rate for emerging countries is likely to be higher than for mature economies. These emerging countries will attract foreign capital at those phases in the business cycle when investors feel confident about the risks of investing in countries about which they know little. This will happen, whatever the domestic policy interest setting. If the authorities try to keep interest rates low, the inflows will be used to buy real assets or equities. So the key point in thinking about interest rates is not that they have to be the *same* as international rates (as implied by the Impossible Trinity), but they *will be higher* over the medium term, and policy has to work around and adapt to this. This is a structural issue, not a cyclical one, so the exchange rate implications of the higher interest rate cannot be sorted out using the Dornbusch (1976) overshooting mechanism. Nor is the exchange rate regime a relevant issue: if the country maintains a fixed rate, the real exchange rate appreciation will come about through faster domestic inflation (e.g., Hong Kong, China, at least over its medium-term history).

Inflows will not only be encouraged by these structurally higher interest rates, but will be further encouraged by the prospect of structural exchange rate gains. This might be explained in terms of the Balassa–Samuelson theorem or may simply reflect the high overall productivity as a rise in the capital/labor ratio as the country moves towards the best-practice production frontier. During this journey, interest rates need to be higher, and the real exchange rate may appreciate. This is an attractive intrinsic environment for capital inflows (for another description, see Lipschitz et al., 2002).

3.1.2 How Does Monetary Policy Work in a Small Well-Integrated Economy?

So much for the medium-term structural forces: superimposed on these are the shorter-term cyclical influences which monetary policy addresses. How does monetary policy work in a globally integrated environment?

Before the 1980s, in a less integrated world, monetary policy worked by constraining the cyclical upswing and its accompanying asset price pressure, either with higher interest rates or credit controls, and impinged mostly on interest-sensitive expenditures such as investment and asset prices. Nowadays, for a small economy with a floating exchange rate and which is well integrated into international financial markets, when the monetary authorities raise the short-term policy interest rate in response to inflation-threatening excess demand, some borrowers are able to move out along the yield curve and obtain their funds at rates which reflect the availability of foreign funding. Essentially, the higher domestic short-term interest rates encourage borrowers to tap into overseas sources of funds to obtain some of their financing at rates which do not fully reflect the rise in the domestic short-term policy rate.[3] Tighter monetary policy induces extra capital inflow, funding the cyclical upswing, at the same time that it is being constrained through higher interest rates. This new exchange rate channel restrains the inflationary impact by providing additional supplies of appreciation-cheapened goods and services via the enlarged current account deficit. Monetary policy works through the exchange rate as well as the interest rate, and the former channel may be more powerful than the latter. Monetary policy is still effective, but it works differently. Excess demand is spilled overseas rather than restrained.

3.2 WHY DO CAPITAL FLOWS CAUSE PROBLEMS?

3.2.1 Macro Problems

Macro problems can be grouped into three: (i) inflation pressures; (ii) exchange rate problems; and (iii) loss of control over, or constraints on the free use of, monetary policy.

3.2.1.1 Inflation

We argued above that capital flow adds as much to supply as it does to demand, so it should not, in itself, be inflationary. It might, however, be inflationary in other ways. If it makes monetary policy less effective or constrains the use of monetary policy, this might be relevant, but we will argue below that competent monetary policy can avoid this threat.

There are two possible inflationary channels. Although capital flow adds to supply, the inflow may be directed mainly at the purchase of existing assets, so the demand pressure is not offset much by the extra supply of cheap foreign goods and services. This asset price inflation is accommodated by the stance of domestic monetary policy, which targets consumer price index (CPI) prices rather than asset prices. Central banks remain uncomfortable with this asset price inflation as it is distortionary while underway, exacerbates the cycle, and is disruptive when the asset bubble eventually bursts. This was certainly the case in a number of East Asian countries in the years leading up to the 1997–98 crisis.

This presents a dilemma for policy: the authorities can raise interest rates, but they refrain from this partly out of the belief that their actions will be to some extent frustrated by extra capital inflows, but mainly because they do not believe they can effectively control asset prices, and they do not want to be blamed for pricking the bubble. They have, moreover, judged themselves to be unable to do more than, at most, lean against the wind, ready to pick up the pieces when the asset bubble bursts. This is unsatisfactory, but represents the imperfect current 'state of the art'.

If the inflow does bid up asset prices, there is a second possible effect. It increases the general investment demand via Tobin's 'q': existing assets are now more expensive than the cost of reproducing them, so investment is boosted. Higher equity prices cheapen funding costs, so thus encourage more investment.

3.2.1.2 What is the analytical model for the exchange rate?

Cyclical pressures on the exchange rate combine with the structural influences to produce an exchange rate which has a strong tendency towards appreciation, and has no clear anchor in the 'fundamentals'. It is possible to explain the cyclical path of the exchange rate in terms of the Dornbusch (1976) overshooting model, just as some cyclical movements may be explicable in terms of the world commodity-price cycle (Gruen and Kortian, 1996). Economic analysis, however, has little to say about the path of the exchange rate during the decades-long journey to the technological frontier. It might be possible to envisage the exchange rate being on a steady trajectory towards the long-term equilibrium, when the economy has reached the technological frontier. But at any point on this path, this exchange rate will be too low for portfolio equilibrium, as the investors face the prospect of higher interest returns and exchange rate appreciation.

We observe that this inflow is not equilibrated by price arbitrage: the foreign and domestic interest rates do not merge together over time. So there must be other forces at work constraining the inflow. One common approach is to explain the enduring interest differential as a 'risk premium'. This might mechanically satisfy some portfolio balance constraint, but is analytically unhelpful unless some explanation can be offered for the risk premium and how it changes over time.

Is there a structural analogue of the cyclical Dornbusch overshooting mechanism? If the exchange rate appreciates and remains above its longer-term equilibrium until some random shock creates the risk of a short-term fall, the prospect of even a small fall in the near future outweighs the interest differential. This would have to be a very random, tenuous, and unstructured equilibrium path because a longer-term investor would not be deterred by this short-term depreciation risk or high-frequency volatility. Investors with a short-term horizon, however, might want to cut their exposure. We might expect to see not only swings in the exchange rate of the recipient country, but in the capital-supplying country as well. This fits well with the experience of Japan during the yen-carry period: the substantial current account surplus together with an undervalued exchange rate punctuated by a sudden sharp appreciation whenever the outflows are in question (October 1998, August 2007) with very large swings (in the range of 80–150 yen/dollar).

This fits with the idea of 'sudden stops'. Some simply call this a 'time-varying risk premium'. The more honest approach is that taken by Krugman (2006), who calls this a Wile E. Coyote process: 'a moment when investors realize that the dollar's value doesn't make sense and that value plunges'. This puts the sophistication of the analysis on the right level: that of a cartoon. The 'search for yield' lasts as long as asset prices are rising and the boom is strong. The most plausible explanation of the Asian contagion in 1997 is Morris Goldstein's 'wake up call': nothing more substantive than a reminder that there was an issue. More often than not, the trigger for outflow is an external policy event rather than a domestic one (Ferrucci et al., 2004). Perhaps an insight can be gained by remembering that the foreign investors usually know very little about the specifics of their investment or even the country they have invested in. The arrival of a small amount of new information can add hugely to their stock of knowledge, and lead to an abrupt change of view.

The markets themselves encompass self-exacerbating processes. They use similar risk models, which signal the same decision-point for all investors. Credit rating agencies set their evaluations by looking in the rear vision mirror, and when they downgrade in response to bad news, investors are forced to sell. Herding or 'correlated errors' cause the investors to cut their investments at the same time, often into 'crowded markets' with a large impact on prices. A fall in the exchange rate is supposed to create the expectation of a subsequent rise ('mean reversion'), but when the exchange rate is unanchored, it can fall greatly without encouraging new inflows (as seen during the 1997–98 crisis). Eventually, however, the fall ends and the underlying interest differential reasserts itself, setting off a new exchange rate cycle.

This creates the likelihood of broad swings in the value of the currency, perhaps following the periodicity of the business cycle. This is not an issue of short-term volatility of the exchange rate, but of sustained departures or misalignment from the equilibrium exchange rate.

It is hardly surprising that policymakers find this world – an overly-appreciated exchange rate with a tendency to sudden gyrations – uncomfortable and unattractive. In most cases in East Asia since the crisis, with flexible exchange rates in place, the policy concern has not been that capital flows threaten price stability, but rather that the inflows set in train this appreciation/instability of the exchange rate.

The appreciated exchange rate undermines international competitiveness, at the cost of slower growth in the tradable sector, often the most dynamic sector of the economy (for argument in favor of under-valued rates see Rodrik, 2007).[4] The greater the appreciation, the larger the fall when the reassessment comes. With the addition of some overshooting in the opposite direction, spill-over into inflation and self-reinforcing capital flight, the stage is set for a crisis.

With the exchange rate subject to this sort of random influence, policymakers face the difficult task of distinguishing between this randomness and the ongoing and continuous changes in the equilibrium, with the danger that they may try to resist the latter as well as the former. However uncomfortable it may be, the authorities in the emerging countries have to accept the need for some appreciation. A capital inflow *should* put upward pressure on the exchange rate, because this is the mechanism through which the real counterpart of the financial capital inflow – the transfer of resources – takes place: the appreciation encourages imports and discourages exports.

This is true whether the capital flow is long-term structural, or cyclical. In both cases the movement of the exchange rate is part and parcel of the adjustment process, and policy should not resist it. Its unwelcome nature is, however, understandable: even if the authorities acknowledge that this sequence – with appreciated exchange rate and current account deficit – is the necessary channel for the capital inflow to operate, they no doubt recall that both these same elements – appreciation and current account deficit – were identified as being central causes of the Asian crisis and often blamed for the problems (see, for example, Feldstein, 2000). Misguided though such criticism might have been, it was important in undermining confidence. Policymakers are understandably reluctant to leave themselves and their countries open to a repeat performance.

We might note in passing how the Impossible Trinity led to a focus on the wrong issue after the crisis. The exchange rate debate focused on the exchange rate regime: specifically on the need for 'corner solutions' (fixed or floating rate). The middle ground of managed rates was out of bounds. Over time, opinion has softened and fuzzed (Fischer, 2001) and now focuses on the dangers of a fixed-but-changeable peg. In the meantime, however, attention was distracted from the possibility that at times the unanchored exchange rate will be significantly away from its equilibrium value and for long enough to do damage. In the fixed/free-float dichotomy, policymakers have no need to think about some notion of the 'right' level of the exchange rate. But if the middle ground of partially managed rates turns out to be the practical reality, then policymakers need a framework in which the value of the exchange rate has some place in their policy consideration.

Of course it is not easy to operationalize such a framework, and many will see this as a distraction from the single-objective approach to monetary policy. However, for countries that are not yet ready to let their shallow and immature foreign exchange market handle the price discovery (see Calvo and Reinhart, 2002), there is a need to have some specific working notion of what is the 'right' exchange rate (if only in terms of a range), and how this might change the cycle structurally over the medium term. They also need some notion of how to reconcile the possibly conflicting signals which the foreign exchange market may be giving to their price stability objectives.

We return to this issue below, when we discuss policy measures. For the moment it is sufficient to observe that exchange rates in emerging countries are not well anchored by widely accepted stable views about the 'fundamentals' or a long track-record which can establish the parameters of a mean-reverting process, and while memories of the huge movements during the 1997 crisis remain, exchange rates will be vulnerable not just to short-term volatility, but to sustained misalignment.

3.2.1.3 Loss of monetary control

The 'Impossible Trinity' was a warning that countries could not simultaneously have open capital markets, a fixed rate, and an independent monetary policy. A floating rate would free up monetary policy, but interest rates and the exchange rate would be governed by uncovered interest parity (UIP): the interest differential had to remain equal to the expected change in the exchange rate. Thus, if interest rates were altered for domestic purposes, the exchange rate would move in response, mapping out the overshooting path prescribed in Dornbusch (1976). The corollary was that the exchange rate could not be influenced without changing the domestic interest rate.

Meanwhile, in the real world, major countries with a high level of integration into world financial markets experienced decade-long periods with substantially different interest rates. The United States (US) and Japan had an average differential of more than 300 basis points for most of the 1990s and 2000s. While these countries had floating rates, there was no sign of the Dornbusch portfolio equilibrating process at work. It would have required a one-off step 'overshooting' depreciation of the yen followed by a steady appreciation. Instead, the cross rate has fluctuated between 90 and 150, with three wide cycles over this period.

East Asian countries have by and large been able to set policy interest

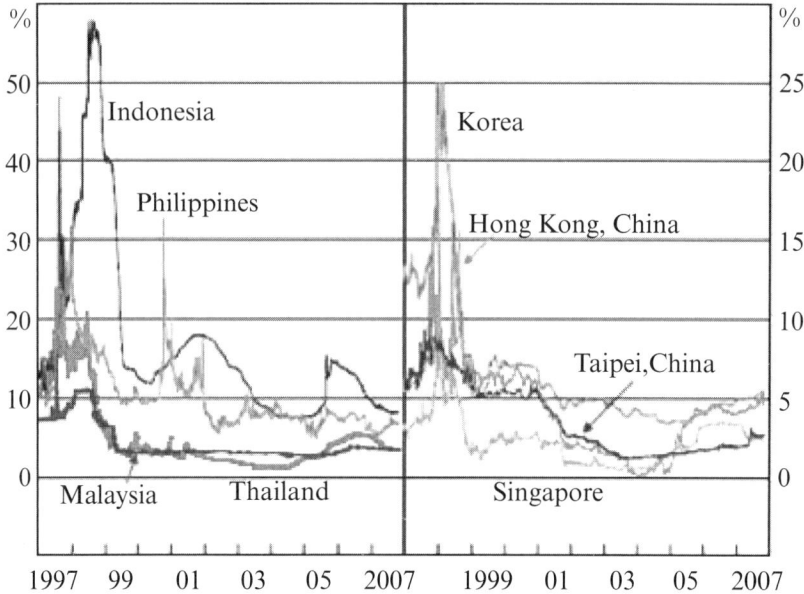

Sources: Reserve Bank of Australia (RBA) (http://www.rba.gov.au/statistics/tables/index.html#interest_rates) and Bloomberg.

Figure 3.1 Asian short-term interest rates

rates where they wanted them, both before the crisis (when the exchange rate regimes were semi-fixed, and interest rates were routinely higher than world rates) and since the crisis (when the regimes are usually classified as a 'managed float') (Figure 3.1). Despite very large capital inflows, interest rates have not equalized, even for countries with relatively small financial sectors. In Thailand, with a fixed rate, foreign savings equivalent to 9 per cent of GDP in the single year of 1996 were insufficient to bring interest rates into line with foreign rates.

Why is reality so far from the message of the Impossible Trinity? First, UIP assumes perfect substitutability between domestic and foreign assets, even when these are denominated in different currencies. This would require not only the absence of capital controls but also well-developed institutional connections, full information, similar tax and legal regimes, similar risk appetites and, above all, a very clear view about the future path of exchange rates.[5]

Secondly, UIP posits a very direct connection between capital inflows and looser monetary policy, because it envisages the credit multiplier

Table 3.1 Change in foreign reserves, money supply (M2) and reserve money (year-on-year, %)

	1999	2000	2001	2002	2003	2004	2005	2006
Indonesia								
Change in foreign reserves	16.4	7.8	4.4	13.7	12.9	0.0	5.2	24.0
Change in M2	11.9	15.6	13.0	4.7	8.1	8.2	16.3	14.9
Change in reserve money	38.8	24.3	15.9	0.9	12.8	1.7	31.0	28.5
Malaysia								
Change in foreign reserves	19.7	7.4	4.2	13.0	31.4	50.3	6.0	17.6
Change in M2	13.7	5.2	2.2	5.8	11.1	26.1	15.6	17.1
Change in reserve money	26.3	9.4	3.3	6.4	6.9	10.0	5.1	10.6
Philippines								
Change in foreign reserves	43.1	1.4	2.9	1.1	2.4	3.9	21.4	25.7
Change in M2	19.3	4.8	6.9	21.0	4.2	10.2	10.3	21.4
Change in reserve money	20.6	6.8	3.5	12.8	5.5	9.8	9.3	61.0
Thailand								
Change in foreign reserves	18.2	6.0	1.1	17.6	8.0	18.5	4.2	28.8
Change in M2	2.1	3.7	4.2	2.6	4.9	5.4	8.2	6.0
Change in reserve money	28.5	18.6	5.7	13.6	11.9	12.4	5.1	2.2
Korea, Republic of								
Change in foreign reserves	42.4	29.9	6.9	18.1	28.0	28.2	5.7	13.6
Change in M2	5.1	5.2	8.1	14.0	3.0	6.3	7.0	12.5
Change in reserve money	37.6	0.9	16.3	15.7	7.3	4.8	11.5	19.9
China, People's Republic of								
Change in foreign reserves	5.7	6.7	28.1	35.0	40.2	50.6	33.7	30.1
Change in M2	14.7	15.4	14.4	16.9	19.6	14.5	16.7	16.9
Change in reserve money	7.3	8.5	9.2	13.3	17.1	11.4	9.3	20.8
India								
Change in foreign reserves	19.5	16.0	21.0	47.5	46.2	28.0	4.2	29.4
Change in M2	17.1	15.2	14.3	16.8	13.0	16.7	15.6	21.6
Change in reserve money	11.4	7.7	10.2	9.3	13.8	16.3	14.9	18.5

Source: International Financial Statistics (IMF).

process as being the basis of monetary policy, whereby a rise in foreign exchange reserves adds to base money, which is multiplied up automatically into credit growth. With financial deregulation, this model is no longer relevant, and it is now feasible, within broad limits, for the authorities to maintain the policy interest rate in the face of capital inflows.[6]

With that background, we can now ask if capital flows cause any loss of control over money supply. First, we can test this against the pre-deregulation common target – base money. This has special resonance for the Impossible Trinity, because this was the channel through which attempts at policy differentials would be frustrated. Table 3.1 shows M2 growth compared with growth in foreign exchange reserves. It is difficult to see any connection. With the possible exception of India, there does not appear to be any close link between additions to net foreign assets and base money.

Why is this linkage so weak? First, the process of sterilization seems to have been quite effective. In practice, it is relatively easy for central banks to sterilize excess base money in a deregulated system, as banks have no alternative use for it if they are already supplying all the loans that are demanded at the going policy-based interest rate. In any case, where the interest rate is the policy instrument, there can be a great deal of slippage between base money and credit. If the authorities have set the interest rate structure, this will determine the rate of credit expansion, and excess base money may not have much effect on credit growth: it remains as unintended excess reserves in the banks' balance sheets (c.f., Japan in 2001–04 and Indonesia in 2005–06).

We can also examine whether the authorities are able to maintain their policy interest rates in the face of a large build-up in foreign exchange reserves. Ho and McCauley (2008) conclude that: 'Central banks with explicit short-term interest rate operating targets or official rate corridors (for example, in India, Indonesia, Republic of Korea, Malaysia, the Philippines and Thailand) were able to manage money market liquidity such that the relevant interest rates did not fall and stay below their announced targets, notwithstanding bouts of foreign exchange purchases.'

It is possible that the authorities would have preferred higher interest rates and trimmed their setting in the hope of discouraging some of the excessive capital inflow. But if they did trim their policy instrument, it does not seem to have stopped them from achieving their final objective – low inflation. So far this century, despite very large capital inflows, inflation has by and large, been contained (although the People's Republic of China (PRC) may represent an unfinished story). Ho and McCauley (2008) conclude:

> All in all, Asia during the period under consideration did not provide evidence for the well-known argument that large-scale reserve accumulation would be inflationary. The top reserve accumulators, be it in absolute terms (PRC and Japan) or in relative to GDP terms (Singapore; Malaysia; Taipei,China; and PRC), did not experience notably larger rises in inflation over the period 2002–2006 compared to economies that accumulated little reserves.
> More strikingly, there is in fact an inverse relationship between reserve accumulation and average inflation performance in Asia over the same period. The top reserve accumulators all had relatively low inflation or even deflation. In contrast, two economies that saw the least reserve accumulation (Indonesia and the Philippines), given currency weakness through 2005, were the ones that over-shot inflation targets and experienced the highest inflation in the region.

This inverse relationship is even more evident if one juxtaposes the inflation rate in 2001 (i.e., the initial condition) with the subsequent degree of reserve accumulation. (p. 11)

Not everyone shares this assessment. The Bank for International Settlements (BIS) 2007 Annual Report, using a wider range of countries, claims to see some relationships between, on the one hand, growth of foreign exchange reserves and, on the other, base money, credit, and inflation. However, these relationships appear tenuous, relying on a couple of outlier countries for their visual impact, with little general explanatory power. The IMF, stuck as usual in a decades-old paradigm, still wants to test the Impossible Trinity in terms of the relationship between base money and credit growth (IMF World Economic Outlook, October 2007).

3.2.2 Flighty Volatile Capital: Sudden Stops

If a flexible exchange rate is not well anchored by expectations and a well-established history of mean reversion around some longer-term trend, 'sudden-stop' capital reversals are a constant danger. As capital leaves in response to a disturbance or change in confidence, it drives down the exchange rate, causing a vicious cycle as more capital leaves in response to this fall.

When these investors flee, they are not easily replaced as few other foreigners can be persuaded to invest by a modest fall in the exchange rate, because the exchange rate is not well anchored and there is no general perception of what the 'right' rate is.[7] Capital inflow in emerging economies is binary: it is either on or off.

Such sudden outflows require a huge and painful adjustment process. When the capital flow is inelastic in response to a lower exchange rate, the adjustment has to take place largely in terms of *income falls* (reduced absorption) which, through reduced imports, are the only path by which the current account can be quickly brought into equilibrium with the now-reduced foreign funding. The exchange rate cannot produce a quick response by 'switching', so the equilibrium has to be achieved by painful 'adjusting'.

To illustrate the point, let us compare Australia and Thailand during the Asian crisis. The fall in the Australian dollar was not, of course, as great as in Thailand, but it was nevertheless very substantial – close to 30 per cent. The relationship between this exchange rate fall and capital flows was, however, quite different, for reasons we will explore in a moment. But first, let us look at the data.

Figure 3.2 shows the huge turnaround in capital flows in Thailand

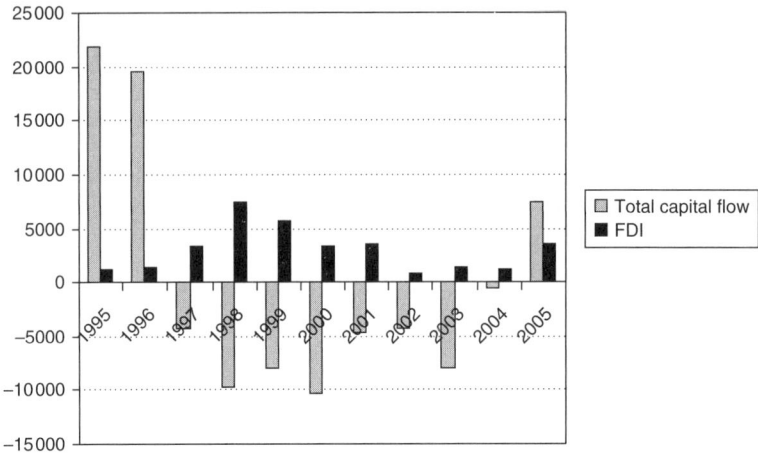

Figure 3.2   Thailand: capital flows

(amounting to well over 20 per cent of GDP, from an inflow of nearly 9 per cent in 1996 to an outflow of 13.6 per cent in 1998).

This contrasts with Australia (shown in Figure 3.3) which shows no sign of any reversal of capital at all, despite the significant fall in the exchange rate: the inflow was actually larger in 1998 than the previous average.[8] Thus the fall in the exchange rate was a threat to inflation, but not to capital flows. Relaxed about the threat to price stability, the Australian central bank was prepared to let the exchange rate fall without raising interest rates in its defense. The result was that the real economy was largely unaffected. The Thai authorities, on the other hand, were forced to raise interest rates in an economy already put in free-fall by the need to trim the current account to the available (hugely reduced) foreign funding. Clearly there is a different relationship between exchange rate weakness and capital flows.

Other countries provide similar comparisons. Caballero et al. (2004) argue that the different behavior of Chile, compared with Australia, was not caused by different views on the inflation danger (the pass-through in both countries is similar), but rather was aimed at pre-empting capital outflow which would be much more likely to happen in Chile (fewer opportunities to diversify risk through derivatives), and do more damage when it did (commercial balance sheets are quite exposed to exchange-rate risk).[9] Hausmann (1999) compares Mexico and Australia: in Mexico's case it is not clear whether the interest rate increase was a response to the inflation threat or designed to encourage capital to remain, but the capital flow behavior in the two cases is clearly quite different.

This difference between Mexico, Chile, and Thailand, on the one hand,

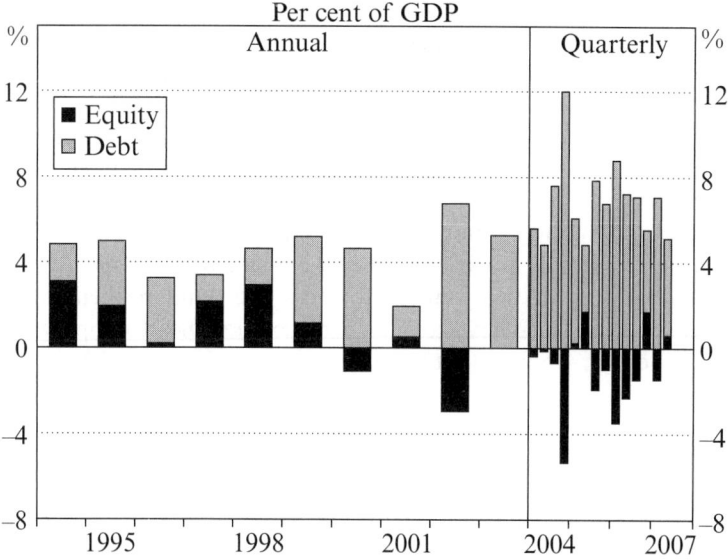

Figure 3.3   Australia: capital flows

and Australia (and similar countries) on the other is the central policy issue: what is it that makes investors prepared to hold their positions[10] in the case of Australia, but not with the other countries? Caballero et al. (2004) identify the difference as 'country trust', as distinct from 'currency trust'.

Others would describe this differently, with different characteristics. They might talk in terms of institutions and the environment of law and governance. Others would emphasize that the central issue is the disparity in size between the financial markets of the emerging countries and those of the mature countries which are the source of the disruptive flows (Volcker, 1999; Richards, 2002; Runchana, 2007). Still others will argue that at each stage of the exchange rate fall in Australia, foreign investors thought that the rate had fallen enough and there was no expectation of a further fall.

3.2.3   Financial System Stability

It is hard to insulate the financial sector from these problems – 'twin crises' are the norm (Kaminsky and Reinhart, 1999). To start with, the capital inflow often comes through the financial sector, intermediated by banks or finance companies. Even where it does not, the banks' customers – the companies whose balance sheets have been seriously damaged by the outflow – have borrowed from the domestic banks and they now routinely default not just on their foreign debts, but their domestic debts as well. Both the vulnerability to capital reversals and the fragility of the financial sector reflect institutional and reputation weaknesses. The policy problem is that reputation and institutions[11] cannot be built quickly or easily. The prescription is simply unattainable in the short or even medium term. While embarking on this journey towards deep and resilient financial markets, policymakers have to put in place strategies to cope with the journey. We turn, now, to that issue.

3.3 HOW SHOULD POLICY RESPOND?

The policy responses might be grouped into two categories: those preventative measures put in place before the crisis, and those used to try to rescue or ameliorate the unfolding crisis. However, some measures substantially overlap, such as foreign exchange market intervention, which will be discussed in a separate section.

3.3.1 Before the Crisis: Prevention

The two broad approaches here are to try to limit the inflow, and to prevent the exchange rate from overshooting in its appreciation.

3.3.1.1 Sand in the wheels

It would be possible to discourage the inflow by introducing various types of 'sand in the wheels': unstable politics, arbitrary administrative or judicial decisions, poorly functioning institutions, obscure information and random market processes, resulting in wide and unpredictable fluctuations in the exchange rate. It goes without saying that policy should be aimed at removing such imperfections, not using them as a policy instrument to solve a problem of excessive inflows. This kind of 'sand in the wheels' is simply inefficient and denies the emerging country the benefit of the cheaper capital available overseas.

We noted in Section 3.2.1.2 above, that maintaining exchange rate uncertainty and volatility is one way of discouraging inflows. While this sort of disruption is widely accepted as the main explanation for time-varying risk, it seems sub-optimal.[12]

There is another price-based mechanism at work. The foreign investment bids up the price of domestic assets (not just equities, but debt and property). This helps foreigners achieve portfolio equilibrium as the yield on the assets is driven down towards the foreign interest rate. There are, however, two disadvantages for the recipient country. First, as asset prices rise, an asset bubble becomes likely. Second, domestic investment is encouraged by the asset price increase (Tobin's 'q' operates), so the stance of monetary policy is undermined.

3.3.1.2 Taxes on inflows

Is there nothing better available in the policy armory to restrain excessive inflows? If we see the problem in terms of a price differential between the return on capital at home and abroad, policy might aim to ration the inflow while at the same time ensuring that the recipient country gets the full benefit of the fact that capital is available more cheaply in the world market. If rationing is needed, then a tax on inflows seems worth exploring, as it does the job and gives the benefit of the price differential to the home country (although, as usual, capacity to administer such a tax is an issue). The first measure might be to ensure that the foreign investment is fully taxed in the recipient country. International tax treaties aimed at avoiding double taxation tend to shift taxation out of the recipient country perhaps to some tax haven. This may be hard to change, but would at least ensure that taxation does not act as a distortion working against macro-economic stability. A comprehensive capital gains tax would seem to have the same virtue. While a rigorously enforced capital gains tax may not prevent an asset bubble from forming, it may exercise some constraint and the revenue will help clean up the damage when it bursts.

One preemptive response to excessive surges of foreign capital might be inflow controls – Chilean-style unremunerated reserve requirements (URR).[13] Mainstream discussion of these still has the flavor that, just as 'real men don't eat quiche', serious countries do not have URR controls. This seems puzzling, as objective assessments show them to have been modestly successful over the policy horizon[14] and they seem closely tailored to the requirement to discourage the least useful and most disruptive form of inflow – short-term funds. The negative consensus surrounding URR has been unhelpful to their effective use. Financial markets, carrying the Impossible Trinity baggage, were unanimously critical when Thailand attempted to introduce URR in December 2006, triggering outflows. If URR are a legitimate policy response, they require more *in principle* support from the IMF. To the extent that they are often thought to be effective only for relatively short periods of time, such measures might be thought of as being relevant to surges and the cyclical issues rather than the structural issue.

3.3.1.3 Prudential controls

To the extent that the foreign inflows are coming through the domestic financial system, there seem many opportunities for stronger prudential controls, driven by the fact, well established by now, that prudential problems in the downswing of the cycle were largely created during the upswing.[15] Policy should be bold enough not only to recognize the incipient problems, but to act on them. There is a good case for prudential regulations preventing or greatly limiting the role of the core financial institutions (banks) in intermediating the foreign inflows. So one answer to the second leg of the 'twin crises' – the collapse of the banking system – may be to prevent the banks (and their subsidiaries) from acting as intermediaries for the inflow, and subject their customers' whole-of-balance-sheet exposures to detailed prudential scrutiny and proper reserving practices.

As often occurs, doctrinal or philosophical views get in the way of good policy. In this case, there is a commonly voiced argument that prudential measures should not be used for macro-economic purposes, but this is a misunderstanding of the nature of the problems: it is a prudential problem which also happens to have macro-economic implications.

A more radical option would be to build a core of narrow banks (i.e., banks which would hold only government securities as assets). This would not only assure the safety of a core group of deposits, but could assure the stability of a basic payments system in the event of a financial crisis (for a proposal along these lines for Indonesia, see Grenville, 2004b). It might be worth noting that the types of deposit insurance widely introduced in Asia after the crisis (where small depositors are covered, but the larger depositors are not protected) would have no effect in ameliorating a systemic crisis (Grenville, 2006).

3.3.1.4 Hedging

In the aftermath of the Asian crisis, there was a strong suggestion that the crisis could have been averted or greatly mitigated if only domestic borrowers had hedged their foreign exchange exposure beforehand.[16] To evaluate this, we need to separate the three different channels that come into play in a crisis. First, the exchange rate falls and this is a threat to inflation. Second, the capital outflow requires an adjustment in the current account position to fit with the new (reduced) availability of external funding. Third, the exchange rate fall administers a balance sheet loss to anyone with a currency exposure.

With these distinctions in mind, we can evaluate the effect of hedging. While it can shift the exposure around, the exchange rate vulnerability remains: if there is large capital inflow, then someone – either domestic or foreign – has taken on a currency mismatch. If hedging shifts the exposure from one resident to another, there would seem to be little macro-effect. If the exposure is shifted to foreigners, this shifts the balance sheet exposure to them and softens the effect of the crisis on domestic corporations. This may mitigate the crisis, but the remaining two effects – exchange rate fall and the need for current account adjustment through the absorption effect – remain, and may even be more severe. Foreigners will attempt to cut their exposure when the currency comes under threat, pushing the exchange rate down and creating the same pressure on inflation and the same need for current account adjustment in response to capital reversal.

A closely related debate goes under the catchy title of 'original sin' (Eichengreen et al., 2005) which puts the currency denomination of foreign debt as the central issue. Hausmann (1999) explains the difference between Mexico and Australia in terms of the ability of Australia to borrow in its own currency, while Mexico (having 'original sin') had to borrow in dollars, leaving its borrowers vulnerable to an exchange rate depreciation. This raises the same issues as discussed in the previous paragraph. Unless it can be shown that foreign investors are more stable holders of currency exposure than domestic borrowers, the vulnerabilities remain, whoever holds the exposure.[17]

Our analysis questions the conventional wisdom of encouraging countries to shift the exchange risk to foreigners, thus ridding themselves of 'original sin'. Certainly, this shifts the balance sheet damage of a depreciation to foreigners. But the country and its investors pay a significant premium for this risk shifting. Just as a Japanese investor would have been much better off by investing in Australian dollars,[18] an Australian borrower would have been significantly better off borrowing in yen over this period. Shifting the currency risk to foreigners gives them the benefit of the difference between the low international rates and the high domestic rates. Why is this universally regarded as good policy?

3.3.1.5 Fiscal surplus

The one policy prescription which seems to achieve wide support in theory if not in practice is to respond to excessive capital inflow by shifting the budget in the direction of surplus.[19] This prescription seems to rely on the Mundell–Fleming IS/LM framework: a budget surplus will shift the IS to the left, lowering interest rates and discouraging capital inflows. This seems to fail on two levels. First, the IS/LM framework no longer captures the way monetary policy operates. The authorities set the short-term interest rate and have no reason to change this in the face of a large budget surplus and a leftward shift of the IS. Longer-term interest rates are set by the Wicksellian natural rate, which does not change. Even if interest rates *did* fall, the capital flows facing the countries of East Asia seem to be fairly interest-inelastic, as they are now dominated by FDI and portfolio flows into equities. If this is the right framework, then the extra savings from the budget will shift the saving/investment balance and, *pari passu*, the current account towards surplus. If the same quantity of capital inflow has to be brought into equilibrium with a smaller current account deficit, this would seem to put upward pressure on the exchange rate, the exact opposite of the desired result.[20]

3.3.1.6 Run current account surpluses

In their broad order of magnitude, the capital inflows into East Asia in the 2000s have been around the same as in the first half of the 1990s, but their absorption has been fundamentally different. In the 1990s, there were corresponding current account deficits, so the capital flows were transferred in terms of real goods and services. But these countries have run current account surpluses since the Asian Crisis, so the net inflows have, roughly speaking, gone straight into official foreign exchange reserves. This makes the countries much less risk prone (see the informal risk ranking in The *Economist* on 17 November 2007, page 76). This has been achieved by a combination of restrained growth, lack-luster investment climate, and exchange rates which have been held down by intervention. This may be a natural reaction and aftermath to the 1997–98 crisis, and a significant reserve build-up can be justified. As a longer-term strategy, however, it is mercantilist and ignores the need for maximizing growth opportunities.

3.3.1.7 Intervention

Can the authorities use foreign exchange market intervention to prevent the exchange rate from rising too much in the pre-crisis period? If it does not rise too much, then it will not fall much. This is where policymakers need some operational notion of what the 'right' exchange rate is. Probably the least palatable message that comes out of this discussion is that the authorities should be ready to allow the exchange rate to appreciate. They need to resist opposing the ongoing underlying structural appreciation and the appreciation which is the normal part of monetary policy during the upswing of the cycle. If they can identify any further overshooting, there is a fair chance that intervention will, at least, do no harm and will turn out to be profitable for the central bank. Topping and tailing the cyclical overshooting of the exchange rate seems not only possible, but desirable. This is not a doctrinal issue, simply one of operational capacity. Whether or not it changes the path of the exchange rate much, it gets policy to focus on the right issue – has the exchange rate overshot? The justifiable concern that the exchange rate may overshoot would suggest some variant on the Williamson basket-band-crawl (BBC) (Williamson, 2000). This has, in a fairly mechanical form, some of the characteristics of the Singapore exchange rate approach, which permits quite aggressive and determined intervention, but normally only when the exchange rate has moved significantly away from what is seen as the medium-term equilibrium.[21]

Of course, any intervention has to be kept consistent with the monetary stance but, as we noted in Section 3.2, this is less difficult in practice than the Impossible Trinity implies.[22] The threat to the stance of monetary policy is more likely to come from a reluctance to keep interest rates at the proper level, rather than the use of intervention in the foreign exchange market.

3.3.2 Managing a Crisis

When prevention fails and the 'sudden stop' is impending or has begun, central banks have three possible responses: raise interest rates, intervene in the foreign exchange market, or impose capital controls.

3.3.2.1 Interest rates

Higher interest rates can help to retain fleeing capital, but not often, and never when the exchange rate fall is accompanied by a financial crisis (Goldfajn and Gupta, 1999). During the Asian crisis, the reversals in Thailand and Indonesia were dramatic, and could not be countered by any realistically acceptable rise in interest rates. At an intuitive level, the central problem is that the prospect of an imminent depreciation will always outweigh the investors' higher running return. We shouldn't have had to learn this lesson in the 1997 crisis: in 1992 the UK was unable to defend the sterling peg because the market knew that an interest rate defense was too politically painful to be maintained, and in the same year Sweden tried to impose 500 per cent interest rates to defend the krona, ultimately unsuccessfully.

3.3.2.2 Intervention

There is very little support for foreign exchange intervention in the academic literature, and it takes a brave central bank to stand against a serious bout of capital outflow. Nevertheless, this is what reserves are for, and if the authorities are not ready to use their reserves, then why bother to have them in the first place? Intervention has (at least) two aims:

- First, to discourage capital outflow by supporting the exchange rate.
- Second, to finance a continuation of the current account position, so as to avoid a forced turnaround which, in turn would force a sharp contraction in GDP.

While in practice these two aims are inexorably interwoven, they should be judged separately. Even if the intervention has no effect on the path of the exchange rate, intervention might well be justified by the extra time it buys for the absorption adjustment process to take place.

Why does intervention get such bad (academic) press? Once again it is tempting to put some of the blame on the strong presumption, held by many analysts, that the market always provides the right answer. Perhaps a stronger reason is that history provides plenty of examples of futile defenses of unsustainable exchange rates. The test, however, is not to lump together all the attempted defenses and to try to distil a single answer on whether intervention 'works', but to identify the circumstances in which intervention *could* work, and test these. This is, unfortunately, not easy: we cannot know the counterfactual path of the exchange rate and there is an intractable identification problem, in that we cannot distinguish between the policy reaction and policy failure.

What we do know is that some central banks have consistently made a handsome profit over time by attempting to 'lop the peaks and fill the troughs' (Andrew and Broadbent, 1994). Others such as Japan have had good (if unacknowledged) success. Whether they succeeded in lopping and filling is impossible to prove, but their profits suggest, at least, that private arbitrageurs are 'leaving money on the table'. The experience of Singapore during the crisis suggests that a well-functioning economy can protect itself against depreciation overshooting through intervention. The key is for the authorities to allow the exchange rate to move a significant distance before attempting a determined and well-resourced defense. This takes a high degree of expertise and experience, backed by good administrative arrangements. Not every country will be able to emulate Singapore's success.

Whatever the arguments about the effectiveness of intervention in influencing the path of the exchange rate, there will still be a case for using reserves to smooth the absorption adjustment in a crisis, and in Section 3.3.3 below we return to the issue of what is a sensible level of reserves to hold for this purpose.

3.3.2.3 Capital controls

The academic literature is similarly unenthusiastic about capital controls, although after the Asian crisis there appeared to be increased support for inflow controls of the Chilean type, as mentioned above. It is hard to find any support at all for outflow controls, and again this may reflect the reality that the loudest voices come from the creditor countries. Despite the frequently heard assertions of the sanctity of debt, it is equally hard to see the philosophical objection: every country has domestic bankruptcy rules to sort out the relative rights of debtors and creditors when the debtor is insolvent. Rapid recognition of bankruptcies in 1997 would have fundamentally altered the way the Asian crisis played out, especially in Indonesia. Private debtors would not have been in a position to buy foreign currency to stave off their creditors. Rather, their balance sheets would have been in the hands of a bankruptcy administrator who, in due course, would have negotiated a settlement with the creditors.

Given the undoubted success of the Korean standstill on bank debt at the end of 1997 and the importance of this in restoring stability and confidence, it might be thought that this would become part of the normal policy armory. Not so. It is treated as a unique occurrence in unusual circumstances. It would have been impossible, it is said, to make deals with all the widespread creditors in the other cases. As a generalization, this is clearly nonsense: it could be done in the same way that domestic bankruptcy administrators work, by an administrator simply announcing that the business is insolvent, and having creditors come forward to register their claims, which are dealt with in good order. This would, however, require some international endorsement to avoid individual creditors jumping ahead in the line, and it has not been possible to get international endorsement of orderly debt resolution even in the far simpler sub-case of sovereign debt restructuring.

There is one further policy measure, related to foreign exchange intervention, which gets little discussion but seems to have been effective in Brazil in 1999 (see Bevilaqua and Azevedo, 2005). Rather than use its foreign exchange reserves to sell into the market, the government can issue debt denominated in dollars. This provides dollar-denominated assets which the market can use to provide currency cover for those who would otherwise have bought dollars in the foreign exchange market. Of course, the government is taking on currency risk, so should try to follow the Brazilian example: only do this if the currency has overshot and is likely to appreciate.

3.3.3 Managing the Central Bank Balance Sheet

We have suggested above that intervention both to constrain overshooting in appreciation before the crisis, and to restrain the depreciation during the crisis, may well be justified. This involves significant foreign exchange reserves, usually on the balance sheet of the central bank. This raises operational and policy issues which we address here.

Large capital inflows lead to intervention and increases in foreign exchange reserves. One measure of the pressure on the exchange rate is shown in Figure 3.4. The reserve build-up presents two problems for the management of a central bank's balance sheet. First, the central bank has a

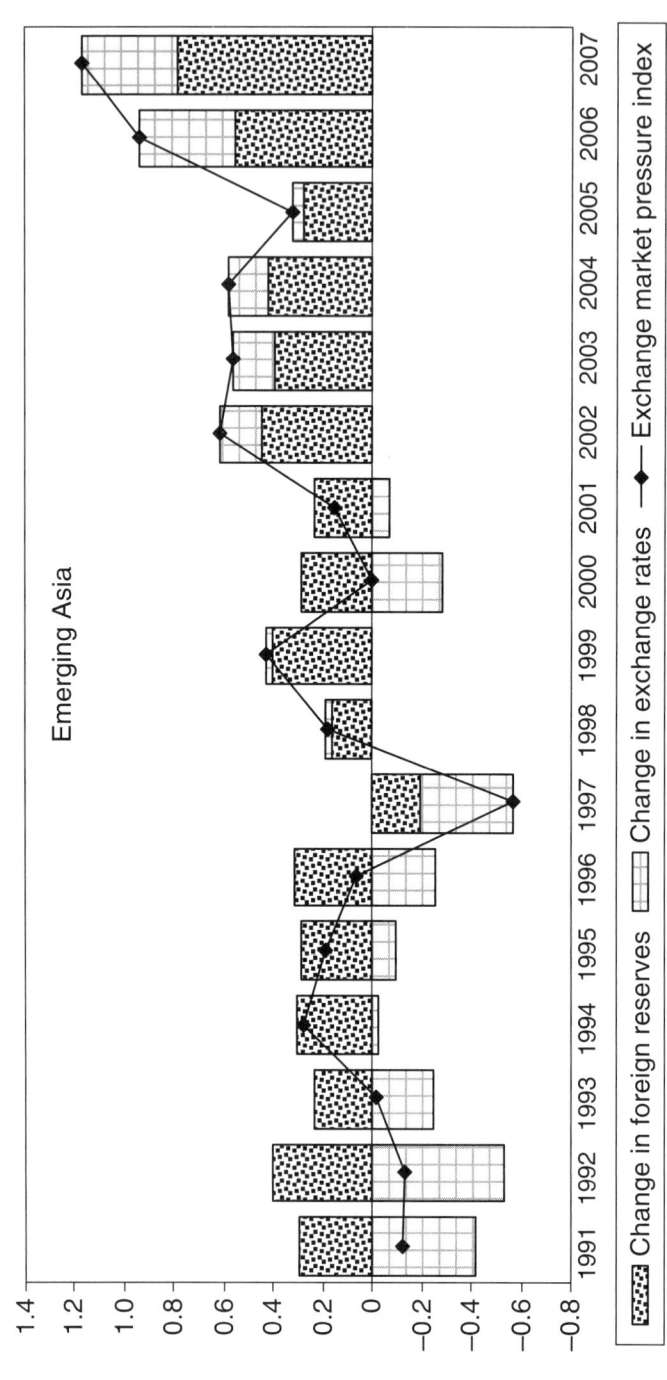

Source: World Economic Outlook (IMF), October 2007.

Figure 3.4 Exchange market pressure index

foreign exchange exposure, which threatens its capital position in the event of appreciation. Second, the earnings on these foreign exchange assets are often smaller than the cost of issuing the sterilization instrument, putting the central bank's profit at risk.

Despite these two potential-cost factors, reserve holding may represent a proper policy choice: even where the central bank makes losses, the country as a whole may make offsetting gains. Alternatively, the investments may be thought of as a sensible self-insurance policy against foreign capital flight. If reserves could have been used to avoid or mitigate a crisis, the return on reserve-holding would be very high. But no central bank wants to go, cap in hand, to the government for a recapitalization if either of these factors puts its solvency in question.

Rodrik (2006) sets out the cost of foreign exchange reserve holding for emerging countries as a whole, putting it at around 1 per cent of GDP. He sees this as a self-insurance policy worth taking. The ongoing cost of financing reserve holdings seems quite modest (smaller than Rodrik's estimates). Ho and McCauley (2008) confirm this view.

The risk of valuation losses in the event of an appreciation seems more substantial. A hypothetical scenario that might provide the broad order of magnitude is to imagine a 20 per cent appreciation of the yuan, impinging on foreign exchange reserves equal to half of GDP. In this case, the accounting loss for the central bank would be equal to 10 per cent of GDP. Table 3.2 sets out some more detailed calculations.

In one sense, these capitalization and profit issues are accounting problems which could be handled by some inventive inter-governmental accounting – through the addition of some government bonds to the central bank balance sheet. Just as central bank losses arising from support of a failing banking system must be swiftly made good by the budget without threatening central bank independence, so too revaluation losses should be made good swiftly and without condition.

This leaves open the more important policy issue of whether these foreign exchange exposures are in the nation's interest, and whether the investment in often low-return assets is sensible. This issue seems unresolved in the literature, although we have moved beyond judging reserve adequacy by comparison with the imports bill (traditionally three months of imports), recognizing that the capital account is now where the threat lies.

One often heard suggestion is the Guidotti Rule (Greenspan, 1999), which proposes that emerging countries should hold foreign exchange reserves equal to the debt that will fall due over the next year. If this is interpreted as the longer-term debt falling due over the next year, it might make some sense as insurance against difficulty in rolling over the

Table 3.2 The cost of foreign exchange reserve holdings in 2006

	Cost of funding the reserves, billion USD (% of GDP)[a]	Cost of a 20% appreciation, billion USD (% of GDP)[b]
Indonesia	2.967 (0.815)	8.221 (2.257)
Malaysia	−1.150 (0.772)	16.426 (11.029)
Philippines	0.087 (0.074)	4.005 (3.407)
Thailand	−0.138 (0.067)	13.058 (6.329)
Korea, Republic of	−0.934 (0.105)	47.776 (5.379)
China, People's Republic of	−27.648 (1.045)	213.698 (8.080)
India	2.640 (0.302)	34.148 (3.909)

Notes:
[a] Total reserves*(yield of 3-month domestic treasury bill – average yield of US Treasury 1–5 years).
[b] Total reserves*0.2.

Sources: International Financial Statistics (IMF); Bloomberg; World Economic Outlook Database.

long-term debt. However, if the reserves are being held against the short-term debt liabilities (which would be the case in East Asia), it raises the issue of why the short-term debt was a good idea in the first place. The Guidotti rule is, however, a reminder that the old rules of thumb connecting recommended reserve holdings with imports are not relevant in a world where the shock comes to the capital account.

A more fruitful argument is found in Jeanne and Ranciere (2006), who note the role that reserves could have played in averting the dramatic fall in absorption which was forced on the crisis countries of Asia as they turned their current account deficits into surpluses in order to meet the funding constraint. They note that, in a large sample of 'sudden stops', the average output loss was 4.5 per cent of GDP in the first year and 2.2 per cent in the second. Their model requires input of parameters covering risk factors and other unknowns and allows for little interaction between the level of reserves and the likelihood of a sudden stop, but seems to be the basis for a sensible approach to assessing reserve levels.

All this does, however, leave a huge policy issue largely unaddressed in this discussion. It might be possible to explain the build-up of emerging economies' foreign exchange reserves in terms of self-insurance against volatile capital flows. But when they amount to more than one-third of GDP for the countries taken together, and for the PRC, to more than half of GDP, is it sensible policy for this to continue? A current account surplus of over 10 per cent of GDP and growing suggests a lack of sustainability, and the size of the potential valuation losses is a reminder that, seen in terms of self-insurance, the premium may turn out to be high. One often proffered answer to upward pressure on the exchange rate – tighten fiscal policy – seems inappropriate for the PRC, with its existing huge saving surplus.[23] Whether the answer is found in further freeing of capital outflow, or stimulus to domestic consumption, or more significant appreciation of the currency, remains in the realm of future policy challenges.

3.4 CONCLUSION

This chapter leaves the policymaker with unanswered operational questions. What precisely is the right level of foreign exchange reserves for self-insurance in a world of unanchored exchange rates and volatile capital flows? Once that level has been reached, what then? Allowing the exchange rate to rise has to be part of the answer, but how far? Can the IMF's renewed interest in exchange rate surveillance fill the gap, based on macro-balance, equilibrium real effective exchange rates and sustainability calculations? Can this be linked into the supposedly deeply embedded relationships of saving and investment, using this as a basis for a view about the appropriate current account balance? If this can be used to identify the appropriate current account position, how can policy maintain capital flows at around this same size?

This chapter does little more than clear the decks and set an agenda for more operationally focused research. Clearing the decks, however, seems important, as analytical thinking about these issues has been severely hampered by doctrinal blinkers. The Impossible Trinity, UIP, and a strong predilection for the 'magic of the market' has meant that in the decade following the Asian crisis, much of the expert advice being offered was simply not listened to. When pure floats are advocated, there is no discussion of how policy should conduct a managed float or manage foreign exchange reserve levels. When prudential rules are limited to micro balance sheet issues, larger macro implications of the behavior of the financial sector are ignored. When free capital flows are doctrinally believed to be optimal, there is no useful discussion of how countries might limit and restrain these flows. A practical research agenda would encompass the design parameters of a managed float, reserve holdings, and intervention policies, including the possibility of using state-contingent assets and government foreign/domestic debt management, as well as conventional reserves. It would provide an analytic framework for judging whether a current account was broadly appropriate. Finally, it would explore taxation constraints on surges of inflow (including URR), stronger (i.e., more intrusive) prudential measures, contingent controls on capital outflows, and better bankruptcy procedures, both domestically and for foreign debts.

There is no likelihood of a 'twin crisis' in East Asia any time soon, as the countries of the region have taken the narrowly conservative path of running current account surpluses and accumulating reserves. This seems neither optimal nor sustainable. With capital flowing 'uphill' and foreign exchange reserves overflowing the coffers, the current conjuncture is not sustainable and increasing globalization will put further pressure on these imbalances over time. When East Asia returns to the more normal configuration of significant current account deficits, the benefits of such crisis preparedness will become apparent.

NOTES

1. In terms of the Swan diagram, the external balance line moves to the right, and absorption increases by the same amount as the capital flow raises demand. A new equilibrium is found with an appreciated exchange rate and non-tradables more expensive compared with tradables.
2. Lipschitz et al. (2002) illustrate this point by calculating physical capital per worker in Eastern Europe, which on average is one-third of the German level. On the bold assumption of the same Cobb-Douglas production function, raising this to the German level would require net investment equal to nearly five times GDP. Even with a combination of domestic and substantial foreign-funded investment, it will take decades to bring the capital stock up to German levels.
3. The borrowers may not feel constrained by the currency risk, as currencies of high interest rate countries tend to appreciate, reducing the costs of their borrowing.
4. Emerging countries are not alone in being reluctant to see their exchange rates appreciate: ECB Chairman Trichet called the appreciation of the Euro in 2004 'brutal'.
5. Despite persistent profitable interest differentials, capital flows have not arbitraged away the differences. Following 15 years of pathetically low returns on yen-denominated investments, Japanese investors still have less than 20 per cent of their bond holdings, and less than 10 per cent of their equity holdings, in the form of foreign assets (IMF *World Economic Outlook*, 2005, Chapter 3).
6. Much of the discussion on sterilized intervention in Asia suffers from anachronism, since it applies measures consistent with quantity targeting to assess the behavior of central banks with interest-rate operating targets (Ho and McCauley, 2008, p. 6).
7. I have described it (Grenville, 2004a) as like trying to sell discount tickets outside a theatre which is already ablaze, with the patrons streaming out.
8. It is worth noting that there was no discernable outflow in the earlier exchange rate 'crisis' in Australia – the 'Banana republic' episode of 1986, when the exchange rate fell 35 per cent without any capital outflow, despite the relative novelty of the exchange rate regime, which had floated only 18 months earlier.
9. 'In Chile there was widespread fear of a capital flow reversal. Net capital outflows could lead to a balance of payments crisis that would turn out to be much more costly than the contraction brought about by high interest rates. Contractionary monetary policy

10. The United States provides a more recent example of stable capital flows. Foreigners' purchases of mortgage-backed securities funded almost one-third of the US capital inflow in 2006. When risk-ratings were re-assessed starting in mid-2007, foreigners sold these assets but continued to hold dollar-denominated assets (IMF Managing Director's speech, October 2007).
11. In the Douglass North (1990) sense of rules and norms which govern relationships between market participants.
12. It might be noted in passing that inducing volatility or uncertainty into market prices is sometimes put forward as a desirable thing. This example from the IMF comes very close to advocating a volatile exchange rate in order to create risk: 'Policymakers should continue to be pragmatic and allow for greater exchange rate flexibility in order to create two-way risk in the foreign currency markets and promote a rebalancing of growth where necessary, limiting any intervention to efforts to reduce volatility and ensure that market conditions remain orderly' (IMF Regional Outlook Asia, October 2006, p. viii).

    This seems perverse: reducing the uncertainty in exchange rate movements would reduce the risk premium, and if this results in too much inflow, it would be better to discourage this through some form of tax (with the revenue benefits) rather than through artificially inflating the risk premium.
13. Because many commentators hold negative views about these, they may conveniently forget that many other countries used this sort of capital control before Chile did: Australia in the 1970s had 'Variable Deposit Requirements' that were so powerful in their effect that they had to be abandoned.
14. The IMF Independent Evaluation Office (2005) concludes that URR temporarily allow domestic interest rates to be higher; that there is no significant effect on exchange rate; that the volume of capital inflow is reduced although this effect diminishes over time; and that the composition of capital inflows moves towards longer maturities.
15. Tight loan-to-valuation ratios, cyclically variable provisioning requirements and limitations on the accepted value of security seem sensible measures. See Borio and Lowe (2002).
16. For a recent example, see IMF (2007): 'these countries had accumulated large unhedged foreign exchange liabilities, as domestic interest rates were higher than international rates and very tightly managed fixed exchange rates had conveyed a false impression of no exchange rate risk' (p. 24).
17. On these issues, see also Goldstein and Turner (2004).
18. A Japanese investor who invested 100 yen at the Japanese official policy rate at the start of 1990 would, by April 2007, have 124 yen. If she had exchanged it into Australian dollars and invested at the corresponding official rate in Australia, by April 2007 her investment, converted back to yen, would have been 265 yen, a return nearly seven-fold the home alternative.
19. See, for example, Schadler et al. (1993).
20. Sometimes this argument is confused with the idea that the capital flow has caused excess demand and thus a fiscal surplus will fix the problem. Of course in a simple Keynesian sense a fiscal surplus reduces demand. But in the context of capital flows, we need a clearer specification of the problem. A capital flow matched by a current account deficit adds as much to supply as to demand, and so does not cause excess demand. The inconvenient aspect of the inflow is the upward pressure on the exchange rate needed to bring about the real transfer, in the form of a current account deficit, and a fiscal surplus would not seem to help here unless it lowers interest rates and discourages inflows.
21. This does not imply, of course, that BBC would necessarily use the exchange rate as the instrument of monetary policy to target inflation, as Singapore does. Australian intervention practices also have some of these characteristics, in that substantial intervention

takes place, but only if the exchange rate has departed significantly from what the RBA judges to be a sensible level. Whether or not a formally defined band is best (neither Singapore nor Australia have such bands) and whether this is made public are purely operational issues. A publicly announced band may help to anchor the exchange rate, but will also constrain the flexibility of the authorities in responding to shocks.

22. The common textbook distinction between 'sterilized' and 'unsterilized' intervention reflects a confusion of operational practice. Any competent monetary authority will routinely sterilize an intervention through its daily liquidity management operations (otherwise system liquidity would be unbalanced). The substantive distinction should be between intervention which is supported by a change in monetary policy and one which is not. Obviously, supported intervention has a greater likelihood of influencing the path of the exchange rate, but the support may not be consistent with domestic monetary objectives.

23. And, for that matter, much of the rest of East Asia.

REFERENCES

Andrew, R. and J. Broadbent (1994), 'Reserve bank operations in the foreign exchange market: effectiveness and profitability', Reserve Bank of Australia Research Discussion Paper No. 9406.

Bevilaqua, A. and R. Azevedo (2005), 'Provision of FX hedge by the public sector: the Brazilian experience', BIS Papers 24, 119–26.

Borio, C. and P. Lowe (2002), 'Asset prices, finance and monetary stability: exploring the nexus', BIS WP114, July.

Caballero, R., K. Cowan and J. Kearns (2004), 'Fear of sudden stops: lessons from Australia and Chile', NBER Working Paper 10519.

Calvo, G. and C.M. Reinhart (2002), 'Fear of floating', *Quarterly Journal of Economics*, **107**(2), May, 379–408.

Dornbusch, R. (1976), 'Expectations and exchange rate dynamics', *Journal of Political Economy*, **84**(6), 1161–76.

Eichengreen, B., R. Hausmann and U. Panizza (2005), 'The pain of original sin', in B. Eichengreen and R. Hausmann (eds), *Other People's Money: Debt Denomination and Financial Instability in Emerging Market Economies*, Chicago: University of Chicago Press, pp. 13–47.

Feldstein, M. (2000), 'Avoiding currency crises', presentation at a conference organized by the Federal Reserve Bank of Kansas City, Jackson Hole, Wyoming.

Feldstein, M. and C. Horioka (1980), 'Domestic saving and international capital flows', *Economic Journal*, **90**, 314–29.

Ferrucci, G., V. Herzberg, F. Soussa and A. Taylor (2004), 'Understanding capital flows to emerging market economies', *BoE Financial Stability Review*, June.

Fischer, S. (2001), 'Exchange rate regimes: is the bipolar view correct?', *Journal of Economic Literature*, **15**(2), 3–24.

Goldfajn, I. and P. Gupta (1999), 'Does monetary policy stabilize the exchange rate following a currency crisis?', IMF Working Paper 99/42, March.

Goldstein, M. and P. Turner (2004), *Controlling Currency Mismatches in Emerging Markets*, Washington: Institute for International Economics.

Greenspan, A. (1999), 'Lessons from the global crisis', remarks made before the World Bank Group and the International Monetary Fund on 27 September 1999.

Grenville, S. (2004a), 'The IMF and the Indonesian crisis', *Bulletin of Indonesian Economic Studies*, **40**(1), April, 77–94.
Grenville, S. (2004b), 'What sort of financial sector should Indonesia have?', *Bulletin of Indonesian Economic Studies*, **40**(3), December, 307–27.
Grenville, S. (2006), 'Financial safety nets: their role and effects on market discipline of banks', in S.-W. Nam and C.S. Lum (eds), *Corporate Governance of Banks in Asia: A Study of Indonesia, Republic of Korea, Malaysia, and Thailand*, Vol. 2, Tokyo: Asian Development Bank Institute, pp. 51–73.
Gruen, D. and T. Kortian (1996), 'Why does the Australian dollar move so closely with the terms of trade?', Reserve Bank of Australia Research Discussion Paper No. 9601.
Hausmann, R. (1999), 'Discussion of Dooley and Walsh, Grenville and Gruen and Brock', in D. Gruen and L. Gower (eds), *Capital Flows and the International Financial System*, Proceedings of a Conference on Capital Flows and the International Financial System, 9–10 August, Sydney: Economic Group, Reserve Bank of Australia, pp. 141–50.
Ho, C., and R. McCauley (2008), 'Resisting appreciation and accumulating reserves in Asia: examining the domestic financial consequences', Hong Kong Institute for Monetary Research Public Seminar Series, January.
IMF (International Monetary Fund) (2007), *Regional Economic Outlook*, October, Washington, DC: IMF.
IMF Independent Evaluation Office (2005), *The IMF's Approach to Capital Account Liberalization*, Washington, DC: IMF.
Jeanne, O. and R. Ranciere (2006), 'The optimal level of international reserves for emerging countries: formulas and applications', IMF Working Paper 2006/229.
Kaminsky, G. and C.M. Reinhart (1999), 'The twin crises: the causes of banking and balance-of-payments problems', *American Economic Review*, **89** (3), June, 473–500.
Keynes, J.M. (1929), 'The German transfer problem', *Economic Journal*, **39** (153), 1–7.
Krugman, P.R. (2006), 'Will there be a dollar crisis?', *Economic Policy*, **22** (51), 435–67.
Lipschitz L., T. Lane and A. Mourmauras (2002), 'Capital inflows to transition economies: master or servant?', IMF Working Paper 02/11.
North, D. (1990), *Institutions, Institutional Change and Economic Performance*, Cambridge: Cambridge University Press.
Richards, A. (2002), 'Big fish in small ponds: the momentum investing and price impact of foreign investors in Asian emerging equity markets', mimeo, Reserve Bank of Australia.
Rodrik, D. (2006), 'The social cost of foreign exchange reserves', NBER Working Paper 11952, Cambridge, MA: National Bureau of Economic Research.
Rodrik, D. (2007), 'The real exchange rate and economic growth: theory and evidence', John F. Kennedy School of Government, Harvard University Cambridge, MA 02138, August.
Runchana, P. (2007), 'Inflation targeting in a small open economy: a challenge to monetary theory', Bank of Thailand Working Paper, June.
Schadler, S., A. Bennett, M. Carkovic and R. Kahn (1993), 'Recent experiences with surges in capital inflows', IMF Occasional Paper No. 108, August, Washington, DC.
Volcker, P. (1999), 'Problems and challenges of international capital flows', in D.

Gruen and L. Gower (eds), *Capital Flows and the International Financial System*, Proceedings of a Conference on Capital Flows and the International Financial System, 9–10 August, Sydney: Economic Group, Reserve Bank of Australia, pp. 11–17.

Williamson, J. (2000), 'Exchange rate regimes for emerging markets: reviving the intermediate option', September, Washington, DC: Institute for International Economics.

4. Managing large capital inflows: taking stock of international experiences

Susan Schadler

4.1 INTRODUCTION

Large capital flows to emerging markets are almost inevitable given the wide disparities between capital per worker in emerging and in advanced countries. When a combination of historical factors in emerging markets has prevented the investment and technological progress needed to catch up to industrial country income levels, removing such constraints on growth should result in a re-equilibrating shift in the global allocation of capital. This is the story since the early 1990s – and the result has been large changes in the global allocation of capital as the world moves from an old equilibrium toward a new one. Shifts to new equilibria seldom happen smoothly and can have many (desirable and undesirable) side-effects. This is the broad framework in which large capital flows should be seen.

In the course of some 20 years' experience with large capital inflows to emerging market countries, four broad perceptions seem to have taken shape.

- Episodes of large capital inflows carry two main risks: that they will feed overheating pressures which effectively undermine the benefits inflows should deliver and that they will end in crisis.
- There are no good macroeconomic policy solutions to the potential overheating problem. The orthodoxy is that restrictive fiscal policy is the most effective response, but it is difficult to implement.[1] Much attention, therefore, focuses on monetary policy options. Some argue that policymakers must ultimately decide between currency appreciation and higher inflation. Others argue that sterilized intervention can guide economies on a low-inflation, low-appreciation path.
- Large inflows are often driven by a sizable short-term (hot) component reflecting investor opportunism. This perception has produced

considerable interest in controls to moderate large inflows and to discourage hot money. But their effectiveness and desirability over more than short periods is subject to doubt.
- Countries experiencing inflows need strategies for protecting themselves during possible hard landings. Many countries see accumulation of large official foreign exchange reserves as one such strategy.

This chapter reviews the experiences of countries in several regions since the early 1990s in search of evidence on these four perceptions and draws conclusions on how countries should prepare themselves for and respond to large inflows in the future. The remainder of the chapter has four sections. The first identifies the episodes of large inflows since the early 1990s, and looks at whether unwanted developments accompanying large inflows – especially excessive real currency appreciation and inflation – have been prevalent. The second examines the main policy responses that have occurred. The third turns the investigation around and asks what the macroeconomic characteristics of the most successful episodes were. The fourth section looks at ways countries have attempted to prepare themselves for possible crises in the wake of inflow episodes. Conclusions are offered in a final section.

4.2   EPISODES OF LARGE INFLOWS

The past 20 years have seen surges in net private capital flows[2] into emerging market countries.[3] The first occurred during 1990–97 and, after a hiatus during 1998–2002, the second during 2003–07 (Figure 4.1). A few general features of this period stand out.

- First, changes in FDI inflows tend to be gradual, rising steadily through the 1990s (from about 0.5 per cent to about 3 per cent of emerging market GDP) before sliding back to about 2 per cent of GDP in 2005–07.
- Second, non-FDI inflows (comprising portfolio and other flows) move sharply. Volatile non-FDI is evident in all regions, but stands out in emerging Asia. In other words, countries experiencing large non-FDI inflows are more vulnerable to sudden stops or reversals.
- Third, synchronization of large inflows is low across all emerging markets. Given relatively stable FDI, the wide variation between maximum and minimum capital inflows for any year suggests quite significantly different behavior across countries of non-FDI inflows in any given year.

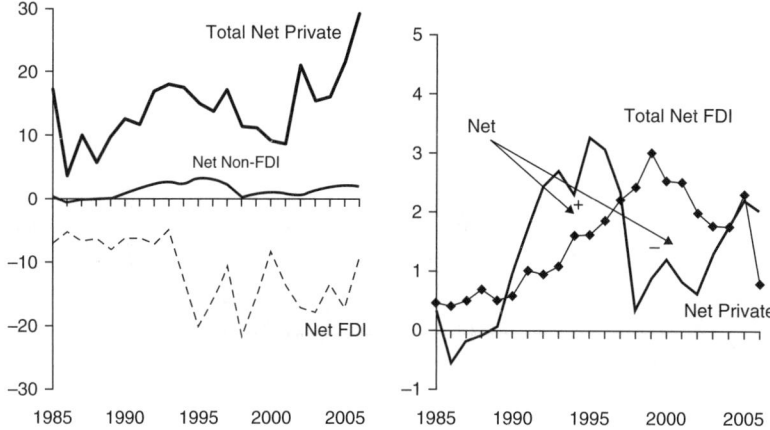

Sources: World Economic Outlook (IMF) and author's calculations.

Figure 4.1 Net private inflows to emerging markets and components, 1985–2006 (% of total emerging market GDP)

These observations point to a key question: what drives non-FDI inflows and what could make them more stable? Regional differences in the pattern and size of net inflows indicate that countries' experiences are shaped importantly by neighborhood. The surge in inflows in the 1990s was dominated by emerging Asia and Latin America.[4] The more recent one centers on emerging Europe and 'other' emerging countries. This pattern raises the question of whether surges in inflows are more the result of regional attractions (for example, countries' adoption of common goals such as accession to the EU or the cyclical position of a major country in the region) than global influences (for example, an increased appetite for emerging market risk or a drop in returns on investments in advanced countries). All things equal, any individual country must therefore expect that when inflows start to come to its region, they will soon be arriving to it. This regional commonality may make it sensible to coordinate responses to inflows.

The 2003–07 inflow episode raises the question whether only net inflows matter or whether surges in gross inflows also matter. Net private inflows to emerging Asia, which at the mid-1990 peak were the largest (relative to GDP) of any region, were in the more recent period well below those to emerging Europe. Gross inflows to emerging Asia, however, have been extremely high. Insofar as macroeconomic effects, in particular overheating, are mainly related to net inflows, large gross inflows alone are unlikely

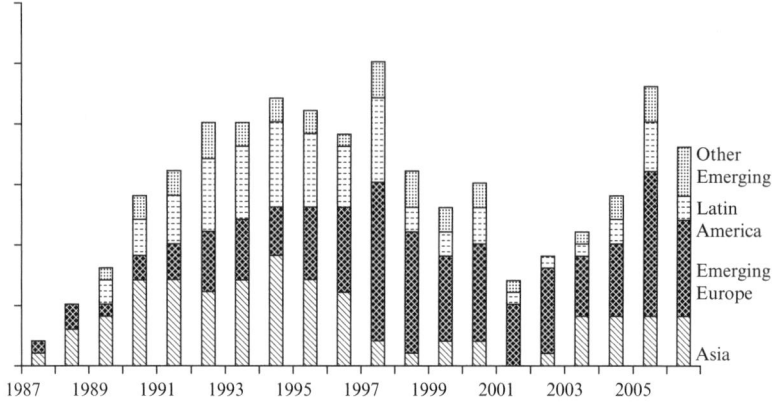

Sources: World Economic Outlook (IMF) and author's calculations.

Figure 4.2 Episodes of large net private inflows to emerging markets, 1987–2006 (number of ongoing episodes)

to arouse the same concerns.[5] Still, it is possible that large gross flows have important distributional effects.[6]

Assessments of macroeconomic issues in countries receiving large inflows should zoom in on episodes of unusually large net inflows to individual countries. The identification of such episodes in the IMF's October 2007 World Economic Outlook (WEO) serves this purpose. Net inflows in any given year must meet one of two criteria to qualify as an episode: the ratio of net inflows to GDP exceeds its trend value plus one standard deviation; or it exceeds a threshold of 75 per cent of the average of the country's region. Applying this methodology produces a list of 109 episodes – some lasting only one year, but most lasting several years. Not surprisingly, developments in the number of large inflow episodes broadly match the overall average and regional distribution of net inflows described earlier in this section (Figure 4.2).

4.2.1 How Serious are the Unwanted Effects of Large Inflows?

While large inflows should be good for an economy as they shift savings from capital-rich to capital-poor countries, facilitate the transfer of technology, and allow residents in countries with strong growth potential to smooth consumption, there is much fear that episodes of large inflows are dominated by volatile 'hot' money that has few of these good effects. Unquestionably, non-FDI flows were an important influence on the

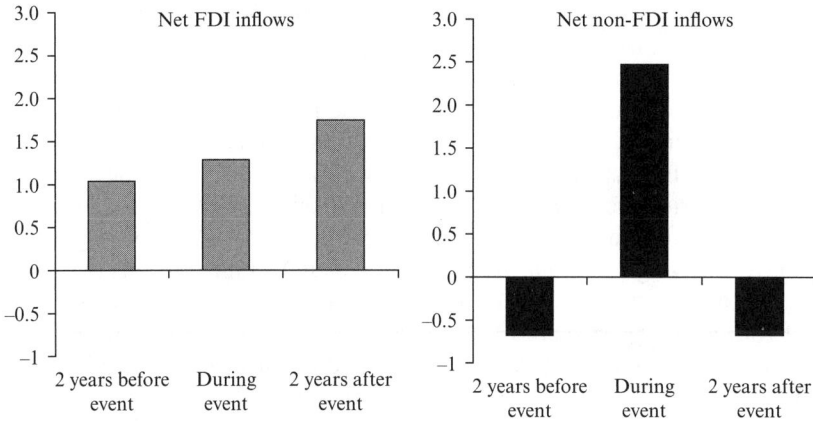

Sources: World Economic Outlook (IMF, 2007) and author's calculations.

Figure 4.3 Net FDI and non-FDI inflows before, during and after episodes (medians for all emerging markets, % of GDP)

pattern of surges. On average, from net outflows prior to episodes, non-FDI inflows rose sharply during episodes and then fell back to negative territory, defining the end of episodes (Figure 4.3). But FDI inflows also played a significant role in the episodes. In particular, FDI inflows on average rose significantly during episodes and remained more or less at the elevated level in the two years after the episode. These patterns underscore the importance of policy efforts to avoid overheating and ward off the threat of crisis in the aftermath of large inflow episodes.

This section asks how large were any adverse effects from surges in inflows. I start with a summary of how episodes ended – whether landings were soft or hard. I then turn to the extent of the overheating pressures in terms of exchange rate appreciation and inflation. Finally, I look for signs that inflows fed excessive credit growth (a possible sign of over-leveraging or asset bubbles). In an effort to focus the analysis, I do not address the benefits conveyed to recipient countries, but these should not be forgotten.

4.2.2 Crises or Hard Landings

Defining the end of inflow episodes as 'soft' or 'hard' is far from an exact science. Though policymakers know when their economy is in a crisis, it is not obvious how to define a crisis empirically.[7] Also, the line between crises and less serious short-term setbacks is blurred particularly because crises since the early 1990s have taken several different forms: crunches on funding a current account deficit; a government's inability to service its domestic and/or external debt; and major domestic bank insolvencies. Establishing a benchmark for any of these is not straightforward. It is, therefore, tempting to define a crisis in terms of a sharp drop in the rate of capital inflows.[8] But such 'abrupt endings' are not necessarily closely related to crises, for example, if a sudden drop in inflows (where inflows are an autonomous influence rather than the result of excessive government borrowing to finance large public deficits) simply curtails excessive growth of investment or consumption fed by previous large inflows.

From a policy perspective, it makes sense to define crises in terms of sharp changes in a key price, fiscal balance, or measure of activity, presumably under duress. A large depreciation is one such indicator. For countries that fix and manage to defend the exchange rate, a 'crisis' might be signaled by a sharp increase in interest rates (for example, in the Baltic countries' defense of currency boards/hard peg in the 1998 Russia crisis). As for policy instruments, a clear sign of crisis is a sharp worsening of the government's balance sheet or a sharp fiscal tightening. More direct signs of a crisis show up in economic activity, such as outright drops in output or demand. Empirically, setting thresholds to delineate crisis is arbitrary – I use a depreciation greater than 20 per cent, a drop in real government primary expenditure relative to GDP by more than 2 percentage points or a drop in output, each within two years after the episode.

On the basis of these three metrics, about 15 per cent of episodes completed by 2004 ended in crisis (Figure 4.4).

In none were all three thresholds crossed. More than half of all crises involved a depreciation of 20 per cent or greater, and of these, most also entailed an output drop. Surprisingly, the share of episodes ending in crisis was not higher for longer duration episodes or for episodes with larger inflows (Figure 4.5). All regions experienced some crises, but proportionately more emerging Asia episodes had hard landings (Figure 4.6).

4.2.3 Overheating and Rapid Growth of Bank Credit to the Private Sector

Apart from the risk of a crisis, overheating during inflow episodes risks derailing growth strategies. Large inflows can provide funding to raise capital labor ratios, import technology, and boost productivity. In this process, they will unavoidably result in some real appreciation, either through nominal exchange rate appreciation or higher inflation. But when exuberance or speculative pressures from inflows result in overheating or excessive leveraging, the cost of instability could outweigh the potential

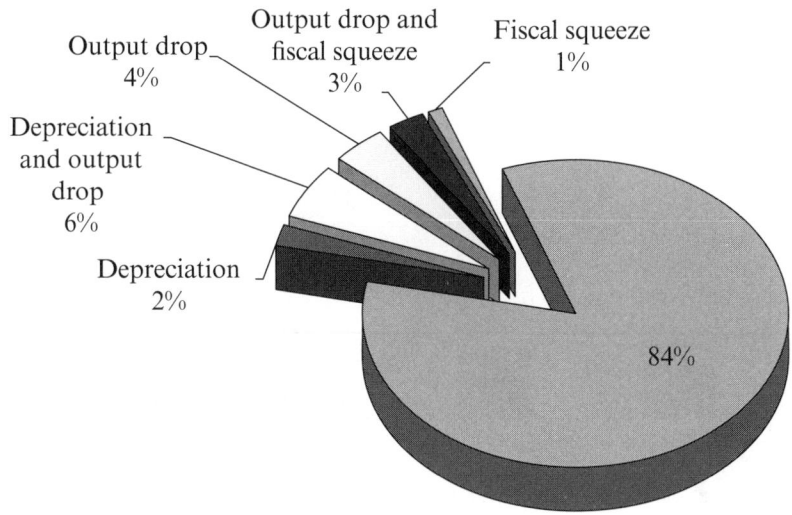

Sources: World Economic Outlook (IMF) and author's calculations.

Figure 4.4 Episodes ending in crisis (% total episodes ending in or before 2004)

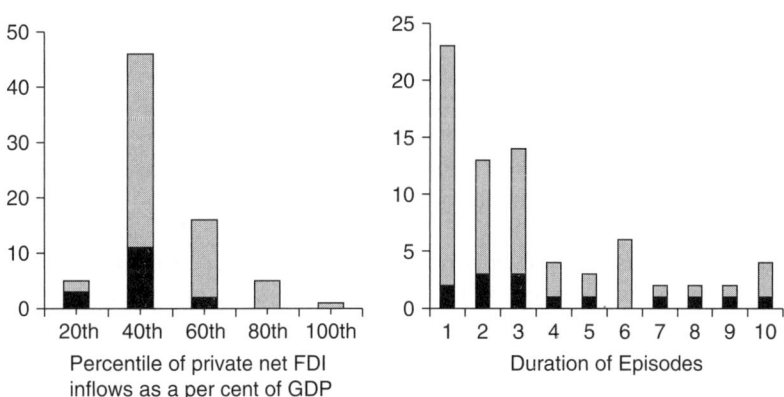

Note: Full bar shows total number of episodes with the specified intensity or duration. Darker portion shows number that ended in crisis.

Sources: World Economic Outlook (IMF) and author's calculations.

Figure 4.5 Episode intensity, duration and crisis (number of episodes with specified characteristics ending in or before 2004)

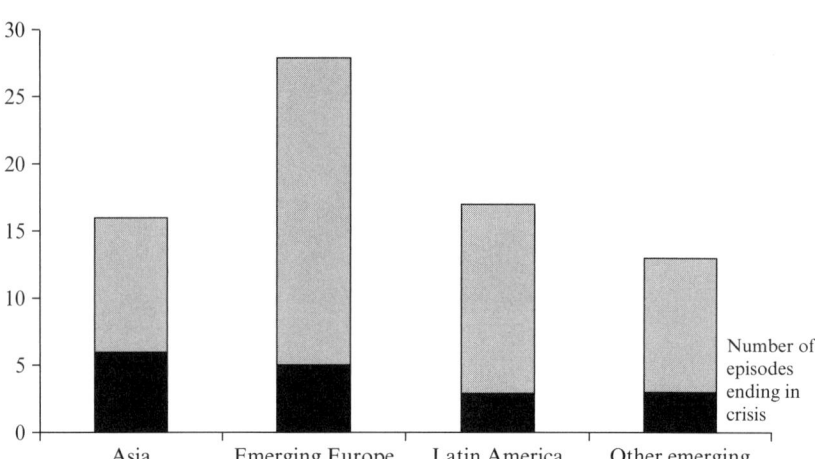

Sources: World Economic Outlook (IMF) and author's calculations.

Figure 4.6 Total episodes and episodes ending in crisis by region (number of episodes)

benefits of inflows. Signs of such developments are rising inflation, real appreciation beyond that consistent with productivity gains, or rapid bank credit growth. How severe have such setbacks been in reality?

Looking first at inflation, the experience since the early 1990s suggests that the effects on average have not been large (Figure 4.7). Median inflation rates fell from an annual average of 8 per cent in the two years prior to inflow episodes to 7 per cent during episodes. This drop reflects the fact that surge episodes were common in major disinflations, particularly during the 1990s and particularly in Latin America.

Typically, a combination of influences (falling global inflation and domestic disinflation policies) raised market confidence in the currency and the growth potential of the economy. Flight capital returned, de-dollarization occurred (both reflected in non-FDI inflows), and FDI inflows rose. Also, in some cases, high domestic interest rates as part of the disinflation program attracted (presumably hotter) capital. Making the case that inflows were inflationary in these circumstances would require a counterfactual indicating that the disinflation would have been faster in the absence of inflows.

The picture on median real appreciations during episodes is not as benign as on inflation, but nor is it alarming. Two kinds of patterns are most clear. First, in Latin America – where countries were typically disinflating during the episodes – real appreciations were high (Figure 4.8).

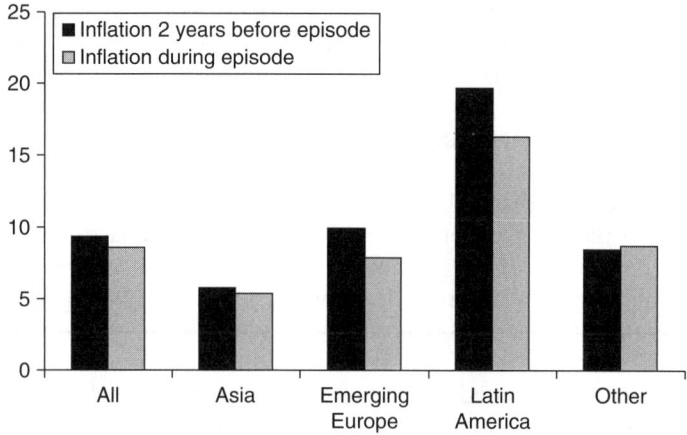

Sources: World Economic Outlook (IMF) and author's calculations.

Figure 4.7 Inflation during episodes (median annual inflation, %)

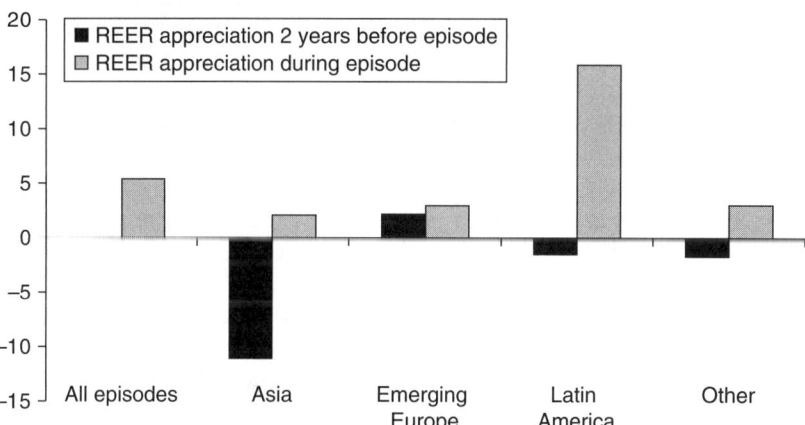

Sources: World Economic Outlook (IMF) and author's calculations.

Figure 4.8 Real effective exchange rate (REER) during episodes (median change, %)

Inflows tended to be accompanied by a slowing of the rate of *nominal* depreciation, so that with high inflation, even if falling, real currency values rose. A second pattern is evident in Asia. Large real depreciations in the two years prior to episodes (many during the late 1980s when *de facto* dollar pegs with a depreciating dollar produced effective depreciations) meant that inflow surges may have resulted in part from relatively low exchange rate valuations.

But the median change in real exchange rates during all episodes looks well within a manageable range: the two years before episodes saw median real effective depreciations of less than 1 per cent, and the episode years saw median cumulative real appreciations of about 5 per cent. And, most countries in the sample were probably experiencing Balassa–Samuelson and other catch-up effects on the equilibrium real exchange rate that would make some real appreciation normal. Of course, averages hide the outliers, some of which experienced serious setbacks in competitiveness.

Inflows feeding rapid growth in bank credit to the private sector have been another serious concern. This issue has received much attention in the ongoing episodes in emerging Europe, where commercial bank borrowing from abroad has been unusually large in both absolute terms and as a share of total inflows. Rapid credit growth was also a prominent characteristic of the episodes in Asia. But in emerging Europe, where inflation has been low, strong expectations of nominal appreciation in the pure floating countries or hard pegs in the currency board countries have made foreign currency borrowing quite attractive. Moreover, on the supply side, banks have actively funded increased lending from parent banks and have been eager to lend in foreign currency so as to avoid taking open foreign exchange positions on their own balance sheets. Two concerns are most pressing in these circumstances.

- First, rapid credit growth appears to be feeding large increases in housing prices in emerging Europe. The question is: how much increase is too much?
- Second, growing household exposures to foreign currency liabilities mean that any large exchange rate change would have severe effects on households' balance sheets and, should defaults increase, banks' balance sheets.

But bank lending and household indebtedness started at extremely low levels following the transition shock of the 1990s in emerging Europe, so even large changes represent small absolute changes in indebtedness. Also, the banks most active in on-lending inflows to households have tended to be banks with the strongest capital positions.[9] And finally, much of the lending is occurring through foreign-owned banks, the parents of which are likely to preserve their reputation by supporting troubled subsidiaries. Nevertheless, large-scale foreign currency lending represents new terrain in the emerging market experience with large inflows.

4.2.4 Current Account Balances – Are Deficits a Problem?

There are two possibilities for using such net capital inflows: (i) effect the transfer (purchase goods for investment or consumption in exchange for the inflow); and/or (ii) take the capital out of the domestic economy (by taxation, saving, sterilization). How should countries choose?

Using foreign capital to raise investment or smooth consumption – both contributing to a widening of the current account deficit during the inflow period – makes sense if the receiving economy is well run, has a financial system capable of intermediating inflows efficiently, and is likely to produce a high return on domestic investment adequate for repayment of debt.[10] Hoarding inflows in foreign exchange reserves makes sense as part of a strategy of absorbing inflows gradually, of responding to inflows that are expected to reverse in a short period of time, or of accumulating a reserve cushion in the face of shocks.

The obvious conclusion is that widening deficits during inflows are not in themselves a problem. Nevertheless, developments vary widely. Episodes in the 1990s and ongoing episodes in emerging markets almost all were/are accompanied by rising current account deficits, whereas recent and ongoing episodes in emerging Asia and Latin America have tended to be accompanied by balanced or even surplus current account positions.

While it is tempting to conclude that countries with balanced or surplus current account positions have a safer strategy than countries with deficits, this would fail to take into account other important considerations related to the growth orientation of the policy environment into which inflows are coming. Large inflows to a strongly performing economy are likely to produce deficits that are the counterpart of growth-oriented saving and investment decisions.

4.3 CONTAINING OVERHEATING – THE ROLE OF MACROECONOMIC POLICIES

This section asks whether and how effectively the trilogy of macroeconomic policies for countering overheating effects from large inflows – sterilized intervention, changes in controls or taxes on capital inflows, and fiscal restraint – have been applied since the early 1990s.

I concentrate on the extent of real effective exchange rate appreciation as an indicator of overheating. It is not a perfect indicator, but others are more flawed. Inflation was generally falling in episodes not because overheating was absent, but because globally, inflation was falling or low. Also several countries' success in disinflation was an important part of the attraction to large inflows. The considerations against using developments in the current account balance were laid out above. And output gaps are based on a critical unknown – potential GDP, or in an emerging market, the viable rate of catch-up to advanced country income levels. This leaves real appreciation as the best standard of comparison across countries. Clearly, it suffers as a measure of overheating from the difficulty of determining the sustainable or equilibrium real appreciation for a catching-up country and from the fact that the more open an economy is, the less this indicator responds to demand pressures.

4.3.1 Sterilized Intervention

Assessing sterilized intervention entails two steps – determining the size of the intervention and determining the amount of sterilization undertaken. Many researchers focus simply on offset coefficients – the parameter relating change in net foreign assets (NFA) to change in net domestic assets (NDA) of central banks or base money. While essential, this does not provide insight on how much sterilized intervention has taken place or how effective it has been in reducing overheating. To do this, more steps are needed. Following IMF (2007b), the following calculations are reproduced below.

- First, an index of exchange market pressure (EMP) – a weighted average of percentage changes in the nominal exchange rate against a major reference currency and of changes in official foreign exchange reserves – is constructed.[11]
- Second, a resistance index is constructed as the change in official reserves as a proportion of the total EMP. The index, which can take on any value, is normalized to fall within the range of 1 (full resistance) to 0 (pure float).
- Third, countries are divided into two groups based on whether they have high or low offset coefficients.[12] Comparing (between the two groups) the effects of intervention on the real exchange rate indicates whether countries that actively sterilize (or for some institutional reasons have higher offset coefficients) have lower real appreciations than those that do not.

The results bear out the general tendency of other research that fails to find a clear effect from sterilized intervention on the real exchange rate (Figure 4.9). Indeed, stronger resistance appears to be associated with larger real appreciations, though the relationship is not statistically significant. Dividing episodes into those of countries with high offset coefficients

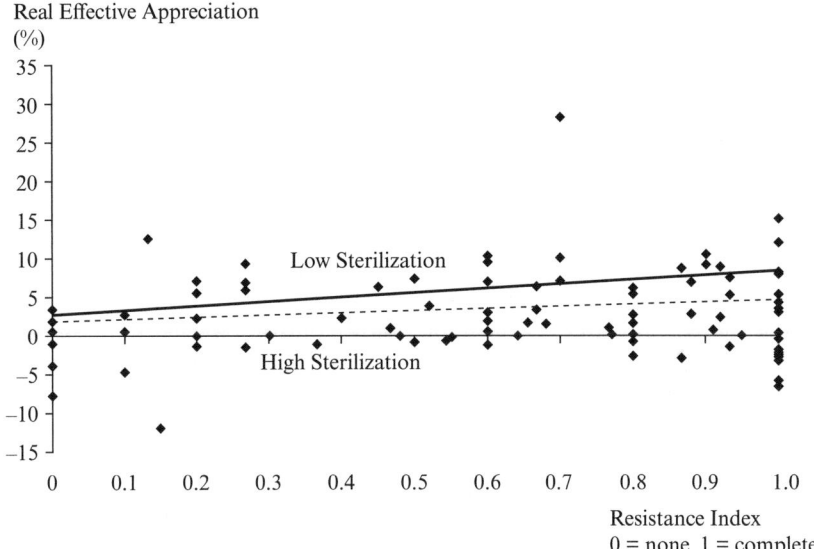

Sources: IMF (2007b) and author's calculations.

Figure 4.9 Real appreciation and intervention (all episodes)

and low offset coefficients produces a slightly less dismal picture of the ineffectiveness of intervention (the regression line shifts slightly clockwise), but it essentially becomes flat rather than downward sloping as interventionists would hope.

This traditional approach to examining the effectiveness of sterilized intervention is not perfectly suited to the emerging markets under review as it was developed for countries with flexible exchange rates. For countries with fixed or highly controlled exchange rates, a commitment to sterilized (or, in the case of currency boards, unsterilized) intervention, in some cases in conjunction with capital controls, is a central pillar in maintaining fixed or crawling nominal exchange rates. The key question for this subset of countries is whether the cost of sterilized intervention in the face of large capital inflows becomes prohibitive as the length of inflow episodes grows.

4.3.2 Capital Controls

The effect of capital controls or taxes on inflows is the subject of much passion, yet continuing ambiguity. Chile's unremunerated reserve requirement (*encaje*) was an explicit effort to prevent real appreciation in the face of rising short-term inflows in the early 1990s and was largely dismantled by 1998.

Evidence on the encaje has been mixed. But the weight of the evidence seems to be that it did not significantly influence the total volume of flows (Chile's episode in this chapter runs from 1988–97) or the change in the real value of the peso.[13] At the same time, evidence on microeconomic costs – disproportionate limitations on small firms' access to borrowing, disintermediation of banking, and reduced market discipline in financial markets and the government – suggests that there is no free lunch.[14] Yet even though much analysis points to limited gains and non-negligible costs, 'Chilean-style' market-based capital inflow controls have been the subject of considerable interest even to the IMF.[15] Indeed, subsequently, when faced with rising inflows several countries (Colombia, Malaysia, Romania, and Thailand to name a few) with relatively liberal capital accounts have introduced reserve requirements on banks borrowing from abroad.

Evidence from across the episodes identified for this chapter does not change this picture. IMF (2007b) reports that relating the size of real appreciation to the average level of controls during episodes gives a small but statistically significant negative relationship. This suggests that tightly controlled systems are more impervious to inflows than more liberalized systems. It also appears that an intensification of restrictions – market-based or outright controls – during a surge episode has no discernable effect on real appreciation. The relationship – though slightly negative (i.e., a tightening of controls on inflows or easing of controls on outflows is associated with lower real appreciation) – is not statistically significant. The relationship between the increase in non-FDI inflows during the episode and the change in capital controls is slightly more negative, though still not statistically significant (Figure 4.10).[16] The implication is that having started down the liberalization path, countries find it difficult to regain control.

The indexes of controls used here do not differentiate types of controls or, therefore, their relative effectiveness. The IMF's index of controls based on the Annual Report on Exchange Arrangements and Exchange Restrictions (AREAER) does not capture many types of prudential changes known as 'market-based' controls. Further progress in understanding possible roles for efficient discretionary use of capital controls and taxes on speculative behavior should be undertaken but will require more finely tuned measures and assessment of micro data.

4.3.3 Fiscal Restraint

Several dimensions of fiscal policy restraint can help in an inflow episode. Most obviously, fiscal restraint works to rein in the growth of domestic

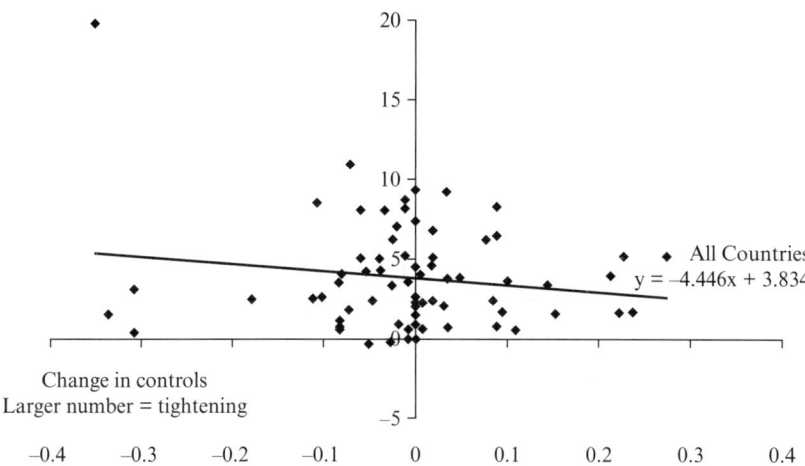

Sources: IMF (2007b) and author's calculations.

Figure 4.10 Non-FDI inflows and changes in capital controls (all episodes)

demand, either directly by slowing the growth of government demand or indirectly by increasing tax receipts from the private sector. Also, by reducing government financing requirements, fiscal restraint also puts downward pressure on interest rates – directly reducing incentives for interest rate-related inflows. And finally, since large inflows almost always occur during periods of domestic cyclical strength, counter-cyclical fiscal policy helps reduce volatility of inflows by ensuring that debt remains at sustainable levels even after surge episodes end. A frequent criticism of this reasoning is that restrictive fiscal policy, by increasing confidence of capital markets in a country's future stability, actually attracts capital. Perhaps it does on a transitory basis, but over time sustainable fiscal policy should help attract the most stable and committed types of capital.

Yet strangely, less empirical work exists on the effects of fiscal policy in episodes of large capital inflows than on other, generally less effective, policy responses. Perhaps because few governments actually respond to large capital inflows with fiscal restraint, it is hard to analyze empirically a policy that is so seldom used. Indeed, Kaminsky et al. (2004) demonstrate that the preponderance of countries receiving large capital inflows have strongly pro-cyclical fiscal (as well as monetary) policy, both during and after the inflow episode.

Following IMF (2007b), the stance of fiscal policy is measured here as

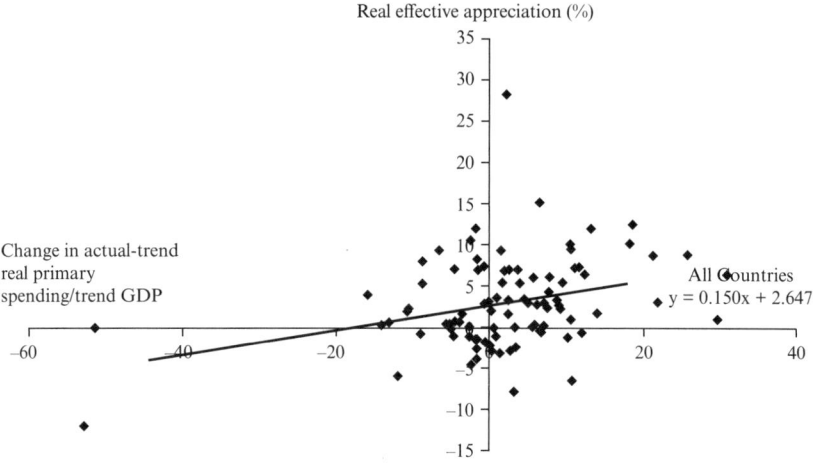

Sources: World Economic Outlook (IMF) and author's calculations.

Figure 4.11 Real appreciations and fiscal expansion during episodes (all episodes)

the change in the gap between actual real primary government expenditure and its trend derived from a Hodrick-Prescott filter: an increase in the gap (or positive number) indicates an expansionary stance. Broader measures based on the cyclically adjusted overall or primary balances would be even better.

Figure 4.11 plots changes in the real effective exchange rates during inflow episodes against changes in the gap between actual and trend spending during the period. Bearing out results in IMF (2007b), relationships are consistently positive (larger cyclical increases in government spending are associated with larger real appreciations). Moreover, changes in the gap between actual and trend spending during episodes are negatively related to post-episode GDP growth – that is, higher pro-cyclical fiscal stimulus during episodes increases the risk of a hard landing (Figure 4.12). Further support for the strength of this relationship is given in IMF (2007b), which reports the results of a regression analysis of the real appreciation and post-episode GDP growth on the main domestic policy variables and key global conditions (interest rates and growth). The evidence points to the conclusion that fiscal policy is the only domestic policy instrument with a significant constraining effect on either real appreciation or augmenting effect on post-episode growth.

Why, then, is the record of using counter-cyclical fiscal policy during

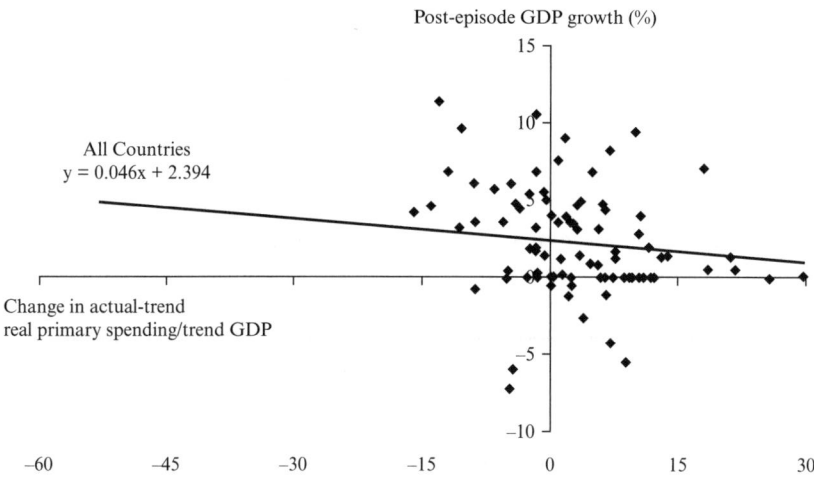

Figure 4.12 Post-episode GDP and expansionary fiscal policy during episodes (all episodes ending in or before 2004)

inflow periods so dismal? There are the obvious political difficulties of undertaking tight fiscal measures when times are good. In addition, it is difficult to distinguish cyclical from underlying changes in the pace of activity. Frequently, countries receiving inflows have experienced changes in the macroeconomic landscape. In these circumstances, the tendency is to overestimate the size of the beneficial effects on potential growth rates. Both of these difficulties are best addressed through governments committing to clear and binding fiscal rules that guide fiscal decisions, most importantly during periods of large change.[17] In this vein, one of the paradoxes in the debate on how to respond to surges in capital inflows is that Chile is so frequently examined for the role of prudential measures in reducing the volatility of inflows. In fact, the more important feature of Chile's experience is its adherence to a fiscal rule that went a long way toward reducing the pro-cyclicality of fiscal policy.

4.4 SUCCESSFUL AND CRISIS ENDINGS: WHAT DIFFERS?

Some countries have done exceptionally well out of their inflow episodes and their experience is at least as instructive as that of countries that have had more difficulty. The goal in this section is to examine episodes from the perspective of these countries, asking how they managed their macro policies and how successful episodes worked out. To do this, I sort the episodes into four groups: those ending in crisis as defined earlier in the chapter; those that had satisfactory endings; those that had strong endings; and those that are ongoing (as of 2007) or ended in 2005 (and therefore cannot be classified by the immediate post-inflow developments). To achieve the greatest symmetry vis-à-vis the definition of crisis, I define successful episodes as those where real GDP growth in the two post-episode years was above trend and the real effective exchange rate depreciated by less than 2 per cent. Episodes where GDP growth in the two post-episodes years was below trend, but was above −2 per cent and where the real effective exchange rate fell less than 20 per cent or even rose are collected in a category called satisfactory.

Basic characteristics of the various groups of episodes were similar, but policy management and results differed significantly. Median duration of the episode, at 2–3 years, was similar, and the groups were not distinguishable in terms of the annual average size of the net inflows during the episodes. Similarities stop there. More successful episodes generally had higher shares of FDI in total inflows, though the most successful group had an (insignificantly) lower share than the group with satisfactory endings. Use of intervention to absorb exchange market pressure was greatest in the group with satisfactory endings and lowest in the group ending in crisis. Similarly, the use of capital controls was lowest in the crisis group, though in all, median capital controls were modest.

The starkest difference in the policy response came in fiscal policy. In contrast to a median fiscal expansion during episodes ending in crisis, the median of episodes ending most successfully saw fiscal contractions. The difference between the average fiscal performance of the group ending in crisis and that of the group ending most successfully is highly statistically significant.

These differences were reflected in less demand pressure during episodes and more robust GDP growth after the episode in the most successful group vis-à-vis others. On the measure of demand pressures, median annual real effective appreciation in the most successful group, at 2.4 per cent, broadly matched many estimates of Balassa–Samuelson and other catch-up effects on the real exchange rate. In contrast, the group of satisfactory episodes saw median appreciation of 5.4 per cent, and the crisis episodes experienced 6.5 per cent annual real appreciation. Post-episode GDP growth and inflation differentials bear out the salutary effects of this restraint.

In this metric, ongoing episodes have both strong and worrying features. Median inflows (relative to GDP) are comparatively large, yet the share of FDI is high. The group of countries with ongoing episodes has low reliance on capital controls and modest inclination to intervention. Of greatest concern is the strikingly lax median fiscal stance according to the measures used here. In turn real appreciations have been sizable. Thus, except for the reassuring developments in FDI, medians point to some cause for concern.

4.5 PROTECTIVE MEASURES

The best way to prepare for post-episode disruptions is to ensure that policies support robust long-term growth. Overheating, asset bubbles, and sharp changes in investor sentiment happen, so mechanisms and cushions to help absorb them are good policy.

In this vein, first thoughts turn to reserve accumulation. The sharp increase in reserve holdings since 2000, dominated by the largest emerging market countries, has taken the reserves relative to almost any standard – imports of goods and services, GDP, foreign currency short-term debt by remaining maturity, or M2 – to exceptionally high levels.[18] But this surge in reserves has been highly concentrated in a few countries. Excluding Brazil, the People's Republic of China, India, and Russia, increases in reserves for regional groupings have on average been more moderate.

The key question is, how much safer are countries with higher reserves, and, if they are safer, at what price does the safety come? While large reserve accumulation is often seen simply as the result of intervention to stem currency appreciation, Obstfeld et al. (2007) argue that it rather fits a rational response of central banks to their lender of last resort function when increases in financial openness and fragility create the potential for internal and external drains on the banking system. A practical question, however, is whether the optimal response to severe disruptions would best be dealt with by using extremely large foreign reserves. Could the existence of such large reserves even create some moral hazard if agents perceive a ready source of funds for bail-outs in the event of crisis? In light of such doubts, questions such as those raised by Rodrik (2006) about the social costs of large reserve holdings take on particular importance.

Reserve sharing arrangements among countries are an obvious way to deal with the preference for having significant levels of reserves when reserve holding is costly. At one end of the spectrum of such arrangements is the IMF; at the other end is the euro area. The euro area effectively combines a reserve-sharing arrangement with a solution to the difficulties of coordination of exchange rate moves within a region of export competitors. The gains for the new members of the European Union (EU) from prospective euro adoption appear to be substantial.[19] Indeed, it appears that simply the prospect of membership within the next seven to eight years has bolstered market confidence in the region's currencies and reduced risk premia on sovereign foreign currency debt.[20] Correspondingly, prospective euro adoption may well be one of the reasons why the new members of the EU, excluding the four currency board/hard peg countries, are among the lowest reserve holders of emerging market countries. Key to the success of any reserve sharing arrangement is, first, political compatibility among participants and, second, clear ground rules on the limits to both fiscal and monetary policy choices.

A promising direction in recent research is exploring the link between domestic financial market structure and institutions and capital inflows, including volatility. A priori, it stands to reason that the more open, deep, transparent, and well regulated a financial system is, the more attractive it should be to foreign capital, though there is little empirical work to establish this contention firmly.[21] Whether these characteristics also contribute to lowering volatility by attracting less 'hot' money and by reducing the skittishness of investors is even less researched, though IMF (2007c) provides a first pass at an answer.

The early results suggest that a range of structural and institutional characteristics of domestic financial markets influence the size and volatility of inflows. Using panel data covering 15 developed and 41 emerging market countries during 1977–2006, IMF (2007c) finds a statistically significant positive relationship between the size of net capital inflows and equity market turnover, financial openness, and corporate governance quality. The study finds that more financial openness is associated with lower volatility of inflows. Equity market turnover, equity market capitalization, and the quality of accounting standards also have negative relationships with volatility, though they are not statistically significant. A more heuristic examination of the bivariate relationship between a number of dimensions of governance (regulatory quality, government effectiveness, rule of law, control of corruption, political stability, and voice and accountability) also reveals systematically negative relationships. The strength of these conclusions needs further examination, but the early message is that countries might be able to significantly reduce the volatility of inflows by targeted development of their financial markets.

Another dimension of financial infrastructure crucial for inflow recipients is supervision and prudential control of banks to protect the domestic banking system from the hazards of rapid credit growth during inflow episodes. Generally, meeting this objective does not open new questions on supervisory practices, so much as it reinforces the need for developing best-practice, independent bank supervision. However, two tricky issues have become quite important, particularly in emerging Europe: first, whether and how to regulate foreign currency lending, particularly to households, which are unlikely to be hedged; and second, whether and how to limit rapid increases in mortgage lending (substantially funded by bank borrowing from abroad) that in some countries risks feeding housing market bubbles. Clear answers exist for neither of these questions. On the first, prohibiting foreign currency (mortgage) lending would be a rather blunt instrument for the basic objective of ensuring that banks' risk management adequately accounts for risk from foreign currency lending. As with many other prudential measures to discourage inflows to banks or credit growth of banks, such instruments run high risks of promoting disintermediation from the domestic banking sector. On the second, more active consideration needs to be given to fiscal instruments of control. For example, in economies where housing prices are rising rapidly enough to raise serious concerns about a bubble, real estate transaction taxes can play a useful role in slowing trades and price increases.

4.6 CONCLUSION

The experience since the early 1990s of emerging market countries with surges in capital inflows confirms some common perceptions but casts doubts on others. Specifically, only a modest portion of the episodes have ended in crisis and overheating pressures have not in general been severe. Volatile non-FDI inflows have been an important determinant behind the shape of surges; but sizable and more stable increases in FDI have also contributed to episodes of large inflows. Policy responses to large inflows are not futile. But whereas much attention is focused on whether sterilized intervention or capital controls are effective, insufficient attention is focused on fiscal policy which is most likely to have a strong and constructive effect. Indeed, fiscal policies have tended to be pro-cyclical, aggravating an already pro-cyclical pattern of capital inflows.

That said, the risk of crisis as financial integration increases will never disappear, and countries must pursue protection from risks of volatility and sudden stops. In this vein, it is far from clear that recent large accumulations of official reserves in some countries are a cost effective defense against serious crises. But strengthening financial sector supervision, and considering fiscal disincentives to excessive asset price increases that could turn into bubbles, makes sense.

This review has raised a number of issues on which further research could push the frontier on the political economy of dealing with large capital inflows. Four are particularly worthy of mention here.

- The impact of fiscal policy responses to surges in capital inflows has not received enough attention in the literature. Three dimensions cry out for further study. First, the evidence to date that fiscal policy in the face of surges in inflows tends to be pro-cyclical is alarming and needs to be subjected to continuing research scrutiny. Second, what would be the most effective types of fiscal policy responses in terms of political feasibility, shortest implementation lags, and effectiveness in countering adverse effects of inflows? What role should fiscal rules play in preparing for inflow episodes? Third, are there synergies between fiscal prudential measures (such as raising transfer taxes on real estate transactions) and fiscal measures for macroeconomic objectives?
- The possibility of co-movements and interdependencies among various categories of capital inflows and outflows should be examined. Most studies have very aggregated classifications of types of flows. This precludes addressing many important questions that should affect the level of concern about the stability of inflows, and characterizing the differences between inflows to countries with more and less open financial sectors.
- Prudential or market-based measures to limit inflows (particularly of 'hot' money) are receiving increasing attention from researchers, but the measurement of such actions is at best imprecise. More work is needed to establish a metric that would allow research on prudential measures outside the confines of case study approaches.
- A key issue both for emerging markets and for lower income countries that are likely to be the next wave of recipients of large inflows is how financial sector development affects the size and volatility of inflows. Is the finding in IMF (2007c) that greater financial sector openness reduces volatility robust to other techniques and data sets? What dimensions of institutional development would have the largest impact on the volatility of inflows?

NOTES

1. See, for example Schadler et al. (1993), Montiel (1999), Reinhart and Reinhart (1998), and IMF (2007b).
2. Net private inflows correspond to the definition in the International Monetary Fund's (IMF) Balance of Payments database, comprising net foreign direct investment, private portfolio flows, and other private flows. Flows are considered 'private' regardless of the source if the recipient is in the private sector.
3. The emerging market countries considered in this paper comprise 43 countries that (i) are included in the World Economic Outlook classification of other emerging market and developing countries or newly industrialized Asian countries and (ii) experienced at

least one episode of unusually large net private capital inflows during 1987–2006 (as per the definition given in this chapter).
4. This distinction is somewhat skewed by the absence of data for many emerging European countries in the first half of the 1990s. But insofar as most were undergoing a highly disruptive exit from central planning during this period, it is unlikely, especially in the early years, that net private inflows were large.
5. One interesting question for countries experiencing large gross inflows, but not large net inflows is whether the inflows are actually the result of residents investing domestically, but channeling funds through foreign investment vehicles. This could occur for reasons related to tax evasion, restrictions on residents' investment or better legal protection from vehicles for foreign investment into the country.
6. IMF (2007d) examines the surge in gross inflows to emerging Asia.
7. Kaminsky et al. (1998) has a taxonomy of definitions of crisis in many empirical studies.
8. See IMF (2007b).
9. See Tamirisa and Igan (2006).
10. Schadler et al. (2006) have an empirical analysis of the interaction of growth and current account positions in Central and Eastern Europe.
11. This approach reflects the work in IMF (2007b). In fact, using the change in the nominal exchange rate as one of the two indicators of exchange market pressure is flawed for the episodes under consideration, where many disinflating countries had depreciating currencies during their episodes even though they were facing (and attempting to limit) exchange market pressures that slowed the pace of depreciation.
12. The offset coefficient is the estimated β in the equation $\Delta NDA = \alpha + \beta \Delta NFA + \mu$ where NDA is net domestic assets and NFA is net foreign assets, both of the central bank.
13. See Cowan and De Gregorio (2005).
14. Forbes (2005) reviews the micro evidence.
15. See Fischer (2001).
16. The measure of capital controls is taken from IMF (2007b). It is based on a summary of the IMF's *Annual Report on Exchange Arrangements and Exchange Restrictions* (AREAER) representing indices on nine dimensions of controls on inward and outward capital flows – on capital and money market instruments, on FDI, and on personal capital movements.
17. See Schadler (2005) for a review of experiences with fiscal rules and fiscal responsibility laws.
18. See Greenspan (1999).
19. See Schadler et al., (2004) for an analysis of costs and benefits of euro adoption for emerging Europe.
20. See Luengnaruemitchai and Schadler (2007) for an empirical model investigating the compression of spreads in the new members of the EU.
21. This is in contrast to the question of whether financial openness and development have benefits for output and investment growth, on which there is a rather substantial body of work, though the results are not particularly clear. See Edison et al. (2004) for a review.

REFERENCES

Cowan, K. and J. De Gregorio (2005), 'International borrowing, capital controls and the exchange rate: lessons from Chile', NBER Working Paper 11382, Cambridge, MA.
Edison, H., M. Klein, L. Ricci and T. Slok (2004), 'Capital account liberalization and economic performance: survey and synthesis', *IMF Staff Papers*, **51**(2), 220–56.

Fischer, S. (2001), 'Exchange rate regimes: is the bipolar view correct?', Distinguished Lecture in Economics and Government, delivered at the Meetings of the American Economic Association in New Orleans, 6 January.
Forbes, K. (2005), 'The microeconomic evidence on capital controls: no free lunch', NBER Working Paper 11372, Cambridge, MA.
Greenspan, A. (1999), 'Currency reserves and debt', Remarks before the World Bank Conference on Recent Trends in Reserves Management, Washington, DC, 29 April, available at: http://www.federalreserve.gov/boardDocs/speeches/1999/19990429.htm.
IMF (2007a), 'Reaping the benefits of financial globalization', IMF Research Department Discussion Paper, available at: http://www.imf.org/external/np/res/docs/2007/067.htm.
IMF (2007b), 'Managing large capital inflows', in *World Economic Outlook*, Washington, DC: International Monetary Fund.
IMF (2007c), 'The quality of domestic financial markets and capital inflows', in *Global Financial Stability Report*, Washington, DC.
IMF (2007d), 'The evolving nature of capital flows in emerging Asia', in *World Economic and Financial Surveys*, Regional Economic Outlook, Asia and Pacific, April.
Kaminsky, G., S. Lizondo and C. Reinhart (1998), 'Leading indicators of currency crisis', IMF Staff Papers, March, Washington, DC.
Kaminsky, G., C. Reinhart and C. Vegh (2004), 'When it rains, it pours: procyclical capital flows and macroeconomic policies', in M. Gertler and K. Rogoff (eds), *NBER Macroeconomics Annual 2004*, Cambridge, MA: MIT Press, pp. 11–53.
Luengnaruemitchai, P. and S. Schadler (2007), 'Do economists' and financial markets' perspectives on the new members of the EU differ?', IMF Working Paper 07/65, Washington, DC: IMF.
Montiel, P. (1999), 'Policy responses to volatile capital flows', unpublished, Washington, DC: World Bank.
Obstfeld, M., J. Shambaugh and A. Taylor (2007), 'Financial stability, the trilemma, and international reserves', NBER Working Paper, Cambridge, MA.
Reinhart, C. and V. Reinhart (1998), 'Some lessons for policymakers who deal with the mixed blessing of capital inflows', in M. Kahler (ed.), *Capital Flows and Financial Crises*, New York: Cornell University Press, pp. 93–127.
Rodrik, D. (2006), 'The social cost of foreign exchange reserves', *International Economic Journal*, **20** (September), 253–66.
Schadler, S. (2005), 'Enhancing the credibility of fiscal policy – the role of fiscal responsibility laws and fiscal councils', remarks at the Belgian IMF/World Bank Constituency meeting, Istanbul, June, available at: http://www.susanschadler.com.
Schadler, S., A. Bennett, M. Carkovic and R. Kahn (1993), 'Recent experiences with surges in capital inflows', Occasional Paper 108, Washington, DC: IMF.
Schadler, S., P. Drummond, Z. Murgosova and R. van Elkan (2004), 'The next step in European integration: euro adoption in the new Member States', Occasional Paper, Washington, DC: IMF.
Schadler, S., A. Mody, A. Abiad and D. Leigh (2006), 'Growth in Central and Eastern Europe', Occasional Paper, Washington, DC: IMF.
Tamirisa, N. and D. Igan (2006), 'Credit growth and bank soundness in the new member states', IMF Country Report No. 06/414, Washington, DC: IMF.

5. Managing recent hot money inflows in Asia
Robert N. McCauley[1]

5.1 INTRODUCTION

Capital inflows into Asia were more puzzling than problematic in the years leading up to the peak of the dollar in early 2002. Into 2002, private capital flows remained mixed, with equity inflows offset to some extent by private firms' repayment of debts to international banks. These private outflows vis-à-vis banks were joined by official outflows in the form of a build-up of foreign exchange reserves. While the inflows took the form of a purchase of risky assets, the outflows amounted to a purchase of safe assets, especially the investment of official reserves in prime securities (McCauley, 2003). Rather than an international exchange of assets resulting in a symmetric sharing of risks, Asia was using the international capital markets to systematically lay off equity risk. Coming on top of generally substantial current account surpluses, Asian economies were battening down the hatches, positioning their international accounts to weather storms.

The flows have shifted since 2002 and, at writing in early 2008, pose an increasing challenge to policymakers. The next section elaborates the differences in the patterns of capital flows. The following sections then take up portfolio equity flows, bond market flows, bank flows, and carry trades. The final section considers policy responses.

5.2 DIFFERENCES IN THE PATTERNS OF CAPITAL FLOWS SINCE 2002

Prospects for the strong performance of Asian economies have led to an acceleration of equity inflows. At the same time, prospects for appreciation, or at least stability, of Asian currencies have led to debt inflows, including flows into local currency bond markets, bank flows, and carry trades.

5.2.1 Accelerating Portfolio Flows

Portfolio inflows into the region have accelerated and have become more volatile. When global markets have experienced sharp downturns and the price of equity options has soared, Asian markets have seen massive withdrawal of foreign capital. The usual view is that developments in peripheral markets reflect developments in major markets and evidence from daily cross-border flows in six Asian economies bears out this view. The image is often used of liquidity spilling over from major markets to smaller ones. But the systematic withdrawal of funds from Asia requires a new image: portfolios in major markets suck up liquidity from Asian markets under stressed conditions.

5.2.2 Indirect Foreign Investment in Local Currency Bonds

Several years ago, local currency bond markets in the region were described as generally parochial affairs (Jiang and McCauley, 2004), but they have become globalized since then. Except in Indonesia, this globalization has not so much taken the form of direct non-resident purchases. Rather, leveraged accounts have become virtual investors through derivatives, and foreign banks within the markets have become important holders, whether to hedge the derivative positions offered to leveraged investors or to hedge forward sales of dollars by exporters.

5.2.3 Return of Bank Inflows

The most evident turnaround in capital flows vis-à-vis Asia since the dollar's peak in early 2002 has been the return of bank inflows. Given the history of the Asian financial crisis, the risk is that these flows are taken as a matter of reflex as hot money. That is, one is tempted to consider bank flows as having responded to interest-rate differentials favoring domestic currencies in the context of 'excessive' or artificial stability of local currencies against the US dollar: in short, currency mismatches (Goldstein and Turner, 2004). But to a considerable extent, the return of bank flows reflects the experience of, or prospects of local currencies gaining against the US dollar, which is different from the pre-crisis motivation of borrowing dollars hoping for exchange rate stability. Where currencies have appreciated considerably, as in the Republic of Korea (hereafter Korea), exporters have sought to hedge future US dollar receipts by selling them against domestic currencies. This has drawn in short-term dollar funding, particularly into foreign bank branches, which is swapped for local currency. Thus the Asian banking systems tend to hold on their books a short-US dollar, long-domestic currency position that squares a forward commitment to buy dollars against local currency.

5.2.4 Carry Trades

Carry trades have certainly gained in importance in the region since 2002, although it is generally not possible to measure the stock of outstanding carry trades with any precision. Certainly, currencies in the region have tended to become more internationalized since 2004, with a greater share of trading taking place offshore, often in non-deliverable form that is less constrained by domestic regulations (Ma et al., 2004; McCauley, 2006b, 2010). A new element is the tendency of market participants to put on carry trade with emerging currencies on both sides of the trade.

5.3 PORTFOLIO EQUITY FLOWS, EQUITY PRICES, AND EXCHANGE RATES

The capital inflows into Asia through purchases of equities have become larger and more volatile over the years. Foreign investors have liquidated holdings of Asian equities in episodes of global volatility in ever larger amounts over the years, as shown in Figure 5.1. The bouts of disinvestment that have occurred since the summer of 2007 have been unprecedented. In the face of losses on mortgage securities, liquidity blockages in major money markets and prospects for decelerating growth, foreign investors liquidated over $12 billion in August and November 2007 in six Asian markets with daily transaction reporting. These liquidations have reached such levels notwithstanding the fact that global volatility (as measured by the VIX index of option prices on the Standard and Poor's index of US equities) has not climbed to the levels reached earlier in the decade or at the time of the Long-Term Capital Management and Russian defaults.

Even before this most recent episode, these flows have drawn much market commentary and such interest led a number of stock exchanges to release daily data on non-resident flows. This has resulted in a number of careful studies that have shed much light on the relationship between capital flows and equity prices. Two of these are reviewed below. Before turning to this analytic work, let us consider the source by geography and type of investor of the flows vis-à-vis Asian equity markets.

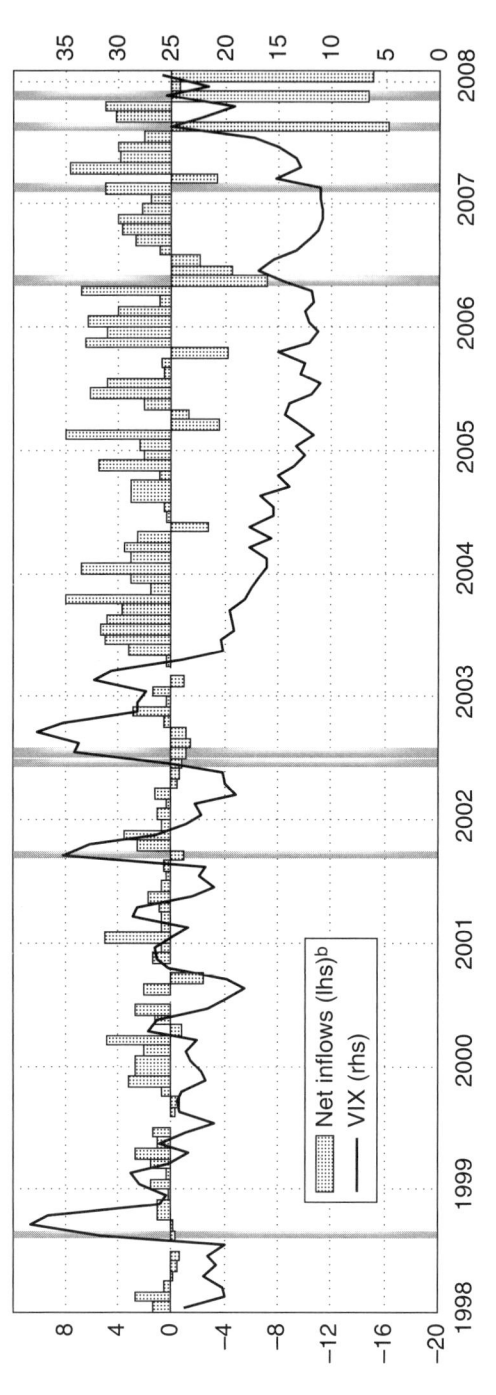

Notes:

[a] Shaded areas refer to seven episodes of rising volatility since 1998: (1) the Russian default (Aug 1998); (2) September 11 (Sep 2001); (3) June–July 2002; (4) the May 2006 sell-off; (5) the February 2007 sell-off; (6) the Bear Sterns hedge fund woes in August 2007; and (7) the subprime-related sell-off in November 2007. Net foreign purchases of equities in India (data start in 1999); Indonesia; Korea; the Philippines; Taipei,China; and Thailand.
[b] In billions of US dollars.

Sources: Bloomberg; CEIC; Korean Stock Exchange; Philippines Stock Exchange; BIS calculations.

Figure 5.1 Global volatility and Asian net equity inflows[a]

Table 5.1 Foreign equity holdings in East Asia, end-2007 ($ billion)

Host	United States	Europe	Japan	East Asia including Japan	Total	East Asian %
PRC	96	59	15	189	389	48.4
Hong Kong, China	120	87	18	64	329	19.4
Indonesia	15	10	1	4	39	10.2
Japan	529	341	–	19	1046	1.8
Korea, Republic of	129	70	6	16	260	6.3
Malaysia	18	13	1	12	54	22.3
Philippines	10	4	–	1	19	8.0
Singapore	56	37	6	14	128	11.2
Taipei,China	81	41	3	11	154	7.0
Thailand	16	14	1	6	47	13.6
Total	1069	675	51	337	2464	13.7
Total ex JP as host	540	334	51	318	1418	22.4
% of total East Asia ex JP	38.0	23.5	3.6	22.4	100.0	

Note: Europe comprises Austria, Belgium, Denmark, Finland, France, Germany, Greece, Iceland, Ireland, Italy, Netherlands, Norway, Portugal, Spain, Sweden, Switzerland, and the United Kingdom. East Asia comprises the named economies.

Source: IMF Coordinated Portfolio Investment Survey.

5.3.1 Source of Inflows into Asian Equity Markets

As for the source of the capital inflows, the national composition points to the importance of the United States and Europe. Flows within Asia, notably from Hong Kong, China, and from Japan and Korea, into the mainland of the People's Republic of China (PRC) have become more important (Table 5.1).

As for the importance of speculative accounts versus real money, the IMF (2007a) has offered evidence that the former has more variable flows. In particular, cumulated inflows captured by Bank of New York, a major depository serving institutional investors like pension funds and mutual funds, in the four years before May–June 2006 proved much stickier in that episode than cumulated overall flows as reported by the stock exchanges. This suggests that hedge funds and proprietary trading desks account for more than their share of the volatility of flows in such episodes. In particular, it appears that such hot money investors disproportionately respond to higher levels of global volatility by liquidating positions in Asian equities.

5.3.2 Earlier Study of the Relationship between Equity Flows and Prices

Richards (2005) analyzed daily non-resident flows in six Asian equity markets and found that the flows both reflected price developments in major markets and affected price developments in the target markets. For Korean, Taiwanese and Thai equities, a buoyant Standard and Poor's led to net purchase of equities by non-residents. And whatever drove the inflows into the six markets studied, he found that they affected the pricing in the target market. Inflows help to boost these asset prices, while outflows tend to lower them.

5.3.3 Chai-anant and Ho and the Exchange Rate Connection

The missing element in this earlier study using Asian daily data was the exchange rate. Market participants were interested to know the tendency of foreign purchases and sales of local equities not only in order to anticipate the trend of the local equity market, but also to assess how such flows could affect the exchange rate. Of course, in view of the style of intervention that leans against short-term volatility – particularly in India, the Philippines, and Taipei,China – one might expect the measured impact of portfolio equity flows on currency values to be weaker (in technical terms, one might expect the effect of large flows to be censored). Chai-anant and Ho (2008) confirm findings of earlier studies that non-residents generally buy into rising regional markets and sell into falling ones. They also find that inflows push up, and outflows push down, currencies (Gyntelberg et al., 2009). Their further finding that net equity flows show strong co-movement across six Asian equity markets (which was implied by Richards, 2005) suggests that equity capital flows may subject Asian economies to common shocks.

5.3.4 Asian Equities as an Option for, and Source of Liquidity to, Global Players?

If foreign investors chase returns in regional equity markets, and affect equity and currency values in the process, some further thinking is required on the procyclical nature of the international risk sharing implied by the substantial global holdings of Asian equities. In a global downturn, global investors do not accept their share of the poor harvest in textbook fashion, but instead head for the exit. This means that the equity risk that

Asia lays off on the rest of the world returns to Asian portfolios under stressed market conditions.

Parallel to questions about the international allocation of Asian equity risk in normal and declining markets are questions about the provision of liquidity by Asia to global portfolios. In stressed markets, when equity markets are falling and credit spreads widening, Asian investors accommodate the liquidity demand of global portfolio managers by repurchasing their own equities. In effect, local investors as a group switch out of risk-free domestic paper into risky equities at times of heightened volatility. To the extent that Asian central banks purchase their own currencies against sales of low-risk US Treasury and agency debt (as they did in August 2007), they enable global investors to switch from risky Asian equities to low-risk paper in the major currencies. It is a strange world in which countries of moderate income provide liquidity to investors in rich countries during times of financial strains.

5.4 NON-RESIDENT INVESTMENT IN LOCAL CURRENCY FIXED INCOME MARKETS

Through the turn in the US dollar cycle in early 2002, it was fair to say that local currency bond markets in East Asia remained generally insular (Jiang and McCauley, 2004). Three developments in the intervening years have served one way or another to open up local currency bond markets. The first was the rise in inflation in Indonesia in 2005, which led to a tightening of policy rates. Short-term rupiah yields rose, leading to inflows by investors willing to bet against a corresponding depreciation of the rupiah. In addition, high bond yields drew in investors seeking both the immediate yield pick-up and an eventual capital gain as subsiding inflation permitted policy rates to return to single-digit levels. The second development took place less visibly in the derivative markets, where non-resident investors gained exposure to fixed income markets in a virtual manner. The third development was the growth of foreign banks in the domestic markets. Under certain conditions, they have emerged as major holders of local-currency government bonds to accommodate the hedging of dollar receipts by exporters. It is not so much that foreign investors have sought out these markets because the impediments, be they withholding taxes or simply illiquidity, have been reduced (Takeuchi, 2006). Rather, foreign investors and banks have become active in these markets despite these impediments, using derivative markets or a local presence to get around the impediments on cross-border flows.

The following sections necessarily rely on different kinds of data to capture the behavior of foreign investors in the region's local currency bond markets. For Indonesia, data on holdings of short-term *Sertifikat Bank Indonesia* (SBI) and government bonds demonstrate how non-resident investors respond to global volatility. For non-resident investment in the rest of the markets, only indirect evidence of virtual investment can be assembled. In particular, the growth of interest-rate swaps and cross-currency swaps suggest the potential for non-resident activity, despite low measured holdings of government bonds.

5.4.1 Non-resident Investment in the Indonesian Fixed Income Market

Foreign investors were drawn to substantial investment in Indonesian bonds only after the mini-crisis of 2005. That year, higher oil prices led to a deterioration of the government budget deficit, given subsidies. In addition, market participants perceived a slow monetary policy response to the inflationary challenge of higher energy prices. Eventually, a vigorous monetary tightening that saw the policy rate rise from less than 8 per cent to 12.75 per cent stabilized the exchange rate. Bonds offering similar yields amid expectations of a return to single-digit inflation and policy rates drew foreign investment despite challenging liquidity and a withholding tax.[2] By end-2005, foreign investors held 8 per cent of Indonesian bonds and 12 per cent of SBIs.

Foreign investors have not monotonically increased their holdings of Indonesian bonds and paper, as one might expect if the globalization of portfolios were the only force at work. Instead, one observes them selling into a declining market at times of global financial market strains. Four episodes have been revealing: mid-2005, May–June 2006, February–March 2007 and July–August 2007.

As noted, in the middle of 2005, the sell-off in the Indonesian market was idiosyncratic, owing to concerns about Indonesian policies. Foreign investors reduced their holdings gradually in the first half. Holdings of SBIs started to recover before the exchange rate bottomed in August 2005 at 12 000 rupiah/dollar, and non-resident bond holdings resumed their expansion in the following month.

The following three episodes were global in origin. They featured sell-offs in equity markets and rises in equity and exchange rate volatility. Investment in Indonesian fixed income instruments responded as one might expect speculative investors to behave in the face of losses elsewhere in their portfolios and/or an increase in risk as measured by such popular metrics as value-at-risk. In May and June 2006, foreign investors reduced their exposure to Indonesian fixed income instruments in a much sharper and more concentrated manner than they had in mid-2005, when Indonesian policies were at issue. The subsequent disturbance of February–March 2007 had a smaller effect in Indonesia (as elsewhere). The decline of holdings in June–August 2007 reflected losses in US mortgage lending, leading to a disabling of leveraged financing more generally.

While different in origins, the latter three episodes send a consistent message. Foreign investment links the Indonesian fixed income market and the rupiah's exchange rate to global equity and credit developments. As with equities above, fixed income inflows respond to global developments and push local market bond prices up. Further, there appears to be an element of stop-loss trading: downward movement of the Indonesian bond market and the rupiah may induce selling, putting further pressure on both.

What is strikingly consistent across all the episodes is that the foreign investment in SBIs is more responsive to uncertainties (whether in Indonesia or globally) than that in government bonds. One is tempted to associate SBI investment with more leveraged hot money investors and bond investment with more sticky 'real money' investors. There may be something to this supposition. But it must also be recalled that the liquidity and thus the overall cost of a cycle of selling and buying differs across money and bond markets. Thus leveraged or real money accounts alike that hold both face a cost incentive to reduce exposure by selling SBIs rather than government bonds.[3]

The evidence of greater heat in the flow into SBIs has led to a debate in Indonesia whether inflows into these securities should be discouraged. The discussion of policy below returns to this debate.

5.4.2 Virtual Bond Investment through Derivatives

While other bond markets in Asia have received little in the way of cash investment from non-residents, the development of fixed-income derivative markets has allowed considerable indirect participation by non-residents in the region's bond markets.[4] A foreign investor who foresees a decline in long-term interest rates in a given market may find it inconvenient, from the standpoint of taxation or liquidity, to buy a local-currency government bond. Much the same position can be taken in the cross-currency swap market: the investor can contract to receive a stream of fixed-rate payments in the local currency against floating-rate payments in US dollars. Should monetary policy be unexpectedly eased and were long-term interest rates to fall (or were long-term rates to fall for any other reason), the position could be closed out at a profit. If the currency exposure were not desired, the investor could use the interest-rate swap market to contract to receive fixed-rate local currency payments

Table 5.2 Turnover of interest-rate swaps and currency swaps in Asia-Pacific currencies (daily averages, $ million)

	Interest rate swaps		Currency swaps	
	April 2004	April 2007	April 2004	April 2007
Australian Dollar	6 609	14 060	1 573	1 824
Chinese Renminbi	n.a.	151	4	133
HK Dollar	3 819	8 778	293	420
Indian Rupee	396	3 329	97	411
Indonesian Rupiah	14	17	24	148
Japanese Yen	35 433	109 682	3 354	3 495
Korean Won	301	3 942	342	1 303
Malaysian Ringgit	26	166	11	37
New Zealand Dollar	1 072	5 550	80	474
Philippine Peso	1	3	4	13
Singapore Dollar	1 588	2 291	54	154
New Taiwan Dollar	355	891	102	99
Thai Baht	96	321	246	59

Source: BIS, Triennial Central Bank Survey, 2005, 2007.

against floating-rate local currency payments. Such positioning would be currency-neutral, but would put downward pressure on domestic long-term interest rates all the same.

Data from the 2007 Triennial Central Bank survey point to generally strong growth of the derivative markets that permit non-resident investors access to Asian markets (Table 5.2). A tripling of daily volumes in currency swap markets was not uncommon. Only in the New Taiwan dollar and Thai baht was a decline in currency swaps observed. Even then, interest-rate swaps in the baht expanded briskly, in line with the trend elsewhere.

The participants in the region's virtual bond markets vary across markets and over time. For instance, at the time of the Thai coup d'état of September 2006, multinationals in Thailand were said to have sold forward their Thai baht profits against US dollars, using the cross-currency swap market. On the other side of the market were hedge funds that were betting that the Bank of Thailand would ease, perhaps before the Federal Reserve, in the face of the appreciating currency and lagging government investment spending.

A more recent example is from the Korean bond market (Carrillo-Rodriguez and Hohensee, 2007) where shipbuilders were said to be hedging US dollar revenues to be earned on deliveries of ships scheduled for two or three years hence (Bank of Korea and FSS, 2008). They were in effect borrowing in US dollars and investing the proceeds in won bonds. Foreign banks in Korea accommodated the shipbuilders' forward sales of dollars by borrowing dollars from affiliates outside of Korea, swapping the proceeds for won and investing the won in the Korean bond market. This is taken up in the next section.

5.4.3 Bond Investment by Foreign Banks

Korea serves as a prime example of a government bond market that has become globalized thanks to the participation of foreign banks. Holdings of Korean bonds by non-residents remain very low, at less than 2 per cent, in contrast to the one-third share that non-residents hold of Korean equities.

It can thus be said that the Korean bond market is not internationalized. At the same time, however, foreign banks in Korea have become significant holders of Korean government paper. Kim and Song (2010) report that foreign investors and foreign bank branches in Korea together hold a quarter of government bonds and monetary stabilization bonds outstanding, totaling over 60 trillion won by end-2007.

In summary, in various ways, the bond markets in East Asia are falling under the influence of global fixed income developments. In Indonesia, the market has hosted significant direct holdings by non-residents (as well as further investment through structures sold offshore by foreign banks with a local presence). In places like Thailand and India, foreign investors have gained access to the local bond market through derivatives to an extent that eludes measurement. And in Korea, foreign bank branches have become important holders of government bonds as they have accommodated the long-term forward sales of Korean exporters.

5.5 RETURN OF BANK INFLOWS

Since the peaking of the dollar in early 2002, the claims of Bank for International Settlements (BIS) area banks on the major Asian economies have bottomed. The rise has been observed across the different categories of foreign claims: cross-border interbank claims, other international claims, and net local claims in local currency (the refinance gap).

In the early years of this decade, one could consider the growth of local claims as a development apart from the evolution of cross-border loans.[5] Indeed, after the crisis, Asian firms and banks repaid cross-border debts while increasing their borrowing in local currency from foreign banks.

And these in turn mobilized local funding to finance the bulk of their local currency assets.

This has changed. As Figure 5.2 shows, the refinancing gap, or the difference between foreign banks' in-country domestic currency assets and liabilities, has grown. In short, at the margin, foreign banks have come to depend heavily on funds borrowed from their affiliates abroad and swapped for local currency. By September 2007, a third of foreign banks' local assets were funded cross-border in these major Asian economies.

5.6 CARRY TRADES

Carry trades refer to positions taken across currencies that seek to profit from interest rate differentials in excess of currency movements over the holding period. Such trades can be defined narrowly to include only speculative positions, or more broadly to include in some sense overweighted positions in high-coupon currencies in 'real money' portfolios.

5.6.1 Measuring Carry Trades[6]

The scale of carry trades eludes measurement. Data on the positioning of different classes of traders in the Chicago currency futures markets are perhaps the most often referenced data. Yet futures trading is a small corner of the overall market for foreign exchange (BIS, 2007). Moreover, given the selection process for participants in this market, which substitutes exposure to the exchange as a whole for individual counterparty exposure, there is no reason to believe that positions taken in futures can be assumed to be representative of broader positioning.

All that said, the Chicago futures data indicate that carry trades were unwound in August 2007. Short positions in the yen and the Swiss franc were cut back sharply, and long positions in sterling and the New Zealand dollar were likewise much reduced.

Within Asia, the positioning by Japanese individuals in forward trades has similarly received much attention. They abandoned long positions in high-yielding Antipodean currencies in August 2007. The decline in margined holdings of New Zealand dollars was very sharp as the currency plunged against the yen (Figure 5.3). This is consistent with a market practice of closing out losing positions automatically rather than issuing margin calls. However, these positions add up to only several hundred billion yen.

Broader efforts to use flows of fund or international banking data from McCauley and von Kleist (1998) to Galati et al. (2007) or Hattori and

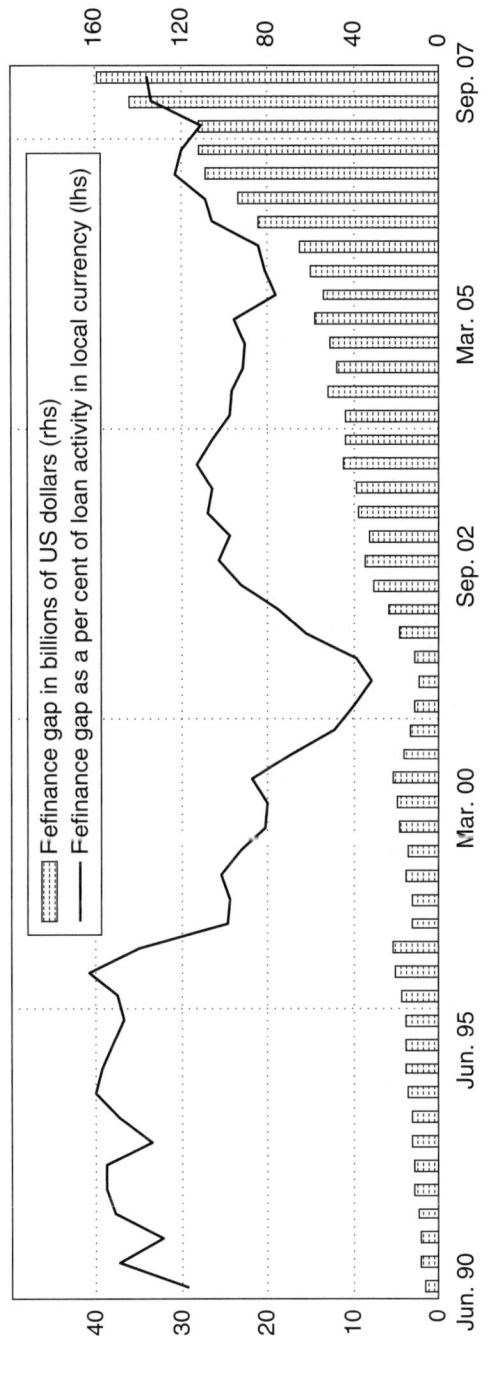

Note: [a] Asian countries include PRC; India; Indonesia; Malaysia; the Philippines; Korea; Taipei,China and Thailand.

Source: Bank for International Settlements.

Figure 5.2 Foreign funding of foreign banks' local currency assets in Asian countries[a]

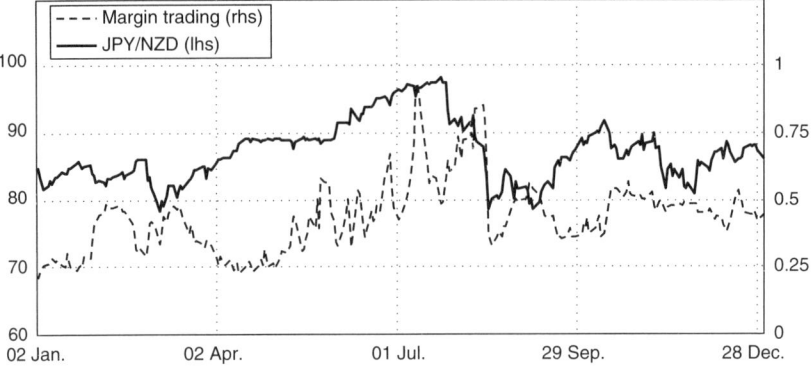

Sources: Tokyo Financial Exchange; BIS.

Figure 5.3 NZD margin positions in Tokyo, 2007 (NZD billion)

Shin (2007) cannot be judged successes if the goal is to provide a convincing measure of the scale of carry trades. The basic difficulty is that, while one can think of a carry trade being constructed through a speculator borrowing yen from a bank and selling it in the spot market in order to buy a higher-yielding asset, in practice the transaction need not take this form and thereby need not leave a yen asset for a bank to report.[7] Large speculative players are more likely to preserve their balance sheets and to achieve much the same end by swapping dollars for yen and then selling the yen spot, in effect setting up a short forward position. A position in the Brazilian real, South African rand or Indonesian rupiah funded with yen can be established with a short position in the yen versus the US dollar and a long position in one of these currencies against the US dollar.

Thus the positions that one can measure through yen loans might be part of a larger position including unmeasured forwards. And, over time, measured positions might be substituting for unmeasured forward positions.[8]

If one widens the definition of carry trade to capture real money overweight positions in high-yielding currencies, then measurement becomes more possible.[9] Thus, data from the Japanese securities firms can be used to measure the outflow of Japanese funds into foreign bond and equity funds. These data show massive outflows into bonds and equities amounting to tens of trillions of yen, not the hundreds of millions into the forward positions examined above (Figure 5.4). Data in late 2007 and early 2008 show a downturn of holdings. This suggests at minimum that new inflows have not offset valuation losses as the yen has appreciated and equity markets have corrected.

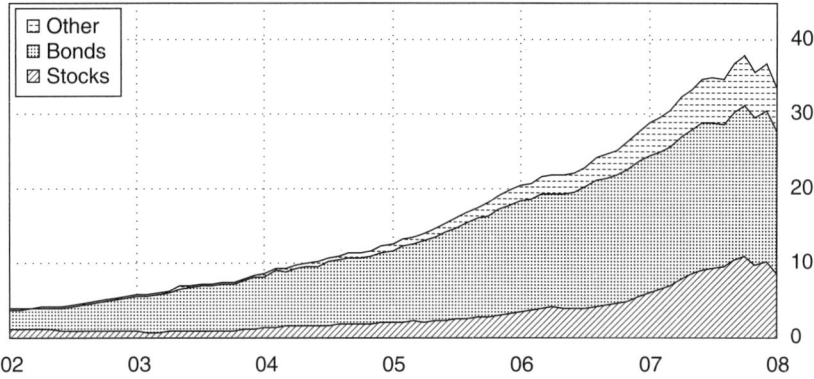

Source: Investment Trusts Association of Japan.

Figure 5.4   Foreign currency investment trusts in Japan (outstanding amount in trillions of yen)

In addition, one can look to the primary market and measure the higher-coupon international bonds that are marketed directly to households and other investors under the Uridashi rules (Nishi and Vergus, 2006). Market participants in Australia and New Zealand track these data against the backdrop of scheduled redemptions for possible pressures on the Australian and New Zealand dollars. In fact, in August 2007 as the AUD/JPY and NZD/JPY sank precipitously, the primary market dried up entirely for new issues for the New Zealand dollar and largely for the Australian dollar (Figure 5.5). Many would presume that the proceeds of maturing bonds were converted into yen and that therefore Japanese investors reduced their exposure to the two currencies. In percentage terms, this decline would be nothing like that observed in the forward trading of Japanese households, but, in value terms, it would be comparable.

5.6.2   Carry Trades across East Asian Currencies

A recently popular form of the carry trade has been to set up positions across emerging market currencies. Such trades are particularly attractive if the currency pairs are seen to react in similar fashion to broader price movements, such as dollar/yen, equity prices or equity volatility. Thus, one trade that was recommended early in 2007 was a long position in Indian rupee against a short position in the Chinese yuan. Since both legs would be set up in nondeliverable contracts, calling the renminbi the 'funding' currency is a figure of speech more than a description. This

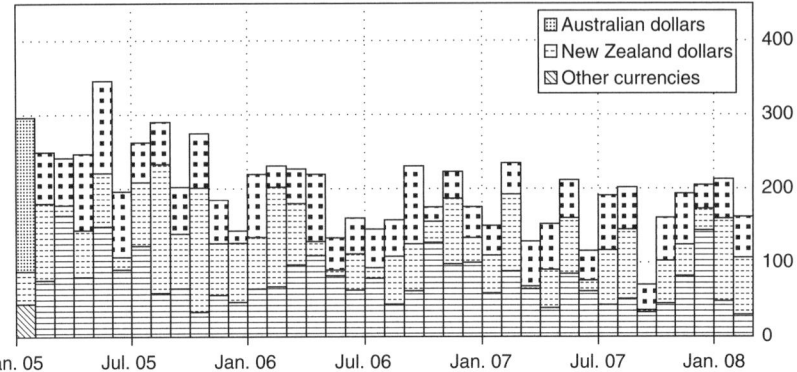

Note: a Derived using average exchange rates in January 2006. Debt issued outside Japan and registered under Japanese securities laws for sale to Japanese investors; in billions of yen.

Source: Bloomberg.

Figure 5.5 Uridashi bond issuance[a] (monthly by currency)

recommendation could be seen as a bet that the Reserve Bank of India would have greater difficulty than the People's Bank of China (PBC) in sterilizing capital inflows amid booming bank lending, very rapid growth of corporate capital spending, and a current account deficit. In the event, of course, the rupee was allowed to rise substantially against the US dollar, while the PBC contained the rise in the renminbi.

More recently, Hohensee (2007) has argued that the persistence of interest rate differentials in East Asia against the backdrop of currencies showing an increasing stability against the currencies of their trading partners creates opportunities for carry trades. The analogy is drawn to the lead-up to monetary union in Europe, when the carry trade was dubbed the convergence trade in light of the commitment to exchange rate stability and inflation and interest rate convergence. Carry trades along these lines would use low-yielding currencies like the Singapore dollar to fund positions in higher yielding currencies like the Indonesian rupiah or Philippine peso.

5.6.3 Evidence from the Triennial Survey

Judging from the results of the April 2007 Triennial Central Bank Survey of foreign exchange markets (BIS, 2007), activity offshore in Asian currencies tended to grow faster than that onshore. As a result, these currencies tended to become more internationalized. While a similar phenomenon is observed across a wide range of currencies, in much of East Asia, this shift occurred in the face of restrictions on deliverability of the currency offshore. This set of observations is consistent with the supposition that carry trades are becoming relatively more important in regional foreign exchange markets.

5.6.4 Inferring Carry Trades from Currency Performance and Global Volatility

If the carry trade cannot be measured, it can be inferred from price action. Cairns et al. (2007) found that when equity market volatility rose sharply, high interest rate currencies sold off against low interest rate currencies. One can think of rises in equity volatility as forcing deleveraging of speculative positions through a number of channels. Higher volatility raises values at risk. Or higher volatility proxies risk aversion. Or higher volatility means lower wealth or capital since volatility tends to rise as equity markets sell off. Whatever the channel, Cairns et al. (2007) found an association between equity volatility and losses on carry trades. This relationship lends itself to graphical presentation (Figures 5.6 and 5.7).

Since the publication of this study, four further spikes have confirmed out of sample that heightened volatility leads to a reversal of carry trades. While the relationship was weak in the spike of volatility in January–February 2008, it proved very strong in the period around the failure of Lehman Brothers in September 2008 (McCauley and McGuire, 2009).

In summary, carry trades defy measurement but form an important class of capital flows into and within East Asia. Our ability to measure speculative positions subject to stop-loss management, such as the forward trading of Japanese households, represents an exception to the general rule of unobservable positions. Still, there are strong indications that carry trades involving Asia-Pacific currencies have been substantial. There are more limited indications that carry trades across emerging market currencies have been gaining in popularity.

5.7 POLICY RESPONSES TO CAPITAL FLOWS

Policymakers in the region have responded in various ways to the challenge of capital inflows (Grenville, Chapter 3, this book). Many economies in the region have responded to the inflow of capital by liberalizing capital outflows. The market timing of such liberalization has tended to work against an immediate strong response by private parties. If domestic asset prices

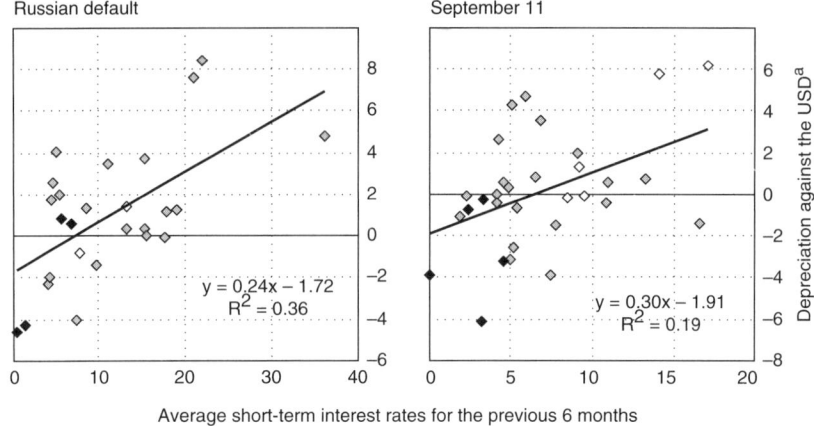
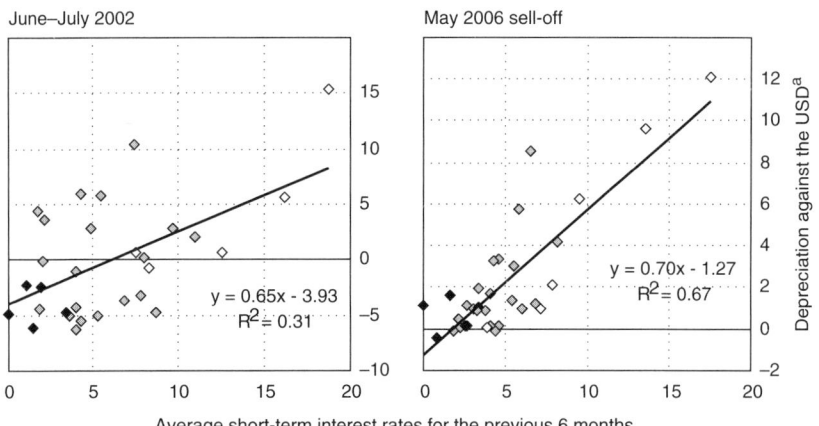

Notes: Black markers represent generally low-yield currencies (JPY, CHF, SGD, TWD and EUR), while white markers represent relatively high-yield ones (TRY, IDR, BRL, RUB, PHP and INR). Currencies with interest rates above 40% and those fixed to the USD are excluded. HKD 12-month forward and CNY 12-month NDF are used to represent HKD and CNY respectively. For Russian default, inclusion of RUB, IDR, TRY, ARS and BRL results in slope of 0.1266 and R^2 of 0.0393. For September 11, inclusion of TRY, ARS and MYR results in slope of 0.1201 and R^2 of 0.2390. For June–July 2002, inclusion of TRY, ARS and MYR results in slope of 0.2399 and R^2 of 0.2735. Interest rates are either money market rates (60b) or treasury bill rates (60c) from the IMF.
[a] As a percentage.

Sources: Bloomberg; IMF, International Financial Statistics; BIS calculations.

Figure 5.6 Unwinding of carry trades: selected episodes during heightened volatility

are performing well and pressure on the currency to appreciate is evident, why invest abroad now? The authorities of a number of major economies have also responded to strong capital inflows by restricting certain capital inflows, particularly bank inflows. Some of these measures are described below and the prima facie evidence of their effects is consulted.

5.7.1 Liberalizing Capital Outflows

In response to strong capital inflows, the authorities in a broad range of Asian economies have liberalized capital outflows. These measures have been taken since the dollar peaked in 2002 but their adoption has accelerated in recent years in Korea, PRC, India, the Philippines, and Thailand. These measures simultaneously signal the authorities' comfort with their international liquidity position and their discomfort with adding to official reserve holdings. The following is by no means an exhaustive account, but describes some of the measures taken.

In mid-2005, Korea's Overseas Investment Activation Plan abolished ceilings on overseas finance and insurance business investment by non-financial institutions and raised the limits on real estate acquisition abroad and overseas direct investment by individuals. The May 2006 Foreign Exchange Liberalization Plan further accelerated the schedule of an earlier plan (announced in 2002) to liberalize foreign exchange transactions by Koreans. In 2007, limits on outward investments were eased further and the process of making such investments was made less burdensome.

In April 2006, the Chinese authorities put in place the Qualified Domestic Institutional Investors (QDII) scheme. Households and firms were allowed to invest in fixed income products through licensed banks and fund managers to the extent permitted by pre-set quotas. A year later, investment in equities was permitted. At the same time, individuals have been allowed to convert renminbi into dollars in an amount up to $50 000 per year (Ma and McCauley, 2007).

Since 2006, India has also eased the limits on various institutions and individuals to invest abroad. Listed companies may invest up to 35 per cent of their net worth in portfolios abroad, mutual funds up to $4 billion and individuals up to $100 000 a year.

In early 2007, the Philippines allowed residents to invest abroad without prior central bank approval, and doubled the limits to $12 million per year (Yap, Chapter 13, this book). Net open position limits on banks' foreign currency holdings were relaxed to allow them to hold substantial long positions in dollars so as to make the foreign exchange market more liquid.

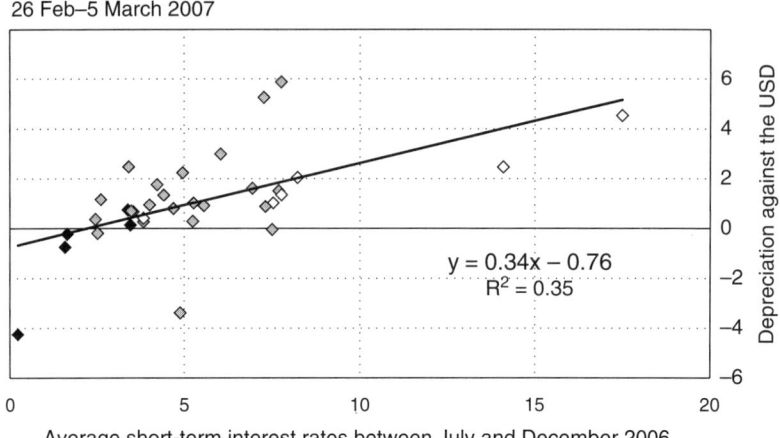

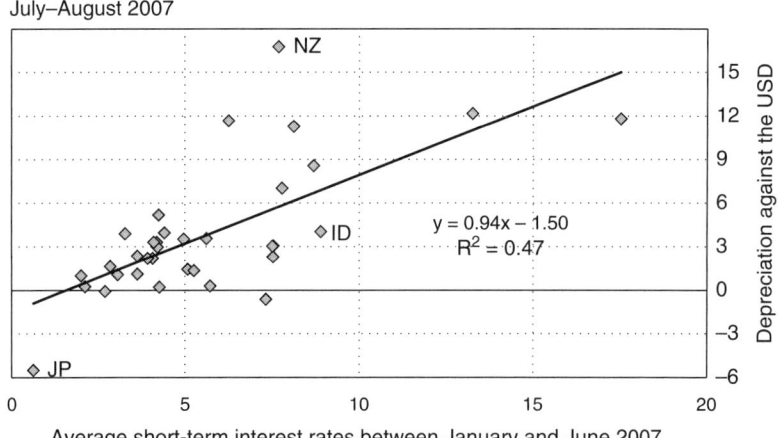

Note: Black markers represent generally low-yielding currencies (JPY, CHF, SGD, TWD and EUR) while white markers represent relatively high-yielding ones (TRY, IDR, RUB, PHP and INR).

Sources: IMF, International Financial Statistics; Bloomberg; DataStream; BIS calculations.

Figure 5.7   Unwinding carry trades in episodes of heightened volatility, 2007–08

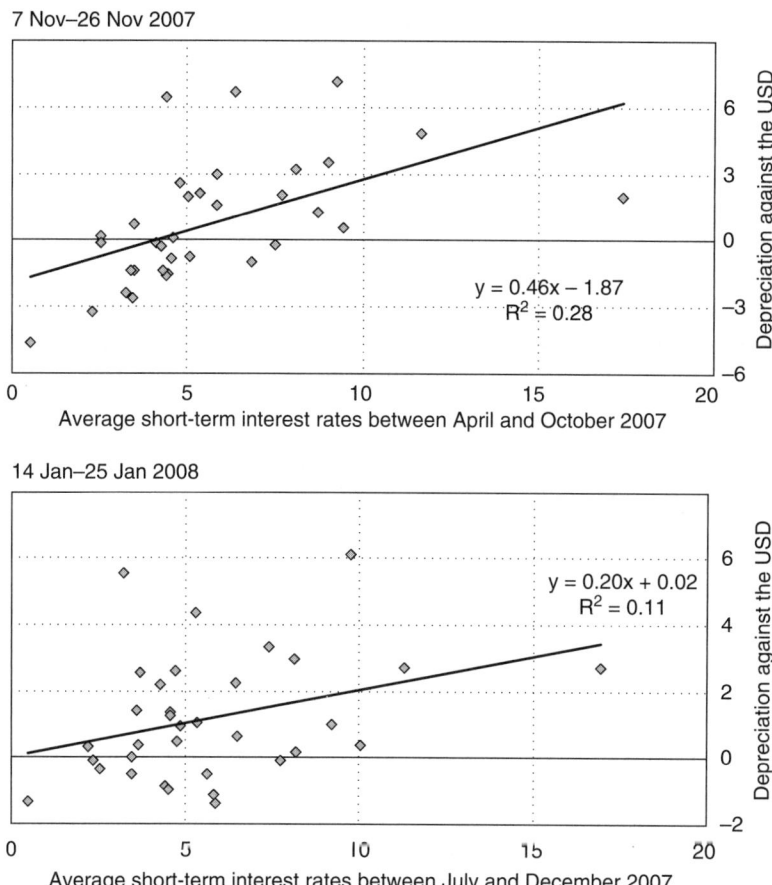

Figure 5.7 (continued)

In the face of a sharp upward move in the baht in July 2007, the Bank of Thailand relaxed regulations on outward capital flows. The measures include the abolishment of the surrender requirement for Thai exporters. With the abolition of the unreimbursed reserve requirement in March 2008 (see below), the Ministry of Finance announced that state-owned enterprises would be encouraged to swap foreign currency debt into baht, and the government pension fund, the social security fund and domestic financial institutions would be encouraged to invest more abroad.[10] The Securities Exchange Commission approved another $12 billion in overseas portfolio investment quotas.[11]

Korea has no doubt enjoyed the greatest success in promoting capital outflows. On top of the fairly steady outflow of direct investment, Korea has recently liberalized portfolio outflows. Outflows favored Chinese and Indian shares. Kim and Yang (Chapter 11, this book) say, 'Equity investment abroad skyrocketed in 2005–06, from $3.6 billion to $15.2 billion.' Net private capital flows recorded an outflow equivalent to 2 per cent of GDP in 2006. Kim and Yang expect the outflows to continue, ascribing them to risk diversification and profit-seeking. While a substantial fraction of the portfolio equity outflows were currency hedged, the scale of the capital outflows is remarkable.[12]

The lesson would seem to be that liberalization of equity outflows has the greatest potential, except for economies with very low short-term rates such as Japan and Taipei,China where strong outflows can favor fixed income investments. On this view, the reluctance of the Chinese authorities to allow outflows into equity markets abroad – in part owing to the risk to local share prices of allowing flows into cross-listed shares trading at a discount in Hong Kong, China – has prevented capital outflows from taking some of the pressure off the currency.

5.7.2 Restricting Capital Inflows

Major Asian economies have responded to strong capital inflows with measures to restrict them. In different ways, authorities have reached back to formerly used measures, made existing restrictions on capital outflows symmetric, and adopted new restrictions or adapted other policies to serve the perceived need for restricting inflows.

The Thai measures to restrict inflows into the Thai bond market in late 2006 do not much differ from policies taken in the PRC, India and Korea. Even in Indonesia, where equity, bond and money markets have *de facto* been among the most open in the region, there is a debate about restricting capital inflows into the money market.

The following sections analyze measures adopted to restrict capital inflows in chronological order: PRC, September 2006; Thailand, December 2006; Korea, April 2007; and India, August 2007. Indonesia's policy debate is also discussed. The reader is reminded that capital inflows that are blocked through one channel can find another channel, so what follows is no more than a partial assessment. That said, the price evidence should probably be given more weight than the flow evidence.

Restrictions on borrowing of dollars by foreign bank branches in the PRC
In response to the turn in the bank flows, the Chinese authorities extended to foreign banks the longstanding restrictions on the ability of domestic banks to borrow dollars abroad to fund dollar assets in the PRC. This

measure has subsequently been reinforced by the requirement that banks meet an increase in bank reserve requirements with US dollar deposits with the central bank. The BIS international banking data suggest that inflows into banks in the PRC leveled off for a half a year in response to the measures (Figure 5.8, left panel). Whether the inflows would have continued to accelerate in the absence of the measures is hard to say.

Notwithstanding the resumption of the growth of claims on banks in the PRC, the restrictions appear effective: US dollar interbank rates there have exceeded those offshore. And along with all the other restrictions, limits on banks' ability to bring dollars into the PRC have allowed interest rates implied by offshore forward transactions in the renminbi-dollar exchange rate to fall far below onshore rates of like maturity (Figure 5.9, left panel).[13]

Unremunerated reserve requirements on fixed income flows into Thailand

In response to a build-up in non-resident holding of baht bank accounts in September 2003, the limits on lending baht to banks offshore that dated to early 1998 were generalized to limits on banks in Thailand borrowing baht from offshore parties. Market participants subsequently attempted to get around these restrictions on baht inflows by creating baht debt securities and marketing them to non-residents. After several efforts to limit particular forms of securities, the Thai authorities announced an unremunerated reserve requirement against portfolio inflows. The subsequent plunge in equity prices led the authorities to apply the reserve requirements only to fixed income inflows.

The measure led to a sharp slow-down in fixed-income portfolio flows as captured in the Thai balance of payments. 'Other loans' had shown an inflow of $2.9 billion in 2006, and then reversed into a net outflow of $0.5 billion in the first three quarters of 2007. Meanwhile, portfolio equity inflows accelerated from $2.4 billion in 2006 to $3.6 billion in the first three quarters of 2007.[14]

In terms of prices, the effect of the measure was very evident in the gap between the onshore and offshore rate of exchange of the baht against the US dollar. A gap of 2–3 baht (6–9 per cent) pointed unsubtly to the effectiveness of the restriction on non-resident holdings in Thailand. The measure led to huge gaps between onshore and offshore interest rates as implied by foreign exchange swaps.[15] The thin offshore market featured higher yields and the absolute value of the gaps hit levels after December 2006 not previously reached in periods of baht weakness before 2002 or periods of baht strength since September 2003.

The Thai authorities removed the unreimbursed reserve requirement as of 3 March 2008, simultaneously taking measures to promote outflows,

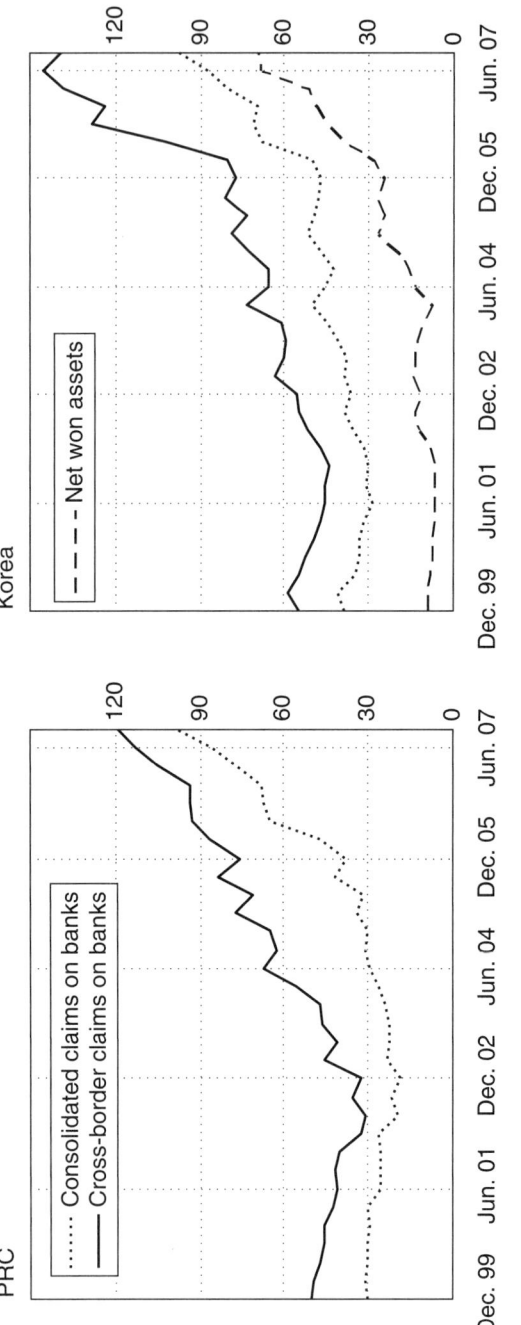

Figure 5.8 Global banks' claims on banks in the PRC and Korea (in billions of dollars)

Source: Bank for International Settlements.

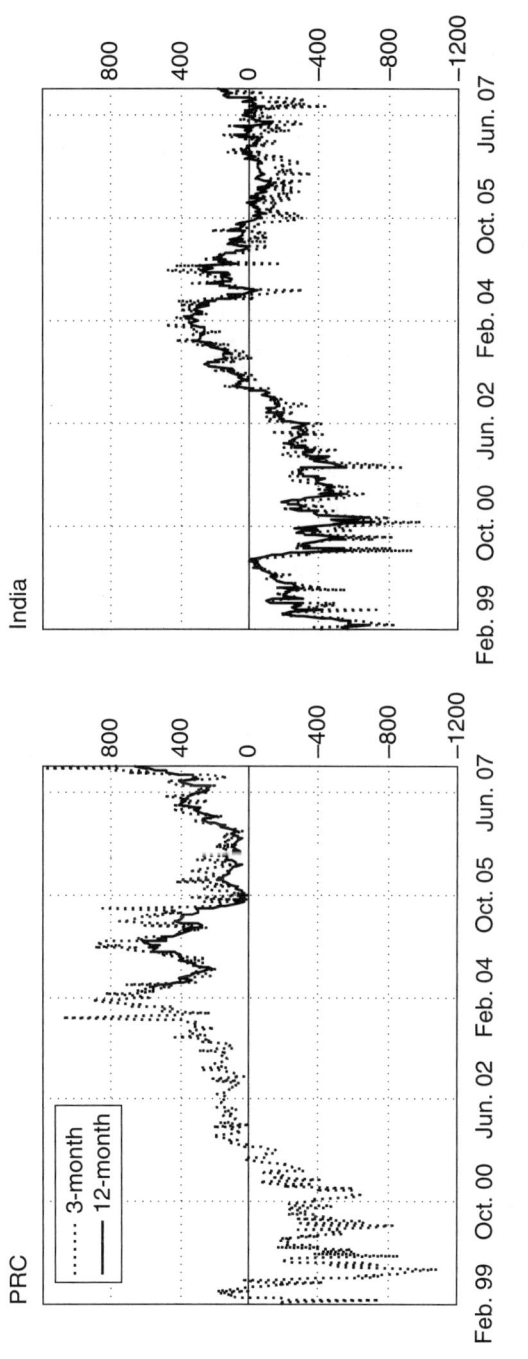

Note: Weekly data. For PRC: 3-month (12-month) NDF, three-month Chibor (one-year PBOC bill auction yield), and 3-month (12-month) Libor. For India: 3-month (12-month) NDF, 91-day (364-day) treasury bill implicit yield, and 3-month (12-month) Libor.

Sources: Bloomberg; CEIC; BIS calculations.

Figure 5.9 *Onshore less offshore NDF-implied yields in the PRC and India (in basis points)*

as described above.[16] The gap between the onshore and offshore exchange rate narrowed in anticipation of the end of the reserve requirement and then disappeared with the policy change.

Restrictions on foreign banks' borrowing dollars from abroad in Korea

Starting in April 2007, foreign banks in Korea were jaw-boned not to respond to strong arbitrage incentives to swap dollars borrowed abroad for Korean won. Moreover, limits on lending in foreign currency to Korean firms, which had been dropped five years ago, were reinstated. Finally, starting in 2008, leverage restrictions originally intended to limit the opportunities for income shifting to offshore affiliates were reduced, as a further measure to limit bank inflows (albeit only borrowings from affiliates).[17]

In terms of the flow of funds, these measures seemed to slow down foreign banks' funding of their branches in Korea. One can see this in the behavior of the three series plotted in Figure 5.8, right panel. After the Korean measures in April 2007, international banks' cross-border claims on banks in Korea, including their own affiliates, leveled off in the second and third quarters of 2007. Also, their offshore funding of their won books has also leveled off.[18] In contrast, consolidated claims on unaffiliated banks in Korea, mostly Korean banks less directly affected by the measures of April 2007, continued to grow.

In price terms, these measures were remarkably effective.[19] Korean won interest rates implied by foreign exchange forwards and imbedded in cross-currency swaps fell to very low levels relative to the domestic market. Thus, a foreign bank that could borrow US dollars abroad and bring them into Korea could lock in a substantial spread by buying central bank paper or a Korean Treasury bond.

Renewed limits on external commercial borrowing in India

In India, the limits on external commercial borrowing, which had been very substantially liberalized over the previous five years (Jadhav, 2005), were tightened in August 2007. While firms remained able to borrow abroad in foreign currency, their ability to convert the foreign exchange into rupees to finance spending in India was limited to $20 million per year, subject to approval (Reserve Bank of India, 2007). This move came toward the end of a half year that saw external commercial borrowing almost double to $10.6 billion from $5.7 billion.

It is too early to assess the effect of the new measure on the dollar volume of external commercial borrowing. But in terms of prices, after August 2007, the gap between onshore Indian interest rates and the yield implied by non-deliverable forwards traded offshore remained modest – at least by the standards of the similar gap for PRC (Figure 5.9; see also McCauley and Ma, 2009).

The debate in Indonesia on policy toward non-resident holdings of SBIs
In Indonesia, the evidence that non-resident holdings of SBIs are the most flight-prone foreign investment has led to suggestions to ban such holdings. Some proposals cite the purpose or essence of SBIs as monetary control in rationalizing such a ban. Others cite the cost of the carry – the 8 per cent plus cost against the returns of 4–5 per cent on the corresponding international reserve assets, and the comfortable position of such reserve holdings. Taken in isolation, the loss of the $3–4 billion of reserves corresponding to non-resident holdings of SBIs would put a modest dent in reserves of over $50 billion.

An outright ban on holdings might have the untoward effect, however, of sending the signal that the Indonesian authorities do not welcome foreign capital to a country with large needs for infrastructure spending. Some critics have pointed to the perversity of the SBIs not attracting a withholding tax, while non-resident investment in government bonds does. This disparity provides a new argument for consolidating the stock of SBIs into government debt (McCauley, 2006a). Such a consolidation would put short- and long-term obligations on the same footing with respect to the withholding tax, without a possibly confusing change of the rules.

5.8 CONCLUSION

Capital has been flowing into East Asia through banks and local bond markets as well as through equity markets and through direct investment. Much of portfolio equity flows and measurable carry trades, such as purchases of short-term Indonesian securities, respond to global volatility in a manner that supports their designation as hot money. But it would be a mistake to understate the role of Asian firms' borrowing dollars in order to protect their cash flow against dollar depreciation. Such corporate hedging has played an important part in drawing funds into the region from the international banking system.

Faced with the upward pressure on currencies from the capital inflows, the authorities in Asia have sought to ease up on restrictions on capital outflows. Over the long haul, more liberal policy toward outflows could lead to a better balance between the private and public sectors' holdings of foreign assets. But in the near term, the outlook for further appreciation of the home currency checks the impulse to invest abroad. Korea's success in encouraging outflows deserves further study and may bear lessons for others in the region.

The authorities in the region have resorted to restrictions on capital inflows to a greater extent than is often recognized. The Thai imposition of unreimbursed reserve requirements in late 2006 is often seen as unique and, with the announcement of their removal in March 2008, short-lived. But it is the burden of this analysis that the authorities in other large Asian economies have extended restrictions on bank inflows (PRC), used moral suasion and tax policy against bank inflows (Korea), and reinstated restrictions on converting external bank loans into local currency (India). While we are awaiting evidence from India, evidence from the other economies points to the technical effectiveness of such restrictions.

It would be wrong to let these measures obscure the impulse in the region toward 'fuller capital account convertibility', as the second Tarapore report was titled (Reserve Bank of India, 2006). Similarly, it would be wrong to ignore the live, albeit conflicted, interest in the internationalization of regional currencies (McCauley, 2006b and 2010). However, faced with unenviable choices among an appreciation widely seen as potentially damaging, further intervention with its risks of exchange rate valuation losses and restrictions on inflows, authorities have not excluded such restrictions.

Progress in Asia toward fuller capital account convertibility, therefore, has the character of two steps forward, one step back, rather than a monotonic process. With US dollar interest rates headed for levels below those in the early 1990s, the choices for policymakers in the region are not getting any easier.

NOTES

1. Senior Adviser, Monetary and Economic Department, Bank for International Settlements. The author thanks Eric Chan for research assistance. Views expressed are those of the author and not necessarily those of the BIS.
2. Ichsan (2007) also cites market participants' view that Indonesia 'might be upgraded to "investment grade" after the 2009 elections'.
3. The fact that government bonds attract a withholding tax, while SBIs do not, works in the same direction. To the extent that the tax liability is managed through structured notes bought offshore from market-makers, unwinding the bond position may require a transaction with the market-maker that produced the structured note, possibly resulting in lower liquidity and higher cost trading than the underlying government bond itself.
4. For a description of derivatives markets in the local bond markets, see Hohensee and Lee (2006). If multinationals contracted to pay fixed-rate baht against receipt of floating-rate dollars (a cross-currency swap), while hedge funds contracted to receive fixed-rate baht against receipt of floating-rate baht (an interest-rate swap), the arranging investment bank would square the deal by selling floating-rate baht against floating-rate dollars (a series of forward sales of baht against dollars or a so-called basis swap).

5. Or even as reflecting different strategies. See McCauley et al. (2002).
6. This section draws on Galati et al. (2007). See also Gyntelberg and Remolona (2007).
7. In the case of carry trades in government bonds, Borio and McCauley (1996) were able to use repo transactions as a measure of the funding of holdings of bonds. Short-term money-market positions can be established, by contrast, with forward positions that cannot be similarly measured.
8. Hattori and Shin (2007) infer an expansion of carry trades from outflows of yen from the Japanese banking system to the rest of the world. Recall, however, that for a time Japanese banks' credit standing was such that they had difficulty borrowing dollars outright and thus resorted to foreign exchange swaps. These put yen into the hands of foreign banks, some of which ended up as deposits with the Bank of Japan. As Japanese banks have regained access to direct dollar funding, foreign banks may have had to obtain yen directly as well. To the extent that on balance-sheet yen borrowing by foreign banks substituted for obtaining yen through swap transactions, the outflow that Hattori and Shin measure may not be associated with an increase in yen funding of carry trades.
9. A wider definition of the carry trade to include portfolio diversification that favors high-yielding currencies is necessary to consider foreign holdings of Bank Indonesia paper as a measure of carry trade activity. That is, included among holders of such paper would be international bond funds for institutional and individual investors, not just leveraged accounts.
10. The Ministry of Finance also pledged to favor baht debt in the financing of the 'megaprojects' for infrastructure. Note that reducing government debt denominated in foreign currency in favor of government debt denominated in baht is similar in its effect on asset stocks to sterilized intervention by the Bank of Thailand.
11. Notwithstanding these measures, Wilaipich and Harr (2008) lowered their forecasts of the dollar/baht rate, indicating a stronger baht was expected.
12. The Bank of Korea and the FSS (2008, p.2) report $13.5 billion in forward sales by investment funds compared to $60.4 billion of forward sales by shipbuilders.
13. On the non-deliverable forward markets, see Ma et al. (2004) and Ho et al. (2005). For more on the comparison of capital account management in China and India, see McCauley and Ma (2009).
14. Net outflows reported by banks in Thailand in 2006–07 must be interpreted with care since the Bank of Thailand uses forex swaps to sterilize its purchase of dollars. Private banks can end up holding a foreign currency claim on the rest of the world matched against a forward sale of dollars to the central bank, in effect a baht asset.
15. For an earlier analysis of this onshore–offshore rate differential, see McCauley (2006c).
16. While Wilaipich (2008) titles her piece, 'BoT lifts capital controls', she describes how the limits on bank lending to non-residents were lifted from B50 million to B300 million, while limits on bank borrowing from non-residents were reduced from B50 million to B10 million.
17. See IMF (2007b), Bank of Korea and FSS (2008), Tebbutt et al. (2008), McCauley and Zukunft (2008) and Committee on the Global Financial System (2009).
18. Holdings of mostly government bonds by foreign bank branches in Korea leveled off in 2007, consistent with their not adding to positions in which they sell dollars forward, borrow dollars spot, and buy Korean government paper spot.
19. See Carrillo-Rodriguez and Hohensee (2007).

REFERENCES

Bank for International Settlements (BIS) (2005, 2007), *Triennial Central Bank Survey of Foreign Exchange and Derivatives Activity*, March and December, Bank for International Settlements.

Bank of Korea and Financial Supervisory Service (2008), 'Joint survey result of "imbalance in supply and demand of FX forward market"' (in Korean), 29 January.
Borio, C.E.V., and R.N. McCauley (1996), *The Economics of Recent Bond Market Volatility*, BIS Economic Paper.
Cairns, J., C. Ho and R.N. McCauley (2007), 'Exchange rates and global volatility: implications for Asia-Pacific currencies', BIS *Quarterly Review*, March, 41–52.
Carrillo-Rodriguez, C. and M. Hohensee (2007), 'The strange case of the USD/KRW basis', Deutsche Bank, Market Strategy, Korea Strategy Update, 16 November.
Chai-anant, C. and C. Ho (2008), 'Understanding Asian equity flows, market returns and exchange rates', BIS Working Paper No. 245, February.
Committee on the Global Financial System (2009), 'Capital flows and emerging market economies', CGFS Publications No. 33, January, Basel: Bank for International Settlements.
Galati, G., A. Heath and P. McGuire (2007), 'Evidence of carry trade activity', BIS *Quarterly Review*, September, 27–41.
Goldstein, M. and P. Turner (2004), *Controlling Currency Mismatches in Emerging Markets*, Washington, DC: Institute for International Economics.
Gyntelberg, J. and E. Remolona (2007), 'Risk in carry trades: a look at target currencies in Asia and the Pacific', BIS *Quarterly Review*, December, 73–82.
Gyntelberg, J., M. Loretan, T. Subhanij and E. Chan (2009), 'International portfolio rebalancing and exchange rate fluctuations in Thailand', BIS Working Papers No. 287, August.
Hattori, M. and H.S. Shin (2007), 'The broad yen carry trade', Institute for Monetary and Economic Studies, Bank of Japan, Discussion Paper No. 2007-E-19, October.
Ho, C., G. Ma, and R.N. McCauley (2005), 'Trading Asian currencies', BIS *Quarterly Review*, March, 49–58.
Hohensee, M. (2007), 'The Asia convergence trade: introduction to the Deutsche Bank Asia Convergence Index', 4 October, Deutsche Bank.
Hohensee, M. and K. Lee (2006), 'A survey of Asian hedging markets: a description of Asian derivatives markets from a practical perspective', in *Asian Bond Markets: Issues and Prospects*, BIS Paper No. 30, November, 261–81.
Ichsan, F. (2007), 'Indonesia's hot money', Standard Chartered Global Research, Special Report: Indonesia, 25 October.
IMF International Monetary Fund (2007a), 'Global financial stability report: financial market turbulence', October.
IMF (2007b), 'Republic of Korea', Staff Report for the 2007 Article IV Consultation, 14 August, IMF Country Report No. 07/344, October.
Jadhav, N. (2005), 'Capital account liberalization: the Indian experience', in W. Tseng and D. Cowen (eds), *India's and China's Recent Experience with Reform and Growth,* Basingstoke: Palgrave Macmillan for the International Monetary Fund, pp. 275–307.
Jiang, G. and R.N. McCauley (2004), 'Asian local currency bond markets', BIS *Quarterly Review*, June, 67–79.
Kim, K. and C.-Y. Song (2010), 'Foreign exchange liberalization and its implications: the case of Korean won', in C. Shu and W. Peng (eds), *Currency Internationalization: International Experiences and Implications for the Renminbi,* Basingstoke: Palgrave Macmillan, pp. 78–111.

Ma, G. and R.N. McCauley (2007), 'Do China's capital controls still bind? Implications for monetary autonomy and capital liberalization', BIS Working Paper No. 233, August.
Ma, G., C. Ho and R.N. McCauley (2004), 'The markets for non-deliverable forwards in Asia', BIS *Quarterly Review*, June, 81–94.
McCauley, R.N. (2003), 'Capital flows in East Asia since the 1997 financial crisis', BIS *Quarterly Review*, June, 45–59, available at: http://www.bis.org/publ/qtrpdf/r_qt0306e.pdf.
McCauley, R.N. (2006a), 'Consolidating the public bond markets of Asia', in *Asian Bond Markets: Issues and Prospects*, BIS Paper No. 30, November, 82–98.
McCauley, R.N. (2006b), 'Internationalising a currency: the case of the Australian dollar', BIS *Quarterly Review*, December, 41–54.
McCauley, R.N. (2006c), 'Understanding monetary policy in Malaysia and Thailand: objectives, instruments and independence', in *Monetary Policy in Asia: Approaches and Implementation*, BIS Paper No. 31, December 172–98.
McCauley, R.N. (2010), 'Internationalizing the Australian dollar', in C. Shu and W. Peng (eds), *Currency Internationalization: International Experiences and Implications for the Renminbi*, Basingstoke: Palgrave Macmillan, pp. 56–77.
McCauley, R.N. and G. Ma (2009), 'Resisting financial globalization in Asia', in *Financial Globalization and Emerging Market Economies, Proceedings of an International Symposium Organized by the Bank of Thailand, Bangkok, Thailand, 7–8 November 2008*, Bangkok: Bank of Thailand: pp. 177–218.
McCauley, R.N. and P. McGuire (2009), 'US dollar appreciation in 2008: safe haven, carry trade, dollar shortage and overhedging', BIS *Quarterly Review*, December, 85–93.
McCauley, R.N. and K. von Kleist (1998), 'Carry trade strategies', BIS *Quarterly Review*, February, 23–24.
McCauley, R.N. and J. Zukunft (2008), 'Asian banks and the international interbank market', BIS *Quarterly Review*, June, 63–79.
McCauley, R.N., J.S. Ruud and P. Wooldridge (2002), 'Globalizing international banking', BIS *Quarterly Review*, March, 41–51.
Nishi, F. and A. Vergus (2006), 'Asian bond issues in Tokyo: history, structure and prospects', in *Asian Bond Markets: Issues and Prospects*, BIS Paper No. 30, November, 143–67.
Reserve Bank of India (2006), *Report of the Committee on Fuller Capital Account Convertibility*, Tarapore Report, July.
Reserve Bank of India (2007), 'Review of external commercial borrowings (ECB) policy', 7 August.
Richards, A. (2005), 'Big fish in small ponds: the trading behavior and price impact of foreign investors in Asian emerging equity markets', *Journal of Financial and Quantitative Analysis*, **40**, March, 1–27.
Takeuchi, A. (2006), 'Identifying impediments to cross border bond investment and issuance in Asian countries', in *Asian Bond Markets: Issues and Prospects*, BIS Paper No. 30, November, 246–60.
Tebbutt, P., H. Chang and M. Kang (2008), 'Korean banks: analysis of their offshore borrowing activities', Fitch Ratings: Banks: Korea Special Report, 21 February.
Wilaipich, U. (2008), 'BoT lifts capital controls', *On the Ground: Thailand*, Standard Chartered, 29 February.
Wilaipich, U. and T. Harr (2008), 'Further implications from the new measures', *On the Ground: Thailand*, Standard Chartered, 4 March.

6. Crises, capital controls and financial integration

Eduardo Levy-Yeyati, Sergio L. Schmukler and Neeltje van Horen

6.1 INTRODUCTION

Since the early 1990s, emerging economies have been rapidly integrating with the international financial system. Financial integration has manifested in many ways, including financial liberalization of previously closed economies, larger cross-border capital flows, entry of foreign banks, and participation of domestic firms in international markets. In particular, as firms go abroad, part of the domestic market activity has migrated to international markets. Capital is raised in international markets and securities are traded in international stock exchanges, in addition to domestic ones.[1] This process of financial integration has been fueled by the belief that it encourages better allocation of resources and risks worldwide, and ultimately promotes higher growth.[2]

Two factors have emerged to threaten this financial integration. Firstly, a series of crises erupted when countries opened up to capital flows, which led to some reservations regarding the net benefits of outright financial liberalization.[3] Secondly, capital controls have emerged as a way to mitigate financial integration.[4] In times of crises, controls on capital outflows have been used to stem reserve losses, currency devaluations, and the collapse of the banking sector. Two such well-known cases are those of Malaysia during the East Asian crisis of 1997–98 and Argentina during its 2001–02 collapse.[5] In tranquil times, controls have been used to avoid the currency and maturity mismatches that short-run foreign flows can produce, and to mitigate the currency appreciation that tends to negatively affect trade balance and domestic production. In fact, Chilean-style controls on capital inflows have regained interest in recent years, with appearances in Argentina, Colombia, Peru, and Thailand.[6]

This chapter analyzes the effects of capital controls and crises on the integration of emerging economies with the international financial system.[7] Specifically, using a large set of firms from emerging economies, we examined the percentage price difference between the stocks that traded domestically and the corresponding depositary receipts (DRs) that traded internationally. We call this price difference the *cross-market premium*. DRs are certificates traded in major financial centers (New York in this case). They are issued by a US depositary bank and they represent shares of ordinary stocks held by a custodian bank in the issuer's home country. The stocks and the DRs represent the same asset traded in two different markets, because underlying stocks can be easily transformed into DRs and vice versa. This characteristic allowed us to measure international financial integration through the law of one price (LOOP), which stipulates that countries are integrated when the DRs in New York and the underlying stock are equally priced.

When there are no barriers to cross-country capital movement, arbitrage is expected to equalize the prices of the DR and the underlying shares. It follows that, in a fully integrated market, the cross-market premium should be approximately zero. However, full integration of capital markets can be disrupted by capital controls and crises.

Effective government controls on cross-country capital movement are expected to segment the markets, widening the cross-market premium. Controls on capital outflows put upward pressure on the underlying stock relative to the depositary receipt, since investors can purchase the security domestically and sell it at a discount in the international market, without having to pay tax to transfer funds outside the country. This positive cross-market premium could not be arbitraged away, because it would imply purchasing the DR in New York, selling it in the domestic market, and transferring the proceeds abroad. However, controls on capital outflows prevent the latter transaction. On the other hand, when the price in New York is higher than the domestic price (implying a negative cross-market premium), arbitrage can take place because investors can purchase the underlying stock domestically, sell it in New York, and transfer the funds back to the country. Note that capital controls limit the cross-border movement of funds, not stocks; therefore, arbitrageurs can transfer the stock from one market to another, with the goal of selling wherever the price is higher, but transferring proceeds from such transactions is governed by capital controls.

Controls on capital inflows have the opposite effect: they push up the relative price of depositary receipts (implying a negative cross-market premium), as investors buy them abroad and sell them domestically, avoiding the tax to enter the country. In this case, the negative cross-market premium could not be arbitraged away, because investors would have to purchase the underlying stock domestically, sell it in New York, and transfer the funds back into the country, but controls on capital inflows prevent the latter transaction. In sum, the cross-market premium reflects the effectiveness of capital controls and the price that investors are willing to pay to hold securities that can be freely transferred across borders when other restrictions are in place.

The impact of financial crises is more ambiguous. In principle, there are no obstacles to arbitrage; therefore, the cross-market premium would fluctuate around zero. However, the risks associated with swapping the underlying stock for the DR (and vice versa) increase due to transfer and convertibility risks, higher exchange rate volatility, and most importantly, reduced liquidity, which in turn induce market players to reduce their open positions at any point in time to a minimum.[8] Consequently, one would expect crises to be associated with a more volatile cross-market premium that oscillates around zero, and that can turn positive or negative depending on the risks involved.

Recently, DRs have been used to assess the impact of capital controls and crises. Rabinovitch et al. (2003) attribute the persistence of return differentials between American Depositary Receipts and stocks in Chile to the presence of capital controls. Melvin (2003) and Auguste et al. (2006) examine the large ADR discounts that built in the midst of the Argentine crisis in early 2002, which Levy-Yeyati et al. (2004) interpret as a reflection of the strict controls on capital outflows and foreign exchange transactions imposed at the time. Pasquariello (2008) presented evidence of large return differentials during crises. In Levy-Yeyati et al. (2009), we investigated the statistical properties of the cross-market premium using linear and non-linear models to measure the no-arbitrage bands, the convergence speed to those bands, and the mean-reverting properties of the premium. We further studied the effect of capital controls and liquidity on the cross-market premium, and analyzed the advantages of this measure of financial integration over alternative ones.

In this chapter, we characterize the behavior of the cross-market premium around crises and changes in different types of capital controls by computing summary statistics and by using an event-study methodology. To do so, we worked with daily cross-market premium for a set of 98 stocks from nine emerging economies: Argentina, Brazil, Chile, Indonesia, Republic of Korea (hereafter Korea), Mexico, Russia, South Africa, and Venezuela. For all countries, except Argentina, we sampled the period 1990–2004. In the case of Argentina, we extended the sample period to 2007 in order to analyze the impacts of the controls on inflows introduced in 2005.

We found that capital controls were able to segment domestic markets from international ones. When binding (that is, when flows move against the controls), controls on outflows resulted in a positive premium, while controls on inflows resulted in a negative premium, as market participants were willing to engage in costly arbitrage only to a limited degree. Crises, on the other hand, while they did not tax arbitrage directly, affected financial integration by increasing volatility and by putting downward pressure on the domestic price, such that the underlying stock on average traded at a discount compared to the DR.

The remainder of the chapter is organized as follows: Section 6.2 discusses the methodology and data, Section 6.3 analyzes the effects of capital controls on the cross-market premium, Section 6.4 illustrates the impact of crises on the premium, and Section 6.5 gives a summary and conclusion.

6.2 METHODOLOGY AND DATA

Depositary receipts (DRs, also known as American Depositary Receipts or ADRs) are shares of non-US corporations traded in the US, while the underlying shares are traded in the issuer's domestic market. DRs are issued by so-called depositary banks in the US and represent a specific number of underlying shares remaining on deposit in so-called custodian banks in the issuer's home country.[9] The depositary bank can create a new DR by depositing the required number of shares in the custodian bank, after which the dividends and other payments will be converted by the depositary bank into US dollars and thus be made available to the holders in the US. The process can simply be reversed by canceling or redeeming the DR. In this way, an underlying stock can easily be transformed into a DR and vice versa.

The cross-market premium, defined as the percentage difference between the dollar price of the stock in the domestic market and its corresponding DR, reflects the deviation between the home market price of the stock and its price in New York. The cross-market premium can be computed by converting the local currency price of the underlying stock to dollars, multiplying it by the number of underlying shares one DR represents, and then dividing it by the DR price.

When there are no barriers to cross-country capital movement between the domestic market and the US, there are no transaction costs. Furthermore, if the two markets close at the same time, arbitrage should be instantaneous and costless, and prices should be equal. If the price of the underlying stock is higher than the price of the DR, investors can make an instant profit by buying the DR, transforming it into underlying stock, and selling it. This will lower the price of the underlying stock and bring the premium back to zero. The reverse holds when the price of the DR is higher. If a shock occurs too late in the day to be arbitraged away, closing prices will differ, but this difference will disappear quickly the next trading day.[10] In reality however, instantaneous and costless arbitrage does not exist. Many factors can affect arbitrage, including capital controls and crises, as mentioned above.

In order to examine how the cross-market premium reacts to capital controls and crises, we conducted event studies. These studies allowed us to determine whether the cross-market premium behaved statistically differently after an event. We did this in two ways: first, we constructed a portfolio of stocks and studied its evolution, then at the stock level, we computed the estimated post-event deviations from the pre-event mean and variance values. We then reported the mean and variance differences and the number of stocks for which these differences were statistically significant.

We analyzed the following events: the imposition and lifting of capital controls, significant relaxations in the intensity of capital controls, and crises. In the case of capital controls, the event date (time zero) is marked as the date capital controls change (i.e., they are introduced, lifted, or relaxed). Six-month windows before and after the event were used to calculate the pre-event and post-event means. In the case of crises, we defined the event as the beginning of a crisis, and studied the behavior of the cross-market premium during the crisis period relative to the pre-crisis mean. The lengths of the post-crisis windows are equal and are determined by the duration of the crisis.

In terms of data, we worked with countries that experienced changes in capital controls or financial crises during the sample period, so that we were able to analyze the effects of both. We also worked with stocks with a long history of DR listings with important trading volume. Thus, we used publicly traded stocks in the US, either on the National Association of Securities Dealers Automated Quotation System (NASDAQ) or the New York Stock Exchange (NYSE). In total, we worked with 102 stocks (out of 133 DRs that trade in the NYSE and NASDAQ) from nine emerging economies: Argentina (8 stocks), Brazil (30 stocks), Chile (20 stocks), Indonesia (2 stocks), Korea (6 stocks), Mexico (23 stocks), Russia (2 stocks), South Africa (8 stocks), and Venezuela (3 stocks). The cross-market premium was calculated only on days when both the underlying stock and the DR were traded.[11]

The data needed to calculate the premium (the dollar price of the stock in the domestic market, the price of the DR in New York, and the number of underlying shares per unit of the DR) came from Bloomberg. For Argentina, Brazil, Chile, and Venezuela we used the closing price both in the domestic market and in New York. For Asian markets, which are already closed when the New York stock market opens, as well as for Russia and South Africa, we instead used the closing price (and the

Table 6.1 Cross-market premium summary statistics

Country	Mean	Median	Std Dev.	5th percentile	95th percentile	Number of observations
Argentina	0.06	0.00	0.72	−0.97	1.35	2138
Brazil	0.11	0.03	1.27	−1.76	2.15	2301
Chile	0.29	0.25	0.73	−0.82	1.54	1617
Indonesia	0.58	0.53	1.89	−2.32	3.88	1315
Korea	1.59	1.17	3.80	−3.76	7.87	972
Mexico	0.19	0.16	0.81	−1.05	1.55	2379
Russia	0.11	0.23	1.52	−2.50	2.30	1371
South Africa	−0.09	−0.13	1.45	−2.33	2.45	2032
Venezuela	0.00	−0.06	2.84	−4.43	4.95	1440
All stocks	0.12	0.12	0.73	−0.74	0.96	2618

Note: The summary statistics are based on all available data excluding crisis periods and periods with capital controls. For Korea, the summary statistics are based on the average cross-market premium of the two stocks that were unaffected by the controls on inflows, Kookmin Bank and Hanaro Telecom.

Source: Data from Bloomberg.

exchange rate) in the domestic market and the opening price in New York, to minimize distortions due to time differences.

Before studying the effects of capital controls and crises on the integration of emerging economies in the next sections, it is useful to observe the behavior of the cross-market premium during tranquil (non-crisis) times when capital controls are absent. Table 6.1 presents summary statistics of the simple average of the cross-market premium of the stocks in each country's portfolio. A positive premium indicates that the price of the underlying stock exceeds that of the DR, while a negative premium indicates otherwise. The table shows that during tranquil times, the premium is generally close to zero. In all cases, except in Korea, the average premium is below 1 per cent. The summary statistics of all stocks show a mean of 0.12 per cent, with a standard deviation of 0.73. In other words, during tranquil times and under no controls, emerging economies seem well integrated with the international capital market.

6.3 CAPITAL CONTROLS ON THE CROSS-MARKET PREMIUM

In this section, we analyze the effects of capital controls on the cross-market premium. Capital controls are diverse, differing across countries in intensity and over time. Furthermore, there are different types of controls; the most notorious difference is between controls on inflows (typically used to discourage short-term flows) and on outflows (to prevent capital flight in the midst of a crisis). Though the effects will depend on the type and intensity of controls, if the introduction of capital control impedes arbitrage and thus effectively segments markets, this should be reflected in the cross-market premium, as the law of one price ceases to hold.

When controls on inflows are in effect, purchasing the underlying stock to sell the DR would require paying an inflow cost to re-enter the funds into the country. As a result, relatively low domestic prices will not be arbitraged away and the underlying stock will be bought at a discount compared to the DR, as investors need to be compensated for the costs they incur by moving capital into the country. Thus, controls on inflows would introduce a negative cross-market premium. Under the presence of controls on capital outflows, an international investor seeking to buy the DR to sell the underlying stock would need to repatriate the proceeds from this sale and incur a cost. This makes it difficult for investors to profit from relatively high domestic prices, introducing a positive cross-market premium. Given that arbitrage takes place mostly within a day (as documented in Levy-Yeyati et al. 2009), we expect that controls would have an effect right after they are imposed (or lifted), not before, even when anticipated.

6.3.1 Brief Chronology of Capital Controls

Periods of capital controls are relatively easy to detect, as governments impose them through laws and a number of public institutions document them. Below we provide a brief summary of the capital controls in the countries under study, during the periods analyzed in this chapter. Six countries in our sample experienced a period in which capital restrictions potentially affected the behavior of stock markets: Argentina, Chile, Indonesia, Korea, South Africa, and Venezuela.[12]

Argentina When the financial and currency crises of 2001 became unsustainable, Argentina introduced controls on capital outflows on 2 December 2001, as well as restrictions on cash withdrawals from commercial banks (the so-called 'corralito'). Both foreign and domestic investors were prohibited from transferring funds abroad, wire transfers required central bank approval, and foreign currency futures transactions were prohibited. Exactly one year later, the corralito was lifted and capital was allowed to leave the country, albeit with some restrictions on capital outflows. Virtually all controls were eliminated in June 2003. However, authorities re-imposed controls on inflows of foreign capital in 2005. These controls consisted of two restrictions: the amount entering the country must remain within Argentina for 365 days and 30 per cent of the total amount must be deposited in a local bank in the form of usable funds for the bank's minimum reserve requirement. These restrictions were enforced when local businesses obtained loans not falling within the exceptions of the decree (such as financing of foreign trade and direct investment), or when foreign investors bought public or private stocks or bonds in the secondary market. These controls were still in effect at the end of the sample period for Argentina.

Chile In 1991, Chile had already introduced controls on inflows in the form of an Unremunerated Reserve Requirement (URR), but these controls only affected the DR market from July 1995 onwards. This was due to a 30 per cent non-earning reserve deposit that had to be paid, with the holding equal to the loan maturity, with a minimum of three months and a maximum of one year. Primary DRs were considered capital additions and were therefore never subject to the URR. With markets in turmoil and the Chilean peso under attack, the reserve requirement was lowered to 10 per cent in June 1998. In August, a few months later, the URR was eliminated for secondary DRs, and in September of the same year, reserve requirements on all inflows were eliminated.[13]

Indonesia The Indonesian capital market was largely liberalized when the first publicly traded DR was introduced by an Indonesian company. However, foreigners were only allowed to purchase up to 49 per cent of all companies' listed shares. In September 1997, this restriction was lifted and foreign investors were allowed to purchase unlimited domestic shares, with the exception of banking shares.

Korea When the first publicly traded DR was introduced in Korea, there were restrictions on foreign investments in the stock markets. In particular, there was a ceiling on the share of foreign investor ownership, which was gradually increased over time. In May 1998, the government lifted the foreign investment restrictions on Korean securities, with the exception of Kepco, Posco, mining and air transportation companies, and information and telecommunication companies. Cross-listed stocks using DRs faced an additional restriction: until January 1999, the conversion of underlying shares into DRs was severely restricted, requiring the approval of the issuing company's board. In November 2000, Korea changed its regulations so that underlying shares could be converted to DRs without board approval as long as 'the number of underlying shares that can be converted into DRs' is less than 'the number of underlying shares that have been converted from DRs'.[14] For four of the stocks in our country portfolio, SK Telecom, Kepco, Posco, and KT Corp, this rule has often prevented arbitrage: in effect, these stocks still faced controls on capital inflows at the end of the sample period (2004). Two other stocks in our portfolio, Kookmin Bank and Hanaro Telecom, were unaffected by the rules during the period covered by our sample, so controls were not effectively in place. These two stocks were not used in the event studies that are presented in the next section. In order to examine the impact of the gradual relaxation of the controls, we divided the control period of Korea into three distinct sub-periods. The first period, which lasted until January 1999, was termed 'very restrictive'. The second period, which lasted from January 1999 to November 2000, when free conversion started to be allowed but conditioned by the rule, was termed 'restrictive'. The third period, which started in November 2000 and lasted until the end of the sample period, was termed 'less restrictive'.

South Africa   A dual exchange rate system that effectively controlled capital outflows was already in place from 1961 to 1995, although it was temporarily abandoned from 1983 to 1985. The dual exchange rate informally existed during the 'blocked rand' system (1961–76) and the 'securities rand' system (1976–79), until it evolved into a formal dual exchange system called the 'financial rand' system (1979–83 and 1985–95).

The 'blocked rand' system introduced restrictions on the repatriation of funds invested in South Africa by non-residents, while residents were prohibited from transferring funds abroad. The proceeds of sales of South African assets by non-residents could not be transferred abroad and instead had to be deposited in 'blocked rand' accounts at commercial banks within South Africa. Therefore, non-residents were able to obtain rands in two ways: the direct channel (the official commercial exchange rate) or by buying 'blocked rands' through the indirect channel.[15] Since the 'blocked rand' exchange rate traded at a discount to the commercial exchange rate, the indirect mechanism was mostly used. The 'securities rand' system did not greatly modify the restrictions imposed on residents, but introduced some changes to boost non-residents' investment in South Africa.[16]

The 'financial rand' system put in place a formal dual exchange rate system with a 'commercial rand' subject to intervention by the monetary authorities and a free-floating 'financial rand', which traded at a discount to the commercial rand. The 'financial rand' was applied to all current account transactions and the 'commercial rand' to capital account transactions for non-residents.[17]

In March 1995, the 'financial rand system' was abolished and all exchange rate controls were lifted. Only then were non-residents able to invest and repatriate funds, and transfer capital and current gains without restrictions.

Venezuela The country experienced two periods of controls on capital outflows. The first one started in June 1994, when the foreign exchange market closed, and controls on capital outflows were introduced to stop the severe speculative attacks against the Bolivar. The controls implied an outright prohibition of capital outflows, including the repatriation of non-resident investment, excluding flows related to the repayment of external debt. Furthermore, the measures restricted the availability of foreign exchange for import payments. In May 1996, these controls were abolished, and by January 2003, exchange rate trading was suspended and limits to dollar purchases were introduced. Originally, the measure was introduced as a temporary measure, but remained in place at the end of our sample period (2004) and was accompanied by a new set of stringent capital controls introduced in January 2003.

6.3.2 Effects of Capital Controls

To examine the impact of capital controls on financial market integration we performed event studies on a stock level basis.[18] Table 6.2 presents the summarized results of the event study tests for capital control events, showing the number of cases in which the post-event mean is significantly different from the pre-event mean. The event studies examined whether the post-event mean was significantly different from the pre-event mean. The event date is marked as the date that capital controls change. Pre- and post-event periods are equal in length and add up to a 260-day window. Event studies were done at the stock level but are presented at the country level, averaging across stocks. The upper row displays event study results with respect to controls on outflows, while the bottom row shows the events with respect to controls on inflows. Mean and variance significance tests were done at a 10 per cent significance level.

In addition, we show the behavior of the average cross-market premium changes in controls on outflows (Figure 6.1) and changes in controls on inflows (Figure 6.2).[19] Figures 6.1 and 6.2 display, by country, the behavior of the cross-market premium before and after the introduction and lifting of capital controls on outflows. The solid line on each graph represents the average cross-market premium across stocks and the dashed line represents the pre- and post-event mean of the average cross-market premium. The horizontal axis represents the number of days prior to or elapsed from the event. For both Figures 6.1 and 6.2, we used a 260-day window.

Table 6.2 Event studies: capital controls

Event	Country	Number of stocks tested	Post and pre event mean difference	Number of stocks w/ positive mean difference	Number of stocks w/ negative mean difference	Post and pre event variance difference	Number of stocks w/ positive variance difference	Number of stocks w/ negative variance difference
Controls on Outflows								
Introduction	Argentina	6	10.13	6	0	56.97	6	0
	Venezuela	1	25.85	1	0	683.92	1	0
Lifting	Argentina	8	−0.81	0	6	−6.53	0	6
	South Africa	3	−15.86	0	3	−21.21	0	3
Controls on Inflows								
Introduction	Argentina	7	−0.63	0	7	−0.72	0	2
	Chile	10	−1.59	0	10	−0.47	1	3
Lifting	Chile	17	2.53	17	0	4.48	9	1
	Indonesia	2	−1.74	0	2	9.28	2	0
Relaxation	Korea							
High to medium		3	11.77	3	0	66.77	2	0
Medium to low		4	0.92	2	1	−14.06	0	3

Notes:
1. Pre- and post-event periods are equal in length and add up to a 260-day window.
2. Event studies are done at the stock level but are presented at the country level, averaging across stocks.
3. The upper panel displays event study results with respect to controls on outflows, while the bottom panel shows the events with respect to controls on inflows.
4. Mean and variance tests are computed at a 10% significance level.

Source: Data from Bloomberg.

Figures 6.1 and 6.2, and Table 6.2 suggest a common pattern. Before capital controls on outflows were introduced, the cross-market premium was close to zero with a very low volatility, but it rose significantly after controls were imposed. For example, in Argentina the average cross-market premium went from −0.02 per cent to 11.54 per cent. In the case of Venezuela, it went from −1.29 per cent to 24.56 per cent. When controls were lifted, the reverse happened; for example, when Argentina removed the controls on capital outflows, the mean of the average premium decreased from 2.33 per cent to 0.76 per cent. In the case of South Africa, the mean of the average premium decreased by 15.79 per cent, from 17.71 per cent to 1.92 per cent. This result is highly consistent across stocks (as noted in Table 6.2). The introduction of capital controls significantly increased the cross-market premium for all stocks tested. The lifting of controls resulted in a drop of the premium in all but two stocks (in the case of Argentina).

Note that the premium during the period of capital controls was not only relatively volatile, but also displayed persistence. This persistence reflects capital flowing into and out of the country, since during the periods shown, the intensity of the controls did not change. That is, given a certain restriction to shift funds abroad, the cross-market premium seemed to reflect the pressure exerted by investors by shifting (or trying to shift) funds abroad in any way possible, which was especially evident in the case of Argentina. The mean of the premium six months after controls were imposed was 11.54 per cent. However, the mean had already dropped to only 2.33 per cent in the six months prior to the lifting of the same controls.[20] When Argentina imposed controls it was in the midst of its crisis, so these controls became very binding, which explained the very large and sudden shift in the cross-market premium (reaching highs of 32.82 on 7 December 2001 and 34.3 on 20 December 2001). When the controls were abolished, the desire to shift funds out of the country was substantially less, explaining the much lower premium at this time.[21]

As expected, the introduction of controls on inflows had exactly the opposite effect compared to the introduction of controls on outflows: the cross-market premium turned negative. In Argentina, the average cross-market premium dropped to −0.31 from 0.21, while in Chile, the drop was even more pronounced as it fell to −1.63 from 0.03.

When controls on inflows were lifted in Chile, the average cross-market premium again immediately started to oscillate around zero. In the case of Indonesia, however, the average cross-market premium fell instead of rising when controls on inflows were lifted. This suggests that the limits on foreign participation may not have been binding at the time, and allowed domestic investors to perform arbitrage. A ceiling on foreign investment

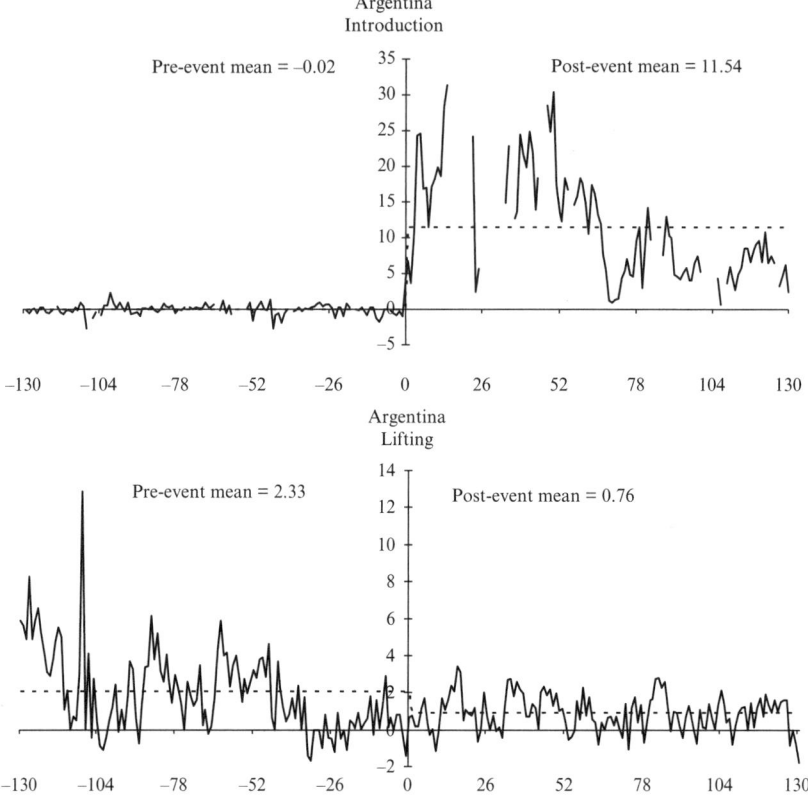

Notes:
1. The event date is marked as time zero, defined as the day controls are introduced in the two upper panels and the day controls are lifted in the two bottom panels.
2. The solid line on each graph represents the average cross-market premium across stocks.
3. The dashed line represents the pre- and post-event mean of the average cross-market premium.
4. The horizontal axis represents the number of days prior to or elapsed from the event.
5. A 260-day window was used.

Source: The data source is Bloomberg and other reports (see main text).

Figure 6.1 Event studies: capital controls on outflows

did not affect arbitrage by foreign investors as long as foreign participation was well below the limit. Moreover, in the case of Indonesia, the restrictions on capital movement did not seem to be binding.[22] In contrast, in Korea, a similar ceiling combined with a rule restricting the convertibility of the DRs impeded arbitrage, regardless of whether the ceiling

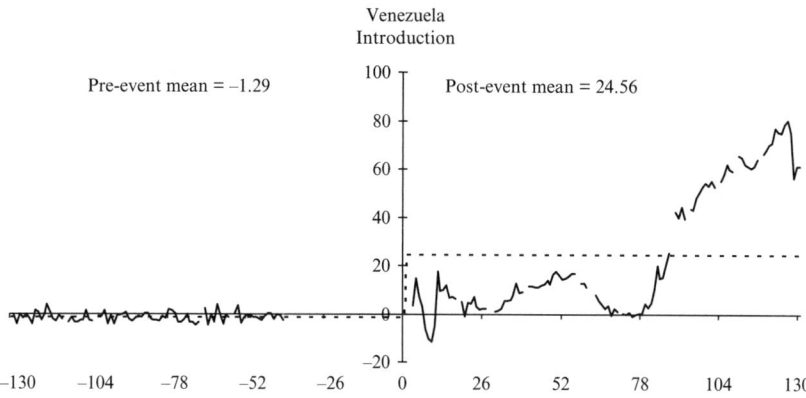

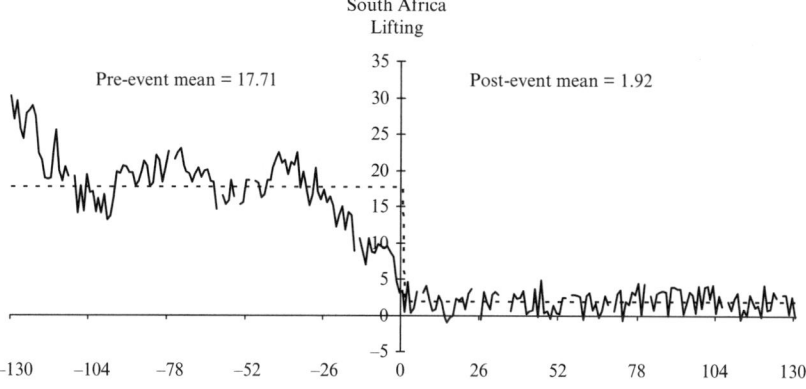

Figure 6.1 (continued)

was binding. However, when controls on inflows were changed to a less stringent level, the cross-market premium in Korea reacted and the discount became smaller. The evidence that the discount was much lower in Argentina and Chile than in Korea directly reflected the different nature of the restrictions: quantitative limits that prevented arbitrage in Korea, and an implicit tax that weakened arbitrage in Argentina and Chile.

Note that 'tax' on inflows effectively decreased the price investors were willing to pay for the underlying stock, as investors add the entry tax to the price of the domestic stock when comparing it to the price of the 'untaxed' DR.

As with controls on outflows, the results were highly consistent across stocks. The introduction of controls on inflows in Argentina and Chile generated discounts for all stocks. On the other hand, the lifting of

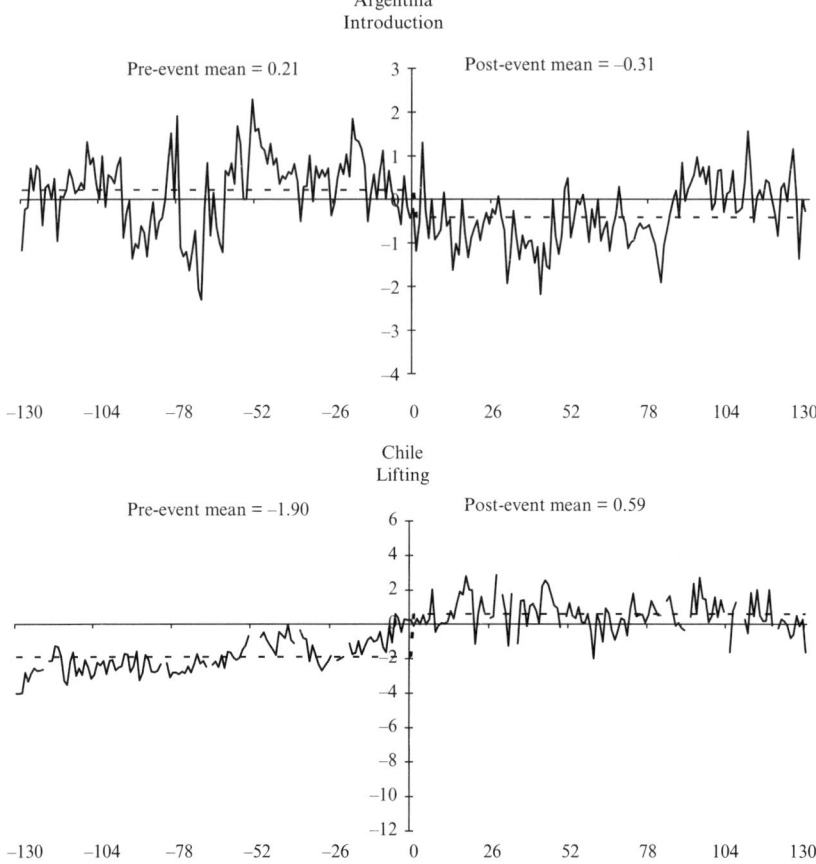

Notes:
1. The event date is marked as time zero, defined as the day controls are introduced, lifted, or relaxed.
2. The solid line on each graph represents the average cross-market premium across stocks.
3. The dashed line represents the pre- and post-event mean of the average cross-market premium.
4. The horizontal axis represents the number of days prior to or elapsed from the event.
5. A 260-day window was used.

Source: The data source is Bloomberg and other reports (see main text).

Figure 6.2 Event studies: capital controls on inflows

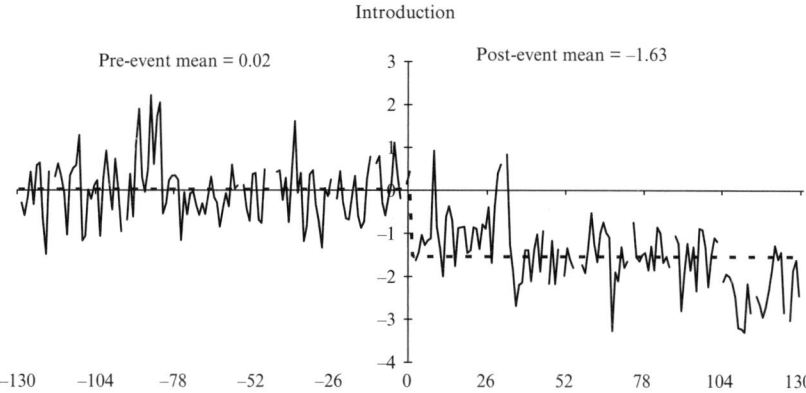

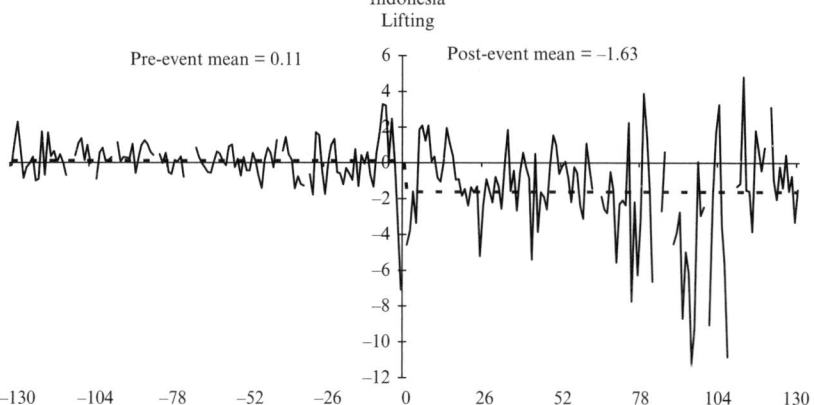

Figure 6.2 (continued)

controls in Chile raised the cross-market premium for all stocks, and the cross-market premium of Indonesian stocks significantly dropped when the controls were lifted. In Korea, the discount for all but two stocks significantly decreased when the intensity of the controls was reduced.

In summary, our results provide evidence that capital controls do affect the size and persistence of deviation of the cross-market premium from zero and cause the law of one price to break down. In other words, regulations on capital movement can prevent investors from engaging in arbitrage-related activities, effectively segmenting the domestic market from the international capital market.

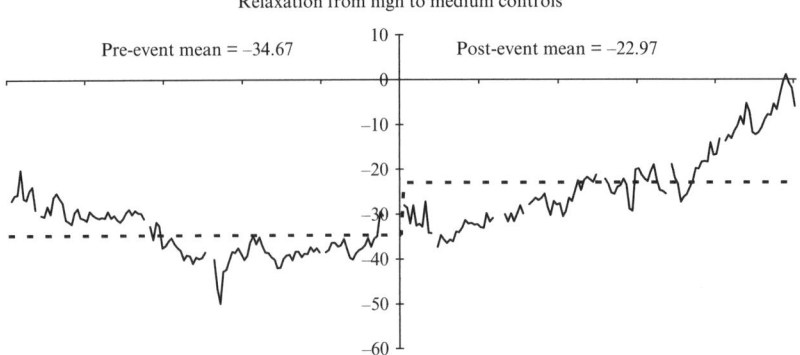

Figure 6.2 (continued)

6.4 CRISES AND THE CROSS-MARKET PREMIUM

The impacts of financial crises are more ambiguous. They can temporarily influence the level of financial integration, as the risk associated with swapping the underlying stock for the DR and vice versa increases due to higher volatility of exchange rates and risks of transfer and convertibility. On the other hand, an increase in the variability of the premium could simply reflect the greater price volatility that characterizes episodes of financial turmoil, even if the degree of arbitrage remains unaltered. However, before studying the effects of crises on the cross-market premium, it is necessary to define crisis periods, which are less trivial than supposed.

6.4.1 Crisis Periods

Times of crises are difficult to pin down. Perhaps what makes this task particularly challenging is the lack of an uncontroversial operational definition of crises. Aside from the problem of not having a uniform definition, as there are various methodologies and ad hoc criteria used to identify crises, the literature concentrates on determining the beginning of crises, but not their end. For our purpose, it was essential to accurately determine the duration of crises in order to correctly specify the periods we wished to analyze.

To define crises, we followed the approach adopted by Broner et al. (2004), which determined *ex ante* certain criteria to identify the beginning and end of crises according to the behavior of certain market indicators.

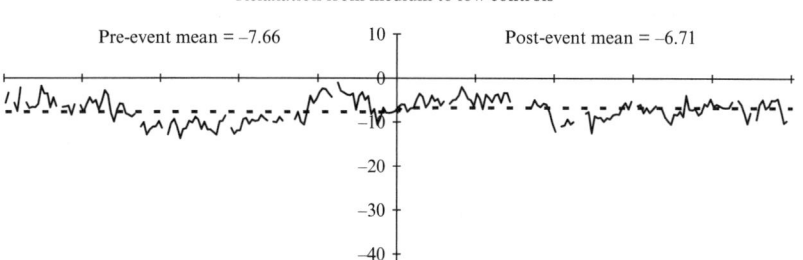

Figure 6.2 (continued)

Their methodology allowed us to distinguish country-specific crisis periods (which could be of domestic or foreign origin), without having to resort to the use of *ex post* data. We used two different procedures to identify crisis periods: one based on the exchange market pressure (EMP) index and the other based on the local stock market index.[23] As crisis dating is arbitrary, we performed a robustness exercise.

The EMP index is computed as the weighted average of the daily changes in the interest rate and the log difference of the exchange rate, with weights equal to the reciprocal of the standard deviation of the respective variables.[24] A crisis initiates when the EMP volatility (its 15-day rolling standard deviation) exceeds a threshold level and remains above that level for at least four weeks, where the threshold is defined as the mean of the EMP volatility plus one standard deviation. A crisis ends the first date after which the EMP volatility drops below the threshold and remains there for three months.

When using stock market prices, crises begin when the stock market index starts a decline of at least five consecutive weeks that reaches a cumulative drop in excess of 25 per cent. A crisis ends on the first date after which the index grows for at least four consecutive weeks.

The exchange and interest rate series came from Bloomberg and Datastream and the local stock market index series came from the Emerging Market Database (EMDB). The interest rates used varied according to data availability; in all cases, however, all available market-determined interest rates behaved similarly over the sample period.[25] Table 6.3 reports the crisis periods identified by both procedures. The EMP crisis period was identified using an EMP index, the weighted average of the

Table 6.3 Crisis periods

	EMP Crises		Stock Market Crises	
	Start date	End date	Start date	End date
Argentina				
Crisis 1			24 Jul. 1998	09 Oct. 1998
Brazil				
Crisis 1	13 Jan. 1999	24 Feb. 1999	07 Aug. 1998	05 Mar. 1999
Crisis 2			17 Aug. 2001	21 Feb. 2003
Indonesia				
Crisis 1	15 Aug. 1997	12 Nov. 1998	08 Aug. 1997	09 Oct. 1998
Crisis 2			16 Jul. 1999	03 Dec. 1999
Mexico				
Crisis 1	20 Dec. 1994	02 Jun. 1995	09 Dec. 1994	15 Mar. 1996
Crisis 2			24 Jul. 1998	16 Oct. 1998
Russia				
Crisis 1	25 May. 1998	11 Nov. 1998	01 May. 1998	16 Apr. 1999
Thailand				
Crisis 1	17 Jun. 1997	08 Jul. 1998	03 Oct. 1997	16 Jan. 1998
Crisis 2			24 Apr. 1998	09 Oct. 1998

Notes:
1. This table uses two different procedures, one based on the exchange market pressure (EMP) index and the other based on the local stock market index.
2. The crises considered do not coincide with periods in which capital control modifications take place.
3. The following rates were used: seven-day interbank rate (Argentina), the bank deposit certificate rate (Brazil), the 30-day CD rate the interbank call money rate (Indonesia, Russia), the 90-day bank deposit rate (Mexico), and the three-month discount rate.

Sources: The exchange and interest rate series came from Bloomberg and Datastream and the local stock market index series came from the Emerging Market Database (EMDB).

daily changes in the interest rate and exchange rate. The crises considered did not coincide with periods in which capital control modifications took place (e.g., Argentina's stock market crisis in 2001–02 coincided with the introduction of capital controls, so this case was excluded from the analysis; the same applies to the 1997 crisis in Korea).

6.4.2 Effects of Crises

As in the case of capital controls, we examined the impact of crises on financial integration by performing event studies. Table 6.4 presents the

Table 6.4 Event studies: crises

Country	Number of stocks tested	Post and pre event mean difference	Number of stocks w/ positive mean difference	Number of stocks w/ negative mean difference	Post and pre event variance difference	Number of stocks w/ positive variance difference	Number of stocks w/ negative variance difference
EMP Crises							
Brazil	11	−1.35	1	4	1.82	2	0
Indonesia	2	−1.75	0	2	12.42	2	0
Mexico	8	−1.39	0	4	8.10	8	0
Russia	2	−2.29	0	2	37.15	2	0
Stock Market Crises							
Argentina	7	−0.03	0	0	1.13	4	0
Brazil (1)	3	0.06	1	0	6.55	3	0
Brazil (2)	17	−0.05	3	5	3.69	6	4
Indonesia (1)	2	−1.94	0	2	11.82	2	0
Indonesia (2)	2	−1.09	0	1	−1.01	0	0
Mexico (1)	9	−0.58	0	5	3.59	8	0
Mexico (2)	12	0.20	3	0	7.03	8	0
Russia	2	−1.98	0	2	26.59	2	0

Notes:
1. The event date is marked as the date the crisis starts.
2. The post-event period used to calculate the mean is equal to the crisis period and the pre-event period is of equal length. The length of the window varies for each country.
3. Mean and variance significance tests were done at a 10% significance level.

Source: The data source is Bloomberg

results of the event study tests for crisis events; it also shows the number of cases in which the post-event mean is significantly different from the pre-event mean. The event studies examined whether the post-event mean was significantly different from the pre-event mean. The pre- and post-event periods are equal to each other, with the length varying on a per country basis. The upper panel displays the event study results when the crisis dates were based on the EMP criteria. The lower panel shows the event study results based on the stock market criteria. Mean and variance significance tests were done at a 10 per cent significance level. The upper panel of the table provides the results using the EMP crisis definition; the lower panel shows the results using the stock market crisis definition (discussed below).

In addition, Figure 6.3 shows the behavior of the average cross-market premium for Brazil, Indonesia, Mexico, and Russia, countries that

Brazil

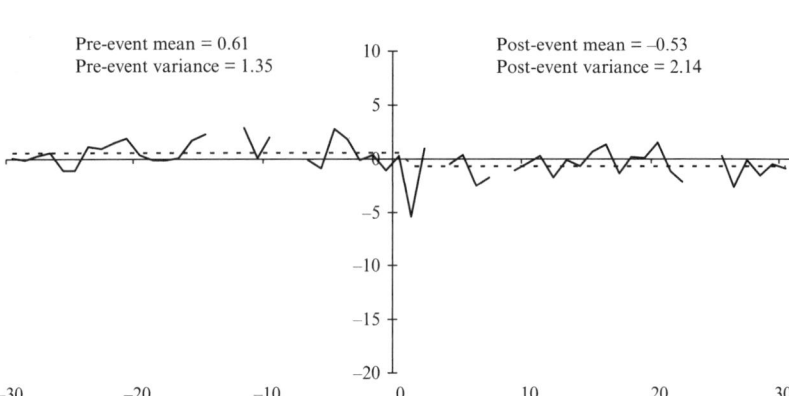

Mexico

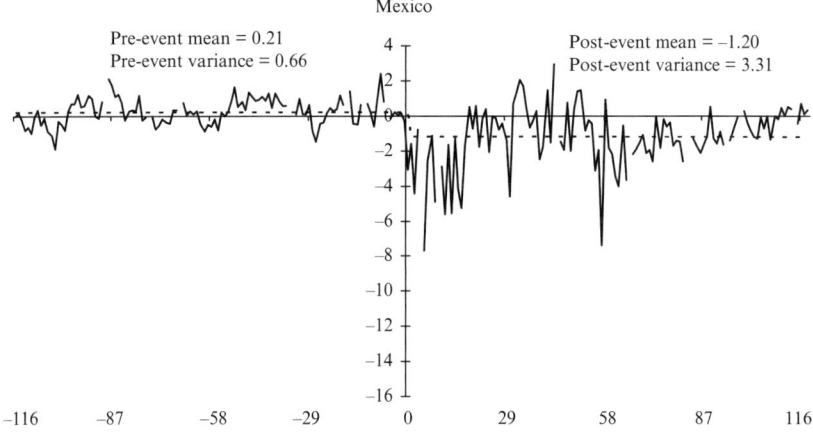

Notes:
1. The solid lines on each graph represent the average cross-market premium across stocks.
2. The dashed lines represent the pre- and post-event mean of the average cross-market premium.
3. The horizontal axis represents the number of days prior to or following the event.
4. Although the length of the window varies, the pre-event and post-event periods are equal for each country.

Sources: The data sources are Bloomberg and other reports (see main text).

Figure 6.3 Event studies: EMP crises

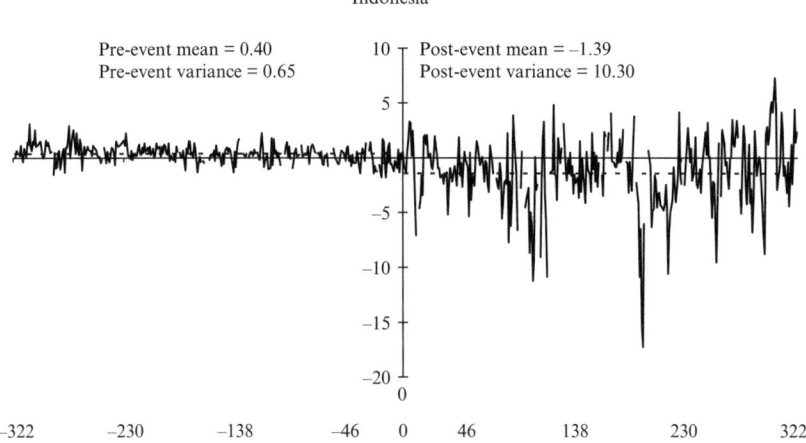

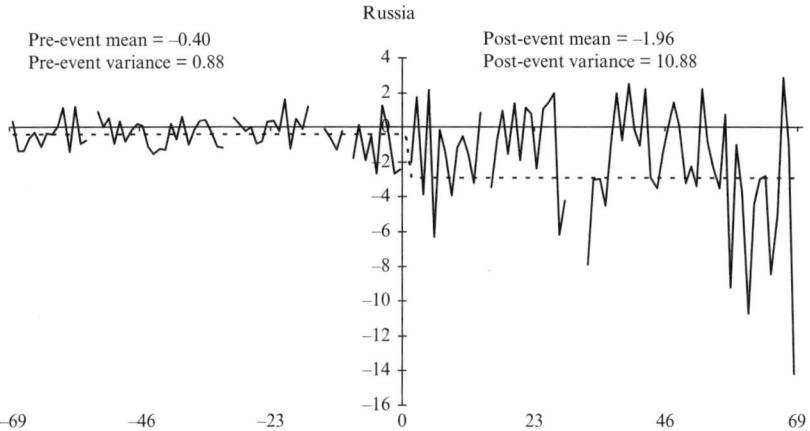

Figure 6.3 (continued)

experienced a crisis (as determined by our EMP definition) during our sample period. Since there was a large change in the variance, Figures 6.3 and 6.4 also report the pre- and post-event variance. They also display, by country, the behavior of the cross-market premium before and during crisis periods. The event date, marked as time zero, is the day the crisis started based on the EMP criteria.

The charts indicate that in all four cases the mean of the cross-market premium becomes negative during the crisis. In Indonesia for example, the pre-event mean equals 0.40, while the post-event mean equals −1.39.

182 Managing capital flows

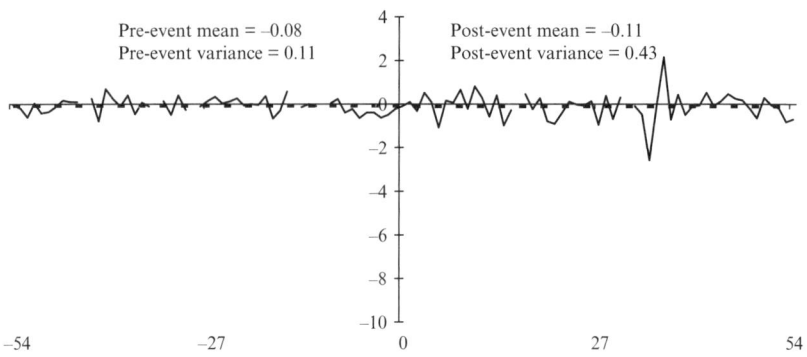

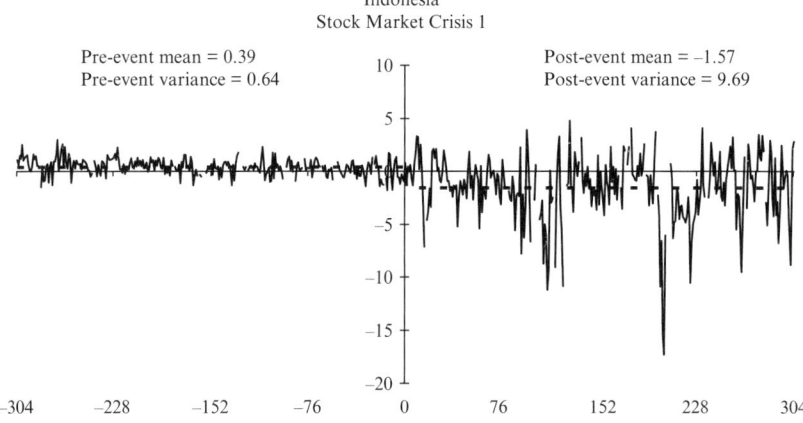

Notes:
1. The solid lines represent the average cross-market premium across stocks.
2. The dashed lines represent the pre- and post-event mean of the average cross-market premium.
3. The horizontal axis represents the number of days prior to or following the event.

Sources: The data sources are Bloomberg and other reports (see main text).

Figure 6.4a Event studies: stock market crises (Argentina, Russia, and Indonesia)

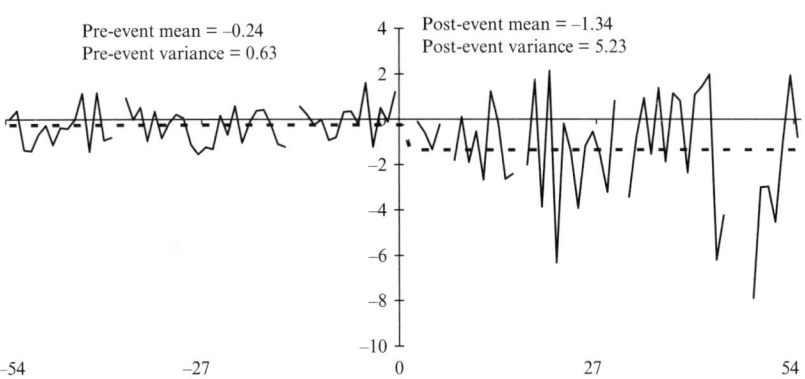

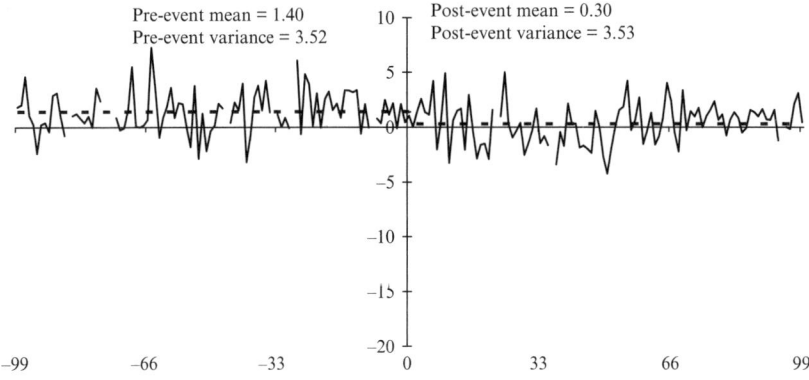

Figure 6.4a (continued)

Similarly, in Mexico the mean of the average cross-market premium dropped to −1.20 during the crisis, compared to 0.21 in the pre-crisis period. The results in the upper panel of Table 6.4 show that most stocks indeed experienced a significant drop in the cross-market premium during the crisis period. The country with the weakest result is Brazil, where only 4 out of 11 stocks showed a significant drop in the mean. This result can be explained by the fact that it was hard to detect a clear crisis period in Brazil, as there was a prolonged period of turbulence, but there was only a limited period of severe exchange market pressure. There was a decrease in the average mean, and compared with tranquil times, the volatility of

184 Managing capital flows

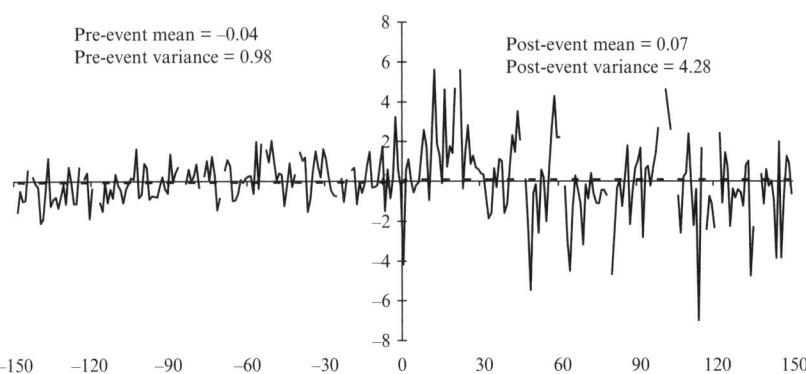

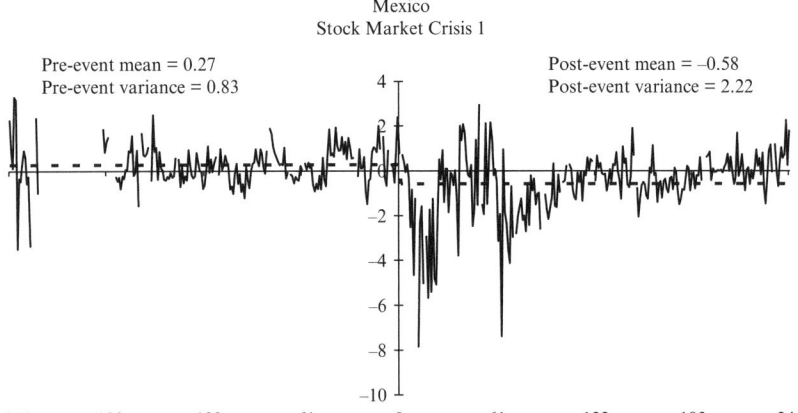

Notes:
1. The solid lines represent the average cross-market premium across stocks.
2. The dashed lines represent the pre- and post-event mean of the average cross-market premium.
3. The horizontal axis represents the number of days prior to or following the event.

Sources: The data sources are Bloomberg and other reports (see main text).

Figure 6.4b   Event studies: stock market crises (Brazil and Mexico)

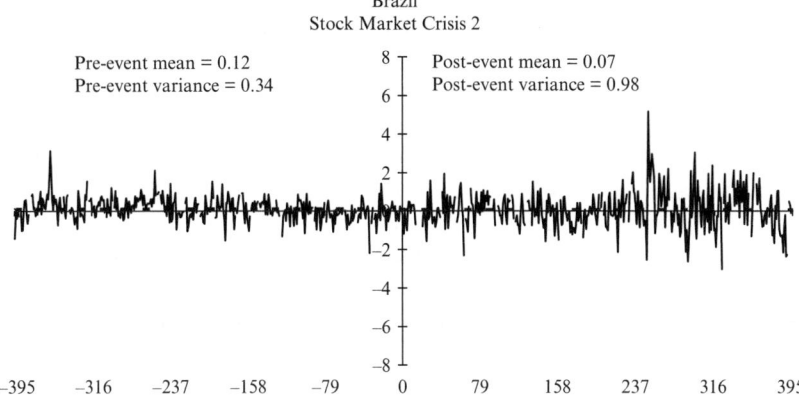

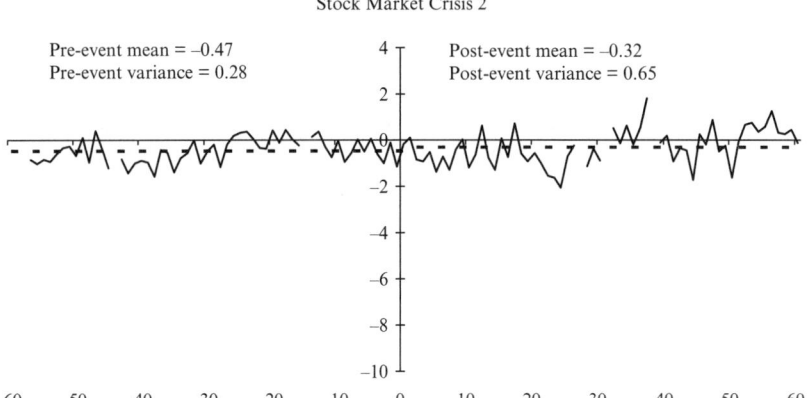

Figure 6.4b (continued)

the premium significantly increased during crises. In Russia for example, the variance increased from 1.67 before the crisis to 38.82 after the crisis. Also in Indonesia, the premium became much more volatile, with the variance increasing from 1.20 to 13.62 (Table 6.4). Volatility also increased in Mexico and Brazil, albeit at a more modest level.

Thus, the results indicate that during crises, the cross-market premium becomes more volatile and continues to oscillate around zero, while the average premium drops. This implies that markets do not segment during crises. However, the risks associated with swapping the underlying stock for the DR and vice versa increased due to exchange rate, transfer, and convertibility risks. Moreover, the typical decline in liquidity in periods of financial distress tended to reduce traders' inventories and added to price volatility, thus inhibiting immediate arbitrage. This is in line with the findings in Levy-Yeyati et al. (2008), where we documented, using an event-study approach, an increase in trading costs (e.g., bid-ask spreads widen) in times of crisis. The negative cross-market premium suggests that these risks are more pronounced for the underlying stock and, as a result, investors demand a discounted price for this stock.

As a robustness test, we performed the same event studies using the stock market crisis definition. The results in the bottom panel of Table 6.4 and in Figures 6.4a and 6.4b, which display, by country, the behavior of the cross-market premium before and during crisis periods, largely confirmed our previous results. During crisis periods, the premium continued to oscillate around zero, indicating that the markets remain integrated. However, volatility substantially increased in all but one case. The results on the drop of the mean of the cross-market premium during crises were, however, less pronounced in this case. Still, in the vast majority of cases, there existed a significant negative difference between pre- and post-event mean.

In summary, the result showed that contrary to the introduction of capital controls, the occurrence of a crisis did not break down arbitrage. However, investors appear to have demanded a risk premium for the underlying stock to compensate them for the risks associated with selling the stock in the local market.

6.5 CONCLUSIONS

This chapter showed that capital controls and crises do affect the integration of capital markets, using data from firms from emerging economies that simultaneously trade their stocks in domestic and international stock markets.

First, the chapter showed that the cross-market premium accurately reflected the effective impact of controls on cross-border capital movement on international arbitrage. More specifically, controls, if effective, affect the size and sign of the difference in prices between the underlying stocks and their DRs in New York. By raising the costs of shifting funds across borders, regulations on capital movement prevent investors from engaging in arbitrage-related activities. Controls on inflows depress the price of the underlying stocks in domestic markets, as investors need to pay a tax to purchase relatively undervalued assets, as opposed to buying the DRs. Conversely, controls on capital outflows increase the price of the underlying stocks, as investors are restricted from transferring the proceeds from the sale of those assets abroad.

These controls on cross-country capital movement have been frequently used to prevent crises and inhibit capital outflows once crises occur. While these controls have been criticized many times for being easy to evade, this paper showed that even when they did not fully preclude cross-border flows, they appear to work as intended and segment markets effectively – where effectiveness is understood as the success in producing the desired market segmentation. Whether or not this segmentation is beneficial to the economy is an altogether different question that exceeds the scope of this paper.

Second, as expected, the chapter showed that crises were reflected in capital markets. When crises erupt, the cross-market premium becomes volatile, reflecting the shocks that markets receive and the difficulties in performing instantaneous arbitrage. Contrary to periods of capital controls however, arbitrage is still possible during crises, as is evident from the fact that the cross-market premium oscillates around zero. Nevertheless, the decrease in the average premium during crises, including the fact that the underlying stock tends to trade at a slight discount, suggests that the risks of holding the underlying stock compared to the DR increases.

Ultimately, the chapter illustrated that cross-market premium could be used as a tool to measure capital market integration, particularly during periods of capital controls and crises. For example, to the extent that there is market segmentation, this measure reflects the intensity of the segmentation and the force of capital flows. As the case of the Republic of Korea proves, the premium diminished when controls on capital outflows became less restricted. Moreover, when investors were pushing to get out of Argentina at the beginning of the 2001 crisis, the cross-market premium sharply increased, and as markets calmed down, the premium subsided. Nevertheless, even when markets are not segmented, this measure can show the shocks markets suffer, as reflected in the crisis periods. In the end, this measure might become a useful tool for policymakers to monitor market sentiment in economies with assets traded both domestically and abroad.

NOTES

1. See Levine and Schmukler (2006 and 2007) and Gozzi et al. (2008 and 2010), and the references therein.
2. See Obstfeld (1994), Acemoglu and Zilibotti (1997), Fischer (1998), Rogoff (1999), and Summers (2000) for arguments in favor of financial integration.
3. See Henry (2006) and Kose et al. (2006) for comprehensive surveys on the literature of

financial integration. See Bhagwati (1998), Rodrik (1998), Soros (2002), and Stiglitz (2002) for arguments against financial integration.
4. See Eichengreen et al. (1998), Cooper (1999), and Stiglitz (2000) for arguments against free capital flows. See Kawai and Takagi (Chapter 2, this book) for a survey on the literature on managing capital inflows. Also, see Grenville (Chapter 3, this book) for a discussion on the macroeconomic consequences of capital inflows and Schadler (Chapter 4, this book) for an analysis of over 90 recent episodes of large capital inflows.
5. See Edison and Reinhart (2001) for a detailed study of the case of Malaysia, and de la Torre et al. (2003) and Perry and Servén (2003) for analyses of the case of Argentina.
6. In 1991, Chile introduced unremunerated reserve requirements (URR) on capital inflows, the encaje, and was followed by Colombia in 1993, Thailand in 1995, and Argentina in 2005. In the midst of a fast appreciation of the Peruvian sol, Peru raised reserve requirements on bank deposits by offshore accounts to 120 per cent in May 2008. Thailand lifted controls in March 2008. Le Fort and Lehmann (2003) and Cowan and De Gregorio (2005) study the Chilean case. In-depth analyses of the more recent episodes of controls on inflows are still missing.
7. We study the effects of crises originated both domestically and abroad.
8. Levy-Yeyati et al. (2008) document the liquidity decline during periods of financial distress.
9. Depositary banks provide all the stock transfer and agency services in connection with a depositary receipt program, and must designate a custodian bank to accept deposits of ordinary shares. A custodian holds the ordinary shares underlying the ADRs in the issuer's home market. When new ADRs are issued, the custodian accepts additional ordinary shares for safekeeping and when ADRs are canceled, the custodian releases the ordinary shares in accordance with instructions received from the depositary. Depositary banks are located in the US whereas the custodian bank is located in the home country of the underlying stock issuer.
10. The same should apply to temporary non-zero premia due to differences in trading hours between the domestic and the US stock market.
11. For a detailed description of which companies are included in the respective portfolios and the period for which the cross-market premium is calculated, see Levy-Yeyati et al. (2008). In that paper, we also discuss the effects of using observations for which trading occurs in only one market.
12. The sources for these measures are: Bloomberg, Clarin (newspaper, Argentina), IFC Emerging Markets Factbook, IMF Annual Report on Exchange Arrangements and Exchange Restrictions, Korea's Financial Supervisory Service's Regulation on Supervision of Securities Business, and Kaminsky and Schmukler (2008).
13. In fact, the URR was set to zero, but the mechanism was left in place until it was finally eliminated in 2002.
14. See Articles 7–9 of the Financial Supervisory Service's Regulation on Supervision of Securities Business.
15. The latter means purchasing South African assets listed in London with foreign currency and selling them in the Johannesburg stock market to obtain blocked rands in order to buy other South African securities.
16. The 'securities rand' was then traded in Johannesburg directly, making it unnecessary to obtain stocks through the London stock exchange.
17. The financial rand applied to the local sale or redemption proceeds of South African securities and other investments in South Africa owned by non-residents, capital remittances by emigrants and immigrants, and approved outward capital transfers by residents.
18. In some cases, the underlying stock or the DR trades very infrequently in either the pre- or post-event period, limiting the number of observations. When less than 15 observations are available to calculate the mean, the stock is not used in the event study.
19. Note that Tables 6.2 and 6.4 show the average change of the mean across stocks (the cross-market premium mean difference is first calculated per stock and then averaged across

stocks per country and event). Meanwhile, the figures display the change of the mean of the average cross-market premium (the cross-market premium is first averaged across stocks per country and then the pre- and post-event mean difference is calculated). As a result, the mean change for each event differs slightly between the table and the figures.
20. The average cross-market premium equals 11.54 between December 2001 and May 2002 (the six-month period after the introduction of capital controls), compared to 2.33 between December 2002 and June 2003.
21. Consider that although controls are in place, investors might find ways to shift funds in and out of the country. For example, in the case of controls on capital outflows, investors can purchase stocks or bonds domestically and sell them abroad. The cross-market premium reflects the implicit price investors pay for these transactions, among other things. See Levy-Yeyati et al. (2008).
22. See Levy-Yeyati et al. (2008).
23. To define crisis periods, Broner et al. (2004) use the 9-year bond spread, which is not readily available for all countries in our sample.
24. Ideally, one would also like to include the change in reserves; unfortunately, these data are not available on a daily frequency for the countries in our sample.
25. The following rates were used: seven-day interbank rate (Argentina), the bank deposit certificate rate (Brazil), the 30-day CD rate (Chile, Venezuela), the interbank call money rate (Indonesia, Korea, Russia), the 90-day bank deposit rate (Mexico), and the three-month discount rate (South Africa).

REFERENCES

Acemoglu, D. and F. Zilibotti (1997), 'Was Prometheus unbound by chance? Risk, diversification, and growth', *Journal of Monetary Economics*, **50**, 49–123.

Auguste, S., K. Dominguez, H. Kamil and L. Tesar (2006), 'Cross-border trading as a mechanism for capital flight: ADRs and the Argentine crisis', *Journal of Monetary Economics*, **53**, 1259–95.

Bhagwati, J. (1998), 'The capital myth: the difference between trade in widgets and dollars', *Foreign Affairs*, **7**(May–June), 7–12.

Broner, F.A., G. Lorenzoni and S. Schmukler (2004), 'Why do emerging markets borrow short term?', Policy Research Working Paper No. 3389, World Bank and Working Paper No. 13076, NBER.

Cooper, R.N. (1999), 'Should capital controls be banished?', in G.L. Perry and W.C. Brainard (eds), *Brookings Papers on Economic Activity No. 1*, Brookings Institution Press, Washington, DC, pp. 89–125.

Cowan, D. and J. De Gregorio (2005), 'International borrowing, capital controls, and the exchange rate: lessons from Chile', Working Paper No. 11382, NBER and Working Paper No. 322, Central Bank of Chile.

De la Torre, A., Levy-Yeyati, E. and Schmukler, S (2003), 'Living and dying with hard pegs: the rise and fall of Argentina's currency board', *Economia*, Spring, 43–107.

Edison, H. and C. Reinhart (2001), 'Capital controls during financial crises: the case of Malaysia and Thailand', in R. Glick, R. Moreno and M. Spiegel (eds), *Financial Crises in Emerging Markets,* Cambridge: Cambridge University Press, pp. 427–56.

Eichengreen, B., M. Mussa, G. Dell'Ariccia, E. Detragiache, G. Milesi-Ferretti and A. Tweedie (1998), 'Capital account liberalization: theoretical and practical aspects', Occasional Paper No. 172, IMF.

Fischer, S. (1998), 'Capital account liberalization and the role of the IMF', in S. Fischer, R.N. Cooper, R. Dornbusch, P.M. Garber, C. Massad, J.J. Polak, D. Rodrik and S.S. Tarapore, *Should the IMF Pursue Capital-Account Convertibility?*, Essays in International Finance No. 207, May, Princeton, NJ: International Economics Section, Princeton University, pp. 1–10.

Gozzi, J.C., R. Levine and S. Schmukler (2008), 'Internationalization and the evolution of corporate valuation', *Journal of Financial Economics*, **88**, 607–32.

Gozzi, J.C., R. Levine and S. Schmukler (2010), 'Patterns of international capital raisings', *Journal of International Economics*, **8**(1), 45–57.

Henry, P. (2006), 'Capital account liberalization: theory, evidence, and speculation', *Journal of Economic Literature*, **45**, 887–935.

Kaminsky, G. and S. Schmukler (2008), 'Short-run pain, long-run gain: the effects of financial liberalization', *Review of Finance–Journal of the European Finance Association*, **12**, 253–92.

Kose, M., E. Prasad, K. Rogoff and S. Wei (2006), 'Financial globalization: a reappraisal', Working Paper No. 06/189, IMF and Working Paper No. 12484, NBER.

Le Fort, G. and S. Lehmann (2003), 'The unremunerated reserve requirement and net capital flows: Chile in the 1990s', *CEPAL Review*, **81**, 33–64.

Levine, R. and S. Schmukler (2006), 'Internationalization and stock market liquidity', *Review of Finance–Journal of the European Finance Association*, **10**, 153–87.

Levine, R. and S. Schmukler (2007), 'Migration, spillovers, and trade diversion: the impact of internationalization on domestic stock market liquidity', *Journal of Banking and Finance*, **31**, 1595–612.

Levy-Yeyati, E., S. Schmukler and N. van Horen (2004), 'The price of inconvertible deposits: the stock market boom during the Argentine crisis', *Economic Letters*, **83**, 7–13.

Levy-Yeyati, E., S. Schmukler and N. Van Horen (2008), 'Emerging market liquidity and crisis', *Journal of the European Economic Association*, **6**(2–3), 668–82.

Levy-Yeyati, E., S. Schmukler and N. van Horen (2009), 'International financial integration through the law of one price: the role of liquidity and capital controls', *Journal of Financial Intermediation*, **18**, 432–63.

Melvin, M. (2003), 'A stock market boom during a financial crisis? ADRs and capital outflows in Argentina', *Economic Letters*, **81**, 129–36.

Obstfeld, M. (1994), 'Risk-taking, global diversification, and growth', *American Economic Review*, **84**, 1310–29.

Pasquariello, P. (2008), 'The anatomy of financial crises: evidence from the emerging ADR market', *Journal of International Economics*, **76**(2), 193–207.

Perry, G. and L. Servén (2003), 'The anatomy of a multiple crisis. Why was Argentina special and what can we learn from it?', Policy Research Working Paper No. 3081, World Bank.

Rabinovitch, R., A.C. Silva and R. Susmel (2003), 'Returns on ADRs and arbitrage in emerging markets', *Emerging Markets Review*, **4**, 225–47.

Rodrik, D. (1998), 'Who needs capital-account convertibility?', in S. Fischer, R.N. Cooper, R. Dornbusch, P.M. Garber, C. Massad, J.J. Polak, D. Rodrik and S.S. Tarapore, *Should the IMF Pursue Capital-Account Convertibility?*, Princeton Essay in International Finance No. 207, May, Princeton, NJ: International Economics Section, Princeton University, pp. 55–65.

Rogoff, K. (1999), 'International institutions for reducing global financial instability', *Journal of Economic Perspectives*, **13**, 21–42.

Soros, G. (2002), *George Soros on Globalization*, New York: Public Affairs.
Stiglitz, J. (2000), 'Capital market liberalization, economic growth, and instability', *World Development*, **28**, 1075–86.
Stiglitz, J. (2002), *Globalization and its Discontents*, New York: W.W. Norton and Company.
Summers, L. (2000), 'International financial crises: causes, prevention, and cures', *American Economic Review*, **90**, 1–16.

7. Managing capital flows: experiences from Central and Eastern Europe*
Jürgen von Hagen and Iulia Siedschlag

7.1 INTRODUCTION

The twelve states that entered the European Union (EU) in 2004 achieved considerable macroeconomic stabilization during the accession process. Given the different initial conditions and economic characteristics of Cyprus and Malta, we focus on the Central and Eastern European (CEE) countries.[1]

The CEE countries went through the transition from central planning to market economies, beginning with severe recessions, high inflation, and financial instability. In due course, the inflation rates came down and nominal interest rates declined. Public debt has been stabilized, though high and persistent deficits and the need for further fiscal adjustments are still critical issues in several cases.

In the years to come, the new EU member states will face two principal challenges in formulating macroeconomic policies. The first is to manage the continued and likely rapid process of further real economic convergence, which will come with high real GDP and productivity growth rates, and large capital inflows. The second is to achieve the degree of nominal convergence required to enter into (the Third Stage of) European Economic and Monetary Union (EMU). These two challenges are not unrelated, as rapid growth and large capital inflows can make it more difficult to achieve nominal convergence, although, as we have argued (von Hagen and Traistaru-Siedschlag, 2006), there are good reasons to believe that real convergence would be easier to manage for some of the countries at least, if they were allowed to adopt the euro immediately. Both challenges relate mainly to fiscal policy: managing capital inflows, because fiscal policy can absorb part of their demand effects; and nominal convergence, because the sustainability of public finances is part of the requirement for entering EMU.

Lifting capital controls and restrictions on foreign currency trade was one of the conditions these states had to meet to qualify for EU

Experiences from Central and Eastern Europe 193

membership. Thus, the CEE countries went from being largely closed to being largely open to international capital flows. This chapter discusses their experience with capital account liberalization and with coping with large capital inflows. We begin in Section 7.2 with a discussion of basic economic characteristics and the real convergence achieved so far. In Section 7.3, we discuss the pace and sequencing of capital account liberalization and the degree of international financial integration[2] achieved so far. In Section 7.4, we analyze trends and patterns of capital inflows in these countries in recent years. Some stylized facts are useful for understanding the macroeconomic implications and policy challenges of coping with large capital inflows discussed in Section 7.5. Finally, we conclude in Section 7.6 with policy implications for emerging Asian countries.

7.2 BASIC ECONOMIC CHARACTERISTICS AND REAL CONVERGENCE

The 10 CEE countries or EU-10 are small open economies. As a group they amount to about 21 per cent of the EU-27 population and 11 per cent of the EU-27 total GDP in Purchasing Power Standards. Figure 7.1 shows that the smallest among them (Estonia, Latvia, Lithuania, Slovak Republic, Slovenia, and Bulgaria) are comparable in economic size to Luxembourg, while the Czech Republic, Hungary, and Romania are similar in size to Ireland, and Poland is similar to the Netherlands. By

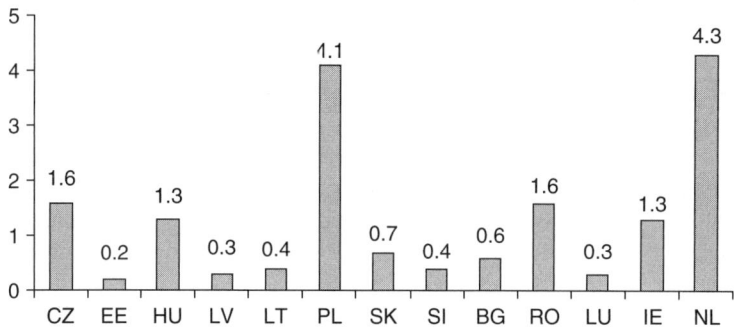

Note: CZ – Czech Republic, EE – Estonia, HU – Hungary, LV – Latvia, LT – Lithuania, PL – Poland, SK – Slovak Republic, SI – Slovenia, BG – Bulgaria, RO – Romania, LU – Luxembourg, IE – Ireland, NL – The Netherlands.

Source: Based on the AMECO Database, European Commission.

Figure 7.1 GDP in PPS, 2006 (% in EU-27)

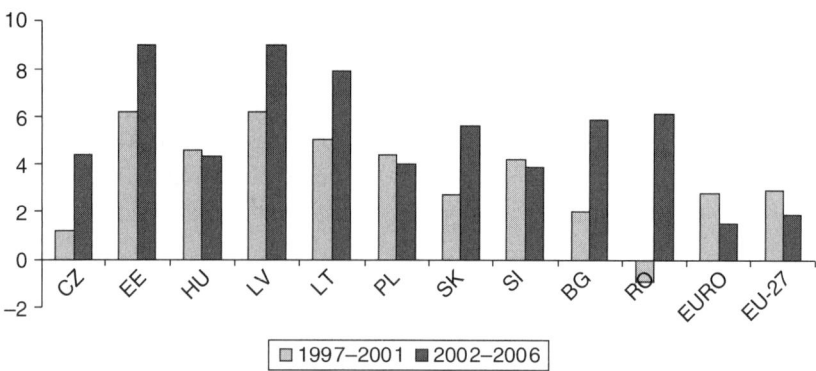

Note: CZ – Czech Republic, EE – Estonia, HU – Hungary, LV – Latvia, LT – Lithuania, PL – Poland, SK – Slovak Republic, SI – Slovenia, BG – Bulgaria, RO – Romania.

Source: European Commission, Economic Forecast, Spring 2007.

Figure 7.2 Real GDP growth rates, 1997–2006

European standards, Luxembourg, Ireland, and the Netherlands are also small open economies.

The EU-10 also have a liberal trade regime. Trade openness, measured as total exports and imports of goods and services as a percentage of GDP, exceeded 100 per cent in 2006, except for Romania and Poland at 76.9 per cent and 81.9 per cent, respectively; the most open is the Slovak Republic at 176 per cent. Gross fixed capital formation as per cent of GDP ranged from 20 per cent in Poland to over 34 per cent in Latvia in 2006, generally higher than the euro area average of 21.1 per cent. Given the low levels of per capita income in these countries, investment rates are expected to remain high in the foreseeable future.

Over the past decade, the CEE countries experienced a strong process of real convergence to the EU in terms of real GDP per capita and productivity levels. As shown in Figure 7.2, real GDP growth rate averaged 3.6 per cent during 1997–2001, and 5.4 per cent during 2002–06, while the euro area grew at 2.8 per cent and 1.5 per cent, respectively. The three Baltic countries – Estonia, Latvia, and Lithuania – experienced the highest growth rates. Over the same period, real growth remained significantly vigorous in the CEE countries even though growth in the euro area slowed down.

There is a significant negative correlation between the level of GDP per capita in 1997 and the average annual growth rates over 1997–2006, as countries with low initial per capita income levels grew faster than richer countries. The three Baltic countries, as well as Bulgaria and Romania, which have the lowest levels of per capita income, are expected to continue to post the highest growth rates among the EU countries.

Between 1997 and 2006 labor productivity growth, measured as the increase in real GDP per person employed, has been much higher in EU-10 than the euro area, with the three Baltic countries again experiencing highest growth rates. Thus, there is a clear tendency for productivity levels to converge as countries with low initial levels of productivity enjoyed higher growth rates in comparison to countries with higher levels.

7.3 CAPITAL ACCOUNT LIBERALIZATION AND INTERNATIONAL FINANCIAL INTEGRATION

In this section, we present an overview of the pace and sequencing of capital account liberalization in the 10 CEE countries before their accession to the EU and analyze the degree of their international financial integration to date.

At the beginning of the transition to market economies, all 10 CEE countries had closed capital accounts. Capital account liberalization was part of their integration into the world economy but the pace was country-specific, reflecting different initial conditions and macroeconomic development.[3] As a first step, current account convertibility was achieved between 1994 and 1996 as part of IMF membership obligations.[4] For the Czech Republic, Hungary, Poland, and the Slovak Republic, the application for the Organisation for Economic Co-operation and Development (OECD) membership in 1993–94 was an additional catalyst for capital account liberalization. But most importantly, the prospect of EU membership and the accession negotiations provided an institutional anchor for capital account liberalization in all CEE countries.

Since the free movement of capital among member states and between member states and third countries is part of the European Commission (EC) Treaty,[5] EU accession required full capital account liberalization. A schedule of steps for capital account liberalization was negotiated between each CEE country and the EC. Deviations from this schedule were allowed only in circumstances that had the potential to undermine the conduct of monetary and exchange rate policies. Transitional arrangements allowing some restrictions to be maintained beyond the entry into the EU were implemented for all CEE countries, mostly with respect to politically sensitive areas such as the acquisition of agricultural and forestry land and real estate.

Three common features can be identified from the experience of the

CEE countries with regard to the sequencing of the process of capital account liberalization: (i) restrictions on FDI were removed before portfolio flows were liberalized; (ii) capital inflows were liberalized before capital outflows; and (iii) long-term capital flows were liberalized before short-term flows. Regarding the pace of capital account liberalization, we can distinguish two groups of countries. First, the Baltic countries and the Czech Republic had abolished most restrictions on capital transactions by 1995. By contrast, Hungary, Poland, the Slovak Republic and Slovenia opened their capital accounts more gradually, achieving full liberalization in 2001–04. We include Bulgaria and Romania in this latter group, as they joined the EU only in 2007. On capital transactions controls in place at the end of 2006 in the 10 CEE countries, the number ranges from two in Romania to eleven in Poland. All 10 countries maintain controls for real estate transactions. With the exception of Hungary, all have specific provisions with respect to commercial banks and institutional investors.[6]

7.3.1 Assessing Capital Account Liberalization

The traditional approach for assessing capital account openness is to look at legal restrictions on cross-border capital flows (*de jure* measures) grouped into direct (administrative) and indirect (market-based) restrictions. The IMF's *Annual Report on Exchange Arrangements and Exchange Restrictions* (AREAER) has been used to construct quantitative measures of capital account openness ranging from binary measures (0/1 dummy variables) (Grilli and Milesi-Ferretti, 1995) to more sophisticated indices of financial openness (Chinn and Ito, 2006; Miniane, 2004; Mody and Murshid, 2005; Quinn, 2003).

However, these *de jure* measures may not accurately capture the extent of capital account openness (Kose et al., 2006). First, the AREAER information is related to foreign exchange restrictions, which do not necessarily limit capital flows. Second, they do not reflect the enforcement of capital controls nor their effectiveness. Finally, other financial regulations, such as prudential caps on the foreign-exchange exposure of domestic banks, restrict capital flows, but they are not counted as capital controls.

An alternative approach to measure capital account openness is to use *de facto* measures that reflect international financial integration (see for example Prasad et al., 2003; Kose et al., 2006; Lane and Milesi-Ferretti, 2006). Such measures are based on actual capital flows and more accurately reflect the capital account openness in practice. To illustrate the extent of capital account liberalization in the CEE countries, we analyze the evolution of the sum of gross external position, i.e., the sum of foreign assets and liabilities, as a ratio to GDP,[7] as an indicator of international

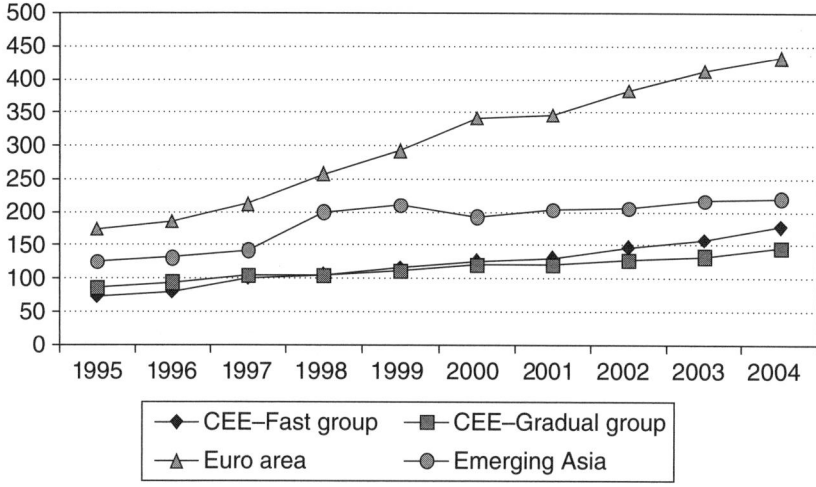

Source: Authors' calculations based on the dataset from Lane and Milesi-Ferretti (2006).

Figure 7.3 International financial integration of the CEE countries, euro area, and emerging Asia, 1995–2004

financial integration. We draw on the database constructed by Lane and Milesi-Ferretti (2006) covering 145 countries from 1970 to 2004, which are able to account for valuation effects and correct for cross-country differences in data definitions and variable construction.

Figure 7.3 shows the evolution of the cross-country average[8] of this indicator over the period from 1995 to 2004 in the 10 CEE countries, the euro area,[9] and the group of emerging Asian economies (EAE).[10] Over the entire period, international financial integration was lower in the 10 CEE countries than in the euro area and the EAE group. The countries that rapidly liberalized their capital accounts experienced a stronger financial integration than gradual liberalizers since 2000.

Over the period from 1995 to 2004, the 10 CEE countries experienced large net capital inflows and, as a consequence, dramatic changes in their net external positions. As shown in Figure 7.4, net capital flows into the CEE countries as a percentage of GDP were significantly larger than in the euro area and EAE. Since 2000, the group of fast liberalizers has experienced larger net capital inflows than the gradual liberalizers. This is in contrast to the improving net external positions of the EAE and the euro area.

The evolution of the composition of gross stocks of foreign assets and liabilities in the CEE countries over the 1995–2004 period reveal

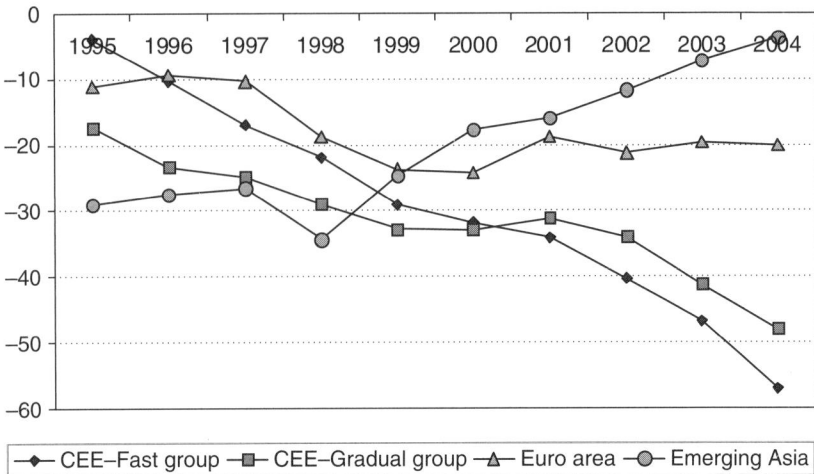

Source: Authors' calculations based on the dataset from Lane and Milesi-Ferretti (2006).

Figure 7.4 Net external positions

a common feature, which is the high share of portfolio debt in foreign assets and liabilities. This reflects the dominant role of the banking sector in financial intermediation and the large size of government securities markets in the CEE countries.[11]

Table 7.1 shows the composition of the stocks of external liabilities in the CEE countries in 1995 and 2004. The low share of portfolio equity in capital inflows in 1995 reflects the low level of capital market development and poor corporate governance in these countries. Only the Czech and Slovak Republics stand out for larger shares of equity in total foreign liabilities. This may be explained by the relative strength of the enterprise sector in these countries and their historical economic and trade links to Germany and Austria. Another factor may have been that the privatization of the industrial sector in these two countries was implemented by giving citizens shares in domestic companies. Note that the Czech Republic is the largest portfolio investor in the Slovak Republic.[12]

With the exception of Latvia, the share of FDI in total liabilities has increased, while that of external debt has decreased in all countries. Compared to the gradual liberalizers, the group of fast liberalizers has a large share of FDI and a small share of debt in total foreign liabilities. Excessive reliance on debt for financing current account deficits is commonly regarded as a sign of vulnerability to financial shocks, while FDI-based financing is perceived as promoting risk-sharing (Kose et al., 2006;

Table 7.1 Composition of stocks of external liabilities in the CEE countries (%)

	1995			2004		
	Equity	FDI	Debt	Equity	FDI	Debt
Czech Republic	9.7	27.0	63.2	8.9	53.5	36.3
Estonia	0.0	46.8	53.2	9.7	50.1	40.1
Latvia	0.4	31.9	67.8	0.9	27.3	71.6
Lithuania	0.7	19.7	79.6	1.1	40.0	58.9
Bulgaria	0.4	4.1	95.5	0.1	36.6	63.3
Hungary	0.5	29.3	70.2	8.6	44.7	44.8
Poland	1.1	13.2	85.7	6.4	41.6	52.0
Romania	0.0	5.8	94.2	3.0	39.8	57.2
Slovak Republic	7.1	16.6	76.3	9.4	38.5	52.1
Slovenia	1.0	27.6	71.4	2.9	27.3	69.7
CEE–Fast group	2.7	31.4	66.0	5.1	42.7	51.7
CEE–Gradual group	1.7	16.1	82.2	5.1	38.1	56.5

Source: Based on the dataset from Lane and Milesi-Ferretti (2006).

Lane and Milesi-Ferretti, 2006). From this point of view, the changes in the composition of gross stocks of foreign liabilities in the CEE countries between 1995 and 2005 seem positive.

Table 7.2 reports the composition of the foreign assets of CEE countries in 1995 and 2004. Foreign exchange reserves and portfolio debt dominate the composition of external assets in these countries. Following the liberalization of capital outflows and increase in cross-border assets trade, the shares of FDI and portfolio equity have surged, particularly in Estonia, Hungary, Slovenia and the Czech Republic. To the extent that the private sector in the CEE countries becomes more internationalized, it is likely that the FDI and portfolio equity outflows will further increase.

7.4 CAPITAL FLOWS: PATTERNS AND DETERMINANTS

As shown in the previous section, net capital flows to the CEE countries have been on a rising trend since the early 1990s. Unlike that in other regions (Asia and Latin America), the surge in capital flows has been associated with large current account deficits. In 2000–06, Estonia and Latvia stood out with deficits exceeding 8 per cent of GDP, both Lithuania and Hungary with 5.6 per cent, and the Czech Republic with 5.1 per cent. While the Czech

Table 7.2 Composition of stocks of foreign assets in the CEE countries (%)

	1995			2004		
	Equity+ FDI	Debt	Reserves	Equity+ FDI	Debt	Reserves
Czech Republic	3.6	49.1	47.4	9.3	47.0	41.3
Estonia	6.8	44.3	48.9	21.5	57.6	20.6
Latvia	14.3	57.2	28.6	3.2	75.5	20.7
Lithuania	0.4	37.2	62.4	6.3	45.8	47.9
Bulgaria	2.0	75.7	22.3	−0.2	41.3	58.8
Hungary	1.0	17.7	81.2	15.9	40.1	38.1
Poland	1.8	48.7	49.5	4.8	49.1	46.1
Romania	1.7	77.2	21.1	1.4	31.4	67.3
Slovak Republic	9.5	57.7	32.8	8.9	32.1	59.0
Slovenia	7.5	66.0	26.6	17.1	42.5	40.4
CEE–Fast	6.3	47.0	46.8	10.1	56.5	32.6
CEE–Gradual	4.0	57.2	38.9	8.0	39.4	51.6

Source: Authors' calculations based on the dataset from Lane and Milesi-Ferretti (2006).

Republic's current account deficit has not been supported by high real GDP growth rates in recent years, it has been accompanied by a high investment rate. Only Slovenia, the first country in this group to join the euro area, has kept its current account close to balance, on average, in recent years. Most new EU member states experienced sizeable real currency appreciations[13] in recent years (Figure 7.5). Thus, their large current account deficits are not an indication of weak currencies; instead, they reflect the large capital inflows these countries have attracted in recent years.

Following their entry into the EU, the experience of these countries has been diverse. Those countries that followed hard exchange rate pegs, namely Bulgaria, Estonia, Latvia and Lithuania, saw a widening of their current account deficits, while those that adopted floats, such as the Czech Republic and Poland, kept their current account deficits at smaller rates of GDP. Capital inflows rose in the former and fell in the latter. Slovenia, which adopted an intermediate peg, had the smallest capital inflows during that period.

The sustainability of persistent, large current account deficits depends in part on the type of capital inflows used to finance these deficits. Generally, direct investment is less vulnerable to sudden capital flow reversals and less fickle than portfolio investment. A high share of direct investment, therefore, results in less exposure to sudden reversals of capital flows that

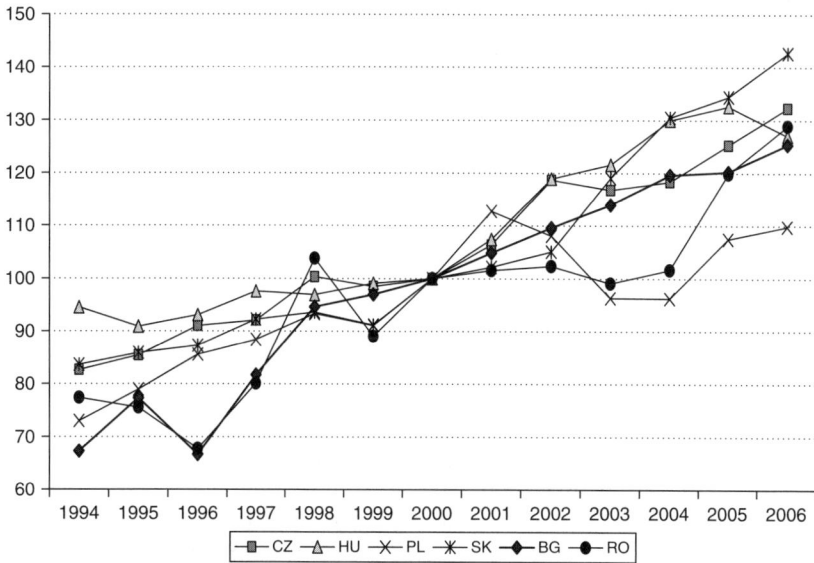

Note: CZ – Czech Republic, HU – Hungary, PL – Poland, SK – Slovak Republic, BG – Bulgaria, RO – Romania.

Figure 7.5 Real effective exchange rates

might occur due to changing expectations and investor confidence in the international capital market.[14]

External performance among new member states showed striking differences in the type of financing from 2000 to 2003. In Bulgaria, the Czech Republic, Poland, the Slovak Republic and Slovenia, net foreign direct investment (FDI) substantially exceeded the current account deficits. The other states, by contrast, took recourse to portfolio and other investment to a much larger extent. As a result, in 2000–06, foreign debt as a per cent of GDP increased significantly, particularly for Estonia, Hungary and Latvia where it hovered over 90 per cent in 2000–03, and exceeded 130 per cent in 2004–06. It is interesting to note that Estonia and Lithuania, which operate currency boards, have relatively low shares of FDI in financing their current account deficits. This suggests that the credibility of a hard peg is not the principal factor in determining the financing conditions.

Following their entry into the EU in 2004, Estonia and Hungary joined the group of countries with FDI exceeding the current account deficit. With the exception of Latvia and Lithuania, the share of direct investment in total capital inflows rose following accession to the EU. This suggests

Table 7.3   Marginal product of capital (multiple of German MPC)

	BG	CZ	EE	HU	LV	LT	PL	RO	SK	SI
1996	n.a.	4.17	10.35	4.87	16.36	9.95	8.07	n.a.	6.08	2.87
2002	10.9	4.08	6.03	3.88	9.80	6.74	5.48	16.0	4.33	2.15

Note: CZ – Czech Republic, EE – Estonia, HU – Hungary, LV – Latvia, LT – Lithuania, PL – Poland, SK – Slovak Republic, SI – Slovenia, BG – Bulgaria, RO – Romania

Source: Authors' estimates.

that the firm commitment to European integration and the assured access to West European markets persuaded international investors to make more long-term oriented investments. Furthermore, EU membership implies a higher degree of legal certainty for investors, and thus induces a reduction in country-risk premiums.

The prospect of further large capital inflows will be an important factor shaping the macroeconomic policies of the new member states in the years to come. As noted by Lipschitz et al. (2002) and Lipschitz (2004), the CEE countries in particular are rich in well-trained labor and poor in capital compared to their main trading partners, implying that their marginal product of capital is relatively high. Table 7.3 reports some 'back-of-the-envelope' estimates of the marginal product of capital relative to Germany in the new member states. Following Lipschitz et al. (2002), they are based on the assumption of Cobb-Douglas production functions with a capital elasticity of 1/3 and equal total factor productivities in all countries.[15] In 1996, the largest relative marginal products of capital estimated in this way were in the Baltic countries, followed by Poland.

EU membership and the adoption of the *acquis communautaire* represent a dramatic improvement in the institutional framework, which, in macroeconomic terms, can be interpreted as a rise in total factor productivity adding to the gap in the marginal products of capital in favor of the new member states.[16] Based on these considerations, Lipschitz estimates the cumulated potential future capital inflows to be between 65 per cent (Slovenia) and 596 per cent of GDP (Lithuania).[17] Obviously, these estimates must be taken cautiously given the uncertainty of the model and potential limits of capital supply.[18] Furthermore, the inflows will be distributed over time. Thus, capital inflows are likely to remain large in the foreseeable future.

Other factors contribute to this tendency (Begg et al., 2003). One is the relatively low level of financial development of the former socialist economies, which limits the extent to which capital investments are financed from domestic sources. Another is the likely increase in the demand for money as inflationary expectations continue to fall. Given the limited size of domestic securities markets, much of that increase will likely be accommodated by an inflow of foreign reserves at the central bank. Finally, Ahearne et al. (2007) show that capital flows within the euro area have responded much more strongly to differences in per-capita incomes or output–labor ratios than capital flows among European countries outside the euro area. This suggests that capital flows to the CEE countries will surge again upon their adoption of the euro.

7.5 MANAGEMENT OF LARGE CAPITAL INFLOWS: POLICY CHALLENGES

While large capital inflows are desirable in principle for relatively low-income countries, they also pose potential risks from two sides: overheating and volatility.

The first risk is that of the (in)famous convergence play, a combination of real appreciation and declining long-term interest rates due to falling inflationary expectations and country-risk premiums, which makes the economies even more attractive for short-term capital inflows and portfolio investment. If the demand financed by capital inflows falls entirely on tradables, it can simply be absorbed by large trade deficits. But the experiences of Italy, Spain and Portugal in the late 1980s to early 1990s showed that convergence play in practice fuels domestic demand for non-tradables where domestic supply is limited, overheating the economic with inflationary pressures.

These conventional demand effects may be augmented by financial market or balance sheet effects (Calvo and Reinhart, 1999; Calvo, 2002, 2003; Calvo et al., 2004), in what Calvo and Reinhart (1999) call the Fisherian channel of the transmission of capital inflows. The real appreciation of the home currency under fixed exchange rate induces a rise in the relative price of non-tradables. The more it rises, the more the central bank tries to stabilize the nominal exchange rate. As a result, producers of non-tradables face a lower ex-post real interest rate and rising cash flows that raise the value of assets that can be collateralized against bank loans. Large capital inflows are, therefore, often connected to asset and real estate price bubbles fuelling credit booms. To the extent that they are absorbed by an expansion of international reserves at the central bank, the ensuing monetary expansion contributes to this development.

We can assess this risk by looking at recent growth rates of narrow money and credit in the new member states. As shown in Table 7.4, growth

Table 7.4 *Annual average real money and credit growth, 1999–2006*

	Real money growth less real output growth		Real domestic credit growth less real output growth	
	1999–2003	2004–2006	1999–2003	2004–2006
Bulgaria	8.9	17.5	n.a.	n.a.
Slovak Republic	7.3	3.6	−1.2	4.8
Poland	6.7	6.4	6.3	−5.0
Czech Republic	6.4	3.4	−1.1	−0.1
Romania	−0.1	n.a.	n.a.	n.a.
Estonia	14.0	11.1	18.5	19.2
Latvia	13.2	15.9	28.0	30.9
Slovenia	12.5	9.1	13.5	15.9
Lithuania	11.3	20.1	12.2	32.3
Hungary	10.2	5.3	7.2	6.7

Notes: Average annual growth rates of narrow money and domestic credit.

Source: Based on IMF, International Financial Statistics.

rates of real money exceeded real GDP growth in almost all countries. Please note that average growth rates of real GDP over the same period are subtracted. Following accession, real money growth rose strongly in Bulgaria and Lithuania, but stabilized somewhat in Hungary and Slovenia. Falling interest rates and declining inflationary expectations may have caused a decline in the equilibrium velocity of money. If the income elasticity of the demand for money exceeds 1, strong real GDP growth adds another explanation. Thus, real money growth rates of 6–8 per cent above real output growth may not be excessive; but may raise cautionary flags.

The ongoing process of financial market development leads to the expectation that credit is growing fast in the new EU member states. Table 7.4 shows four countries – Estonia, Latvia, Lithuania, and Slovenia – with clear signs of strong credit booms. In the past, these four countries also put the largest weight on stabilizing their exchange rates among the countries in this group (von Hagen and Zhou, 2004; Backé and Thimann et al., 2004).

To prevent the large capital inflows from excessively fuelling domestic demand, many central banks, especially those with exchange rate pegs, have tried to sterilize them, resulting in rising foreign assets of central banks. However, this sterilization can be costly as foreign assets typically have interest rates below domestic-currency denominated assets. The

Table 7.5 Volatility of capital inflows

Bulgaria	Czech Republic	Estonia	Hungary	Latvia	Lithuania	Poland	Slovak Republic	Slovenia
8.2	4.6	3.6	5.0	5.6	3.0	2.8	2.6	4.4
0.6	0.7	0.3	−1.5	−5.4	−2.0	−1.4	−1.5	0.9
−12.1	−11.2	−6.5	−19.9	−5.8	−6.1	−3.8	−2.3	−9.9
(1996)	(1997)	(1997)	(1996)	(2002)	(1999)	(2001)	(1997)	(2003)

Notes: Standard deviations for Poland and Czech Republic: 1994–2002; for Slovak Republic: 1994–2000. All entries are in per cent of GDP.

Source: Authors' calculations based on IMF, International Financial Statistics.

resulting interest payments can be a substantial budget burden. Hauner (2005) estimates the costs of sterilizing capital inflows at 0.5–0.6 per cent of GDP annually for the CEE countries.

On the central bank net foreign assets accumulation, for Hungary, a country with pegged currency, the ratio of net foreign reserves to reserve money was stable or slightly increasing in 1994–2006, indicating that central bank money growth was primarily driven by foreign-exchange policies. Over the same period, floating-rate countries (Czech Republic, Poland, Romania and Slovak Republic) experienced a rising trend in the ratio of net foreign reserves to reserve money, indicating that their central banks purchased foreign assets on a large scale, presumably to keep their currencies from appreciating faster. Thus, large capital inflows fuelled monetary expansion even in countries that did not officially peg their exchange rates.

The second risk connected with large capital inflows is their volatility as experienced by new EU member states to date. Table 7.5 reports the standard deviation of annual capital inflows relative to GDP between 1994 and 2003. This ratio varied between 2.6 per cent of GDP for the Slovak Republic and 5.0 per cent of GDP for Hungary. The table also shows that several countries in this group experienced large reversals of capital inflows, what Calvo and Reinhart (1999) call 'sudden stops'.

Between 1999 and 2000, capital inflows slowed down in most countries except for the Czech Republic, Estonia, and Slovenia. Between 1994 and 2003, eight of the ten countries experienced at least one year in which capital inflows declined by more than 5 per cent of GDP, while four experienced a decline of almost 10 per cent or more. This confirms the observation by Calvo and Reinhart (1999) that large capital inflows are often followed by sudden stops and reversals. Obviously, they have affected countries with very different exchange rate regimes, supporting Calvo's

(2003) argument that exchange rate policies are of secondary importance for the incidence of sudden stops. Note also that the largest reversals occurred around the year 2000, confirming the observation in Calvo and Reinhart (1999) and Calvo et al. (2004) that sudden stops are bunched in time and across countries.

Sudden stops create macroeconomic problems through the same channels discussed above in reverse (Calvo and Reinhart, 1999). A sudden stop contracts current account deficit or the money supply or both, which in turn contracts aggregate demand. The ensuing real currency depreciation drops the relative price of non-tradables. Producers of non-tradables now face higher ex-post real interest rates and lower asset values than anticipated, including those assets they can use as collateral for borrowing from banks. Deteriorating loan quality prompts banks to cut lending. The resulting credit crunch makes the recession more pronounced and longer lasting. This financial effect can be avoided by a large nominal currency depreciation, which, however, increases the foreign currency debt burden on the government and the private sector.

Coping with large capital inflows is a difficult task for macroeconomic policy. The obvious response is to tighten monetary policy to prevent aggregate demand from overheating with varying consequences under fixed and flexible exchange rate regimes. Episodes of large capital inflows into small open economies generate a preference for low exchange rate variability, even if the official exchange rate regime allows for a high degree of flexibility, dubbed the 'fear of floating' in recent literature. The reason is that, since emerging-market countries typically cannot borrow internationally in their own currency, large capital inflows lead to a mounting stock of foreign debt denominated in foreign currency. Exchange rate variations then expose the government and private sector to fluctuations in their balance sheets. Hausmann et al. (2001) show that fear of floating is strongly associated with a country's borrowing in foreign currency and the degree of exchange rate volatility it allows.[19]

If this is true for the new EU member states, they will show a tendency to tightly manage their exchange rates as the capital inflows continue to persist. As of 2006, Bulgaria, Lithuania, and Estonia have currency boards; Hungary and Latvia have intermediate pegs; Poland, Romania, the Slovak Republic and the Czech Republic have floating currency; and Slovenia has joined the euro area. They may even decide to enter the Exchange Rate Mechanism-2 (ERM-2) for that reason, hoping that it will offer more credibility to their commitment to exchange rate targets.[20] Yet, the comfort offered by an exchange rate peg in this situation can be quite deceptive. As the risk of exchange rate variability seems to be low, private borrowers and the government are more inclined to borrow in foreign currencies than they would be otherwise, which increases the exposure to sudden stops and exchange rate crises. As long as the capital inflows continue to be large, the exchange rate peg brings a monetary and credit expansion that aggravates the tendency for overheating. Once the capital flows dry up, the peg may come under speculative attacks, which, unless they can be successfully defended, are costly and more disruptive than the adjustment under a floating rate.

The ERM-2 may offer some relief and credibility in such a situation due to the financial support for interventions it provides, but the history of the early 1990s suggests that its usefulness is limited at best. The experience teaches that European exchange rates tend to become objects of politics, especially in situations where there is market tension. The countries exposed to convergence play failed to adjust their exchange rates in a timely way in the late 1980s and early 1990s, and this contributed to the size of the later devaluations and currency crises. For instance, when Germany asked for a revaluation of the deutschmark to absorb the post-unification capital inflows, other governments and central banks were unwilling to grant it. It is not clear a priori that the new member states would not see similar resistance against repeated devaluations of the euro against their currencies, which might be required to counteract inflationary tendencies if capital inflows continued during their ERM-2 membership. Thus, the multilateral nature of the ERM-2 does not obviously add to its economic rationality. It is equally uncertain that the multilateral political negotiations required for devaluations can be completed fast enough in the case of a sudden stop. The multilateral political framework may, in contrast, create ambiguities and rumors in the markets, which can undermine the credibility of the pegs.

Since a sudden stop of capital inflows is equivalent to a cut in international credit to the home economy, the appropriate response by the central bank is to expand credit to the private sector. This can be done through open market operations or loans to the banking system under a flexible exchange rate and entail a nominal depreciation of the currency. The latter also reduces the need for the relative price of non-tradables to fall, but increases the domestic value of the foreign debt burden on the government and the private sector to the extent that foreign debt is denominated in foreign currency. Maintaining an exchange rate peg, in contrast, allows one to avoid the valuation effect, but the loss of international reserves at the central bank leads to a monetary contraction that makes the credit crunch more severe. Thus, sudden stops create a monetary policy dilemma.

As recent literature has noted, euro-ization offers a partial way out of this dilemma.[21] First, it eliminates the valuation effect on the affected country's debt denominated in euros. Second, the supply of bank credit is no longer limited by the domestic central bank's supply of bank reserves but by the European Central Bank's (ECB's) supply of bank reserves. This makes the credit contraction less severe, as monetary policy will not add to it. As a result, countries facing large (and volatile) capital inflows should have a preference for either floating exchange rates or euro-ization, but avoid soft pegs, especially if, as in the case of the ERM-2, they are unprotected by capital controls.

Fiscal policy is the more appropriate policy instrument for dealing with capital flows. In the face of large inflows, tightening the fiscal stance helps reduce the risk of economic overheating. If tightening is achieved by raising tax rates, the result is buoyant tax revenues and, therefore, a strong temptation to expand fiscal spending. At the same time, initiatives to cut spending in the face of a strong economy will not be very popular. Furthermore, Calvo (2003) points out that, by raising distortionary taxes, the government may reduce the economy's growth potential and thus precipitate a sudden stop. It is important to achieve tightening by cutting government expenditures rather than by raising taxes. This makes the role of planning institutions and strict budget implementation especially important.[22]

As most of the new EU member states need to tighten their fiscal policies to meet the requirements of EMU, managing capital inflows and meeting these requirements are complementary goals for them. However, the countries with the tightest fiscal stance in recent years are also those that have experienced the strongest credit expansions. For them, a further tightening of fiscal policy to fend off the macroeconomic effects of large capital inflows may be asking too much (Jonas, 2004).

Managing large capital inflows also involves prudential supervision and banking regulation. Recent empirical studies show that large credit booms and strong real appreciations are among the best indicators of the risk of currency and banking crises.[23] Banking regulation can help to prevent capital inflows from spilling over into domestic credit booms (Begg et al., 2003).

One important feature of the financial opening of the CEE countries in this regard has been the transformation of banking sectors. At the beginning of this process in the early 1990s, the banking sectors consisted largely of a few incumbent institutions emerging from the socialist monobank systems in each country. The exception was the Baltic countries. Banking systems were generally quite weak, and they went through a series of crises. In the late 1990s, foreign banks were given permission to move into the CEE countries and quickly established a presence there.

In 2006, the market share of foreign-owned banks was at least 50 per cent in all the CEE countries, and over 80 per cent in Hungary, the Slovak

Republic, Czech Republic, Lithuania and Estonia (EBRD, 2006). This added significantly to the stability of the financial sector of these countries, as the parent banks have provided liquidity and capital support during banking crises, enabling their local subsidiaries to maintain lending when local banks had to cut back their own. Furthermore, the presence of foreign banks has added to the quality of banking supervision, since, under EU rules, supervisors in the parent banks' home countries are responsible for the consolidated institutions. It is, therefore, likely that the presence of foreign banks has strengthened the CEE countries' ability to cope with the macroeconomic challenges posed by large capital inflows.

7.6 LESSONS AND POLICY IMPLICATIONS FOR ASIA'S EMERGING ECONOMIES

Between 1995 and 2005 the 10 CEE countries achieved a high degree of market integration and macroeconomic stabilization as part of their accession process. Capital account opening formed part of the increasing integration of these countries into the world economy. EU accession and OECD membership were two important institutional anchors for their international financial integration.

As a consequence of large capital inflows in recent years, the net external position in the 10 CEE countries has changed dramatically from the mid-1990s. In 2004, their average net external position as a percentage of GDP was significantly larger than the average for the euro area and the group of emerging Asian countries. Since 2000, the group of fast liberalizers has experienced larger net capital flows than the gradual liberalizers.

While large capital inflows are in principle desirable for relatively low-income countries, they also pose the potential risk of sudden stops leading to large economic and financial imbalances. Coping with large capital inflows is a difficult task for macroeconomic policy. Since the underlying reason is real, there is not much monetary policy can do. The obvious response is to tighten monetary policy to prevent aggregate demand from overheating. With a fixed exchange rate, inflationary pressures result in a real appreciation, a loss in international competitiveness, and a widening current account deficit. With a flexible exchange rate, the central bank may be more successful in keeping inflation low, but at the cost of a nominal appreciation of the currency, with the same effect on competitiveness and the current account. We argue that fiscal policy is the more appropriate policy instrument for dealing with large capital inflows. Tightening the fiscal stance helps to reduce the risk of economic overheating. Further, in our view, more effective spending controls and improved budgeting procedures rather than higher taxes will best promote macroeconomic stability.

There is also a role for prudent banking and financial market supervision in steering clear of credit booms and asset price bubbles that make such scenarios more likely, but also for reducing the vulnerability of the financial sector and the exposure of the government to implicit liabilities that can result from a capital account crisis. Governments would be well advised to keep substantial safety margins with regard to both deficits and debt to assure that they can respond to a sudden stop with the necessary financial rescue of the banking system and a fiscal expansion to partly absorb the fall in aggregate demand.

NOTES

* This chapter is an updated and extended version of the authors' paper 'Macroeconomic adjustment in the new EU member states', SUERF Studies 2006/4, Vienna: SUERF – The European Money and Finance Forum, December 2006, which was originally presented at the SUERF/Central Bank of Malta Seminar on 'The Adoption of the Euro in New Member States: Challenges and Vulnerabilities on the Last Stretch' on 4–5 May 2006 and is reprinted with SUERF's permission.
1. The CEE countries are Bulgaria, Czech Republic, Estonia, Hungary, Latvia, Lithuania, Poland, Romania, Slovak Republic, and Slovenia.
2. Throughout this paper the terms 'international financial integration', 'capital account liberalization' and 'financial openness' are used interchangeably.
3. Árvai (2005) discusses in detail the capital account liberalization in eight of the new EU member states (Czech Republic, Estonia, Hungary, Latvia, Lithuania, Poland, Slovak Republic, and Slovenia).
4. Article VIII.
5. The relevant provisions are under Articles 56 EC to 60 EC.
6. Some of these provisions are prudential measures and their aim is not necessarily to control capital flows.
7. Stock-based measures are less affected by short-term economic fluctuations (IMF, 2007; Kose et al. 2006).
8. Unweighted cross-country averages.
9. The euro area includes Austria, Belgium, Finland, France, Germany, Greece, Italy, the Netherlands, Portugal, and Spain. Ireland and Luxembourg are not included as they are extreme outliers due to their positions as major offshore centers.
10. People's Republic of China, India, Indonesia, Korea, Malaysia, Philippines, Singapore, Thailand, and Viet Nam.
11. For a discussion of the composition of capital flows to CEE countries, see also Árvai (2005) and Lane and Milesi-Ferretti (2007).
12. See Lane and Milesi-Ferretti (2007).
13. Von Hagen and Traistaru-Siedschlag (2006) discuss in detail the extent and causes of real currency appreciation in the new EU member states.
14. Note, however, that even foreign direct investment inflows could be reversed quickly, if foreign investors could sell their assets in liquid domestic securities or equities markets (Buiter and Grafe, 2002).
15. Let $y_i = A_i (k_i)^\alpha$ be output per employed worker in country i, with k_i the capital–labor ratio, A_i total factor productivity, and $\alpha = 1/3$ the capital elasticity. The marginal

product of capital is $MPC_i = \alpha A_i(k_i)^{-(1-\alpha)}$. The capital–labor ratios are computed using output in PPP dollars from the World Economic Outlook 2004 database and labor force and unemployment data from the World Bank's World Development Indicators.
16. IMF (2003) presents empirical evidence that institutional quality affects economic growth. Studying growth patterns in transition economies, Grogan and Moers (2001) find that institutional improvements lead to higher growth and stronger foreign direct investment. Alfaro et al. (2003) find that, in a sample of 50 countries, institutional weakness is an important hindrance against capital inflows to poor countries.
17. Lipschitz does not give estimates for Cyprus and Malta.
18. Jonas (2004) notes that global capital flows to emerging market economies surged in 2003, but predicts that they will be reduced in the coming years.
19. Detken and Gaspar (2004) show that fear of floating could also stem from the combination of inflation targeting and a specific monetary-policy rule in a neo-Keynesian model.
20. The Exchange Rate Mechanism (ERM-2) is the official framework of the ECB within which EU countries can choose to peg their currencies to the euro. It stipulates a central parity which can be adjusted by agreement between the ECB and the respective country, and bands of +/− 2.25%. Importantly, it does not stipulate a requirement for the ECB to intervene in support of a participating currency. Countries that wish to join the euro area are required to participate in the ERM-2 for at least two years without devaluing their currencies on their own initiative.
21. See Begg et al. (2003) and the literature discussed there.
22. Kopits (2000) also notes the usefulness of credible medium-term fiscal plans ('rules' in his terminology) to avert currency crises in emerging market economies.
23. For banking crises, see Borio and Lowe (2004) and Ho and von Hagen (2007). For currency crises, see Kaminsky and Reinhardt (1999).

REFERENCES

Ahearne, A., B. Schmitz and J. von Hagen (2007), 'Current account imbalances in the euro area', Mimeo, University of Bonn and Bruegel, Brussels.

Alfaro, L., S. Kalemli-Ozcan and V. Volosovych (2003), 'Why doesn't capital flow from rich countries to poor countries? an empirical investigation', Working Paper, University of Houston.

Árvai, Z. (2005), 'Capital account liberalization, capital flow patterns, and policy responses in the EU's new member states', IMF Working Paper 05/213.

Backé, C. and C. Thimann (team leaders), O. Arratibel, O. Calvo-Gonzalez, A. Mehl and C. Nerlich (2004), 'The acceding countries' strategies towards ERM II and the euro: an analytical review', European Central Bank Occasional Paper No. 10.

Begg, D., B. Eichengreen, L. Halpern, J. von Hagen, and C. Wyplosz (2003), 'Sustainable regimes of capital movements in accession countries', CEPR Policy Paper 10, London: CEPR.

Borio, C. and P. Lowe (2004), 'Securing sustainable price stability: should credit come back from the wilderness?', BIS Working Paper No. 157.

Buiter, W.H. and C. Grafe (2002), 'Anchor, float, or abandon ship: exchange rate regimes for accession countries', Working Paper, European Bank for Reconstruction and Development.

Calvo, Guillermo (2002), 'Globalization hazard and delayed reform in emerging markets', *Economía*, **2**, 1–29.

Calvo, G. (2003), 'Explaining sudden stop, growth collapse, and BOP crises. The case of distortionary output taxes', *IMF Staff Papers*, **50**, 1–20.
Calvo, G. and C. Reinhart (1999), 'When capital inflows come to a sudden stop: consequences and policy options', Working Paper, University of Maryland.
Calvo, G., A. Izquierdo and L. F. Mejía (2004), 'On the empirics of sudden stops: the relevance of balance sheet effects', NBER Working Paper 10520.
Chinn, M. and H. Ito (2006), 'What matters for financial development? Capital controls, institutions and interactions', *Journal of Development Economics*, **81** (1), 163–92.
Detken, C. and V. Gaspar (2004), 'Fearless floating: maintaining price stability in a small open economy', mimeo, European Central Bank.
EBRD (European Bank for Reconstruction and Development) (2006), *Transition Report 2006*, London: EBRD.
Grilli, V. and G.M. Milesi-Ferretti (1995), 'Economic effects and structural determinants of capital controls', *IMF Staff Papers*, **42**(3), 517–51.
Grogan, L. and L. Moers (2001), 'Growth empirics with institutional measures for transition countries', *Economic Systems*, **25**, 323–44.
Hauner, D. (2005), 'A fiscal price tag for international reserves', IMF Working Paper 05/81.
Hausmann, R., E. Stein and U. Panizza (2001), 'Why countries float the way they float', *Journal of Economic Development*, **66**, 387–414.
Ho, T.K. and J. von Hagen (2007), 'Money market pressure and the determinants of banking crises', *Journal of Money, Credit, and Banking*, **39**(5), 1003–35.
IMF (International Monetary Fund) (2003), *World Economic Outlook*, Washington DC: International Monetary Fund.
IMF (2007), 'Reaping the benefits of financial globalization', IMF Discussion Paper, No. 06/07, June, Research Department.
Jonas, J. (2004), 'Comments on Jürgen von Hagen, fiscal positions and sustainability – policy challenges for EU accession countries', IMF-CNB Conference on Euro Adoption, Prague, February.
Kaminsky, G. and C. Reinhardt (1999), 'The twin crises: the causes of banking and balance-of-payments problems', *American Economic Review*, **89**, 473–500.
Kopits, G. (2000), 'How can fiscal policy help avert currency crises?', IMF Working Paper 00/185.
Kose, M.A., E. Prasad, K. Rogoff and S.J. Wei (2006), 'Financial globalization: a reappraisal', IMF Working Paper 06/189.
Lane, P.R. and G.M. Milesi-Ferretti (2006), 'The external wealth of nations mark II: revised and extended estimates of foreign assets and liabilities, 1970–2004', IMF Working Paper 06/69.
Lane, P.R. and G.M. Milesi-Ferretti (2007), 'Capital flows to Central and Eastern Europe', *Emerging Markets Review*, **8**(2), 106–23.
Lipschitz, L. (2004), 'Real convergence, capital flows, and monetary policy: notes on the European transition countries', mimeo, IMF.
Lipschitz, L., T. Lane and A. Mourmouras (2002), 'Capital flows to transition economies: master or servant?', IMF Working Paper 2/11.
Miniane, J. (2004), 'A new set of measures on capital account restrictions', *IMF Staff Papers*, **51**(2), 276–308.
MNB (National Bank of Hungary) (2003), *Annual Report for 2002*, Budapest: MNB.

Mody, A. and A.P. Murshid (2005), 'Growing up with capital flows', *Journal of International Economics*, **65**(1), 249–66.
OECD (2004), *Economic Survey of the Slovak Republic*, Paris: Organisation for Economic Co-operation and Development.
Prasad, E.S., K. Rogoff, S.J. Wei and M.A. Kose (2003), 'Effects of financial globalization on developing countries: some empirical evidence', IMF Occasional Paper No. 220.
Quinn, D. (2003), 'Capital account liberalization and financial globalization, 1890–1999: a synoptic view', *International Journal of Finance and Economics*, **8**(3), 189–204.
von Hagen, J. and J. Zhou (2004), 'Exchange rate policies on the last stretch', in G. Szapari and J. von Hagen (eds), *Monetary Strategies for Accession Countries*, Cheltenham, UK and Northampton, MA, USA: Edward Elgar, pp. 41–73.
von Hagen, J. and I. Traistaru-Siedschlag (2006), 'Macroeconomic adjustment in the new EU member states', SUERF Studies No. 2006/4, Vienna: European Money and Finance Forum.
World Bank (2006), *Global Development Finance Report*, Washington DC: World Bank.

PART III

Country Studies

8. Managing capital flows: the case of the People's Republic of China
Yongding Yu

8.1 INTRODUCTION

Since 1979 the economy of the People's Republic of China (PRC) has grown at an average annual rate of 9.7 per cent, making the PRC the world's fourth largest economy, just behind the US, Japan, and Germany. Surprisingly, the PRC economy has a very liberal trade regime and a trade/GDP ratio surpassing 67 per cent, much higher than either the US or Japan. The PRC is also the world's third largest recipient of foreign direct investment (FDI), with inflows of about $50–60 billion per annum, and the third largest capital exporting country with a current account surplus of about $200 billion in recent years.

The successful management of cross-border capital allowed the uninterrupted growth of the PRC's economic miracle. For example, despite the PRC's fragile financial system, the yuan escaped attacks by international speculators during the Asian financial crisis owing to capital controls. The PRC has also achieved an average growth rate of over 10 per cent for five consecutive years since 2002 while keeping inflation under control, despite the great pressure on the yuan to appreciate. However, the macroeconomic situation has changed since 2007. The PRC's internal and external imbalances and inflation have worsened; and asset markets have become increasingly volatile.

This chapter argues that the adequate management of cross-border capital flows is the key to the PRC's stable growth path. It aims to provide a comprehensive account of the evolution of the PRC's management of capital flows and to analyze possible trajectories for the management of capital flows in the future. The chapter is organized as follows. Following the introduction, Section 8.2 reviews the changing pattern of cross-border capital flows. Section 8.3 describes the evolution of capital controls, and Section 8.4 discusses the imbalances of international balance of payments (BOP) and exchange rate policy. Section 8.5 discusses the interaction between macroeconomic stability and capital flows management under the present situation. Finally, Section 8.6 concludes.

8.2 CAPITAL FLOWS IN THE PRC

The single most important feature of capital flows in the PRC is the overwhelming domination of FDI since the start of economic reforms. However, from 2003, cross-border capital flows in the PRC have taken a much more complicated shape.

8.2.1 The Changing Pattern of Capital Flows

The pattern of capital flows has gone through roughly three stages: (i) 1979 to 1991; (ii) 1992 to 2002; and (iii) 2003 to the present. In the first two stages, the changes in the pattern of capital flows basically involved FDI inflows. In 1979, when reform and opening up had just been launched, FDI inflows were a negligible $0.08 million. At the same time, the PRC faced two major constraints in its development: shortage of capital and shortage of foreign exchange reserves. Based on Deng Xiaoping's personal instructions, four Special Economic Zones were established, and were given power to use special policies aimed at attracting FDI. Later, more special regions and cities were opened to foreign investors. From 1984 to 1991, FDI grew at an annual rate of 20 per cent.

The reform and opening up process intensified following Deng Xiaoping's tours of South China in 1992. As a result, FDI inflows increased from $4.4 billion in 1991 to $11 billion in 1992; they slowed when the Asian financial crisis struck in 1997 but soon recovered in 2001 when the PRC joined the World Trade Organization (WTO). FDI inflows reached $52.7 billion in 2002, making the PRC the largest FDI recipient in the world.

In 2003, the economy finally broke loose from the spell of deflation, after seven years of expansionary monetary and fiscal policy. At the same time, both the current account and capital account surpluses rose significantly, causing strong pressure for appreciation of the yuan, which was placed on a *de facto* peg to the US dollar following the 1997–98 Asian financial crisis. The expectations for the yuan appreciation exercised a strong influence on the pattern of cross-border capital flows in the PRC.

Figure 8.1 shows that there have been several changes in the pattern of cross-border capital flows since then, and variations in capital account as a whole and in some sub-accounts in particular have also increased significantly.

The new pattern can be summarized as follows. First, while FDI still

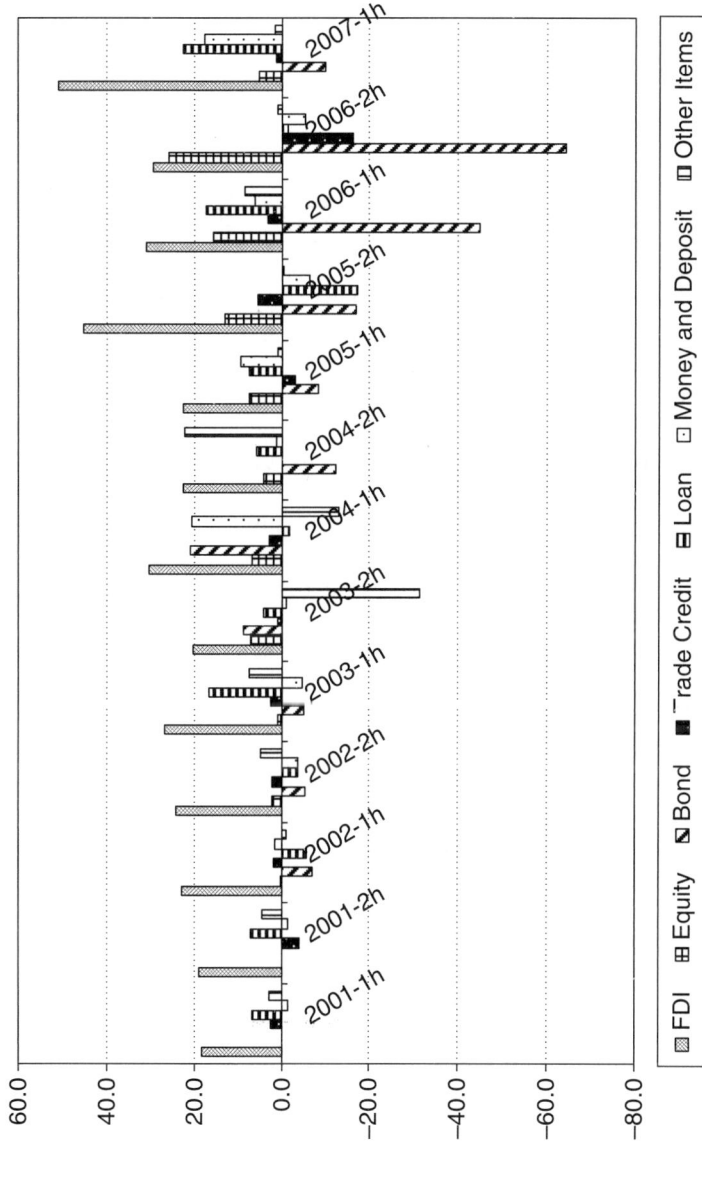

Source: State Administration of Foreign Exchange (SAFE).

Figure 8.1 Cross-border capital flows in the PRC, 2001–07 ($ billion)

Table 8.1   The PRC's debts, 2001–07 ($100 million)

	Gross external debt		Short-term external debt			Trade credits		
	Balance	Growth %	Balance	Growth %	Share %	Balance	Ratio to ST debt %	Ratio to gross debt %
2001	1848	26.8	653	399.0	35.3	363	55.6	19.6
2002	1863	0.8	708	8.4	38.0	413	58.3	22.2
2003	2088	12.1	922	30.2	44.2	517	56.1	24.8
2004	2475	18.5	1232	33.7	49.8	654	53.1	26.4
2005	2811	13.6	1561	26.7	55.6	908	58.2	32.3
2006	3230	14.9	1836	17.6	56.9	1040	56.6	32.2
2007Jun	3278	10.0	1849	11.2	56.4	1111	60.1	33.9

Source: State Administration of Foreign Exchange (SAFE), October 2007.

accounts for the bulk of capital inflows, other forms of capital inflows such as debt flows have increased significantly (Figure 8.1 and Table 8.1). Second, the account of errors and omissions has turned from negative balances into positive ones. Until the second half of 2001, there had always been concern about capital flight, which was mainly reflected in a negative balance in the errors and omissions account. However, since 2003 capital flight has ceased to be an issue. The errors and omission account deficit has narrowed and turned positive in 2004 and 2007.

Third, despite the fact that the PRC was a net capital exporter for more than one and a half decades, it consistently ran investment account deficits. However, in 2005, it began to run an investment income account surplus. Similarly, the PRC's transfer account surplus has also increased materially. Fourth, the purchasing of foreign bonds has increased since 2005. The increase in the first half of 2007 was quite dramatic (Figure 8.1). Commercial banks and non-bank financial institutions have increased their purchases of foreign bonds and equities to improve the quality of their assets.

In many recent studies, it is pointed out that 'unexplained' changes in foreign exchange reserves have increased significantly. In other words, a large proportion of the increase in foreign exchange reserves can no longer be explained by the trade surplus and FDI inflows. By contrast, in the past, the sum of FDI and trade surplus was roughly equal to the increase in foreign exchange reserves, and the residual would fall into the category of errors and omissions. The 'unexplained changes' in foreign exchange reserves are not an entry in the balance of payments sheet. The increase in 'unexplained changes' in foreign exchange reserves reflects the diversification and complication of cross-border capital flows in the PRC today.

Many in the PRC believe that because of the abundant opportunities for interest rate and exchange rate arbitrage and speculation on capital gains in the PRC's bubbling real estate market and equity market, the large trade surplus was deceiving, and a large proportion of the trade surplus is nothing but hot money in disguise, aimed at evading capital controls. Similarly, a large amount of FDI inflows is believed to be not FDI in its true sense. In other words, these FDI inflows are also arbitrage and speculative capital in disguise. There is some anecdotal evidence to support this conjecture. However, due to the lack of statistical evidence, no firm conclusions on the exact amount of hot money inflows via those channels can be drawn.

8.2.2 Factors Affecting the Pattern of Cross-border Capital Flows

The literature categorizes factors contributing to capital flows into developing countries as 'push' (economic conditions outside the host country) and 'pull' (the economic conditions of the host country) factors. It seems fair to say that the large and persistent FDI inflows into the PRC are attributable mainly to pull factors. The reason why FDI long dominated the pattern of cross-border capital flows can be found in government policies. Learning from the Latin American crisis experience in the 1980s, the PRC government decided that the form of foreign capital should be FDI and that indirect capital inflows were better avoided. Hence preferential policies towards FDI were adopted from the very beginning. These policies, roughly in order of implementation, included income tax exemptions and reductions, tariff exemptions and reductions, value-added tax rebates, preferential loans, and so on.

The government shifted its policy focus from attracting FDI to fulfilling its commitments toward liberalization after its WTO entry in 2001. The liberalization measures included: (i) relaxing local content requirements; (ii) relaxing export requirements; (iii) liberalizing the current account, which basically was done before the PRC's entry into the WTO; (iv) dismantling the requirement for self-balancing of foreign currency; (v) easing restrictions on foreign ownership; and (vi) dismantling barriers to highly profitable and sensitive sectors, especially the four most important sectors: telecommunication, banking, insurance, and professional services. Inherent factors of the PRC economy have also played important roles in attracting FDI inflows, such as low-cost skilled labor, a huge domestic market, decent infrastructure, and political stability (Yu, 2006).

As mentioned earlier, the pattern of cross-border capital flows in the

PRC has become much more complicated and elusive since 2003. Hence, explanations of the new pattern have also become much more difficult.

First, one possible reason for the surge in foreign borrowing is that, due to expectations for an appreciation of the yuan exchange rate, short-term borrowings are used for the purposes of locking in foreign exchange rate risks as well as arbitraging. Second, a major cause of the surge of equity inflows was initial public offerings (IPOs) by the PRC enterprises in overseas equity markets, especially the Hong Kong stock exchange.

Indeed, foreign equity investment in the PRC increased significantly in 2006, especially in the second half of the year, as revitalization followed the successful reform of the PRC's equity market, which had been characterized by the separation of shares of the same listed company between floating and non-floating shares. By the end of 2004, 64 per cent of shares in the PRC's share markets were non-floating, and state-owned shares accounted for 74 per cent of the non-floating shares. As a result of the separation, the rights of owners of the same shares became extremely unequal. The owners of floating shares have no say in the governance of the enterprises. The owners of non-floating shares, as majority share owners, often issue new shares at the expense of the interest of floating share owners. As a result of the reform, non-floating shares are floated, after appropriate compensation is given to existing owners of floating shares. As a result of the change, confidence returned to the equity market, and share prices started to soar. In early 2006, the equity price index in the Shanghai Stock Exchange was just above 1000 points. In March 2007, it rose to more than 3000 points.

To take advantage of the bull market, foreign security companies started to buy A shares via formal channels (Qualified Foreign Institutional Investment – QFII) as well as informal channels. This flow subsided in the first quarter of 2007, because, perhaps, most foreign investment had decided that the PRC's equity prices were already too high, and unwound their long position. At that time, the mood in the PRC's equity markets was changing, and fear of a major crash was taking hold of the market. The PRC's equity markets may have been perceived as too risky by foreign investors. Unless a major crash does indeed take place, and prices come to be seen as really cheap, large scale capital inflows into the PRC's equity markets seem unlikely in the near future.

Third, the fact that the PRC's investment account has changed from negative to positive can be attributed to the accumulation of foreign exchange reserves. This is likely the case. The PRC has accumulated $1.6 trillion in assets vis-à-vis its accumulated FDI stock of about $700 billion. Despite this, the yields on the PRC's foreign exchange reserves are low compared to the profitability of FDI.

Fourth, the purchasing of foreign bonds increased in 2006 even more significantly. This may be the result of the measures taken by the People's Bank of China (PBOC) to liberalize the restrictions on commercial banks' purchases of foreign bonds and other debt instruments to encourage outflows of funds so as to reduce pressure for yuan appreciation.

Fifth, the negative sign of 'other items' in 2004 may be attributed to PBOC's capital injection into the commercial banks (Figure 8.1). After receiving capital injections, commercial banks have been maintaining their new capital in the form of foreign assets, and are not allowed to convert these assets into yuan. They have had to keep these foreign exchanges in overseas accounts for a certain period of time. Since 2005, commercial banks have sometimes been engaged in currency swaps. The increases in inflows of the money and deposits account in 2007 (Figure 8.1) are related to the unwinding of previous positions by commercial banks.

Six, a large proportion of the 'unexplained' capital outflows in 2006 can be explained by IPO repatriations, options with Central Huijin (a state-owned financial controlling company that nominally owns all three big commercial banks that have received capital injections in 2003), and speculative inflows into the PRC's foreign exchange reserves. Hence, speculative capital may not have been a major contributor to capital outflows in the year. The same facts can be used to account for the 'unexplained capital inflows' in 2007. However, a large portion of the foreign exchange reserve increase still remains unexplained, after the trade surplus, FDI, interest income, IPO repatriations, and the exercise of options with Central Huijin are taken into account. Hence, speculative capital inflows betting on the rise in the PRC's currency, property, and equity prices are the likely suspects for the rest of the increase. Although there are no reliable statistics available, my sense is that the main driver of the unexplained increase in foreign exchange reserves in 2007 is the unwinding of previous positions by commercial banks. The role of the carry trade and speculative capital inflows in the increase in foreign exchange reserves seems also very important.

8.3 THE EVOLUTION OF THE PRC'S CAPITAL CONTROLS

This section discusses two aspects of the management of cross-border capital flows: the long-run aspect and short-run aspect. The long-run aspect is related to capital controls and liberalization. The short-run aspect is related to macroeconomic stability. The literature on capital account liberalization is comprised of two main parts: the costs and benefits of capital account liberalization and the sequencing of capital flow liberalization. The two components are basically answers to two questions: why capital flows should/should not be liberalized and how they should be liberalized.

8.3.1 Arguments For and Against Capital Controls

The benefits of capital mobility seem unquestionable. In the literature, the main arguments for the free movement of capital include: (i) greater international investment opportunities; (ii) increased opportunities for portfolio diversification; (iii) capital controls are ineffective and give rise to corruption and favoritism; and (iv) individuals should be allowed to dispose of their own wealth and income as they see fit.

Then why does the PRC government still impose capital controls? First, they are necessary to maintain monetary policy independence while the PRC is still preparing to adopt a floating exchange rate regime. Second, the PRC's financial system is fragile and its economic structure rigid. Sudden changes in the direction of cross-border capital flows can severely destabilize the economy. With a more flexible exchange rate, capital inflows will cause large appreciations. The lack of financial instruments for hedging renders the PRC enterprises vulnerable to exchange rate risks. Third, the PRC's economic reform has not been completed and property rights issues remain. Ambiguous ownership may encourage money laundering and asset stripping, which can lead to social tension. Fourth, the government hoped to prevent the introduction of the wrong type of capital. The wrong incentives created by the current fiscal system allow local governments to use foreign capital inflows of any type regardless of long-term consequences to the country as a whole. And fifth, given the huge foreign exchange reserves, an open capital account would attract predatory attacks by international speculators. Thus a firewall of capital controls is needed to protect the PRC.

8.3.2 Some Important Features of the PRC's Capital Controls

The regime of capital controls that was adopted from the PRC's opening up until the mid-1990s comprises the following important features.

First, all inward FDI had to be approved by and registered with both the planning and foreign trade departments of the government. Approved investors could remit foreign exchange into the PRC but the conversion of foreign exchange into the yuan required advance approval from the SAFE or its provincial branches. Self-balancing of foreign exchanges was required for virtually all foreign-funded enterprises. Meanwhile, investors of approved outward FDI must register their investment with foreign exchange authorities before remitting foreign exchanges to the host country of investment.

Second, foreign investors were in general prohibited from using the yuan to invest in the stock exchanges inside the PRC. They were only allowed to use foreign exchange to invest in so-called B shares.

Third, the issuers of bonds abroad were limited to 10 authorized window institutions in addition to the Ministry of Finance and the state policy banks. With the exception of SAFE-authorized financial institutions engaged in foreign borrowing and large-size enterprise groups, the PRC residents were not allowed to buy foreign securities of any kind.

Fourth, the entities eligible for borrowing from foreign banks and other foreign financial institutions were financial institutions authorized by the SAFE and industrial and commercial enterprises or groups of enterprises approved by the SAFE. The PRC residents were not allowed to borrow from foreign banks or other foreign financial institutions without receiving prior approval by the government.

8.3.3 The PRC's Capital Account Liberalization

Capital controls have become very costly and increasingly difficult to implement, placing an unbearable workload on the government, due to the opening of the country's financial service sector and liberalized trade regime. They also caused great inconvenience to enterprises and banks. Moreover, the WTO entry adds a new dimension to the urgency of capital liberalization. On the one hand, it is clear that the PRC needs to liberalize its capital account. On the other hand, an all-at-once liberalization is out of the question. Therefore, the question concerns the proper sequencing so as to strike a balance between improving resource allocation by capital account liberalization and maintaining financial stability in order to minimize the welfare losses during transition (Yu, 2007).

The PRC's capital account liberalization has followed roughly the sequence depicted in Figure 8.2. The first important step in liberalization took place in 1986, when foreign exchange controls were relaxed for foreign-funded enterprises. FDI firms were allowed to use their yuan earnings to finance export production or to convert the earnings into foreign exchanges in swap markets that were opened in 1985. The most significant development in the liberalization of capital flows was the realization of currency convertibility for current account transactions in 1996, which significantly increased FDI. After the merger of the PRC's official foreign exchange market with the swap market in 1994, a unified but significantly depreciated yuan vis-à-vis the US dollar was achieved. The government

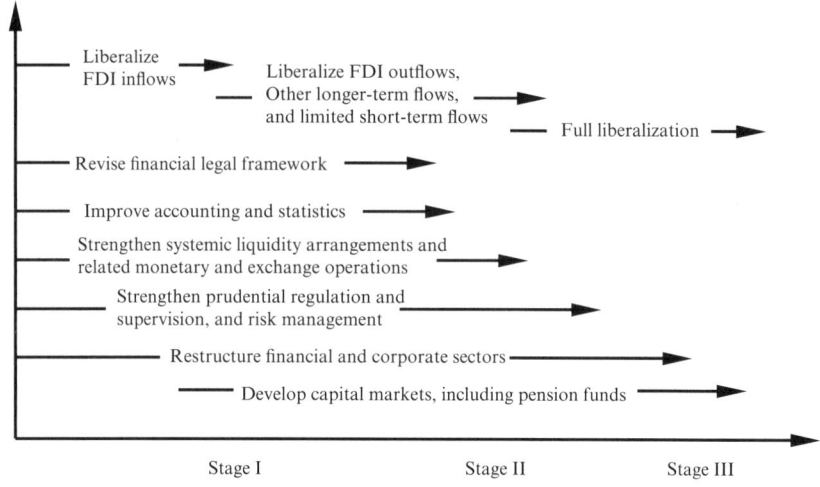

Source: Ishii and Haberneirer (2002).

Figure 8.2 A stylized representation of sequencing

then proceeded to further liberalize the capital account but the process was abruptly halted in 1997 due to the Asian crisis, when tight controls were put in place on both the current and capital accounts to prevent capital flight.

In October 1998, the PRC's Supreme Court carried out a crackdown on illegal foreign exchange transactions. The government sent tens of thousands of auditors to enterprises and financial institutions to track down and recover illegally transferred money. Consequently, the capital flight was brought under control and the official foreign exchange reserves returned to their normal growth level in the fourth quarter of 1998.

As the PRC had to liberalize its financial service sector entirely within five years of entry into the WTO, several measures were undertaken toward this end. FDI flows were liberalized entirely. Requirements for foreign investors such as self-balancing of foreign exchanges were abolished. Application and approval processes were greatly simplified. Foreign commercial banks and non-financial institutions were allowed to operate with only minimum restrictions. The government also re-launched capital account liberalization, and since 2003 the process has been significantly accelerated.

The impetus behind the speed-up is the desire of the government to reduce pressure for yuan appreciation.

Table 8.2 Summary: the PRC's capital controls as of 2008

		Inflows	Outflows
Money market	Non-residents	No permission	No permission
	Residents	Prior approval by the PBOC and SAFE is required	No permission for residents, except authorized entities
Stock market	Non-residents	B shares and QFII	Sell B shares, repatriate QFII
	Residents	Sell H (or N or S) share abroad, repatriate of QDII	QDII
Bonds and other debts	Non-residents	QFII	No permission, except for some international finance entity, repatriate QFII
	Residents	Prior approval by the PBOC and SAFE is required. Bonds issued abroad must be incorporated into the State external debt plan.	No permission for residents, except authorized entities
Derivatives and other instruments	Non-residents	No permission	No permission
	Residents	Operations in such instruments by financial institutions are subject to prior review of qualifications and to limits on open foreign exchange position.	Operations in such instruments by financial institutions are subject to prior review of qualifications and to limits on open foreign exchange position.

The main features of the PRC's capital controls after more than two decades of evolution are summarized in Table 8.2. Calculations, based on the IMF formula, show that as of 2008 80 per cent of the PRC's capital account has been liberalized.

8.4 BALANCE OF PAYMENT IMBALANCE AND EXCHANGE RATE POLICY

The PRC has been running capital account surpluses almost every year since the early 1980s, except in 1998 owing to the 1997 Asian crisis, and has run a current account surplus consistently since the early 1990s (Figure 8.3).

The persistent 'twin surpluses' have resulted in a continuous increase in foreign exchange reserves. By the end of 2007, the PRC's foreign exchange reserves surpassed $1.6 trillion. As discussed, the main contributor to the PRC's accumulation of foreign exchange reserves in the past was the capital account surplus, or more precisely, FDI inflows. However, since 2005, the current account surplus has superseded FDI to become the most important contributor to the increase in foreign exchange reserves.

8.4.1 Current Account Surplus, FDI, and Savings

One popular explanation for the PRC's current account surplus is the saving–investment gap. This means that the saving rate is higher than the investment rate, which has been the case since the mid-1990s. There appears to be a co-movement between the current account surpluses and the saving–investment gap, but it is difficult to establish a causal relationship between the two.

As discussed above, prior to the WTO entry in 2001, the large current account surplus was mainly due to the government's export promotion policy, which particularly favored the processing trade to take advantage

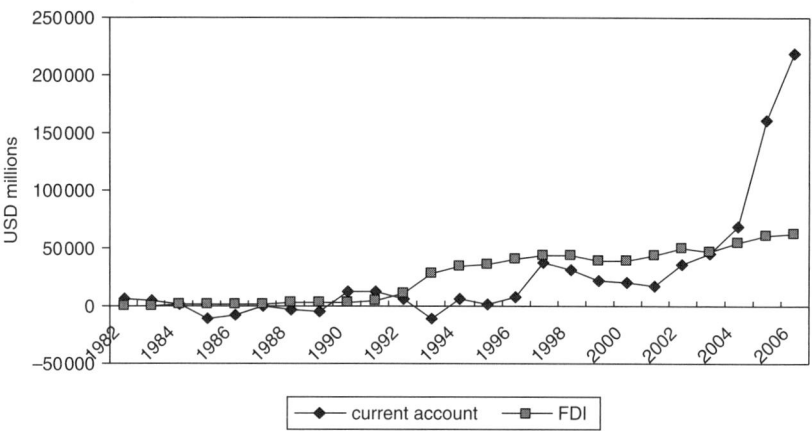

Figure 8.3   The PRC's international balance of payments, 1982–2006

of the low labor costs. The export-promotion policy had extremely tight capital controls to prevent any possible crisis in the balance of payments (BOP). FDI had to be export-oriented to minimize trade deficit. As a result, the processing trade dominates the PRC's trade sector.

The PRC's export promotion policy coincided with the formation of international production networks (IPN), and its trade pattern was to a large extent shaped by FDI. The bulk of FDI is channeled into manufacturing sectors that tend to involve IPN. The PRC became a processor and assembler in the IPN. The PRC's trade growth expansion is increasingly being dominated by the processing trade, which in turn means that the PRC must run a current account surplus.

According to Corden's (2006) Parking Theory 'it seems perfectly rational to invest some of the extra savings abroad given the inefficiency so far of the financial system in allocating funds'. Another explanation he offers is 'the deliberate pursuit of export-led growth'. This chapter argues that both explanations are relevant to the PRC and are interrelated. If the PRC runs only a current account surplus, 'parking' can be regarded as a second best solution, because the PRC does not have the ability either to translate its current account surplus as capital account deficit or to use the funds for domestic investment. In other words, the PRC has to settle with low-yield but safe treasury bills. But the PRC's situation is worse than that, as it runs both current and capital account surpluses (Yu, 2007).

To run twin surpluses persistently for over 15 years is a reflection of a gross misallocation of resources. First, as the 100th poorest country in per capita terms, the PRC should not be the third largest capital exporting country in the world. Second, as the third largest FDI hosting country, it should translate capital inflows into trade deficits. Third, as a net creditor for over 15 years, the PRC has been running negative investment incomes for most years until 2005, when its foreign exchange reserves surpassed $800 billion. Fourth, considering the continued devaluation and defaults on US securities, US assets are no longer a good place for the PRC to park its savings. All in all, the irrational structure of the international balance of payments should be corrected as soon as possible.

8.4.2 The Adjustment of the Growth Strategy and Exchange Rate Policy

The government's 11th five-year program, formulated in 2005, called for a balanced trade account by the end of 2010. As of 2007 several corrective measures have been undertaken, such as the elimination of favorable treatments of export industries, in terms of tax rebates, taxes, access to bank loans, and use of land. However, concerns on reduced employment in exporting industries have made the government very reluctant to allow the yuan to appreciate. Although the yuan has appreciated by some 10 per cent against the US dollar since the de-peg in July 2005, its nominal effective exchange rate has barely moved because of the huge appreciation of the euro against the US dollar.

At the same time, the PRC has gone a long way toward participation in IPN. Trade/GDP ratio has surpassed 75 per cent and processing trade accounted for over 60 per cent of total trade. The de-pegging in July 2005 resulted in a surge of trade surplus while FDI inflows have continued unabated. The rapid increase in the twin surpluses further increased foreign exchange reserves. Thus, reducing the pressure has become the single most important guiding principle for the management of capital flows in the PRC.

8.5 MACROECONOMIC STABILITY AND CAPITAL FLOWS MANAGEMENT

In 2003, when the debate on the need for yuan appreciation had just begun, critics feared the possible deflationary effect on the economy. But signs of overheating began to surface as early as 2004 when the annual growth rate reached 11.5 per cent. Capital inflows in 2006 and early 2007 contributed to the equity bubble. Prices on the equity index soared and housing prices persistently increased. By 2007, an overheating economy was undeniable. In this regard, this section explores the role of capital flows management under the current macroeconomic situation in 2007.

8.5.1 Capital Flows and Overheating

The current overheating in 2007 is reflected in the following important indicators:

- A high annual growth rate of 11.5 per cent vis-à-vis the commonly accepted potential growth rate of 9 per cent;
- An annualized inflation of 6.7 per cent in November;
- Soaring prices on the equity index;
- Persistent high growth rate of housing prices; and
- Annual growth rate of investments of more than 20 per cent in nominal terms and a high investment rate of more than 45 per cent of GDP.

The question here is to what extent cross-border capital flows have contributed to the overheating in general, and asset bubbles and inflation in

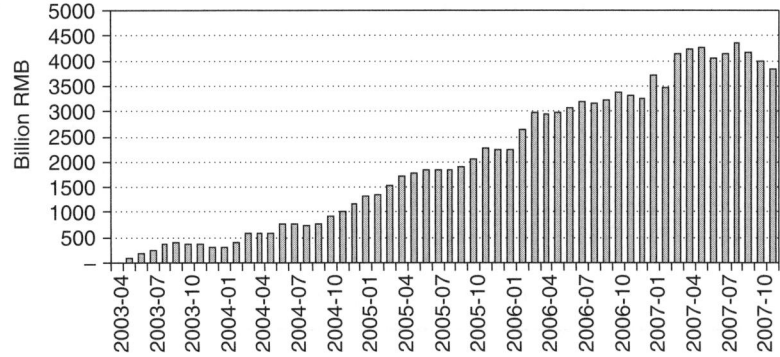

Notes: Our assumption is that the balance of central bank notes is zero at the end of 2002. The highest balance from April 2004 to November 2007 was 4.3 trillion yuan in August 2007.

Sources: http://www.chinabond.com.cn. and author's calculation.

Figure 8.4   Central bank bills balance in the PRC, 2003–07

particular. The direct impacts of capital inflows on the real estate bubble were obvious in 2003 and 2004. In this period, large amounts of unspecified foreign capital flowed into the PRC's real estate market via different channels in the international BOP, attracted by relatively low housing prices and the great potential for rising prices. Excess liquidity from cross-border capital flows, in turn, leads to asset bubbles and inflation.

To maintain price stability and contain asset bubbles, the PBOC has carried out a large-scale sterilization operation, mainly by issuing central bank bills (CBB), to mop up excess liquidity.

Figure 8.4 shows that the balance of the CBBs has been steadily increasing, but decreased in the third quarter of 2007. Taking into consideration commercial banks' total assets of 50.6 trillion yuan, the share of low-yield CBBs in the total bank assets is just below 10 per cent.

Another important sterilization policy is reserve requirements. Since September 2003, the PBOC has increased the reserve requirements 15 times, reaching 14.5 per cent at the end of 2007 from 7 per cent in 2003.

As a result of the sales of CBBs and the raising of the reserve requirements, the share of low-yield assets now accounts for over 20 per cent of banks' total assets. Although the sterilization policy has created serious problems for commercial banks as they had to buy low-yield CBBs and deposit an increasing proportion of their cash with the central bank, it has been mostly successful in mopping up excessive liquidity. According to PBOC documents, as of October 2007, high-powered money created by PBOC intervention was 11 trillion yuan. Through sales of central bank bills (CBBs) of 5 trillion yuan and the raising of reserve requirements by 3 trillion yuan, a total amount of 8 trillion yuan were sterilized. The remaining 3 trillion spread over five years was just enough to respond to the need to support the growth of broad money. In other words, the growth of the monetary base was largely in line with the historical experience. Because the PRC's nominal economic growth rate was more than 16–17 per cent, and the growth rate of M2 was 17–18 per cent, the growth rate of broad money M2 was not widely off the mark. Although with the benefit of hindsight, it should have been lower. The same can be said of the growth rate of credit.

But the PRC's financial system is still flooded with excess liquidity. Otherwise, asset prices would not be soaring, and inflation would be tamed. Where does the excess liquidity come from? The answer lies in the fact that excess liquidity is not only a money supply issue, but also involves money demand. Financial innovation can also lead to the introduction of new liquidity into the banking system by influencing the demand for money. Greed, ignorance, and 'irrational exuberance' can also create excess liquidity by enticing the public to exchange their money for risky financial assets. Hence, if the money supply remains constant, excess liquidity comes in the form of lower demand for money.

Since the fourth quarter of 2006, market exuberance has encouraged a fall in money demand and a flight of bank deposits into stock exchanges. The PRC's M2 to GDP ratio stands at 160 per cent, the highest in the world. According to monetary theory, if M2 growth is consistently greater than GDP, inflation should rise sharply. In the past, this has not materialized because of the PRC's savings rate. The past excess money supply has come back to haunt the economy.

The lack of demand for money is the key challenge for policymakers. There are two fundamental reasons behind the drastic decline. First, developments in capital markets have given normal savers the opportunity to diversify their assets. Rising stock market share prices owing to reforms in 2004–06 and capital inflows encourage households to shift their deposits away from banks into stocks. The increase in share prices in turn encourages further flight and asset price inflation, ultimately creating a vicious cycle. Second, even if the preference of citizens for savings deposits has not changed, interest rate gains are being outpaced by price increases, making it difficult to save in the form of savings deposits.

8.5.2 Managing Capital Inflows for Macroeconomic Stability

Three factors are linked to the creation of excess liquidity: the twin surpluses, intervention in the foreign exchange markets to prevent the yuan appreciation, and the inability of the PBOC to fully sterilize the increase in the monetary base resulting from the intervention in the foreign exchange market.

The management of cross-border capital flows can play important roles in the maintenance of macroeconomic stability. First, it can reduce the need for intervention in the foreign exchange market by the PBOC, by discouraging unwanted capital inflows. The preferential policy aimed at attracting FDI should be scrapped as soon as possible. Of course, at the same time trade promotion policy should also be eliminated. The aim of the policy adjustment is to reduce the twin surpluses, and in fact, over the past several years, preferential policies have been abolished gradually. Of course, during this adjustment, the yuan should be allowed to appreciate more vigorously. Given the exchange rate policy, on top of the policy adjustment, which is beyond day-to-day macroeconomic management, the management of cross-border capital flows has played the role of stopping arbitrage and speculative capital inflows, which are slipping into the PRC via different legitimate channels such as the trade account, FDI, and investment account, as well as through illegitimate channels such as money transfers via underground financial institutions and smuggling. The recent crackdown on short- term borrowing by real estate developers in Hong Kong, China is a case in point. To prevent the real estate bubble from ballooning further, the PBOC has succeeded in blocking capital inflows destined for the PRC's real estate market.

The most important challenge for the PBOC is how to stop flows of hot money disguised as trade surplus and FDI. In practice it is very difficult to distinguish between legitimate money flows and hot money. There are two ways to face this difficulty: liberalization of capital accounts and improvement of the management of cross-border capital flows. In the eyes of many PRC economists, capital controls do not work in today's environment. Liberalization can at least make capital flows more transparent and reduce the incentive for arbitrage and rent-seeking, which in turn can improve the PRC's macroeconomic management and resource allocation. However, this option appears too risky. Despite the serious technical difficulties involved in the micro-management of capital flows, the development of IT technology should be able to help the government to obtain timely information on capital flows and take prompt actions to deal with hot money. Even if the cost is high, it is worth trying.

The PRC's management of cross-border capital flows has always been asymmetrical. In the past, the practice was 'easy in, difficult out'. Now the situation has been reversed, because of the abundant foreign exchange reserves and excess liquidity. Since 2003, the practice has become 'easy out, difficult in'. The problem with the approach is that, under expectations of a yuan appreciation, such policies are ineffective. The unattractiveness of investment via so-called Qualified Domestic Institutional Investors (QDII) is clear evidence of a lack of demand for outflows. Furthermore, the 'easy out' policy cannot actually reduce capital inflows, but instead attracts more capital inflows. If it is easy to run away, meaning that the risk premium is low, why not come and have a try?

Under the current circumstances, it is likely that two kinds of capital will be eager to utilize the opportunities provided by the 'loosening control over capital outflows' to flow out of the PRC. The first kind is the unwinding of speculative capital. The second is capital related to 'assets stripping'. The first type of capital outflow is common to all countries. However, the second type requires elaboration. On top of the usual problems with the capital outflows of developing countries, the PRC is a country without clearly defined property rights. A great portion of public assets has been quietly stolen by so-called stealth privatization, and the stolen money channeled to destination such as the Virgin Islands or Cayman Islands. For enterprises which are owned by the state both in name and in practice, the lack of appropriate incentive mechanisms and low morality make managers very careless about whether other people's money will be lost. In short, before further institutional reform is accomplished, and correct corporate governance is put in place, encouraging capital outflows for the purpose of relieving the pressure on yuan appreciation is indeed 'putting the cart before the horse'. Legitimate outbound investment and remittances of investment incomes have already found channels to move over borders without undue difficulties. However, even this legitimate outbound investment needs to be carefully monitored and supervised. The PRC should not repeat Japan's painful experience since the Plaza Accord. Without careful monitoring and supervision, the results of the disorderly outflow of the PRC capital could be much worse than the outcome for the Japanese who went on a buying spree in the second half of the 1980s.

Last but not least, capital controls are the PRC's last defense and should not be eased until financial reforms are complete. Growth is cyclical, and sudden changes in the economic situation can prompt massive capital flight. If there are no restrictions to buffer the blow, the effects on the PRC's economy may be disastrous. As pointed out by Goldstein (2004), for a number of reasons, the PRC households may decide to diversify a proportion of their savings, say 5 per cent, into foreign assets abroad. If the PRC liberalizes its restrictions on capital outflows to permit that diversification to take place before its financial house is put in order, the 5 per cent swing of household saving deposits may be sufficient to trigger a currency crisis.

Some economists in the PRC argue that capital controls are ineffective and therefore pointless. The PRC's capital controls are indeed extremely leaky. However, one should not underestimate the effectiveness of capital control altogether, when the authorities are determined to make it effective. At the very least, the government can do something to increase the transaction cost for illegitimate cross-border capital flows. The evaluation of the effectiveness of the PRC's management of cross-border capital flows has an important bearing on the PRC's macroeconomic policy.

To mop up excess liquidity, the PBOC needs to encourage households to hold onto their money stocks as well as to slow the growth rate of money supply. There are only two feasible methods for doing this: hiking interest rates or lowering inflation. Naturally, hiking rates is another way to control inflation so it will likely be the key policy instrument in the near future. Balancing returns in different asset classes is the only way to strengthen demand for money, easing the effects of disintermediation. However, the PBOC is inhibited by its lack of freedom in setting rates. There is concern that higher rates will increase the chances of greater capital inflows and bring in new liquidity from the supply side. As such, the central bank will be forced to abandon sterilization. This is a classic 'Mundell Impossible Trinity' problem. The PBOC has been fighting on two fronts: hiking interest rates to stabilize the demand for money (to slow the velocity of monetary circulation) and using open market operations and raising the required reserve ratio to mop up excess liquidity created by the 'Impossible Trinity'. However, fundamentally, if cross-border capital flows are not manageable, this policy will be ineffective because tightening monetary policy implies higher interest rates, which in turn will attract more inflows to neutralize the effect of the monetary tightening.

Over the past several years, based on the exchange rate policy decided by the State Council, the PBOC has been very cautious about tightening monetary policy, especially its interest policy. The main concern of the PBOC has been the carry trade, which has cast its shadow over interest rate policy since 2005. The PRC government's intention was to allow the yuan to appreciate at an annual rate of 3 per cent, so that enterprises could have sufficient time to make adjustments. To realize this goal, the government encouraged the formation of appreciation expectations of 3 per cent in the markets by repeatedly rejecting any suggestion of faster appreciation. Given the US interest rate, the PBOC tried hard to adjust the PRC interest rate to maintain a 3 per cent spread vis-à-vis the London Inter-Bank Offered Rates for the US dollar (LIBOR USD). As noted by McKinnon (2006, p. 9), 'Investors in renminbi assets were willing to accept a lower return because they expected the renminbi to appreciate a little over 3 per cent. This interest differential of 3 per cent or so will continue as long as investors project that the renminbi will continue to appreciate by that amount.' The PBOC's cautious approach towards monetary tightening was based on the assumption that capital controls were ineffective, and the management of cross-border capital flows cannot prevent the carry trade and other unwanted forms of capital inflows.

However, experience during the past several years seems to show that the significance of the interest rate differential for capital inflows into the PRC has been exaggerated. There are ample reasons to believe that those bringing in funds are looking for more than a 1.5–2.5 per cent expected appreciation minus interest spread, and would most likely be interested in getting hold of an asset which added another 10–20 per cent a year to the return. In other words, Uncovered Interest Parity (UIP) does not necessarily apply in the PRC. This is attributable to the fact that capital flows cannot move freely across borders, capital markets are not efficient in the PRC, and there is a home bias for foreign investors. In other words, capital controls in the PRC are still working and the management of cross-border capital flows can serve to maintain macroeconomic stability. Hence the PRC may not need to worry too much about hot money in general and the carry trade in particular, as long as it refuses to give up capital controls and manage cross-border capital flows carefully, when it is tightening monetary policy and raising interest rates. In fact, in 2007 the PBOC raised the reference interest rates[1] on commercial bank loans and household savings deposits, despite the fact that the interest rate spread between the PRC and the US had been narrowing in recent months. Of course, if the interest rate spread between the PRC and American assets narrows further and moves in favor of the US (as has happened recently), the carry trade is likely to become more active, along with other forms of capital inflows as well. Then the PBOC will have to decide whether hot money can be prevented from inundating the economy by improving the management of capital flows. It is reasonable to assume that the improvement will give the PBOC more freedom to use monetary policy to stabilize the economy. Otherwise, there will be no alternative but to allow the yuan to appreciate with a large margin.

8.6 CONCLUDING REMARKS

The PRC faces three colossal tasks in the area of open macroeconomic reform: reform of the exchange rate regime; capital movement liberalization; and financial system reform. The PRC is making preparations for a transfer from a *de facto* exchange rate regime to managed floating in a true sense. It needs to speed up the process of financial reform. However, this will be a long-term process and the completion of reform cannot be expected for many years to come. A complete liberalization of the capital account will be dangerous, if the fragile financial system has not been strengthened. The PRC needs to adjust its strategy to make its growth more efficient and sustainable. To achieve this objective, a well-functioning foreign exchange market should be established so that exchange rates can be determined on the basis of the fundamental internal and external equilibrium. To facilitate the regime change, partial capital account liberalization, namely, the liberalization of some more items of the capital account, is necessary. In short, the liberalization of the capital account and changes in the exchange rate regime should go in tandem.

The management of cross-border capital flows is an indispensable element of macroeconomic stability. In order to cool the overheating economy, the PRC government will continue to implement a tight monetary policy. Faced with possible cuts in the US interest rate, the PRC's monetary tightening will become increasingly difficult. Hence, the PRC must maintain capital controls whenever possible and improve its management of cross-border capital flows, to enable the PBOC to implement an independent monetary policy.

The main conclusion of the paper is that the management of cross-border capital flows should be treated as part of the PRC's long-term program of economic reform and opening up, and should not be subject to the need for reducing pressure for yuan appreciation. There is still a long way to go before the complete convertibility of the yuan is achieved. Careful management of capital flows will be not only useful but also essential for the maintenance of macroeconomic stability in the PRC.

NOTE

1. Commercial banks are allowed to have certain leeway in deciding the rates around the reference rates.

REFERENCES

Corden, W.M. (2006), 'Those current account imbalances: a skeptical view', Working Paper No. 13/06, Melbourne Institute Working Paper Series, Melbourne University, August, pp. 6–7.
Goldstein, M. (2004), 'Adjusting China's exchange rate policies', paper presented at the IMF Seminar on China's Foreign Exchange System, Dalian, China, 26–27 May.
Ishii, S. and K. Haberneirer (2002), 'Capital account liberalization and financial sector stability', IMF Occasional Paper 211, Washington, DC: IMF.

McKinnon, R. (2006), 'Why China should keep its exchange rate pegged to the dollar: a historical perspective from Japan', October, Stanford University, pp. 1–26, available at: http://www.stanford.edu/~mckinnon/papers/International%20Finance%20China%20peg.pdf.

Yu, Y. (2006), 'The experience of FDI recipients: the case of China', in S. Urata, C.S. Yue and F. Kimura (eds), *Multinationals and Economic Growth in East Asia: Foreign Direct Investment, Corporate Strategies and National Economic Development*, New York: Routledge, pp. 423–52.

Yu, Y. (2007), 'Global imbalances and China', *Australian Economic Review*, **40**(1), 3–23.

9. Managing capital flows: the case of India

Ajay Shah and Ila Patnaik

9.1 INTRODUCTION

In the early 1990s, India faced a balance of payments (BOP) crisis. This crisis was followed by an IMF structural adjustment program, economic reforms, and liberalization of the trade and capital accounts. Policymakers were, however, very cautious about opening up the economy to debt flows.

The experience of the BOP crisis as well as the lessons learned from other developing countries suggested that debt flows, especially short-term debt flows, could lead to BOP difficulties if the country faced macroeconomic imbalances and had an inflexible exchange rate. The emphasis was, therefore, on foreign investment – both foreign direct investment (FDI) and portfolio investment. Even these were opened up slowly and a system of capital controls remained in place (see Shah and Patnaik 2007a for a detailed treatment of the easing of capital controls in the 1990s).

This chapter on managing capital flows in India is organized into six sections. Following the introduction, Section 9.2 is a discussion of types of capital flows and controls in India. Section 9.3 compares India's capital controls and degree of openness to capital flows with those of major economies, using international measures. The next section is devoted to portfolio flows, owing to their increasing importance in the capital account. Section 9.5 examines the macroeconomic impacts of capital flows, and finally Section 9.6 offers policy recommendations.

9.2 CAPITAL CONTROLS AND TYPES OF CAPITAL FLOWS

9.2.1 Inbound FDI

India opened up slowly to FDI in the 1990s. The limits on the share of foreign ownership were gradually eased in every sector. By 2000, while most sectors were opened up to 100 per cent, sectors where FDI was restricted include retail trading (except single brand product retailing), atomic energy, and betting.

While inbound FDI investors have the ability to repatriate capital, so far, in the Indian experience, this reverse flow of capital has been tiny. As an example, in 2006–07, it was 0.01 per cent of GDP. Hence, for all practical purposes, inbound FDI has been a one-way process of capital coming into the country.[1] The easing of capital controls, coupled with strong investment opportunities, gave impetus to FDI flows into India: from 0.14 per cent of GDP in 1992–93 to 0.53 per cent in 1999–2000 and then to 2.34 per cent of GDP in 2006–07, suggesting strong growth. From April 2000 to August 2007, $44.4 billion came into India through FDI, of which 44.7 per cent or $17.4 billion came from Mauritius. The reason for this is that India has a preferential tax treaty with Mauritius. In terms of sectoral composition of inbound FDI, services attracted the highest amount at $8.1 billion or 20.6 per cent in the same period, followed by computer software and hardware which attracted $6.2 billion (16 per cent). The next four sectors, each with less than 10 per cent of inbound FDI, were telecom, automobile, construction, and power.

9.2.2 Portfolio Flows

In the early 1990s, India opened up to portfolio inflows through 'foreign institutional investors' (FIIs), part of a policy framework to substantially reform the equity market. FII equity investment involves two main constraints: (i) shareholders of a company can limit aggregate foreign holding; and (ii) the ownership cap is set at 10 per cent for one foreign portfolio investor in a company. Both limits are further subject to applicable 'sectoral limits' imposed by the government.

Nonetheless, unlike the People's Republic of China's (PRC) Qualified Foreign Institutional Investment (QFII) framework, portfolio investors are free to bring capital in and out of India without requiring permissions. Over a thousand global firms are now registered in India as 'FIIs'. By November 2007, the value of listed firms where trading takes place on at least two-thirds of the days of the year stood at $1.6 trillion from $0.11 trillion in November 1997. The two Indian exchanges (National Stock Exchange of India Limited (NSE) and Bombay Stock Exchange Limited (BSE)) have been ranked third and fifth in the world by the number of transactions.

In many emerging markets, issuance on the American Depository Receipts/Global Depository Receipts (ADR/GDR) markets has been an important vehicle for financial globalization. In the case of India, the ADR/GDR market was significant in 1994–97 because in 1993, when

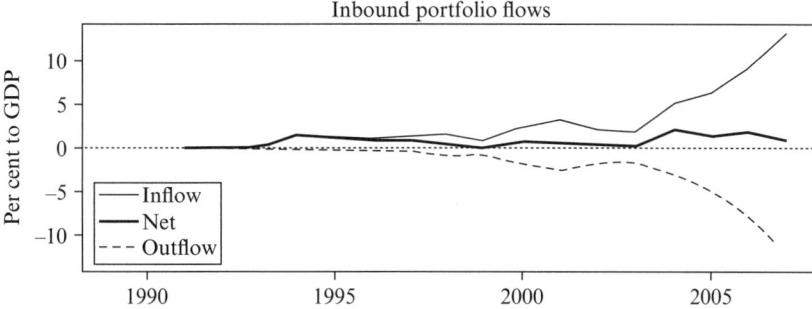

Source: Handbook of Statistics and Monthly Review, Reserve Bank of India (various issues).

Figure 9.1 Inbound portfolio flows

FII investment into India first surged, the settlement system collapsed. Issuance on the ADR/GDR markets was seen as a way to avoid the weak institutions of the domestic stock market. However, by 1997, domestic equity market reforms had made substantial progress.

The flow of issuance on the ADR/GDR markets as a fraction of the stock market capitalization at the end of the year showed large values averaging 1.08 per cent over the period 1993–97. By 1997, the Indian equity market reforms had started falling into place, reducing the annual issuance on the ADR/GDR market to 0.4 per cent of market capitalization from 1998 to 2007. In this respect, India's experience has been different from that of many emerging markets, where deepening financial globalization has often been accompanied by a substantial scale of offshore listing.

The combination of easing capital controls, strong investment opportunities in India, and the sophistication of the domestic equity market led to sharp growth in portfolio inflows, increasing from 0.11 per cent of GDP in 1992–93 to 0.84 per cent in 2006–07.

Figure 9.1 shows the time-series of inbound portfolio flows, expressed as per cent to GDP. Unlike FDI, a remarkable feature of portfolio flows has been substantial inbound and outbound flows, which leave a small net inflow. This reflects the *de facto* convertibility that has been granted to foreign portfolio investors on the equity market.

In 2007, the government introduced fresh capital controls against 'participatory notes', which are over-the-counter (OTC) derivatives sold by a FII-registered financial firm to an investor who is not registered, to reduce capital inflows and facilitate the implementation of the pegged exchange rate. However, this particular capital control neither changed net portfolio purchases by FIIs, nor the role of FIIs in the domestic market.[2]

Table 9.1 The importance of quasi-sovereign borrowing

Stock of debt (billion $)	1992	2000	2007
Sovereign debt	48.62	45.98	47.24
Quasi-sovereign debt	15.96	25.63	45.26
Private debt	20.71	26.65	62.54
Total debt	85.29	98.26	155.04
Ratios (in per cent)			
Sovereign debt to GDP	20.20	11.30	6.08
Sovereign + quasi sovereign debt to GDP	26.83	17.59	11.9
Private debt to GDP	8.60	6.55	8.05
Private debt to total debt	24.28	27.12	40.34

9.2.3 Sovereign Debt

One element of the policy framework of the early 1990s was to encourage equity flows but hamper debt inflows. Technically, the Government of India has no sovereign debt program and aid flows are miniscule. A $1.5 billion cap exists on the stock of ownership of government bonds by FIIs. Practically, FII investment into rupee-denominated government bonds is zero.

However, from time to time, banks have borrowed abroad depending on the government's assessment of the adequacy of foreign exchange reserves. One form of foreign borrowing is through bank deposits of Non-Resident Indians (NRIs) (Gordon and Gupta, 2004). The interest rates on these deposits are set by the Reserve Bank of India (RBI) and fluctuate according to whether the government wishes to encourage or discourage inflows. Three-quarters of Indian bank deposits are with government-owned banks, which are explicitly guaranteed by the government. Thus, the borrowing of Indian banks is visibly backed by the government.

The authorities claim that a massive reduction in offshore debt, particularly offshore sovereign debt, took place in the 1990s. By the official classification, the external debt of GOI stagnated at between $45 billion and $50 billion over 1998–2007. However, a more accurate rendition of the situation requires addressing a phenomenon that we term 'quasi-sovereign' debt.

Table 9.1 shows statistics for quasi-sovereign borrowing, based on a reclassification of the detailed statistics for debt stock. While sovereign debt measured in dollars has stagnated, implying a rapid decline in sovereign debt expressed as per cent of GDP (from 20 per cent in 1992 to 6 per cent in 2007), this decline is exaggerated by keeping quasi-sovereign debt out of this reckoning.

Until 2000, private sector debt accounted for about a fourth of the total

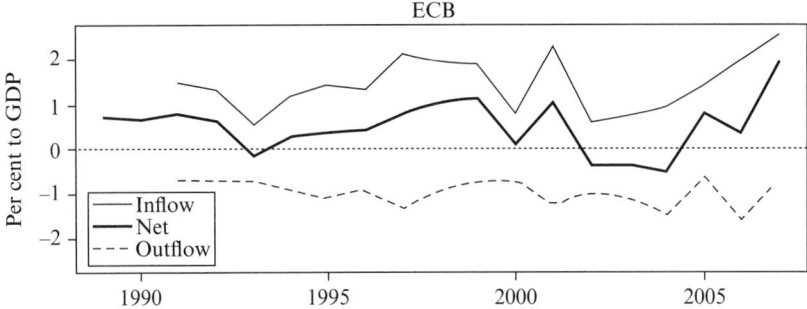

Source: Handbook of Statistics and Monthly Review, Reserve Bank of India (various issues).

Figure 9.2 External commercial borrowing

but this rose to roughly 40 per cent in 2000–07, reflecting the liberalization of external commercial borrowing (ECB). However, its economic significance was limited, as the private debt to GDP ratio in 2007 was below the level seen in 1992.

9.2.4 Debt of Firms

Firms are allowed to borrow abroad through ECB. Borrowing includes loans or bond issues abroad that are foreign currency-denominated. Small transactions are processed by the government with 'automatic approval', and bigger transactions require permission. Under the present policy framework, a three-year maturity is required for external borrowings by firms for amounts below $20 million and five years for amounts beyond. Borrowing of up to $500 million by a firm for certain specified end-uses is allowed without requiring permissions.

Figure 9.2 shows the evolution of ECB, expressed as per cent of GDP. The borrowing of a given year inevitably induces repayment in the following years; the net inflow on account of ECB reflects the combination of fresh issuance of the year and repayments owing to older transactions. Apart from ECB, FIIs can buy rupee-denominated corporate debt on the domestic market but a cap on ownership of corporate bonds by all FIIs put together is set at $2.5 billion.

9.2.5 Capital Outflows

Outward capital flows primarily take two forms. The first and massive mechanism is the purchase of US treasury bills and other foreign assets by

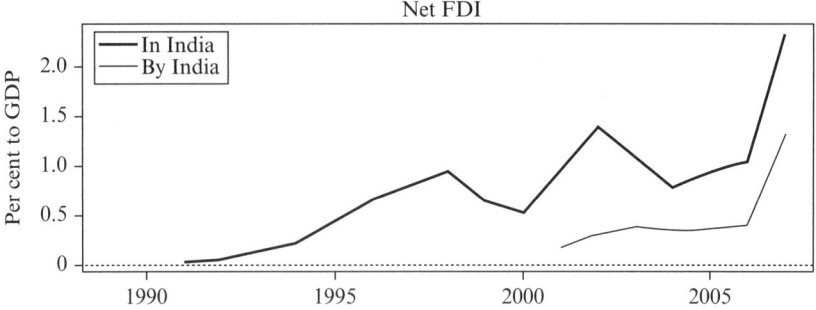

Source: Handbook of Statistics and Monthly Review, Reserve Bank of India (various issues).

Figure 9.3 Inbound and outbound FDI

RBI when it builds reserves. Foreign reserves have grown since 1991, from $5.8 billion to over $300 billion in 2008 (RBI, 2009).

Outbound FDI by Indian companies has also become important in recent years, rising sharply since 2004 when Indian companies were allowed to invest in entities abroad up to 200 per cent of their net worth in a year. This was a result of the liberalization of India's overseas investment policy in 1992 to provide Indian industry access to new markets and technologies with a view to increasing their competitiveness.

In response, thousands of Indian firms have embarked on turning themselves into multinational corporations. Approvals for investment abroad jumped to 1395 in 2005–06 from 290 in 1996–97. But in 2006–07, 870 approvals were granted to Indian companies, worth over $6 billion, compared to 822 approvals worth $1.2 billion in the previous year.

Figure 9.3 juxtaposes inbound and outbound (net) FDI flows, both expressed as per cent of GDP. Outbound flows have risen sharply, to a level of over 1 per cent of GDP a year. In 2007 the flow of outbound FDI as a percentage of gross fixed capital formation in India rose to 2.1, gross outbound FDI rose to 1.5.

Software firms were among the first Indian firms that used overseas acquisitions as a way to better access the US market, followed by pharmaceutical firms to penetrate regulated overseas markets like Europe and the US. The share of the primary sector in overseas investment is still low; it consists of natural resource seeking companies that have sought to get control over oil resources in several countries. Mining of coal and metals has also attracted investment by Indian companies. Three-quarters of outbound investment from India between 2000 and 2007 went to developed countries, mainly the US and Europe.

A third front on which capital controls have been eased in recent years has been on outbound portfolio flows. There has been some response to these as various funds are now offering international diversification to the Indian customer. In addition, individuals are now permitted to take $200 000 per person per year out of the country. However, so far, the magnitudes have been negligible.

9.3 CAPITAL CONTROLS IN AN INTERNATIONAL CONTEXT

India has retained strict control over the capital inflows that are permitted into the country. Since 1993 these controls have mainly been eased, but there have been instances when they have also been tightened, as in 2007 when the pressure on the currency increased.

9.3.1 *De Jure* Capital Controls

The 'Chinn–Ito Index', a measure of capital account openness, is an index of capital controls available for many countries, for many years (Chinn and Ito, 2006). It is based on processing responses of countries to the International Monetary Fund's Annual Report on Exchange Arrangements and Exchange Restrictions (AREAERs). The Chinn–Ito Index shows the state of *de jure* convertibility. Their measure is a stringent one, where a need to obtain permission constitutes a restriction, even if the permission is 'usually' or even 'always' given.

Their focus is on measuring the extent to which governments are trying to be involved in the capital account. Countries with a score of 2.6 have complete unquestioned capital account convertibility.

Figure 9.4 shows some summary statistics from the Chinn–Ito database. India's score has been stable at −1.1 all through the period under examination.[3] The top left graph shows the opening up of emerging markets juxtaposed against the world mean. The top right graph shows that members of the 'Group of 20' have had a greater level and pace of opening the capital account when compared with the world mean. The bottom left graph computes the fraction of countries that are as closed as India, or worse. It suggests that in roughly 1980, India's closed capital account was roughly the median among countries in the world; by the end of this period, roughly 60 per cent of countries were more open than India. Finally, the right hand bottom graph shows the experience of a few countries which undertook substantial reforms of capital controls: these trajectories are quite unlike those seen for India.

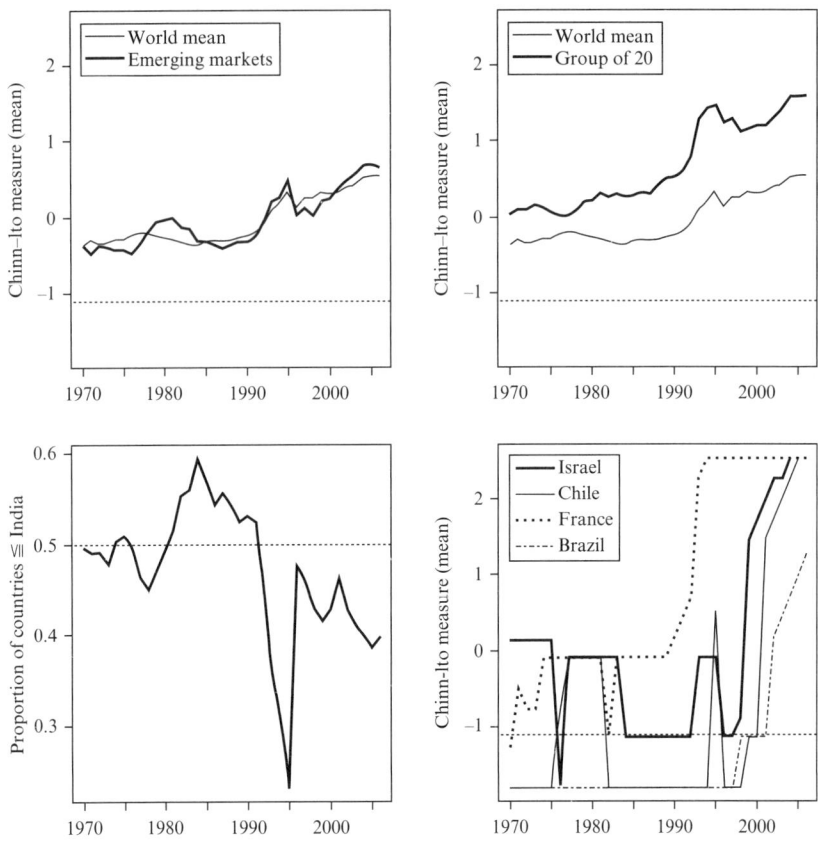

Source: Chinn and Ito (2008).

Figure 9.4 India's de jure *opening in the context of the Chinn–Ito measure*

Comparisons for India are most interesting against large countries. Hence, we focus on the biggest 25 countries of the world by nominal GDP, the smallest of which is Austria. Among these countries, the Chinn-Ito Index takes values from −1.1 to 2.6. There are three countries at the bottom of the table – the last holdouts of nonconvertibility – with a score of −1.1: Turkey, India, and the PRC. Amongst these top-25 countries, the average score is 1.467 and half of them are above 2.33. Key peers to India are ahead in opening the capital account: Brazil is at 0.21, Russia is at −0.06, Mexico is at 1.23, and Indonesia is at 1.23. When we go beyond these 25 countries to the full database of 180 countries, the median score is 0.18: much better than India's −1.1.

9.3.2 Evolution of Openness

We now summarize the structure of net capital flows into India, expressed as per cent of GDP. Net capital flows stagnated at roughly 2.5 per cent of GDP from 1993 to 2000, and have since risen sharply to 5.4 per cent of GDP by 2007. This has partly reflected a rise in equity flows, which were encouraged by policymakers, and went from 0.25 per cent of GDP in 1993 to 1.24 per cent of GDP in 2000 to 1.87 per cent of GDP in 2007.

India's policymakers have believed that debt flows are dangerous, and at first, debt inflows dropped from 3 per cent of GDP in 1993 to 0.9 per cent of GDP in 2000. However, by 2007, debt inflows were back to 3 per cent of GDP.

We now focus on gross flows as a metric of integration with the world economy. The familiar trade/GDP ratio sums up merchandise imports and exports, and expresses them as per cent of GDP: it is used as a measure of merchandise trade integration. We sum up gross flows on the current and capital accounts, and express them as per cent to GDP. This gives us three measures of integration.

All these measures show a massive increase in international integration. Gross flows on the current account rose from 25.9 per cent in 1993 to 34.1 per cent in 2000 and rose sharply to 60.6 per cent in 2007. Gross flows on the capital account stagnated at roughly 18 per cent from 1993 to 2000, but then rose sharply to 49.4 per cent in 2007. Putting these together, the overall integration metric went from roughly 50 per cent of GDP over the 1993–2000 period to roughly 110 per cent of GDP in 2007, suggesting a rapid pace of globalization in the post-2000 period.

This change, of 60 percentage points of GDP in the post-2000 period, was an unprecedented one. For a comparison, total flows stagnated at roughly 20 per cent of GDP in 1956–57 and 1986–87. The reforms of the early 1990s led to a much bigger value of 49.9 per cent in 1996–97. This was followed by a dramatic expansion to 110 per cent of GDP in 2006–07. This suggests a rapid and unprecedented globalization of the Indian economy (Kelkar, 2004).

9.3.3 *De Facto* Openness Exceeds *De Jure* Openness

One element of this openness lies in remittances. A survey of banks found that roughly half of remittance flows were used for acquiring financial assets. In recent years, the correlation coefficient between the rupee–dollar interest rate differential, and remittance inflows, prove to be as high as 0.8. This emphasizes the extent to which capital account considerations shape what is apparently a current account transaction. In terms of absolute magnitude, remittance flows have been roughly as big as net capital inflows. This suggests that if the capital inflows component of remittances were correctly measured, net capital inflows might need to be revised upwards by roughly 50 per cent.

The other major source of openness is the current account. Indian and global firms with operations in India are able to move capital across the boundary through misinvoicing. A firm that is prevented from obtaining offshore debt by the system of capital controls could contract debt overseas under the name of an offshore subsidiary, and transfer-price this capital into India. Similar processes could be used for repayment. Given that gross flows on the current account are over 60 per cent of GDP, if misinvoicing of 10 per cent on average takes place in a single direction, this could add roughly 6 per cent to net capital flows.

9.4 DETERMINANTS OF PORTFOLIO FLOWS

The most interesting element of capital flows into India is portfolio flows. The reason for this is twofold. First, this was the earliest element to be opened up (in the form of convertibility for foreign institutional investors), and ample data is available from a mature policy regime. Second, capital flowing in and out of the country on account of portfolio flows is large; this is the biggest single component of gross flows on the capital account.

9.4.1 The Decline of Home Bias against India

Table 9.2 shows that over the 2001–07 period, home bias against India declined. The Intertemporal Capital Asset Pricing Model (ICAPM) weight for India went from being 11.8 times bigger than the actual in March 2001 to being 6.47 times bigger in March 2007. The market value of shares held

Table 9.2 Change in home bias against India

	March 2001	March 2007
ICAPM weight of India	0.42	1.53
Actual weight of India	0.04	0.24
Home bias metrics		
1 - (actual/ICAPM)	0.92	0.85
ICAPM /actual	11.8	6.47

Source: Shah and Patnaik (2007b).

by portfolio investors went up by 12.8 times over this six-year period: from $9.67 billion to $124.2 billion or over 10 per cent of GDP. These stylized facts demand exploration.

9.4.2 Time-series Evidence

Monthly data on net portfolio inflows from foreign institutional investors is available in India from 1996 onwards.[4] A key difficulty in dealing with this data lies in finding an appropriate parametrization, as portfolio flows measured in million dollars per month were small in 1996 and have become large in 2007. In order to stabilize the distribution, we focus on the net portfolio inflow of each month expressed as per cent of the broad market capitalization of that month.[5] At the end of 2007, broad market capitalization was $1.6 trillion. Hence, in this parametrization, a one percentage point of broad market capitalization corresponds to a net inflow in one month of $16 billion.

In previous work (Shah and Patnaik, 2007a), currency expectations – measured by the covered interest parity (CIP) deviation – have been found to be useful in explaining portfolio flows. However, the CIP deviation takes on some extreme values and there is a danger of regression results being distorted as a consequence.[6] Hence, robust regressions are utilized.[7]

Table 9.3 shows a model that explains net FII inflows (expressed as per cent of broad market capitalization).[8] The results of the robust regression are not unlike those found using an ordinary least squares (OLS) method.[9]

The key features of this model are:

Table 9.3 Explaining monthly net FII flows

Parameter	Value	t statistic
Intercept	0.2837	4.26
CIP Deviation	0.0235	3.57
CIP Deviation squared	0.0017	3.58
Lagged monthly returns on Nifty:		
1 month	0.0075	3.80
2 months	0.0038	1.86
3 months	0.0047	2.36
4 months	0.0030	1.55
CMIE Cospi P/E	−0.0061	−1.86
VIX	−0.0032	−1.48

- Currency expectations, measured by the CIP deviation, matter strongly. If the CIP deviation shifts from 0 to 5, this induces additional portfolio inflows of 0.03 per cent of the broad market capitalization, indicating that expectations of currency appreciation attract portfolio flows into India. By end-2007, this corresponded to $0.5 billion in one month.
- Nifty is the main stock market index of India. Lagged Nifty returns of 1 through 4 months matter but contemporaneous Nifty returns are not utilized in this regression given the potential impact of portfolio inflows on the stock market index. Since monthly Nifty returns are roughly random, it is possible to get an estimate of the total impact of a 1 per cent shock to Nifty in a month, over the coming four months, by summing up the coefficients. This yields a rough estimate of 0.019. If Nifty returns prove to be 10 per cent in a month, this induces additional inflows of 0.19 per cent of the market capitalization spread over the coming four months. By end-2007, 0.19 per cent of market capitalization amounted to $3 billion.
- Foreign investors are deterred by a high value of the broad market price-earnings (P/E) ratio, and vice versa. When the market P/E ratio is high, foreign investors expect it to go down and therefore flows fall.
- Finally, high levels of the VIX[10] deter portfolio flows into India. The VIX reflects what the market thinks volatility of the S&P 500 index, the stock market index for the biggest 500 US companies, will be over the next one month.[11] A low level of VIX implies that returns from the global market will lie within a narrow band. When the VIX goes up, it suggests that returns on stock prices are likely to be in a much higher band, in other words, much more volatile. When the VIX goes up, people are less willing to take risks. A higher level of the VIX therefore results in lower portfolio flows into an emerging economy like India.

Variables which might have been expected to have an impact on portfolio flows into India but are *not* statistically significant in this regression include: the Indian short rate, the US short rates and the spreads between the two, industrial production growth, S&P 500 returns, the US long rate, the US Baa corporate bond rate, Nifty volatility, INR/$ currency volatility, the US term spread, and the US credit spread.

9.4.3 Explaining the Decline in Home Bias

Recent literature has examined the characteristics of firms in emerging markets which are able to internationalize their shareholding (Claessens and Schmukler, 2006). Shah and Patnaik (2007b) obtain insights through the following decomposition of F, the value of foreign ownership of shares in an emerging market. Let $F = g(1 - p)M$, where M is the market capitalization of the country; p is the insider shareholding and g is the fraction of outsider shareholding that is held by foreigners.[12] Total differentiation yields:

$$\Delta F \approx M(1 - p)\Delta g + g(1 - p)\Delta M - gM\Delta p$$

The first term, $M(1 - p)\Delta g$, can be interpreted as the change in F associated with a change in g holding other things constant. This corresponds to traditional home bias explanations. The second term, $g(1 - p)\Delta M$, measures the rise in foreign ownership owing to a higher M, holding other sources of home bias unchanged. It reflects foreign investors preserving their ownership of $g(1 - p)$ on a larger M, reflecting ICAPM-style reasoning while ignoring changes in world market capitalization. The third term, $-gM\Delta p$, may be termed a 'Stulz effect', reflecting the drop in foreign ownership associated with a rise in insider ownership p, while holding other things constant.

This decomposition is not an economic model explaining the dynamics of F. Rather, it represents an attempt at accounting for the changes in F and obtaining a quantitative sense of the importance of the three forces at work. Shah and Patnaik (2007b) show these calculations with Indian data. As an example, in 2005, F went up by Rs.622 billion. This change breaks down to three elements: Rs.317 billion owing to traditional explanations of home bias, Rs.501 billion owing to bigger Indian market capitalization and *a decline* of Rs.182 billion since insiders *increased* their ownership share in 2005.

This focuses interest on understanding g, the fraction of outside shareholding that is held by foreigners, estimated using firm-level data. Modeling this requires a two-stage 'Heckman-style' model, because there is a large clump of firms with zero foreign ownership. This implies a distinction between selectivity and propensity effects.

The key finding of Shah and Patnaik (2007b) concerns the importance of year characteristics after controlling for firm characteristics. After controlling for firm characteristics, year fixed effects on the OLS equation exhibit little year-to-year fluctuation.

This suggests that the recent surge of foreign investment into India was largely induced by modified firm characteristics, and not a change in sentiment about India as a whole. The growth of the economy and successful reforms transformed the situation in terms of firm characteristics. With these modified characteristics in place by 2007, firms were much more attractive to global investors than was the case in 2001.

9.5 MACROECONOMIC IMPACT OF CAPITAL FLOWS

RBI has generally emphasized a 'multiple objectives' framework, where the goals of monetary policy are not specified, and the market does not know a monetary policy rule. The goals of monetary policy change from time to time but are not effectively communicated to the market. Dincer and Eichengreen (2007) score the transparency of central banks. On a scale of 0 to 15, Asian central banks have been improving as a whole, scoring 5.1 in 2005, compared to 3 in 1998. The PRC's transparency improved to 4.5 from 1. RBI has stagnated at a score of 2 throughout.[13]

This approach towards monetary policy has come under stress in the context of a pegged exchange rate and increasing *de facto* openness. In this section, we examine the macroeconomic impact of capital flows. Our treatment runs from the pegged exchange rate regime, to currency intervention by RBI, to the extent to which sterilization is achieved, the loss of monetary policy autonomy, and its impact on inflation.

9.5.1 The Backdrop – A Pegged Exchange Rate

According to RBI, the rupee is a 'market determined exchange rate', in the sense that there is a currency market and the exchange rate is not administratively determined. However, RBI actively trades on the market with the goal of 'containing volatility' and influencing the market price.

In India, as in most developing countries, there has been a distinction between the *de facto* and the *de jure* currency regime. Patnaik (2007) shows that the Indian Rupee (INR) is *de facto* pegged to the dollar. As is typical with such an exchange rate regime, the nominal INR/US$ exchange rate has had low volatility, while other exchange rates with respect to the rupee have been more volatile.

While the INR currency regime has been *de facto* pegged to the dollar, the extent of pegging has varied significantly through this period. The exchange rate regression, popularized by Frankel and Wei (1994), involves regressions of weekly percentage changes of the exchange rate of the INR against the Swiss Franc (a numeraire) against weekly percentage changes against the same numeraire for the US dollar, pound sterling, the euro, and the Japanese yen. The residual volatility of this regression is a measure of exchange rate flexibility. A mechanism for identifying structural breaks in the exchange rate regime that is consonant with this regression is required. Zeileis et al. (2007) have identified the following phases of the Indian currency regime.

Period 1: 2 April 1993 to 17 February 1995

This was the period when trading in the INR began. For most of this period, there was strong pressure to appreciate, which was blocked by purchases of dollars by the RBI, giving a *de facto* fixed exchange rate at Rs.31.37 per dollar.

Period 2: 18 February 1995 to 21 August 1998

This period, which included the Asian crisis, had the highest-ever currency flexibility in India's experience. Even though the RBI made public statements about 'managing volatility on the currency market', they were hardly credible given the small size of foreign exchange reserves. In January 1998, the short-term interest rate was raised by 200 basis points (bps) to defend the INR.

Period 3: 22 August 1998 to 19 March 2004

This was a period of tight pegging, with low volatility and some appreciation. A substantial reserves accumulation took place, which led to considerable distortion of monetary policy.

Period 4: 20 March 2004 to 31 January 2008

This period has greater currency flexibility than Period 3 but lower than Period 2. With massive reserves and a hectic pace of reserves accumulation, the risk of a large depreciation was absent.

The evolution of the currency regime reflected compulsions rooted in monetary policy and the evolution of capital controls (Patnaik, 2005). In turn, the difficulties of implementing the exchange rate regime have shaped tactical details of the evolution of capital controls. Since the evolution of the exchange rate regime is essential to understanding capital flows and monetary policy, the vertical light line of Figure 9.5 dates structural change of the exchange rate regime. The pegged exchange rate regime has required a massive scale of trading on the currency market by the RBI.

In the early and mid-1990s, there was a motivation for building reserves in order to insure against adverse shocks. As demonstrated in Patnaik (2003), by the late 1990s, reserves were more than adequate for self-insurance, and currency purchases were primarily motivated by the implementation of the pegged exchange rate. Over the 2003–08 period, reserves were between eight to nine months of imports of goods and services, well in excess of what is considered safe. Total short-term external debt was between 10 per cent and 15 per cent of reserves over this period, well below what is considered dangerous.

This increase in net foreign exchange assets of the RBI would lead to

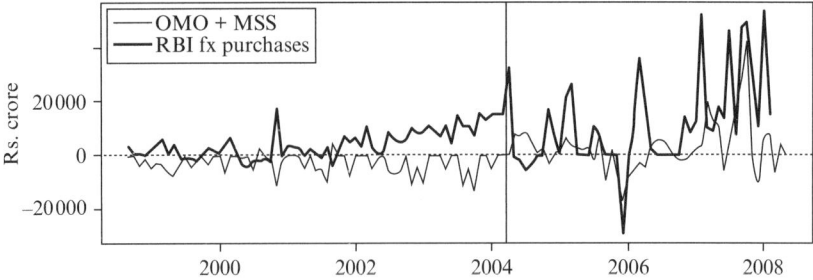

Source: *Handbook of Statistics and Monthly Review*, Reserve Bank of India (various issues).

Figure 9.5 Incomplete sterilization

a sharp increase in the monetary base. To prevent this from happening, sterilization has been attempted.

9.5.2 Extent of Sterilization

Figure 9.5 juxtaposes currency trading against sterilization. When sterilization is effective – as was the case from 2000 to 2004 – the two curves in the graph appear to be roughly mirror images.

The RBI ran out of government bonds for the purpose of sterilization in late 2003. From January 2004 onwards, a new mechanism for sterilization – the Market Stabilization Scheme (MSS) – was put in place. The MSS authorizes RBI to sell bonds on behalf of the government. The government would not utilize the proceeds obtained by the sale of these bonds, so as to ensure there was no impact on the monetary system. There was an initial ceiling on the MSS at Rs.0.6 trillion, which was raised to Rs.2.5 trillion.

A key strength of MSS lies in the fact that it makes the cost of sterilized intervention more transparent. Interest payments for MSS have risen, and these expenses face scrutiny in the budget process. This may have helped keep MSS bond issuance in check.

As Figure 9.5 shows, in Period 4, the two curves are generally not mirror images. This underlines the limited sterilization which has taken place: it was not possible to decouple RBI's currency trading from monetary policy, and the implementation of the pegged exchange rate has had implications for reserve money.

9.5.3 Loss of Monetary Policy Autonomy

The incomplete sterilization that is visible in Figure 9.5 in the post-2004 period has led to a pronounced acceleration of reserve money growth. One method through which high M_0 growth can be confronted is to raise reserve requirements of banks. While reserve requirements have been raised in India (thus reversing a decade-long effort at phasing out reserve requirements, which were seen as a tax on banking), they have not been able to prevent a significant acceleration in M_3 growth.

9.5.4 Impact on Inflation

The flip side of the coin of this atmosphere of unsterilized intervention and high money supply growth is low interest rates. Real rates in India have been low when compared with other Asian countries. With low real rates, the stance of monetary policy has been expansionary. On the other hand, inflation in India has risen after 2004, and has remained stubbornly high when compared with the aspirations of politicians and policymakers.

9.5.5 Summary: Pegged Rate Induced a Loss of Monetary Policy Autonomy

In the Indian case, the strategies which have been attempted for regaining monetary policy autonomy while pursuing a pegged exchange rate include:

Augment mechanisms for sterilization MSS bonds were created, to augment the capability for sterilization.

Enhanced reserve requirements Reserve requirements on banks were increased, so as to prevent accelerated M_0 growth from spilling into higher M_3 growth.

Capital controls RBI has advocated a significant reversal of liberalization of the capital account. However, this reversion would hurt the interests of many participants in the democratic decision making process. In addition, the autarkic policy goals of RBI have been out of tune with the broad consensus in India about moving forward towards becoming a mature market economy that is integrated into the world economy. As a consequence, capital controls that have been attempted were not harsh enough to solve the difficulties described above.

Currency flexibility Episodes of currency flexibility have taken place when the implementation of the exchange rate regime was difficult. The exchange rate regime in Period 4 has greater currency flexibility when compared with that in Period 3.

These strategies have not been adequate. The RBI has repeatedly argued that the Impossible Trinity is not a constraint: that it is possible to have both a pegged exchange rate and monetary policy autonomy. However, despite the use of these four mechanisms, the scale of currency trading required for implementing the pegged exchange rate regime has impacted upon monetary policy to a substantial extent. Monetary policy in India is now acted out on a day-to-day basis in RBI's currency trading room.

9.6 APPROPRIATE POLICY RESPONSES

This paper has suggested that there is a substantial mismatch between the needs of India, a fast-growing and fast-globalizing trillion dollar economy, and the present policy framework of capital controls and monetary policy. The present policy framework, which served India well in the 1980s and 1990s, is under increasing stress. There is a significant possibility of experiencing an external sector crisis owing to the inherent contradictions of this policy framework. In addition, upholding this policy framework involves significant costs.

The appropriate strategy for policy involves two key elements: monetary policy reform and a rapid movement to convertibility.

9.6.1 Monetary Policy Reform

The most important weakness of the Indian policy environment is the monetary policy framework which lacks defined goals of the central bank. This policy has come under tremendous stress owing to the combination of exchange rate pegging and increasing *de facto* openness. Sound monetary policy involves attributes such as independence, transparency, predictability, rules rather than discretion, anchoring of inflationary expectations in the eyes of economic agents, and accountability. All these principles are violated in India (Mistry, 2007; Shah, 2008).

When monetary policy is structured with these attributes, many important benefits are harnessed. Sound monetary policy stabilizes the business cycle, and is made effective by a properly functioning monetary transmission. Sound monetary policy is 'speculation proof' in that the central bank completely controls the short-term interest rate but is not otherwise involved in trading on financial markets. A sound monetary policy framework stabilizes capital flows, and (in turn) is not attenuated by fluctuations of capital flows.

9.6.2 Full Convertibility

India is globalizing at a frenzied rate. Gross flows in the current account and capital account stand at 110 per cent of GDP, and have grown by 60 percentage points in a decade. Under this environment, capital controls have become increasingly ineffective.

However the planning approach employed is still reminiscent of the central planning that India once employed in industrial policy. A greater skepticism about this 'industrial policy approach' to capital controls is called for. The analytical foundations of such a policy are weak or nonexistent, and the ingenuity of the private sector in dodging the system of capital controls is remarkable.

At this point in India's progression towards integration into the world economy, the rapid dismantling of capital controls appears to be the best strategy. The first elements where full decontrol is immediately feasible are: FDI, portfolio flows, and rupee-denominated debt. In the case of FDI and portfolio flows, there is already convertibility, and all that needs to be done is to remove procedures and frictions. Rupee-denominated debt does not involve 'original sin' and should also feature in the early stages of opening up. This opening up needs to be accompanied by a monetary policy reform, a shift towards greater exchange rate flexibility, and the creation of currency derivatives markets. Once these are in place, liberalization of foreign currency debt and outflows can take place.

NOTES

1. There are four kinds of gross flows in the case of FDI. There are inbound flows, and repatriated capital, for FDI in India by foreigners. There are outbound flows, and then repatriated capital in the reverse direction, for outbound FDI from India. Some BOP statements for India show net FDI inflows into India as a single net number summing up these four components. In this paper, we are careful to separate out the net capital flows associated with two distinct phenomena: FDI in India and FDI by India. The latter is discussed in Section 9.2.5 as one of the mechanisms for outward capital flows.
2. For a discussion about participatory notes, see Singh (2007). For a treatment of this episode of capital controls against participatory notes, see http://ajayshahblog.blogspot.com/2007/10/middle-muddle.html on the world wide web.
3. The database released by Chinn and Ito shows a spike where India's score rose in 2000 and then dropped back to −1.1. This appears to be related to some difficulties in the data. A careful examination of India's experience with capital controls in 2000 suggests no important change took place in that year that was reversed in the next year.
4. Two time-series are available, the above mentioned series from RBI, and a shorter series

from SEBI. The correlation coefficient between the two series is 0.866. The results in the text are based on the longer RBI time-series. These results are qualitatively similar to those obtained with the shorter data from SEBI, and are available from the authors on request.
5. The CMIE Cospi index is used as the broad market index.
6. Section 13.5.2 of Shah and Patnaik (2007a) explains the unique interpretation of the deviation from CIP in India as a measure of currency expectations. Figures 13.3 and 13.4 there suggest that there may be difficulties with influential observations when using CIP deviation in a regression.
7. We use robust regression using an M estimator, as implemented by Venables and Ripley (2002).
8. This model is an improved version of Table 13.13 of Shah and Patnaik (2007a), which pertains to a shorter time-series.
9. Details are available from the authors on request.
10. VIX is the symbol for Chicago Board Options Exchange Volatility Index.
11. Options on the S&P 500 are traded on the Chicago Board Options Exchange (CBOE). The option prices seen on the market imply a value for the future volatility that traders must have on their mind when trading the options. This value is reverse engineered out of the observed option prices, thus giving the VIX in real time.
12. Stulz (2005) has emphasized that insider ownership limits the extent to which home bias can go down.
13. Poirson (2008) analyzes the difficulties of transparency at RBI and offers proposals about how this can be improved.

REFERENCES

Chinn, M.D. and H. Ito (2006), 'What matters for financial development? Capital controls, institutions, and interactions', *Journal of Development Economics*, **81**(1), 163–92.
Chinn, M.D. and H. Ito (2008), 'A new measure of financial openness', *Journal of Comparative Policy Analysis: Research and Practice*, **10**(3), September, 309–22.
Claessens, S. and S. Schmukler (2006), 'International Financial Integration through Equity Markets: Which Firms from which Countries Go Global?', Technical Report, World Bank.
Dincer, N.N. and B. Eichengreen (2007), 'Central bank transparency: where, why, and with what effects?', Working Paper 13003, National Bureau of Economic Research, available at: http://www.nber.org/papers/w13003.
Frankel, J. and S.J. Wei (1994), 'Yen bloc or dollar bloc? Exchange rate policies of the East Asian countries', in T. Ito and A. Krueger (eds), *Macroeconomic Linkage: Savings, Exchange Rates and Capital Flows*, NBER-EASE Vol. 3, Chicago, IL: University of Chicago Press, pp. 295–333.
Gordon, J. and P. Gupta (2004), 'Nonresident deposits in India: in search of return?', Technical Report, IMF Working Paper No. 04/48.
Kelkar, V. (2004), 'India: on the growth turnpike', Technical Report, Australian National University; K.R. Narayanan Memorial Lecture, available at: http://rspas.anu.edu.au/papers/narayanan/2004oration.pdf.
Mistry, P. (2007), 'Making Mumbai an International Financial Centre', Committee Report, Sage Publishing and Ministry of Finance, Government of India, available at: http://finmin.nic.in/mifc.html.
Patnaik, I. (2003), 'India's policy stance on reserves and the currency', Technical

Report, ICRIER Working Paper No. 108, available at: http://www.icrier.org/pdf/wp108.pdf.

Patnaik, I. (2005), 'India's experience with a pegged exchange rate', in S. Bery, B. Bosworth, and A Panagariya (eds), *The India Policy Forum 2004*, Washington, DC: Brookings Institution Press and New Delhi: National Council of Applied Economic Research, pp. 189–226, available at: http://openlib.org/home/ila/PDFDOCS/Patnaik2004_implementation.pdf.

Patnaik, I. (2007), 'India's currency regime and its consequences', *Economic and Political Weekly*, available at: http://openlib.org/home/ila/PDFDOCS/11182.pdf.

Poirson, H.K. (2008), 'Monetary policy communication and transparency', in *India: Selected Issues*, Washington, DC: International Monetary Fund.

RBI (Reserve Bank of India) (2009), 'Half-yearly report on foreign exchange reserves: 2008–2009' (covering the period of up to March 2009), Mumbai, July 16, available at: http://rbidocs.rbi.org.in/rdocs/Publications/PDFs/IHYRFRMAR09.pdf

Shah, A. (2008), 'New issues in Indian macro policy', in T.N. Ninan (ed.), *Business Standard India 2008*, New Delhi: Business Standard Books, pp. 26–54, available at: http://www.mayin.org/ajayshah/PDFDOCS/Shah2008_whatchanged.pdf.

Shah, A. and I. Patnaik (2007a), 'India's experience with capital flows: the elusive quest for a sustainable current account deficit', in S. Edwards (ed.), *Capital Controls and Capital Flows in Emerging Economies: Policies, Practices and Consequences*, Chicago, IL: University of Chicago Press, pp. 609–43, available at: http://www.nber.org/papers/w11387.

Shah, A. and I. Patnaik (2007b), 'What makes home bias abate? The evolution of foreign ownership of Indian firms', Technical Report, NIPFP.

Singh, M. (2007), 'Use of participatory notes in Indian equity market and recent regulatory changes', Technical Report 07/291, IMF, available at: http://www.imf.org/external/pubs/cat/longres.cfm?sk=21508.0.

Stulz, R.M. (2005), 'The limits of financial globalisation', *Journal of Finance*, **LX**(4), 1595–638.

Venables, W.N. and B.D. Ripley (2002), *Modern Applied Statistics with S*, 4th edn, New York: Springer.

Zeileis, A., A. Shah and I. Patnaik (2007), 'Exchange rate regime analysis using structural change methods', Report 56, Department of Statistics and Mathematics, Wirtschaftsuniversität Wien, Research Report Series, available at: http://epub.wu-wien.ac.at/dyn/openURL?id=oai:epub.wu-wien.ac.at:epub-wu-01_c48.

10. Managing capital flows: the case of Indonesia
Ira S. Titiheruw and Raymond Atje

10.1 INTRODUCTION

A close look at Indonesia's economy after the East Asian financial crisis reveals a mixed picture of its performance. On the one hand, various macroeconomic indicators show that the economy is doing fairly well. The government has done a good job in maintaining macroeconomic stability and sound fiscal performance: inflation is down, although it is still high compared to other emerging economies in the region, and the fiscal deficit was only slightly above 1 per cent of GDP in 2006. In addition, the financial sector is stable, with the banking sector in better shape compared to the pre-crisis period: capital adequacy ratio (CAR) remains high (around 20 per cent) and non-performing loans (NPLs) are on a declining trend. The capital account is in surplus and in 2007 foreign reserve was over $50 billion.

On the other hand, GDP growth and the investment rate remain low compared to before the crisis. Capital flows into Indonesia tumbled following the crisis and the net inflow of foreign direct investment (FDI) turned positive only in 2004. There are a number of factors that may explain this phenomenon. One of the often-mentioned factors is the unfavorable investment climate, which, in turn, depends on a host of other factors, such as inadequate infrastructure, lack of contractual enforcement, draconian labor regulations, and so on. As for the portfolio investment, it is reported that foreign investors dominate trading in the Jakarta Stock Exchange (JSX), lured in by lower dollar prices of the stocks traded there. In short, different forces and constraints are at work to channel the flows of different types of capital into various directions.

Also, as noted, 10 years after the crisis, Indonesia's investment rate was still below the pre-crisis rate (ADB, 2007). One reason is the fall in the real prices of capital goods and shifts in the composition of output but the reduction is insufficient to explain the prolonged decline in investment. As for the change in the structure of the economy, it is noted that in Indonesia, services have overtaken industry in contribution to GDP growth. Arguably, services require less investment than industry. However, a more recent claim, yet to be confirmed, suggests that the restrictive labor law mentioned above has actually driven investment away from labor intensive industries and toward more capital intensive industries.

The next section discusses post-Asian financial crisis capital flows in Indonesia. Section 10.3 discusses the determinants of capital flows in Indonesia while section 10.4 provides an analysis of the impact of capital inflows on financial and asset prices. Section 10.5 reviews the authorities' responses to surges in capital inflows and discusses the mini-crisis in 2005. The last section concludes.

10.2 POST-ASIAN FINANCIAL CRISIS CAPITAL FLOWS TO INDONESIA

The overall balance of payments (BoP) has recorded a surplus since 2002 with the exception of the 'mini crisis' period in 2005; the surplus was contributed by both current account and capital account surpluses. But since 1998, the current account was already in surplus and, recently, it has been supported by record-level exports which partly resulted from booming world commodity prices. The current account surplus was expected to reach 2.5 per cent of GDP (approximately $10.8 billion). The capital and financial account remains positive since 2004 due to a large surplus in public/government account, reflecting excess proceeds from government sales of securities after the government decided to make early repayment to the IMF in 2006. A small deficit was booked for capital and financial accounts in July–August 2007 due to portfolio investment outflow; the same period when the US subprime mortgage crisis started to unfold. Both accounts produced an accumulated $52.8 billion in net international reserves at the end of September 2007.

Looking back to the 1990s, the capital account surplus dominated the overall BoP up to the 1997–98 crisis. Both domestic demand and imports increased strongly. Meanwhile, the current account was in deficit for most of the decade. The subsequent crisis in 1997–98 set off flight of foreign (and domestic) capital out of the country. At the same time, huge depreciation of the rupiah suppressed import demand, and, as a result, the current account has been in surplus since 1998.

Figure 10.1 demonstrates the recent buildup of foreign reserves fueled by the current account surplus and (occasionally) by net capital inflows. While the current account surplus had been more or less stable on the positive side, net capital flows have had a rather mixed performance to date.

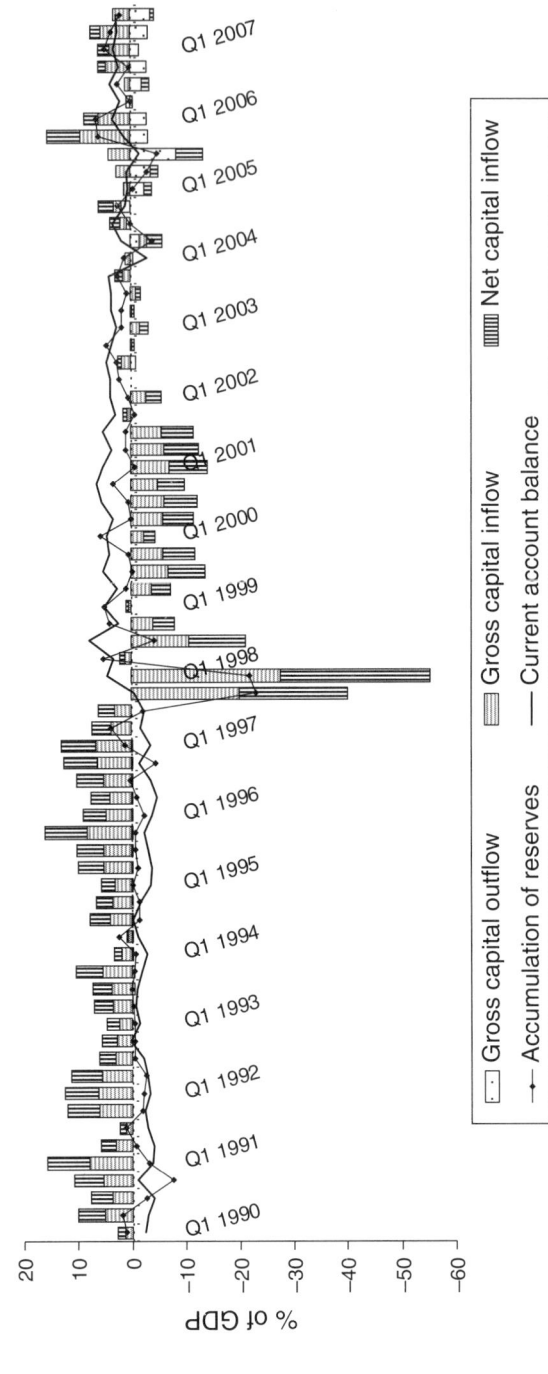

Sources: International Financial Statistics (IMF) and Bank Indonesia.

Figure 10.1 Indonesia: gross capital flows, current account balance, and reserve accumulation, 1990–2007 (% GDP)

In 2002, net capital inflows recorded positive numbers for the first time in the post-crisis period. Net capital inflows slumped in the third quarter of 2005. Rising expectations that the country's macroeconomic environment would deteriorate due to its heavy subsidy on domestic oil prices[1] resulted in significant gross capital outflow. As of 2007, net capital inflows are still below pre-Asian financial crisis level.

On the inflow side, the dominance of other investment inflows (e.g., external debt and loan repayment from both private and public sectors) in the 1990s has been taken over by FDI and portfolio investment flows after 2005. Post-crisis portfolio investment inflow was initially recorded in 2002. Although FDI inflow started to grow in 2004 and remained more or less on a positive trend, the overall picture of capital inflows is still dominated by portfolio (and other) investment flows.

Gross capital outflows seemed to be recorded improperly until 2004. As can be gathered from Table 10.1, capital outflows were mainly attributed to transactions in other investment assets (records of external debt transactions from corporate and banking sectors). The huge deficits in other investment assets in 2005 ($10.4 billion) were due to increased assets (currency and deposits) holdings by the private sector[2] in foreign countries, particularly in the second and third quarters of 2005. Similar events took place in July–August 2007, whereby other investment assets in the private sector increased from $486 million (end of September 2006) to $2.6 billion (end of September 2007). The increase in other investment assets was due to increased deposits in foreign countries by domestic banks (bank's nostro/foreign exchange account in foreign correspondence banks).

Figure 10.3 presents the breakdown of the net financial account. Before the 1997–98 period, capital (and financial) account transactions depended on FDI and external borrowings (as reflected in net other investment flow). In the post-crisis period, the composition shifted more towards portfolio investment in the form of securities (equity) and bonds (debt) issued by government and corporate sectors.

10.2.1 Public Sector Financial Account

In the public (government and monetary authority) financial account, the portfolio investment liabilities consist of government bonds (SUN) and SBI net purchases by foreign investors. Public portfolio investment transactions dominated the private counterpart in the overall financial account. Since their issuance in 2002,[3] government bond holdings by the banking sector remained the largest, ranging between Rp259.92 billion and Rp348.40 billion for the period 2002–07. They peaked in 2002 and dropped to the lowest level in July 2007. Bank Indonesia (BI) started

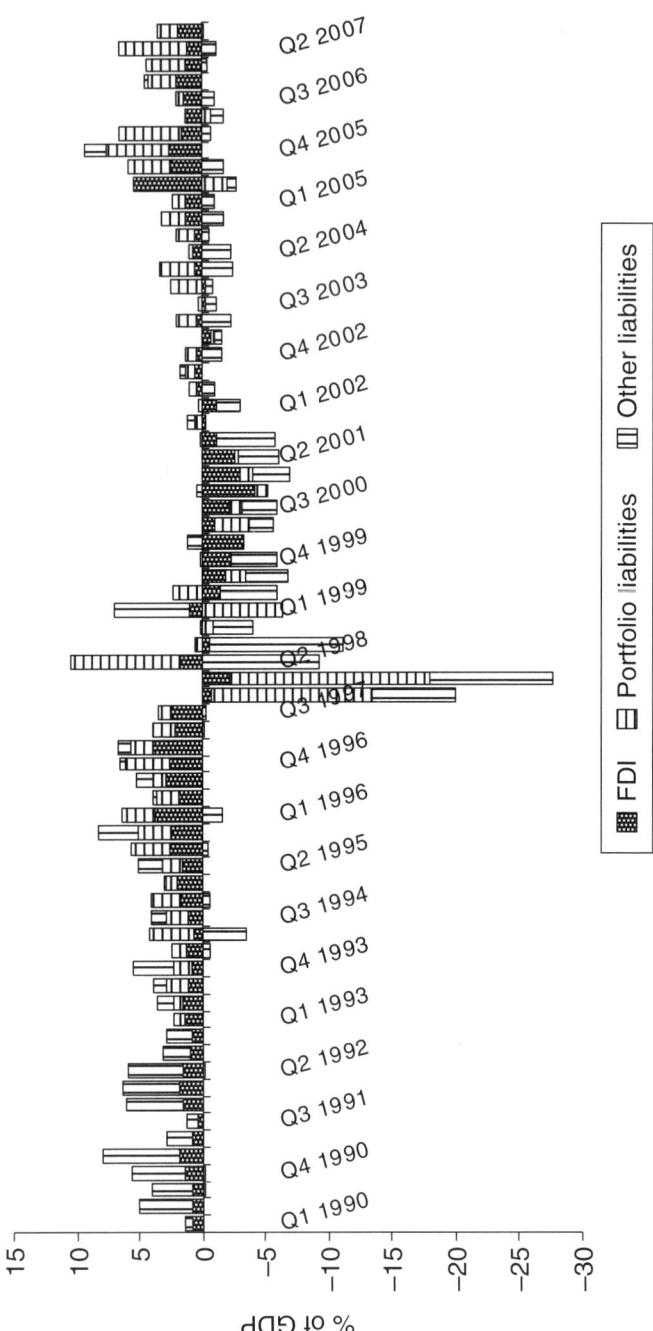

Sources: International Financial Statistics (IMF) and Bank Indonesia.

Figure 10.2 Indonesia: gross capital inflow, 1990–2007 (% GDP)

Table 10.1 Indonesia: gross capital outflow, 2004–07 (% GDP)

Year/Quarter	Direct investment abroad	Portfolio investment asset	Other investment assets
2004:1	−0.57	0.06	−1.21
2004:2	−2.04	−0.39	0.06
2004:3	−1.04	0.09	0.86
2004:4	−1.66	0.77	1.75
2005:1	−0.95	−0.50	−0.92
2005:2	−0.87	−0.09	−2.57
2005:3	−1.23	−0.64	−6.48
2005:4	−1.21	−0.28	−2.04
2006:1	−0.77	−0.46	−1.89
2006:2	−0.58	−0.50	1.63
2006:3	−1.39	−0.35	−0.51
2006:4	−0.21	−0.80	−2.04
2007:1	−1.13	−0.28	−0.28
2007:2	0.48	−0.90	−2.96
2007:3	−1.22	−0.33	−2.31

Sources: International Financial Statistics (IMF) and Bank Indonesia.

taking ownership of the government bonds in 2005, in amounts ranging from Rp7.54 billion to Rp14.86 billion.

As regards the government bond ownership by non-bank institutions, from 2002 until 2004, mutual fund institutions steadily held government bonds in amounts ranging from Rp35.72 billion to Rp53.98 billion. In 2006–07, among non-bank institutions, foreign investors constituted the largest ownership of government bonds. The amount reached approximately Rp80 trillion at the end of October 2007. The purchase of government bonds to date has helped to finance budget deficits necessary to accelerate priority sector spending, mainly infrastructure, health and education.

10.2.2 Private Financial Account

On the private sector side, the tendency since early 2007 has been to offset gross capital inflow with gross outflow – leaving a negligible amount of net private capital inflow to the country. The outflow from private financial accounts was mainly other investment assets – domestic banks' currency and deposit holdings in foreign countries. FDI was the single largest component of private capital inflow. Since FDI is a relatively stable part of the

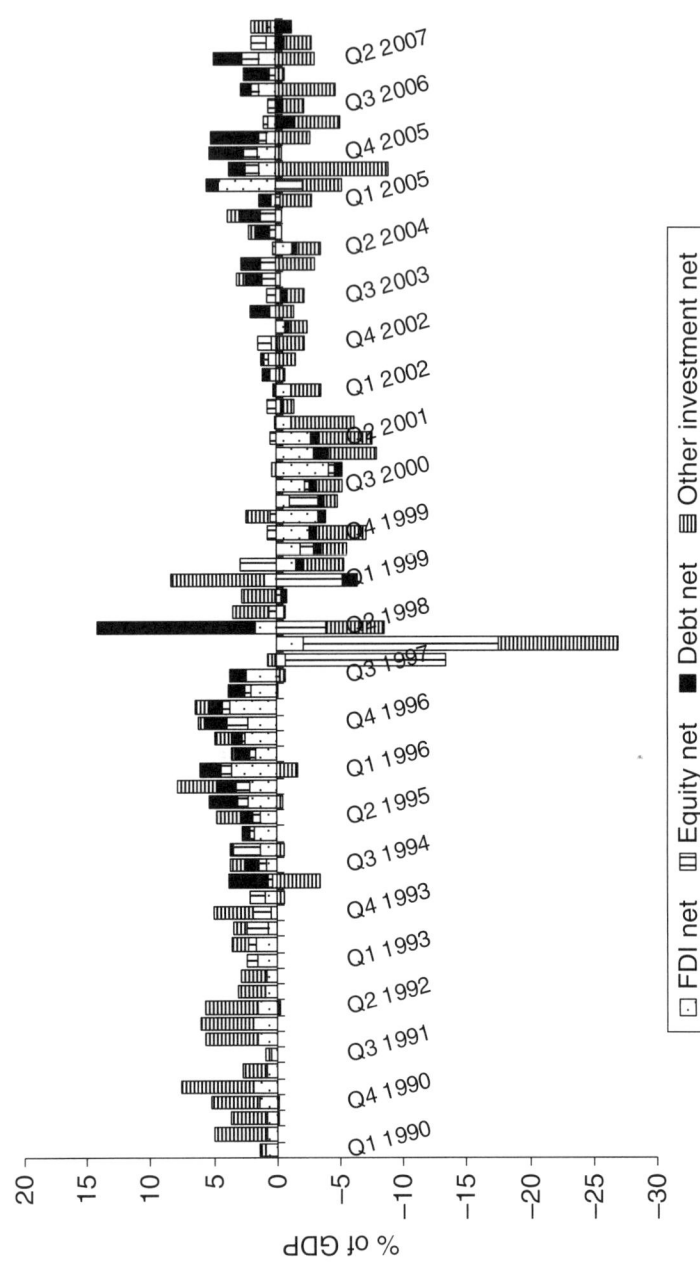

Sources: International Financial Statistics (IMF) and Bank Indonesia.

Figure 10.3 Indonesia: net financial account, 1990–2007 (% GDP)

The case of Indonesia 267

inflow, it certainly is good news for government efforts to build a more solid base for long-term growth.

10.3 DETERMINANTS OF CAPITAL FLOWS TO INDONESIA

There are a number of 'pull factors' attracting capital inflows to Indonesia. Some are related to fundamental reasons such as improved macroeconomic conditions. Compared to other East Asian countries adversely affected by the financial crisis in 1997–98, Indonesia experienced the largest decline in economic growth. GDP growth recovered slowly in 1999, posting 0.8 per cent in its y-o-y figure. Since then, economic growth rates started to climb and remain at the 4–5 per cent range.

Other macroeconomic indicators performed fairly well during the 10-year period. Inflation declined from 78 per cent in 1998 to 6.4 per cent in 2004. The inflation rate began to rise in 2005 and a 114 per cent increase in fuel prices in October pushed the inflation rate to over 17 per cent at the end of the year. In 2006, inflation decelerated rapidly and was back on track to record 6.6 per cent at the end of the year. However, in 2007, there was growing concern (again) over rising oil and food prices. Up to October 2007, the consumer price index posted a 6.7 per cent increase.

Fiscal deficits had narrowed from above 4 per cent of GDP in 1998 to 0.5 per cent in 2005. However, the deficit widened to 0.9 per cent of GDP in 2006, and it was expected to widen further in 2007 (reaching up to 1.5 per cent of GDP). The Ministry of Finance (MoF) had projected the deficits to expand to 1.9 per cent of GDP in 2008.

Another 'pull factor' related to macroeconomic fundamentals is reduced external debts. By the end of 2006, total external debt to GDP had declined to 33 per cent of GDP. External debt was split evenly between government and private debt. While the trend in external government debt[4] seems to be declining over the years, private debt is on the rise.

Growth in some economic sectors could also be considered a driver of another type of capital inflows: FDI. However, due to the possibility of structural changes, some of which have occurred since the 1997–98 crisis, the post-crisis FDI level has remained at 70 per cent of the pre-crisis level. For the decade before the financial crisis struck (1986–96), Indonesia's annual GDP growth exceeded 8 per cent – driven mainly by growth in industry (including manufacturing, mining, utilities, and construction) that contributed to more than 47 per cent of output. The manufacturing industry alone contributed 31 per cent. Agriculture and service sectors contributed 9.5 per cent and 43.2 per cent, respectively (Hayashi, 2005).

Post-crisis period (1997–2006) data on sectoral sources of GDP growth showed that agriculture, industry, and the services sectors contributed 15.3 per cent, 37.5 per cent, and 47.2 per cent, respectively, to GDP growth. The services sector has overtaken the industry sector as the largest contributor to GDP growth in the post-1997 crisis. Since industry (a comparatively more capital-oriented sector) has had a slower growth rate after the crisis, it is safe to expect a lower investment ratio than that in the pre-crisis period.

Another 'pull factor' has to do with the short-term profit-making opportunity due to high interest rates in Indonesia. Compared to other economies in Southeast Asia – particularly Malaysia, the Philippines, Singapore, and Thailand – Indonesia offered the highest yield in domestic currency investment from 1997 to the end of 2006.

During 2007, the yield spread between the Indonesia global bond and the US treasury notes (T-notes) for the two-year tenor stood at around 3 per cent from January to May, before it fluctuated slightly and landed at 5.7 per cent in November 2007. Meanwhile, the 10-year tenor spread between the Indonesia global bond and US T-notes was higher than the two-year tenor, but it experienced a similar spread trend to that of the two-year tenor. A higher yield provided an incentive for foreign investments.

10.4 IMPACT OF CAPITAL INFLOWS ON FINANCIAL AND ASSET PRICES

Foreign capital inflows can have substantial macroeconomic and financial benefits. The inflows could provide investment funding for capital-constrained countries. In the long term, inflows, particularly in the form of FDI, could speed up technology transfer and managerial practices in order to bolster domestic productivity. However, large capital inflows produce difficulties in managing macroeconomic stability due to the pressure on domestic currency appreciation and demand-induced inflation. This could reduce the country's competitiveness.

Below are some macroeconomic implications of capital flows in Indonesia.

Exchange rate movement After net capital inflows showed up in 2002, the rupiah appreciated in real terms by approximately 6 per cent (Figure 10.4). However, in the second half of 2007 the rupiah was pressured downward due to capital outflows as foreign investors began to withdraw capital due to uncertainty in the global financial markets precipitated by the US sub-prime financial crisis.

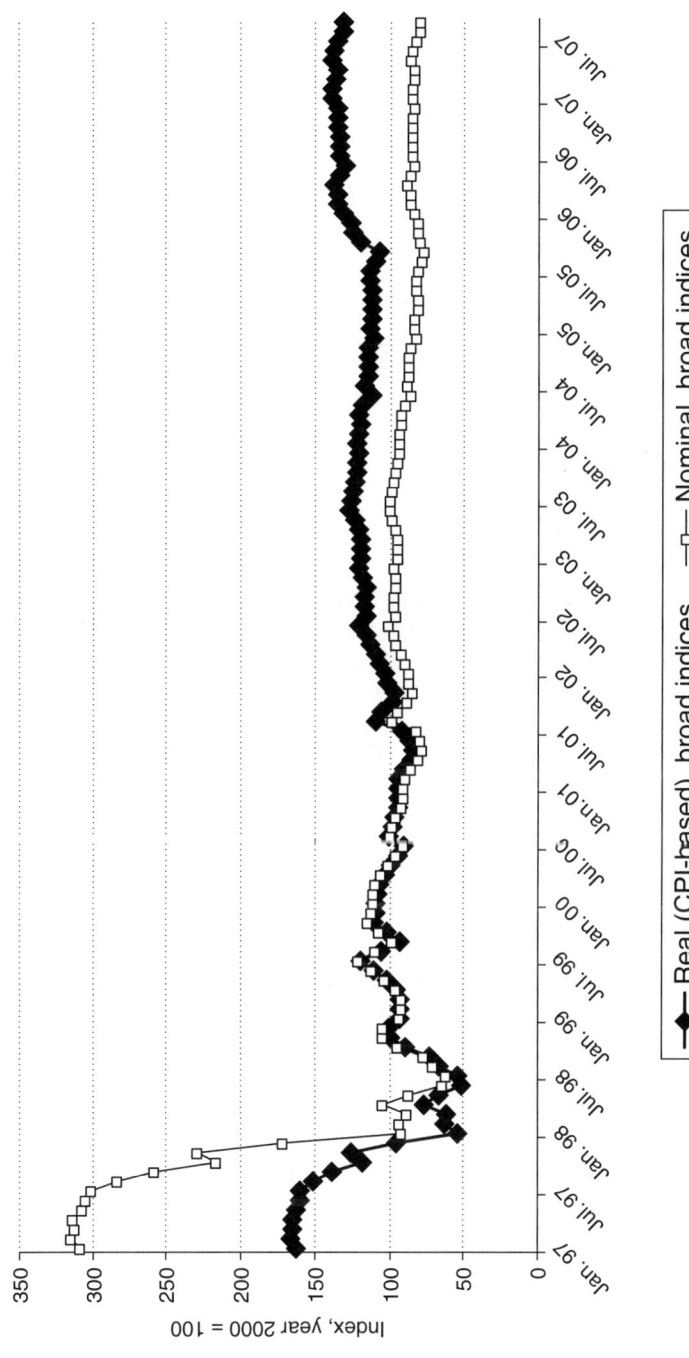

Source: BIS.

Figure 10.4 Indonesia: real effective exchange rate, 1997–2007

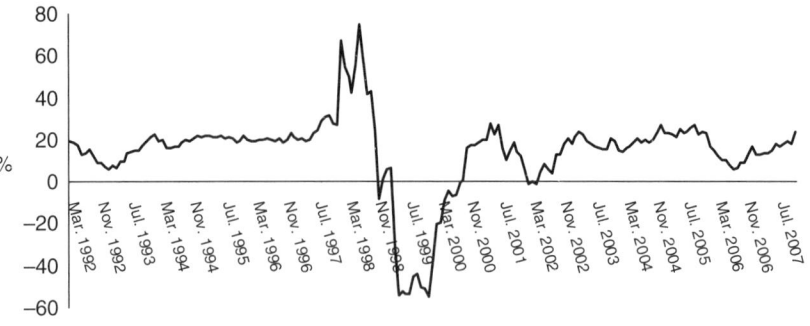

Source: CEIC.

Figure 10.5   Indonesia: banks' commercial loan growth, 1992–2007 (% year-on-year)

Inflation   The inflation rate declined from 77.5 per cent in 1998 to 6.4 per cent in 2004, but it rose in 2005 to 17.1 per cent due to the 114 per cent increase in fuel prices. In 2006 inflation decelerated rapidly to 6.6 per cent. However, in 2007, there was growing concern again over rising oil and food prices that could raise the inflation rate to a higher level in the following year. It should be noted that the recent rising trend in inflation is not due to demand-induced pressure (which, if anything, has been suppressed by the government's tight fiscal policy) as suggested in the event of large foreign capital inflows. The supply-side pressures (increasing international commodity prices and problems in real sectors such as the high-cost economy, lack of infrastructure, and labor problems) have been pointed to as the culprit. These problems have already created difficulties in channeling excess liquidity in the domestic economy.

Banking sector   Capital inflows contributed to increased exposure of domestic banks to foreign exchange risk through external debt and (indirectly) through accelerated credit growth. At the end of September 2007, the outstanding external debt of banks stood at 1.2 per cent of GDP. The ratio of outstanding external debt to GDP was approximately 32 per cent in the third quarter of 2007, divided into private sector external debt at 13 per cent of GDP, and the government's external debt at 19 per cent of GDP. It is noteworthy that the ratio of outstanding external debts to private banks to outstanding international reserve declined from more than 80 per cent in 1997 to slightly above 10 per cent in September 2007.

Figure 10.5 shows commercial bank loan growth, which returned to positive territory in 2001 and remained elevated except in two episodes

Table 10.2 Residential property price index, 2002–07 (1999 = 100)

	2002	2003	2004	2005	2006	2007
Mar	133.22	110.58	118.52	124.97	135.67	143.38
June	135.56	113.31	120.33	127.33	136.71	145.91
Sep	137.63	115.89	121.81	128.37	139.62	146.93
Dec	139.86	117.35	122.76	132.42	142.6	

Source: Property Survey, Bank Indonesia.

that occurred in 2002 and 2006. Meanwhile, the gross NPLs ratio declined rapidly from more than 25 per cent during the 1997–98 crisis to less than 10 per cent since 2003. Post-crisis restructuring in the banking sector is expected to build more robust banks.

Asset prices Large capital inflows could result in inflated asset prices. One of many indicators of inflated asset prices is the stock market price index. The increasing trend of the JSX Index reflected a surge in Indonesian stock prices, particularly after 2004.

In 2007, the JSX Index grew 52 per cent. On one side, macroeconomic fundamentals provided strong support to the increase of the JSX Index. But on the other side, corporate sector growth (the micro foundations) has not been strong enough to actually create a very bullish trend in stock prices. Growth in listed companies' Price Equity Ratio (the PER) for December 2007 (approximately 18.5) could not entirely keep pace with the soaring JSX Index. These numbers do not necessarily indicate that asset bubbles have been established and could burst any time soon. However, the short-term nature of portfolio investment generates concerns that it could be withdrawn from the country quickly and lead to the collapse of asset prices and depletion of reserves.

Domestic investors occupied a more dominant position than foreign investors in the stock market. This is indicated by the small proportion of foreign net buy (to market capitalization) in the JSX.

Another indicator to check inflated prices is the property price index. The BI has been conducting a quarterly property survey since 1999. Table 10.2 shows that property prices have gradually (less than 10 per cent) moved up. According to the survey, however, the increase has been attributed to higher prices of materials and the high cost of obtaining a construction license.

10.5 POLICY RESPONSES

After learning hard lessons from the Asian financial crisis, the government has worked to improve Indonesia's macroeconomic fundamentals and tightened financial sector regulation and supervision. Combining this with a more flexible exchange rate regime, Indonesia has become less vulnerable to external shocks like those that occurred during 1997–98. The US subprime mortgage problem, which caused problems for major world financial institutions, appeared to have limited impacts on domestic financial markets. This is partly due to strong macroeconomic fundamentals and sound financial and corporate sectors.

Responding to the influx of capital flows, Indonesia did not opt for capital control measures. Besides being quite confident about its macroeconomic fundamentals and significant amount of reserve accumulation, Indonesia has improved prudential regulations[5] and supervision,[6] as well as upgrading corporate governance regulations and practices. With regard to the foreign exchange market, the BI has moved to limit rupiah transactions and foreign exchange credit in order to restrict speculative movement. In addition to these policies, the authorities decided to proactively develop financial markets and instruments to avoid heavy concentration in either the banking sector[7] or traditional financial instruments such as Bank Indonesia Certificates. On banking development, the BI focused on consolidation in the banking sector by raising minimum capital requirements for banks. The so-called 'Single Presence Policy' expects some mergers and acquisitions. Regulation on this policy was issued in October 2006 to limit bank shareholders to having a controlling interest in only one bank. It is expected that by the end of 2010, bank owners with controlling interest in more than one bank will have to submit their respective plans (i.e., undertake merger, establish a holding company, or sell one and keep the other with controlling interest). Yet implementation has been delayed and substantial amendments are expected. Another development was related to reducing the amount of insured deposits (from Rp1 billion to Rp100 million) in March 2007, which was implemented without a hitch.

Since the BI has committed to the inflation targeting (IT) monetary framework in 2005, available policy options to manage the impact of capital inflows are: allowing the exchange rate to appreciate, reducing the interest rate to curb inflows, and introducing administrative measures to help manage capital flows. The impact of these policies could lead to a deterioration in export competitiveness (in turn, it would have adverse implications for external balance) and in case of excessive appreciation, undershooting of inflation targets. Another policy option for managing potentially disruptive capital inflows is to reduce the interest rate. However, interest rate reduction may also trigger acceleration in the banking sector's credit growth and increase pressure on short-term inflation targets.

The Indonesian monetary authority did allow the exchange rate to absorb the impact of capital inflow. The policy has been in line with the BI's IT monetary framework. However, from time to time, the BI has been more likely to be confronted by depreciation threats rather than appreciation. So far, policies to manage capital outflow have performed quite well (see 2005 mini-crisis episode, below). The government and the BI continue to work toward a more sustainable foreign capital supply, for example by improving the investment climate, expanding sources of current account surpluses (reducing heavy reliance on surging commodity prices), and strengthening financial institutions and regulations.

Two major investment-related packages were introduced in late 2005 and early 2006. The infrastructure package was announced in November 2005 (Presidential Regulation No. 67/2005 on Cooperation between the Government and Enterprises in Infrastructure Procurement – revoking the previous Public–Private Partnership (PPP) in Presidential Decree No. 7/1998). The package attempted to assure private investors that the PPP process will be fair, open, competitive, and transparent; while, at the same time, it recognized that projects must be based on mutual benefit of investors and the public. In other words, the new regulation deals with risk management and government support for infrastructure projects. In May 2006, the Ministry of Finance issued a regulation on the Technical Directives for Controlling and Managing Risks of Infrastructure Development (Regulation No. 38/MK/2006), which basically allows the government to offer financial or other forms of compensation to private enterprises participating in infrastructure projects subject to political, project performance (including land acquisition problems[8]), and demand risks exposure.

Following the general PPP framework provided by this regulation, the various industry sectors have their own set of relevant laws and regulations to facilitate private investment in sector projects – laws on toll roads, water supply and sanitation have been enacted while draft laws for ports, airports, and railroads have been submitted to the parliament. These laws will phase out the monopoly of state-owned enterprises (SOEs) in the provision of infrastructure services in those sectors. In addition, the government has sought to improve the regulatory framework for various infrastructure sectors by unbundling the regulatory functions from main government entities operating the businesses in the sector. For instance, for toll roads, the government has unbundled regulatory functions from the main SOE (Jasa Marga) and transferred the responsibility to a new regulatory body. Oil and gas, electricity and telecommunication sectors have undergone a similar transformation. To reaffirm its commitment to infrastructure development and its stance on PPP, the government held its second annual infrastructure conference in November 2006 to boost investor confidence in the PPP program for infrastructure development.

The package launched in March 2006 aimed at improving the investment climate. The package involved a total of 85 individual action items that focuses on five areas: general investment policies/procedures; customs, excise and duties policies; taxation; labor; and small and medium enterprises finance. The reform package included the planned submission of a new investment law, completion of new tax law deliberation[9] and revision of a labor law[10] for parliamentary deliberation. Fifty-four of these items specified a target date for completion, ranging from March to December 2006. To date, 42 (or 78 per cent) of these items were completed by the end of 2006.

The most important achievement in the package is the approval of the Investment Law in March 2007. The Law provides, among other things, equal treatment for domestic and foreign investors, binding international arbitration, the elimination of forced divestiture (considered a guarantee against nationalization), land use rights up to 95 years (from 35 years previously), and extended residency permits for foreign investors. In accordance with the Investment Law, the government plans to develop clearer, simpler, and more transparent criteria for a negative investment list.

In July 2007, the government issued Presidential Instruction (Inpres) No. 6/2007 which included major initiatives in streamlining business start-up and licensing procedures, cutting value-added tax refund time, launching a pilot project for National Single Window at the main port, improving risk profiling for customs clearance, and establishing 43 small taxpayer offices.

The Case of the 2005 Mini-crisis

A 'mini crisis' occurred in Indonesia in 2005, due mainly to concerns over sustainability of the government budget to deal with rising world oil prices. Investors easily lost confidence as the government and the BI did not appear to respond to their concerns. Figure 10.6 shows both the rupiah/dollar exchange rate and the JSX Index movements on a daily basis in 2005.

In fact, the rupiah had been under pressure since the US Federal Reserve began raising its key interest rate in 2004. Pressures also came from increased imports for consumption and investment activities that had been sustained since late 2004. However, the government and monetary authority seemed to think that rupiah depreciation was a global

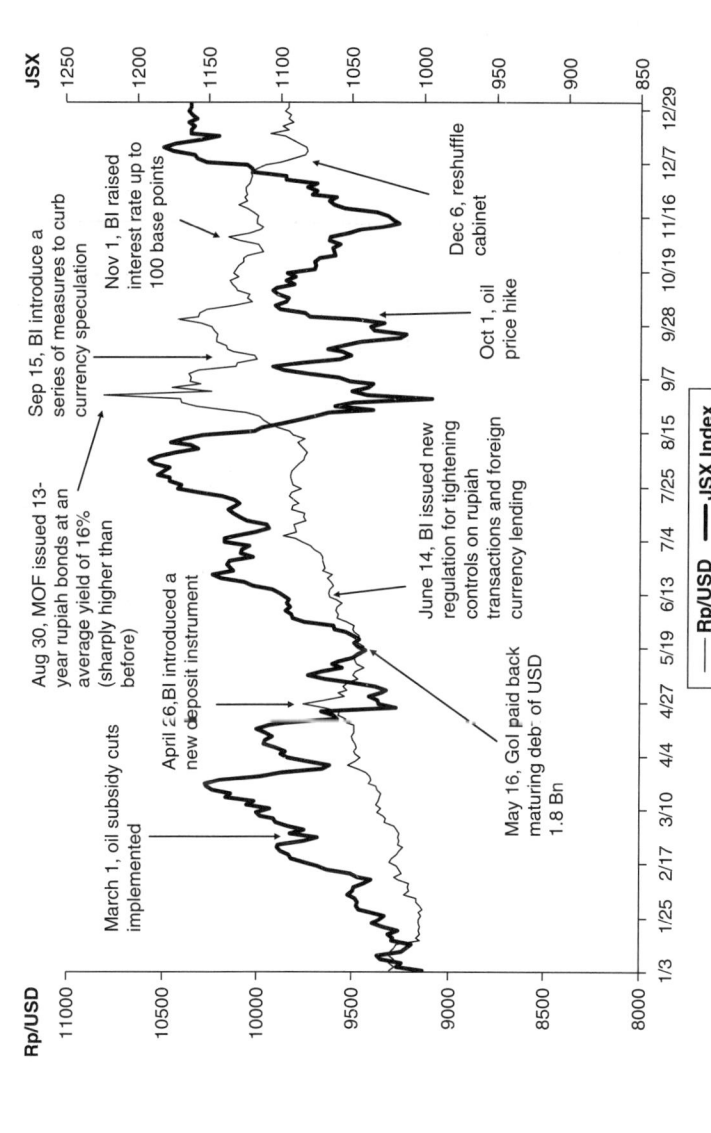

Sources: Bank Indonesia and Indonesia Stock Exchange.

Figure 10.6 Indonesia: daily movement of exchange rate and JSX Index, 2005

phenomenon in which major currencies such as the euro and yen also depreciated. After the world oil price soared to $70/barrel in March 2005, the government and the BI finally moved to respond to this changing external environment. The government decided to raise domestic fuel prices by 29 per cent on average. Joint efforts of the BI and the government sought to curb pressures in the foreign exchange market by compelling SOEs (most importantly, Pertamina) to coordinate with the BI to buy dollars. In April, the BI issued a regulation to reduce the Net Open Position of the banking sector from 30 per cent to 20 per cent. It also introduced the Fine Tuning Contraction (FTC) instrument which offered maturities of 1–14 days. The FTC rate was set at 5.75 per cent for a four-day deposit, and 3.6 per cent for the two- and three-day rates.[11] Another short-term instrument available at the time was a seven-day Fasilitas Bank Indonesia (FASBI) deposit facility (the FASBI seven-day rate was increased to 7.25 per cent in early April), and one-month and three-month Bank Indonesia Certificates (interest rate was set at 8.25 per cent and 8.05 per cent, respectively). The BI also resumed a weekly auction of SBI in May 2005 in order to soak up excess liquidity in the market. In the following month, the BI issued a regulation, effective 14 July 2005, to restrict rupiah transactions and foreign currency lending. Besides limiting foreign exchange derivative transactions against the rupiah to $1 million and putting a ceiling on dollar purchases for forward transaction and swaps to $1 million, the BI also imposed a three-month minimum investment hedging period on foreign exchange transactions. As a result of implementation of PBI No. 7/14/PBI/2005, swap transaction volume was reduced to an average of $410 million/day for the second half of 2005 – the previous half recorded an average volume of $1.06 billion/day.

In another move to defend the rupiah, the government and the BI agreed to supply dollar needs of Pertamina for oil imports directly out of the country's foreign exchange reserves (Policy Package 5 July 2005). Both also agreed to make SOEs place their foreign exchange earnings from exports in local banks.[12] To strengthen foreign exchange reserves, the government and the BI agreed to increase its participation in Bilateral Swap Arrangement.[13]

Despite all these efforts, the rupiah continued to lose value against the dollar. It hit as low as Rp10 030/dollar on 22 August 2005 – only days after the President delivered his speech on the draft of the 2006 State Budget. The fact that there were no dramatic changes in the government's fiscal priority the next year brought market distrust and uncertainty over policy direction. The government assumed average oil prices for the next year to be $40/barrel, thus the fuel subsidy was budgeted around Rp68.5 trillion. This was seen as utterly unrealistic as the market assumed that oil prices would climb to $55/barrel the next year, and therefore, the government would be unable to maintain fiscal sustainability, endangering the country's balance of payments. A policy package was launched on 30 August 2005 to stabilize the rupiah, including increasing banks' statutory reserve (Bank Indonesia Regulation (PBI) No. 7/29/PBI/2005), regulating derivative transactions (PBI No. 7/31/PBI/2005), and on hedging swap transactions (PBI No. 7/36/PBI/2005). The BI also issued a regulation to further minimize banks' foreign exchange risk exposure by classifying the Net Open Position (NOP) item into two: NOP on the balance sheet and overall NOP (PBI No. 7/37/PBI/2005). Each was set at 20 per cent.

Confidence returned to the domestic financial market after the government increased domestic fuel prices by 114 per cent on 1 October 2005. The headline inflation rate shot up to reach 17.1 per cent at the end of 2005, with core inflation remaining reasonable at 9.7 per cent. It was expected that inflationary pressure would ease quickly in the first quarter of 2006. In November 2005, the President managed to do a cabinet reshuffle to boost credibility. Indeed, the 'mini crisis' was a case of poorly managed escalating negative sentiment that turned into a self-fulfilling prophecy.

10.6 CONCLUDING REMARKS

The Government of Indonesia has been a staunch supporter of capital account liberalization. Since 1970, the government has imposed no restriction on movement of foreign capital – underlining the importance of foreign capital flows since its early stage of economic development. During the 1970s to 1980s, official development assistance was the largest single component of foreign capital inflow. Then, throughout the 1990s up to the point of the 1997–98 crisis, it was overtaken by other types of capital, FDI, and corporate/bank lending, which were recorded as other investment items. The overall BoP was characterized by a negative current account and a positive capital account, since foreign capital inflows on the latter side created pressure for the domestic currency to appreciate, resulting in a negative current account balance.

Foreign capital flows started to return to the country in 2002 in the form of portfolio investment. As the government tried to reduce its reliance on foreign currency denominated debt, it shifted its development financing towards the issuance of domestic currency denominated government bonds, which has attracted foreign capital inflows. FDI also began to record positive figures two years later, but the overall level of foreign capital inflows has not reached its pre-crisis level. Nevertheless, the nature of the foreign capital flows remains volatile, which became more apparent during the mini crisis in 2005. Indeed, the government has been striving to maintain a balance between attracting foreign capital flows and managing their volatility.

As of 2008 the government and the monetary authority directed their attention towards achieving more solid economic fundamentals such as maintaining fiscal restraint and controlling inflation. The conduct of macroeconomic stability by credible policymakers would attract foreign capital inflows as well as reduce their volatility. In addition, the government and the monetary authority also focused on enhancing governance in the banking and corporate sectors through the adoption of international standards such as capital adequacy requirements, provisions of NPLs for banks and corporate governance principles for private/public companies.

Finally, the monetary authority has undertaken some measures to improve the management of capital flows into and out of the country. For example, people are now required to notify the relevant authority when they bring in or take out of the country a certain amount of capital. Before the 1997–98 crisis, this was not the case. The main purpose of this requirement is to allow the monetary authority to monitor capital flows in both directions and, presumably, to improve its capability to react in a timely manner to any eventuality. It remains to be seen whether such a policy will indeed be effective.

NOTES

1. International oil prices reached $70/barrel in the first quarter of 2005. This created a confidence crisis toward net oil importing countries.
2. Other investment assets by the private sector account for $9.6 billion while the public sector's other investment assets amount to approximately $850 million.
3. The government issued its first bonds, named 'recap bonds', to help ailing banks during the crisis.
4. Including official development assistance (ODA), non-ODA and commercial securities held by non-residents.
5. See IMF (2004), 'Assessing Indonesia's Banking Sector Reforms', in *Indonesia: Selected Issues* (Washington DC).
6. For example, Bank Indonesia's Circular Note No. 7/22/DLN/2005 regulates External Debt Reporting Requirement.
7. As of 2008 Indonesia's financial system remained dominated by the banking system – more than 75 per cent.
8. Due to the importance of the land acquisition problem, the government amended the presidential regulation that provides a legal basis for the government to acquire infrastructure project land (and compensate landowners to an amount based on fair market valuation) – Presidential Regulation no. 65/2006).
9. The Tax Administration Law has been passed recently.
10. The government has put on hold revision of the manpower law due to pressure from labor unions.
11. These rates were capped at a one-week FASBI rate. At the time, it was below the rate

for a two-day rupiah deposit (5–6 per cent in interbank money market). The instrument was used in particular by some banks that could not enter the interbank market due to risk limits.
12. The regulation did not apply to private sector exporters since they could undermine or circumvent the regulation by under-invoicing their exports.
13. Bilateral swap arrangements (BSAs) by Indonesia with Japan and the People's Republic of China were agreed in May 2005. A BSA with Korea has been signed since December 2003. Since 2000, Indonesia has participated in a liquidity support mechanism at regional level under the Chiang Mai Initiative, which involves the establishment of BSAs and the extension of the ASEAN swap arrangement.

REFERENCES

Asian Development Bank (2007), 'Ten years after the crisis: the facts about investment and growth', *Asian Development Outlook 2007*, March, available at: http://www.adb.org/Documents/books/ADO/2007/part01-ten-years-after.pdf.

Bank Indonesia (various years), *Laporan Perekonomian Indonesia*, various annual publications.

Bank Indonesia (various years), *Statistik Ekonomi dan Keuangan Indonesia*, various monthly publications.

Bank Indonesia (various years), *Tinjauan Kebijakan Moneter*, various monthly publications.

Hayashi, M. (2005), 'Structural changes in Indonesian industry and trade: an input–output analysis', *The Developing Economies*, **43**(1), March, 39–71.

International Monetary Fund (various years), *Global Development Finance*.

International Monetary Fund (2005–07), *Global Financial Stability Report*.

International Monetary Fund (various years), *International Financial Statistics*.

11. Managing capital flows: the case of the Republic of Korea

Soyoung Kim and Doo Yong Yang

11.1 INTRODUCTION

Since 1980 the Republic of Korea (hereafter Korea) has experienced huge capital flows, increasing almost 39 times from $2.3 billion in 1980 to $91.8 billion in 2006.[1] In the 1980s and early 1990s, bank loans and transfers were the primary source of capital flows, accounting for more than half of all private capital inflows into the Korean economy. However, the recent huge capital surge into Korea is portfolio investments, making up to 80 per cent of total private capital inflows.

The surge in capital inflows into Korea has been induced by both 'pull' and 'push' factors related to Korea's new economic environment that emerged following the currency crisis. With low interest rates and dropping asset investment returns due to the economic slowdown in advanced economies, investors' demand for investment in emerging market portfolios began to soar. To these international investors, Korea is seen as a primary investment point. In recent years, the favorable global liquidity condition has contributed to increased capital inflows into emerging market economies including Korea. At the same time, Korea, like other major East Asian countries, relaxed its regulatory measures on foreign portfolio investment through capital market/account liberalization, further spurring the portfolio inflows.

We investigate the effects of capital inflows on the Korean economy, paying particular attention to asset prices. In Section 11.2, we provide a brief summary of capital account liberalization, followed by an analysis of the patterns of capital flows and some explanation of the recent surge in capital inflows, with a special focus on portfolio inflows. In Section 11.4, we discuss the effects of portfolio inflows on asset prices and exchange rates. In Section 11.5, we perform an empirical investigation of the effects of capital flows in the economy based on a vector autoregression (VAR) model. In the last section, we identify lessons from the Korean experience on managing capital flows, policy challenges, and appropriate policy responses.

11.2 BRIEF SUMMARY OF CAPITAL ACCOUNT LIBERALIZATION IN KOREA

Capital flows in Korea are to a large extent related to the openness of capital markets, as in other emerging market economies. Since the 1980s, the government has continued to open capital markets to foreign investors, as well as to allow domestic agents to invest abroad. Since the 1997 crisis, most capital flow restrictions have been liberalized and as a result, capital flows into and out of the Korean economy are market-determined.

Throughout the 1980s, the policy of the Korean government on capital flows depended on the current account balance. Under the pegged exchange rate regime, the capital inflows were used to accommodate the overall balance of payments (BOP). Therefore, the overall BOP fluctuated around a net zero balance, and the current account and capital account moved in opposite directions (Kim et al. 2004). In 1988, the Korean government formally accepted the obligations of Article VIII, Section 2-4 of the IMF's Articles of Agreement and abolished its remaining restrictions on payments and transfers for current account transactions.

With the intention to join the Organisation for Economic Co-operation and Development (OECD), Korea accelerated its capital account liberalization in the early 1990s. In 1992, foreign investors were given permission to purchase Korean stocks of up to 3 per cent of outstanding shares of each company per individual, but no more than 10 per cent of a company in total. In June 1993, the Korean government put forth a blueprint for the financial sector liberalization that would ease restrictions on foreign exchange transactions, such as widening the daily won/dollar trading margins, expanding limits on foreign investments in the stock market, and permitting long-term commercial loans. Further capital account liberalization became inevitable when Korea joined the OECD in 1996. However, the Korean government was not without reservations. In the OECD membership negotiations, Korea was reluctant to liberalize its capital account out of concern that foreign capital inflows would increase dramatically due to the interest rate differentials between home and abroad. The government had thus planned to delay the capital account liberalization until the interest rates converged significantly.

Following futile attempts to defend the rapid depreciation of the won after the baht flotation on 2 July 1997, the Korean government widened the won's trading band from 2.25 per cent to 10 per cent on 19 November, before allowing the won to float on 16 December. The floating exchange rate system was accompanied by the acceleration of the ongoing capital account liberalization plan. Under the IMF program, Korea undertook bold liberalization measures and completely opened the capital markets to foreigners in 1998. All regulations on foreign purchases of debt securities were removed in December 1997. Ownership ceilings were completely lifted and short-term money market instruments, such as commercial papers and trade bills were fully liberalized on 25 May 1998. As of that date, all domestic enterprises, regardless of size, were allowed to borrow without limit from overseas, as long as the maturity did not exceed one year.

The liberalization of capital movements was accompanied by a relaxation of rules on foreign exchange. The Foreign Exchange Transactions Law that went into effect in April 1999 replaced the positive list system with a negative list system, which allowed all capital account transactions except those expressly forbidden by law. While foreign exchange dealings in the past had to be based on *bona fide* real demand, speculative forward transactions were now permitted. The new system was set to be implemented in two stages, in April 1999 and at the end of 2000, in order to allow sufficient time to improve prudential, regulatory, and accounting standards before full liberalization. The first stage of the new system eliminated the one-year limit on commercial loans while liberalizing various short-term capital transactions by corporations and financial institutions. Moreover, foreign exchange dealing was opened to all eligible financial institutions. In 2006, the Korean government announced its decision to advance the implementation schedule of the ongoing foreign exchange liberalization.

Although all direct restrictions on original transactions of current and capital transactions have been removed, the ceiling of $3 million on overseas real estate investments remains.[2] Procedural restrictions on original transactions still exist: for example, some capital transactions must be reported to the Ministry of Finance and Economy and the Bank of Korea. As for foreign exchange transactions, or the settlement of original transactions, only overseas transactions using abnormal means of transfer that bypass banks, such as exchange manipulation, are required to be reported to the Bank of Korea in order to restrict unlawful transactions.

11.3 CAPITAL FLOWS IN KOREA

From 2000 to 2006 Korea, like other emerging market economies, has experienced huge capital inflows. The profit-seeking activities and diversification of risks by domestic and multinational financial institutions were the main contributors to increased cross-border capital flows. Cross-border capital flows in general grew rapidly from the 1980s, because institutional investors began to show a high tendency to diversify their international portfolios in order to lower risks. With the turn to the 1990s, capital inflows on a global scale started to take multiple forms, as investors from advanced economies diversified their assets internationally. In addition, the development of information and communication technology enabled global investment and broadened opportunities for investors to manage risks through investment in diversified financial assets across countries. In line with this, the changes in the form of capital flows in emerging market economies have been induced by both push and pull effects. In other words, with lower returns on domestic capitals due to sluggish economic growth in the advanced economies, investors' demand for investment in emerging market portfolios began to soar. At the same time, major emerging market economies relaxed their regulatory measures on cross-border capital flows.

11.3.1 Total Gross Capital Flows

Korea has experienced different types of capital flows since 1980. The total gross capital flows increased from $2.3 billion in 1980 to $91.8 billion in 2006. The share of total gross capital flows to GDP rose from 2 per cent to 5.5 per cent in the same period. In terms of type of gross capital flows, bank loans were the dominant form in Korea. Since the beginning of the 1980s, bank loans have made up most of the capital flows in Korea. However, in the second half of the 1980s, FDI flows increased, beginning with the government's liberalization of FDI inflows, and became a primary source until the currency crisis in 1997. Although equity investment caught up with FDI investment after the crisis, FDI is expected to continue to remain an important source of capital flows in Korea. As a result, equity-related capital flows now dominate capital flows. In 2003, the equity gross flows made up 50 per cent of the total gross flows.

Unlike equity, debt financing is not an important component of capital inflows in Korea. In particular, the rudimentary development of the bond market has been cited as one of the main reasons for the Asian crisis. Ideas for promoting regional bond markets have been proposed and are under close examination.

Gross debt inflows have increased from $6.7 billion in 2001 to $28.9 billion in 2006. The increase is mainly due to purchases by domestic financial institutions of domestic bonds from overseas. This is regarded as non-resident purchases of domestic bonds since transactions by domestic financial institutions located outside of the territory are recorded as non-resident. At the same time, domestic financial institutions have invested heavily into foreign long-term bonds since 2001, and this has caused huge portfolio outflows in terms of long-term bonds. This is why bond flows

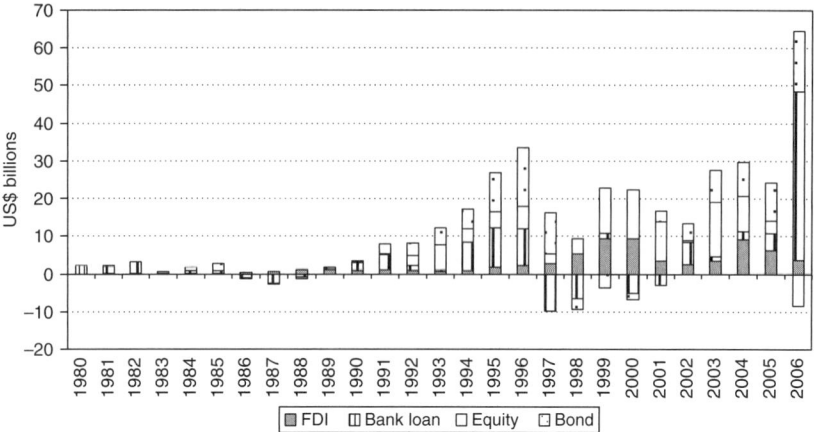

Source: Balance of Payments Statistics, IMF.

Figure 11.1 Pattern of capital inflows in Korea ($ billion)

recently seem to have become a dominant form of capital flows in Korea. Bank financing has had the most volatility. It has plummeted twice, in 1986 and after the 1997 currency crisis. Since then, it has accounted for only a negligible amount of capital flows in Korea.

Capital inflows The total amount of capital inflows into Korea has increased almost 32 times from $2.2 billion in 1980 to $68.8 billion in 2006 (Figure 11.1). In the early 1980s, bank loans were the most important capital inflows along with transfer payments. Since most other types of capital inflows were prohibited, the Korean government encouraged domestic banks to borrow from abroad in order to fill the current account deficit. Foreign investors were only allowed to participate in the equity market through investment trust funds such as the Korea Fund, which was listed on the New York Stock Exchange from 1981.

In 1990, foreign equity investment in the Korean stock market was allowed, with limitations on the share purchased by foreign investors, and since 1998 these limitations on holdings have been removed. Following these liberalization measures, the equity inflows were increasing before the crisis and have increased steadily since then (after the drop in 1997). As equity was seen as a candidate for resolving the currency crisis, the government removed most barriers to investment in the equity markets in early 1998. As a result, equity financing increased rapidly in 1999, but its momentum was reversed in 2000 due to the global burst of the information

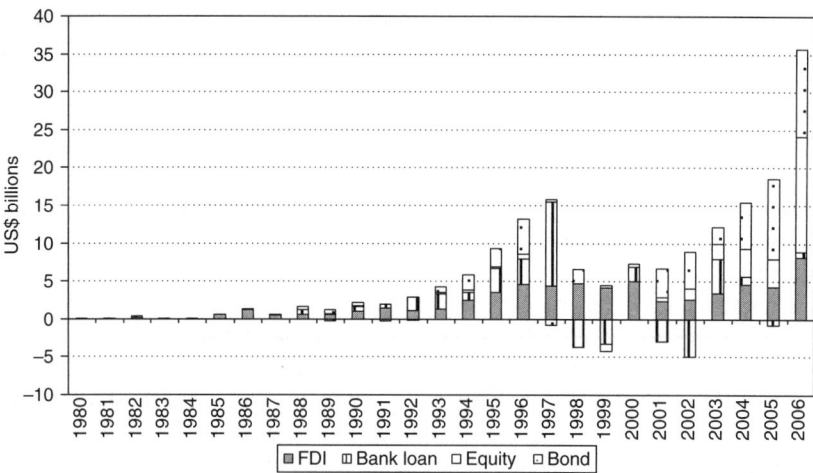

Source: Balance of Payments Statistics, IMF.

Figure 11.2 Pattern of capital outflows in Korea ($ billion)

technology bubble. In 2003, foreign investment in the domestic equity market reached a record high of $14.4 billion, but declined significantly from 2005 due to global deleveraging in response to the evolving US subprime mortgage crisis. FDI flows have shown a relatively steady increasing pattern from 1991 to 2000. As foreign banks have been extremely cautious in their cross-border lending in Korea, bank loans have shown a negative value from 1998 to 2001, implying that foreign banks have repatriated their loans since the crisis.

Capital outflows Gross capital outflows reached $34.3 billion in 2006, increasing nearly 5 times over the previous 10 years (Figure 11.2). FDI investments have been the major components of outflows, increasing at a steady pace until 2000. Since the late 1990s, FDI into the People's Republic of China (PRC) has rapidly increased. But since 2001, portfolio investments have made up more than 60 per cent of capital outflows in Korea, reflecting the liberalization of resident investment abroad. Equity investment abroad skyrocketed in 2005–06, from $3.6 billion to $15.2 billion. This trend is expected to continue for some time since overseas fund investments are increasing due to risk diversification and profit-seeking behavior by individual and institutional investors in Korea.

Since capital outflows have been increasing from 2004, net capital inflows into the Korean economy actually decreased in 2005–06. In 2006 in particular, net capital inflows recorded −$19.7 billion mainly due to a fall in net portfolio inflows, which was driven by a surge in Korea's outward investment in equity reaching $23.6 billion in 2006. Meanwhile, net capital inflow maintained a stable level in terms of historical average, hovering at 1.4 per cent of GDP since the crisis.

From capital importer to capital exporter Traditionally, Korea has been a capital importing country which financed domestic investment. The resulting high economic growth and increasing domestic investment led to a current account deficit before the crisis averaging 2.5 per cent of GDP except in the years 1986 to 1989. Since the crisis, the rapid devaluation of the won/dollar exchange rate, fall in domestic investment and imports, and increase in exports, have resulted in a current account surplus. As discussed above, Korea became a capital exporter due to its more recent increase in gross capital outflows, especially equity outflows, in 2006. The trend is expected to continue in the next few years. This implies that the foreign capital inflows are no longer functioning to provide capital for domestic investment.

Exporting risky assets and importing safe assets The patterns of capital flows show that Korea has exported risky assets to developed economies and imported safe ones from advanced countries. The yearly average amount of cross-border bond purchases by domestic investors was $5.5 billion from 2001 to 2005. On the other hand, the yearly average amount of cross-border equity purchases by domestic investors was $2.2 billion during the same period. This reveals risk-averse behavior of domestic investors, as they consider equities to be riskier assets than bonds. Korea's portfolio inflows, however, are heavily concentrated into equity flows. With the exception of 2005 and 2006, domestic equities have been the dominant portfolio investments by foreign investors since the crisis. Furthermore, comparing the foreign holdings of domestic equities and bonds, the share of foreign equity holdings to the total market capitalization in Korea was very high, at 35.2 per cent in 2006, while the share of foreign bond holdings was a mere 0.59 per cent in the same year.

FDI as a stable and primary source of capital FDI inflows in Korea have proven to be a stable and steady source of capital inflows. Unlike other types of capital inflows, FDI inflows have increased steadily from the early 1980s. FDI began to play a dominant role in total capital flows in the mid 1990s. The government also promoted increased FDI inflows, providing special incentives to foreign firms to set up companies. The coefficient of variation of FDI flows in Korea at 1.45 is lower than that of other capital flows – 4.4 for equity, 5.6 for bank loans, and 2.04 for debt. This confirms the view that FDI flows are considered cold money which is generated by the long-term considerations of foreign investors. In contrast, portfolio investments are seen as unstable hot money, which is triggered by short-term considerations of the foreign investors.

11.4 EFFECTS OF CAPITAL FLOWS ON THE DOMESTIC ECONOMY

In this section, we examine the impacts of capital flows and current transfers on the domestic economy.

11.4.1 Trends in Asset Prices

Since the 1997 crisis, equity prices in Korea have increased significantly with a very clear upward trend, interrupted only during the burst of the IT bubble in 2000. From March 2003 to March 2007, the Korea Stock Price Index quadrupled, reaching about 2000. As shown in Figure 11.3, foreign investment in the domestic stock market increased along with the stock price hike until 2000 before reversing in 2000 with the burst of the global IT bubble. In 2003, foreign investment in the domestic equity market reached a record high of $14.4 billion but since 2006, the equity inflows have declined significantly due to the global rebalancing from the sub-prime mortgage crisis in the US.

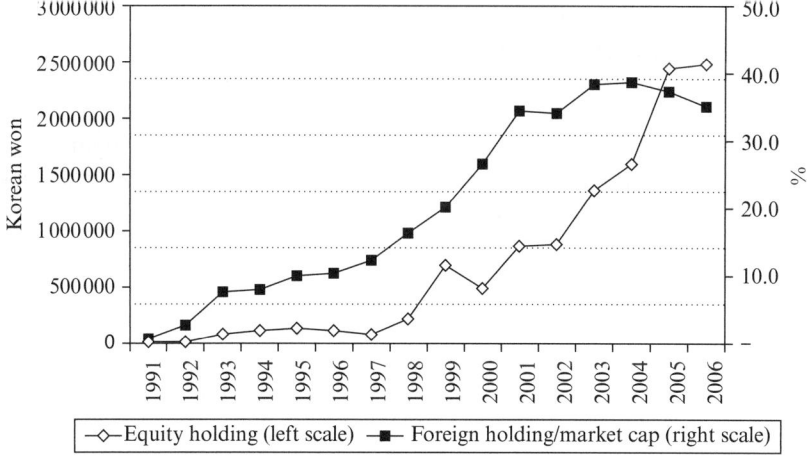

Figure 11.3 Foreign equity holdings

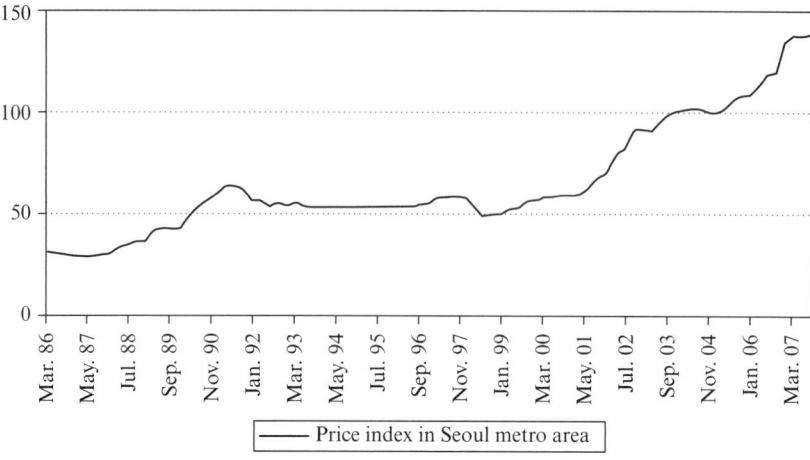

Source: Bloomberg.

Figure 11.4 Land price index of Seoul metro area

While the upward trend in stock prices began on a large scale in 1998, a downward trend in bond yields generally started in late 1999, which may be, among others, a spillover effect of the equity markets. Most foreign capital flows enter the stock markets, partly due to Korea's few developed domestic bond markets. However, as stock prices rise, expected returns on equities drop and bonds become more attractive to local investors, who bid up bond prices, lowering bond yields.

The real estate market has also been influenced by the equity market boom since the crisis. Like the bond market, the real estate market substitutes equity investment for a better rate of returns. At the same time, the wealth effects from equity price hikes and liquidity effects from portfolio inflows contribute to the price hike in the real estate market. Figure 11.4 shows the land price index of the Seoul metro area. Since late 1999, the real estate price has increased steadily. The price index has rapidly increased from 2004 to 2007, up to almost 40 per cent in 2007.

11.4.2 Exchange Rate, Liquidity, and Foreign Reserves

Portfolio inflows are closely tied to the movements of exchange rates. Under a floating exchange rate regime, foreign portfolio inflows can directly affect the demand for domestic currency assets, leading to an appreciation in the nominal exchange rate. Combined with the sticky price, the real exchange rate can also appreciate. On the other hand, if

Source: Bank of Korea.

Figure 11.5 Won/dollar exchange rate and real effective exchange rate

the monetary authority intervenes in the foreign exchange market, the nominal appreciation can be avoided in a managed floating regime. However, the real exchange rate may still appreciate. Consumption and investment booms are likely to increase the price of non-traded goods more than the price of traded goods because the supply of non-traded goods is more limited. Therefore, it can be argued that increases in asset prices and exchange rate appreciation in Korea are the result of capital inflows. To roughly check this hypothesis, we examine the trends in various macroeconomic variables.

The won/dollar exchange rate has shown a long-term downward trend since the crisis. The nominal exchange rate has appreciated steadily since 2003, however, the real appreciation started from 2004 (Figure 11.5).

Figure 11.6 shows Korea's foreign exchange reserves and money supply. Foreign exchange reserves have increased rapidly since the crisis based on a precautionary demand for foreign reserves. Furthermore, while Korea has been running sizeable surpluses on its current accounts, it has also accumulated large capital inflows as seen in the previous section. The bulk of the current account surpluses and capital inflows have been sterilized and added to reserves, as in other countries that want to stabilize either the nominal or real effective exchange rate with the objective of maintaining

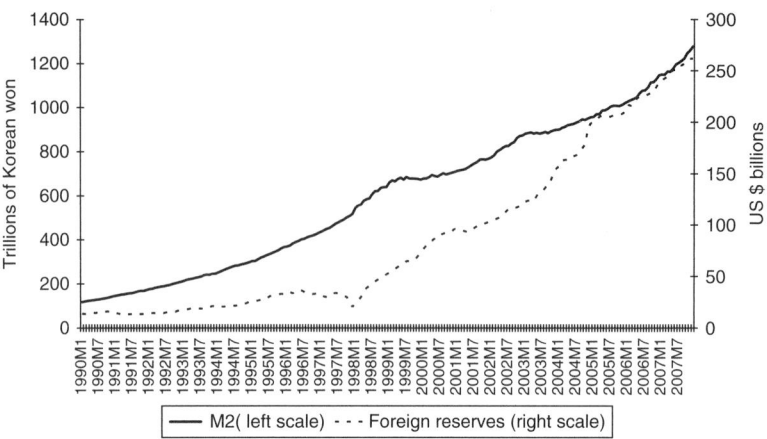

Source: Bank of Korea.

Figure 11.6 Foreign reserves and money supply (M2)

their export competitiveness. Although the sterilization of reserve accumulation was substantial, money supply (M2) also seems to have increased sharply in Korea, which may imply that the sterilization was only partial.

The data provide some support for the hypothesis that surges in portfolio inflows led to increases in the asset prices and nominal exchange rate appreciation in the 2000s. During the same period, although foreign exchange reserves increased, which suggests some sterilization, money supply also increased, which suggests that sterilization was only partial. There was an economic boom, although without consumption and investment booms. Monetary expansion, along with portfolio inflows and the economic boom, may have contributed to the increase in the asset prices. The nominal exchange rate appreciation can be attributed to capital inflows. However, some other factors may explain the asset price increases and exchange rate appreciation in the Korean economy. The recovery from the crisis and improved economic prospects may have also led to asset price increases. Monetary expansion and low interest rates, beginning from the recession in the late 1990s and early 2000s, may have contributed to asset price booms. The won's appreciation against the US dollar may be due to the massive US current account deficit and debt problems.

11.4.3 Issues of Portfolio Inflows

There are three important issues related to current capital flows in Korea. First, we identify the problems and the effects of concentrated equity-related capital flows. Even though net capital flows are either nearly balanced or negative in Korea, current capital flows have been dominated by equity-related flows. This has further contributed to the asset price hike, and in return influenced other capital markets such as the bond and real estate markets.

Second, global expectations of the dollar depreciation due to global imbalances create downward pressure on the won/dollar exchange rate. As a result, capital gains from investment in Korea are expected to increase. Moreover, foreign investors in the equity market do not generally hedge the currency risk from their investments in Korea as long as the downward pressure on the won/dollar exchange rate exists. This will reinforce the appreciation of the won against the dollar.

Third, since 2006 Korea has been experiencing a surge in short-term borrowing by foreign banks due to the expectation of the won's appreciation and mismatches in the forward market. Domestic exporters face full currency risks, since most trade transactions are in US dollars. Therefore, they purchase forward contracts in order to fix their cash flows in terms of the Korean won reducing forward swap rates. On the other hand, banks, which intermediate these contracts, are in the opposite position of selling forward contracts to buyers of forward contracts. Since foreign banks have an advantage on dollar-denominated funding in the global market, the interest rate differential between Korea and the US creates risk-free arbitrage profits by borrowing from abroad and trading forward contracts in the domestic forward market. This will lead to a further appreciation of the won.

11.5 EMPIRICAL ANALYSIS

11.5.1 VAR Model

Here, we examine the effects of foreign capital inflows on various economic variables, especially asset prices, using a VAR (vector autoregression) model. VAR models provide a useful methodology for investigating this issue. First, they are data-based models with a relatively small number of restrictions. This empirical framework is useful for documenting empirical facts. Second, the effects are expected to be inherently dynamic. For example, foreign capital inflows may affect different types of asset markets with different timing. VAR models are useful for inferring dynamic effects.

11.5.2 Empirical Model

In the basic model, the data vector, y_t^i, is {Y, P, R, CAP_OUT, CAP_IN, X} where Y is the log of a measure of output, P is the log of the measure of price level, R is the interest rate, CAP_OUT is capital outflows or portfolio outflows, CAP_IN is capital inflows or portfolio inflows (as a ratio to trend GDP), and X is the domestic variable under consideration.[3] For X, we consider the following set of variables: the log of the KOSPI index (KOSPI), the log of the Korean Securities Dealers Automated Quotations index (KOSDAQ), the log of the won/dollar exchange rate (ERUS), the log of the won/yen exchange rate (ERJ), the log of the won/euro exchange rate (ERE), the log of the nominal effective exchange rate (NEER), the log of the real effective exchange rate (REER), the log of apartment price (APT), the log of housing price (HOUSE), the log of foreign exchange reserves (FRES), the log of monetary base (MB), the log of M1 (M1), and the log of M2 (M2). We included CAP since they are the main variable of our interest. Y and P are included to control for the factors that can affect X, including asset prices.

The factors or variables affecting domestic variable X can be divided into three types.

1. Certain factors affect X mostly through changes in foreign capital inflows. For example, a policy change toward a more open foreign capital market would affect capital flows and then affect X.
2. Certain factors affect a domestic variable X mostly through channels other than foreign capital inflows. For example, an increase in the price level (which may be the result of a monetary expansion) may increase domestic asset prices, a case where capital inflows are not likely to have an important role.
3. There are factors that affect X through changes in foreign capital flows and other channels. For example, a change in the domestic economic condition may induce foreign capital inflows, which affects the domestic variable X, which in turn influences domestic investments and asset prices.

The first type of factor affects X mainly through the changes in capital inflows. Therefore, to analyze the effects of capital inflows, it is unnecessary to control for this type of factor in the model. However, the second type of factor should be controlled because there may be an omitted variable bias if the model excludes an important factor. We also try to control some of the third type of factors. If we exclude this type of factor in the model, all the effects of this factor, including the effects through channels other than changes in capital inflows, may be captured as the effects of foreign portfolio inflows.

As a second type of factor, we control for the aggregate price level. The aggregate price level shows the nominal and monetary condition of the economy, which can also affect X, for example, asset prices. As a third type of factor, we control for the domestic interest rate and aggregate output. Aggregate output is the most important variable representing the domestic economic condition, which may affect X both through changes in foreign capital inflows and through other channels. A change in the interest rate may affect asset prices directly, and also affect capital inflows. On the other hand, it may not be necessary to control some second types of foreign factors because their indirect effects are already captured in the control variables. For example, a change in the US real economic condition may affect the domestic economy through real economic linkages, not by changes in capital flows. But if a variable reflecting the domestic economic condition (Y in our model) is controlled, such indirect effects can be controlled at least to some extent. Finally, we also control for capital outflows since capital outflows and inflows are sometimes inter-related, and we would like to separate the effects of capital inflows only.

Regarding the ordering of the variables, all the control variables are assumed to be contemporaneously exogenous to capital inflows in order to take out all the inter-related effects from capital inflows shocks. On the other hand, capital inflows are assumed to be contemporaneously exogenous to X. In order to make the assumption more reliable, the data is constructed as of the end of the period value. Consequently, capital inflows are a flow variable that represents the activities during the period while X represents the value at the end of the period. Therefore, the assumption that other variables such as capital inflows are contemporaneously exogenous to X is a reasonable one.[4]

Finally, we note that the ordering among Y, P, R, CAP_OUT does not matter when we examine the effects of shocks to capital inflows.[5] Monthly data is used for the estimations. The estimation period is from January 1999 to September 2007. We exclude the period prior to 1999 since economic behavior before and after the Asian crisis may be considered different within the framework of our study. A constant term and three lags are assumed. As a measure of output, we use price level, the interest rate, industrial production, CPI, and the call rate. To construct capital inflows and outflows, we exclude FDI since its effect may be somewhat different from the effects of usual capital flows.

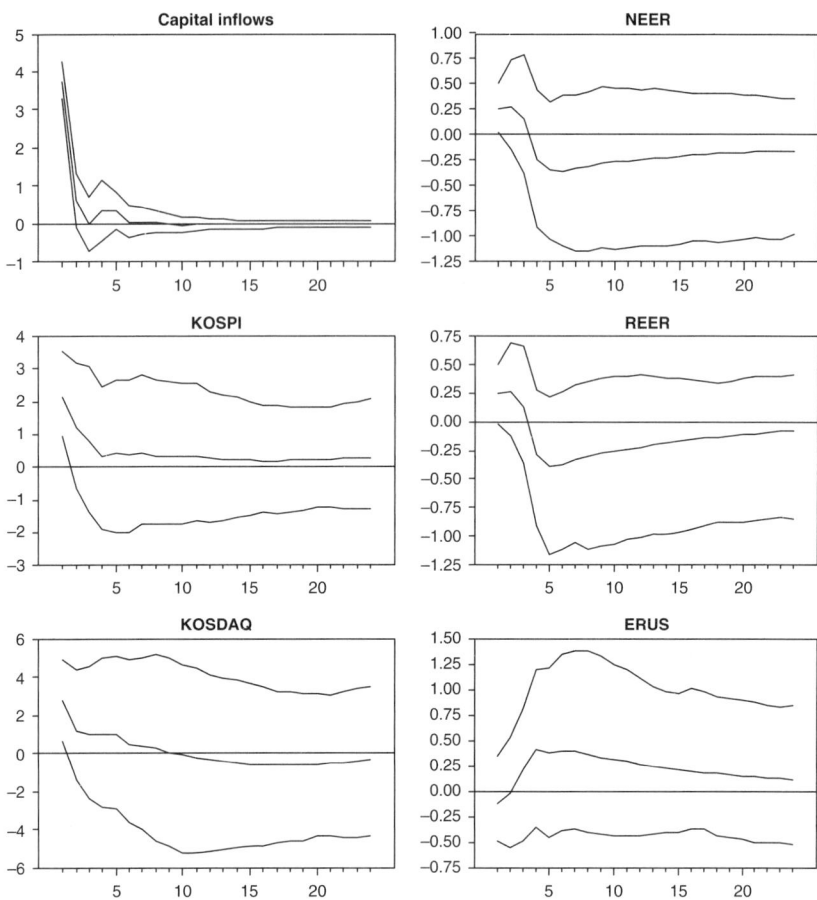

Figure 11.7   Impulse responses to capital inflows shocks

11.5.3   Results

Figures 11.7 and 11.8 report the impulse responses, with 90 per cent probability bands for the two-year horizon, of each variable to capital inflows shocks and portfolio inflows shocks, respectively. The names of the responding variables are reported at the top of each graph.

First, to discuss the nature of capital inflows or portfolio inflows shocks, we examine the impulse responses of capital inflows or portfolio inflows. Typical capital inflows shocks involve an approximate 4 per cent (as a ratio to trend GDP) immediate increase in capital inflows while a typical portfolio inflow shock involves an approximate 2.5 per cent (as a ratio to trend

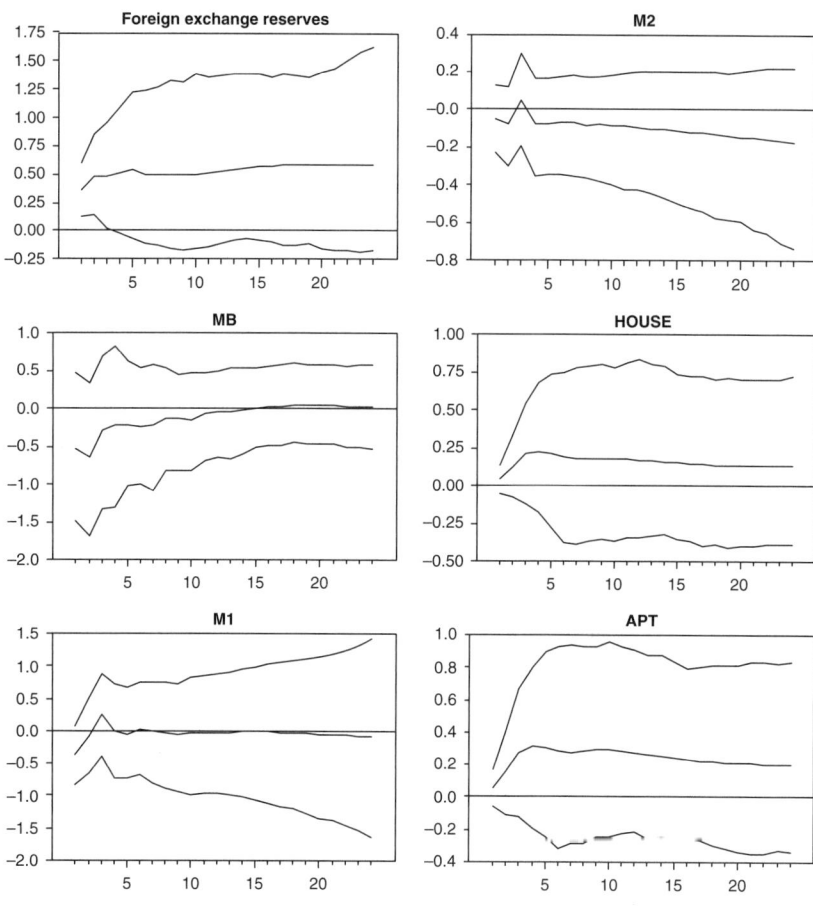

Figure 11.7 (continued)

GDP) immediate increase in capital flows. In both cases, the responses return the flows to the initial level very quickly, but the responses of portfolio inflows are a bit more persistent.

Both types of capital inflow shocks increase stock prices sharply on impact, but the effects of portfolio inflows are larger and more persistent. Capital inflow shocks increase the KOSPI index about 2 per cent on impact while portfolio inflows increase it by about 3 per cent. The KOSPI index returns to the initial level about four months after the capital inflow shock, and returns to the initial level about one year after a portfolio inflows shock. The effects on the KOSDAQ index are also large and significant. Capital inflow and portfolio inflow shocks, on impact, increase the KOSDAQ

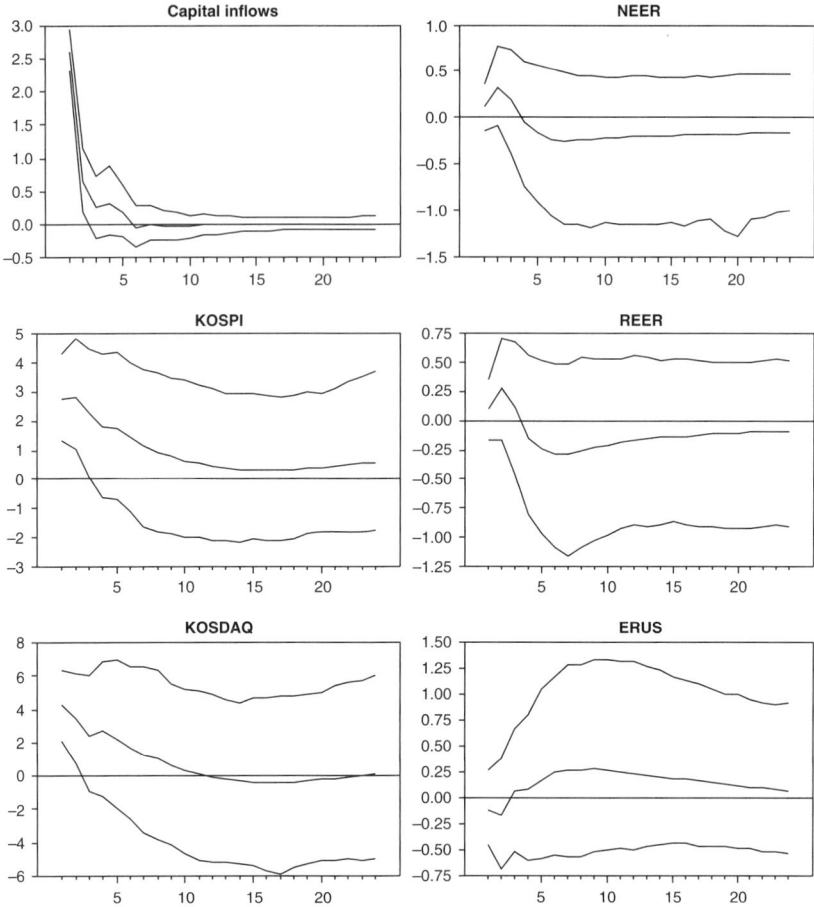

Figure 11.8 Impulse responses to portfolio inflows shocks

index by about 2.5 per cent and 4 per cent, respectively. The effect of portfolio inflow shocks is more persistent than that of capital inflows shocks.

On the other hand, the effects on housing and apartment prices are moderate and insignificant. The point estimate shows that the size of the change is relatively small, far below 5 per cent. In addition, the 90 per cent probability bands include zero responses in all cases. These small effects may be related to recent government policy measures for regulating the housing market in Korea.

The nominal and real effective exchange rates tend to appreciate in the very short run. In the case of capital inflows, the impact effects of

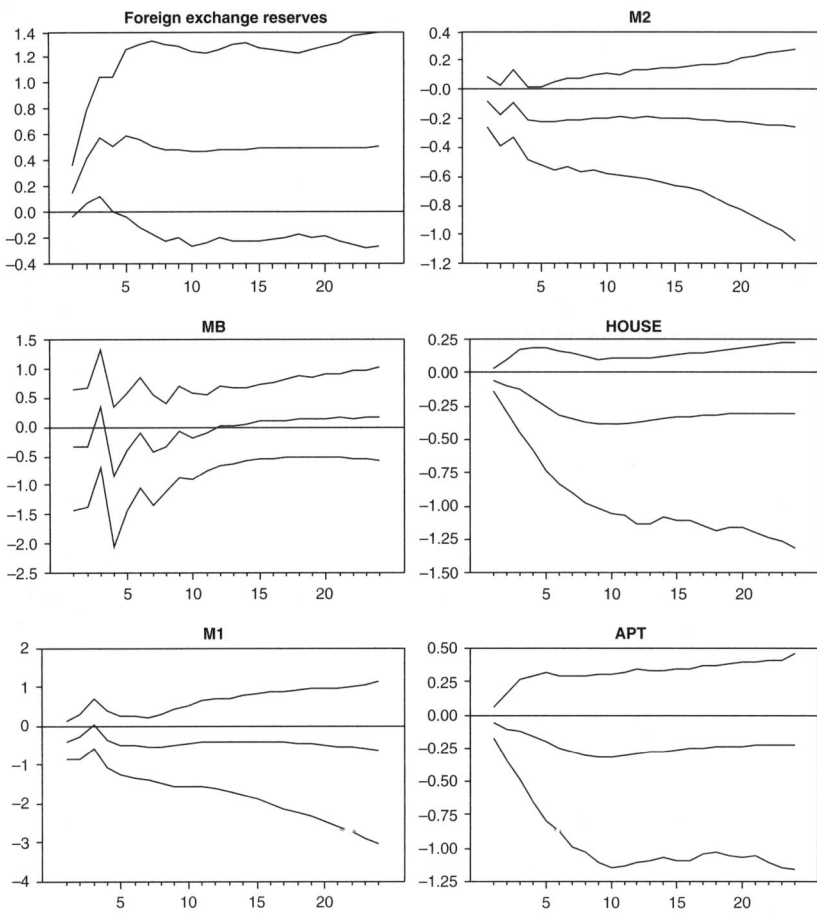

Figure 11.8 (continued)

the approximate 0.25 per cent appreciation are marginally significant. However, in the case of portfolio inflows, the probability bands are very wide, including zero responses. In both cases, the effects on the won/dollar exchange rate are also very small and insignificant. This seems to be mostly related to the foreign exchange intervention to accumulate foreign exchange reserves. In both cases, foreign exchange reserves increase significantly. In response to capital inflows shocks, foreign exchange reserves increase about 0.35 per cent on impact and then increase up to about 0.5 per cent within two or three months after the shock. In response to portfolio inflows shocks, foreign exchange reserves increase about 0.2 per cent on impact and then increase to about 0.5 per cent three months after the shock. As a result, the monetary aggregates like monetary base, M1 and M2 do not increase significantly.

11.5.4 Determinants of Capital Inflows

Here, we briefly examine the determinants of capital inflows by modifying the empirical model. To evaluate the role of various factors, we include various factors explicitly in the model. In the previous model, four pull factors (domestic interest rate, price level, domestic output, stock price) were explicitly included. We also included two important push factors, world interest rate and world output. On the other hand, we excluded capital outflows; capital outflows were included in the model to isolate the effects of capital outflows shocks, and now we exclude it to preserve the degree of freedom.[6] As a result, we construct a model of {Y*, R*, Y, P, R, CAP_IN, SP}, where Y* and R* are world output and world interest rate, respectively, and we order the contemporaneously exogenous ones first.

In the model, we assume that world variables are contemporaneously exogenous to Korean variables since the Korean economy can be regarded as a small open economy that cannot affect world variables much. We also assume that output and the price level are contemporaneously exogenous to the interest rate since aggregate variables tend to move sluggishly but financial variables tend to respond to information instantaneously.[7,8] In the estimation, we use the US variables as proxies for world variables.

To discuss the role of each factor, we report the variance decomposition of capital inflows and portfolio inflows in Table 11.1. From the result, no single dominant factor emerges; each shock plays some role (about 5–10 per cent) in explaining capital and portfolio inflow fluctuations. The role of two push factors is not very large: about 10% of capital and portfolio inflows fluctuations are explained by the two push factors. The role of each pull factor tends to be larger than that of each push factor. For capital inflows fluctuations, output shocks explain about 10 per cent. For portfolio inflows fluctuations, stock price shocks explain about 10 per cent.

11.6 POLICY OPTIONS

The Korean government has implemented a variety of policy measures to deal with large capital inflows, including the mitigation of currency appreciation pressure by implementing sterilization methods, prepayment of foreign debt, encouragement of capital outflows, and tightening of credit growth by increasing lending rates and required reserves. Here, we assess

Table 11.1   Forecast error variance decomposition of capital inflows

	6 months	12 months	24 months	48 months
	Capital inflows			
Y*	5.0 (3.3)	5.5 (3.4)	6.0 (3.7)	6.8 (4.4)
P*	4.0 (2.6)	4.5 (2.8)	4.6 (2.9)	4.9 (3.1)
Y	9.6 (4.9)	10.2 (4.9)	10.8 (5.1)	11.2 (5.5)
P	6.7 (3.9)	7.0 (3.8)	7.2 (3.9)	7.6 (4.1)
R	5.7 (3.1)	6.4 (3.2)	6.9 (3.5)	7.2 (3.8)
CAP_IN	65.9 (7.2)	62.6 (7.7)	59.4 (8.9)	56.0 (11.2)
SP	3.1 (2.3)	3.9 (2.6)	5.1 (3.6)	6.5 (5.3)
	Capital outflows			
Y*	4.1 (2.7)	4.4 (2.8)	5.0 (3.3)	5.9 (4.7)
P*	4.4 (2.8)	4.8 (2.9)	5.0 (2.9)	5.2 (3.1)
Y	6.6 (4.0)	7.1 (4.2)	7.7 (4.5)	8.2 (5.0)
P	5.4 (3.5)	6.0 (3.7)	6.4 (3.7)	6.9 (4.0)
R	5.8 (3.1)	6.2 (3.2)	6.5 (3.5)	6.9 (3.9)
CAP_IN	64.6 (7.4)	61.8 (7.9)	59.1 (8.9)	55.6 (11.2)
SP	9.1 (4.7)	9.7 (4.8)	10.3 (5.1)	11.2 (6.4)

the effectiveness of existing policies and measures adopted by the Korean authorities to manage capital flows and domestic liquidity.

11.6.1   Exchange Rate Policy

The effects of capital inflows may vary depending on the exchange rate regime. Although real exchange rate appreciation pressures may increase under a floating or fixed exchange rate regime, the adjustment under a floating regime is more direct and less costly. This is due to the availability of measures under each type of regime. The primary measure for adjustment under a fixed regime is a rise in inflation which naturally occurs as inflows stimulate domestic activity. Under a floating regime, nominal exchange rate appreciation is an option that can be used to augment adjustment with the additional benefit of discouraging inflows by reducing their returns in terms of foreign currencies. On the surface, adjustment under a floating regime tends to be less stable because of the utilization of the nominal exchange rate in adjustment; however, the effects of these measures may be less detrimental in larger and deeper financial markets.

One way to enhance monetary autonomy is through the implementation of a floating exchange rate regime, which enables monetary authorities to handle fluctuations in monetary aggregates resulting from fluctuations in capital flows with greater flexibility. In addition, the central bank may intervene in the event of a capital flow reversal, curbing financial instability as a safety net lender.

To deal with increasing capital inflows, countries must move more into flexible exchange rate regimes. This would enhance the maneuvering room for monetary authorities in a world of volatile capital flows. However, increasing the flexibility of exchange movements alone cannot cool down an overheating economy or prevent the development of asset bubbles. Allowing more flexibility in the exchange rate is one option, but not the only one. Even though Korea has allowed the exchange rate appreciation, capital inflows still increased in the 2000s.

11.6.2 Monetary Policy

One way of dealing with capital inflows is to lower interest rates. Lower interest rates tend to reduce capital inflows and reduce appreciation pressures by making interest arbitrage less attractive. However, cutting interest rates may further boost liquidity and add to inflationary pressures, making this option less attractive if inflation is already elevated. At the same time, if asset prices are increasing, lowering the interest rate may boost asset bubbles.

On the other hand, in a time of surges in asset prices, the central bank may indeed consider raising interest rates. How monetary policy reacts to asset prices is highly controversial in general, both from an academic point of view and from a policy perspective. There is wide debate over whether monetary policy should target asset prices.

It is not obvious that Korea should implement monetary policies that target asset prices in general. However, Gochoco-Bautista (2008) shows that asset price booms matter in East Asia because they affect the probability of the occurrence of adverse macroeconomic development, and insists that pre-emptive monetary policy is required to deal with asset price appreciations in the region. In addition, recent experiences in the United Kingdom, Australia, and New Zealand suggest that it is possible to react to the formation of bubbles through a moderate and gradual monetary policy tightening without causing a financial and economic crash.

Korea tightened its monetary policy in 2006 to moderate housing prices. Even though inflation pressures persist due to economic recovery and high oil prices, the Bank of Korea (BOK) raised the benchmark call rate by 25 basis points from 4.25 per cent to 4.5 per cent in August 2006. This implies that even if the BOK is not targeting asset prices directly, it is indirectly considering potential inflationary pressures stemming from asset price appreciations.

However, monetary tightening is a limited policy option in emerging Asian economies since higher interest rates can stimulate portfolio inflows and create more pressure in liquidity expansion. At the same time, exchange rates will also appreciate reducing export price competitiveness. In the presence of strong external inflows, many countries use sterilized foreign currency market intervention to neutralize appreciation pressures on the exchange rate. However, sterilized intervention may not be completely effective, and can lead to increases in domestic liquidity conditions which can feed into asset markets. Even if ineffective, sterilized intervention has some important effects on domestic asset markets. First, the domestic interest rate will be higher than otherwise. With inflows into the domestic bond markets, interest rates will tend to fall but sterilization will at least partially offset the drop. Thus, any gap between foreign and domestic interest rates will persist, encouraging capital inflows to continue. Second, sterilization increases outstanding domestic government bonds, which may increase the size of the public debt. This can undermine the credibility of macroeconomic policy, setting up a potential reversal in capital flows. Third, with sterilization, the monetary authority increases the holdings of foreign currency assets but decreases the holdings of domestic government bonds. This can be very costly because the domestic bonds are likely to provide higher interest payments than foreign currency assets. Fourth, sterilized intervention may hamper further financial reforms. Commercial banks will hold up the central bank's debts. To cut down the cost, a lower interest rate may be applied to the debts. It may eventually increase the burden of commercial banks or turn out to be a control over domestic interest rates.

The monetary authority may increase reserve requirements or the discount rate to prevent the increase in the money supply from reserve accumulation. However, these policies also involve some problems. They can be viewed as more regulation on financial markets – countering financial market liberalization. In addition, they can distort the banking system, for example, if participants discover counterproductive ways to bypass regulations. Indeed, the BOK increased the average reserve requirement ratio from 3 per cent to 3.8 per cent in December 2006. This led to a slight lowering of the liquidity expansion, as the capacity of financial institutions to provide credit weakened in accordance with the increase in their required reserves.

In general, like other Asian economies, Korea has limited monetary policy options to mitigate the adverse effects of huge capital inflows, and potential difficulties lie on complicated policy objectives, since there are trade-offs between domestic and external objectives. In order to assuage the surges of capital inflows, lowering interest rates may be a good candidate. However, this will increase domestic liquidity and the formation of asset bubbles. At the same time, to cool down an asset price hike, monetary tightening can be considered, but this will put pressure on the exchange rate and exports will be adversely affected.

11.6.3 Fiscal Policy

The government can tighten fiscal policy to calm an overheating economy in order to counter some of the effects of capital inflows. In addition, decreasing government spending can reduce the relative price of non-tradables and relieve the appreciation pressure on the real exchange rate.

In East Asian economies that have high inflationary pressure, a fiscal contraction may be an important option since an alternative contraction policy (i.e., a monetary contraction) can cool down the economy but may further attract capital inflows and appreciate exchange rates. Most East Asian economies including Korea have displayed a generally balanced fiscal position for decades. Therefore, it seems that fiscal contraction is not necessary for reducing the fiscal burden. However, tightening fiscal policy can reduce the impact of portfolio inflows by contracting domestic demand, and therefore limiting inflation and real appreciation.

On the contrary, the policy authority should be very careful in implementing fiscal contraction. Fiscal policy is subject to long decision lags, compared with very volatile and unpredictable capital flows.

11.6.4 Encouraging Capital Outflows

Korea has encouraged overseas investment by financial institutions and individuals to mitigate the negative effects of the huge capital inflows into the domestic capital market. In 2007, a temporary three-year tax exemption will be applied to capital gains generated from overseas stock investment by domestic investment trust and investment companies. The government has also eased regulations in order to boost overseas real estate investment through indirect investment. For example, the acquisition limit on overseas real estate by domestic residents for investment purposes will be raised from $1 million to $3 million.[9]

11.6.5 Financial Market Regulation and Supervision

If a government cannot directly control capital inflows and is concerned about an excessive appreciation of asset prices, strengthening financial regulation and supervision should be considered in order to prevent asset bubble bursts. When there is excess liquidity with lower interest rates in the market, it is highly plausible for economic agents to take risky investments. The government should access and influence risk-taking behaviors by financial institutions through a range of qualitative and quantitative methods. These measures include restrictions on portfolio composition, risk-based capital requirements, loan loss provisions, and stress testing of market risk exposures. Concerns can then be addressed using regulatory measures directed at specific asset markets. This will be all the more effective if a large portion of the funds flowing into asset markets derives from domestic agents. In general, a more targeted approach may reduce the chance of unintended macroeconomic effects of broad-based monetary, fiscal, or exchange rate policies – or even capital controls. To the extent that the banking sector is funding speculative investments in stock and real estate markets, exposures can be closely monitored or reduced through selective imposition of higher reserve requirements, higher down-payment requirements for real estate purchases, or higher reserve margins for equity investments. However, effective financial market regulation and supervision requires well-trained professionals with independence, a professional code of standards, and the ability to engage sophisticated market players. Therefore, Korea, which has experienced current surges in capital inflows, should expand its risk management policies on credit expansion into the equity and real estate market.

NOTES

1. Gross capital flows are defined as investments by residents (outflows) and non-residents (inflows), limited to direct investment, equity investment, bank loans and bond investment. Transfers are not included since transfer payments are very small in Korea.
2. Professor Shinji Tagaki has pointed out that, according to the liberalization index of Chinn and Ito (2008), Korea's liberalization procedure went backward just before and after the crisis. It is strange that the index shows a temporary setback, indicating a smaller degree of liberalization during the 1996–2000 period. However, the general picture is of Korea moving toward greater liberalization.
3. A linear trend in GDP is assumed. Assuming different types of trend such as a quadratic trend does not affect the results much.
4. Exceptions are: housing price, apartment price, and nominal and real effective exchange rate. We could not obtain the end of period value for these data series.
5. See Christiano, Eichenbaum, and Evans (1999).
6. The results on the determinants of capital flows are similar in the model with capital outflows.
7. This type of assumption is widely used in past studies. See, for example, Sims and Zha (2006), Kim (1999), and Kim and Roubini (2000).
8. We also assume that domestic output is contemporaneously exogenous to domestic price level based on the idea that real variables are more fundamental than nominal variables. At any rate, the results are similar under the assumption that domestic price level is contemporaneously exogenous to domestic output. On the other hand, we assume that domestic variables are contemporaneously exogenous to capital inflows, but that there

can be a simultaneity between domestic variables and capital inflows. We leave it to a more rigorous future study to resolve the issue.
9. In Korea, foreign real estate purchases by domestic residents have been permitted since May 2006.

REFERENCES

Chinn, M.D. and H. Ito (2008), 'A new measure of financial openness', *Journal of Comparative Policy Analysis: Research and Practice*, **10**(3), September, 309–22.

Christiano, L., M. Eichenbaum and C. Evans (1999), 'Monetary policy shocks: what have we learned and to what end?', in J.B.Taylor and M. Woodford (eds), *Handbook of Macroeconomics*, Vol. 1A, North-Holland, Amsterdam, pp. 65–148.

Gochoco-Bautista, M.S. (2008), 'Asset prices and monetary policy: booms and fat tails in East Asia', BIS Working Papers 243, February, Bank for International Settlements.

Kim, S. (1999), 'Do monetary policy shocks matter in the G-7 countries? Using common identifying assumptions about monetary policy across countries', *Journal of International Economics*, **48**(2), 387–412.

Kim, S. and N. Roubini (2000), 'Exchange rate anomalies in the industrial countries: a solution with a structural VAR approach', *Journal of Monetary Economics*, **45**, 561–86.

Kim, S., S.H. Kim and Y. Wang (2004), 'Macroeconomic effects of capital account liberalization: the case of Korea', *Review of Development Economics*, **8**(4), 634–49.

Sims, C.A. and T. Zha (2006), 'Does monetary policy generate recessions?', *Macroeconomic Dynamics*, **10**, 231–72.

12. Managing capital flows: the case of Malaysia
Kee Kuan Foong

12.1 INTRODUCTION

The Malaysian economy has recovered solidly since the 1997–98 financial crisis; the recovery was made possible by numerous reforms as well as favorable external conditions. Ongoing reforms in the financial sector have made the economy more resilient. Operation of the securities markets is more efficient and the level of corporate governance enhanced. The banking system's delinquencies and exposure to double mismatches have been reduced. Smaller banks were merged with larger and more capitalized ones. Better risk management and prudential regulations were also implemented.[1] Distressed firms were either shut down or merged with stronger ones. Moreover, the exchange rate is increasingly flexible (McCauley, 2002).

From 1999 to 2007, Malaysia has generated a current account surplus, attracted a fair amount of foreign capital, and accumulated large international reserves. The last factor may act as a precautionary device to prevent speculative attacks on Malaysia's currency, given its highly opened economy. While the running of a positive current account may tend to replace depleted foreign exchange reserves after the crisis, a recurrent current account surplus of more than 10 per cent of GDP may indicate excess savings over investment. This is also evident by the downward trending loan–deposit ratio of the banking system. A persistent current account surplus also shows that the economy is driven by exports, with the domestic sector being anemic. A more dynamic domestic sector would lead to a smaller current account surplus through higher domestic consumption and investment.

While strong economic growth and healthy corporate and household sectors, as well as continued global search for yields, have led to massive inflows of capital into Asia, these inflows have posed both benefits and risks.[2] Inflows contributed to Malaysia's resilience by entering productive activities in the real economy and by confronting external shocks through the build-up of reserves. Nevertheless, Malaysian regulators need to pursue active monitoring and intervention to prevent excessive domestic liquidity, credit growth, a volatile or misaligned exchange rate, inflation, and possible overheating of the economy.

In addition, prolonged global imbalances could jeopardize the Malaysian economy. Large capital inflows combined with a current account surplus could exert upward pressure on the ringgit exchange rate, which would tend to erode the level of competitiveness. To moderate currency appreciation pressure, the monetary authority has intervened in the foreign exchange market, as well as through bond issuance to absorb excess liquidity generated by large foreign inflows.[3] This trend is expected to continue at least in the medium term, given ample global liquidity and a greater degree of risk-taking by investors. Global liquidity remains high due to structural weakening of the US economy and its financial assets, and the rising trend in carry trades encourages capital to flow into high-yielding emerging Asian economies.

Thus, it is timely to discuss how the monetary authority should manage surges in capital flows, while maintaining prudent macroeconomic and financial stability. Failing this, is there any scope for regional cooperation initiatives? The chapter is organized as follows. Section 12.2 discusses issues pertaining to capital flows under a fixed exchange rate regime. Policy measures are also evaluated. The study of capital flows and policies under a managed float exchange rate regime is the subject of Section 12.3. Section 12.4 examines alternative policy measures to manage capital flows and Section 12.5 concludes.

12.2 CAPITAL FLOWS 1999–2005

Appendix Box 12A.1 gives a summary of policy milestones since 1999. This section highlights issues regarding capital flows and corresponding policy action between 1999 and 2005, when the ringgit was pegged to the US dollar (USD) at 3.80.[4]

12.2.1 Trends

Throughout this period, Malaysia experienced consecutive years of current account surplus, on average around 11.8 per cent of GDP (Table 12.1).[5] Current transfers deteriorated over the same period, in particular over 2004–05. Higher overseas remittances by foreign workers and expatriates, and education payments were the main reasons. Malaysia also attracted a reasonable amount of net direct investment and accumulated international reserves.

Table 12.1 Balance of payments (US$ billion)

	1999	2000	2001	2002	2003	2004	2005
Current account balance	12.6	8.5	7.3	8.0	13.3	15.1	20.0
As a % of GDP	15.9	9.4	8.3	8.4	12.8	12.8	15.3
of which: Current transfers	−1.7	−1.9	−2.2	−2.8	−2.4	−3.9	−4.5
Credit	0.8	0.8	0.5	0.7	0.5	0.4	0.3
Debit	2.5	2.7	2.7	3.4	3.0	4.3	4.8
Financial account balance	−6.6	−6.3	−3.9	−3.1	−3.2	4.9	−9.8
Direct investment	2.5	1.8	0.3	1.3	1.1	2.6	1.0
Outward	−1.4	−2.0	−0.3	−1.9	−1.4	−2.1	−3.0
Inward	3.9	3.8	0.6	3.2	2.5	4.6	4.0
Portfolio investment, net	−1.2	−2.5	−0.6	−1.7	1.1	8.5	−3.7
Other investment, net	−7.9	−5.6	−3.5	−2.7	−5.4	−6.2	−7.0
Official sector	1.8	1.0	1.9	1.2	−2.9	0.6	−0.8
Private sector	−9.7	−6.6	−5.4	−4.0	−2.4	−6.8	−6.2
International reserves, net	30.9	28.7	29.9	33.7	44.2	66.2	70.2

Sources: Department of Statistics, Malaysia; author's calculation.

The financial account, which measures total net capital flows, was in deficit from 1999 to 2003. During 1999 to 2002, portfolio outflows were small due to the negative sentiment generated by the imposition of graduated exit levies on 15 February 1999.[6] Since the levy was applicable only at the time of repatriation, it could not be offset by double taxation agreements. The 10 per cent levy on profits was seen as discouraging portfolio inflows. The higher levy of 30 per cent, applicable on gains on investments of less than one year's duration, attracted heavy criticism because potential investors would apply the higher levy rate of 'last in, first out' principle. The higher levy was eliminated on 21 September 1999, leaving in place only a single rate of 10 per cent on capital gains regardless of duration of investment. In a further relaxation, the 10 per cent levy on capital gains was retained only for capital with a duration of less than one year in the country. This rule took effect on 1 February 2001 but was revoked on 2 May 2001.

The graduated system was successful in managing volatile portfolio flows. The levy lowered the expected rate of return on equity to foreign investors, and hence, increased the required pre-levy yield necessary relative to other countries. This was an effort intended to discourage casual entry into Malaysia, and to ensure that capital would enter only based on economic fundamentals.

Total net capital flows improved only in 2004, supported by a surge in net portfolio funds of $8.5 billion. In fact, portfolio investment started its

Table 12.2   Domestic liquidity and credit

	1999	2000	2001	2002	2003	2004	2005
	\multicolumn{7}{c}{Level (MYR billion)}						
M3	436.2	458.4	471.7	504.2	553.1	621.2	672.8
NFA	124.7	122.2	125.8	134.0	167.4	258.0	259.9
NDA	445.8	476.3	495.1	534.0	578.2	592.2	631.5
Public sector	−16.8	−11.8	−12.8	−1.1	11.9	−4.7	−9.9
Private sector	462.7	488.1	508.0	535.1	566.3	596.9	641.4
	\multicolumn{7}{c}{Annual growth rate (%)}						
M3	8.6	5.1	2.9	6.9	9.7	12.3	8.3
NFA	31.7	−2.0	2.9	6.6	24.9	54.1	0.7
NDA	−0.9	6.8	4.0	7.8	8.3	2.4	6.6
Public sector	−20.0	−29.7	8.5	−91.7	−1,213.0	−139.7	110.4
Private sector	−1.7	5.5	4.1	5.3	5.8	5.4	7.5

Source: Bank Negara Malaysia.

upward trend in 2003 when non-residents put their funds in local equities and bonds to speculate on the ringgit's appreciation. However, the ringgit appreciated only gradually vis-à-vis the USD in late 2005, which explained the reversal in portfolio capital in 2005, and thus, the outflow of $9.8 billion in the financial account.

It is worthwhile to analyze the position of the net other investment more closely since it accounted for most of the variation in total net capital flows (IMF, 2007). Over 1999–2005, the average other investment to GDP ratio was around minus 5.6 per cent. This was due partly to the influence of carry trades, as well as the repayment of public external debt by the central government, notably from 2003 to 2005.

12.2.2   Impacts

Rapid movement in capital flows and current transfers may affect the growth of domestic liquidity and credit, the exchange rate, inflation, and the performance of the real and financial sectors.

12.2.2.1   Domestic liquidity and credit

Domestic liquidity, as measured by M3, grew by an average of 7.7 per cent over the period 1999–2005 (Table 12.2). Money supply started its upward trend from 2001 and peaked at 12.3 per cent in 2004. This was due to large expansion in net foreign assets (NFA) and to a lesser extent on

Table 12.3 Average NEER and REER indices of the MYR (2000 = 100)

	1999	2000	2001	2002	2003	2004	2005
				NEER			
Level	98.06	100.00	106.15	105.86	100.45	96.73	96.18
Change (%)	0.12	1.98	6.15	−0.27	−5.11	−3.70	−0.57
				REER			
Level	98.49	100.00	105.58	105.90	99.88	95.26	95.29
Change (%)	1.17	1.53	5.58	0.31	−5.69	−4.63	0.03

Sources: BIS; author's calculation.

net domestic assets (NDA). NFA started to increase from 2001 due to a steady net inflow of capital. However, an NFA slowdown in 2005 reflected outflows in portfolio investment. On the other hand, NDA expanded from 2001 to 2003 as the intermediation of capital inflows by banks led to a rise in credit growth to the private sector. NDA declined in 2004 possibly due to a sterilization effect by the monetary authority aimed at neutralizing the impact of large portfolio inflow speculating on the currency. NDA resumed its upward growth in 2005, which resulted in higher credit growth.

12.2.2.2 The exchange rate

Volatility, as measured by the average standard deviation of the monthly bilateral exchange rate, was zero from 1999 to 2004. This is not surprising as the currency was pegged to the USD from 2 September 1998 to 21 July 2005. As noted earlier, there were net portfolio inflows over 2003–04 speculating on the ringgit's appreciation. These inflows reversed in 2005 since the degree of appreciation was small, as reflected in the small rise in volatility to 0.02.

The nominal effective exchange rate (NEER) appreciated from 2003–04 owing to large inflows of portfolio investment. With inflation relatively benign over this period, the NEER appreciation also translated into appreciation of the real effective exchange rate (REER). However, the capital reversal in 2005 did not result in depreciation in either NEER or REER (Table 12.3).

12.2.2.3 Price inflation

(a) Consumer prices Headline inflation started to rise in 2004 after a one-year lag from the inflow of short-term portfolio funds (Table 12.4).

Table 12.4 Consumer price inflation (2000 = 100), annual change in %

	1999	2000	2001	2002	2003	2004	2005
Headline	2.8	1.6	1.4	1.8	1.1	1.4	3.1
Core	1.8	1.4	1.8	2.4	1.0	1.0	2.8
Of which: Transport & Communication	0.5	2.1	3.6	6.6	1.6	0.8	4.4

Note: The weight used in computation of 'core' inflation is 66.2, while that of the 'transport & communication' is 18.8.

Source: Department of Statistics, Malaysia.

Table 12.5 Asset price inflation, annual change in %

	1999	2000	2001	2002	2003	2004	2005
KLCI (1977=100)	38.6	−16.3	2.4	−7.1	22.8	14.3	−0.8
MHPI (2000=100)	−2.4	6.0	1.1	2.5	4.0	4.8	2.4

Sources: KLCI (Bursa Malaysia); MHPI (NAPIC, Department of Valuation and Property Services).

Both core inflation and its component, namely, transport and communication, increased only in 2005, which coincided with rising global crude oil (and other commodities) prices.[7]

(b) Asset prices The Kuala Lumpur Composite Index (KLCI), which measures the performance of the top 100 companies, rose in 2003 and 2004, but fell in 2005 (Table 12.5). This was consistent with the trend of portfolio investment over the same period. Meanwhile, the Malaysia House Price Index (MHPI), which measures nationwide house prices, also followed the movement of the KLCI.[8]

12.2.2.4 The real sector
On average, non-resident capital, in the form of inward direct investment into the manufacturing sector, was around $4.1 billion over the period 1999–2005. Moreover, foreign capital appeared to be more important than domestic capital during 1999–2002 for manufacturing growth.

12.2.2.5 The financial sector
The depth of the financial sector is measured by the sum of the ratios of liquid liabilities (M3) and equity market capitalization to GDP. From Table

Table 12.6 Financial sector deepening, 1999–2005 (as % GDP)

	1999	2000	2001	2002	2003	2004	2005
Liquid liabilities	144.9	128.6	133.8	131.6	132.1	131.0	129.5
Equity market capitalization	183.6	124.7	131.9	125.7	152.9	152.3	133.8
Financial depth	328.5	253.3	265.7	257.2	285.0	283.4	263.4

Source: World Development Indicators (World Bank).

12.6, it is not obvious that capital inflows contributed to the deepening of the financial sector. The lack of evidence on financial depth could be due to the effects from the imposition of various policy controls on capital flows.

12.3 CAPITAL FLOWS 2006–2007

This section examines policy challenges associated with capital flows when Malaysia adopted a managed float exchange rate regime, and implemented various liberalization measures on capital outflows. On the external front, greater risk-taking by investors in the face of high global liquidity resulted in large capital flows into emerging Asian economies.

12.3.1 Trends

In 2006–07, Malaysia continued to run a current account surplus and accumulated foreign reserves (Table 12.7). Higher remittances abroad by foreign workers and expatriates continued to depress current transfers. To mitigate the adverse effects of capital inflow, Malaysia encouraged local firms to invest abroad. Outward direct investment almost doubled to $6 billion in 2006 from 2005, which negated the amount of inward direct investment.

Investment opportunities improved in 2007 following numerous liberalization measures in financial, plantation, and property sectors. The introduction of investment incentives covering taxation, more liberal foreign equity participation, and employment of expatriates raised the attractiveness of Malaysia as an investment destination. These factors led to higher direct capital inflows in the first half of 2007. However, the trend on outward direct investment also accelerated resulting in a small net direct inflow. By progressively relaxing controls on capital outflows, excess liquidity is drained out of the financial system and pressure on the ringgit reduced. Some caution has to be taken to ensure that outflows are

Table 12.7 Balance of payments (US$ billion)

	2005	2006	1Q06	2Q06	3Q06	4Q06	1Q07	2Q07
Current account balance	20.0	25.5	5.5	5.0	7.4	7.7	5.7	6.9
Of which: Current transfers	−4.5	−4.6	−1.3	−1.1	−1.2	−1.1	−1.1	−1.1
Credit	0.3	0.3	0.1	0.1	0.1	0.1	0.1	0.1
Debit	4.8	4.9	1.3	1.1	1.2	1.2	1.2	1.2
Financial account balance	−9.8	−11.9	−1.4	−0.1	−4.9	−5.5	0.8	2.2
Direct investment	1.0	0.0	−0.3	−0.1	−0.3	0.8	0.2	0.0
Outward	*−3.0*	*−6.0*	*−1.3*	*−1.6*	*−1.7*	*−1.4*	*−1.4*	*−3.3*
Inward	*4.0*	*6.0*	*1.0*	*1.5*	*1.4*	*2.2*	*1.6*	*3.3*
Portfolio investment, net	−3.7	3.5	2.2	−0.3	0.1	1.5	7.3	4.6
Other investment, net	−7.0	−15.4	−3.3	0.2	−4.6	−7.8	−6.7	−2.4
Official sector	*−0.8*	*−2.2*	*−0.3*	*−0.1*	*−0.7*	*−1.1*	*−0.1*	*−0.3*
Private sector	*−6.2*	*−13.2*	*−3.0*	*0.3*	*−3.9*	*−6.7*	*−6.7*	*−2.1*
International reserves, net	70.2	82.5	73.4	78.8	79.5	82.5	88.6	98.4

Sources: Department of Statistics, Malaysia; author's calculation.

of a reasonable amount that does not lead to a threatening fall in official reserves.

A greater appetite on the part of investors and strengthening macroeconomic fundamentals led to large inflows of portfolio funds into domestic equities and bonds during the first quarter of 2006. While equity and bond prices were driven higher by capital inflows, there were also some signs of speculative activity in the exchange rate. Repricing of risk premium attached to riskier securities investment due to a deteriorating global inflation outlook led to portfolio outflows in May to June 2006. Inflows resumed in the second half of 2006 as the risk–reward outlook improved again.

Strong economic growth, and healthy corporate and household sectors led to a surge in portfolio inflow in the first half of 2007, despite several bouts of volatility. However, policies may not be effective in circumventing volatile capital flows. Sound macroeconomic conditions, financial sector sophistication, and transparent policies may lower chances of capital reversal, but external pressures and a contagion effect may lead to sudden outflows (Grenville, 2006). While there is a sizeable amount of outward direct investment, the corresponding amount is negligible in terms of portfolio investment. The main reason is domestic investors' reluctance to invest abroad, possibly due to lower returns as well as a lack of requisite investment skills by domestic financial institutions.

More recently, net inflow of direct investment amounted to $2 billion in the third quarter of 2007.[9] The bulk of the capital was channeled into manufacturing, industrial (oil and gas), and services sectors. Outward direct investment was about $2 billion. Meanwhile, portfolio funds recorded a net outflow of $6.5 billion due to liquidation of domestic securities by non-resident investors in August, following tightened global credit conditions. Inflows resumed in September 2007.

Meanwhile, other investment continued to record a large net outflow in 2006–07 due to intensified carry trades. However, this may be subject to heightened risk aversion, repricing of credit risk, and prolonged global financial turmoil that could lead to sharp reversal (ADB, 2007). Repayment of public external debt can also contribute to the decline in net other investment. In addition, it also reflected better portfolio diversification of the domestic banking sector following liberalization of restrictions on capital outflows.

12.3.2 Impacts

In a liberalized environment, rapid capital inflows could raise domestic liquidity and credit, leading to an unstable currency appreciation and inflation that could possibly derail economic activity.

12.3.2.1 Domestic liquidity and credit

Domestic liquidity (M3) expanded by 13 per cent in 2006 supported by rapid expansion in NFA and to a lesser degree on NDA (Table 12.8). To some extent, the growth in NFA also captured higher portfolio diversification as banks placed more assets abroad. Massive net inflow of portfolio funds, arising from high global liquidity and increased risk-taking by investors, generated a rise in liquidity in the financial system. To overcome inflationary pressure and to stabilize interest rates, the monetary authority conducted sterilization operations. In turn, this action, together with prudential lending procedures, led to a lower credit growth.

Alternatively, swap arrangements can also stabilize domestic money supply and interest rates without issuing central bank securities. When foreign reserves accumulate beyond a desired level, the monetary authority can sell some of them to domestic financial institutions in exchange for domestic currency. The buyers are required to invest the acquired funds overseas for a specified period. At the end of the period, the regulator

Table 12.8 Domestic liquidity and credit

	2005	2006	1Q06	2Q06	3Q06	4Q06	1Q07	2Q07	3Q07
	\multicolumn{9}{c}{Level (MYR billion)}								
M3	672.8	760.3	690.8	700.5	716.3	760.3	789.2	788.6	804.2
NFA	259.9	312.6	268.3	284.1	297.9	312.6	345.6	388.1	370.2
NDA	631.5	674.5	639.8	642.5	646.7	674.5	680.7	676.0	719.5
Public sector	*−9.9*	*−1.6*	*−7.2*	*−19.2*	*−21.5*	*−1.6*	*−0.6*	*−21.3*	*−10.7*
Private sector	*641.4*	*676.1*	*646.9*	*661.7*	*668.2*	*676.1*	*681.3*	*697.4*	*730.3*
	\multicolumn{9}{c}{Annual growth rate (in per cent)}								
M3	8.3	13.0	6.7	6.6	8.3	13.0	14.2	12.6	12.3
NFA	0.7	20.3	−5.0	−1.8	4.5	20.3	28.8	36.6	24.3
NDA	6.6	6.8	8.2	8.1	6.9	6.8	6.4	5.2	11.3
Public sector	*110.4*	*−83.9*	*−49.0*	*7.0*	*−3.6*	*−83.9*	*−91.5*	*11.3*	*−49.9*
Private sector	*7.5*	*5.4*	*6.9*	*8.1*	*6.5*	*5.4*	*5.3*	*5.4*	*9.3*

Source: Bank Negara Malaysia.

reimburses the buyers for any loss resulting from the interest rate differential between domestic and foreign markets, as well as any loss from changes in the exchange rate. In this respect, central bank swap arrangements also provide an avenue for increasing outward portfolio investment, which is lacking in Malaysia. The money supply continued to record double-digit growth in 2007, supported by growth in NFA with NDA picking up in the third quarter due to higher credit expansion.

12.3.2.2 The exchange rate

The average standard deviation of the monthly exchange rates remained small in 2006, despite net inflow of short-term capital. These inflows emerged because of good domestic macroeconomic fundamentals as well as market expectations of further appreciation of the ringgit. However, these factors were negated by strong demand for foreign currencies for outward direct investment, repayment of external loans (other investment, net), and the repatriation of profits and dividends (current account balance). To some extent, the observed small volatility also reflected sterilization efforts by the monetary authority aimed at maintaining competitiveness.

Since Malaysia operated a large overall payment surplus due to large inflow of foreign capital, a flexible exchange rate policy would lead to an appreciation of the ringgit. By allowing (gradual) appreciation, the

Table 12.9   Average NEER and REER indices of the MYR (2000 = 100)

	2005	2006	1Q06	2Q06	3Q06	4Q06	1Q07	2Q07	3Q07
					NEER				
Level	96.18	98.55	98.27	98.92	98.15	98.84	101.83	102.89	100.59
Change (%)	−0.57	2.46	4.74	4.00	0.92	0.30	3.63	4.02	2.49
					REER				
Level	95.29	98.81	98.38	99.23	98.35	99.28	102.65	102.64	100.16
Change (%)	0.03	3.70	5.97	5.43	2.08	1.47	4.34	3.43	1.84

Sources: BIS; author's calculation.

regulator can mitigate the cost of sterilization. If appreciation is not ongoing, the magnitude of capital inflow may be reduced via an increase in the rate of expected depreciation. The relative success of this also depends on sequential liberalization of the external financial account, and strong domestic financial institutions with good regulation and enforcement (Kawai, 2005).

In 2007, the path of the exchange rate was subjected to numerous rounds of portfolio liquidation exercises in February, March, May, August, and November. Despite this, volatility was relatively small due to foreign exchange interventions by the central bank to maintain orderly market conditions.

As capital inflows continued in 2006 up to the second half of 2007, both NEER and REER appreciated (Table 12.9). The trend in both NEER and REER started to fall in the third quarter of 2007 when investors began liquidating portfolio positions in the face of the deepening US subprime turmoil.

12.3.2.3   Inflation

(a)   Consumer prices   Net portfolio inflows began in the first quarter of 2006 and continued until the second quarter of 2007, with a respite in the second quarter of 2006 (Table 12.10). Inflation and its components surged in the first quarter of 2006 and peaked in the next quarter, before trending downwards until the second quarter of 2007.[10] Higher global oil prices and their resulting inflationary impact in the first half of 2006 prompted the central bank to raise interest rates, which led to the subsiding effect on inflation until the first half of 2007. With oil prices persistently hovering at high levels in the third quarter, the risk of higher inflation prevails. Some reduction in inflationary pressure may permeate through an increasingly flexible exchange rate and the gradual pace of appreciation.[11]

Table 12.10   Consumer price inflation (2005 = 100), annual change (%)

	2004	2005	2006	1Q06	2Q06	3Q06	4Q06	1Q07	2Q07	3Q07
Headline	1.5	3.0	3.6	3.8	4.1	3.6	3.0	2.6	1.5	1.8
Core			3.8	3.6	4.5	3.6	3.0	2.5	1.0	1.4
Of which: Transport	0.7	6.3	11.0	11.5	13.9	10.0	8.7	6.1	1.1	1.1

Note: The weight used in the calculation of 'core' inflation is 68.6, while that of 'transport' is 15.9.

Source: Department of Statistics, Malaysia.

Table 12.11   Asset price inflation, annual change (%)

	2005	2006	1Q06	2Q06	3Q06	4Q06	1Q07	2Q07	3Q07
KLCI (1977=100)	−0.8	21.8	6.3	3.0	4.3	21.8	34.6	48.1	38.1
MHPI (2000=100)	2.4	1.9	2.4	1.4	2.1	4.8	4.3	3.2	

Sources: KLCI (Bursa Malaysia); MHPI (NAPIC, Department of Valuation and Property Services).

(b) Asset prices Large inflows of short-term capital have entered into Malaysian securities markets – equities, bonds, and properties – since the first quarter of 2006. This has somewhat resulted in asset price inflation, as measured by the growth in KLCI (Table 12.11). The movement in MHPI was weaker compared to that of the KLCI because restrictions in the property market were relaxed only in late 2006 stretching into 2007. Nevertheless, the monetary authority needs to monitor this trend, given the repercussions of asset price inflation on the economy. Persistently rising asset prices may lead to bubbles with huge economic cost. Furthermore, heightened risk aversion, as exemplified by the recent US subprime turmoil, may lead to massive capital outflow.

12.3.2.4   The real sector

Similar to 1999–2005, investment in the manufacturing sector by non-residents was highly volatile in 2006 to the third quarter of 2007 (Table 12.12). Moreover, the domestic share of total investment approvals seemed to be higher in 2006.[12]

For the first nine months of 2007, the main recipient of inward direct

Table 12.12 Manufacturing investment approvals

	2005	2006	1Q06	2Q06	3Q06	4Q06	1Q07	2Q07	3Q07
				Domestic					
Level(USD billion)	3.5	7.0	0.4	1.9	3.5	1.2	0.7	3.4	1.0
Annual change (%)	−15.1	101.8	−16.0	55.1	330.8	23.9	90.3	79.4	−72.3
				Non-Resident					
Level(USD billion)	4.7	5.5	1.0	0.8	1.9	1.8	1.1	3.1	2.1
Annual change (%)	37.1	16.5	562.6	−48.8	84.4	−9.7	9.3	285.3	10.5

Source: Malaysian Industrial Development Authority (MIDA).

Table 12.13 Financial sector deepening, 2005–07 (as % GDP)

	2005	2006	1Q06	2Q06	3Q06	4Q06	1Q07	2Q07	3Q07
Liquid liabilities	129.5	132.8	512.2	499.3	481.3	511.8	546.5	512.3	487.0
Equity market capitalization	133.8	148.2	543.4	514.4	500.9	571.3	682.1	707.0	624.4
Financial depth	263.4	281.0	1055.6	1013.7	982.3	1083.1	1228.6	1219.3	1111.4

Source: World Development Indicators (World Bank).

capital was the electrical and electronic products subsector. This industry continued to attract sizeable capital inflows, in particular for reinvestment and expansion of existing operations in Malaysia. The investments involved the production of semiconductors, fabricated wafers, substrates for the semiconductor industry, and printed circuit boards. This is beneficial to the real economy as it results in technological diffusion and innovation necessary for sustaining long-term economic growth. On the other hand, this industry is also highly sensitive to the health of the global economy, and in particular the US. Hence, any sign of global downturn may adversely affect export growth in Malaysia and may result in capital reversal. Apart from this industry, foreign capital also flowed into the energy subsector – petroleum refineries and products, and chemicals and chemical products.

12.3.2.5 The financial sector

The trend in net portfolio capital contributed to the deepening of the financial market, as measured by the equity market capitalization to GDP ratio (Table 12.13). However, it is not apparent that capital inflows affect financial intermediaries (measured by liquid liabilities ratio) or the financial sector collectively (measured by financial depth indicator).

12.4 ALTERNATIVE POLICY MEASURES

This section discusses various policies to manage capital flows. Some may be more effective than others depending on the state of the economy and the financial sector.

First, fiscal policy may be useful in controlling capital inflows. By running a budget surplus, inflation pressure and appreciation of the real exchange rate can be lowered. A reduction in government expenditure has the same effect as a decrease in demand for loanable funds because it can lower interest rates. However, this policy has to be balanced with the development responsibility of the government. Moreover, fiscal policy has long lags. Thus, it may not be effective in managing short-term speculative capital inflows.

There is some indication that Malaysia is trying to use the above measure in conjunction with sterilization to handle surges in foreign capital (Ministry of Finance Malaysia, 2007). To mitigate lower government expenditure on infrastructure, a private financing initiative was strongly encouraged. The progress was slow, however, given current financial volatility.

Policies aimed at strengthening domestic consumption and investment may be useful in lowering dependency on the volatile external sector. The high level of national savings could be directed to productive investment activities as well as encouraging more consumption. However, prudential regulations should be employed to prevent an unsustainable boom in consumption and investment.

Private investment, which grew by 7 per cent in 2006, is expected to remain on an upward trend, accelerating by 10 per cent in 2008 and 11.4 per cent in 2009 (Figure 12.1). To attain 6 per cent in GDP growth over the Ninth Malaysia Plan (9MP) period from 2006 to 2010, higher private investment growth of 11.2 per cent per year would be needed.

There are three measures to encourage faster private investment growth in Malaysia. First is the reduction in the corporate tax rate from 27 per cent in 2007 to 26 per cent in 2008. By lowering the corporate tax rate, the level of competitiveness in Malaysia is enhanced. Corporate earnings will be higher and in turn, this may lead to higher reinvestments by local economic agents. Moreover, a lower corporate tax rate may also encourage more inflows of direct investment into strategic industries in Malaysia.

The second measure entails a revamped public delivery system to ease the cost of doing business in Malaysia. Although there were some

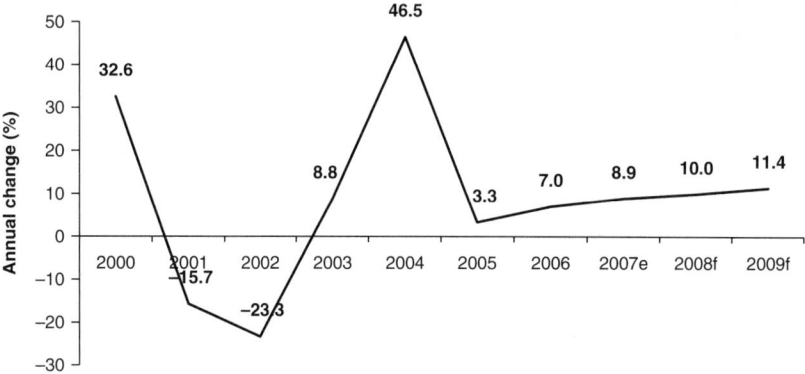

Source: Department of Statistics, Malaysia.

Figure 12.1 Private investment growth

improvements in expediting the public sector delivery procedure, more measures may be required to ensure faster implementation of public projects under the 9MP.

The first two drivers mentioned above seek to address concerns raised by Guimaraes and Unteroberdoerster (2006). The third measure centers on industry clusters to raise the rate of private investment. More specifically, the government has recently launched five regional economic corridors in Malaysia (Table 12.14). These economic corridors are expected to target a combined sum of around $343.8 billion investment over the period 2006 to 2030.

When domestic policies are not effective in dealing with massive capital flows, troubled countries may seek regional assistance from the Chiang Mai Initiative (Ariff, 2007). Although the available funding is still small, it may be better than being subjected to tough IMF conditionalities.

Finally, with little progress in the international financial system, Asian economies have continued to amass foreign reserves. Large reserves may be useful in the face of large capital reversal. With high import covers and low exposure to foreign debts, Asian countries have been able to weather the recent financial contagion without much difficulty.

12.5 CONCLUSION

The paper has reviewed policies taken to address capital flows in Malaysia from 1999 to 2007. Strong macroeconomic fundamentals and a

Table 12.14 Comparison of the five economic corridors

	Peninsula Malaysia			East Malaysia	
	(1) IDR (Iskandar Development Region)	(2) NCER (Northern Corridor Economic Region)	(3) ECER (Eastern Corridor Economic Region)	(4) SDC (Sabah Development Corridor)	(5) SCORE (Sarawak Corridor of Renewable Energy)
Concept	Creation of new catalyst developments	Enhancing key industries as catalysts	Eradication of poverty	Capturing high-value economic activities	Focused development on natural resources
Member states	Southern Johor	Kedah, Perlis, Penang, Northern Perak	Kelantan, Terengganu, Pahang, East Johor	Sabah	Sarawak
Population	3.2 million	4.3 million	3.9 million	Not available	2.5 million
Period	20 years	18 years	12 years	18 years	22 years
Investment	USD 119.4 billion; mainly FDI	USD 55.3 billion, purely domestic	USD 35.0 billion, all domestic	USD 32.8 billion, mainly FDI	USD 104.4 billion, FDI and local funding
Infrastructure	USD 1.3 billion	USD 15.6 billion	USD 15.0 billion	Not available	Not available
Key drivers	Property, infrastructure, FDI	Electrical & electronics, manufacturing, agriculture, tourism	Oil & gas, agriculture, tourism	Agriculture, tourism, manufacturing, logistics	Energy resources
Authority	Iskandar Regional Development Authority	Northern Corridor Implementation Agency	Development Council	Sabah Economic Development Investment Authority	Regional Corridor Development Authority

global search for yields will continue to shift more capital into Asia. This trend is expected to prevail at least in the medium term, given structural weakness in the US. However, capital flows are sensitive to any change in risk appetite. Accordingly, the national monetary authority may need to pursue active monitoring of capital flows. Having sound policies, financial sector resilience, large reserves, a flexible exchange rate, and a strong domestic sector may be useful in facing increasingly volatile capital flows.

NOTES

1. For further discussion on financial sector reforms, see Bank Negara Malaysia (2007).
2. Note that some of these pull factors may not hold, given the ongoing global credit crunch and subprime issues. Some of the economies in Asia are facing economic slowdown, while others are more successful in weathering the financial turmoil. Nevertheless, Asia as a whole still receives a considerable amount of capital inflows, notably in high interest rate economies.
3. For a review of other sterilization measures on capital flows, see Obstfeld (1982), Kumhof (2004), and Kawai and Takagi, Chapter 2 of this book.
4. The ringgit exchange rate was fixed at 3.80 per USD on 2 September 1998 and remained until 21 July 2005. Selective exchange controls were introduced on 1 September 1998 to protect the financial system from external influences, effectively shutting down the offshore ringgit market. For further discussion, see Bank Negara Malaysia (1999) and Ariff (2007).
5. Note that Malaysia adopted the Fifth Edition of the Balance of Payment Manual of the IMF in 1999. Hence, figures prior to 1999 are not comparable to those from 1999 onwards.
6. For funds already in Malaysia, there was a price on exit inversely proportional to duration of stay. Capital that had entered the country more than one year was free to leave at a zero exit price. For funds yet to come in there was a levy only on profits, which exclude dividends and interest, also graduated by length of stay. Investments in the newly established, over-the-counter equity market, MESDAQ, were exempted. See Bank Negara Malaysia (1999) for further discussion.
7. Vector autoregression (VAR) or threshold VAR is useful to analyze transmission lags from capital flows to inflation and its components. The paper did not pursue this exercise, given the small sample size of the data.
8. Note that this is based only on observation. More thorough econometric exercises may be needed to confirm it. Moreover, during 1999–2005, Malaysia practiced some non-resident restrictions on the property (housing) sector. Some of these rules were progressively relaxed in late 2006 and in 2007.
9. The third quarter figures were based on the Cash BOP System, where retained earnings and investment in the form of imported machinery and equipment are excluded.
10. Note that the computation of consumer price inflation differs between Table 12.4 and Table 12.10. The former combined transport and communication using a weight of 18.8, while the core inflation was 66.2. To focus on the impact of high global crude oil prices on transportation, Table 12.10 used a weight of 15.9 for transport and core inflation of 68.6. Thus, these figures should be interpreted with caution.
11. In order to investigate the impact of capital flows on inflation and the exchange rate, the use of VAR and Granger-causality tests may be needed. This was not possible, given the small time period of the sample concerned.

12. Note that, due to data limitation, detailed analysis of capital inflows into various sectors of the economy is not possible. The analysis in this subsection uses data based on a cash basis, which differs from the methodology adopted in the Fifth Edition of the Balance of Payment Manual of the IMF. Accordingly, results should be interpreted cautiously.

REFERENCES

ADB (Asian Development Bank) (2007), *Asia Bond Monitor*, November.
Ariff, M. (2007), Comment on 'Asian currency crisis and the IMF, 10 years later: overview', *Asian Economic Policy Review*, **2**(1), 50–51.
Bank Negara Malaysia (1999), *Annual Report 1999*.
Bank Negara Malaysia (2007), *Financial Stability and Payment Systems Report 2006*.
Grenville, S. (2006), 'Ten years after the Asian crisis: is the IMF ready for the next time?', Sydney: Lowy Institute for International Policy.
Guimaraes, R. and O. Unteroberdoerster (2006), 'What's driving private investment in Malaysia? Aggregate trends and firm-level evidence', IMF Working Paper WP/06/190, Washington, DC.
IMF (International Monetary Fund) (2007), *Regional Economic Outlook, Asia and Pacific*, October.
Kawai, M. (2005), 'East Asian economic regionalism: progress and challenges', *Journal of Asian Economies*, **16**, 29–55.
Kumhof, M. (2004), 'Sterilization of short-term capital inflows – through lower interest rates?', *Journal of International Money and Finance*, **23**(7–8), 1209–21.
McCauley, R.N. (2002), 'Setting monetary policy in East Asia: goals, developments, and institutions', *SEACEN Occasional Paper*, No. 33.
Ministry of Finance Malaysia (2007), *Economic Report*.
Obstfeld, M. (1982), 'Can we sterilize? Theory and evidence', *American Economic Review*, **72**(2), 45–50.

APPENDIX

BOX 12A.1 POLICY MILESTONES

1999

4 January	Banking institutions were instructed to achieve a minimum loan growth of 8 per cent by the end of 1999.
10 January	BNM took control of MBf Finance Berhad, the biggest finance company (with assets amounting to about $5 billion, one-fourth of total assets of all finance companies) on grounds of weak management.
4 February	The 12-month holding rule on repatriation of foreign portfolio capital was replaced with a three-tier exit levy on the principal and profit.
18 February	Repatriation of funds relating to investment in immovable property was exempted from the exit levy.
26 May	BNM raised $1 billion through a global bond issue. The issue was oversubscribed by 300 per cent.
29 July	BNM unveiled a plan to combine the country's 58 financial institutions (22 commercial banks, 11 merchant banks and 25 finance companies) into six large banking groups.
7 August	Residents were allowed to grant overdraft facilities in ringgit not exceeding RM200 million for intra-day and not exceeding RM500 for overnight to foreign stockbroking companies subject to certain conditions.
9 August	BNM's intervention rate was reduced from 7 per cent to 5 per cent.
21 September	The three-tier levy on repatriation of portfolio capital was replaced with a flat 10 per cent levy on profit repatriated.
21 October	Commercial banks were allowed to enter into short-term currency swap arrangements with non-resident stockbrokers for a maturity period not exceeding five working days with no rollover option.

2000

14 March	Funds arising from sales of securities purchased by non-residents on the CLOB market were permitted to be repatriated without paying exit levy.
30 September	Licensed offshore banks in the Labuan Offshore Financial Center were allowed to invest in ringgit assets from their own account only and not on behalf of clients. The investment could not be financed by ringgit borrowing.
27 October	Profit earned from foreign portfolio investment in Malaysia for a period of more than one year was exempted from the 10 per cent repatriation duty.
15 December	The 10 per cent levy on profits earned from foreign portfolio investment repatriated within one year was abolished.
20 December	Licensed commercial banks were allowed to extend intra-day overdraft facilities not exceeding RM200 million and overnight facilities not exceeding RM10 million to foreign stockholding companies and foreign custodian banks.

2001

6 January	All controls on the trading of futures and options on the Malaysian stock exchange were abolished.
21 November	Licensed banks were allowed to extend credit facilities to non-residents up to an aggregate of RM5 million to finance projects undertaken in Malaysia.

2002

12 March	RM10 000 ceiling on foreign currency loans to residents for investment overseas was removed. The requirement for using only ringgit for settlement of transactions on ringgit-denominated assets between residents and non-residents and between non-residents was abolished.
3 August	Banks were permitted to extend ringgit overdraft facilities not exceeding RM500 000 in aggregate

to non-residents provided the credit facilities are fully covered at all times by fixed deposits placed by the non-resident customer with the lending bank.

2003
4 January

The maximum amount of repatriation of profits, dividends, rental income and interests on all bona fide investment without prior approval was increased from RM10 000 to RM50 000 or its equivalent in foreign currency. Residents who have foreign currency funds were permitted to invest freely in any foreign currency products offered by onshore licensed banks. The ceiling on bank loans to non-residents (excluding stockbroking companies, custodian banks and correspondent banks) was raised from RM200 000 to RM10 000 000.

2005
1 April

(a) investment in Malaysia by non-residents

- there is no restriction on repatriation of capital, profits, dividends, interest, fees or rental by foreign direct investors or portfolio investors
- ringgit assets purchased by residents from non-residents may be settled in ringgit or foreign currency, other than restricted currency

(b) investment abroad by residents

- licensed onshore bank and approved merchant banks may invest abroad as long as they comply with the Banking and Financial Institution Act 1989 or Islamic Banking Act 1983 and their approved foreign currency net open position limit. Remittances for investment abroad must be made in foreign currency, other than restricted currency

	(c) residents, companies and individuals with no domestic borrowing are free to invest abroad. The investment may be made through the conversion of ringgit or from foreign currency funds retained onshore or offshore.
21 July	BNM announced abolition of the ringgit peg to the dollar in favor of a managed floating system tied to a basket of currencies.

2007

1 April — Foreign exchange administration rules are liberalized to:

(a) expand the scope of licensed onshore banks' foreign currency business

- abolish net open position limit of licensed onshore banks which was previously capped at 20 per cent of the banks' capital base
- abolish the limit imposed on licensed onshore banks for foreign currency accounts maintained by residents
- allow investment banks in Malaysia to undertake foreign currency business subject to a comprehensive supervisory review on the capacity of the investment banks

(b) facilitate investments in ringgit assets by non-residents

- further flexibility for non-resident stockbrokerages and custodian banks to obtain ringgit overdraft facility from licensed onshore banks to avoid settlement failure due to inadvertent delays
- abolish the limit on the number of residential or commercial property loans obtained by non-residents

- allow licensed onshore banks to appoint overseas branches of their banking group as a vehicle to facilitate the settlement of any ringgit assets of their non-resident clients
- remove the restriction on Labuan offshore banks to transact in ringgit financial products on behalf of non-resident clients to enhance the role and scope of business of the Labuan offshore banks

(c) enhance business efficiency and investment opportunities

- increase the limit of foreign currency borrowing that can be obtained by resident corporations from licensed onshore banks and non-residents as well as through issuance of onshore foreign currency bonds, to RM100 million equivalent in aggregate and on corporate group basis from the previous RM50 million equivalent
- allow residents to hedge foreign currency loan repayment up to the full amount of underlying commitment
- enhance flexibilities for resident individuals and corporations to invest in foreign currency assets
- increase the limit for resident institutional investors to invest in foreign currency assets
- allow resident corporations to lend in foreign currency, the proceeds arising from listing of shares on foreign stock exchanges to other resident corporations within the same corporate group in Malaysia

- abolish restrictions on payments in foreign currency between residents for settlement of foreign currency financial products offered onshore
- allow resident individuals to open and maintain joint foreign currency accounts for any purpose

(d) to facilitate development of the capital market to support the initiatives to expand the pool of high quality stocks and to provide diversity of offerings and promote cross-border linkages with other markets, the following foreign exchange administration rules are liberalized:

- allow non-resident corporations to utilize abroad the proceeds arising from the listing of shares through initial public offering on the main board of Bursa Malaysia

Allow resident corporations to utilize proceeds arising from the listing of shares through initial public offering on the main Board of Bursa Malaysia for offshore investment purposes.

1 August — The individual reporting threshold for transactions between residents and non-residents is increased to RM200 001 or its equivalent in foreign currency from RM50 001 per transaction.

1 October — The liberalization covers the following areas:

(a) the abolition of five registration requirements

- forward foreign exchange contracts by residents
- ringgit-denominated loans to non-residents for purchase or construction of immovable properties in Malaysia

- investment in foreign currency assets by residents
- foreign currency borrowing by residents
- prepayment or repayment of foreign currency borrowing by residents

(b) granting greater flexibility for Islamic funds managed onshore
(c) providing greater flexibility on hedging of ringgit exposure by non-residents.

28 November Resident companies with export earnings are allowed to pay another resident company in foreign currency for the settlement of purchases of goods and services. The objective of this liberalization is to enhance Malaysia's competitiveness by reducing the cost of doing business for resident companies.

13. Managing capital flows: the case of the Philippines
Josef T. Yap

13.1 INTRODUCTION

The global financial instability that was spawned by the 1997 East Asian financial crisis generated a broad consensus that the international financial architecture (IFA) had to be reformed. The proposed reforms had two wide-ranging objectives (Griffith-Jones and Ocampo, 2003): (i) to prevent currency and banking crises and better manage them when they occur; and (ii) to support adequate provision of net private and public flows to developing countries, particularly low-income ones. Much progress has been made in terms of reforming the IFA between 1997 and 2007. However, the progress has been uneven and asymmetric and in certain areas patchy (Griffith-Jones and Ocampo, 2003; Wang, 2004; Kawai, 2005; World Bank, 2005; and Kawai and Houser, 2007). For example, while the ASEAN+3 nations agreed to pool the region's vast foreign currency reserves in May 2007, the urgency of architectural reform in the G-7 countries has receded considerably (Wang, 2004). As long as the structural problems on the supply side of international capital such as volatile capital movements and G-3 exchange rate gyrations persist, the East Asian countries will remain vulnerable to future crises.

There are many indications of the inadequacies in the reform of the IFA. For example, in 2006, aggregate net resource flows into developing countries reached $566 billion, of which $316 billion comprised foreign direct investment (FDI) and $94 billion comprised portfolio equity or 'hot money'. The latter was three times its peak level in 1997. The development is largely brought about by a situation of excess global liquidity, which is related to the global macroeconomic imbalances problem. With the abundance of global liquidity, investors are lured into emerging markets which offer higher returns. The resulting inflow of capital has created 'important challenges for policymakers because of their potential to generate overheating, loss of competitiveness, and increased vulnerability to crisis' (IMF, 2007a).

In this chapter, the experience of the Philippines with regard to managing capital inflows – or more generally foreign exchange inflows – from 1987 to 2007 is reviewed, with a focus on the post-1997 period, since earlier work (Lamberte, 1995) has adequately analyzed pre-crisis experience. Following the introduction, the impacts of foreign exchange inflows and the policy responses, particularly those of the country's central bank (Bangko Sentral ng Pilipinas (BSP)), will be evaluated in the succeeding sections. The last section offers some policy recommendations.

13.2 CAPITAL INFLOWS INTO THE PHILIPPINES: 1987–2007

13.2.1 Trends and Composition

Net capital flows to the Philippines have been fairly steady from 1989–97, except for a blip in 1996 when net capital flows jumped to $14.7 billion (Table 13.1). FDI was a constant contributor, although the level was much lower compared with neighboring countries with a similar level of development, i.e. Malaysia, Thailand and Indonesia. Portfolio investment surged in 1995 and 1996 following the global trend during this period. Meanwhile, transactions classified as 'other investments' were the largest source of flows during this period, and this category largely explains the jump in capital inflows in 1996. Data indicate that this was attributable mainly to the increase in net foreign assets of commercial banks.

Between 1998 and 2007, which is the period after the East Asian financial crisis, net capital flows to the Philippines fell sharply (Table 13.2). The only exceptions were in 1999 when there was a fairly large amount of foreign investment in debt securities, and in 2005 when there was a surge in portfolio investment. In 1999, there was an increase in borrowers availing themselves of medium and long-term loans largely in response to the adverse effects of the crisis. The category 'other investments' also increased sharply in 2005 although this was followed by a turnaround in 2006.

Despite the slowdown in capital inflows after the 1997 crisis, foreign exchange inflows remained strong owing to remittances of Filipinos working abroad, which are the main component of current transfers. Net current transfers in 2006 were 11.3 per cent of GDP at $13.2 billion (Table 13.2). However, historical comparison should be approached with caution. While data on capital account are still loosely comparable, the same is not true for current transfers, as adjustments to the balance of payments (BOP) data have been applied only since 1999. The percentage share of current transfers in GDP jumped in 2001 and increased steadily

Table 13.1 Current transfers and net capital flow in the Philippines ($ million)

		1989	1990	1991	1992	1993	1994	1995	1996	1997
2	Current transfers (3)−(4)	830	714	827	816	699	936	880	589	1080
3	Credit: receipts	832	717	828	825	746	1041	1147	1185	1670
4	Debit: payments	2	3	1	9	47	105	267	596	590
5	Capital and financial account (6)+(9)	1354	2057	2927	3209	3267	5120	5309	14767	5648
6	Capital account (7)−(8)	0	0	0	1	0	0	0	0	0
7	Credit: receipts	0	0	0	1	0	0	0	0	0
8	Debit: payments	0	0	0	0	0	0	0	0	0
9	Financial account (10)+(13)+(20)+(23)	1354	2057	2927	3208	3267	5120	5309	14767	5648
10	Direct investment (12)−(11)	563	530	544	228	864	1289	1079	1335	1086
11	Debit: assets, residents' investments abroad	0	0	0	0	374	302	399	182	136
12	Credit: liabilities, non-residents' investments in the Phil.	563	530	544	228	1238	1591	1478	1517	1222
13	Portfolio investments (17)−(14)	280	−50	110	40	−52	269	1190	5317	591
14	Debit: assets, residents' investments abroad (15)+(16)	14	0	15	115	949	632	1429	−191	9
15	Equity securities	0	0	0	0	n.a.	n.a.	n.a.	−21	−30
16	Debt securities	14	0	15	115	949	632	1429	−170	39
17	Credit: liab., non-residents' investments in Phil.(18)+(19)	294	−50	125	155	897	901	2619	5126	600
18	Equity securities	0	0	0	0	n.a.	n.a.	n.a.	2101	−406
19	Debt securities	294	−50	125	155	897	901	2619	3025	1006

20	Financial derivatives (22)–(21)	n.a.	n.a.	n.a.	n.a.			n.a.	n.a.
21	Debit: assets, residents' investments abroad	n.a.	n.a.	n.a.	n.a.			n.a.	n.a.
22	Credit: liabilities, non-residents' investments in the Phil.	n.a.	n.a.	n.a.	n.a.			n.a.	n.a.
23	Other investments (25)–(24)	511	1577	2273	2940	2455	3562	3040	8115	3971
24	Debit: assets, residents' investments abroad	0	0	0	0	0	0	0	−1745	425
25	Credit: liabilities, non-residents' investments in the Phil.	511	1577	2273	2940	2455	3562	3040	6370	4396

Source: Bangko Sentral ng Pilipinas.

Table 13.2 Current transfers and net capital flows in the Philippines ($ million)

1		1998	1999	2000	2001	2002	2003	2004	2005	2006	Q1 2007	Q2 2007
2	Current transfers (3)–(4)	435	5784	5643	6860	7680	8386	9160	11391	13243	3452	3527
			7.837756	7.784013	9.996349	10.34707	10.83206	10.83631	11.86308	11.3		
3	Credit: receipts	758	5969	5909	7119	7948	8626	9420	11711	13511	3529	3635
4	Debit: payments	323	185	266	259	268	240	260	320	268	77	108
5	Capital and financial account (6)+(9)	–1135	6474	–1537	–1094	933	–951	160	11063	–1467	181	77
6	Capital account (7)–(8)	0	163	138	62	27	54	17	40	138	15	–21
7	Credit: receipts	0	270	168	86	50	82	46	58	181	28	29
8	Debit: payments	0	107	30	24	23	28	29	18	43	13	50
9	Financial account (10)+(13)+(20)+(23)	–1135	6311	–1675	–1156	906	–1005	143	11023	–1605	166	98
10	Direct investment (12)–(11)	2127	1114	2115	335	1477	188	109	1665	1983	626	–2462
11	Debit: assets, residents' Investments abroad	160	133	125	–140	65	303	579	189	103	72	2990
12	Credit: Liabilities, Non-Residents' investments in the Phil.	2287	1247	2240	195	1542	491	688	1854	2086	698	528

13	Portfolio investments (17)−(14)	−928	3662	−553	40	733	563	−574	3301	2360	310	964
14	Debit: assets, residents' investments abroad (15)+(16)	603	603	812	57	628	818	862	145	1567	1592	−244
15	Equity securities	184	55	42	−30	8	48	15	4	−1	−5	16
16	Debt securities	419	548	770	87	620	770	847	141	1568	1597	−260
17	Credit: liab., non-residents' investments in Phil. (18)+(19)	−325	4265	259	97	1361	1381	288	3446	3927	1902	720
18	Equity securities	264	489	−202	125	227	501	518	1465	2388	1010	1418
19	Debt securities	−589	3776	461	−28	1134	880	−230	1981	1539	892	−698
20	Financial derivatives (22)−(21)	n.a.	8	44	−15	−21	−64	−27	−43	−138	−60	−90
21	Debit: assets, residents' investments abroad	n.a.	−51	−166	−83	−85	−54	−58	−98	−159	−30	−11
22	Credit: liabilities, non-residents' investments in the Phil.	n.a.	−43	−122	−98	−106	−118	−85	−141	−297	−90	−101
23	Other investments (25)−(24)	−2334	1527	−3281	−1516	−1283	−1692	635	6100	−5810	−710	1686

Table 13.2 (continued)

		1998	1999	2000	2001	2002	2003	2004	2005	2006	Q1 2007	Q2 2007
24	Debit: assets, residents' investments abroad	809	−1051	2455	761	−256	743	−907	−4791	3512	397	1455
25	Credit: liabilities, non-residents' investments in the Phil.	−1525	476	−826	−755	−1539	−949	−272	1309	−2298	−313	3141

Note: Data on current transfers from 1999 onwards are not comparable to data prior to 1999.

Source: Bangko Sentral ng Pilipinas.

until 2006. This implies that while remittances are relatively high, it would be difficult to attribute the sharp rise in the peso's value in 2006–07 to a 'surge' in remittances.

Capital inflows to the Philippines are largely due to 'push' factors. The ebb and flow generally follow global patterns, particularly in the case of portfolio flows. Meanwhile, remittances respond to both pull and push factors, and are largely pro-cyclical and driven by investment motives (Tuaño-Amador et al., 2007). The peso appreciation could also be considered a pull factor, wherein larger dollar remittances are required to sustain a specific standard of living. On the other hand, the main push factor would be more employment opportunities and higher remuneration abroad.

13.2.2 Impact on the Macroeconomy: Econometric Results

Large inflows of capital can lead to accumulation of reserves, real appreciation of the local currency, expansion in domestic liquidity, increase in the price level, and reduction in the domestic interest rate, which, in turn, affect consumption, investment, and government spending. On the other hand, some of these variables constitute the host of 'pull' factors that determine capital flows – such as improved macroeconomic performance and exchange rate regime – that attract investor confidence and encourage capital inflows. Hence, the apparent endogeneity of capital inflows and other macroeconomic variables warrants the use of a non-structural multi-equation approach to analyze the impact of inflows of capital on the macroeconomy.

Before proceeding with the choice of estimation methodology, the time series properties of the variables were first checked since estimations of the nonstationary series are known to be spurious. Given the expected impact of capital inflows in the economy, we include, apart from the measure of capital inflows – using net capital and financial account of the BOP – reserves, 91-day Treasury (T-bill) rate, real effective exchange rate (REER), M3, consumption, investment, and government expenditures in the set of variables. The results of the augmented Dickey-Fuller tests (ADF) indicate that all the variables are stationary in levels except for M3 and consumption which are integrated, of order two.

The nonstationarity of M3 and consumption implies that it is legitimate to search for a cointegration relationship among the variables. In performing cointegration tests using the approach of Johansen (1991), we consider the foregoing set of macroeconomic variables. Results of the Johansen cointegration tests provide evidence that a unique cointegrating vector exists among the above-mentioned set of variables. The existence of cointegration relationship among the four groupings of variables warrants the use of a vector error correction model (VECM), in lieu of an unrestricted vector autoregression (VAR).[1]

The impulse response functions (IRF) derived from the various versions of the VECM could provide indications of the impact of capital flows on the macroeconomic variables included in the groupings. However, IRF results using Cholesky decomposition could be sensitive to the ordering of the variables in VECM. Since our analysis focuses on the impact of capital flows on the macroeconomy, the measure of capital flows is placed first in the ordering. The surge of capital flows could lead to accumulation of reserves, so the reserves are placed second in the ordering. Meanwhile, the central bank is expected to respond to capital inflow shocks using its policy instruments which could influence market rates (Berument and Dincer, 2004). Hence, the 91-day T-bill rate enters the VECM as the third variable. Moreover, exchange rates could respond to the increase in the market rates via the interest parity condition.

In addition, exchange rates could react to capital inflows because the latter could increase reserves and the money supply. Therefore, the real exchange rate and M3 follow the 91-day T-bill rate. Meanwhile, the resulting expansion in money supply could lead to an increase in the price level; hence, the consumer price index (CPI) is placed next. Finally, other variables in the real and fiscal sectors react to changes in the market rate and the real exchange rate so that consumption, investment, and government expenditures are placed at the end of the ordering. Although frowned upon by practitioners, a dummy variable was added to temper the impact of the 1997 financial crisis.

IRF results from the VECM indicate that capital inflows, in aggregate, could lead to an increase in reserves, with the impact reaching its highest magnitude in the second quarter after the capital inflow shock (Figure 13.1). However, the impact of a positive capital flow on the 91-day T-bill rate appears insignificant. Meanwhile, capital inflows tend to lead to a real appreciation of the peso against the basket of major trading partners' (MTP) currencies. Nevertheless, the positive impact of the capital inflow shock seems to dissipate in the second quarter after the shock so that the real exchange rate reverts to its pre-shock value in the seventh quarter but appears to appreciate again thereafter. The broadly positive results from the impulse response functions relating to M3 and CPI indicate the capital inflows could lead to an expansion in domestic liquidity and an increase in inflation. Meanwhile, the impact of capital flows on consumption, investment, and government expenditure appear insignificant.

The estimated VECM was likewise utilized to generate IRFs resulting from a positive shock to reserves. An interesting result is that the reserves shock leads to a real appreciation of the peso against the basket of MTP

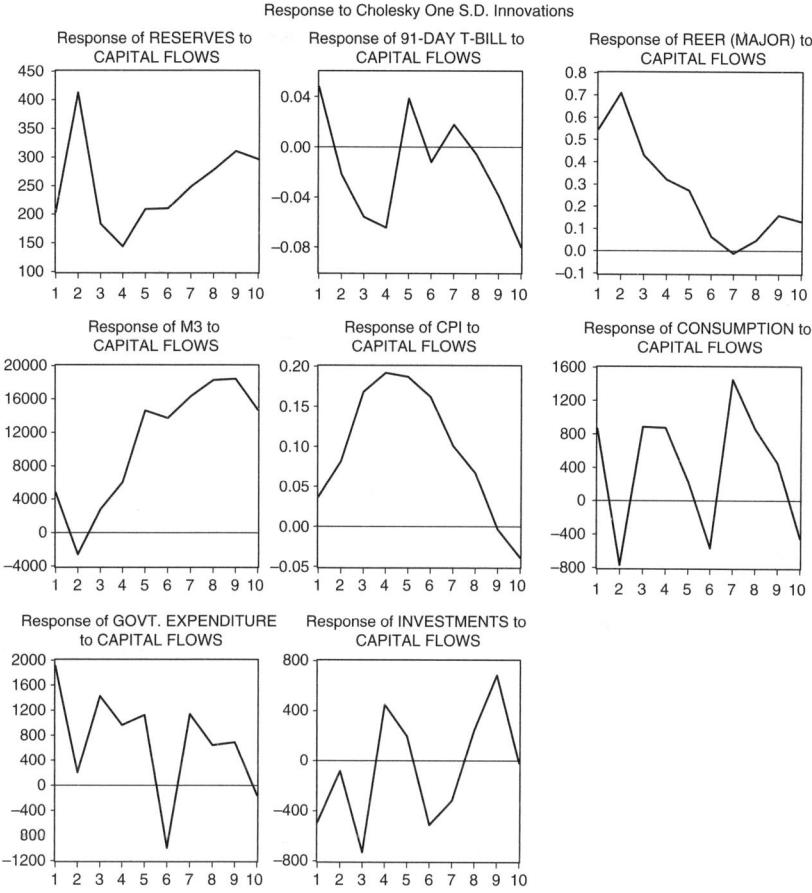

Figure 13.1   *IRFs from shock to capital inflows*

currencies, which appears to be counterintuitive given the precautionary nature of reserves in the Philippine economy (Figure 13.2).

Different versions of the VECM were likewise estimated with the aggregate capital flows variable replaced by its direct investments and portfolio investments components and by current transfers as well. IRFs derived from a positive shock in direct and portfolio investments are either insignificant or counterintuitive.[2] This is due perhaps to the volatility of direct and portfolio investments over the 1989 Q1 to 2007 Q2 sample period with coefficient of variation of 177.9 and 307.0, respectively. Meanwhile, results from the VECM using the current transfers variable, which has a coefficient of variation of 94.3, indicate that a positive shock to current

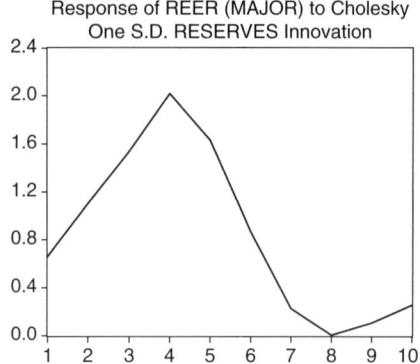

Figure 13.2 IRF of REER (major) from shock to reserves

transfers leads to a rise in the level of reserves, the 91-day T-bill rate, CPI, and government expenditure (Figure 13.3). Generally insignificant results were derived from IRFs relating to the real exchange rate, M3, consumption, and investment.[3] Overall, capital flows and current transfers seem to have minimal impact on the real sector. This is likely because the monetary authority may have sterilized the impact, or exchange rate movements may have diluted any potential real effects.

13.3 IMPACT OF CAPITAL INFLOWS IN THE PHILIPPINES

This section looks at the experience of the Philippines from 1987 to 2007 and determines whether the possible adverse outcomes of surges of foreign exchange inflows were realized. The analysis refers to the econometric results in the previous section when relevant. Basic macroeconomic indicators of the Philippines are shown in Table 13.3. This investigation will help in the analysis of the impact of foreign exchange inflows on the economy and also in the evaluation of selected policy responses.

13.3.1 Real Sector

The results of the VAR analysis indicate that foreign exchange flows have limited impact on investment. The level of FDI investment in the Philippines has been historically low, reaching a maximum of 3.4 per cent of GDP in 1998. A study by Mirza and Giroud (2004) revealed that in several Southeast Asian economies including the Philippines, FDI had

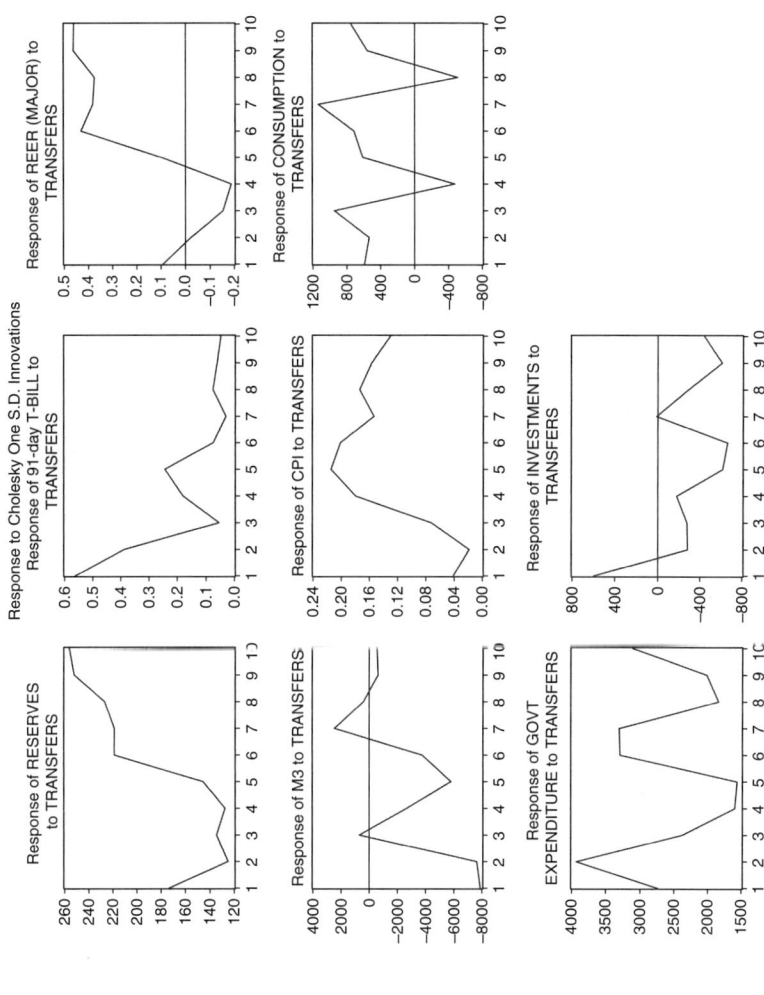

Figure 13.3   IRFs from shock to transfers

Table 13.3 Basic macroeconomic indicators, Philippines

	Current account (% of GDP)	Overall budgetary surplus/ deficit, central government (% of GDP)	Inflation rate (2000=100) (%)	M3 growth rate (%)	91-day Treasury bill rates (%)	Imports / GDP (%)
1987			4.00		11.40	28.77
1988	(1.03)	(2.90)	14.10	22.61	14.40	32.25
1989	(3.42)	(2.11)	12.00	27.98	19.30	34.97
1990	(5.79)	(3.45)	12.30	18.36	23.40	37.35
1991	(1.91)	(2.11)	19.40	15.48	21.40	37.14
1992	(1.62)	(1.18)	8.60	11.04	16.10	40.24
1993	(5.55)	(1.48)	6.70	24.64	12.30	43.93
1994	(4.60)	0.96	10.50	26.50	13.60	48.19
1995	(4.45)	0.58	6.70	25.31	11.30	53.37
1996	(4.77)	0.29	7.50	15.76	12.40	58.91
1997	(5.28)	0.06	5.60	20.95	13.10	63.56
1998	2.37	(1.88)	9.30	7.37	15.30	54.53
1999	(3.77)	(3.75)	5.90	19.27	10.20	51.27
2000	(2.93)	(4.00)	4.00	4.56	9.86	50.44
2001	(2.45)	(4.05)	6.80	18.32	9.86	50.72
2002	(0.36)	(5.32)	3.00	9.28	5.43	51.29
2003	0.36	(4.63)	3.50	4.16	6.03	54.98
2004	1.87	(3.84)	6.00	10.23	7.34	54.58
2005	2.01	(2.70)	7.60	10.32	6.36	53.19
2006	5.02	(1.07)	6.20	21.40	5.40	51.38
2007			2.80		5.35	
2007 Q1	5.70	(3.42)	2.90	24.59	2.97	45.38
Q2	5.20	0.69	2.30	20.88	n.i.	45.77
Q3	1.80	0.06	2.57	12.37	3.76	48.58

Sources: ADB; BSP.

only direct effects while spillover effects in terms of technology transfer were minimal.

However, the negligible impact of current transfers on investment and consumption is not consistent with earlier studies. Lamberte (1995) finds remittances to be a significant determinant of personal consumption but not of investment. A modified form of his regressions was estimated using data from 1999 to 2006 (Table 13.4) showing that remittances significantly affect both investment and personal consumption, but both FDI and portfolio investment are insignificant. The reason for the difference with Lamberte's study in terms of the impact on investment may be the size

Table 13.4 Effects of portfolio investment, foreign direct investment, remittances and savings on investment and personal consumption (logarithmic form)

	Investment		Personal Consumption	
Constant	8.60 (7.95)*	8.53 (7.79)*	8.04 (7.82)*	7.95 (7.73)
Portfolio investment	0.00 (−0.52)		0.00 (−0.46)	
Foreign direct investment		0.00 (0.38)		0.00 (0.43)
Remittances	0.36(5.51)*	0.36(5.47)*	0.64(10.33)*	0.65(10.39)*
Savings	0.01(0.21)	0.01(0.22)	−0.05(−1.04)	−0.05(−1.01)
R-squared	0.58	0.58	0.85	0.85
Durbin-Watson	1.73	1.74	1.27	1.28
Sample period	(Quarterly) First Quarter 1999–Fourth Quarter 2006			

Notes:
T-statistics in parenthesis.
* Significant at 1% level.
All variables are in levels and expressed in logarithmic form. The equations were estimated using the iterative Seemingly Unrelated Regression technique.

of the remittances and the behavior of households. The latter may have become sophisticated over time in managing remittances, thereby using them more productively.

A study based on the 2003 Family Income and Expenditure Survey (FIES) finds evidence that households receiving remittances tend to spend more conspicuously in terms of consumer items but also invest more on education, housing, medical care, and durable goods (Tabuga, 2007). Unfortunately, FIES data do not include capital outlays, hence the impact on investment was not considered.

Meanwhile, a study by Yang (2005) also used FIES data but focuses on the impact of exchange rate shocks on migrant income on a range of investment outcomes in Philippine households such as child schooling, child labor, and entrepreneurial activity. The study finds that favorable exchange rate movements – from the perspective of the overseas worker – lead to greater child schooling, reduced child labor, and increased educational expenditure in Philippine households. Favorable exchange rate shocks also lead to differentially more hours worked in self-employment, and to differential entry into relatively capital-intensive enterprises by households receiving remittances.

The analysis indicates that remittances have the potential to be a more robust source of sustainable economic growth if they are channeled to productive investments. More micro-level studies should be conducted to determine the factors that can bring this about. However, the negligible impact of remittances on consumption based on the VAR analysis, is suspect. This can be considered inconclusive until such time that a consistent data series on current transfers is extended to years prior to 1999.

13.3.2 What is Driving the Exchange Rate?

The most controversial aspect of foreign exchange inflows, arguably, has been the sharp appreciation of many Asian currencies in nominal and real terms from 2004 up to 2007.[4] The peso started appreciating sharply vis-à-vis the US dollar only in December 2005 and it was the most rapidly appreciating currency during the period 2003–07 in Asia (28.2 per cent). The peso had the fastest nominal appreciation in 2007 (18.8 per cent); the literature attributed this knee-jerk reaction to a surge in foreign exchange inflows.

Available data on the ratio of BOP components to GDP during the period 2004–06 for various Asian countries suggest that foreign exchange inflows might have a less prominent role in the appreciation of Asian currencies than assumed. There was no indication of a surge in current transfers among them except for the Philippines. However, Singapore and Malaysia did have substantial current account surpluses but the Singapore dollar and ringgit have significantly lower rates of appreciation.

Meanwhile, the balance in the capital and financial accounts were fairly moderate except for relatively large surpluses in the Philippines and Thailand in 2005. While important, it would be incorrect to cite a surge in foreign exchange inflows as the primary cause of the peso's recent sharp appreciation. Instead, the following factors can be considered in the context of the Philippines:

1. At the 'lowest' points of the various regional currencies, the peso experienced the second largest depreciation in both nominal and real terms. Hence a faster appreciation during the recovery period after the crisis is expected. However, Indonesia's sharp depreciation as a result of the 1997 crisis and net nominal depreciation during the period 2003–07 weakens this argument.
2. Instead of a drawn out process, the peso's recovery was bunched up over the period December 2005 to 2007. This is largely explained by the prevailing fiscal difficulties up to that time. The Philippine government implemented stringent and decisive fiscal reforms beginning in 2005 and their success boosted investor confidence, which was reflected in the peso's strong appreciation in 2006–07.

3. Compared to other central banks in the region, the BSP did not intervene as much in terms of accumulating foreign exchange reserves. The extent of intervention was comparable to the five years preceding 2007. However, this argument is also tempered by Indonesia's experience where the degree of intervention was even lower.
4. A prevailing current account surplus since 2003 has also pushed up the peso's value, recorded at surplus of 5 per cent of GDP in 2006 (Table 13.3). This is largely due to a fall in the investment rate causing ratio of imports to GDP to drop from 63 per cent in 1997 to 46 per cent in the first three quarters of 2007 (Table 13.3).

Rather than surges in foreign exchange inflows, the strength of Asian currencies vis-à-vis the US dollar is largely attributable to the latter's overall weakness. The US dollar depreciated by 38 per cent against the euro during the period 2003–07. This is about 10 percentage points higher than the peso's appreciation against the dollar.

13.3.3 Dollarization and De-Dollarization

Dollar denominated assets held by residents have been increasing over time consistent with the economic liberalization and reflects the degree of dollarization (Table 13.5). Using the IMF standard, an economy is considered highly dollarized if the ratio of foreign currency deposits (FCDs) to money supply is greater than 30 per cent. The Philippines exceeded this level at 41 per cent in 2000, but the ratio fell to 26.4 per cent in October 2007.

The trend towards de-dollarization can be partly explained by the general decline in capital inflows after the 1997 crisis and at a certain point is largely driven by the peso appreciation. In this context, making FCD/M3 an indicator of de-dollarization becomes an exercise in tautology.

Between 2006 and 2007, there was a jump in withdrawals in FCDs, which is a more reliable indicator of de-dollarization. Another indication of de-dollarization is the ratio of FCDs to foreign exchange reserves, which has fallen sharply between 2004 and 2007. Perceptions of dollar weakness prompted economic agents to withdraw from their FCDs and convert them to pesos in anticipation of its appreciation. This action in itself has contributed to the peso's appreciation.

13.3.4 Stock Prices

Foreign portfolio investment has been the main driver of the local stock market. The stock market index surged from 1000 in 2003 to more than

Table 13.5 Ratio of FCDs to broad money aggregates, foreign exchange reserves, and FCD withdrawals

	FCDs (million peso)	FCD/M 3 (%)	FCD/M 4 (%)	FCD withdrawals (million US$)	FCD/ Reserves (%)
1987	–	–	–		–
1988	–	–	–		–
1989	43.85	17.27	14.73		142.37
1990	63.81	21.23	17.51		283.95
1991	77.23	22.25	18.20		86.58
1992	94.46	24.51	19.69		84.08
1993	136.16	28.35	22.09		107/38
1994	158.79	26.13	20.72		99.55
1995	206.69	27.15	21.35		125.66
1996	317.56	36.03	26.49		120.43
1997	433.43	40.66	28.91		201.54
1998	477.94	41.05	29.46	40.64	126.02
1999	521.66	38.21	27.65	42.74	100.57
2000	585.99	41.05	29.10	26.11	101.30
2001	599.19	35.48	26.19	54.89	87.19
2002	643.65	34.87	25.86	28.89	93/57
2003	695.45	36.17	26.56	28.57	93.96
2004	786.61	37.12	27.07	29.12	107.02
2005	787.72	33.69	25.20	25.25	89.79
2006	849.13	29.92	23.03	29.60	82.63
2007 Oct	772.924	26.38	20.87	37.23	61.39

Source: BSP.

3500 in October 2007, which was accompanied by the resurgence of non-residents' investment in equity securities. The results of the VECM analysis and regressions in Table 13.4 indicate, however, that portfolio flows have had an insignificant impact on investment and consumption.

13.4 POLICY RESPONSES

The role of policymakers is to implement measures that will mitigate the adverse impact of foreign exchange inflows. This section provides an inventory of such measures with emphasis on the role of the BSP.

13.4.1 1987–97

The surge in the capital account that lasted between 1993 and 1997 led to a persistent nominal appreciation of the peso between October 1993 and November 1994, and in real terms between April 1995 and June 1997. Inflation, interest rates, and money supply growth were generally higher prior to the crisis. In response, the government implemented measures that can be classified into four categories: (i) reducing the supply of foreign exchange inflows (e.g., cutting back on its requests for loan rescheduling under the Paris debt program); (ii) increasing the demand for foreign exchange (e.g., advancing the phasedown of the forward exchange cover extended to oil firms to add to demand for foreign exchange); (iii) strengthening prudential regulations; and (iv) reducing the cost of production for exporters (e.g., allowing direct and indirect exporters access to foreign currency loans offered by foreign currency deposit units (FCDUs)).

13.4.2 1998–2007

After the crisis, the BSP embarked on an 'aggressive and wide-ranging reform process' of the domestic financial system (Tetangco, 2005). The BSP 'adopted changes in the regulatory and supervisory framework to be able to effectively meet the demands and challenges of globally integrated financial markets and the growing sophistication of financial products and services.'[5]

Measures to improve monitoring and transparency of capital flows were also introduced. The Philippines started subscribing to the IMF's Special Data Dissemination Standards (SDDS) in 1996, and by January 2001, it was in full compliance with the SDDS in the dissemination of the relevant data. The Philippines has also been participating in the formulation of Reports on the Observance of Standards and Codes (ROSCs) to assess the extent to which the Philippines conforms to various key international standards and codes that are relevant to the effective functioning of its economic and financial system. To complement the activities under ROSCs, the Philippines has also been participating in the IMF–World Bank Financial Sector Assessment Program (FSAP) to provide a comprehensive assessment of the strengths, risks, and vulnerabilities of the financial system.

Apart from its effort at reforming the domestic financial system in 1987–97, the BSP also liberalized private sector capital outflows to reduce the inflows and reserve accumulation. This involved the following:[6]

1. Encourage investments by overseas Filipinos (OFs) by facilitating remittances,

2. Encourage private sector capital outflows through further liberalization of foreign exchange transactions,
3. On other capital account transactions, the allowable outward investments by residents without prior BSP approval and registration were increased from $6 million per investor per year to $12 million.

On current account transactions, the limit on allowable foreign exchange purchases by residents from banks to cover payments to foreign beneficiaries for non-trade without supporting documents was increased from $5000 to $10 000.

13.4.3 A Closer Look at BSP Intervention

During the period 1998–2007, the BSP continued to intervene in the foreign exchange market. The latter involves the purchase of foreign currency with domestic currency, which changes the monetary liabilities of the monetary authority, and thus the monetary stance. Typically, intervention aims at the following (IMF, 2007b): (i) influence the level of the exchange rate; (ii) dampen exchange rate changes; (iii) smooth exchange rate flexibility; and (iv) accumulate reserves.

While not as heavy as in other countries, based on a calculated exchange market pressure (EMP) index, the intervention was heavier after the crisis (Figure 13.4 and Figure 13.5).[7] The bars in the figure divide the exchange market pressure on the positive axis into the need to allow the currency to appreciate and a rise in reserves to prevent the appreciation. A useful comparison is the behavior of EMP during the surge of capital flows in 1996 and the surge in 2005.

In 1996, the maximum value of EMP was only 1.3 (August), while in 2005 the maximum value was 4.7 (February), even reaching 9.1 in January 2006. The chart clearly shows that positive changes in international reserves contributed substantially to exchange market pressure.

Not only has the BSP intervened more heavily after the crisis, sterilization has apparently been more pronounced (Table 13.6). The sterilization coefficient for the period 1998–2007 is much higher compared to the coefficient between 1987 and 1997.[8] The coefficient has also been steadily increasing, which can be observed by comparing the regressions for three periods: (i) January 2002–December 2004 when inflation targeting (IT) was initiated; (ii) January 2005–August 2007 the period of heavy capital inflows; and (iii) the period from January 1998–August 2007.

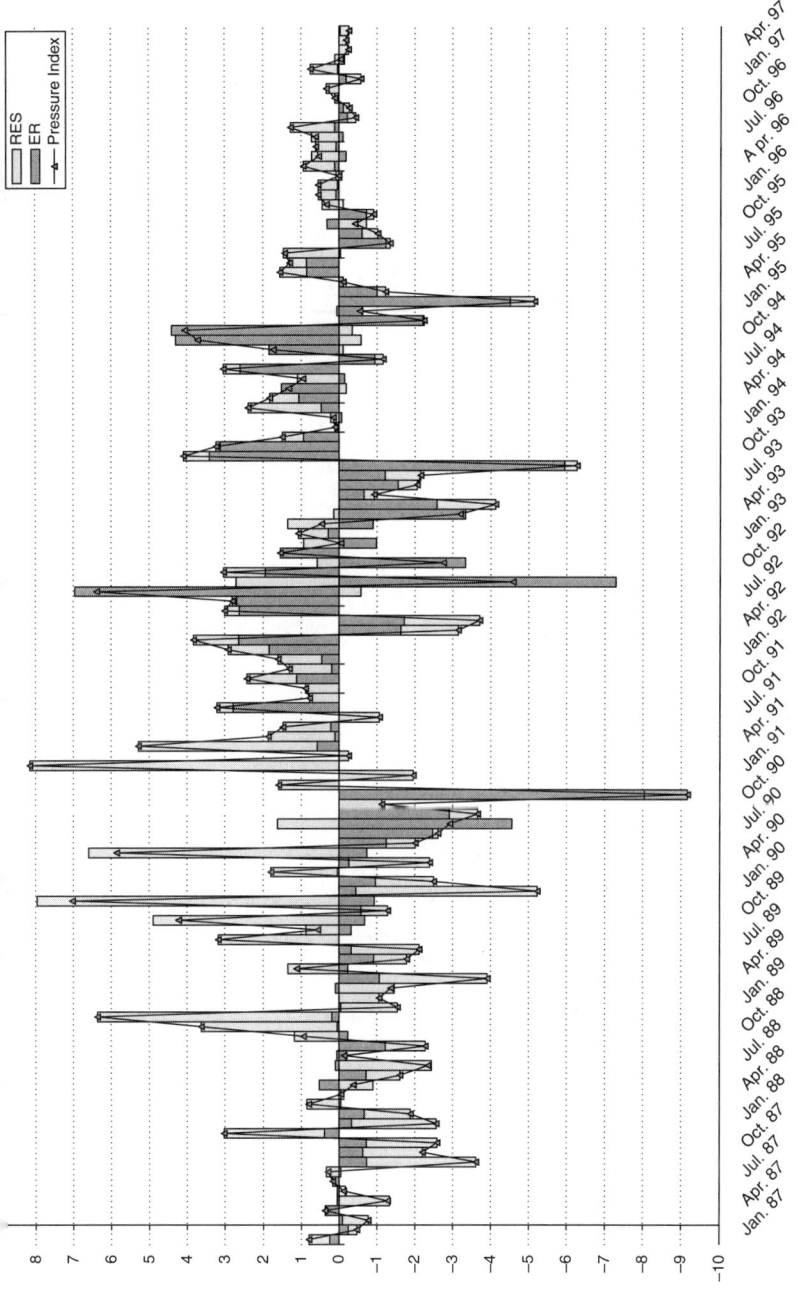

Sources: Bangko Sentral ng Pilipinas and the International Monetary Fund.

Figure 13.4 Pressure index, 1987–97

Sources: Bangko Sentral ng Pilipinas and the International Monetary Fund.

Table 13.6 Degree of sterilization

Dependent variable: ΔNDA
Explanatory variable: ΔNFA
Frequency of data: monthly

Time period	Coefficient of ΔNFA	T-statistic	Adjusted R^2	D.W. Stat
1987.1–2007.8	−0.714	13.4	0.419	2.32
1987.1–1997.6	−0.242	4.2	0.119	2.09
1993.1–1996.12	−1.02	5.6	0.392	2.50
1998.1–2007.8	−0.924	11.5	0.533	2.16
2003.1–2007.8	−1.05	8.6	0.568	2.00
2002.1–2004.12	−0.931	5.6	0.466	2.44
2005.1–2007.8	−1.10	6.9	0.605	1.74

Source: BSP Key Indicators.

13.5 EVALUATION OF POLICY RESPONSES

13.5.1 Has Intervention Worked?

As described earlier, the BSP has engaged in both sterilized and unsterilized intervention. A simple correlation analysis indicates that intervention had a modicum of success in reducing exchange rate volatility in the Philippines between 1993 and 1996, as measured by the percentage of international reserves, and has limited impact on the exchange rate level, percentage change, and volatility (Table 13.7).[9] Meanwhile, intervention prevented a rise in the exchange rate (measured in $/peso) after the 1997 crisis, particularly during the period 2003–07. In many instances the results are counter-intuitive, i.e. the positive correlation coefficient, similar to the result of the impulse response function shown in Figure 13.2.

The empirical results differ from those reported by the IMF (2007b) for the Philippines. However, the IMF study does find limited evidence of systematic links between sterilized intervention and exchange rates in the Philippines, Indonesia, India, the Republic of Korea, and Thailand. The general result is somewhat unexpected given the low degree of substitutability of emerging market assets and the large size of interventions relative to currency market turnover in emerging markets. The IMF attributed the results to persistent structural factors obscuring any effect of intervention beyond a short period; hence preventing the domestic interest rate from adjusting (especially downwards) such that the interest rate differentials remained, thereby failing to alleviate upward pressure on the currency.

Table 13.7 Effectiveness of intervention[a]

Period	ER[b]	%ER[b]	Volatility[c]	ER(+1)[d]	%ER (+1)	Volat (+1)
87.1–97.6	0.116	0.049	−0.018	0.103	0.058	−0.067
93.1–96.12	−0.053	0.216	−0.346*	−0.115	0.113	−0.238*
98.1–07.10	−0.220*	0.091	−0.165	−0.251*	0.211	0.039
03.1–07.10	−0.433*	0.076	0.190	−0.402*	0.092	0.366

Notes:
(a) Figures are the correlation coefficient between monthly data for %RES and the variable indicated at top of column. Note that since ER is defined as $/peso, a significant negative correlation indicates effective intervention. %RES is month-on-month percentage change of foreign exchange reserves; using ΔRES yields similar results.
(b) %ER is month-on-month percentage change of ER; ER is defined as $/peso.
(c) Volatility is the standard deviation of ER (peso/dollar) based on daily data.
(d) ER(+1) is exchange rate one period ahead.

Source: BSP.

Some studies (e.g. Lamberte, 1995) support the relatively large offset coefficient of sterilized intervention in the Philippines. However, as noted earlier, the persistent appreciation of the Philippine peso should also be viewed in the general context of the weak US dollar.

On its part, the BSP argues that the impacts of its intervention policy should be judged by size, nature of shocks, and financial vulnerability. Amid higher volatility of capital flows, BSP intervention needs to be commensurately large to maintain orderly market conditions. The Philippine foreign exchange market expanded more than fivefold in terms of the daily turnover between 1997 and 2007 and the gross foreign exchange flows through the financial system have correspondingly also grown in magnitude.[10]

Moreover, the BSP has been accumulating reserves as a form of precautionary reserves balance, as a first line of defense against future financial crises given the country's relatively high debt burden vis-à-vis other developing countries. Intervention should therefore be adjusted for passive intervention.[11] The BSP argues that the analysis should distinguish between more permanent flows such as exports and remittances and those driven by cyclical trends (such as higher cross-border flows) as a result, for instance, of diversification by central banks and sovereign wealth funds (SWFs) and structural portfolio adjustments in the private sector as home bias declines worldwide. If cyclical factors are driving the trends in the inflows, intervention may be necessary to moderate the macroeconomic imbalances that could result from such large inflows.

While the Philippines' international reserves rose significantly between 2005 and 2007, the relative size of the stock of reserves remained considerably smaller compared to other countries in the region classified as independent floaters. This is the same observation made by Ho and McCauley (2007). The BSP cites the IMF (2007b) study which shows that for 2000–07, the BSP's intervention has been effective in tempering the volatility of exchange rate movements. This is precisely the principle behind the BSP's intervention policy: reducing volatilities rather than swaying the exchange rate in one direction or changing the path of the exchange rate.

It should also be noted that money supply growth in the third quarter of 2007 fell to 12.4 per cent without any significant rise in interest rates (Table 13.3). However, intervention and the subsequent sterilization have financial costs and other central banks are facing similar circumstances. This is another reason why the BSP has built up its capital reserves. These accumulated surpluses now serve as a buffer for losses that the BSP is incurring in its stabilization efforts.

13.5.2 Has Inflation Targeting been Undermined by Foreign Exchange Inflows?

In January 2002, the BSP formally shifted to an inflation targeting framework from a monetary aggregate targeting approach in formulating monetary policy. The shift in the BSP's policy framework from a monetary aggregate targeting approach to inflation targeting was prompted by the observation that the historical relationship between inflation and money supply had weakened.

With more open capital accounts, many countries – including the Philippines – decided that a flexible exchange rate framework is better suited to cushioning domestic economic performance from external disturbances than fixed nominal exchange rates. In this context, the inflation target, rather than the fixed exchange rate, performs the role of a nominal anchor. The BSP is expected to intervene less in the foreign exchange market, allowing the exchange rate to absorb shocks induced by capital flows.

The discussed results indicate that the BSP may be having difficulty in implementing the inflation targeting framework. Surges in foreign exchange inflows – from both the current and capital accounts – seem to have compelled the BSP to intervene in the exchange rate market and revert to targeting monetary aggregates. Whether this has reduced the effectiveness of inflation targeting is yet to be analyzed.

The BSP argues that attention is given to monetary and credit aggregates which are information intensive, in its consideration of the factors that should underpin policy action under an inflation targeting framework. Some evidence suggests that persistently high growth of money and credit aggregates may provide useful 'early warnings' of emerging financial imbalances and may serve as leading indicators of pressures on aggregate demand and on inflation expectations that matter for overall underlying price stability. The growth of monetary aggregates that are beyond the requirements of the economy will tell in the long run on the future evolution of prices.[12]

Meanwhile, an accurate representation of BSP's treatment of the exchange rate in the inflation targeting framework is the willingness to tolerate a significant degree of variability in the exchange rate and to be sufficiently disciplined to participate in the foreign exchange market only in well-defined circumstances. As noted earlier, the BSP intervenes in the market only to temper wide swings in the exchange rate that can lead to disorderly market conditions. However, it is important to underscore that in responding to capital flows, the BSP follows a package of policy measures. This policy mix includes, apart from exchange rate stability, the build-up of international reserves and the prepayment of external obligations. The BSP has been encouraging the shift in the borrowing mix of the government in favor of domestic borrowing. Capital account liberalization, specifically through easing of regulations on non-trade transactions and outward capital investments, continues to be pursued, not for the sake of supporting the peso, but because of the economic gains it can bring by way of portfolio diversification and improved risk management.

13.5.3 Reserve Accumulation: Another Interpretation

The relatively benign effects of reserve accumulation – or central bank intervention in the foreign exchange market – have contributed to the favorable assessment of the BSP, particularly with regard to inflation targeting. However, economic slack and consequently low domestic interest rates in Asia, including the Philippines, contributed largely to the non-manifestation of the usual effects of reserve accumulation (Ho and McCauley, 2007). In this context, Ho and McCauley suggest that reserve accumulation should not be viewed as an exogenous policy with consequences, but rather as a consequence of particular economic circumstances. In particular, the strong efforts to resist currency appreciation in Asia can be seen as a response to weak post-crisis recovery in investment.

A related view is that the accumulation of reserves is largely a consequence of the low investment rate which in turn is a direct result of the uncertainty spawned by the 1997 financial crisis. For example, Genberg et al. (2005) argued that market liberalization appeared to have weakened investment demand throughout East Asia as financial institutions became more reluctant to finance long-term and risky investment projects out of concern for the quality of their asset portfolios. Despite favorable conditions for a recovery in investment in East Asia (Asian Development Bank (ADB), 2007), the sluggish investment performance was attributed by the ADB to increased uncertainty and risk, consistent with the argument of Genberg and colleagues.

The sharp fall of the investment rate can partly explain the present Philippine macroeconomic situation wherein the rapid inflow of foreign exchange is accompanied by an accumulation of reserves, an appreciating currency, a current account surplus, rising money supply growth, stable interest rates and inflation, and an improving fiscal balance. This situation is markedly different from the pre-crisis years. In this context, the following arguments can be made:

- IMF's (2007a) proposal to stem currency appreciation through fiscal restraint is not applicable to the Philippines because the fiscal situation improved markedly between 2005 and 2007 and the fiscal restraint was in the context of correcting a current account deficit.
- The Philippines should instead stimulate private investment to increase imports which would reduce current account surplus and stem the peso appreciation.
- The accumulation of reserves and subsequent sterilization has not undermined the policy of inflation targeting.
- Reserve accumulation is a direct result of weak investment growth which puts a cap on interest rates by lowering the demand for credit. The low interest rate, low credit growth scenario then provides leeway for the BSP to successfully sterilize the rise in foreign exchange reserves.

13.6 THE WAY FORWARD

13.6.1 Measures to Increase Private Investment

The first set of policy recommendations should deal with stimulating private investment in the Philippines. According to a World Bank study (Bocchi, 2008), the key to sustaining growth lies in improving the quality and performance of key institutions that influence investor perceptions about uncertainties, risks, and the costs of doing business; these include addressing issues on governance, contract enforcement, corruption, crime and security, and poor infrastructure.[13]

A more direct mechanism to ease pressure on the current account would be to channel workers' remittances to more productive investment projects. The econometric evidence clearly shows a link between remittances and investment but the latter should go beyond housing and small-scale transportation which are the more popular options at present.

13.6.2 The Heart of the Matter

Despite the substantial progress that has been made, the Philippine economy is still having difficulty coping with a rapidly appreciating peso. The latter is argued to be largely a result of the weak US dollar, the volatility of which between 2003 and 2007 was a manifestation of problems in the IFA.

The uneven and asymmetric progress in the reform of the IFA – particularly the inability 'to guarantee a more coherent macroeconomic policy approach at the global level' – is a manifestation of the unipolar world of finance which has been characterized as unjust and unsustainable.[14] This is an extension of Triffin's dilemma.

In the present global financial system, US dollars dominate trade and reserves. The US can pay for its external deficits by printing dollars and appropriating seigniorage that is created by expanding world trade and cross-border capital flows. The US has been able to combine a widening current account deficit with an appreciation in the real effective exchange rate – or at least one that is relatively stable – because of huge capital inflows. This has been referred to as the trans-Pacific macroeconomic imbalance.

However, the US current account deficit reached $857 billion in 2006 and has become the world's largest debtor nation at $2.7 trillion as of 2005. Another major cause for concern is the annual balance of net income on domestic and foreign investments in the US which turned negative (−$1 billion) for the first time in 2006. If 'net investment income' continues to deteriorate, it will add to the current account deficit and increase the risk of a major reduction or reversal in the capital inflows into the US.

In this context, fixed investment in East Asia may actually be constrained by the need to support the trans-Pacific macroeconomic imbalance and prevent the sharp fall of the dollar.[15] However, the sharp depreciation of the US dollar, particularly since March 2006 and a pending US economic recession may be an indication of a difficult adjustment process.

In order to partly address the inequity caused by a unipolar financial system, the expanded use of Special Drawing Rights (SDRs) was recommended. Other recommendations include an international currency (Mundell, 2003) and an international clearing agency (ICA) (D'Arista,

2007). This ICA could be based on a proposal by John Maynard Keynes to serve as the institutional platform for a new global payments system that would foster egalitarian interactions and more balanced outcomes. The new ICA would clear transactions denominated in members' accounts. These clearing accounts would, in fact, constitute the international reserves of the system, held for the member countries by the ICA and valued using a trade-weighted basket of all members' currencies.

13.6.3 Regional Monetary and Financial Cooperation

Regional financial and monetary cooperation in East Asia is at a critical juncture. The way forward has tremendous implications for the IFA. The 'easy' phase of the reform process in East Asia is at its tail end. Policymakers in the region now have to agree to a blueprint for financial sector development in the foreseeable future, the long-term objective of which Kuroda (2004) succinctly identified as the establishment of a single currency in East Asia. This would cover the need to channel more East Asian savings to infrastructure and investment projects in the region.

The main elements of the blueprint are: (i) the structure of regional financial cooperation in terms of reserve pooling and exchange rate coordination; (ii) the relationship between regional cooperation and the domestic financial system, including required domestic economic reforms; (iii) the institutional set-up in the region that will underpin implementation of the blueprint; and (iv) the non-economic objectives of regional financial cooperation.

The inability of East Asia to effectively speak with one voice hampers real reforms of the IFA. A case in point is the proposed measures to address the trans-Pacific macroeconomic imbalance. Current policy proposals are focused on revaluing the yuan. However, the PRC is not large enough an economy to be responsible for the US deficits or to be able to correct them. Between 1997 and 2004, the US current account deficit deteriorated by $529 billion, and, over the same period, the PRC's current account position improved by only $35.6 billion (Genberg et al., 2005).

Another important issue is that of capital controls, which have proven to be effective in several economies (see for example Epstein et al., 2004). This is evident with the behavior of the Malaysian ringgit compared to other currencies in the region. However, with the advent of greater financial integration, capital controls, particularly on inflows, have to be endorsed at the international level in order to be effective (Grenville, 2007). Given that international backing of any form of capital controls is unlikely, an endorsement at the regional level would be a second best solution. A united East Asian front would be able to throw its weight towards

NOTES

1. The empirical results are available upon request. The four groupings refer to the types of capital flows used in the estimation. One is a combination of FDI and portfolio investment. The second and third are FDI and portfolio investment, respectively, and the fourth is remittances.
2. Tables and results are omitted here but are available upon request.
3. The results are likely to change, particularly for consumption and REER, if a consistent series for current transfers is obtained.
4. An empirical study on the effects of the peso appreciation is beyond the scope of this chapter. Tuaño-Amador et al. (2007) allude to evidence of Dutch Disease in the Philippines, which is also manifest in the deceleration of the manufacturing sector simultaneously with the rapid growth of GDP. Manufacturing sector growth fell to 3.3 per cent in 2007 from 4.6 per cent a year before whereas GDP growth surged to 7.3 per cent in 2007 compared to 5.4 per cent in 2006. However, a more important undertaking would be to determine whether the peso is overvalued at the current exchange rate.
5. Quoted from Tetangco (2005), pages 253–54. The details of the reforms are contained in the same paper.
6. Information was sourced from the BSP.
7. The EMP is calculated as

$$\Delta\%er_t + \frac{\sigma_{\Delta\%er}}{\sigma_{\Delta res}}\Delta res_t.$$

The exchange rate is defined as $/peso, and %er and res are the percentage month-on-month change of the exchange rate and international reserves, respectively. The EMP normalizes the size of the intervention, therefore making comparisons across time valid.

8. The sterilization coefficient is the coefficient from a regression on the contribution of net domestic assets to reserve money growth on the contribution of net foreign assets to reserve money growth.
9. The correlation results were supported by regression analysis using the two-stage least squares procedures applied by the IMF (2007b) as described in Box 3.2 'The effectiveness of intervention: additional tests', page 39.
10. The views of the BSP, as contained in this paragraph and the next two, were expressed by Dr. Cyd Tuaño-Amador, Managing Director for Research of the BSP, during the ADBI workshop in Tokyo on 11–12 December 2007.
11. Dr. Tuaño-Amador cited the fact that the IMF mission recognizes that BSP needs to build up reserves. In the 2006 Article IV consultation report, IMF staff noted that ' . . . reserve cover remains low compared to other emerging markets . . . Some further intervention to build reserves therefore seems justified.' Former IMF Managing Director Rodrigo De Rato in a speech in Thailand in 2007 stated that 'There is a place in managing capital inflows for intervention, especially where inflows of capital appear to be a short-term surge rather than a long-term trend' . . . and that 'the Fund recognizes that intervention can be an appropriate tool of macroeconomic management.'
12. The views in this paragraph and the next were also expressed by Dr. Tuaño-Amador during the ADBI workshop on 11–12 December 2007.
13. A recent World Bank Study explains the dilemma of rising economic growth and declining investment: see Bocchi (2008).

14. A large part of this section is lifted from Agarwala (2004).
15. The more appropriate term is 'global macroeconomic imbalances' since the US also has a deficit with the EU. This issue and the possibility of East Asian investment being constrained by the need to support the US dollar is discussed thoroughly in *Global Imbalances and the US Debt Problem – Should Developing Countries Support the US Dollar?*, edited by J.J. Teunissen, Fondad, The Hague, December 2006; and *Global Imbalances and Developing Countries: Remedies for a Failing International Financial System*, edited by J.J. Teunissen, Fondad, The Hague, June 2007. The books contain relevant policy recommendations on how to address the unipolar financial system.

REFERENCES

ADB (Asian Development Bank) (2007), 'Ten years after the crisis: the facts about investment and growth', in Asian Development Bank (ed.), *Beyond the Crisis: Emerging Trends and Challenges*, Mandaluyong City: Asian Development Bank, pp. 1–20.

Agarwala, R. (2004), 'Reserve Bank of Asia: an institutional framework for regional and monetary cooperation in Asia', in Nagesh Kumar (ed.), *Towards an Asian Economic Community: Vision of a New Asia*, Singapore: Institute of Southeast Asian Studies, pp. 176–203.

Berument, H. and N.N. Dincer (2004), 'Do capital flows improve macroeconomic performance in emerging markets? The Turkish experience', *Emerging Markets and Trade*, 40(4), July–August, 20–32.

Bocchi, A.M. (2008), 'Rising growth, declining investment: the puzzle of the Philippines', Policy Research Working Paper No. 4472, East Asia and Pacific Region, World Bank.

D'Arista, J. (2007), 'A more balanced international monetary system', in J.J. Teunissen and A. Akkerman (eds), *Global Imbalances and Developing Countries: Remedies for a Failing International Financial System*, The Hague: Fondad, pp. 133–40.

Epstein, G., I. Grabel and K.S. Jomo (2004), 'Capital management techniques in developing countries: an assessment of experiences from the 1990s and lessons for the future', UNCTAD G-24 Discussion Paper Series No. 27, March.

Genberg, H., R. McCauley, Y.C. Park and A. Persaud (2005), *Official Reserves and Currency Management in Asia: Myth, Reality and the Future*, Geneva: International Center for Monetary and Banking Studies.

Grenville, S. (2007), 'Globalization and capital flows: unfinished business in the international financial architecture', Lowry Institute for International Policy Perspectives, February.

Griffith-Jones, S. and J.A. Ocampo (2003), 'What progress on international reform? Why so limited?', paper prepared for the Expert Group on Development Issues, available at: http://www.un.org/esa/desa/ousg/presentations/2002_finref.pdf.

Ho, C. and R.N. McCauley (2007), 'Resisting appreciation and accumulating reserves in Asia: examining the domestic financial consequences', Bank for International Settlements, manuscript, 27 December.

IMF (International Monetary Fund) (2007a), 'Managing large capital inflows', in IMF (ed.), *World Economic Outlook*, October, Washington, DC: IMF, Chapter 3.

IMF (2007b), 'Sterilized intervention in emerging Asia: is it effective?', in IMF (ed.), *Regional Economic Outlook, Asia and the Pacific*, October, Washington, DC: IMF, Chapter III.

Johansen, S. (1991), 'Estimation and hypothesis testing of co-integration vectors in gaussian vector autoregressive models', *Econometrica*, **59**, 1551–80.

Kawai, M. (2005), 'East Asian economic regionalism: progress and challenges', *Journal of Asian Economics*, **16**, 29–55.

Kawai M. and C. Houser (2007), 'Evolving ASEAN+3 ERPD: from peer reviews to due diligence', paper presented at the international conference The First OECD-Southeast Asia Regional Forum: Peer Review Mechanism for Policy Reform, organized by OECD with the ASEAN Secretariat and ADB, Jakarta, 23–24 January.

Kuroda, H. (2004), 'Transitional steps in the road to a single currency in East Asia', Statement at the seminar 'A single currency for East Asia – lessons from Europe', organized by Asian Development Bank, Jeju, 14 May.

Lamberte, M.B. (1995), 'Managing surges in capital inflows: the Philippine case', *Journal of Philippine Development*, **XXII**(1) (First Semester), 43–88.

Mirza, H. and A. Giroud (2004), 'Regionalization, foreign direct investment and poverty reduction: lessons From Viet Nam in ASEAN', *Journal of the Asia Pacific Economy*, **9**(2), 223–48.

Mundell, R.A. (2003), 'The international monetary system and the case for a world currency', Distinguished Lecture Series No. 12, Leon Koźmiński Academy of Entrepreneurship and Management, 23 October.

Tabuga, A.D. (2007), 'International remittances and household expenditures: The Philippines case', Philippine Institute for Development Studies Discussion Paper 2007-18.

Tetangco, A.M. Jr. (2005), 'The composition and management of capital flows in the Philippines', *Globalisation and Monetary Policy in Emerging Markets*, BIS Papers No. 23, May, 242–59.

Tuaño-Amador, M.C.N., R.A. Claveria, V.K. Delloro and F.S. Co (2007), 'Philippine overseas workers and migrants' remittances: the Dutch Disease phenomenon and the cyclicality issue', paper presented at the 45th Philippine Economic Society (PES) Meeting, 14 November.

Wang, Y. (2004), 'Prospects for financial and monetary cooperation in Asia and monetary cooperation in Asia', in Nagesh Kumar (ed.), *Towards an Asian Economic Community: Vision of a New Asia*, Singapore: Institute of Southeast Asian Studies, pp. 155–75.

World Bank (2005), 'International financial architecture: a progress report', information note by the World Bank staff, July, available at: http://www.worldbank.org/ifa/IFAprogressreport2005.pdf.

Yang, D. (2005), 'International migration, human capital, and entrepreneurship: evidence from Philippine migrants' exchange rate shocks', World Bank Policy Research Working Paper Series No. 3578, February. http://ssrn.com/abstract=546483, retrieved 6 August 2007.

14. Managing capital flows: the case of Singapore
Hwee Kwan Chow

14.1 INTRODUCTION

There has been much discussion on the state of the regional economies coinciding with the tenth anniversary of the Asian financial crisis. As has been widely noted, the Asian economies recovered quickly from the crisis and are now amongst the fastest growing in the world. Since Asia has not experienced further crises in the past decade, can one infer that the region is now less vulnerable to the destabilizing effects of unfettered international capital flows? After all, considerable efforts have been undertaken to build buffers and reduce vulnerabilities. Compared to the pre-crisis period, the Asian economies are now run more conservatively, have strengthened current accounts, and have significant buildups in foreign reserves. Meanwhile, the financial systems in the region have become more resilient, with the restructuring of balance sheets and the enhancement of surveillance.

However, there has been a resurgence of private capital flows into Asia since 2003. This resurgence has largely been attributed to the search for high-yielding investments arising from low interest rates in developed countries.[1] In view of the pro-cyclicality of such capital flows (Kaminsky et al. 2004), some question whether the region's exposure to a capital flow reversal will lead to yet another financial crisis. It is clear that structural reforms and stronger economic fundamentals have increased Asia's robustness towards such financial shocks. In contrast to the 1997–98 Asian crisis, the region has greater capacity to accommodate the capital outflows so that a liquidity crunch or balance of payments crisis is improbable. Nonetheless, should there be a sudden large-scale reversal of capital flows and undermining of investor confidence, financial market distress and other risk scenarios could ensue (Khor and Kit, 2007). In particular, the attendant sharp corrections in asset prices would have an adverse impact on the economy, especially through indirect channels.

The purpose of this chapter is to present Singapore's experience in managing the risks posed by capital flows as well as the retention of control over exchange rates and monetary conditions. At the outset, we note that Singapore has the support of strong economic fundamentals including persistent budget surpluses, huge foreign exchange reserves, substantial current account surpluses, high savings rates, low inflation, robust institutions, a sound financial system, and a stable currency. In this chapter, we address three key issues: Singapore's exchange rate-centered monetary policy framework, monetary policy operations since the crisis, and the non-internationalization of the Singapore dollar. We consider how these three broad areas, along with a framework of consistent macroeconomic and microeconomic policies, contribute towards defending Singapore against instability arising from free capital mobility.

14.2 TRENDS IN CAPITAL FLOWS[2]

A key feature of the Singapore economy is its extreme openness to trade and capital flows. The size of total imports and exports has been approximately three times that of GDP over the past three decades. In relation to capital flows, almost all forms of capital controls and foreign exchange restrictions have been dismantled since 1978. As a consequence of its small open nature, the Singapore economy has often been buffeted by shocks from the external environment such as the downturn in the global electronics industry in 1996–97, the Asian crisis in 1997–98, and the burst of the information technology bubble in 2001.

Notwithstanding the fluidity of the economic environment and free capital mobility, Singapore has persistently recorded current account surpluses and exported capital abroad (Figure 14.1). With the lone exception of 2001, the overall balance of payments (BOP) has remained positive since 1990. In fact, the overall BOP surplus has been growing in recent years, reflecting the expansion in the current account surplus over the same period. Concomitantly, the excess of national savings over investment has allowed Singapore residents to acquire foreign assets abroad. This includes the Singapore government investing public sector budget surpluses abroad.

To differentiate amongst the various types of capital flows, Figure 14.2 provides a breakdown of the financial account into foreign direct investment (FDI), portfolio investment, and other investment. From 1996 to 2006 we observe a general pattern that net positive FDI is consistently offset by net outflows in portfolio and other investment accounts.

Direct investment inflows have been on a general upward trend since the early 1990s. In comparison, with the exception of 2001, direct investment

The case of Singapore 363

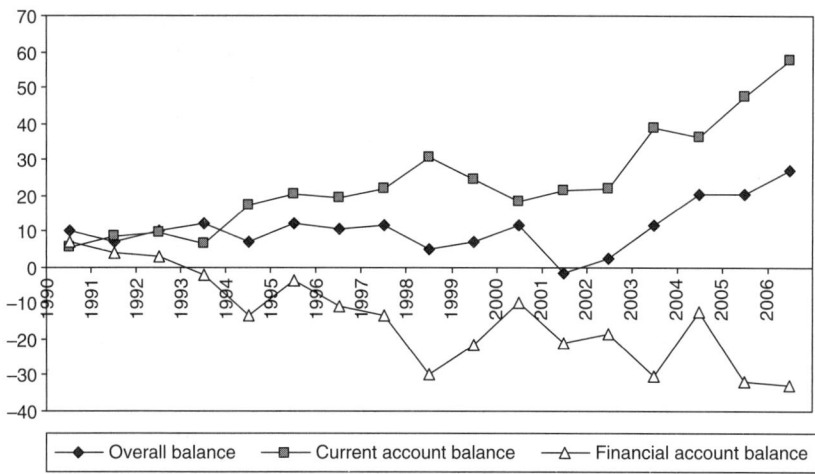

Note: Flows in the capital account have been negligible, being dominated by those in the financial account.

Source: Singapore Department of Statistics.

Figure 14.1 Overall balance of payments (S$ billion)

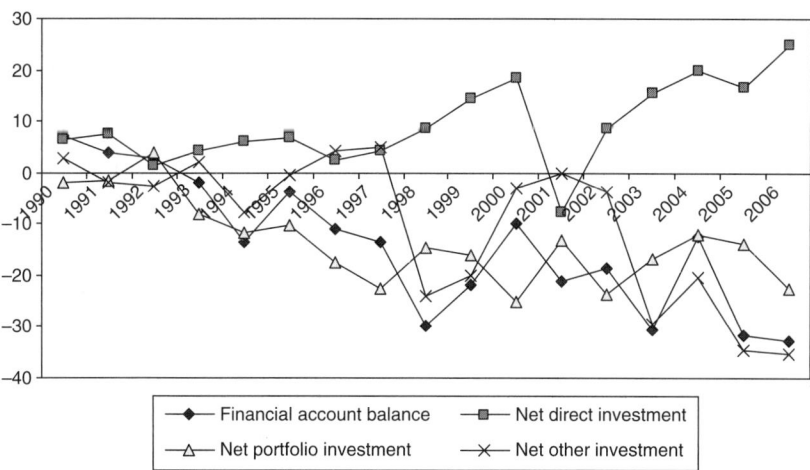

Source: Singapore Department of Statistics.

Figure 14.2 Components of financial account (S$ billion)

outflows have been hovering around S$10 billion.[3] The strong inflows of FDI reflect Singapore's commitment to attract multinational corporations to aid its economic growth. In terms of sectoral distribution, the financial services, manufacturing, and commerce sectors are the major recipients of the FDI inflows, accounting for 38 per cent, 33 per cent, and 16 per cent of the total FDI stock at end-2005, respectively. As is well recognized, such long-term inflows are a relatively stable form of finance; they have undoubtedly been beneficial for the development and growth of the Singapore economy.

In comparison, the portfolio investment account has consistently recorded net outflows. Portfolio inflows have generally been on the rise in the post-crisis period, partly reflecting a return of foreign investors to the local stock market since 2003. However, this is more than offset by the large portfolio outflows, which capture both government and private sector investment in foreign equity and debt markets. Portfolio flows tend to be volatile as investors have the flexibility to shift from one financial instrument into another as these instruments are traded. Indeed, portfolio investment has a tendency to accentuate crises (Dobson and Hufbauer, 2001). In this regard, the low volume of portfolio inflows (relative to FDI inflows) helps to reduce Singapore's vulnerability to capital flow reversal.

The main components of the other investment account include loans, and currency and deposits (C&D). The high volume of capital flows reflects a lively interaction between domestic banks and foreign financial institutions (and other non-residents). As in the portfolio investment account, we observe an increase in both inflows and outflows in the recent period, with the latter exceeding the former. Bank lending[4] is, by conventional wisdom, considered to be more liable to reversal than all the other forms of capital flows including portfolio investment. In the case of portfolio flows, adjustments in the volume are mitigated by price adjustments of the relevant assets (Williamson, 2005). After the 1997 crisis, bank lending has been considerably reduced in net terms.

In total, gross capital inflows have not only recovered after the crisis but have exceeded the pre-crisis peak level (Figure 14.3). The recent surge in capital inflows poses several interesting questions. In particular, how do the various types of capital inflows affect the domestic economy? What are the factors that serve to attract stable long-term capital flows while inhibiting volatile speculative inflows? What policies and measures has the government adopted to meet with the challenges posed by volatile capital flows? These issues are examined in the following sections.

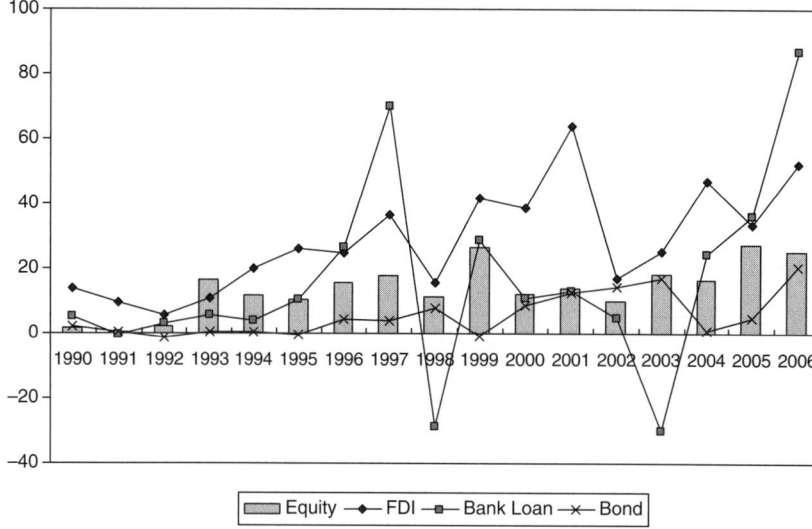

Note: The negative values for inflow of loans refer to the repatriation of loans by foreign banks.

Source: Singapore Department of Statistics.

Figure 14.3 Gross capital inflows (S$ billion)

14.3 OVERVIEW OF MONETARY AND FINANCIAL DEVELOPMENTS

It has been observed that large capital inflows often give rise to increases in money supply and domestic liquidity, appreciation of both nominal and real exchange rates, and acceleration in asset prices. Hence, a country experiencing excessive capital inflows usually has to face the challenges of inflationary pressures, loss of a competitive exchange rate (which could undermine the international competitiveness of its manufacturing sector) and misallocation of capital into unproductive projects. In what follows, we provide an overview of monetary and financial developments in Singapore since 1990.

Domestic liquidity has been growing since the 1990s with the monetary aggregates rising steadily until quarter one of 2006,[5] after which they exhibited a sharp acceleration. Indeed, in 2006–07 the year-on-year (y-o-y) monetary growth rates (Figure 14.4) exceeded the y-o-y nominal GDP growth, which averaged 10 per cent only over the same period. The

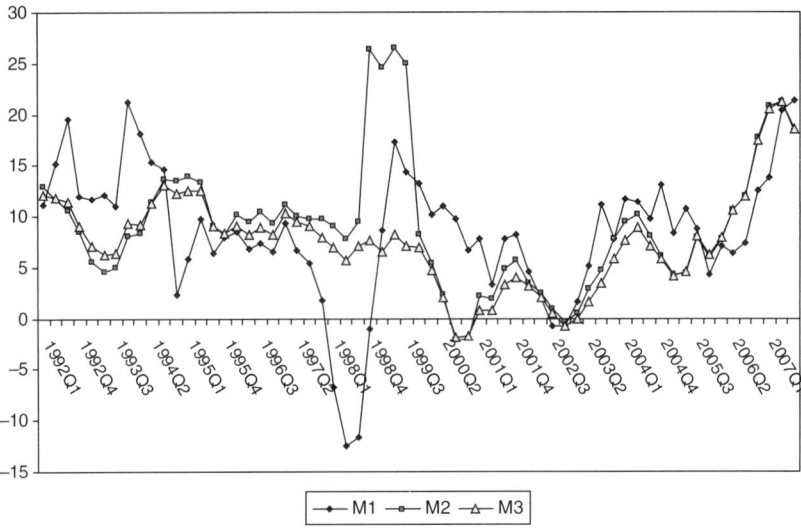

Source: Singapore Department of Statistics.

Figure 14.4 Monetary aggregates (year-on-year growth rates)

various short-term interest rates – overnight, 1-month, and 3-month interbank rates – moved in tandem, staying below 4 per cent after the temporary spike to 6–7 per cent during the 1997 crisis.

Turning to exchange rates, we see from Figure 14.5 that the Singapore nominal and real effective exchange rates (NEER and REER, respectively) exhibited an upward trend before the Asian crisis, reflecting the Balassa–Samuelson effect. The NEER leveled off after the weakening of the currency during the crisis. Nonetheless, an appreciation in the NEER is discernible in the most recent period, reflecting a return of the Singapore dollar to an appreciation path against its major trading partners. By comparison, the REER continued its depreciation path for some time after the Asian crisis, reflecting deflationary trends in domestic wages until the most recent period. Correspondingly, while the consumer price inflation stayed low, growth rates of unit labor cost have frequently been negative in the post-crisis.

By contrast, stock prices have risen rapidly since 2003 (Figure 14.6) in tandem with the increase in portfolio inflows to the local stock market. A similar surge in property prices started only in the later period, with rising foreign investor interest in the high-end residential segment of the property market.

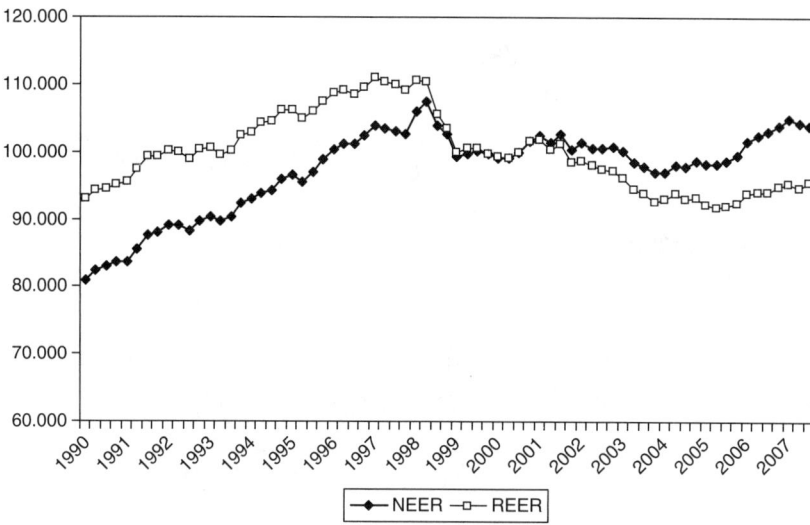

Source: International Financial Statistics (IMF).

Figure 14.5 Nominal and real effective exchange rates: 1990: Q1–2007: Q3 (2000 = 100)

Concomitantly, we observe a pickup in the trend for loans to the construction sector in the recent period. Meanwhile, loans to the commerce and financial sectors also registered a rise in the corresponding period. However, loans to the manufacturing sector mostly remained steady (Figure 14.7).

As for the real economy, the FDI inflows into the various sectors of the economy have boosted the growth of these sectors. Manufacturing, financial and commerce sectors all exhibited relatively faster growth rates since 2004, no doubt benefiting from direct investment flows into their industries.

14.4 EXCHANGE RATE-CENTERED MONETARY POLICY FRAMEWORK

14.4.1 Exchange Rate as Key Monetary Policy Instrument

Despite the increase in capital flows since 2004, Singapore's NEER has been relatively stable. To advance our understanding of how the central bank retains control over the exchange rate, we consider the monetary

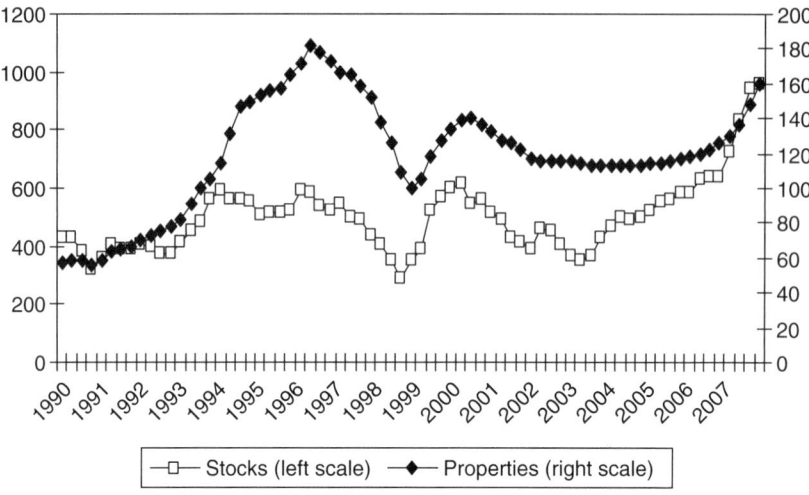

Source: Singapore Department of Statistics.

Figure 14.6 Stock price and residential property price indices: 1990: Q1–2007: Q3

policy framework. A unique feature of Singapore's monetary policy framework is the use of the exchange rate instead of the more conventional benchmark policy interest rate as the key policy operating tool. Singapore, as an international financial center, has opted for free capital mobility. With reference to the open-economy trilemma,[6] it follows that the central bank can choose to use as its key policy instrument only one nominal variable of the three: the exchange rate, the interest rate, or a monetary aggregate. The Monetary Authority of Singapore (MAS) has chosen to use the exchange rate as an intermediate target since the early 1980s.

The rationale of this decision is clear. A high-import content of about 60 per cent in domestic consumption, as well as being a price taker in the international markets, implies that Singapore is highly susceptible to imported inflation. It is thus unsurprising that the exchange rate is considered to be a more effective tool than the interest rate for stabilizing inflation. The other main influence on domestic cost pressures has been labor supply. While the tightness of the labor market has been somewhat eased by immigration policies, the exchange rate policy has helped to dampen aggregate demand, thereby reining in wage inflation. In a study on Singapore's monetary transmission mechanism, Chow (2005) found that the exchange rate has a highly significant impact on the level of economic activity. Such a result is not in the least unexpected in view of the

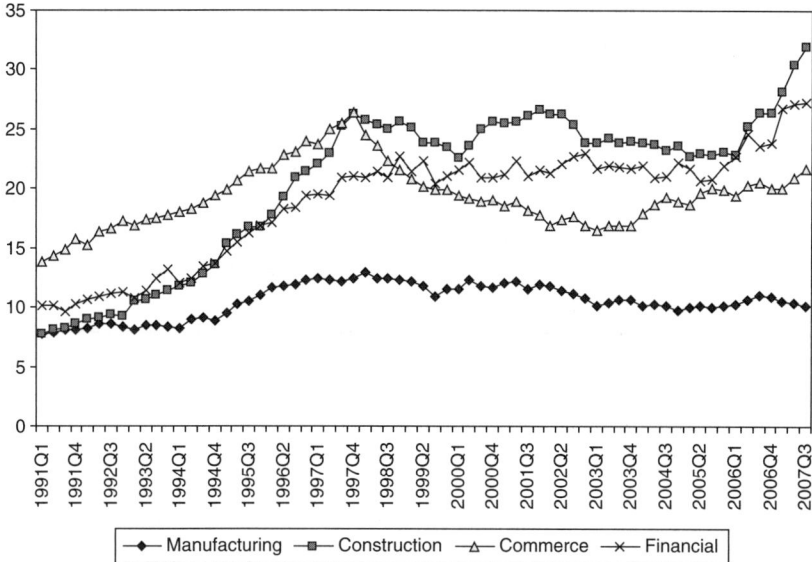

Source: Monetary Authority of Singapore.

Figure 14.7 Loans to key sectors of the economy, 1991: Q1–2007: Q3 (S$ billion)

substantial contribution of external demand to growth – exports account for around two-thirds of total demand.

By contrast, the Singapore economy is less sensitive to interest rates. Firstly, domestic investment is not very sensitive to the interest rate because Singapore's heavy reliance on FDI limits the impact of the cost of domestic borrowing. Secondly, a decline in housing wealth, plausibly caused by a rise in mortgage rates, does not seem to have significant dampening effects on aggregate consumption, even though houses are a major component of personal wealth in Singapore (Abeysinghe and Choy, 2004). This rather unusual finding has been attributed to the illiquid nature of Singapore's housing assets, as well as the strong bequest motives of Singaporean households (Phang, 2004). It is thus unsurprising that interest rates are deemed to have a relatively weaker effect than exchange rates on price stability, which is the final policy target.

Given the economy's vulnerability to external shocks, it is pertinent for Singapore's monetary policy to play a counter-cyclical role in minimizing the impact of these and other shocks on the domestic economy. Parrado (2004) investigated the counter-cyclical nature of Singapore's monetary policy through the use of a monetary reaction function. A variant of the Taylor rule (Taylor, 1993) was estimated, using changes in the exchange rate instead of the interest rate as the policy variable to reflect the use of the exchange rate as the key monetary policy instrument. The two target variables were inflation and output gap measures. The results suggest that monetary policy in Singapore does have a forward-looking orientation aimed at dampening inflation and output volatility. This finding concurs with the stated objective of the monetary policy of the MAS, which is 'to ensure low inflation as a sound basis for sustained economic growth.'

In a related study by McCallum (2007), a similar Taylor type policy rule was estimated. In that study, deviations of the real exchange rate from its equilibrium were included as an additional target variable. While the real exchange rate deviation variable turned out to have no explanatory power, the inflation variable remained highly important and the output gap variable was significant. The empirical evidence suggests that the real exchange rate does not play a role as an independent macroeconomic objective, but that adjustments in the policy variable are consistent with a policy designed to stabilize inflation and output around their desired target levels. In other words, Singapore's monetary policy framework is like a variant of inflation targeting.

The past track record of low inflation and prolonged economic growth attests to the effectiveness of using the exchange rate as a key policy instrument for an ultra-open economy like Singapore, albeit with the support of flexible factor markets and strong institutions.

14.4.2 Basket-Band-Crawl Exchange Rate Regime

In implementing the exchange rate-centered monetary policy, the MAS manages the Singapore dollar under a basket-band-crawl (BBC) system (Khor et al., 2004; Williamson, 1999). Under this intermediate exchange rate regime, the MAS monitors the value of the Singapore dollar in terms of a basket of currencies. Given Singapore's diversified trade pattern, targeting a currency basket instead of a single foreign currency will result in a more stable effective exchange rate. The currency basket, termed the trade-weighted index (TWI), is a trade-weighted average of the currencies of Singapore's major trading partners and competitors. These represent the various sources of imported inflation as well as competition in the export markets, with the basket weights reflecting their degree of importance. Neither the constituent currencies nor their assigned weights in the basket are made public by the MAS.

The MAS uses a prescribed policy band centered at a parity, which is the target exchange rate for the TWI. The target rate reflects the long-run equilibrium exchange rate and is allowed to adjust gradually over time, keeping the policy band in tandem with Singapore's slowly changing long-term economic fundamentals. It is critical not to make parity changes in occasional large steps, as in an adjustable peg exchange rate regime, as this attracts large capital flows speculating on an impending change. The crawl circumvents the emergence of a situation where the currency becomes significantly misaligned. It thereby reduces the incentive for speculative attacks against the currency. Notably, MacDonald (2004) and Lee (1999) amongst others have found no sustained deviation of Singapore's real exchange rate from its equilibrium level even when the equilibrium value of the currency is measured using different approaches.

The TWI is allowed to float within the prescribed policy band to allow for short-term fluctuations in the foreign exchange markets. Like the central rates, the band limits are undisclosed. The MAS can directly influence the value of the currency and defend the band by carrying out intervention operations in the foreign exchange markets. When the TWI approaches or exceeds the boundaries of the policy band, the MAS may carry out intervention to 'lean against the wind', which means resisting the recent trend of the exchange rate, thereby preventing the bounds from being breached. Such intervention operations always resist misalignments and push the TWI towards its estimated equilibrium value, as in the reference rate proposal (Williamson, 2007). Additionally, the MAS can also intervene within the band to smooth out short-term exchange rate volatility as the latter could impair confidence in the currency.

We highlight two key features regarding the policy band that help to discourage one-sided bets and speculative attacks. First, the band is sufficiently wide so that market participants cannot be sure of making a profit even when they correctly speculate on an impending change. Second, a BBC with hard bands, whereby the central bank is obliged to carry out intervention whenever the limits are reached, is avoided. This type of exchange rate regime is akin to a crawling band and, based on empirical evidence, could provoke a crisis. Hence, the authorities can either blur the edges of the bands or not disclose them at all.

Under the managed float system, it is pertinent to have large foreign reserves ready for use to defend the currency. The Singapore dollar is more than fully backed by foreign reserves. In any case, the central bank enjoys high credibility earned from its track record in maintaining low inflation and a strong domestic currency. Consequently, most market participants are convinced that the MAS is committed to enforcing the policy band and they thus tend to keep within the bounds. Such market discipline in turn reduces the need for frequent central bank intervention operations (Krugman, 1991). Contrary to the conventional wisdom at the time of the

Asian crisis that intermediate exchange rate regimes are not viable, the MAS has deterred speculators from attacking the domestic currency and has successfully maintained a managed float since the 1980s.

14.5 MONETARY POLICY OPERATIONS SINCE THE ASIAN CRISIS

14.5.1 Policy Reactions during the Asian Crisis

Notwithstanding a generally sound domestic environment, contagion from neighboring crisis-hit countries could mean that the fallout from volatile capital flows is unavoidable. A case in point is the Asian crisis, when Singapore's GDP dropped by 0.9 per cent while both the equity and property markets plunged. The Straits Times Index of stock prices fell by 60 per cent from a high of 2055.44 in January 1997 to 856.43 in September 1998. Meanwhile, the private property price index suffered a drop of 40 per cent from 270 in quarter one of 1997 to 163.7 in quarter four of 1998 (Chan and Ngiam, 1998). Aware that the rigidity of the exchange rate was a channel of vulnerability, Singapore accepted market-driven depreciations in the wake of, and amid the deepening of, the crisis in tandem with deteriorating fundamentals. The Singapore dollar fell by 18.3 per cent against the US dollar (USD) from S$1.43 per USD the day before the float of the baht, to S$1.75 per USD on 7 January 1998 (Kapur, 2005).[7]

The immediate market-driven depreciations brought about a sufficiently depreciated Singapore dollar that reduced the gains from further speculation. This lowered the incentive for currency speculators to engineer an over-depreciation in the domestic currency (Yip, 2005). Had Singapore adhered to a fixed currency peg and defended the currency from the beginning, greater adjustments – and thus, higher volatility in the real economy – would have been necessary. Instead, the MAS widened the boundaries of the policy band as it met with increased uncertainty during the crisis to allow for greater flexibility in managing the exchange rate. Subsequently, when the volatility in the regional markets subsided, the width of the band was narrowed. The quick reaction of the authorities as well as the flexibility in the exchange rate system have been advantageous in aligning the domestic currency with changing economic fundamentals and allowing the new equilibrium to emerge rapidly. No doubt, this contributes to the credibility of Singapore's exchange rate system and is one of the factors that helped to lessen the severity of the crisis.

The depreciation of the Singapore dollar during the 1997 Asian crisis (as well as during other major economic downturns) was accompanied by wage cuts in the form of downward adjustments in the contribution rates to the Central Provident Fund (CPF), which is a government-administered compulsory saving scheme. Prior to the crisis, employees and employers were each required to contribute 20 per cent of the employees' income to the CPF. With the outbreak of the crisis, the employer's CPF contribution rate was reduced to 10 per cent coupled with a two-year wage restraint to bring down labor costs. In addition, other administrative policy measures such as cost-cutting and budgetary measures were employed.

Such coordination of wage adjustments and cost-cutting measures with the concurrent depreciation of the domestic currency alleviates the need for a bigger NEER depreciation targeted at preserving Singapore's international competitiveness edge. In this way, monetary policy in Singapore is complemented by a proactive and flexible wage policy, whereby real depreciations in the Singapore dollar are partly effected through deflationary wage and price adjustments when the economy is hit by severe negative shocks.

14.5.2 Monetary Policy during the Post-Asian Crisis Period

We next examine the conduct of monetary policy during the post-crisis period. Prior to 2001, the MAS would disclose the general thrust of its exchange rate policy stance via occasional policy announcements made by senior central bank officials. In early 2001, the MAS formalized the announcement of the exchange rate policy stance through a *Monetary Policy Statement* in conjunction with its semi-annual exchange rate policy cycle. Box 14.1 traces Singapore's exchange rate policy stance since the Asian crisis.

We observe from the table the various forms of adjustments to the TWI allowed by the BBC exchange rate regime. First, changes to width of the band can be carried out (as announced in the 11 September 2001 statement) in response to periods of heightened volatility. Second, there can be a re-centering of the policy band (as announced in the July 2003 statement) and third, a change to the slope of the crawl in the central parity can be effected (as announced in the October 2007 statement). These different ways of adjustments demonstrate the flexibility accorded by the exchange rate system, which allows the MAS to use the exchange rate to accommodate shocks to as well as structural changes in the economy (Khor et al., 2007).

Since the BBC exchange rate system has functioned well for Singapore, a natural question arises as to whether it should be recommended for the other regional economies. To adopt this exchange rate arrangement, credible political commitment from the authorities is necessary. Countries

BOX 14.1 TRACING SINGAPORE'S EXCHANGE RATE POLICY STANCE

Late 1990s	Against the backdrop of subsiding inflation and stalling economic growth, MAS ended the decade-long trend of appreciation of the TWI and eased policy to a neutral setting with the policy band centered on a zero appreciation path.
Early 2000	Against a backdrop of a favorable external environment and a strong rebound in the domestic economy, MAS tightened policy by inducing a gradual appreciation of the TWI.
January 2001	MAS maintained a gradual appreciation of the TWI to keep inflationary pressures in check.
July 2001	Against a backdrop of a weak external environment, global electronics downturn, and subsiding inflationary pressures, MAS eased policy to a neutral setting with the policy band centered on a zero appreciation path.
11 September 2001	Against a backdrop of an uncertain external environment and downside risks to the domestic outlook, policy bands were widened. When a degree of calm returned to the foreign exchange market, the narrower bands were restored but the neutral stance was maintained.
July 2003	In view of the downside risk in the external environment, MAS lowered the policy band by re-centering it at the then current level of TWI, while maintaining a zero appreciation path.
April 2004	Against a more favorable growth outlook for the domestic economy, and the risk

	of rising inflationary pressures, MAS announced a shift towards a gradual and modest appreciation of the TWI.
October 2007	Against a backdrop of rapid expansion of the domestic economy and rising inflationary pressures, MAS increased slightly the slope of the TWI policy band while maintaining a modest and gradual appreciation of the TWI policy band.

should also have the capacity required to operate the system. This involves a good sense of what the equilibrium exchange rate level is and how it is evolving; the ability to resist intervention within a sufficiently wide policy band; having the latitude to carry out prompt large-scale intervention operations to defend the band; and possessing good judgment of what market conditions require policy band widening. Nevertheless, it is still possible that the flexibility accorded by the BBC regime may not be sufficient to deal with extremely severe external shocks. A case in point is Indonesia, which had to abandon its BBC regime when hit by contagion from Thailand during the Asian crisis (Williamson, 2007).

14.5.3 Management of Domestic Liquidity

What impact do foreign exchange interventions – carried out mostly to moderate the appreciation of the Singapore dollar – have on domestic liquidity? Defending appreciations usually leads to an increase in foreign reserves and a rise in the monetary base, thereby raising inflationary pressures in the domestic economy unless the central bank carries out sterilization. Indeed, excessive credit growth and the high costs of sterilized foreign exchange interventions are well-recognized challenges posed by large capital inflows.

However, instead of having to manage excess domestic liquidity and withdraw funds, the MAS is generally in the position to supply funds to the domestic banking system. The first reason for this is prudent fiscal management – the Singapore government has continued to run budget surpluses averaging around 5 per cent of GDP since the crisis. As the government's financial agent, the MAS is in receipt of public sector surpluses from the government, which in effect removes liquidity from the domestic economy. The second reason is that the contributions to the CPF tend to be in excess of withdrawals, and these positive net contributions to the CPF also effectively represent a withdrawal of funds from the domestic financial system. In fact, both the public funds transfers and the CPF net contributions channel substantial liquidity out of the economy, causing the money supply to shrink and putting pressure on the Singapore dollar to appreciate.

The MAS can actively offset this liquidity drain through foreign exchange operations that use the Singapore dollar to purchase the US dollar. In this way, funds are channeled back to ensure an appropriate level of liquidity in the domestic banking system, thereby offsetting the effect on the exchange rate. In fact, the MAS can achieve a wide range of exchange rate appreciation or depreciation by controlling the amount of liquidity re-injection. By the same token, the MAS can exert a limited degree of control over domestic interest rates by varying the amount of liquidity re-injections, particularly when the TWI is 'floating' within the prescribed policy band. For instance, if the economy is deemed to be overheating, less liquidity could be re-injected into the market. The relative reduction in the money supply would raise domestic interest rates, which would in turn help to cool the economy. Conversely, if the economy is slowing down, the MAS could re-inject more liquidity into the economy with an attendant reduction in the domestic interest rates, which would help to stimulate the economy.

Domestic interest rates in Singapore are generally lower than US interest rates, reflecting investor expectations of an appreciation of the domestic currency. However, Figure 14.8, which depicts the ex-post three-month uncovered interest differential, reveals that the differentials are quite different from zero, and, as pointed out by Yip (2003), they are substantially larger in magnitude compared with corresponding figures from Hong Kong, China. Hence, the fluctuations in the differentials are indicative of some autonomy in the interest rate policy, albeit to a rather limited extent. This is because Singapore's extensive network of international financial and trade linkages results in such huge and rapid capital flows that domestic interest rates are largely determined by foreign interest rates and market expectations of the future value of the Singapore dollar.[8]

To complement its exchange rate policy, the MAS conducts money market operations in order to foster orderly money market conditions. The MAS adds or withdraws funds from the market using instruments such as foreign exchange (reverse) swaps, direct lending to or borrowing from banks, direct purchase or sales of Singapore Government Securities (SGS), and repurchase agreements on SGS (MAS, 2003). With the use of such money market operations, the MAS is able to pump in or mop up liquidity from the domestic banking system on a massive scale in response

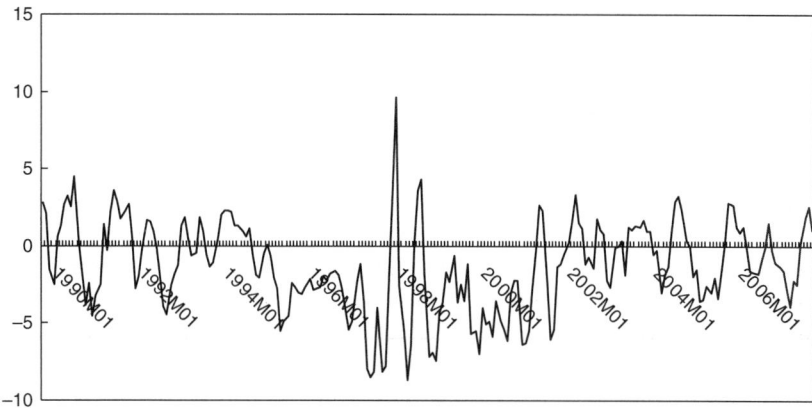

Source: Monetary Authority of Singapore.

Figure 14.8 Ex-post three-month uncovered interest differential, 1990: M01–2007: M12 (per cent)

to economic and financial developments. For instance, the MAS injected S$2.5 billion into the domestic banking system in the immediate aftermath of the September 11 terrorist attacks to forestall turmoil in the local financial markets.

14.6 NON-INTERNATIONALIZATION OF THE SINGAPORE DOLLAR

Arising from the use of the exchange rate as a benchmark policy instrument, the policy of non-internationalization of the Singapore dollar was adopted in the early 1980s as a rather limited form of capital control. Singapore has eradicated all exchange controls since 1978 in order to promote the development of its offshore financial markets. Hence, residents and non-residents are free to remit Singapore dollar funds in and out of Singapore and are also free to purchase or sell Singapore dollars in the foreign exchange market. Singapore's role as an international financial center has also led to the development of a large offshore banking sector, the Asian Dollar Market (ADM), whose assets are denominated in foreign currencies. There are no controls on capital flows between the ADM and the domestic banking system, so holders of Singapore dollars can easily convert their funds into foreign currency deposits and vice versa.

However, the absence of capital restrictions means that speculative attacks on the Singapore dollar could compromise the conduct of the exchange rate-centered monetary policy. The non-internationalization policy, which restricted the international use of the domestic currency, essentially protected the Singapore dollar from speculative attacks to facilitate the effective conduct of monetary policy. At the same time, the policy ensured that the growth of the Singapore dollar market was in line with the development of the economy. Under the non-internationalization policy, safeguards were put in place to prevent a buildup of offshore deposits of the currency that could be used by speculators to short the Singapore dollar. These included allowing bank credit in the Singapore dollar to be extended to non-residents only in cases where borrowing was meant for funding real economic activities. Additionally, restrictions were imposed on inter-bank Singapore dollar derivatives to limit access to liquidity in the onshore foreign exchange, currency, and interest rate swaps and options markets in order to hinder leveraging or hedging of Singapore dollar positions. These restrictions mainly took the form of consultative requirements to limit speculative activities in Singapore's financial markets, and did not seem to have impeded trade and capital mobility (Lee, 2001).[9]

Nevertheless, the restrictions became overly binding as the Singapore economy became more globalized and its financial industry matured. In the first place, increased demand by corporate players and financial institutions for the Singapore dollar and its derivatives for commercial transactions called for the liberalization of the policy. Secondly, the non-internationalization policy hampered the development of Singapore's capital markets, particularly the bond market. For instance, short-sales of securities and access to domestic currency credit lines are essential to deepen market liquidity (see Gobat, 2000). Hence, under the imperative to foster greater financial sector diversification the restrictions on the non-internationalization of the Singapore dollar were progressively relaxed. Four major reviews were undertaken after the Asian crisis, resulting in the lifting of restrictions to avert obstruction of market activities. Box 14.2 traces the evolution of the non-internationalization policy.

The current policy has only two core requirements, as stated in the revised *MAS Notice 757 of 28 May 2004*. First, financial institutions may not extend Singapore dollar credit facilities exceeding S$5 million to non-resident financial entities where they have reason to believe that the proceeds may be used for speculation against the Singapore dollar. Second, for a Singapore dollar loan exceeding S$5 million to a non-resident financial entity or for a Singapore dollar equity or bond issue by a non-resident entity that is used to fund overseas activity, the Singapore dollar proceeds must be swapped or converted into foreign currency before use

BOX 14.2 EVOLUTION OF THE NON-INTERNATIONALIZATION POLICY

1983 The policy codified into MAS Notice 621, whereby access to the Singapore dollar is restricted for both residents and non-residents.

1992 Amendment is made to MAS Notice 621 to lift the consultation requirement for extension of Singapore dollar credit facilities of any amount where the funds are to be used to support economic activities in Singapore.

1998 In conjunction with an extensive financial sector liberalization program, the new MAS Notice 757 replaces MAS Notice 621, whereby all restrictions on residents are lifted; some restrictions on non-residents in relation to arranging Singapore dollar equity listings and bond issues of foreign companies are relaxed.

1999 To foster the development of Singapore capital markets, banks are allowed to engage in a wider range of activities – namely, to transact all Singapore dollar interest rate derivatives with non-residents freely and arrange Singapore dollar equity listing for foreign companies.

2000 Only measures to limit access to the Singapore dollar for speculative activity remain. Banks are allowed to freely extend Singapore dollar credit facilities to non-residents for investment purposes in Singapore and to fund offshore facilities provided the proceeds are first swapped into foreign currency before remitting abroad.

2002 All individuals and non-financial institutions are exempted from the Singapore dollar lending restrictions. Non-resident financial entities are permitted to engage in a wide range of derivative transactions.

2004 Non-resident non-financial issuers of Singapore dollar bonds and equities are no longer required to swap their Singapore dollar proceeds into foreign currencies before remitting them abroad.

outside Singapore. These restrictions do not apply to non-resident financial institutions and there is currently a large offshore market in Singapore dollars abroad. Nevertheless, the MAS deems the current policy useful to deter offshore speculators from accessing liquidity in Singapore's onshore foreign exchange swaps and money markets (MAS, 2002).

On the first restriction, there is clearly an element of judgment involved in determining whether a client intends to engage in speculative activities. In the words of the MAS,

> Financial institutions are expected to institute appropriate internal controls and processes to comply with this restriction . . . [these] include [obtaining] written confirmation from the non-resident financial institution specifying the purpose of funding . . . and [executing a] formal evaluation process of the client profile, which provides a clear basis for assessing that the client is unlikely to use the Singapore dollar proceeds for currency speculation. (MAS, 2006, p. 3)

In view of MAS's tough reputation, financial institutions are expected to err on the side of caution when implementing this policy. As for the second restriction, which has been in effect since 28 May 2004, non-resident non-financial issuers of Singapore dollar bonds and equities are no longer required to swap their Singapore dollar proceeds into foreign currencies before remitting them abroad. The amendment to the policy relieves foreign issuers from incurring the additional cost of swapping, thereby removing an advantage in directly issuing foreign currency bonds. For non-resident financial institutions, however, the requirement is retained.

With the lifting of the various restrictions, there is no longer a non-internationalization policy *per se*. Rather, the policy has been reduced to a lending restriction and is now known as MAS policy on lending Singapore dollars to non-resident financial institutions. Has the liberalization of the non-internationalization policy resulted in the Singapore dollar being at risk of speculative attacks, or has the policy outlived its purpose? The past restrictions by themselves are unlikely to have been the single most important factor in protecting the Singapore dollar against speculative attacks. Rather, it is the maintenance of both internal and external macroeconomic balance as well as the absence of balance sheet vulnerabilities that offers little incentive for speculators to wage attacks against the currency or to circumvent the restrictions for speculative purposes. Furthermore, the MAS places great emphasis on the prudential supervision of financial institutions, ensuring sound credit practices and a strong capital position.[10] In addition to its strong banking system, Singapore continues to develop deep and liquid capital markets for the efficient intermediation of financial flows, thereby enhancing the resilience of its financial system to shocks.

14.7 CONCLUSION

In summary, Singapore's experience with capital flows after the Asian crisis appears to have been somewhat benign. Clearly, it is the overall package of policies – including strong economic fundamentals and a robust financial system, prudent policy management on both the fiscal and monetary side, and credible exchange rate policy aligned with underlying fundamentals – that serves to increase Singapore's resilience towards disruptive swings in capital flows. In addition, the government also relies on direct credit controls when appropriate, such as in curbing surging residential property prices due to availability of easy credit. In view of the destabilizing effects of sudden shifts in capital flows, particular emphasis has been placed on having the latitude to react promptly and on a sufficiently large scale to economic and financial developments.

Pronounced shifts in capital flows, regardless of whether they are triggered by misguided policies or contagion, are often associated with the loss of foreign investor confidence in the prospects for the domestic economy. Ocampo (2003) found that the variations in capital flows can be attributed primarily to shifts in risk evaluation. We have highlighted the need for disciplined macroeconomic and financial policies as well as the crucial role of strong mature institutions, strong human resource capacity, and strong governance in order to bolster the confidence of investors and other market participants. In this regard, it is important for the regional economies to continue the process of building a sound and efficient domestic financial system, and installing an effective system of prudential supervision.

Domestic financial development is often achieved through prudent external financial liberalization, which tends to catalyze both financial deepening and broadening. Chow and Kriz (2007) pointed out that the extent of domestic financial development and the scope of capital account liberalization need to be managed holistically, as interactions between them present both opportunities for growth and potential risks.[11] On the one hand, sufficiently developed domestic financial sectors are necessary to absorb and allocate capital inflows to their most efficient uses. On the other, domestic financial markets cannot fully realize their potential without exposure to international capital markets. For instance, partial international liberalization exerts pressure to overcome entrenched interest and policy inertia to reforms that are necessary to establish core institutional infrastructure. Further, opening the domestic sector to foreign financial institutions often leads to capacity building and increases the pressure to strengthen supervisory and regulatory frameworks.

Smooth responses to fluctuating capital flows not only require accelerated institutional reforms in individual countries but also an upgraded regional financial infrastructure. Although it is the domestic authorities and institutions that are ultimately responsible for a country's financial development and stability, regional cooperation over policy measures can play a supportive role during the liberalization process. For instance, technical assistance, human capital training programs, and the increased availability of financial information can increase the ability of financial systems to absorb fluctuations in capital flows. Given that some countries in Asia are too small to have liquid domestic capital markets, the region could also proactively integrate the financial markets in order to benefit from economies of scale and liquidity agglomeration effects.

Furthermore, regional financial cooperation efforts such as the Chiang Mai Initiative, regional reserve pooling initiatives, and regional financial surveillance help to build the resilience of the region to financial shocks. Emergency crisis management procedures designed through an explicit regional institution will help slow the spread of any potential financial contagion that might arise. Development of such 'financial circuit breakers' can give policymakers the time to locate the specific cause of a given crisis and the opportunity to find an appropriate resolution (Chow and Kriz, 2007).

Is it possible for a country whose financial system is not yet well developed to reap the potential advantages of capital movements without the costs of crises? Closing the capital account, at one extreme, would mean foregoing the potential benefits that capital mobility could bring. At the other extreme, complete capital account convertibility inevitably results in instability. A way forward is for such a country to strike a middle ground, by imposing selective restrictions to alter the composition of capital inflows. The capital controls (provided they can be effectively enforced) should be targeted at curbing excessive inflows of short term loans that are prone to reversal. However, this may deter some investors from investing at all in the country, resulting in a reduction in the other more beneficial forms of capital inflows. As pointed out by Williamson (2005), this calls for a judicious balance between the volume and stability of capital flows.

NOTES

1. Calvo et al. (1993) showed the dominant role for push factors, particularly the state of liquidity in the developed countries, as a driving force for capital flows to emerging markets.
2. All balance of payment data described in this section are obtained from the Singapore Department of Statistics.

3. The huge direct investment outflow in 2001 is due to the two large foreign acquisitions by the local telecommunications company Singtel and the Development Bank of Singapore (DBS).
4. Trade credits, which are relatively stable despite their short tenor, form a separate component in the other investment account.
5. The trend break in the levels of M2 and the corresponding hikes in M2 growth rates at the end of 1998 are due to the incorporation of the Post Office Savings Bank (POSB) into the banking system when it was acquired by the DBS. From November 1998, POSB's data has been incorporated in M1 and M2, and not as a non-bank financial institution under M3.
6. Obstfeld et al. (2004) provide a treatise on the open economy trilemma.
7. With the onset of the Asian crisis, the Singapore dollar actually strengthened on a trade-weighted basis, despite having depreciated against the USD. This was due to a sharp depreciation of the regional currencies such as the Indonesian rupiah, Thai baht, and Malaysian ringgit.
8. The MAS (2000) found that covered and uncovered interest parity tended to hold between Singapore and US one- and three-month inter-bank rates, respectively, in the 1990s before the Asian crisis.
9. We note that none of the restrictions had been imposed on the liability side of the bank balance sheet which means non-residents are free to build up Singapore dollar holdings by converting foreign currency into Singapore dollars and then place them with the domestic banking unit.
10. Since the end of 1997, the MAS has shifted its supervisory regime from a one-size-fits-all regulation to a risk-based approach.
11. The authors suggested a policy-driven paradigm for financial liberalization in emerging open economies: management of the 'financial liberalization trilemma' which states that the extent of any two of the following three components, namely domestic financial development, exchange rate flexibility and capital market openness, should determine the proper course of action for the third.

REFERENCES

Abeysinghe, T. and K.M. Choy (2004), 'The aggregate consumption puzzle in Singapore', *Journal of Asian Economics*, **15**(3), 563–78.

Calvo, G., L. Leiderman and C. Reinhart (1993), 'Capital inflows and real exchange rate appreciation in Latin America: the role of external factors', *International Monetary Fund Staff Papers*, **40**(1), March, 108–51.

Chan K.S. and K.J. Ngiam (1998), 'Currency crisis and the modified currency board system in Singapore', *Pacific Economic Review*, **3**(3), 243–63.

Chow, H.K. (2005), 'A VAR analysis of Singapore's monetary transmission mechanism', in W.T.H. Koh and R. S. Mariano (eds), *The Economic Prospects of Singapore*, Singapore: Addison Wesley, pp. 274–98.

Chow, H.K. and P. Kriz (2007), 'Financial liberalization trilemma and regional policy cooperation: fresh perspectives for emerging markets in East Asia', paper presented at Singapore Economic Review Conference, 2–4 August, Singapore.

Dobson W. and G. Hufbauer (2001), *World Capital Markets: Challenges to the G-10*, Washington: Institute for International Economics.

Gobat, J. (2000), 'Singapore–financial sector development: a strategy of controlled deregulation', *Singapore–Selected Issues* 00/83, Washington, DC: IMF.

Kaminsky G.L., C.M. Reinhart and C.A. Vegh (2004), 'When it rains, it pours:

procyclical capital flows and macroeconomic policies', NBER Working Paper No. 10780.
Kapur, B.K. (2005), 'Capital flows and exchange rate volatility: Singapore's experience', NBER Working Paper No. 11369.
Khor H.E. and W.Z. Kit (2007), 'Ten years from the financial crisis: managing the challenges posed by capital flows', MAS Staff Paper No. 48.
Khor, H.E., E. Robinson and J. Lee (2004), 'Managed floating and intermediate exchange rate systems: the Singapore experience', MAS Staff Paper No. 37.
Khor H.E., J. Lee, E. Robinson and S. Saktiandi (2007), 'Managed float exchange rate system: the Singapore experience', *The Singapore Economic Review*, **52**(1), 7–25.
Krugman, P. (1991), 'Target zones and exchange rate dynamics', *Quarterly Journal of Economics*, **106**(3), 669–82.
Lee, J. (1999), 'Singapore: competitiveness issues', *Singapore – Selected Issues* 99/53, Washington, DC: IMF.
Lee, J. (2001), 'Evolution of the policy on noninternationalization of the Singapore dollar', *Singapore – Selected Issues* 01/177, Section IV, Washington, DC: IMF.
MacDonald, R. (2004), 'The long run real effective exchange rate of Singapore – a behavioral approach', MAS Staff Paper No. 43.
MAS (Monetary Authority of Singapore) (2000), 'Financial market integration in Singapore: the narrow and the broad views', MAS Occasional Paper No. 20.
MAS (2002), 'Singapore: policy of non-internationalization of the S$ and the Asian dollar market', paper presented to BIS/SAFE Seminar on Capital Account Liberalization, 12–13 September, Beijing, China.
MAS (2003), 'Monetary Policy Operations in Singapore', MAS Monograph.
MAS (2004), *Notice 757 of 28 May*.
MAS (2006), *Frequently Asked Questions on MAS Notice 757 and Equivalent Notices*.
McCallum, B.T. (2007), 'Singapore's exchange rate-centered monetary policy regime and its relevance for China', MAS Staff Paper No. 48.
Obstfeld, M., J.C. Shambaugh and A.M. Taylor (2004), 'The Trilemma in history: tradeoffs among exchange rates, monetary policies, and capital mobility', mimeo, University of California, Berkeley and Dartmouth College, March.
Ocampo, J.A. (2003) 'Capital account and countercyclical prudential regulations in developing countries', in R. Ffrench-Davis and S. Griffin-Jones (eds), *From Capital Surges to Drought: Seeking Stability for Emerging Economies*, Basingstoke: Palgrave Macmillan for the United Nations University/World Institute for Development Economics Research, pp. 217–44.
Parrado, E. (2004), 'Singapore's unique monetary policy: how does it work?', MAS Staff Paper No. 31.
Phang, S. (2004), 'House prices and aggregate consumption: do they move together? Evidence from Singapore', *Journal of Housing Economics*, **13**(2), 101–19.
Taylor, J.B. (1993), 'Discretion versus policy rules in practice', *Carnegie-Rochester Conference Series on Public Policy*, **39**(1), 195–214.
Williamson, J. (1999), 'Future exchange rate regimes for developing East Asia: exploring the policy options', paper presented to a conference on Asia in Economic Recovery: Policy Options for Growth and Stability, Institute of Policy Studies, 21–22 June, Singapore.

Williamson, J. (2005), 'Curbing the boom-bust cycle: stabilizing capital flows to emerging markets', Washington, DC: Institute of International Economics.
Williamson, J. (2007), 'The case for an intermediate exchange rate regime', *Singapore Economic Review*, **52**(3), 259–307.
Yip, S.L. (2003), 'A re-statement of Singapore's exchange rate and monetary policies', *Singapore Economic Review*, **48**(2), 201–12.
Yip, S.L. (2005), *The Exchange Rate Systems in Hong Kong and Singapore, Currency Board vs. Monitoring Band*, Singapore: Prentice Hall.

15. Managing capital flows: the case of Thailand

Kanit Sangsubhan

15.1 INTRODUCTION

The Thai economy showed an impressive growth path for over a decade before the Asian financial crisis in 1997–98. The current account deficit barely exceeded 5 per cent and high growth generated budget surpluses for many years. At the same time, massive capital inflows were accumulated progressively along with a high interest rate differential and under a fixed exchange rate regime, including capital account deregulation.

Thailand opened up for a higher degree of capital liberalization in the early 1990s. The Bangkok International Banking Facility (BIBF) scheme was set to facilitate the process. This out–in facility became a new channel for gaining low interest rate funds from abroad. In addition to the BIBF, monetary policies such as defense of domestic currency and high interest rate policy encouraged capital inflows by introducing low currency risk for investors and returns higher than those of the international market. As a result, foreign funds poured into the country to take advantage of the high interest rate differential and to gain from the baht depreciation. Massive short-term borrowing abroad, primarily to finance long-term projects, led to currency and maturity mismatches.

In 1996, the short-term foreign liabilities had exceeded international reserves. As soon as the baht was floated, foreign debt in local currency overshot and the sovereign rate decreased, adversely affecting investors' sentiments. Thailand's impressive growth path for over a decade before the 1997–98 financial crisis and relatively stable exchange rate naturally led both borrowers and lenders to underestimate the risk of their foreign currency exposure. The large unhedged and mostly short-term foreign debt left the country vulnerable to capital flight and sharp devaluation.

This chapter on managing capital flows in Thailand is organized as follows: Section 15.2 discusses Thailand's experience of the 1997–98 Asian financial crisis. Section 15.3 discusses the type of capital flows in Thailand since the Asian financial crisis. Section 15.4 assesses the impacts of capital inflows on the financial system and the real sectors. Section 15.5 discusses current measures and policy implications; and Section 15.6 lays out policy challenges for Thailand and the Asian region for managing capital flows.

15.2 THE 1997–98 ASIAN FINANCIAL CRISIS: THE THAI EXPERIENCE

In many Asian countries where equity and debt markets are relatively undeveloped, bank financing has historically played a leading role in economic development. To build investor confidence, currency pegging was used in the region before the Asian financial crisis, but this alone cannot explain Asia's emergence in the world capital market. By the mid-1990s, most Asian economies including Thailand had opened up their capital account to some extent, to attract foreign capital. Because of greater capital account deregulation, high interest rate differential, and the belief that the fixed exchange rate regime would be sustained, Thailand experienced huge success in accumulating short-term foreign capital in foreign currency (mainly US dollars), while investing in long-term projects, which generated returns in local currency. The average size of capital inflows expanded from 7 per cent of GDP in 1988 to 13 per cent in 1995 (Edwards, 1999). By 1996, total capital inflows as a percentage of GDP was 11.5 (Cavoli and Rajan, 2005), while international reserves as percentage of GDP were 89.6. These numbers were comparable to other Southeast Asian countries.

Part of the capital inflows into Thailand was portfolio investment, which in 1993 increased ten fold over the 1987 level (Akrasanee, 1999). Calvo et al. (1995) warned that such massive portfolio inflows could create problems for policymakers as capital flows might not be 'intermediated efficiently' and sudden reversal could turn the country's economic fortunes upside down overnight. Because reckless portfolio investment can easily be pulled out, such investment contributes little to productivity but creates rapid credit expansion, thereby strengthening the boom-bust business cycle and building up financial vulnerability (McKinnon and Pill, 1996). Although the stock market started to take a downturn after its 1994 peak and the number of Bangkok's unoccupied houses increased to twice the annual demand, no one anticipated the depth of the financial distress to come.

The larger part of capital inflows came in the form of commercial bank borrowing. Due to an underdeveloped swap market, inadequate internal risk evaluation, and government implicit guarantees for banks against failures, foreign debts made by banks and private businesses were mostly unhedged (Sangsubhan, 1999). The total external indebtedness surpassed 50 per cent of GDP even prior to the baht flotation (Rudolph, 2000), and the short-term bank loans exceeded twice the volume of gross international reserves by the end of 1996 (Yoshitomi and Shirai, 2000). Moreover, a large proportion of these were non-performing loans (NPLs): 10 per cent and 13 per cent of total lending in Malaysia and Thailand, respectively. These figures were incredibly high considering that Hong Kong, China and Singapore's figures were at the 3–4 per cent level (Edwards, 1999).

15.3 CAPITAL FLOWS SINCE THE ASIAN FINANCIAL CRISIS

The Asian financial crisis caused massive outflows of foreign capital and caused dramatic Thai baht depreciation in a short period of time. Thus, it is important to take a closer look at the path of development of the foreign exchange flows, in general, and capital flows, in particular, in Thailand since the 1997–98 crisis. There are five major channels of foreign exchange flows: current account, foreign direct investment (FDI), equity securities, debt securities, and loans, when the equity and debt securities are accounted as portfolio investment (Table 15.1).

15.3.1 Composition of Capital Flows

The major flows come from the large magnitude of the current account, while the steadiest flow is observed in the FDI flow. Nevertheless, fluctuations occurred in every type of capital flow in 2005–07.

Current account The current account, which has a high proportion of the trade balance, changed from negative to positive values after the depreciation of the Thai baht in July 1997, except in 2005. Competitiveness was generated via the currency depreciation as the volume of exports consistently increased over time, while the volume of imports showed a huge decline in the first year of the depreciation. The current account balance remained positive and fluctuations became stronger after 2003 with evidence of increasing imports. But basically, the changes in the current account were mostly caused by changes in the trade balance.

Foreign direct investment Net FDI comprises a large proportion of capital flows in the economy. Between 1998 and 2000, net FDI declined substantially as uncertainty arising from the Asian financial crisis drove FDI away from the local economy. Then it rebounded in 2001, reaching $4.8 billion,

Table 15.1 Annual capital inflows in Thailand, 1997–2007

Annual flow of foreign currency (million USD)	1997	1998	1999	2000	2001	2002	2003	2004	2005	2006	Jan.–Aug. 2007
Current account	−3110	14291	12466	9328	5114	5114	4784	2767	−7852.17	3240.46	7356.68
FDI	3180	5019	3218	2761	4793	4793	4608	4952	7297.18	9562.99	5310.77
Equity securities	3987	265	946	897	17	17	583	180	2157.60	4743.99	3907.59
Debt securities	563	118	−555	−791	−660	−660	−827	17	487.26	−266.52	−1269.62
Others (corp & gov loans + trade credits)	−11282	−9211	−4894	−7056	−5527	−5527	−9293	−7232	3042.47	3757.69	−1863.56
Total USD inflow	−6662	10482	11181	5139	3737	3737	−145	684	5132.34	21038.61	13441.86

Source: FPRI (2007).

and it stayed at around that level up until 2004. In 2005 and 2006 net FDI rose significantly, reaching $7.3 billion and $9.6 billion respectively. The sharp rise in net FDI in 2006 and 2007 indicated a return of confidence in the Thai economy owing to the government's efficient policy management (Sangsubhan and Vorawangso, 2007). With a higher level of FDI inflows, the Thai baht became stronger vis-à-vis the US dollar. It is to be noted that the magnitude of Thai direct investment going abroad remained low in 2005 and 2006, which partly contributed to the big increase in net FDI in these years. The expectation of more baht appreciation might have discouraged Thai investors from investing abroad.

Portfolio investment through equity securities Equity net flows had a consistent trend from 1998 to 2004 where the magnitude stayed at a low level. After the baht depreciation, the magnitude of equity investment, both inflow and outflow, consistently declined to a very low level, especially in 2000. In 2001, net equity flows became negative. The government introduced a tight monetary policy and a high rate of interest at the onset of the 1997 financial crisis in order to restore confidence and to stabilize the exchange rate. But given the lack of confidence in the Thai economy, the sustained high interest rate only adversely affected the firms' ability to repay their loans, which led to a credit crunch and an eventual economic recession. This discouraged foreigners from investing in the Thai stock exchange, as is shown in the decreasing trend of equity securities investment. Interestingly, the magnitudes of equity inflows and outflows have expanded significantly since 2005.

Portfolio investment through debt securities This channel exhibited a negative net flow from 1999 to 2005 along with minor fluctuations from time to time. The volume dropped after the crisis in July 1997, reaching a negative level after the baht depreciation, but temporarily bounced up in 1998. From 2005, the volume of debt inflow increased, but with variability; and the magnitude of flows was less than those of other capital flow accounts. From November 2006 to August 2007, the magnitude of the debt inflow declined, eventually becoming negative. One possible explanation is the Bank of Thailand's (BOT) imposition of the 30 per cent reserve requirement on foreign capital inflows issued on 18 December 2006, which discouraged investment in bonds. The massive sales pushed down the rate of return on 10-year government bonds by 0.32 per cent in one day. By the end of the month, the return on 10-year and 19-year government bonds jumped by 0.52 per cent and 0.63 per cent, respectively. The policy was reversed in the case of the equity market but not in the bond market, where activities remained very slow.

Loans and others This type of capital flow has decreased since the onset of the 1997–98 financial crisis. The sudden baht depreciation right after the crisis hiked up the net flow of foreign loans in terms of US dollars (USD), which eventually severely compromised the liquidity of the commercial bank sector. After the crisis, the flows to BIBFs stayed at a negative level before trending upward, and since 2001 have swung within a small range. The negative net flows to BIBFs were dominated by changes in liabilities, which were greater than changes in assets. The magnitudes of flows dropped rapidly in 2005 with considerable fluctuations.

Changes in loans' magnitudes could be attributed to changes in interest rate, and also changes in exchange rate, if one considers these changes in terms of foreign currency (USD). Interestingly, the outflows of foreign loans increased gradually since the beginning of 2007 after a sharp drop in the middle of 2006. This change might be related to the Thai baht appreciation. With a higher value of the baht, it is cheaper to borrow money from abroad, especially in view of the lower value of the USD. On the other hand, the net flow of Thai loans had remained relatively steady with low volumes of both inflow and outflow while the magnitude of outflows had outweighed the magnitude of inflows.

15.4 IMPACTS OF CAPITAL INFLOWS

15.4.1 Financial System

Exchange rate In Thailand, since the beginning of 2005, capital inflows have increased over time. Despite the fluctuations, capital inflows remained positive which led to the gradual appreciation of the baht. In part, this may be due to the USD depreciation against some currencies around the world, which has pushed up the value of the baht and led to persistent capital inflows into the Thai economy. The baht appreciated by about 8 per cent of its 2006 value, reaching 32.22 baht per USD on 13 July 2007. In response, the Bank of Thailand (BOT) intervened in the foreign exchange market, buying mostly USD at the spot rate, to absorb the rapid buildup of USD in a short period of time; this measure led to the rapid increase in foreign reserves.

According to the Fiscal Policy Research Institute's (FPRI) exchange rate monitoring system, the positive capital flows from the current account and equities channels have been observed from 2006 to 2007, and excess USD supply has existed since the beginning of 2007 (FPRI, 2007a).

Figure 15.1 illustrates the BOT's exchange rate intervention in both the forward and spot foreign exchange markets. A positive value shows

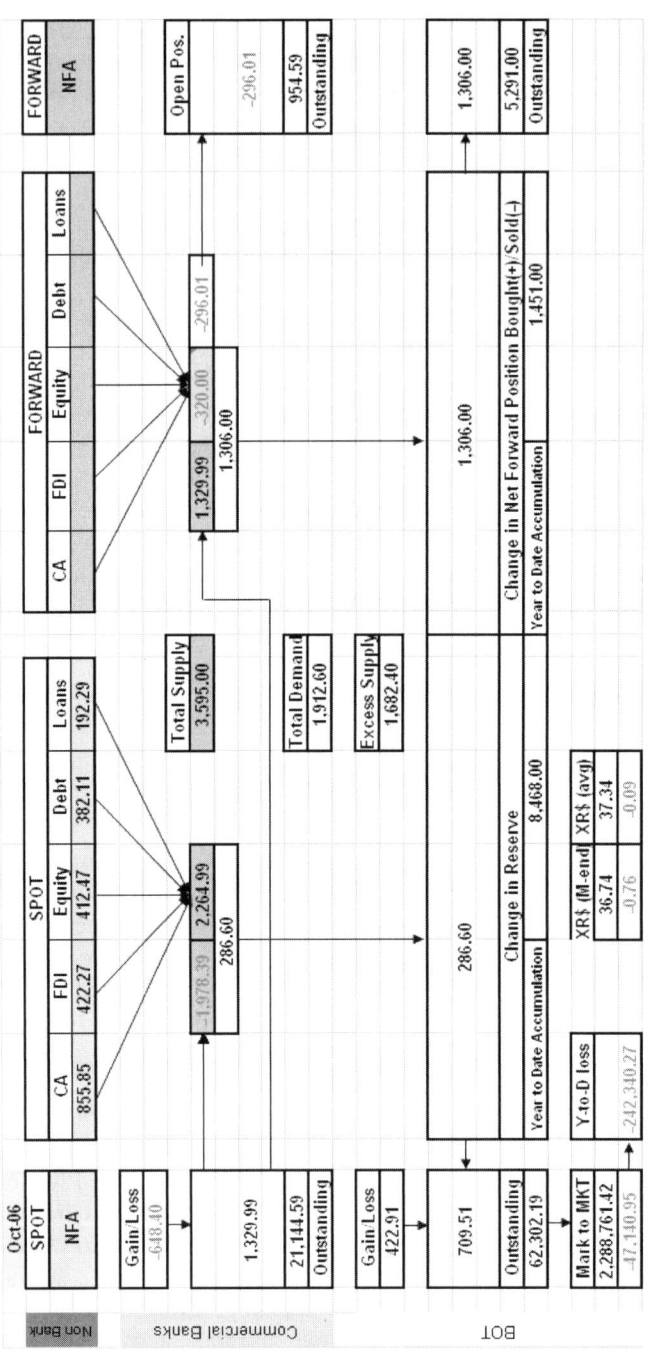

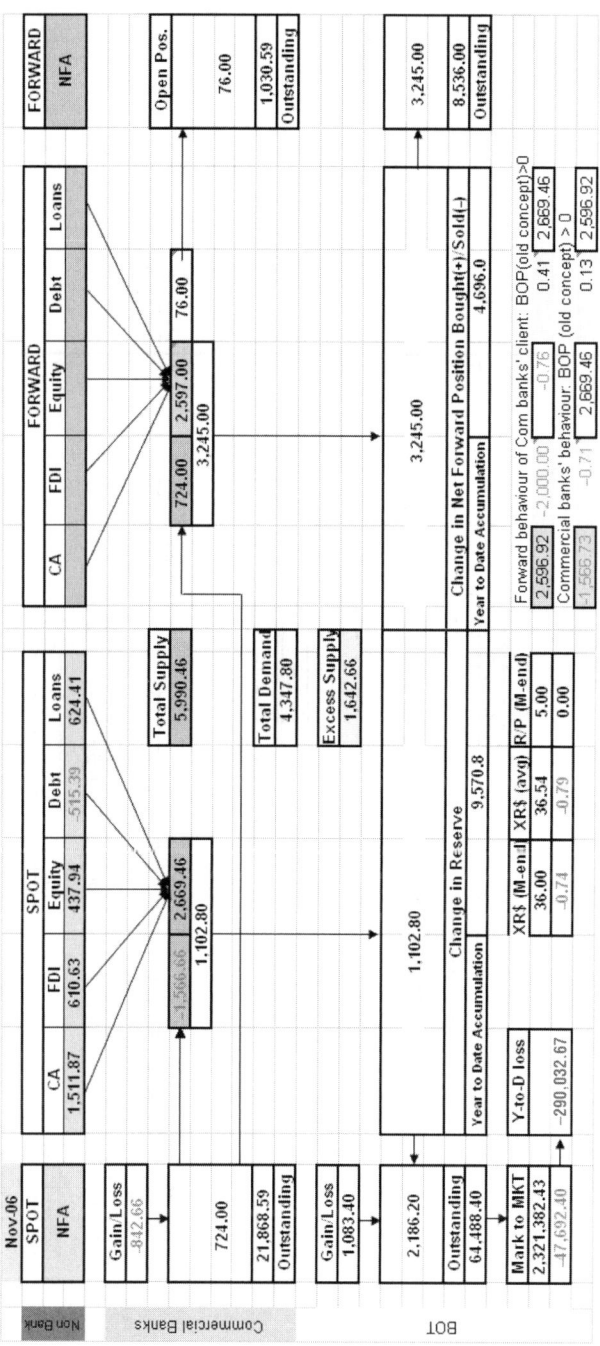

Source: Fiscal Policy Research Institute (2007a).

Figure 15.1 Exchange rate intervention

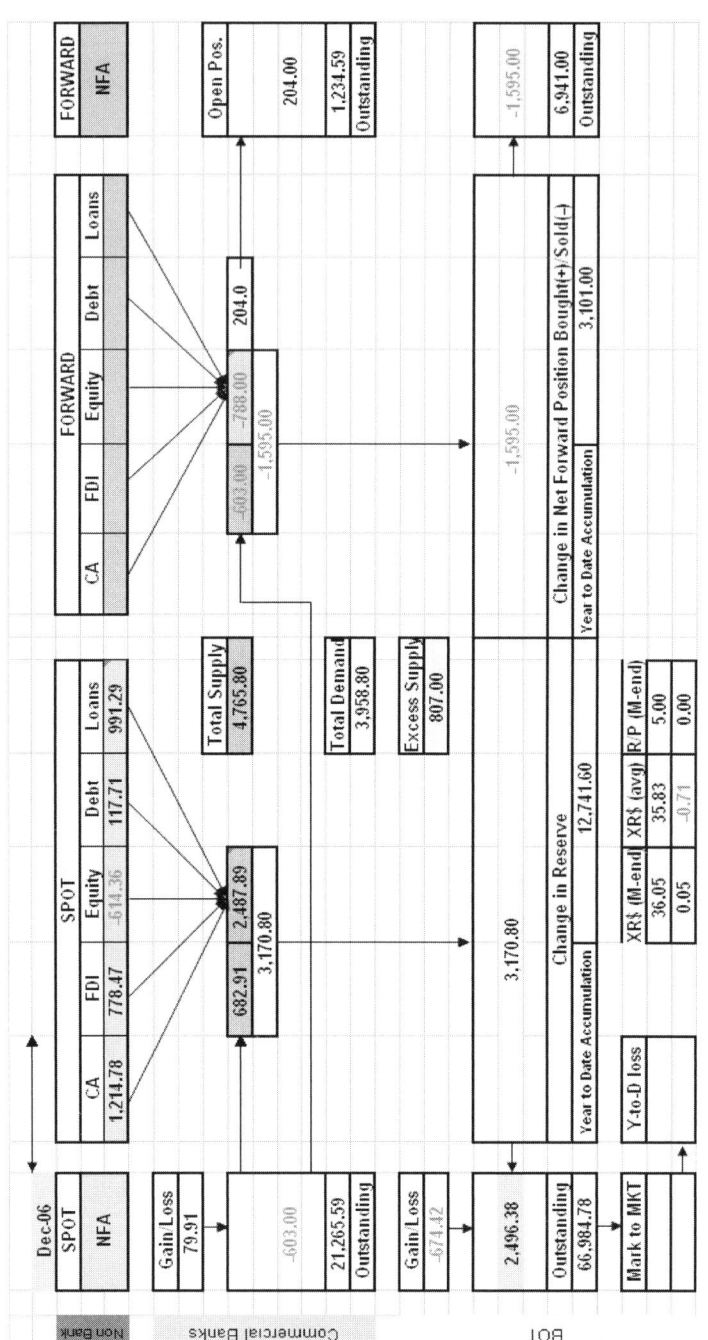

Figure 15.1 (continued)

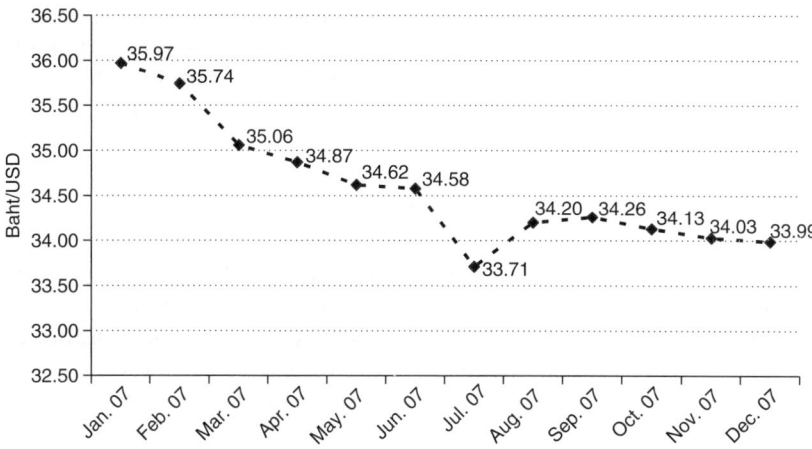

Figure 15.2   Average exchange rate in 2007 (baht/USD)

forward purchasing while a negative value shows forward selling by the BOT in October, November and December of 2006. Capital inflows into commercial banks in the spot market dropped significantly in August 2007 before rebounding. At this turning point, reserves increased rapidly, reflecting currency intervention in the foreign exchange market. With a considerable increase in reserves during August and September 2007, the BOT sold foreign currency in the forward market for hedging purposes.

Figure 15.2 demonstrates the trend of the average exchange rate in each month of the year 2007. After the Thai baht reached its strongest value in July 2007, foreign currency intervention was launched. As a result, the exchange rate began to stabilize thereafter.

Although a slight decrease in the US dollar value against the baht price occurred after September 2007, this did not mean that the BOT had stopped its intervention. Foreign capital that entered the spot and forward markets reached $671 million (FPRI, 2007b). This amount could have caused a dramatic appreciation in Thai baht, but there was in fact only a slim change in the exchange rate, which implied government intervention in the foreign currency market. Nevertheless, the locals, especially exporters, continued selling USD in the forward market due to the lack of confidence in the USD, while some buying of baht occurred in the spot market because of foreigners' demand to invest in the stock market.

Looking at the direction of the onshore exchange rate movement, the trend suggests an improvement of the baht value after the government intervened in July 2007, through the lowering of the repurchase rate by

0.25 per cent, the relaxation of foreign exchange regulations on foreign currency deposit, the expansion of foreign investment funds, and the support for refinancing and foreign loans in baht. Figure 15.3 shows the change of direction in the onshore foreign exchange rate (THB/USD) due to government regulations.

But the offshore exchange rate is another story. Figure 15.4 shows that the baht appreciated continually in the offshore market. This reflects the real market situation without government intervention.

With the continual increase in foreign reserves and signs of growing demand for foreign currency in the spot market, the BOT should capitalize on this opportunity for foreign reserve management. It could sell foreign currency instead of treasury bonds to absorb the baht from the system. Doing so, the BOT need not incur interest payments and may even earn some profit.

Nevertheless, another concern has come into view, as the baht appreciated against only the USD, while actually depreciating against other major currencies, such as the euro and the Japanese yen. The BOT cannot afford to ignore this important point in attempting to maintain the baht's stability.

Interest rate   The repurchase (RP) rate plays a crucial role in the financial market since it is a part of the commercial banks' transaction costs. The RP rate is related to the interbank rate and the commercial banks' deposit and loan interest rates. Needless to say, changes in the RP rate affect all other rates. From the beginning of 2007, the RP rate decreased gradually, reaching 3.25 per cent in October 2007. Although the RP rate became lower, the volume of capital flows declined only slightly, and the baht still continued to appreciate. This indicates that perhaps Thailand still needs more interest rate management to reduce further the differential between domestic and foreign interest rates to stem capital inflows and prevent further currency appreciation. On 18 December 2006, the BOT imposed capital controls on equity, bond and currency transactions. The Thai stock market shrank by more than 12 per cent in a single day, prompting the BOT to reverse immediately the restrictions on equity investments while keeping the 30 per cent unremunerated reserve requirement (URR) in place for currency and bond transactions. This suggests that it is better to explore alternative strategies to reduce pressure on the baht. Indeed, the ability to identify the channels of capital flows could certainly shed some light on the matter.

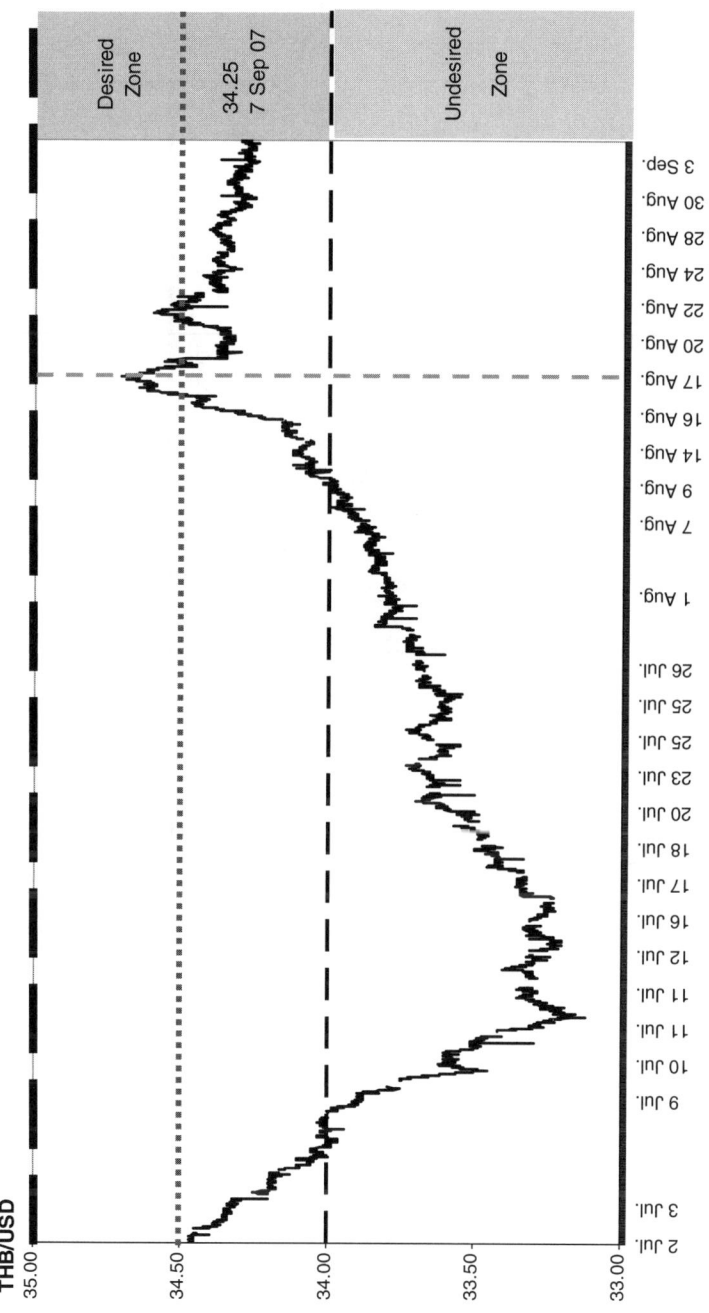

Source: FPRI (2007a).

Figure 15.3 Movement of the onshore baht exchange rate in July to September 2007

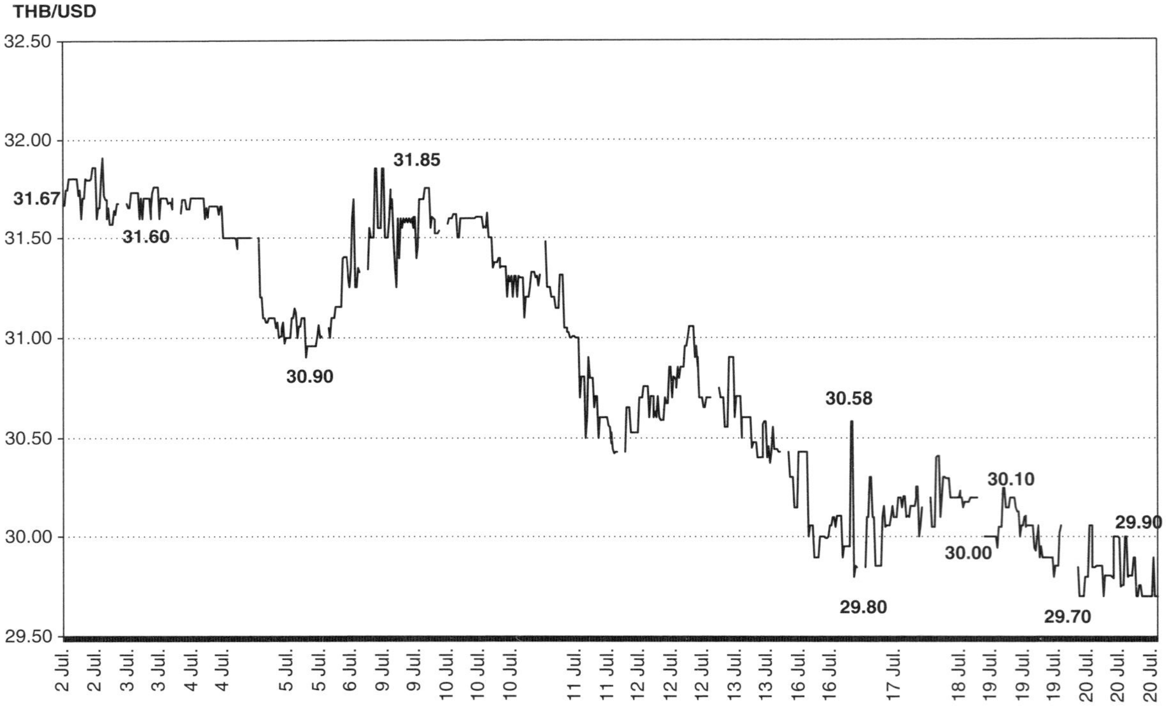

Source: FPRI (2007/a).

Figure 15.4 Movement of the offshore baht exchange rate in July 2007

Table 15.2 Impacts of capital flows on the real sector (%)

	Key ratios			Cost
	Wage/ VA	Capreturn/ VA	Export/ Total revenue	Capital return
Agriculture	42.83	57.17	7.37	−0.9
Mining & quarrying	17.71	82.29	20.00	−4.7
Food manufacturing	43.16	56.84	31.26	−21.1
Textiles	61.66	38.34	30.29	−17.6
Saw mills & wood products	63.13	36.87	48.42	−21.4
Paper & printing	44.07	55.93	21.62	4.3
Rubber, chem, and petroleum	40.81	59.19	40.57	−0.8
Non-metallic product	44.04	55.96	41.11	−23.6
Metal, metal products and machinery	47.02	52.98	55.34	−14.8
Automobiles	46.08	53.92	14.47	1.7
Other manufacturing	58.72	41.28	46.92	−20.2
Public utility	29.47	70.53	3.02	−0.4
Construction	47.06	52.94	1.47	9.7
Trade	51.25	48.75	0.94	−0.5
Services	55.59	44.41	5.86	−1.1
Transport & communications	36.73	63.27	19.55	−10.6
Other services	47.32	52.68	62.07	−28.0

Note:
Change in exchange rate: −12.00%.
Change in total cap return: −6.37%.

Source: FPRI (2007).

15.4.2 Real Sector

The FPRI has constructed a model to assess the impact of a sharp appreciation of the baht on the real sector. It is estimated that a 12 per cent appreciation of the baht (January–August 2007) decreases the profit (total capital return) of the real sector by about 6.4 per cent. Upon disaggregating the real sector, results show that the labor intensive sectors (for example, agriculture, food manufacturing and textiles) tend to be adversely affected by a change in the exchange rate (Table 15.2). On the other hand, high-import content sectors, such as paper and printing, automobiles and construction, tend to benefit from baht appreciation. This demonstrates that baht appreciation is a double-edged sword. It benefits exporters with a high volume of imports and a low volume of exports, for example electricity plants and the iron industry, because most of their revenues are in local currency, while their import costs are lowered. On the other hand, exporters with high levels of exports and low levels of imports, such as textiles, agriculture, and tourism, lose their advantages. In response to cries for government support to maintain export competitiveness, the BOT intervened in the foreign exchange market in July 2007 and announced six regulations to prevent further appreciation, and to enhance local competitiveness and flexibility in foreign exchange management, including balancing foreign currency flows across borders.

15.5 CURRENT MEASURES AND POLICY IMPLICATIONS

15.5.1 Thailand's Capital Controls

Since 1985, Thailand has maintained relatively open current and capital accounts, with liberal treatment of FDI and portfolio investments. Exchange controls, however, still apply to the repatriation of interest, dividends, and principal of portfolio investment. Foreign borrowing by Thai residents is allowed but subject to registration at the BOT. By the end of 1994, Thailand was free of foreign exchange restrictions on current account transactions, and had a very open and favorable regime for foreign investment. Foreign investors were still subject to some restrictions on ownership, particularly with regard to listed companies on the Stock Exchange of Thailand (SET), and on real estate. Restrictions also apply to investments of Thai financial intermediaries and banks overseas.

The capital controls currently employed in Thailand are the results of the following regulations: (i) Exchange Control Act B.E. 2485; (ii) Ministerial Regulation and Notification of the Ministry of Finance (MOF), and (iii) Notices of the Competent Officer. Most of the restrictions fall into the category of direct controls.

Most capital controls employed by Thailand are imposed on non-residents with the intention of reducing speculative attacks. These controls are generally aimed at reducing non-resident holding of the baht (without underlying trade and investment) and eliminating the offshore baht market, which could otherwise provide ammunition for speculators looking for opportunities to attack the baht. Examples of this type of control are the limit on holding of non-resident baht accounts to 300 million baht, as well as the 50 million baht rule on short-term lending to and borrowing from non-residents. Other types of controls are imposed on residents to limit foreign currency risk exposure, both on short-term borrowing and investment abroad. However, the BOT has gradually relaxed its restrictions on in–out portfolio investment since 2002 through a series of special schemes, such as the Foreign Investment Fund (FIF), allowing residents to invest abroad through mutual funds since mid-2003, and Qualified Domestic Institutional Investor (QDII) schemes. Moreover, Thai state enterprises are allowed to hedge freely against foreign currency debts regardless of maturity. Since July 2003, six types of financial institutions have been allowed to invest in sovereign, quasi-sovereign, and investment-grade debt securities. The scope was widened in 2005 to include investment units of foreign unit trusts that are supervised by the members of the International Organization of Securities Commission (IOSCO). Table 15.3 provides a summary of the changes in regulations on capital flows between 2005 and 2007.

Currently, the BOT's framework in dealing with macroeconomic stability involves monitoring seven potential sources of financial imbalances that, if left unchecked, can threaten macroeconomic stability (Box 15.1). If any potential imbalance is identified, the BOT will act using monetary policy tools along with prudential regulations to correct the situation.

Because international capital flows increasingly play a greater role in each of the seven areas, traditional macroeconomic policies may not be enough to ensure the safety and soundness of the economy. Thailand's experience with extensive liberalization of the capital account in the early 1990s shows how easily a small open economy without adequate safeguards can fall victim to massive speculative inflows. Sound macroeconomic fundamentals and a well-regulated financial system are no longer sufficient conditions for financial stability.

15.5.2 Assessing Policies after the 1997–98 Asian Financial Crisis

Allowing more outflows by residents   Inflows from non-residents inevitably mean foreign currency liabilities for Thailand. Allowing residents to invest more in foreign securities and assets can reduce the risk concentration and diversify Thailand's holdings of assets. Specifically, the BOT and various regulators allow more in–out investments after the crisis, such as increasing the scope of securities eligible under the QDII scheme or increasing the quota for the FIF scheme. This is a very important step to give local financial institutions the opportunity to familiarize themselves with international markets. Simultaneously, continuous reforms to enhance the attractiveness of domestic capital markets should be undertaken to mitigate the potential problem of a widening savings-investment (S-I) gap. Because of increasing globalization, more and more Thai businesses may seek to engage in FDI in other countries. This creates business

Table 15.3 Changes in regulations on capital flows in Thailand (2005–07)

2005	2006	2007
(As of 31 December 2005) Foreign capital may be brought into the country without restriction, but proceeds must be surrendered to authorized financial institutions or deposited in foreign currency accounts with authorized financial institutions in Thailand within 7 days of receipt	A limit of 50 million baht applies on the amount that non-residents may lend to domestic financial institutions. This limit applies to loans granted by non-residents without underlying transactions with maturities not exceeding 3 months. The non-resident's head office, branches, representative office, and affiliated companies are counted as one entity Foreign investors required to deposit 30% of investment in foreign currency. The deposited account will be returned if investment in question does not flow out of the country for 1 year	Capital control policy – 30% reserve requirement imposed on foreign capital inflows – issued by BOT on 18 December 2006. The policy reversal was made in the case of the equity market, but not in the bond market Increased flexibility for Thai businesses in managing their foreign currencies
(As of 31 December 2005) Investment exceeding $10 million (or equivalent) a year requires BOT approval	Only authorized banks are allowed to grant financial credits to non-residents, subject to the rule of net foreign exchange position. Without approval from the BOT, residents may grant loans of only up to $10 million (or equivalent) a year to their affiliated companies, provided they own at least 10% of total shares in the company Direct loans in Thai baht were allowed to be made to entities in neighboring countries (i.e. Cambodia, southern parts of the People's Republic of China, Lao PDR, Myanmar, and Viet Nam) under specified conditions and with prior BOT approval Financial institutions are allowed to extend direct loans in baht	Relaxed the regulation on foreign portfolio investment by the institutional investors by allowing them to invest in the form of deposits with financial institutions abroad without seeking approval from the Competent Officer. Nevertheless, the deposited amount is counted as part of the total amount allowable for investing abroad according to the foreign exchange regulations

Table 15.3 (continued)

2005	2006	2007
	with collateral to non-resident natural persons permitted to work in Thailand for not less than 1 year	
(As of 31 December 2005) Purchases of shares under employment stock option plans exceeding the equivalent of $100 000 a year are allowed without BOT approval. Sale or issues locally by non-residents require the approval of the MOF, BOT and SEC		On 24 July 2007, provided Thai residents, both juristic persons and individuals, with greater flexibility in depositing foreign currencies with financial institutions in Thailand Adjusted the limit of fund remittances by Thai residents
(As of 31 December 2005) Foreign equity participation is limited to 25% of the total amount of shares sold in locally incorporated banks, finance companies, credit finance companies, and asset management companies. Foreign equity participation is limited to 49% for other Thai corporations		Allowed companies registered in the Stock Exchange of Thailand, most of which are high-performance businesses and subject to supervision by government agencies, to purchase foreign currencies to invest abroad in an amount up to $100 million per year

Table 15.3 (continued)

2005	2006	2007
Foreign investors are all allowed to hold more than 49% of the total shares sold in local financial institutions for up to 10 years, after which the amount of shares will be grandfathered, and the non-residents will not be allowed to purchase new shares until the percentage of shares held by them is brought down to 49%. Foreign investors are allowed to hold 100% for other Thai corporations with the approval of the BOT. For sales or issues abroad by residents, approval is required under the regulations governing domestic issuance		
The 50 million baht limit on baht credit from non-residents that was imposed on commercial banks and other financial	.	

Table 15.3 (continued)

2005	2006	2007
institutions extended to securities firms		
Reporting requirement on all fund transfer by non-residents imposed on financial institutions		

Source: Bank of Thailand (2007).

opportunities for Thai financial institutions. Financing FDI of local companies would help Thai financial institutions improve their competitiveness internationally.

Strengthening prudential regulations Key internal reforms to strengthen prudential regulations include the partial deposit insurance scheme through the Deposit Insurance Agency, the formalization of consolidated supervision through the Financial Institution Business Act (FIBA), and the introduction of Basel II. Partial deposit insurance to replace full government guarantee was expected to be implemented in 2008. The third draft of the FIBA has been submitted to the MOF and is pending approval by the relevant parties. By the end of 2008, banks are to begin new basic Basel II capital charges (Standardized Approach and Foundation Internal Rating-Based) and by the end of 2009, to begin advanced Basel II capital charges (Advanced Internal Rating-Based and Advanced Measurement Approaches).

Strengthening foreign exchange management Rebounding from the 1997–98 crisis, capital flows in East Asia are becoming more volatile as international investors (especially hedge funds) are chasing higher returns. Thus, it is important for policymakers to decide how they want to finance investment needs, and how much and what type of foreign capital is required. External financing may put further pressure on the current account, but is easy to obtain. However, unregulated capital inflows leave the economy vulnerable to the double mismatch problem and financial volatility. It would be best for Thailand to proceed with care by selecting

BOX 15.1   SEVEN SOURCES OF MACROECONOMIC IMBALANCE

1.	External position	Freer capital flows mean more inflows could come during good times. Yet if short-term capital keeps flowing in, the external position of the country would be weakened and sudden capital outflows may arise leading to volatility in the economy.
2.	Non-financial corporation's financial conditions	Greater inflows of capital can lead to a sharp appreciation of REER, diminishing the corporate sector's price competitiveness. Direct borrowing from the private sector is a possible source of imbalance.
3.	Household financial conditions	Inflows of capital, if channeled to household credit, can lead to higher household debt.
4.	Credit growth	Inflows of capital might be channeled to lending in certain speculative sectors, such as the real estate and stock markets.
5.	Stock market	Inflows that manifest in real estate and stock markets can lead to asset price bubbles.
6.	Real estate sector	
7.	Fiscal position	Unlikely to be directly affected by capital flows (except if the government borrows heavily in foreign currency with short maturity).

Source: Bank of Thailand (2005).

only the less risky capital inflows, such as longer maturity loans or direct investments, and screen out the types of flows that can potentially destabilize the economy. Meanwhile, Thailand should also develop its financial markets so as to be able to absorb shocks, should familiarize itself with outward investment, and should diversify its asset holdings into other foreign markets to reduce risk concentration.

15.5.3 Reducing Short-term Inflows of Non-residents

Because short-term inflows, especially 'hot money', come with a great risk of destabilizing the economy, they should be discouraged. Both public and private short-term borrowing should be restrained. There should be measures that will monitor and limit financial institutions' risk exposure, as well as additional tools to hedge foreign currency risk, such as swaps or loan underwriting, to be developed and used by financial institutions. For example, issued bonds should have higher maturities or be denominated in the baht. Moreover, the BOT should maintain measures to limit the internationalization of the baht and arbitrage activities to prevent currency speculations.

To complement these measures, both the MOF and the BOT should keep a watchful eye on short-term capital flows in order to prevent unnecessary buildup of imbalances in all relevant sectors, and so that corrective policies can be issued promptly. Parallel to this, the scope and scale of inflows allowed should be matched to the state of Thailand's economic conditions and the level of financial markets' development.

15.6 POLICY CHALLENGES – WHAT LIES AHEAD?

15.6.1 Policy Challenges for Thailand

Appropriate intermediate instrument to stabilize long-term inflation
Thailand's monetary policy is conducted in pursuit of price level and exchange rate stability. However, exchange rate stability can conflict with the goal of stabilizing inflation. McCauley (2001 and 2006) suggests that assigning the monetary authority to achieving price stability and managing the exchange rate is harder to sustain in more open economies as the greater will be the effect of the exchange rate relative to the interest rate in setting monetary conditions (i.e., large effective exchange rate changes could lead to an undesirable inflation). Moreover, emerging economies' experience on inflation targeting shows a significant association between large effective exchange rate changes and missed inflation targets (Ho and McCauley, 2003). Perhaps the time has come to question the extension of the link of exchange rate targeting to effectively stabilizing long-term inflation. Given the openness of the Thai economy, interest rates move in accordance with the international rates. Inflation in Thailand has effectively been mainly

imported inflation, so the exchange rate as intermediate target should be a better instrument to stabilize inflation.

Capital outflows management The rise in the level of Thailand's international reserve implies an excess of capital inflows over outflows that led to the appreciation of Thai baht, which in turn adversely affected Thai exporters. By the end of 2007, the BOT's intervention in the exchange rate market cost over $600 million. Moreover, capital flow management – by balancing the inflows and the outflows – has helped Singapore and Malaysia to stabilize their local currencies. This indicates that these countries have successfully encouraged outflow of capital in response to massive capital inflows.

In the case of Thailand, several channels of capital outflows are suggested as tools for capital outflow management – imports for investment, outward FDI, domestic business credit, and international portfolio management. It is commendable that the BOT clearly states its objectives of intervention. The 2007 introduction of capital measures is mostly for balancing capital flows, providing investment opportunities for residents, risk management, and reduction of transaction costs. The relaxation of some restrictions on capital outflows would facilitate international investment including international portfolio investment for Thai investors. At the same time, it allows access to other possible markets for investment. Moreover, coordination of fiscal and monetary policies contributes to the effectiveness of capital outflow management. Monetary policy should be conducted to stabilize long-term inflation through intermediate instruments, that is, the exchange rate. That said, efficient capital outflow management poses another challenge in economic and financial stabilization.

15.6.2 Policy Challenges for the Region: the Future of Regional Cooperation

Regional financial architectures Several steps have been initiated by the ASEAN+3 group to enhance the regional financial architecture, although progress has been slow. For instance, bilateral swap arrangements now exist to combat the short-term liquidity shortage problem; talks are promoted on regional exchange rate coordination to bolster exchange rate stability; and the regional bond market initiative (Asian Bond Market Initiative) was launched to facilitate the utilization of East Asian savings for productive investments in the region.

Exchange rate arrangement The strong investment–production–trade ties in Asia can be disrupted by currency fluctuation. To reduce currency risks from the current triangular currency exchange, direct exchange – price quotation and currency unit – in local currency should be promoted. Some form of Asian currency arrangement might be a good step towards an Asian Currency Unit (ACU) in the future.

Interest rate policy and investment alternatives in the region As a high growth region, Asia attracts capital inflows that could lead to currency appreciation. There are two ways to maintain stability in this particular situation. First, lower the regional interest rate to the point that the real return from capital inflows is no longer attractive. Second, Asia might consider transforming capital surplus into physical and social investment necessary for future sustainable growth. These investments may mean increasing imports and reducing current account surplus while creating new infrastructure projects to generate demand for investment funds of a high rate of return.

Asian bond market development The development of an Asian bond market can facilitate regional investment with a long-term financial instrument. One advantage for holders of long-term bonds denominated in local currency is their lower currency and maturity risks. Compared with the redemption of bank loans, bonds have a secondary market to insulate issuers from massive redemption before maturity. Moreover, Asian bonds could help manage foreign currency given the issue of global imbalance. If Asia is to move to establish some form of currency cooperation, an Asian bond market could be utilized to stabilize a new exchange rate regime.

REFERENCES

Akrasanee, N. (1999), *Thai Economy: 10 Years of Mis-Management* (in Thai), Bangkok Infomedia Corporation.
Bank of Thailand (various years), Press Releases on Exchange Rate Regulations, available at http://www.Bot.Or.Th/Bothomepage/General/Pressreleasesandspeeches/Pressreleases/News2550/Thai/Urrexperiences.Doc.
Calvo, G., L. Leiderman and C. Reinhart (1995), 'Capital inflows to Latin America with reference to Asian experience', in S. Edwards (ed.), *Capital Controls, Exchange Rates, and Monetary Policy in the World Economy*, Cambridge: Cambridge University Press, pp. 339–82.
Cavoli, T. and R.S. Rajan (2005), 'The capital inflows problem in selected Asian economies in the 1990s revisited: the role of monetary sterilization', SCAPE Working Paper Series No. 2005/18, National University of Singapore.
CEIC Data Company Ltd (2006), CEIC Databases.
Edwards, S. (1999), 'On crisis prevention: lessons from Mexico and East Asia', NBER Working Paper, Cambridge, MA.

FPRI (Fiscal Policy Research Institute) (2007a), 'The Bank Of Thailand and 8-Week baht monitoring', (in Thai), *Capital Flows Weekly Focus*, 27 August–19 October.
FPRI (2007b), 'International Reserve Monitoring' (in Thai), *Capital Flows Weekly Focus*, 19–23 November.
Ho, C. and R.N. McCauley (2003), 'Living with flexible exchange rates: issues and recent experience in inflation targeting emerging market economics', BIS Working Papers 30, February, Bank for International Settlements.
McCauley, R. (2001), 'Setting monetary policy in East Asia: goals, developments, and institutions', in R. McCauley, *Future Directions for Monetary Policies in East Asia,* Sydney: Reserve Bank of Australia, pp. 7–55, available at: http://www.Rba.Gov.Au/Publicationsandresearch/Conferences/2001/Mccauley.pdf. Also published as SEACEN Centre Occasional Paper, No. 33, 2003.
McCauley, R. (2006), 'Understanding monetary policy in Malaysia and Thailand: objectives, instruments, and independence', *Monetary Policy in Asia: Approaches and Implementation*, BIS Paper No. 31, December, 172–98.
McKinnon, R. and H. Pill (1996), 'Credible liberalizations and international capital flows: the over-borrowing syndrome', in T. Ito and A. Krueger (eds), *Financial Deregulation and Integration in East Asia*, Chicago: Chicago University Press, pp. 7–50.
Rudolph, J. (2000), 'The political causes of the Asian crisis', in U. Johannen, J. Rudolph and J. Gomez (eds), *The Political Dimensions of the Asian Crisis*, Singapore: Select Books, pp. 13–93.
Sangsubhan, K. (1999), 'Capital account crisis: some findings in the case of Thailand', mimeo.
Sangsubhan, K. and C. Vorawangso (2007), 'From crisis to recovery in Asia: strategies, achievements, and lessons', paper presented at the Bangkok Conference on Advancing East Asia Economic Integration: Building the Institutional and Financial Foundations Of Economic Growth and Integration in East Asia, Bangkok, 22–23 February.
Yoshitomi, M. and S. Shirai (2000), 'Technical Background Paper for Policy Recommendations for Preventing another Current Account Crisis', Asian Development Bank Institute, 7 July.

16. Managing capital flows: the case of Viet Nam
Tri Thanh Vo and Chi Quang Pham

16.1 INTRODUCTION

Viet Nam officially launched its *Doimoi* (Renovation) in 1986, but only started a radical and comprehensive reform package aimed at stabilizing and opening the economy in 1989. During 1996–99, market-oriented reforms were somewhat stalled. Since 2000, a new wave of economic reforms has been stirred up with emphasis on structural reforms (state-owned enterprise (SOE) and financial reforms, and development of the private sector) and further trade and investment liberalization. The years 2000–07 witnessed a boom in the private sector and deeper international economic integration.

Experiences from various countries and the current position of Viet Nam are drawing attention to how Viet Nam can sustain economic growth and sound financial development while mitigating financial risks. This chapter seeks to address the issue, taking into consideration the whole period 1995–2007; that is, from before the Asian crisis, but with a focus on the more recent financial and policy developments.

The chapter is structured as follows. Section 16.2 briefly describes the changes in Viet Nam's economic fundamentals and financial sector development. Section 16.3 analyzes in greater detail the capital flows and their impacts on real economic activities as well as on macroeconomic stability. Section 16.4 then reviews recent macroeconomic policy responses to the surge in capital inflows and assesses the strengths and weaknesses of those policies. Section 16.5 makes some policy recommendations for sustaining high economic growth and sound financial development in the country while mitigating possible financial and inflation risks.

16.2 ECONOMIC FUNDAMENTALS AND FINANCIAL SECTOR DEVELOPMENT

16.2.1 Movement of the Major Macroeconomic Variables

Viet Nam has recorded quite high economic growth over 1990–2007, averaging 7.4 per cent per annum during the period (Table 16.1). It had been successful in combating inflation but since 2004, inflation has emerged as a major concern. After a spike in 2004–05, inflation began moderating progressively and consequently peaked at 12.6 per cent in 2007.

The structure of the economy has changed towards industrialization. The share of manufacturing in GDP increased from 12.3 per cent in 1990 to 21.4 per cent in 2007. The contribution of services and the financial sector to GDP did not change correspondingly; there was, however, an impressive contribution by the financial sector to GDP in 2006 and 2007, at 1.9 per cent and 2.0 per cent respectively, reflecting rises from the steady state level of 1.8 per cent during 2000–05.

The rather high economic growth corresponded with a significant increase in investment as well as public and private savings. Growth has been driven to a large extent by state investment (which is still inefficient), though its ratio in total investment has tended to decline from a high of 60 per cent in 2001 to less than 50 per cent in 2007.[1] However, since 2000, the savings–investment gap has been widening as the investment ratio is increasing while the savings ratio has tended to stagnate.

16.2.2 Development of the Banking System

Key policy reforms
In 1988, Viet Nam shifted from a mono-banking system to a two-tier system, with four state-owned commercial banks (SOCBs) created to assume the State Bank of Vietnam's (SBV) commercial banking activities while the SBV retained the central banking responsibilities. Given the state-driven nature of the Vietnamese economy, up until the recent economic reforms, the SOCBs traditionally focused on lending to the SOEs.

Barriers to entry were reduced in 1991, opening the market to competition to both foreign players (subject to strict restrictions) and joint stock commercial banks (JSCBs). As of 2007 there are over 75 banks operating in Viet Nam, comprising five SOCBs, one policy bank (VSPB), 34 JSCBs, 31 wholly owned branches of foreign banks, and five joint venture banks, and more than 900 people's credit funds (PCFs). In addition, there are 47 representative offices of foreign banks operating in Viet Nam.

In 2006, Viet Nam's top 15 banks together controlled 92.4 per cent of

Table 16.1 Economic size, GDP growth, inflation, investment, and domestic savings

	1990	1995	1996	1997	1998	1999	2000	2001	2002	2003	2004	2005	2006	2007
GDP (VND bil.)	41.9	228.9	272	313.6	361	399.9	441.6	481.3	535.7	613.4	715.3	837.8	973.7	1144
GDP ($ bil.)	6	21	25	27	27	29	31	33	35	40	45	53	61	71
GDP per capita ($)	98	288	337	361	361	374	402	415	440	489	554	635	715	835
GDP growth (%)	5.1	9.4	9.3	8.2	5.8	4.8	6.8	6.9	7.1	7.3	7.7	8.4	8.2	8.5
Share of GDP (current price)	100	100	100	100	100	100	100	100	100	100	100	100	100	100
Agriculture	38.7	27.2	27.8	25.3	25.8	25.4	24.5	23.2	23.0	22.5	21.8	21.0	20.4	20.0
Industry-Const.	22.7	28.8	29.7	32.1	32.5	34.5	36.7	38.1	38.5	39.5	40.2	41.0	41.5	41.8
Manufacturing	12.3	15.0	15.2	16.5	17.1	17.7	18.6	19.8	20.6	20.5	20.3	20.7	21.3	21.4
Services	38.6	44.1	42.5	42.2	41.7	40.1	38.7	38.6	38.5	38.0	38.0	38.0	38.1	38.2
Fin. Institutions	1.2	2.0	1.9	1.7	1.7	1.9	1.8	1.8	1.8	1.8	1.8	1.8	1.9	2.0
Inflation (%)	67.5	12.7	4.6	3.6	9.2	0.1	–0.6	0.8	4.0	3.0	9.4	8.4	6.7	12.6
Total investment	14.4	27.1	28.2	28.3	29.1	27.6	29.6	31.2	33.2	35.4	35.6	38.9	41.0	41.2
Domestic savings	2.9	18.2	17.2	20.1	21.5	24.6	27.1	28.8	28.7	27.4	28.5	30.3	31.3	31.2
Budget saving	3.4	1.5	3.2	2.2	2.5	3.1	3.3	3.4	4.3	5.0	6.0	5.3	5.6	3.9
Other savings	–0.5	16.7	14.0	17.9	19.0	21.5	23.8	25.4	24.4	22.4	22.5	25.0	25.7	27.3

Note: All data for 2007 in this chapter are estimates.

Sources: General Statistics Office of Viet Nam (various issues) and data provided by Ministry of Planning and Investment (MPI), and the authors' calculations.

Table 16.2 Total credits and deposits (VND trillion)

	1996	1999	2000	2001	2002	2003	2004	2005	2006	2007
Broad Money (M2)	64.7	160.4	222.9	279.8	329.0	411.2	532.3	690.7	922.7	1 282.6
% change	22.7	56.6	39.0	25.5	17.6	24.9	29.5	29.7	33.6	39.0
% of GDP	23.8	40.1	50.5	58.1	61.4	67.0	74.4	82.4	94.8	112.1
Credit to economy	50.9	112.7	155.7	189.1	231.1	296.7	420.0	553.1	693.8	943.6
SOE share (%)	52.7	48.2	44.9	42.1	38.7	35.5	34.0	32.8	31.4	31.5
Others share (%)	47.3	51.8	55.1	57.9	61.3	64.5	66.0	67.2	68.6	68.5
% change	20.1	55.0	38.2	21.5	22.2	28.4	41.6	31.7	25.4	36.0
% of GDP	18.7	28.2	35.3	39.3	43.1	48.4	58.7	66.0	71.2	82.5

Note: Credit figures in 2007 have been adjusted by the latest SBV estimates.

Source: IMF (2006, 2007).

market share by assets (excluding foreign bank branches). In 2006, the SOCBs' shares still accounted for nearly 70 per cent of total deposits and 65 per cent of total credits. However, since 2006, the role of the JSCBs has changed significantly and in 2007, they already accounted for 30 per cent in total deposits and 29 per cent in total credits.

Financial depth has also changed significantly (Table 16.2). Fast growing credit with an annualized average growth rate of 33.4 per cent, fueled by strong credit demand from both the corporate and retail markets since 2004, promoted financial deepening. As a result, in 2007, there were sharp increases in financial deepening with indicators such as the credit/GDP ratio and M2/GDP reaching 82 per cent and 112 per cent, respectively.

From 2005 to 2007 the banking industry significantly developed its financial strength as capital adequacy improved and SOCBs' non-performing loans (NPLs) had been reduced from 13 per cent in 2000 to about 3 per cent in 2006.[2]

Due to increasing competitive pressure from deepening integration, especially after the VN–US bilateral trade agreement (BTA) and WTO accession, Viet Nam's local banks have rushed into expanding their business operations by setting up new branches and developing retail banking activities. Moreover, mergers and acquisitions have boomed in recent years, especially since 2006. This trend has been led mostly by large state corporations intent on acquiring small/rural JSCBs and making them dependent entities.

In 2005–07 there were also a lot of marriages between the JSCBs and foreign financial institutions. In December 2007 and January 2008, the SBV approved in principle the setting-up of nine new JSCBs and the licensing of branches of three new foreign banks. Furthermore, the SBV is reviewing the granting of full licenses to three foreign banks (HSBC, ANZ, and Standard Chartered) to set up wholly owned banks in Viet Nam.

16.2.3 Stock Market Evolution and 2006–07 Boom

Key policy reforms

The State Securities Commission (SSC) was established in 1995, followed by the creation of two securities trading centers, the Ho Chi Minh City Securities Trading Centre (HOSTC) in 2000 and the Hanoi Securities Trading Centre (HASTC) in 2005.[3] To promote stock market development, several policy measures were introduced, including improvements to the legal framework on listing conditions, information transparency and exposure, and supervision. The financial markets have also been gradually opened to foreign participants.

Evolution of the stock market: the boom and shrink

After a short-lived surge up until June 2001 (peak of VN-Index=571), trading in the HOSTC had cooled off. Up to 2005, the stock market was generally very weak and ailing on both the supply and demand sides. In 2006 and 2007, it skyrocketed in terms of market capitalization, number of listed companies and investors' accounts, participation of securities companies, and investment management funds. The boom began in the second half of 2006. The VN-index rose by 144 per cent in 2006 and 40 per cent in the first quarter of 2007, reaching a peak of 1170 on 12 March 2007. It has since fluctuated within the range of 900–1100, but has tended to decline from October 2007. Similar trends could also be observed at the HASTC. As of early March 2008, the VN-index and HASTC-index stood at below 600 and 200, respectively.

Key factors behind the market boom in November 2006–March 2007, *inter alia*, were: (i) Viet Nam's high economic growth period and the country's bright prospects after the accession to the WTO; (ii) firms' rapid response following the tax incentive in 2006; (iii) exuberance and sizeable foreign participation, including overseas Vietnamese in Russia and Eastern Europe; and (iv) herding behavior spread amongst local short-term individual investors in the context of insufficient information disclosure and transparency. On the other hand, the sharp decline of the stock market price indices can be attributed to various factors, namely, tightening of lending by commercial banks due to stock investment and monetary policies, high inflation rate and higher VND deposit interest rates, and a possible recession of the US economy. However, while local (individual) investors have tried to avoid the market, foreign investors have been more interested in buying rather than selling the stocks they own. On 6 March 2008, the State Capital Investment Corporation (SCIC) was forced to intervene in the stock market by purchasing several stocks (mostly blue chip) to prevent further decline in stock prices.

16.2.4 Development of the Bond Market

Policy measures
According to the State Budget Law of 1993, the government can no longer finance the budget deficit by printing money. Since the mid-1990s, it has paid more attention to the issuance of bonds for financing budget deficit and development needs. However, improvement of the legal framework for bond market development has been rather slow. The first decree on the issuance of government bonds was only in 2000 and it was amended in 2003.

Characteristics of the bond market
Viet Nam's bond market remains relatively underdeveloped despite a recent expansion. At the end of 2007, there were 570 outstanding bonds in the securities market, with a market value of about VND 115.660 trillion, or 10.1 per cent of GDP. Most of them are government bonds (85 per cent).

Despite continuing improvement, the market is still illiquid as investors hold the bonds to maturity. Beginning in the second half of 2006, foreign buyers started to show an interest in Vietnamese bonds, as many think that they are being undervalued and are ripe for higher returns. Foreign participation has created a new liveliness in the bond markets, especially on the HASTC. Forty-four government bond tenders took place in 2007, which helped raise VND 18.939 trillion in capital. The secondary bond market in Hanoi has also experienced rather strong growth.

16.3 CAPITAL FLOWS AND THEIR IMPACTS

16.3.1 Foreign Direct Investment Inflows

The Foreign Investment Law was passed in December 1987. During 1988–2007, Viet Nam attracted 9492 FDI projects with committed capital of $83.2 billion in total, 52.7 per cent of which were realized.[4] After reaching a peak in 1996, FDI inflows into Viet Nam declined due to the Asian financial crisis. However, since the second half of 2004, FDI has expanded rapidly, reaching more than $10 billion and $21.3 billion in terms of commitments in 2006 and 2007, respectively. The sudden increase of FDI in these recent years reflects investors' confidence in Viet Nam's reform, international integration process and development prospects, as well as the effect of FDI restructuring in Asia, with investment in some labor-intensive industries moving from the PRC to Viet Nam.

In the 1990s, FDI was concentrated in import substitution industries. However, since 2000, there has been a trend towards the export manufacturing and services sectors.

16.3.2 Official Development Assistance

Official development assistance (ODA) was resumed in 1993 and, together with FDI, has also significantly contributed to investment and GDP growth in Viet Nam. From 1993–2007, total committed ODA for Viet Nam reached $41.2 billion, of which $30.7 billion (or 74.5 per cent) was signed, and $19.7 billion (or 47.9 per cent) was disbursed. In the years from 1993 to 2005, ODA represented about 11.4 per cent of the total investment and 50 per cent of the investment from the State budget (MPI, 2005).

16.3.3 Portfolio Investment Flows

The development and outlook of Viet Nam's economy and securities market has attracted the attention of many foreign investors. Foreign portfolio investment (FPI) inflows, together with the presence of a number of foreign investment funds, were a new phenomenon in 2006. FPI inflows accounted for 2.2 per cent and 10.4 per cent of GDP in 2006 and 2007, respectively (Appendix Table 16A.1). In 2006, there was around $1.3 billion of FPI in Viet Nam, of which 70 per cent was invested in stocks, bonds, and real estate, and 30 per cent was held as deposits in the banking system. In 2007, FPI increased sharply to $7.4 billion.

The exuberant and sizeable foreign participation, including overseas Vietnamese in Russia and Eastern Europe, has contributed to the financial boom and increased investments in the real estate market. Since the second half of 2006, the appetite of foreign investors has shown more favor towards both government and corporate bonds. The participation of foreign investors has contributed to the growth of a secondary government bond market in Hanoi. In May 2007, foreigners accounted for 25 per cent of HOSE capitalization.

The increase of FPI can be further explained by the transfer items on the balance of payments (BOP). Private remittances increased substantially, from 0 per cent of GDP in 1990 to 5.1 per cent in 2000, 6.2 per cent in 2006 and 8.7 per cent in 2007 (Appendix Table 16A.1). Anecdotal evidence suggests that a large proportion of remittances were used for investment in real estate and the stock market in 2006–07.

16.3.4 Capital Inflows and Macroeconomic Stability

In the last five years, there were high trade deficits but much less current account (CA) deficit compared to mid-1990s levels. An exception is 2007, which had a very high CA deficit, reaching 9.9 per cent of GDP. Furthermore, the mode of financing trade deficits has also changed. In the mid-1990s, trade and CA deficits were largely funded by FDI. But since 2005, remittances and portfolio inflows have played an increasing role in financing trade deficit. Also, as a result of huge capital inflows, foreign exchange reserves have accumulated rapidly, increasing from $3 billion in 2000 to $11.5 billion in 2006, and further to a record high of around $23 billion (32.3 per cent of GDP) by the end of 2007.

There are, however, some concerns:

- Debt-induced financing has constituted a majority of capital inflow, and hence, the costs of financing CA deficit may increase;
- FDI inflow has also entailed considerable commercial loans;
- Capital utilization efficacy, especially in the public sector, is low; and
- Errors and omissions in the BOP are high due to statistical errors which may reflect shortcomings in controlling short-term capital flows.

It should be noted that a surge in capital inflows, especially during 2006–07, was also associated with domestic credit expansion, higher inflation and rising asset prices. But the outcomes, to a significant extent, have been dependent on responses of key macroeconomic policies.

16.4 MAJOR FINANCIAL ISSUES AND 2007 POLICY RESPONSES

16.4.1 The Banking System

The first issue concerns the non-performing loans (NPLs) of the banking industry. Although NPLs have gone down significantly in recent years, they could still rise in the future. The inefficiency of large SOEs and public investments, and the conflict of interest issues related to the lending of funds raised through bond issuances of SOEs, could result in the loss of repayment capability of those borrowers. Moreover, the risks associated with real estate and securities-related loans, which were substantial in several JSCBs, are quite high in the context of high inflation and an asset bubble. Obviously, one of the key measures in conjunction with restructuring the banking system is to reform the SOE sector.

The banking industry has also faced a prolonged double mismatch problem (maturity mismatch and currency mismatch). Normally, short-term deposits account for 75 per cent of total deposits, but the share of medium and long-term loans in total credit rose from 22 per cent in 1995 to about 40 per cent in recent years (this figure is much higher for some JSCBs in 2007). At the same time, commercial banks have only been allowed to use about 25–30 per cent of short-term deposits to make medium and long-term loans. The risks seem to be magnified in the presence of direct lending and conflict of interest issues, especially when related to loans of questionable real estate deals and other big projects.

The currency mismatch was most severe during 1999–2002 due to sharp increases in foreign currency deposits and a decrease in foreign currency loans, measured as shares in total deposits and total loans, respectively (Figure 16.1). It has recently been narrowed, but remains problematic due to its sensitivity to the exchange rate and interest rate fluctuations, especially in the context of a rather high degree of dollarization.[5] The SBV has attempted to gradually eliminate dollarization. However, this is no easy task as some contradictory policies continue to be in place (such as policies for encouraging remittances), in the context of having capital flows.

The problem of macroeconomic policy consistency should be looked into for greater clarity. Consistency between monetary and exchange rate policies is approached as, according to Johnston and Otker-Robe (1999), the relationship between exchange rates (ERs) and interest rates at a point in time and the sustainability of these policy mixes over time. The consistency at a point in time can best be demonstrated by the conditions of covered and uncovered interest rate parities (CIP and UIP). These two parities indicate the interdependent relationship between the domestic

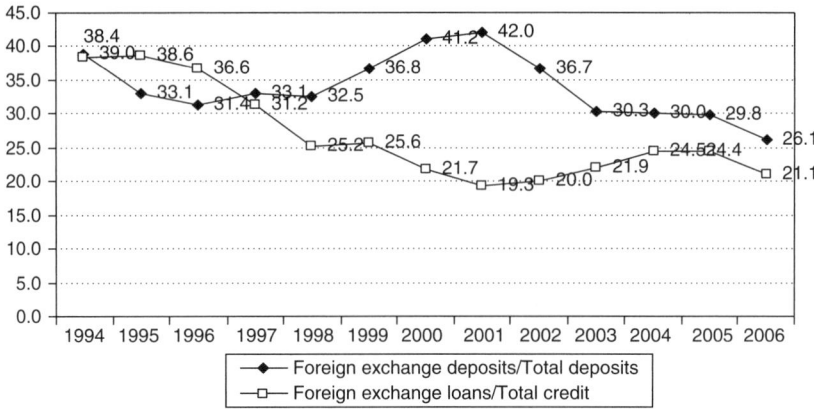

Sources: SBV and authors' estimates.

Figure 16.1 Ratios of FX deposits to total deposits and FX loans to total credit

interest rate and ER at a point in time, when investors consider different returns on various financial assets to maximize return on their portfolios. The policy consistency over time determines the sustainability of the chosen policy mix. The risks and costs of this kind of policy inconsistency are ineffectiveness of monetary policy and encouragement of speculative activities. This point can be illustrated by two case studies: the intensification of dollarization during 1998–2001, and the 'mini-crisis' in 1996–97 (Box 16.1).

The present situation seems to be reversed due to the weakening USD and increasing VND-denominated interest rates (Table 16.3). The VND became more attractive than the USD (a reason for the declining degree of dollarization). This has contributed to the encouragement of VND-based foreign exchange investments in local bonds, real estate, equity markets, and foreign currency borrowings for imports (given high inflation and expectation of stability/appreciation of nominal ER). Some of these investments can also be speculative.

Another issue is that the management capability at both the macro- and micro-levels cannot keep pace with the new development dimensions of the banking sector. In fact, there are still shortcomings in the banking industry as much as there is still a weak financial capacity of commercial banks (low capital adequacy ratio, reserves and loan quality) and weak risk management. Furthermore, the underdevelopment of a regulatory framework, and the limited supervision and monitoring capacity of the

BOX 16.1 DOLLARIZATION, DOUBLE MISMATCHES, AND SPECULATIVE ACTIVITIES

Following the UIP condition, it can be observed that during 1997–2001, given the expectation of further exchange rate (ER) depreciation and lower VND-denominated interest rates, the public had shifted from the preferred portfolio in favor of USD (Table 16.3). This was particularly the case in 2000 when the US Federal Reserve brought the prime rate to higher levels. Due to capital controls, commercial banks attempted to attract foreign currency deposits for deposits abroad to earn the differential spread. The deposits abroad rose remarkably, from $537 million in 1998 to $2.088 billion in 2000 and $1.197 billion in 2001 (Appendix Table 16A.1). In other words, the macroeconomic policy inconsistency in favor of holding USD was a major underlying determinant of the dollarization intensification during 1999–2001, and in certain circumstances this encouraged commercial banks to speculate on currency gains rather than focus on productive investments.

The mini-crisis in 1996–97 is another illustration of the danger of macroeconomic policy inconsistency and problem of double mismatch. In 1996, the very high VND-denominated interest rates attracted a substantial increase in banking deposits, while credits hardly expanded due to the high lending rates and tight regulations on credit ceilings. Reserves in commercial banks rose substantially and many banks had excessive reserves (some banks even refused to accept more deposits). This situation created incentives for banks to evade government controls. A letter of credit (LC) was one important channel for evasion since up to that time, LCs were excluded from credit ceilings. LCs were seen as an off-balance sheet activity of banks, generating opacity on their balance sheets.

Firms also attempted to evade regulations on limits of foreign currency borrowings (only importers and other import-related activities can obtain loans in foreign currencies). Although at that time, Viet Nam had imposed certain restrictions on CA and KA, the flows of funds from abroad through deferred payments on LCs had been outside those restrictions. Domestic enterprises were allowed to have their trade credit guaranteed by commercial banks through deferred LCs. In fact, this was equivalent to enterprises borrowing short-term foreign currency loans from abroad through domestic commercial banks. Moreover, in an environment of a very high VND interest rate and limited foreign currency loans, but with stability and rigidity of exchange rates as an implicit government guarantee against foreign exchange risk, there was a strong incentive for domestic firms to borrow from abroad. Thus, both commercial banks and firms had incentives to lend and borrow through LCs.

As a result, domestic firms (both SOE and private enterprises) borrowed a large amount of short-term USD loans. The amount of LCs was estimated to have accumulated to $1.5 billion by early 1997. Net flows on short-term debt increased significantly, from about $120 million in 1993 and 1994 to $311 million in 1995 and $224 million in 1996. It had become thereafter largely negative in 1997.

The consequences were severe. First, it widened the CA deficit at an alarming level (Appendix Table 16A.1). Second, a large part of this short-term borrowing was channeled into a speculative real estate market, resulting in a market boom. But the market turned into bust in early 1997, when those firms could not pay back the debt. Third, it weakened the banking system and the financial sector as a whole. Around 40 per cent of the LCs (equivalent to 3 per cent of the GDP) guaranteed by commercial banks became bad debts.

As a result, the SOCBs and some other JSCBs defaulted on these guaranteed short-term debts, leading to concern about the level of foreign exchange reserves and about Viet Nam's commitment to international financial arrangements. The SBV had to use foreign reserves to bail out these commercial banks. It was estimated that the stock of foreign reserves fell by the equivalent of five weeks of imports. Viet Nam's sovereign credit rating was lowered from Ba3 to C.

Moreover, the evasion of banks weakened the effectiveness of the monetary policy because the direct control mechanism was eroded, distorting monetary aggregates. In addition, it generated upward pressure on the exchange rate. Due to a sharp increase in demand for foreign exchange by the end of 1996 and early 1997, the SBV broadened the band between selling and buying rates of foreign exchange from 1 per cent to 5 per cent in February 1997. In addition, in mid-1997, the SBV set strict limits on the amount of deferred LCs and tightened controls over commercial banks' LC guaranteeing. To import goods on the restricted goods list, a deposit equivalent of 80 per cent of each LC was required instead of the previous 0–30 per cent level. As a result, during the second half of 1998, the value of late LC payments fell from around USD 350 million to some USD 200 million at the end of 1998.

Table 16.3 *Annual savings interest rates of USD and VND, 1992–2007 (%)*

Year	CPI-based inflation (1)	VND depreciation rate (2)	VND savings interest rate (3)	Real VND savings rate (4)=(3)−(1)	Return on VND in USD (5)=(3)−(2)	USD savings interest rate (6)	Difference in rates (7)=(5)−(6)
1992	17.5	−8.13	34.10	16.60	42.23	4.05	38.18
1993	5.2	2.62	20.40	15.20	17.78	3.20	14.58
1994	14.5	1.92	16.80	2.30	14.88	3.50	11.38
1995	12.7	−0.33	16.80	4.10	17.13	4.50	12.63
1996	4.5	0.33	9.60	5.10	9.27	4.80	4.47
1997	3.6	11.57	9.60	6.00	−1.97	5.00	−6.97
1998	9.2	12.70	9.60	0.40	−3.10	5.00	−8.10
1999	0.1	0.89	5.25	5.15	4.36	4.70	−0.34
2000	−0.6	3.54	4.45	5.05	0.91	4.43	−3.52
2001	0.8	3.90	5.95	5.15	2.05	3.00	−0.95
2002	4.0	2.11	7.20	3.20	5.09	2.50	2.59
2003	3.0	2.20	7.40	4.40	5.20	2.50	2.70
2004	9.4	0.40	7.70	−1.70	7.30	2.60	4.70
2005	8.4	0.90	8.40	0.00	7.50	4.20	3.30
2006	6.7	0.87	8.80	2.10	7.93	4.70	3.23
2007	12.6	−0.20	9.10	−3.50	9.30	5.00	4.30

Note: The end of period ER is used to calculate the depreciation rate.

Sources: Nguyen (2002) for the data up to 2001 and authors' estimates for the 2002–07 data.

key regulatory bodies – SBV, Ministry of Finance (MOF), and SSC – make banking activities less transparent and more fragile.

16.4.2 The Stock and Bond Markets

During a stock market boom, the greatest concern of the Vietnamese authorities has been how to control speculative activities that make the stock market too volatile and at the same time, how to facilitate long-term investment for the development of the economy as a whole. Facing such challenges, the SSC has repeatedly warned investors of risks associated with overheating in the market's development, and the SBV introduced a measure to restrain loans to bank-backed securities companies in December 2006. Within a few days, the SSC promulgated several measures to improve regulation and monitoring of the securities market's operations, including, among others, postponing the lifting of maximum shares of listed companies permitted to foreign investors; cooperating with the SBV to monitor lending for security investment, repo transactions, and other transactions related to security collateralization of commercial banks; and promoting further information disclosure so that investors can make better-informed, rational investment decisions. However, the reaction of the stock market proved that such policy measures were not significantly effective. There has not yet been a clear sign of market fever relief. To address concerns that stock-collateralized loans could become NPLs, in April 2007 the SBV decided to impose a 3 per cent ceiling on total lending for stock-collateralized loans (Direction 03/QD-NHNN), designed to protect the stability of the banking system in particular, and the financial system as a whole. As a result, the VN-Index still fluctuated but with a declining trend.

Development of the stock market in Viet Nam is obviously very much dependent on the SOE reform process. The government focused on reforming large SOEs with a determined action plan. According to the plan that was publicly announced, there are about 2100 SOEs, of which about 1500 have been or will be equitized over 2006–10. This suggests that close to 80 corporations and large firms will have to go public.

There are also some concerns about the role of the SCIC, which was set up in 2005 modeled after Singapore's Temasek Holdings. Although the SCIC has a profit oriented mandate, whether it could be a market stabilizer remains questionable. Risks due to the principal–agent relationship can arise if there is no effective supervision over the SCIC. Moreover, the SCIC does not have sufficient expertise in dealing with complex financial activities.

The bond market in Viet Nam is still very modest and lacks necessary components including the following:

- An appropriate legal framework with an effective judicial system;
- High quality of information and adoption of strict accounting and disclosure standards;
- The presence of independent risk-rating and other information generating agencies;
- An efficient and reliable clearing and settlement arrangement; and

- Some forms of tax incentives during the initial stage of development.

Moreover, the bond market in Viet Nam is heavily dominated by government bonds. It is necessary, however, to strengthen the role of the government as the primary issuer.

With the opening of the economy, full participation in the regional and international bond markets is unavoidable.

16.4.3 Foreign Capital Inflows[6]

Viet Nam continues to be on the right track for attracting FDI with a more liberal and neutral investment environment. Recently, the government has moved towards unifying domestic and foreign investment regulations, aiming to establish a level playing field for both domestic and foreign investors. Commitments to the WTO, especially those of the services sector, are quite broad and deep and are in favor of FDI. Major obstacles, however, still exist, such as red tape and corruption, an inconsistent and barely transparent system of legal documents, and unpredictable policy changes. The slow pace of FDI realization[7] has also revealed major bottlenecks preventing the efficient flow of FDI including weaknesses in the infrastructure and a shortage of skilled workers.

ODA inflow has been the result of the gradual strengthening of a set of common commitments between the Vietnamese government and the donor community in line with the Hanoi Core Statement (HCS) on aid effectiveness. However, some shortcomings in this field such as the modest effectiveness of anti-corruption programs and the lack of capacity for monitoring and evaluation, especially at local levels, necessitate more radical solutions. Last but not least, transparent and effective public–private partnership (PPP) schemes are still wanting.

Foreign invested enterprises (FIEs) were allowed to be transformed into shareholding companies from 2004. The government also provided guidance for purchasing and selling securities by foreigners at the Stock Trading Center (STC). Moreover, the Ordinance on Foreign Exchange Management issued in December 2005 gave permission for individuals to obtain overseas borrowings and for domestic economic entities to lend overseas if they meet necessary conditions. Soon after, external debt monitoring problems arose, leading the SBV to delay the process by issuing a circular guiding the implementation of the Ordinance. Although the capital account (KA) is now relatively open for capital inflows, Viet Nam still has to consider the sequencing of full KA liberalization in conjunction with improvements in the financial supervision system.

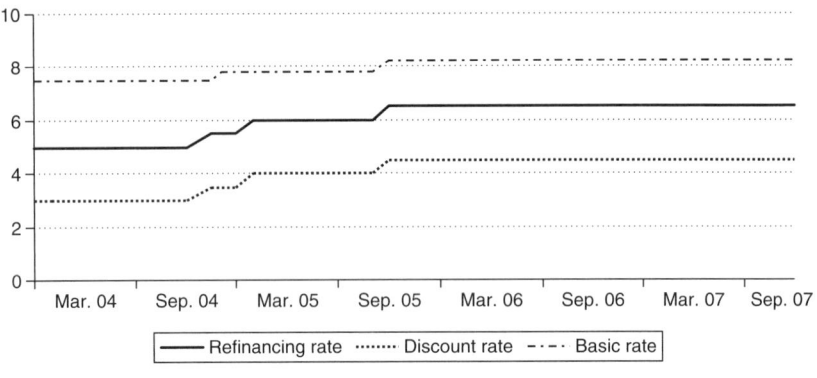

Source: SBV.

Figure 16.2   Evolution of the interest rate policy set by SBV (% year)

16.4.4   Macroeconomic Policies

SBV's conduct of monetary policy of late faced two problems, namely, increasing macroeconomic policy inconsistencies and the 'impossible trinity' as capital inflows surged, especially in 2007. The SBV has had to consider a trade-off between exchange rate stability and inflation targeting policy. There have been two main arguments over the dilemma facing the SBV. The first is that appreciation can hurt exports and economic growth; historically the SBV has pursued a rather weak VND policy in order to promote exports. The second is to let VND appreciate, which seems to be in line with macroeconomic fundamentals and the foreign exchange behavior of many other East Asian economies. Moreover, it could be a signal for the economy that the VND is no longer only in a position of depreciation (JP Morgan, 2007). So what is the choice for the SBV in practice?

In general, the SBV and the government are more concerned about the possible negative impact of appreciation on exports and the slowdown of economic growth. In January 2007, the SBV widened the trading band of the VND/USD from ± 0.25 per cent to ±0.5 per cent around its daily reference rate. The VND/USD appreciated in nominal terms of only 0.2 per cent for the whole year of 2007. At the same time, the SBV kept all official interest rates such as refinancing, and discount and basic rates unchanged from early 2006 in order to provide a stable signal to the market, although the rates set by commercial banks increased slightly (Figure 16.2). While stabilizing the nominal ER, the SBV quickly built up its foreign exchange reserves, which increased from $11.5 billion in 2006 to $23 billion by the end of 2007.

As inflation accelerated in the first half of 2007,[8] the SBV only attempted to sterilize the excess liquidity through its open market operation (OMO) and increases in reserve requirements. It is reported that the SBV regularly withdrew up to VND 11 000–14 000 billion ($688–875 million) per week from circulation from May 2007. At the end of the year, this figure rose to as much as VND 15 000–16 500 billion ($938–1.031 million) (World Bank, 2007). Since June 2007, the SBV has raised its reserve requirements. For VND deposits under 12 months, the compulsory reserve rate increased from 5 per cent to 10 per cent; for VND deposits between 12 and under 24 months, from 2 per cent to 4 per cent. Correspondingly, rates for foreign currency deposits rose from 8 per cent to 10 per cent and from 2 per cent to 4 per cent.

But the sterilization was ineffective and costly (CIEM, 2008). The money supply (both M2 and domestic credit) expanded sharply in 2007 in comparison with that of previous years since 2003, which was already high. The inflation rate jumped from 6.7 per cent in 2006 to 12.6 per cent in 2007. The SBV was recognized by the government to be 'perplexed' in conducting monetary policy, which was considered a major cause, together with cost-push and demand-pull reasons, of higher inflation. Moreover, in the context of the weakening USD and increasing international commodity prices, keeping the stability of the nominal VND/USD also meant a significant import of international inflation.

To control the money supply, the SBV introduced several policy measures:

- By the end of December 2007, the trading band of the VND/USD was cautiously widened to ± 0.75 per cent and as a result, the nominal VND/USD appreciated by 0.3 per cent over the first two months of 2008;
- In January, lending restrictions for stock investment changed from 3 per cent of total loans outstanding to 20 per cent of charter capital, which limits potential growth in such investment credit;
- Since 1 February 2008, the rates of compulsory reserve requirements have been raised to 11 per cent (from 10 per cent) for VND and foreign currency deposits under 12 months, and to 5 per cent (from 4 per cent) for those deposits between 12 months and under 24 months;
- Also since 1 February 2008, all official interest rates have been increased, from 6.5 per cent to 7.5 per cent for the refinancing rate, from 4.5 per cent to 6.0 per cent for the discount rate, and from 8.25 per cent to 8.75 per cent for the basic rate; and
- In particular, in the second week of February 2008, the SBV decided to issue by 17 March 2008 365-day-bills worth VND 20 300 billion

with a coupon of 7.8 per cent and requested a compulsory purchase by 41 commercial banks.

In the following days, some JSCBs with maturity mismatch problems did not have sufficient liquidity to meet the new policy measures. The inter-bank market became too heated with overnight rates of 25–30 per cent. As a result of the 'liquidity chaos', the SBV was forced to pump out VND 33 000 billion. Those banks were, however, in a difficult position in terms of liquidity because they held T-bills/bills issued by the SBV. They increased their annual VND deposit interest rates to 14.6 per cent to attract deposits. The race for higher deposit interest rates among commercial banks began. It calmed down only by the end of February 2008 as the SBV issued a directive requesting all commercial banks to cap annual deposit interest rates at 12 per cent and to meet the liquidity needs of the banking system through the inter-bank market at reasonable rates.

The liquidity chaos once again showed the high costs of keeping the nominal stability of ER in conjunction with maturity mismatch problems in the banking system or of even just among some commercial banks (due to weak supervision) and inappropriate policy actions. The fact that the SBV had to use some administrative measures to control the situation will have higher costs due to distortions in resource allocation. This action, though temporary and necessary, can be seen as a step backward in the process of improving monetary instruments.[9] The movements of some key macroeconomic variables in the first two months of 2008 will make the policy option more complicated. Inflation rose by more than 6 per cent.[10] The rise in deposit interest rates by banks could soften the liquidity problem but it imposes a higher risk for several banks.

Fiscal tightening can be a good response to capital inflows. It contains inflationary pressure, reduces pressure on real appreciation and increases interest rates. However, up to now, Viet Nam is not seriously considering using fiscal policy to complement monetary and ER policies in response to capital inflows. For a long time, fiscal policy has followed the 'golden rule', meaning that fiscal revenues must at least cover current expenditures, and that budget deficit cannot be financed by seigniorage.

Scope for reducing the rather large budget deficit seems to be limited (Table 16.4). Budget revenue still relies heavily on crude oil exports and import tariffs. The former item has fluctuated widely, and because of some technical problems, the volume of crude oil exports will not increase unless new oil resources are found. Important tariffs have significantly decreased over time due to trade liberalization. There is also uncertainty about the impact of tax reforms on the budget revenue. On the expenditure side, the government is facing increasing pressure for infrastructure development

Table 16.4 Budget revenues and expenditures, 2001–07 (%)

	2001	2002	2003	2004	2005	2006	2007
	\multicolumn{7}{c}{Proportion of total revenues}						
Total revenues	100.0	100.0	100.0	100.0	100.0	100.0	100.0
Crude oil revenues	24.5	21.4	18.6	21.6	27.5	29.5	21.97
Trade taxes (import tariffs)	21.4	25.5	19.6	15.5	17.0	15.7	18.12
	\multicolumn{7}{c}{Proportion of total expenditure}						
Total expenditures	100.0	100.0	100.0	100.0	100.0	100.0	100.0
Investment expenditure	31.0	30.5	28.5	25.8	27.2	27.1	27.6
Current expenditure	55.8	53.1	49.8	44.5	55.8	51.3	55.9
Grants and interest payments	11.5	13.4	13.2	13.4	13.1	12.8	13.4
	\multicolumn{7}{c}{Ratio in terms of GDP}						
Total revenue	22.3	23.1	28.2	31.4	26.8	27.8	27.4
Total expenditure	27.0	27.7	31.4	35.8	31.6	32.8	32.4
Budget balance	−4.7	−4.5	−3.3	−4.3	−4.9	−5.0	−5.0

Note: The IMF's latest Article IV estimated a fiscal deficit of 6.9% in 2007 (cited from ANZ, 2008).

Sources: Ministry of Finance and authors' estimates.

and upward adjustment of salaries for public servants (because of higher inflation rates, the government was forced to raise public salaries several times, by 10 per cent–20 per cent, during 2004–08). Nevertheless, investment expenditure is recognized as inefficient in terms of selecting projects and disbursements (at least 20–30 per cent of investment expenditure can be saved).

16.5 POLICY RECOMMENDATIONS

The prospect for Viet Nam's development is bright according to a number of forecasts: the economy will likely continue to grow at an annual rate of 8–9 per cent in the coming years. There exist, however, enormous challenges to Viet Nam in achieving its development goals and in realizing its potential for financial development. The country is still in transition and needs to strive for industrialization. Weaknesses and vulnerabilities persist in some critical areas, such as the SOEs, the financial system, efficiency of public investment, and others.

At the same time, the reform process is becoming more complicated as it touches the production factor markets and the large SOEs, which are socio-economically sensitive and have a socialist orientation. Moreover, macroeconomic instability and financial vulnerabilities are still a threat, and have become more apparent as the country integrates into the world economy.

Obviously, Viet Nam needs to have a broad approach to economic and financial reform as well as more specific policy measures to deal with the present macroeconomic instability. Some ideas for this policy package are discussed below.

16.5.1 Directions for Broader Reforms[11]

The first and most important reform direction for Viet Nam is to continue undertaking a decisive institutional reform – one that will transform the existing state-led economic institutions into efficiency-enhancing entities. This is not only about making the legal framework more consistent with a market-based economy and international commitments, but more importantly, it is also about reforming the large SOEs and establishing an efficient and effective administrative and enforcement system.

The second is to start moving up along the value chain, while fully utilizing traditional comparative advantages. It is essential for Viet Nam to: (i) diversify export products and strengthen non-price competitiveness; (ii) attract efficient FDI; and (iii) improve infrastructure (especially the transportation system and electricity supply) and labor and management skills (at both the macro and micro levels) since these two present bottlenecks for development. What Viet Nam needs to do now is to maximize the benefits of efficient FDI inflows.

The third is to strengthen surveillance and financial supervision capacity. This necessitates amendments and improvements to the existing regulatory framework to cope with the new dimensions of financial activities and development.[12] The key regulators could be unified into a single body to detect vulnerabilities associated with the financial sector and capital movements. It could be more cost-effective, but issues of effectiveness are likely to remain.

The fourth is to develop a healthy financial system. As the capital markets are only at an early stage of development, having a sound banking system is vital. Together with strengthening financial supervision capacity, there is a pressing need to improve risk management, apply international auditing and accounting standards, recapitalize commercial banks, and enhance human resources capacity.

16.5.2 Macroeconomic Policy Responses to Present Instability

The macroeconomic policy options become ever more complex due to the presence of serious policy inconsistencies (high inflation, high VND nominal interest rates, weakening USD with rather low interest rate, and high pressure on nominal appreciation). In this context, any policy response can have an undesirable side effect, and a combination of various macroeconomic policies could be a better, though not a perfect option.

To begin with, a strong commitment to stabilizing the economy should be the focal point in combating high inflation. Macroeconomic stability is a prerequisite for sustaining economic growth. In that sense, stabilization is consistent with the goal of achieving relatively high economic growth. There may be, however, a short-run trade-off between the two. The key risk is that the government would go for high growth over price stability. Experience has shown that too much concern about a slowdown in economic growth can make the conduct of policies more inconsistent, and in the end, this can slightly change inflation expectations.

As money supply growth was very high in 2004–07, and this is associated with inflation, tightening monetary policy was necessary. But it was far from sufficient. Not only was it unsustainable as the ER is kept stable, but also strong monetary policy measures could create a liquidity problem for the whole banking system.

A more flexible ER policy needs to be an option. Greater ER flexibility can reduce pressure on monetary intervention and sterilization. More importantly, in the context of a weakening USD, it could significantly constrain the import of international inflation. At first, however, the widening band of ER fluctuation could lead to nominal ER appreciation and hence, encourage short-term speculative activities. But this need not always be the case. Rather, flexibility is meant to introduce two-way risks and thereby discourage speculative capital inflows, if the SBV can manipulate policy appropriately, especially when inflation is under control.

A natural question to be asked then is whether there is room for nominal appreciation without posing any serious threat to export competitiveness? To measure the price competitiveness of goods, the real effective exchange rate (REER) is usually used.[13] Despite a relatively high inflation rate, the price of Vietnamese exports seems to remain competitive as the REER has depreciated compared to the equilibrium level (Figure 16.3). This is attributed to the depreciation of the USD compared to currencies of Viet Nam's main trading partners, and to the peg of the VND to the USD.

The permission granted by the Prime Minister on 3 March 2008 to the SBV to widen the trading band of VND/USD to ± 2.0 per cent should be seen as a positive move in making ER more flexible.

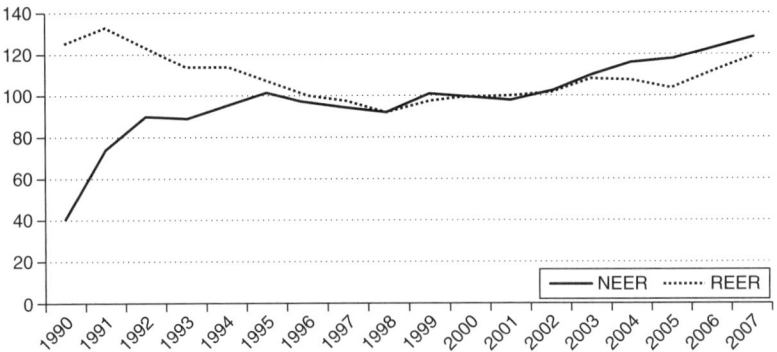

Note: The calculation is based on IMF's *International Financial Statistics* (exchange rates and CPI), and GSO's trade statistics (trade weights). The base year is 2000. Nineteen largest trading partners, accounting for 85.65 per cent of Viet Nam's total trade from 2000 to 2007, were included in partner weights. An upward trend means real depreciation.

Source: Cited from Dang (2008).

Figure 16.3   Evolution of the real and nominal effective exchange rate

Fiscal tightening is another good complementary policy option. It can lessen pressure on real exchange rate appreciation (by limiting increases in the relative price of non-tradable goods) and interest rate hikes. Fiscal policy, however, has several limitations as a response to capital inflows. Fiscal action needs legal approval, which may take a long time. Moreover, fiscal flexibility may be limited to begin with, especially when there is a lack of political will. For Viet Nam, fiscal tightening can be seen as an opportunity for the government to make budget expenditures more transparent and to cut back decisively on inefficient public investment projects.

It is worth noting that policies for the relaxation of capital flows are under consideration by the government. The impact of this measure depends on whether there is sufficient pent-up demand for foreign assets. If not, making it easier to repatriate funds may even lead to additional net capital inflows. Experience has also shown that financial trouble can follow an inappropriate sequencing of financial and KA liberalization. Therefore, consideration of further liberalization of capital flows, if any, needs to focus first on the relaxation of some conditions for FDI outflows and a possible increase in the proportion of foreign equity investors in manufacturing and some services sectors.

In short, measures to sustain economic growth and sound financial development while mitigating the possible financial risks in Viet Nam are critically dependent upon both longer term reform processes and the implementation of necessary macroeconomic policies. This study therefore recommends a broad reform package that aims to: (i) tackle persistent bottlenecks in the economy (weaknesses in economic institutions, infrastructure and human resources); (ii) modernize the SBV; and (iii) strengthen risk management in the banking sector and financial supervision systems. The focus is also on capital market development based on the improvement of its fundamentals and the reform of large SOEs. In particular, this study recommends a firm commitment to combating high inflation, and a combination of tightened monetary and fiscal policies with a more flexible exchange rate policy. The scope and scale of the macro-policy mix should avoid policy shocks in order to test the market for necessary adjustments. Given the evident policy inconsistencies, prudential regulations and monitoring should be strengthened to prevent speculative financial activities.

NOTES

1. State investment includes investment from budget, state credit, and SOEs' retained profit investment. Note also that about 28 per cent and 38 per cent of GDP are accounted for by the SOE and state sectors, respectively.
2. There are, however, some problems with the officially announced NPLs. Some suggest that the figures for NPLs would be three times higher if the estimates were based on rigorous international accounting standards.
3. The HOSTC was transformed into Ho Chi Minh City Stock Exchange (HOSE) in May 2007.
4. The figure for implemented/realized FDI is different from that of FDI in BOP.
5. Measured as ratio of foreign currency deposits to M2, dollarization in Viet Nam remained stable at 20–23 per cent in the mid-1990s. It started to increase in 1997 to reach a peak of 31.7 per cent in 2001, before dropping to 24.4 per cent in 2005 and less than 20 per cent in 2007.
6. Decree 22/1999/ND-CP is the first legal document on FDI outflows. Since then there has been some relaxation on foreign exchange transactions and borrowings for overseas direct investment purposes.
7. The realized FDI as a share of the total FDI commitment in 2006 and 2007 was only 41.0 per cent and 37.8 per cent, respectively. These figures are much lower than that in 2005 (84.7 per cent) and the average during 1988–2007 (52.7 per cent).
8. During 2007, the price of petroleum increased four times – in January, March, May and November, and decreased once, in August. As a result, the price/liter increased from VND 10 500 to VND 13 000 (or 23.8 per cent).
9. Basically, the SBV liberalized foreign currency and VND interest rates in 2001 and 2002.
10. Inflation is often high during the months before and after the Lunar New Year. But inflation at 6 per cent is still high by normal standards. The impact of the most recent monetary measures can be observed with a lag. Note that in January the Government again increased public salaries by 20 per cent and the petroleum price from VND 13 000/liter to VND 14 500 (or 11.5 per cent).
11. Some ideas are taken from Vo (2007).
12. Two laws, the SBV Law and Credit Institutions Law, have been substantially revised and amended.
13. Basically, REER is an overall index of international price competitiveness with weights

reflecting the importance of each trading partner. The REER may not be a good indicator of price competitiveness of Vietnamese commodities due to the vertical structure of exports. Viet Nam has to import a lot of raw and intermediate materials to produce products for export. In addition, Viet Nam's main competitors are not the US, Japan and the EU but Asian countries such as the PRC, Thailand and Indonesia. Therefore, it is necessary to focus on bilateral REER between Viet Nam and these countries.

REFERENCES

ANZ (2008), 'Tackling inflation in Vietnam', *ANZ Economics*, 13 February.
(CIEM) Central Institute for Economic Management (2008), *Vietnam Economy 2007*, Hanoi: Financial Publishing House.
Dang, D.A. (2008), 'Impacts of Vietnam's WTO membership on economic structure and macroeconomic stability', Activity Code HOR-9, Hanoi: Multilateral Trade Assistance Project Vietnam II (MUTRAP II).
General Statistics Office of Vietnam (various issues), *Statistical Yearbook*, Hanoi: Statistics Publishing House.
(IMF) International Monetary Fund (2006), *Country Report – Vietnam: Selective Issues*.
IMF (2007), *Report on the Article IV consultation in Vietnam 2007*, August (draft).
Johnston, B.R. and I. Otker-Robe (1999), 'A modernized approach to managing the risks in cross-border capital movements', IMF Policy Discussion Papers, PDP/99/6.
JP Morgan (2007), 'Vietnam equity strategy update', Asia Pacific Equity Research, 6 December, available at: http://atpvietnam.com/library/doc/JPMorgan-VN-Market-06Dec2007.pdf.
(MPI) Ministry of Planning and Investment of Vietnam (2005), *Strategic Framework on ODA Mobilization and Utilization for 2006–2010*, Hanoi: MPI (Viet Nam).
Nguyen, T.H. (2002), 'Dollarization of financial assets and liabilities of the household sector, the enterprise sector and banking sector in Vietnam', in SBV and JICA (eds), *Dollarization and its Effect on Monetary and Foreign Exchange Rate Policies and the Development of Financial Systems: Vietnam, Lao PDR and Cambodia*, Proceedings of Joint Research Project Workshop, Hanoi, July, SBV/JICA, pp. 13–32.
(SBV) State Bank of Vietnam (various years), *Annual Report*, Hanoi: VinaCapital, Banking Sector Report.
Vo, T.T. (ed) (2007), *Economic Growth and Industrialization and Modernization in Vietnam: Question of Capital Mobilization and Utilization* (in Vietnamese), December, Hanoi: Social Science Publishing House.
World Bank (2007), 'Taking stock – an update on Vietnam's recent economic developments', report for the Annual Consultative Group Meeting for Vietnam, Hanoi, 6–7 December.

APPENDIX

Table 16A.1 Balance of payments of Viet Nam (1990–2007) in million dollars

	1990	1995	1996	1997	1998	1999	2000	2001	2002	2003	2004	2005	2006	2007
1. Trade balance	**−41**	**−2345**	**−2775**	**−1247**	**−989**	**972**	**377**	**481**	**−1054**	**−2581**	**−3854**	**−2439**	**−2776**	**−10360**
Exports (FOB)	1731	5198	7255	9135	9361	11540	14448	15027	16706	20149	26485	32447	39826	48561
Imports (FOB)	1772	7543	10030	10432	10350	10568	14072	14546	17760	22730	30339	34886	42602	58921
Imports (CIF)											31969	36761	44891	62682
2. Services	**55**	**159**	**−61**	**−623**	**−530**	**−547**	**−550**	**−572**	**−749**	**−778**	**61**	**−219**	**−8**	**−894**
Exports	55	2074	2243	2530	2616	2493	2702	2810	2948	3272	3867	4176	5100	6030
Imports	0	1915	2304	3153	3146	3040	3252	3382	3697	4050	3806	4395	5108	6924
Adjusted for F&I												1500	1832	3009
3. Investment income	**−411**	**−236**	**−384**	**−543**	**−677**	**−429**	**−451**	**−477**	**−721**	**−811**	**−891**	**−1219**	**−1429**	**−2168**
Receipts	28	96	140	136	127	142	331	318	167	125	188	364	668	1093
Payments	439	332	524	679	804	571	782	795	888	936	1079	1583	2097	3261
Of which scheduled interest payments	237	262	340	379	303	371	462	345	288	286		443	541	626
(Actual payments)	53	128	281	248	246	276	328	345	288	286		443	541	626
4. Transfer (net)	**138**	**290**	**1200**	**885**	**1122**	**1181**	**1732**	**1250**	**1921**	**2239**	**3093**	**3380**	**4049**	**6430**
Private sector	0	140	1050	710	950	1050	1585	1100	1767	2100	2919	3150	3800	6180
Government sector	138	150	150	175	172	131	147	150	154	139	174	230	249	250

Table 16A.1 (continued)

	1990	1995	1996	1997	1998	1999	2000	2001	2002	2003	2004	2005	2006	2007
A. Current account (Excluding private transfer)	−259	−2132	−2020	−1528	−1074	1177	1108	682	−603	−1931	−1591	−497	−164	−6992
											−4510	−3647	−3964	−13172
B Capital account	121	2360	2624	1944	1129	509	−754	220	1980	2533	2753	3087	3088	18771
5. FDI	120	1956	2395	2220	1671	1412	1298	1300	1400	1450	1610	1889	2315	6600
FDI in Viet Nam												1954	2400	6700
Viet Nam FDI abroad												65	85	100
6. Medium and long-term loans	−47	93	37	356	228	2	65	139	−51	457	1162	921	1025	2043
Disbursements Scheduled	233	433	772	1145	952	1036	1348	958	1049	1540	2047	2031	2260	3480
Amortization	280	340	735	789	724	1034	1283	819	1100	1083	885	1110	1235	1437
(Actual payments)	166	272	508	639	544	582	979	668	990	1083	885	1110	1235	1437
7. Short-term loan	48	311	224	−520	−233	−118	−29	−22	7	26	−54	46	−30	91
Disbursements	338	1381	1747	1006	478	239	333	370	377	418	1001	1046	1070	902
Scheduled Amortization	290	1070	1523	1526	711	357	362	392	370	392	1055	1000	1100	811
(Actual payments)	290	1092	1523	1526	711	357	362	392	370	392	1055	1000	1100	811
8. Portfolio investments												865	1313	7414
9. Currencies and deposits			−32	−112	−537	−787	−2088	−1197	624	1372	35	−634	−1535	2623
C. Errors and omissions	−4	−51	−628	−280	−278	−917	−676	−862	−1020	777	−279	−459	1398	−1611

D. Overall balance	-142	177	-24	137	-224	769	-322	40	357	2151	883	2131	4322	10168
E. Financing	142	-177	24	-137	224	-769	322	-40	-357	-2151	-883	-2131	-4322	-10168
10. Change in NFA (-, incr)	-156	-357	-262	-318	-13	-1317	-116	-191	-467	-2151	-883	-2131	-4322	-10168
Change in NFA (-, incr)	-156	-448	-440	-277	30	-1285	-90	-253	-519	-2097	-810	-2076	-4289	-10143
Use of IMF credit	0	91	178	-41	-43	-32	-26	62	52	-54	-73	-55	-33	-25
Purchases	0	91	178	0	0	0	0	106	106	0	0	0	0	0
Repurchases	0	0	0	41	43	32	26	44	54	54	73	55	33	25
11. Change in arrears and rescheduling	298	180	286	131	237	548	438	151	110					0
Change in arrears							0	0	0					0
Rescheduling							438	151	110					0
% of GDP														
1. Trade balance	-0.68	-11.17	-11.10	-4.62	-3.66	3.35	1.22	1.46	-3.01	-6.45	-8.56	-4.60	-4.55	-14.59
4. Transfer (net)	2.30	1.38	4.80	3.28	4.16	4.07	5.59	3.79	5.49	5.60	6.87	6.38	6.64	9.06
Private sector	0.00	0.67	4.20	2.63	3.52	3.62	5.11	3.33	5.05	5.25	6.49	5.94	6.23	8.70
A. CA balance	-4.32	-10.15	-8.08	-5.66	-3.98	4.06	3.57	2.07	-1.72	-4.83	-3.54	-0.94	-0.27	-9.85
B. KA balance	2.02	11.24	10.50	7.20	4.18	1.76	-2.43	0.67	5.66	6.33	6.12	5.82	5.06	26.44
5. FDI (net)	2.00	9.31	9.58	8.22	6.19	4.87	4.19	3.94	4.00	3.63	3.58	3.56	3.80	9.30
6. M-L term loan (net)	-0.78	0.44	0.15	1.32	0.84	0.01	0.21	0.42	-0.15	1.14	2.58	1.74	1.68	2.88
7. ST loan (net)	0.80	1.48	0.90	-1.93	-0.86	-0.41	-0.09	-0.07	0.02	0.07	-0.12	0.09	-0.05	0.13
8. Portfolio investments	0.00	0.00	0.00	0.00	0.00	0.00	0.00	0.00	0.00	0.00	0.00	1.63	2.15	10.44
C. Errors and omissions	-0.07	-0.24	-2.51	-1.04	-1.03	-3.16	-2.18	-2.61	-2.91	1.94	-0.62	-0.87	2.29	-2.27

Index

Abbreviations used in the index:
CEE = Central and Eastern Europe
EAEs = emerging Asian economies

absorptive capacity 48, 50
administrative capacity and capital controls 58
aggregate demand 206, 209, 354
Ahearne, A. 203
Alfaro, L. 211
American depositary receipts (ADR) 161–2, 162
  India 240–41
Annual Report on Exchange Arrangements and Exchange Restrictions (AREAER) 12
arbitrage 161–4, 187
Argentina, capital controls 166–7
  and cross-market premium 171
Árvai, Z. 210
ASEAN+3 39, 43, 408
  finance ministers 39
Asian Bond Markets Initiative (ABMI) 39, 408, 409
Asian Currency Unit 409
Asian Dollar Market (ADM) 377
Asian financial crisis
  and Australia 85–6
  and Singapore 372–3
  and Thailand 85–6, 387–8
Asian Financial Stability Dialogue 44
Asian Policy Forum 55
asset price booms 290, 300
asset price bubbles 34, 51, 210, 406
asset price inflation 77–8
  Indonesia 271
  Korea 287–8, 290, 300–302
  Malaysia 316
Auguste, S. 162
Australia and the Asian crisis 85–6

baht appreciation 391, 399–400
balance sheet effects 203
balance sheet management, central banks 95–9
Balassa–Samuelson effect 76, 114, 122
Bangko Sentral ng Pilipinas (BSP) 26, 347–8, 351–4
Bangkok International Banking Facility (BIBF) 386
bank borrowing 17, 114
  Thailand 387–8
bank flows, Asia 130–31, 139–40
Bank Indonesia (BI) 25–6, 263–5, 272–3
  and mini-crisis of 2005 274–7
Bank Indonesia Certificates (SBI) 26, 236–7
Bank for International Settlements (BIS) 85
Bank of Korea (BOK) 26, 300, 301
Bank Negara Malaysia 26
Bank of Thailand (BOT) 27, 391–6, 401
banking sector
  CEE countries 208–9
  Indonesia 270–71, 272
  regulation 208
  supervision 124–5, 208–9, 210
  Viet Nam 412–15, 419–23
Basel II and Thailand 405
basket-band-crawl exchange rate regime, Singapore 370–72, 373–5
Bekaert, G. 47
BI, *see* Bank Indonesia
big-bang approach to capital account liberalization 53–4
bilateral swap arrangements 276, 408

blocked rand system 168
BOK (Bank of Korea) 26, 300, 301
Bombay Stock Exchange Limited, *see* BSE
bond market flows, Asia 135-4
bond markets
  Asia 409
  and foreign banks 139
  Viet Nam 416, 424-5
Borio, C.E.V. 157
BOT (Bank of Thailand) 27, 391-6, 401
Brazil, crises and cross-market premium 179-86
Broner, F.A. 176
BSE (Bombay Stock Exchange Limited) 240
BSP (Bangko Sentral ng Pilipinas) 26, 347-8, 351-4
budget deficit reduction, Viet Nam 428-9
Bulgaria 193, 195, 196, 200, 201, 204, 206
business cycle 76, 79, 256, 387
Bussiere, M. 53

Caballero, R. 86, 87
Cairns, J. 145
Calvo, G. 66, 203, 205, 205-6, 208, 382, 387
capacity building 44
capital account 13, 28, 40, 47-8, 50, 53-6, 58, 65-6, 97-8, 118, 156, 168, 195-7, 209, 218, 224, 226, 228-9, 239, 245-8, 257, 260-61, 277, 282, 331-2, 334, 347-8, 353, 363, 382, 386-7, 400, 425, 436
capital account liberalization 2, 4, 12, 36, 39, 40, 45-7, 49, 65-6, 193, 223-4, 233, 237, 239, 255, 277, 280, 354, 381, 401
  CEE countries 195-9
  China 28, 32, 225-7
  impact on growth 46-8
  Korea 281-2
  measurement 196-9
  pace and sequencing 53-6
  Thailand 386
  Viet Nam 33

capital controls 28-33, 39-40, 56-8, 117-18, 166-9
  China 223-7
  and cross-market premium 169-72
  and financial market integration 169-75
  India 239-48, 255
  and macroeconomic stability, China 230-36
  regional cooperation, East Asia 357-8
  as response to crisis 94-5
  Thailand 400-401
capital flow reversal 9, 51, 85-7
capital flows
  CEE countries 199-203
  China 218-23
  emerging Asian economies 12-17
    impact 18-23
  and equity prices 131-5
  India 239-45
  macroeconomic impact 252-6
  Korea 282-7
    impact on economy 287-91
  Malaysia 306-18
  Singapore 362-4
  Thailand 388-91
  Viet Nam 417-18
  see also capital inflows; capital outflows
capital inflow controls 39-40, 56-8, 161-2
capital inflows
  Asia 129-56
  CEE countries 201-3
  characteristics 46-53
  China 218-23
    and macroeconomic stability 232-6
  controls 39-40, 56-8, 161-2
  determinants of, Korea 298
  EAEs 14-17
  India 239-41, 247
  Indonesia 261-7
    determinants 267-8
    impacts 268-71
  Korea 284-5
    effects on economy 287-98
  long-term capital flows 196, 364
  macroeconomic measures 59-61

and macroeconomic stability
  China 232–6
  Viet Nam 418
 management, *see* policy responses to capital flows
 Philippines 331–46
 risks 50–53
 Singapore 362–4
 structural measures 61–2
 Thailand 387–8, 391–400
capital mobility, benefits of 46–8
capital outflow controls 160, 161, 166
 Argentina 166
 Venezuela 169
capital outflows
 China 223, 234
 controls 161
 EAEs 14, 17
 easing restrictions 40–41, 62
 India 243–5
 Indonesia 263
 Korea 285–6, 302
 Thailand 408
capital reversals 9, 51, 85–7
carry trades 131, 140–45
Central and Eastern Europe (CEE) 192–210
 bank credit 114
 capital account liberalization 195–9
 capital flows 199–203
 economic characteristics 193–5
 managing capital flows 203–10
central bank bills
 People's Bank of China 24, 231–2
 State Bank of Vietnam 27
central banks
 balance sheet management 95–9
 and capital flows 75–100
 net foreign assets, CEE countries 205
Central Provident Fund, Singapore 26, 373, 375–6
Chai-anant, C. 134
Chiang Mai Initiative (CMI) 39, 319
Chiappe, M.L. 43
Chile 86
 capital controls 117–18, 167
  and cross-market premium 171, 173–5
 Chilean-style controls 160
 fiscal policy 121

China, *see* People's Bank of China; People's Republic of China
Chinn, M.D. 12
Chinn–Ito Index 245
Chow, H.K. 368, 381
Chuhan, P. 49
collective policy action 42–4; *see also* regional cooperation
commercial rand system 168
consumer price index, Philippines 338
consumer prices, impacts of capital flows, Malaysia 309–10, 315
consumption, effect of remittances, Philippines 342–4
consumption volatility 48
controls on capital inflows 39–40, 56–8, 161–2
controls on capital outflows 160, 161, 166
 Argentina 166
 Venezuela 169
convergence play 203, 207
convertibility, India 257
cooperation, regional 43–4, 357–8, 382, 408–9
Corden, W.M. 229
corner solutions 80
corporate tax reduction, Malaysia 318
'corralito' 166
counter-cyclical policy 43, 120–21
 Singapore 269–70
Covered Interest Parity (CIP) deviation, India 249–50
covered interest rate parity, Viet Nam 419–20
CPF (Central Provident Fund), Singapore 26, 373, 375–6
credit boom 203, 204, 208
credit contraction 208
crises
 definition 109–10, 176–8
 effects on financial integration 160–87
 global 16–17, 33
 mini-crisis, Indonesia 274–7
 mini-crisis, Viet Nam 421–3
 US subprime mortgage crisis 20, 261, 272, 285
cross-border capital flows, China 220–23

and macroeconomic stability 233–6
  management 223–7
cross-border claims 152, 154
cross-currency swap market 137–9
cross-market premium 161–2
  and crises 176–86
  effect of capital controls 162–75
currencies
  carry trades, *see* carry trades
  effect of portfolio equity flows 134
  see also exchange rates
currency appreciation 58–9
  baht 391, 399–400
  collective 43
  effects of large inflows 112–14
  as indicator of overheating 115–16
  peso, Philippines 344–5
  yuan 235
currency board 110, 114, 117, 124, 201, 206
currency bond markets 130, 135–9
currency flexibility, India 256
currency mismatches 52
  Viet Nam 419
currency regime, India 252–4
current account, Thailand 388
current account deficits 115
  CEE countries 199–201
  Viet Nam 418
current account surpluses 92
  China 228–9
  Malaysia 305
current transfers, Philippines 331
cyclicality of capital flows 49
Cyprus 192, 211
Czech Republic 193, 195, 196, 198, 199–200, 201, 205, 206, 209

de-dollarization, Philippines 345
de facto measurement of capital account liberalization 12
de jure capital controls, India 245–6
de jure measurement of capital account liberalization 12
De Rato, R. 358
debt flows
  China 220
  India 243, 247
  Korea 283–4
  Thailand 390–91

debt securities flows
  EAEs 17
  Thailand 390
depositary receipts (DRs) 161–2, 163
  India 240–41
derivatives 4, 16, 29, 86, 130, 135, 137–9, 156, 227, 241, 257, 276–7, 333, 335, 378–9
Desai, M. 57
Detken, C. 211
Detragiache, E. 52
Dincer, N.N. 252
direct investment
  and current account deficit sustainability 200–201
  Malaysia 313, 316–17
  Singapore 362–4
  see also foreign direct investment
dollarization
  Philippines 345
  Viet Nam 421
domestic liquidity
  Malaysia 308–9, 313–14
  Singapore 365–6, 375–7
Dooley, M. 57
Doraisami, A.G. 53
Dornbusch over-shooting model 76, 78, 81
double mismatch, Viet Nam 421

EAEs, *see* emerging Asian economies
economic and financial imbalances 209
economic fundamentals 4–5, 50, 58, 278, 307, 361–2, 371–2, 381, 411
economic growth, *see* growth
Edwards, S. 57
Eichengreen, B. 56, 252
EMEAP (Executives Meeting of East Asia-Pacific Central Banks) 43
emerging Asian economies (EAEs)
  capital flows 12–17, 107–8
  challenges 33–4
  growth rates 9–10
  impact of capital flows 18–23
  policy responses to capital flows 23–33, 34–44
  see also individual countries
emerging economies 2–3, 10, 33, 45, 76, 85, 98, 160–62, 164–5, 186, 209, 260, 407

emerging Europe, *see* Central and Eastern Europe
EMP, *see* exchange market pressure
encaje 117–18
equity markets
  Asia 131–5
  and carry trades 145
  China 222
  Korea 284–5
  Thailand 390
equity prices, impact of capital flows 20, 23
ERM-2 (Exchange Rate Mechanism-2) 206–7
ERPD 38
Estonia 193, 194, 199, 200, 201, 204, 205, 206, 209
EU-10, *see* Central and Eastern Europe
euro adoption 123–4, 207–8
euro-ization 207–8
European Economic and Monetary Union (EMU) 192
European Union 4, 123, 192
event studies
  impact of capital controls on cross-market premium 164–75
  impact of crises on financial integration 178–86
excess liquidity
  China 232
  global 330
exchange market pressure
  Philippines 348
  volatility 177
exchange rate appreciation, *see* currency appreciation
exchange rate arrangement, Asia 408–9
exchange rate flexibility 60–61
Exchange Rate Mechanism-2 (ERM-2) 206–7
exchange rate-centered monetary policy framework, Singapore 367–72
exchange rate policies
  CEE countries 206–7
  China 229–30
  Korea 299–300
  Singapore 367–72
  Viet Nam 431

exchange rates
  analytical model 78–81
  and equity markets 134
  impact of capital flows 18–19, 112–14
  India 252–4
  Indonesia 268
  Korea 288–90, 296–7
  Malaysia 309, 314–15
  Philippines 344–5
  Thailand 391–6
  and mini-crisis, Indonesia 274–7
  Singapore 366
  Viet Nam 426
Executives' Meeting of East Asia-Pacific Central Banks (EMEAP) 43
export promotion policy, China 228–9
external commercial borrowing, India 243
external debt 33, 39, 55, 110, 169, 198, 227, 242, 253, 263, 267, 270, 308, 313, 425
external liabilities 198–9

FDI, *see* foreign direct investment
Feldstein/Horioka paradox 75
financial account 261, 263, 265–6, 307–8, 312, 315, 332, 334, 337, 344, 362–3
financial depth, Viet Nam 414
financial development 6, 202, 365, 377, 381–3, 411, 429, 432
financial globalization 240–41
financial instability, risk of 9, 51
Financial Institution Investment Act (FIBA) and Thailand 405
financial integration 12, 44, 47, 65, 125, 160–91, 193, 195–7, 209–10, 357
financial intermediation 43, 60, 198, 318, 400
financial market effects 203
financial market regulation, Korea 302–3
financial market strengthening 39
financial openness 160–87
  measurement 12
  and volatility of inflows 124
financial rand system 168

444   *Index*

financial sector
  impacts of capital flows
    Malaysia 310–11, 317–18
    Thailand 391–6
  reform 61–2
  regulation 272
  stability 87–8
  supervision, Viet Nam 430
  see also banking sector
financial shocks 198, 361, 382
financial stability risk 9, 51
Fine Tuning Contraction (FTC) 276
fiscal policy
  Korea 302
  and large capital flows 118–21,
    122–3, 126, 208, 209–10
  Malaysia 318
Fiscal Policy Research Institute (FPRI)
    391, 399
fiscal policy tightening 41
fiscal restraint 118–21
fiscal stance 2, 123, 208–9
fiscal surplus 91–2
fiscal tightening 41, 61
  Viet Nam 428, 432
fixed exchange rate 5, 101, 203, 209,
    253, 299, 306, 353, 386–7
fixed income 135–7, 139, 147, 150–51
fixed-income flows 137, 151
fixed-but-changeable peg 80
flexible exchange rates 80, 117
Forbes, K. 57
foreign banks, bond investment 139
foreign currency deposits, Philippines
    345, 347
foreign currency liabilities 114, 401
foreign currency trade 192
foreign direct investment (FDI)
  CEE countries 198–9, 201
  China 218, 221, 229
  EAEs 14–16
  impact on growth 48
  Korea 283
  Philippines 331
  Singapore 362–4
  Thailand 388–90
  Viet Nam 417, 425
foreign direct investment inflows 106,
    109
  China 218

India 239–40
Indonesia 265–7
Korea 286–7
Philippines 340–43
foreign direct investment outflows
  India 244
  Korea 285
foreign equity investment
  China 222
  Korea 284–5
foreign exchange 24–5, 29, 31, 140,
    154, 169, 223–7, 282, 347, 378,
    422, 426
foreign exchange flows 340, 352, 388
Foreign Exchange Liberalization Plan,
    Korea 147
foreign exchange management,
    Thailand 405–7
foreign exchange market 1, 20, 23–7,
    34, 41, 52, 81, 88, 92–3, 95, 144–5,
    147, 169, 225, 232–3, 237, 272,
    276, 279, 306, 348, 352–4, 371,
    374, 377, 391, 395, 400
foreign exchange market intervention
    23–7, 92–3, 93–4
  Bangko Sentral ng Pilipinas 26, 348,
    351–4
  Bank Indonesia 272
  Reserve Bank of India 24–5
foreign exchange reserves 19–20, 95–9
  CEE countries 199
  China 220–21, 222
  Korea 289–90, 297–8
foreign exchange restrictions 196, 362,
    400
Foreign Exchange Transaction Law,
    Korea 282
foreign institutional investors (FII)
  China 32
  India 240–41, 249–50
foreign invested enterprises (FIEs),
    Viet Nam 425
Foreign Investment Fund (FIF),
    Thailand 401
foreign investment in local currency
    bonds
  Asia 130
  Indonesia 136–7
foreign portfolio investment (FPI)
  Philippines 345–6

Viet Nam 417–18
see also portfolio flows
Frankel, J. 252

Gaspar, V. 211
GDP growth
  EAEs 9–10
  Indonesia 267–8
Genberg, H. 354
Giroud, A. 340
global allocation of capital 105
global depository receipts, India 240–41
global financial and economic crisis 16–17, 33
global imbalances 291, 306, 409
global liquidity 20, 280, 306, 311, 313, 330
global policy solutions 42–3
global solution 37, 42
globalization 100, 130, 136, 240–41, 247, 401
Gochoco-Bautista, M.S. 300
Goldstein, M. 234
government bonds 137
  India 242
  Indonesia 136, 137, 263–5
  Korea 139, 390
  Viet Nam 416, 418
government expenditure 5, 120, 208, 318, 337–8, 340
Government of India (GOI) 24, 242
gradualist approach to capital account liberalization 53
graduated exit levy 307
Grilli, V. 47
Grogan, L. 211
growth
  CEE countries 194–5
  EAEs 9–10
  Indonesia 267–8
  Viet Nam 412
Guidotti Rule 97–8
Guimaraes, R. 319

Hanoi Securities Trading Centre (HASTC) 415
hard landings 109–10; *see also* crises
hard peg 200, 201

Hattori, M. 157
Hauner, D. 205
Hausmann, R. 86, 91, 206
Hayashi, M. 267
hedging 90–91
Henry, P.B. 47
herd behaviour 50
Ho, C. 84–5, 97, 134, 353, 354
Ho Chi Minh City Securities Trading Centre (HOSTC) 415
Hohensee, M. 144
home bias decline, India 248–51
hot money 108, 124, 126, 129–56
  China 233
  Korea 287
  Philippines 330
household indebtedness 114
Houser, C. 330
housing prices, effects of inflow shocks, Korea 296
Hungary 193, 195, 196, 199, 201, 204, 205, 206, 208

Ichsan, F. 156
Impossible Trinity 80, 81, 83, 235, 256
impulse response to inflow shocks
  Korea 294–8
  Philippines 338–9
India 239–57
  capital controls 32–3
  liberalizing capital outflows 147
  restricting capital outflows 154–5
  see also Reserve Bank of India
Indonesia 260–78
  capital controls 167
    and cross-market premium 171–2, 175
  crises and cross-market premium 179–86
  currency bond markets 135–7
  restricting capital inflows 155
  see also Bank Indonesia
inflation
  effects of capital flows 20, 112
  India 255
  Indonesia 267, 270
  Malaysia 309–10, 315–16
  Viet Nam 412, 427
inflation stabilization, Thailand 407–8

inflation targeting
  Indonesia 272
  Philippines 353–4
inflow controls 28–33, 89
  effects on cross-market premium 165, 171–5
  see also capital controls
inflows, *see* capital inflows
information technology (IT) bubble 16, 287, 362
initial public offerings 222
instantaneous arbitrage 187
integrated approach to capital account liberalization 54–5
integration 2–4, 12, 38, 43–5, 47, 65, 81, 125, 160–91, 193, 195–7, 202, 209, 247, 257, 357, 411, 414, 417
interest rate policy 27–8, 75–6, 93
  Asia 409
  Korea 300
interest rates
  China 235–6
  Singapore 369, 376
  Thailand 396
international clearing agency (ICA) 356–7
international competitiveness 80, 209, 365, 373
international financial architecture (IFA) reform 330
international financial integration
  CEE countries 195–9
  India 247
  measurement 12
International Monetary Fund (IMF) 10, 12, 48, 54, 85, 89, 99, 101, 108, 118, 123, 126, 195–6, 227, 239, 245, 261, 281, 319, 345, 347, 351
internationalization of the baht 407
intervention in foreign exchange markets 23–7, 92–3
investment
  Indonesia 273–4
  Malaysia 316–17
  Viet Nam 412
Investment Law, Indonesia 274
investment ratios 10
investor-based controls 58
Ito, H. 12, 245

Jakarta Stock Exchange (JSX) Index 271
Japan, carry trades 140–43
Jeanne, O. 98
Jinjarak, Y. 53
Johansen, S. 337
Johnston, R.B. 58
joint stock commercial banks (JSCBs) 412, 414
Jomo, K.S. 52–3
Jonas, J. 211
JSX (Jakarta Stock Exchange) Index 271

Kaminsky. G. 119
Kawai, M. 2, 9, 40, 46, 58, 330
Kim, S. 5, 26, 32, 150, 280–81, 303
Kimball, D. 58
Kopits, G. 211
Korea 280–303
  bank financing 17
  bond investment by foreign banks 139
  capital controls 167–8
  capital controls and cross-market premium 172–3, 175
  liberalizing capital outflows 147, 149–50
  restricting capital inflows 154
  virtual bond market 138–9
  see also Bank of Korea
Korea Fund 284
Korea Stock Price Index 287
KOSDAQ index 295–6
Kose, M.A. 48
KOSPI index 295
Kriz, P. 381
Krugman, P.R. 79
Kuala Lumpur Composite Index (KLCI) 310
Kuroda, H. 357

labour productivity growth, CEE countries 195
Lamberte, M.B. 342
Lane, P.R. 12, 197
large capital inflows, *see* surges in capital inflows
Latin America, exchange rates and inflow surges 112–13

Latvia 193, 194, 199, 200, 201, 204, 206
law of one price 161, 175
Lee, J. 371
letters of credit (LC), Viet Nam 421
leveraging 110, 378
levy on capital gains, Malaysia 307
Levy-Yeyati, E. 162, 186
liberalization
    capital market 167, 280
    China 221
    India 247
    and volatility of inflows 124
    see also capital account liberalization
liberalizing capital outflows 147–50
    Philippines 347–8
limiting capital inflow 88–93
Lipschitz, L. 100, 202
liquidity
    Korea 288–90
    Malaysia 308–9, 313–14
    Singapore 365–6, 375–7
    Viet Nam 428
Lithuania 193, 194, 199, 200, 201, 202, 204, 206, 209
loans
    loan loss provisions 303
    loan–deposit ratio 305
    Singapore 367
    Thailand 391
loss of monetary control 81–5

M3, domestic liquidity
    Malaysia 308–9, 313–14
    Philippines 338
MacDonald, R. 371
macroeconomic impact of capital flows 77–85
    India 252–6
    Philippines 337–46
macroeconomic policies 59–61
    and large capital inflows 203–9
    and overheating 115–21
    Viet Nam 426–9, 431–3
macroeconomic policy consistency, Viet Nam 419–20
macroeconomic risks 9, 51, 77–85
macroeconomic stability and capital flows
    China 230–36
    Viet Nam 418

Magud, N. 57
Malaysia 305–21; *see also* Bank Negara Malaysia
Malaysia House Price Index (MHPI) 310
Malta 192, 211
manufacturing sector, *see* real sector
marginal product of capital, CEE countries 202
market integration 3, 169, 187, 209
market segmentation 187
Market Stabilization Scheme (MSS), India 24–5, 254
MAS (Monetary Authority of Singapore) 26–7, 368, 370, 375–7, 380
maturity mismatches 52
McCallum, B.T. 370
McCauley, R.N. 84–5, 97, 157, 353, 354, 407
McKinnon, R. 235–6
Melvin, M. 162
Mexico 86, 179–86
Milesi-Ferretti, G.M. 12, 47, 197
mini-crisis
    Indonesia 274–7
    Viet Nam 421–3
Mirza, H. 340
misinvoicing 248
Moers, L. 211
monetary aggregates
    Philippines 353–4
    Singapore 365–6
monetary authorities 1, 23, 27, 41, 77, 168, 299–300
Monetary Authority of Singapore (MAS) 26–7, 368, 370, 375–7, 380
monetary control, loss of 81–5
monetary cooperation, East Asia 357–8
monetary policy
    in globally integrated economy 76–7
    Korea 300–302
    and large capital flows 209
    loss of autonomy, India 255–6
    reform, India 256–7
    Singapore 367–77
Monetary Policy Statement, Singapore 373

monetary reaction function, Singapore 370
Monetary Stabilization Bonds (MSBs) 26
money market operations, Singapore 376–7
money supply control, Viet Nam 427–8
money supply growth 20
Mulder, C. 53
multinational corporations, India 244
Mundell–Fleming IS/LM framework 91–2

narrow banks 90
NASDAQ 164
neighbourhood effect 50
net capital flows, Philippines 331–7
net domestic assets (NDA), Malaysia 309
net external position 197–8, 209
net foreign assets (NFA), Malaysia 308–9
New York Stock Exchange (NYSE) 164
Nifty 250
nominal convergence 192
nominal effective exchange rate (NEER)
  Malaysia 309
  Singapore 366
non-FDI inflows 106, 107, 108–9
non-internationalization, Singapore dollar 377–80
non-performing loans (NPLs)
  Thailand 388
  Viet Nam 414, 419
non-resident baht accounts 400
non-resident investment 134, 135–9
  India 242
  Indonesia 136–7, 155
  Korea 283
  Malaysia 310, 316–17
  South Africa 168
  Thailand 151, 407
NYSE (New York Stock Exchange) 164

Obstfeld, M. 123
Ocampo, J.A. 43, 330, 381

official development assistance (ODA), Viet Nam 417, 425
offshore baht accounts 400
offshore exchange rate, Thailand 396
offshore listing 241
onshore exchange rate, Thailand 395–6
open economy trilemma 368
open market operation, Viet Nam 427
openness, *see* liberalization
original sin 91
outbound FDI, *see* foreign direct investment outflows
outbound portfolio flows, *see* portfolio outflows
outward capital flows, *see* capital outflows
outward direct investment, Malaysia 311, 313
over-the-counter derivatives 241
overheating 110–14, 203–5
  China 230–32
  and macroecoomic policies 115–21
overseas Filipinos 347
Overseas Investment Activation Plan, Korea 147

Parking Theory 229
Parrado, E. 369–70
participatory notes 241
Pasquariello, P. 162
Patnaik, I. 58, 251
People's Bank of China (PBOC)
  capital injection into commercial banks 223
  foreign exchange market intervention 24
  interest rate policy 28
People's Republic of China 217–37
  capital controls 28, 32
  liberalizing capital outflows 147
  reducing savings 42
  restricting capital inflows 150–51
peso appreciation 337, 338–9, 344–5
Philippines 330–38
  interest rate policy 28
  liberalizing capital outflows 147
  see also Bangko Sentral ng Pilipinos
Poirson, H.K. 258
Poland 193, 194, 195, 196, 200, 201, 202, 205, 206

Index

policy-experiment approach 47
policy responses to capital flows 34–44, 23–33, 63–5, 88–99, 121–3, 145–66, 209–10
  CEE countries 203–9
  China 230–36
  India 256–7
  Indonesia 272–7
  Korea 298–303
  Malaysia 318–19
  Philippines 346–55
  Singapore 367–80
  Thailand 400–408
  Viet Nam 429–33
  see also capital controls; exchange rate policy; fiscal policy; monetary policy; sterilized intervention
portfolio debt
  CEE countries 198, 199
  EAEs 17
portfolio equity 198–9, 330
portfolio equity flows 129, 131, 134, 155
portfolio equity inflows 16–17, 151
portfolio equity outflows 150, 199
portfolio flows 131–5
  Asia 130
  CEE countries 198, 199
  EAEs 16–17
  India 240–41, 245, 248–51
  Indonesia 263–5
  Malaysia 312–13
  Philippines 331, 345–6
  Singapore 364
  Thailand 387, 390
  Viet Nam 417–18
portfolio inflows
  Korea 291, 294–8
portfolio investment 14, 30–31, 55, 149, 200, 203, 239, 260, 263, 265, 271, 277, 280, 285–7, 307, 309–10, 313–14, 324, 331–2, 335, 339, 342–3, 345, 362–4, 387–8, 390, 400–402, 408, 436–7
portfolio investment inflows 16, 263, 417
portfolio outflows
  India 245
  Korea 285

Prasad, E. 47, 48
PRC, *see* People's Republic of China
precautionary demand for foreign reserves 289
private financial accounts, Indonesia 265–7
private investment
  Malaysia 318
  Philippines 355–6
private sector
  capital outflow liberalization, Philippines 347–8
  debt, India 242–3
property price index, Indonesia 271
protective measures 123–5
prudential controls 90
prudential regulations 57–8
  Thailand 405
public–private partnership, Indonesia 273–4
public sector financial account, Indonesia 263–5
pull factors 49
  Indonesia 267
push factors 49

Qualified Domestic Institutional Investor (QDII) scheme
  China 32, 147, 234
  Thailand 401
Qualified Foreign Institutional Investors (QFII) 32, 222
quasi-sovereign debt, India 242
Quinn, D. 47

Rabinovitch, R. 162
Ranciere, R. 98
rapid credit growth 114
RBI, *see* Reserve Bank of India
real currency appreciation 106, 200, 210
real economic convergence 192
real effective exchange rate (REER)
  Malaysia 309
  Singapore 366
  Viet Nam 431
real exchange rate appreciation 58–9
real money growth, CEE countries 203–4

real sector, impact of capital flows
   Malaysia 316–17
   Philippines 340–44
   Singapore 367
   Thailand 399–400
rebalancing growth 41–2
regional cooperation 43–4, 357–8, 382, 408–9
regional exchange rate coordination 43
regional financial market integration 2, 38, 44
regional financial market surveillance 44
Reinhart, C.M. 57, 59, 66, 203, 205–6
Reinhart, V.R. 59
Reisen, H. 48
remittances
   India 247–8
   Philippines 342–4
Reports on the Observance of Standards and Codes (ROSCs), Philippines 347
repricing of risk premium 312
Republic of Korea, *see* Korea
repurchase (RP) rate, Thailand 396
reserve accumulation 19–20, 123
   Philippines 352–3, 354–5
Reserve Bank of India (RBI) 24–5, 28, 255–6
reserve requirements
   China 24, 231–2
   India 25, 255
   Korea 26, 301
   Viet Nam 27
   see also unremunerated reserve requirements
reserve sharing 123–4
reserves 1, 3, 5–6, 9, 18–21, 27, 34–5, 39, 49, 51–2, 57, 62, 64, 67, 83–5, 92–100, 106, 115–16, 123, 125, 129, 155, 189, 199–200, 203, 205, 207–8, 218, 220, 222–4, 226, 228–30, 233, 242, 244, 253, 261–2, 271, 276, 288–90, 292, 295, 297–8, 301, 305–7, 311–13, 319, 321, 330, 337–41, 345–6, 348, 351–8, 361–2, 371, 375, 386–8, 391, 395–6, 418, 420–22, 426
restricting capital inflows 150–55
retail trading 240

Richards, A. 134
risks
   capital flow reversal 9, 51, 85–7
   capital flows 9, 50–53
   financial instability 9, 192, 300, 330
   risk-based capital requirements 303
   risk diversification 48, 62
   risk-sharing 198
Rodrik, D. 47, 97
Romania 193, 194, 195, 196, 205, 206
ROSC (Reports on the Observance of Standards and Codes), Philippines 347
Roubini, N. 303
Russia, crisis and cross-market premium 179–86
Ryan, C. 58

sand in the wheels 88–9
savings, China 42, 228–9
savings-investment gap, Thailand 412
SBIs, non-resident holdings, Indonesia 26, 136–7, 155
SBV (State Bank of Vietnam) 27, 426–8
SCIC (State Capital Investment Corporation), Viet Nam 424
securities rand system 168
sequencing 54–5
Shah, A. 58, 251
Sheng, A. 53
Shin, H.S. 157
short-term capital flows, volatility, EAEs 17
Singapore 26–7, 361–82
Singapore dollar, non-internationalization 377–80
Single Presence Policy, Indonesia 272
Slovak Republic 193, 194, 195, 196, 198, 201, 205, 206
Slovenia 193, 196, 199, 200, 201, 202, 204, 205, 206
small open economies 193–4, 206, 298, 401
Soto, M. 48
South Africa, capital controls 168–9
   and cross-market premium 171
sovereign debt, India 242–3
sovereign wealth funds (SWFs) 352

Special Data Dissemination Standards (SDDS) 347
special deposit account (SDA) 26
Spilimbergo, A. 52
State Administration of Foreign Exchange (SAFE) 219, 220
State Bank of Vietnam (SBV) 27, 426–8
State Capital Investment Corporation (SCIC), Viet Nam 416
state-owned commercial banks (SOCBs), Viet Nam 412–14
state-owned enterprises (SOEs) 42, 149, 273, 411
State Securities Commission (SSC), Viet Nam 415
stealth privatization 234
sterilization
   capital inflows, CEE countries 204–5
   reserve accumulation, Korea 290
sterilized intervention 34, 39, 59–60, 116–17
   China 231–2
   India 254
   Korea 26, 301
   Philippines 348, 351–2
   Viet Nam 427
Stock Exchange of Thailand (SET) 31, 400, 403
stock markets
   and crisis definition 177
   liberalization 41
   Philippines 345–6
   Viet Nam 415–16, 423–4
structural interest differentials 75–6
structural measures to manage capital inflows 61–2
Stulz, R.M. 258
sudden stops 79, 85–7, 205–6
   central bank responses 93–5
surges in capital inflows 105–26
   emerging markets 106–15
   Korea 284, 291–8
   management of 203–9
swap arrangements 408
   Indonesia 276
   Malaysia 313–14
swap markets 137–9
   China 225
systemic financial crises 10, 90

T-bill rate, Philippines 338
Tagaki, S. 2, 9, 40, 46, 58, 303
taxes on inflows 89, 117–18
Tesar, L.L. 66
Thailand 386–409
   and the Asian crisis 85–6
   capital account liberalization 55
   liberalizing capital outflows 149
   restricting capital inflows 150, 151, 154
   virtual bond markets 138
   see also Bank of Thailand
threshold effect 48
time-varying risk premium 79
total factor productivity 202, 210
total net capital flows 307–8
trade liberalization 62
   CEE countries 194
Trade openness 194
trade surplus, China 220–21, 230
trade-weighted index (TWI), Singapore 370–71
tranquil times, cross-market premium 165
trans-Pacific macroeconomic imbalance 356
transfer-price 248
transfer problem 75
transaction-based capital controls 57
transparency 42–3
Treasury bill rate, Philippines 337, 338
Triennial Bank Survey of foreign exchange markets 144–5
Triffin's dilemma 356
Tuaño-Amador, M.C.N. 358
twin crises 87–8
twin surpluses, China 228–9, 230

uncovered interest parity (UIP) 81–3
   Viet Nam 419–20
unexplained capital flows, China 223
unipolar financial system 356
United States current account deficit 356
unremunerated reserve requirements (URRs) 56–7, 89
   Chile 167
   Thailand 396
Unteroberdoerster, O. 319

valuation effects 44, 197
VAR model, effects of capital inflows, Korea 291–8
vector error correction model (VECM) 338–40
Venezuela, capital controls 169
  and cross-market premium 171
Viet Nam 411–33
  capital controls 33
  interest rate policy 28
  State Bank of Vietnam (SBV) 27, 426–8
virtual bond investment 137–9
VIX, and portfolio inflows, India 250
volatility
  of consumption 48
  of equity markets 145
  of exchange rates, Malaysia 309
  of inflows 124
  of large capital inflows, CEE countries 205–6
  of net short-term capital flows, EAEs 17
vulnerabilities in balance sheets 52

Wei, S.J. 57, 252
Wicksellian 'natural' interest rate 76, 91
Wilaipich, U. 157
Williamson, J. 92–3

Xiao, F. 58

Yang, D. 343
Yip, S.L. 376
yuan appreciation 235

Zeilis, A. 252–4
Zhang, Z. 57